SIPRI Yearbook 2010
Armaments, Disarmament and International Security

STOCKHOLM INTERNATIONAL PEACE RESEARCH INSTITUTE
Signalistgatan 9
SE-169 70 Solna, Sweden
Telephone: +46 8 655 97 00
Fax: +46 8 655 97 33
Email: sipri@sipri.org
Internet: www.sipri.org

SIPRI Yearbook 2010

Armaments, Disarmament and International Security

**STOCKHOLM INTERNATIONAL
PEACE RESEARCH INSTITUTE**

OXFORD UNIVERSITY PRESS
2010

OXFORD
UNIVERSITY PRESS

Great Clarendon Street, Oxford OX2 6DP

Oxford University Press is a department of the University of Oxford.
It furthers the University's objective of excellence in research, scholarship,
and education by publishing worldwide in

Oxford New York

Auckland Cape Town Dar es Salaam Hong Kong Karachi
Kuala Lumpur Madrid Melbourne Mexico City Nairobi
New Delhi Shanghai Taipei Toronto

With offices in

Argentina Austria Brazil Chile Czech Republic France Greece
Guatemala Hungary Italy Japan Poland Portugal Singapore
South Korea Switzerland Thailand Turkey Ukraine Vietnam

Oxford is a registered trade mark of Oxford University Press
in the UK and in certain other countries

Published in the United States
by Oxford University Press Inc., New York

© SIPRI 2010

*Before 1987 the Yearbook was published under the title
'World Armaments and Disarmament:
SIPRI Yearbook [year of publication]'*

British Library Cataloguing in Publication Data
Data available

Library of Congress Cataloging in Publication Data
Data available

Typeset and originated by SIPRI
Printed in Great Britain on acid-free paper by
CPI Antony Rowe, Chippenham, Wiltshire

ISSN 0953–0282
ISBN 978–0–19–958112–2

Contents

Part I. Security and conflicts, 2009

Part II. Military spending and armaments, 2009

Appendix 5B. The reporting of military expenditure data

NOEL KELLY

6. Arms production

SUSAN T. JACKSON

Part III. Non-proliferation, arms control and disarmament, 2009

Preface

With pride and a tinge of regret, I am honoured to pen this preface to the 41st edition of the SIPRI Yearbook. It has been my privilege to serve as the Chairman of the SIPRI Governing Board for 10 years, and now, owing to term limits stipulated in the institution's statutes, I will step down in 2010.

Over the course of the past decade SIPRI has monitored and analysed tumultuous developments on the world scene. Globalization, while bringing many benefits to mankind, has also exacerbated fault lines between civilizations, cultures and communities. Today, we watch with concern as leading countries of the world struggle to recover from financial and economic calamities which seem not to have precluded continued growth in military spending and investments in conventional and strategic weaponry. While this edition of the SIPRI Yearbook tracks the effects of both of these problematic trends, it starts on an optimistic note, with an essay on the practicalities of achieving complete nuclear disarmament. In addition, the Yearbook also continues its longstanding and globally recognized tradition of providing authoritative assessments of the past year's developments on questions of international security, armaments and disarmaments.

The SIPRI Yearbook, while one of the most important contributions of the institute to the international community, is surely not SIPRI's only contribution. Over the past 10 years, under three different directors, SIPRI has moved from strength to strength, diversifying its output and operations and targeting its research and analysis to benefit an increasing number of governments, humanitarian organizations, and civil society actors around the globe concerned with improving the conditions for a more stable and secure world. SIPRI has done so in the face of some difficult challenges, but has only solidified its position as one of the world's leading research institutions.

I thank SIPRI's management as well as the entire staff of the institution, past and present, for their dedication and insight which has consistently kept SIPRI in a league apart. In passing the chairmanship to my successor, I wish also to thank my fellow Governing Board members—a stellar international assemblage of remarkable stature—for their leadership and commitment. Finally, I thank SIPRI's many supporters and friends who recognize and benefit from the value of this remarkable institution. It has been a great honour and truly a privilege to work with all of you, and I look forward to continuing my association with you in different capacities in the years ahead.

Rolf Ekéus
Chairman, SIPRI Governing Board
May 2010

Acknowledgements

The preparation and publication of the SIPRI Yearbook is a remarkable task accomplished through the efforts of a host of remarkable people. I would like to begin by giving a special note of gratitude and admiration to the Chairman of the SIPRI Governing Board, Ambassador Rolf Ekéus, for his dedicated service to Sweden and the world, as well as to SIPRI. While he will step down as our Chairman in 2010, we at SIPRI look forward to continuing our association with him.

I also thank all the authors for their expert contributions to this volume. In addition, grateful thanks go to the ever-superb editors, David Cruickshank, Joey Fox, Jetta Gilligan Borg and Caspar Trimmer, for their tireless work to assure the excellence of the Yearbook. For their exceptional support for SIPRI's work, I give special thanks to Daniel Nord, Deputy Director, Ian Anthony, Research Coordinator, Elisbet Rendert, SIPRI Chief Financial Officer, Nenne Bodell, Director of the Library and Documentation Department, Gerd Hagmeyer-Gaverus, Director of the Information Technology Department, and Cynthia Loo, Executive Assistant to the Director and Chairman. Thanks too to Anna Helleday, who in mid-2009 retired from her position as head of SIPRI's Finance and Administration Department after many years of dedicated service to SIPRI. I am also grateful to the SIPRI Governing Board, and to our many institutional supporters, for their guidance and commitment.

Dr Bates Gill
SIPRI Director
May 2010

Abstracts

SIPRI Yearbook 2010: Armaments, Disarmament and International Security

Oxford University Press, Oxford, 2010, 580 pp.
(Stockholm International Peace Research Institute)
ISSN 0953-0282
ISBN 978-0-19-958112-2

Goodby, J. E., 'A world without nuclear weapons: fantasy or necessity', *SIPRI Yearbook 2010*, pp. 17–34.

Thinking about how to achieve a word without nuclear weapons is a high priority. The 2010 New START treaty opens the door to deeper Russian–US reductions in nuclear weapons. Other states that possess nuclear weapons will have to be involved early on if momentum is to be sustained. Supporting agreements will be necessary that will block the acquisition of nuclear weapons by additional states and the development of alternative threats, such as biological weapons. Deterrence will remain in the forms of reconstitutable nuclear forces and of modern conventional capabilities. The ability of the UN Security Council to enforce compliance and the authority of regional institutions will also require strengthening.

Part I. Security and conflicts, 2009

Stepanova, E., 'Armed conflict, crime and criminal violence', *SIPRI Yearbook 2010*, pp. 37–60.

Continuing proliferation of criminal violence in armed conflict settings and the growing links between crime and conflict underscore the need to more actively integrate the study of organized crime and criminal violence into the analysis of organized collective violence. In 2009 this was illustrated by the case of piracy rooted in the weak, conflict-torn state of Somalia and the interaction between the opium economy and conflict in Afghanistan. Even in the absence of classic armed conflict, systemic criminal violence, such as drug-trafficking-related violence in Mexico, may match conflict in scale and intensity and threaten to undermine human security and social order.

Wiharta, S. and Blair, S., 'Civilian roles in peace operations', *SIPRI Yearbook 2010*, pp. 87–106.

Civilians play an ever more central role in multidimensional and integrated peace-keeping and peacebuilding operations. Although the civilian dimension has been strengthened by a range of recent institutional innovations, peace operations are plagued by the persistent challenges of deploying the appropriate people at the right time and in the appropriate numbers. The UN Mission in Sudan (UNMIS) illustrates the importance of addressing the civilian capacity gap, while taking into account the interrelation of such factors as financing peace operations and recruitment. It also highlights the need for a critical analysis of the purpose and objectives of each civilian function in order to avoid duplication of tasks within missions.

Bailes, A. J. K. and Cottey, A., 'Euro-Atlantic security and institutions: rebalancing in the midst of global change', *SIPRI Yearbook 2010*, pp. 149–74.

The main Euro-Atlantic institutions—the EU, NATO and the OSCE—are challenged by recent security setbacks, still-evolving threat patterns and shifts in global power relations. Burdened by the Afghanistan operation, NATO needs to revisit the more general balance between its tasks abroad and safety at home. The EU has belatedly strengthened its security governance with the Lisbon Treaty but remains a weak military actor and divided in other critical dimensions. Interest in pan-European cooperation appears higher than for some years. Europe–US relations are smoother under President Barack Obama but may grow more distant as other world powers demand greater attention.

Part II. Military spending and armaments, 2009

Perlo-Freeman, S., Ismail, O. and Solmirano, C., 'Military expenditure', *SIPRI Yearbook 2009*, pp. 177–200.

World military expenditure reached $1531 billion in 2009, a 6 per cent real-terms increase. The global economic crisis had little noticeable impact on military spending, with increases by 14 of the 15 top spenders. The new Obama Administration has not halted rising US military spending, although there has been some change in focus. In many developing regions, increased natural resource revenues have contributed to rapidly increased military spending, although falls in commodity prices slowed this trend in 2009. The conflict in Afghanistan is proving increasingly costly for countries involved.

Jackson, S. T., 'Arms production', *SIPRI Yearbook 2010*, pp. 251–71.

Despite the global financial crisis and economic recession, the arms industry continued to see high levels of arms sales in 2008 and, according to initial assessments, in 2009. Arms sales of the SIPRI Top 100 reached $385 billion in 2008. These increases were in part due to sales of military equipment and services for the conflicts in Afghanistan and Iraq and to force modernization efforts (e.g. in Russia). While the number of large acquisitions fell in 2009, there was more consolidation in the Israeli, Russian and US industries as well as a continued pattern of arms-producing companies diversifying into the security industry.

Holtom, P., Bromley, M., Wezeman, P. D. and Wezeman, S. T., 'International arms transfers', *SIPRI Yearbook 2010*, pp. 285–305.

The volume of deliveries of major conventional arms was 22 per cent higher in 2005–2009 than in 2000–2004. The five largest suppliers—the USA, Russia, Germany, France and the UK—accounted for 76 per cent of exports. China, India, South Korea, the United Arab Emirates and Greece were the largest recipients. A pattern of reactive arms acquisitions is emerging in several regions. In North Africa a significant increase in the volume of Algerian arms imports has been followed by large Moroccan orders; this is likely to influence Libyan plans. The rebuilding of Iraq's armed forces has been affected by the economic crisis and declining oil prices.

Kile, S. N., Fedchenko, V., Gopalaswamy, B. and Kristensen, H. M., 'World nuclear forces', *SIPRI Yearbook 2010*, pp. 333–66.

At the start of 2010 eight nuclear weapon states possessed more than 7500 operational nuclear weapons. The overall decline in the number of nuclear weapons in 2009 was due primarily to reductions by Russia and the USA in order to meet the limit set by the 2002 SORT Treaty. However, many of the withdrawn warheads have been placed in storage and could be redeployed. Despite signs of a further resurgence of public interest in nuclear disarmament in 2009, all of the legally recognized nuclear weapon states appeared determined to retain their nuclear arsenals for the indefinite future and were either modernizing their nuclear forces or had announced plans to do so.

Part III. Non-proliferation, arms control and disarmament, 2009

Kile, S. N., 'Nuclear arms control and non-proliferation', *SIPRI Yearbook 2010*, pp. 379–401.

In 2009 progress was made in advancing nuclear disarmament and non-proliferation efforts. Russia and the USA opened negotiations on a new strategic arms reduction treaty. The UN Security Council adopted a resolution aimed at enhancing nuclear security practices and addressing the threat of nuclear terrorism. Two new nuclear weapon-free zone treaties entered into force, one covering Central Asia and the other Africa. The nuclear programmes of Iran and North Korea continued to raise proliferation concerns. North Korea conducted a second nuclear test explosion and resumed the production of plutonium for nuclear weapons. In Iran the International Atomic Energy Agency remained unable to resolve questions about Iranian nuclear activities with possible military dimensions.

Hart, J. and Clevestig, P., 'Reducing security threats from chemical and biological materials', *SIPRI Yearbook 2010*, pp. 403–24.

During 2009 states continued to develop strategies for countering threats from the misuse of chemical and biological materials. Meetings of the states parties to the Chemical Weapons Convention and the Biological and Toxin Weapons Convention focused on universality and national implementation strategies. The EU and the USA presented new chemical, biological, radiological and nuclear (CBRN) policies that emphasize the importance of enhancing international assistance and cooperation on related technologies for peaceful purposes. Other trends were the move towards dealing with misuses of the life sciences and emerging technologies and recognition of the importance of existing public health infrastructure to address international disease surveillance challenges and threats such as the H1N1 pandemic.

Lachowski, Z., 'Conventional arms control', *SIPRI Yearbook 2010*, pp. 425–46.

Endeavours to rejuvenate European conventional arms control intensified in 2009. The European security dialogue continued stressing the need to revitalize arms control and military confidence and security building. The proposal by Russia for a European security treaty gave hope for progress. The 1990 Treaty on Conventional Armed Forces in Europe, however, has remained in abeyance since December 2007. Further steps were taken to make the Western Balkans subregional arms control framework more self-reliant. Efforts to control so-called inhumane weapons continued in 2009, although with less dynamism than demonstrated in 2008 by the 'Oslo process' on cluster munitions.

Bauer, S. and Mićić, I., 'Controls on security-related international transfers', *SIPRI Yearbook 2010*, pp. 447–66.

Non-proliferation efforts have shifted focus from physical movement of goods to analysis of the elements of a transaction that should be subject to control. The main export control forums attempt to effectively control exports of items that may be used in nuclear, biological and chemical weapons and in their missile delivery systems. They also discuss intangible transfers of technology, enforcement, good practices and engagement with non-participating states. The EU has increased cooperation with non-EU countries through technical assistance programmes. In 2009 it adopted a strengthened regulation to control transit and brokering of dual-use items that may be intended for use in connection with weapons of mass destruction. A new directive to facilitate the movement of defence goods inside the EU also entered into force in 2009.

Abbreviations and conventions

ABM	Anti-ballistic missile	CEEAC	Communauté Economique des Etats de l'Afrique Centrale (Economic Community Central African States, ECCAS)
ACV	Armoured combat vehicle		
AG	Australia Group		
ALCM	Air-launched cruise missile		
APC	Armoured personnel carrier	CFE	Conventional Armed Forces in Europe (Treaty)
APEC	Asia–Pacific Economic Cooperation		
APM	Anti-personnel mine	CFSP	Common Foreign and Security Policy
APT	ASEAN Plus Three	CICA	Conference on Interaction and Confidence-building Measures in Asia
ARF	ASEAN Regional Forum		
ASAT	Anti-satellite		
ASEAN	Association of Southeast Asian Nations	CIS	Commonwealth of Independent States
ATT	Arms trade treaty	COPAX	Conseil de Paix et de Sécurité de l'Afrique Centrale (Central Africa Peace and Security Council)
ATTU	Atlantic-to-the Urals (zone)		
AU	African Union		
BMD	Ballistic missile defence		
BSEC	Organization of the Black Sea Economic Cooperation	CSBM	Confidence- and security-building measure
BTWC	Biological and Toxin Weapons Convention	CSCAP	Council for Security Cooperation in the Asia Pacific
BW	Biological weapon/warfare	CSDP	Common Security and Defence Policy
CADSP	Common African Defence and Security Policy		
CAR	Central African Republic	CSTO	Collective Security Treaty Organization
CBM	Confidence-building measure	CTBT	Comprehensive Nuclear-Test-Ban Treaty
CBRN	Chemical, biological, radiological and nuclear	CTBTO	Comprehensive Nuclear-Test-Ban Treaty Organization
CBSS	Council of the Baltic Sea States		
CBW	Chemical and biological weapon/warfare	CTR	Co-operative Threat Reduction
CCM	Convention on Cluster Munitions	CW	Chemical weapon/warfare
		CWC	Chemical Weapons Convention
CCW	Certain Conventional Weapons (Convention)	DDR	Disarmament, demobilization and reintegration
CD	Conference on Disarmament	DPKO	UN Department of Peacekeeping Operations
CDS	Consejo de Defensa Suramericano (South American Defence Council)	DPRK	Democratic People's Republic of Korea (North Korea)

DRC	Democratic Republic of the Congo
EAEC	European Atomic Energy Community (Euratom)
EAPC	Euro-Atlantic Partnership Council
ECOWAS	Economic Community of West African States
EDA	European Defence Agency
ENP	European Neighbourhood Policy
ERW	Explosive remnants of war
EU	European Union
FMCT	Fissile material cut-off treaty
FSC	Forum for Security Co-operation
FY	Financial year
FYROM	Former Yugoslav Republic of Macedonia
G8	Group of Eight (industrialized states)
GCC	Gulf Cooperation Council
GDP	Gross domestic product
GLCM	Ground-launched cruise missile
GNEP	Global Nuclear Energy Partnership
GNI	Gross national income
GNP	Gross national product
GTRI	Global Threat Reduction Initiative
GUAM	Georgia, Ukraine, Azerbaijan and Moldova
HCOC	Hague Code of Conduct
HEU	Highly enriched uranium
IAEA	International Atomic Energy Agency
ICBM	Intercontinental ballistic missile
ICC	International Criminal Court
ICJ	International Court of Justice
ICTR	International Criminal Tribunal for Rwanda
ICTY	International Criminal Tribunal for the former Yugoslavia
IED	Improvised explosive device
IGAD	Intergovernmental Authority on Development
IGC	Intergovernmental Conference
IMF	International Monetary Fund
INDA	International non-proliferation and disarmament assistance
INF	Intermediate-range Nuclear Forces (Treaty)
IRBM	Intermediate-range ballistic missile
ISAF	International Security Assistance Force
JCG	Joint Consultative Group
JCIC	Joint Compliance and Inspection Commission
JHA	Justice and Home Affairs
LEU	Low-enriched uranium
MANPADS	Man-portable air defence system
MDGs	Millennium Development Goals
MER	Market exchange rate
MIRV	Multiple independently targetable re-entry vehicle
MOTAPM	Mines other than anti-personnel mines
MTCR	Missile Technology Control Regime
NAM	Non-Aligned Movement
NATO	North Atlantic Treaty Organization
NBC	Nuclear, biological and chemical (weapons)
NGO	Non-governmental organization
NNWS	Non-nuclear weapon state
NPT	Non-Proliferation Treaty
NRF	NATO Response Force
NSG	Nuclear Suppliers Group
NWFZ	Nuclear weapon-free zone
NWS	Nuclear weapon state

OAS	Organization of American States	SALW	Small arms and light weapons
OCCAR	Organisation Conjointe de Coopération en matière d'Armement (Organisation for Joint Armament Cooperation)	SAM	Surface-to-air missile
		SCO	Shanghai Cooperation Organization
		SCSL	Special Court for Sierra Leone
ODA	Official development assistance	SECI	Southeast European Cooperative Initiative
OECD	Organisation for Economic Co-operation and Development	SLBM	Submarine-launched ballistic missile
		SLCM	Sea-launched cruise missile
OIC	Organization of the Islamic Conference	SORT	Strategic Offensive Reductions Treaty
OPANAL	Organismo para la Proscripción de las Armas Nucleares en la América Latina y el Caribe (Agency for the Prohibition of Nuclear Weapons in Latin America and the Caribbean)	SRBM	Short-range ballistic missile
		SRCC	Sub-Regional Consultative Commission
		SSM	Surface-to-surface missile
		SSR	Security sector reform
		START	Strategic Arms Reduction Treaty
OPCW	Organisation for the Prohibition of Chemical Weapons	TLE	Treaty-limited equipment
		UAE	United Arab Emirates
OPEC	Organization of the Petroleum Exporting Countries	UNASUR	Unión de Naciones Suramericanas (Union of South American Nations)
OSCC	Open Skies Consultative Commission	UAV	Unmanned aerial vehicle
OSCE	Organization for Security and Co-operation in Europe	UCAV	Unmanned combat air vehicle
P5	Five permanent members of the UN Security Council	USAID	US Agency for International Development
PFP	Partnership for Peace	UN	United Nations
PPP	Purchasing power parity	UNDP	UN Development Programme
PRT	Provincial reconstruction team	UNHCR	UN High Commissioner for Refugees
PSC	Private security company	UNODA	UN Office for Disarmament Affairs
PSI	Proliferation Security Initiative	UNROCA	UN Register of Conventional Arms
R&D	Research and development	WA	Wassenaar Arrangement
SAARC	South Asian Association for Regional Co-operation	WEU	Western European Union
SADC	Southern African Development Community	WMD	Weapon(s) of mass destruction

Conventions

. .	Data not available or not applicable
–	Nil or a negligible figure
( )	Uncertain data
b.	Billion (thousand million)
kg	Kilogram
km	Kilometre (1000 metres)
m.	Million
th.	Thousand
tr.	Trillion (million million)
$	US dollars, unless otherwise indicated
€	Euros

Geographical regions and subregions

Africa	Consisting of North Africa (Algeria, Libya, Morocco and Tunisia, but excluding Egypt) and sub-Saharan Africa
Americas	Consisting of North America (Canada and the USA), Central America and the Caribbean (including Mexico), and South America
Asia and Oceania	Consisting of Central Asia, East Asia (with South East Asia), Oceania and South Asia (including Afghanistan)
Europe	Consisting of Eastern Europe (Armenia, Azerbaijan, Belarus, Georgia, Moldova, Russia and Ukraine) and Western and Central Europe (with South Eastern Europe); in discussions of military expenditure, Turkey is included in Western and Central Europe
Middle East	Consisting of Egypt, Iran, Iraq, Israel, Jordan, Kuwait, Lebanon, Syria, Turkey and the states of the Arabian peninsula

Introduction

International security, armaments and disarmament in 2010

Chapter 1. A world without nuclear weapons: fantasy or necessity?

Introduction
International security, armaments and disarmament in 2010

BATES GILL

I. Overview

Assessing the past year

While the past year saw some encouraging steps in relation to nuclear disarmament and in the resolution of some regional conflicts, overall the world faced continuing and growing challenges to security, stability and peace. The financial crisis and economic recession that affected most of the globe appeared to have little effect on levels of military expenditure, arms production or arms transfers. On the other hand, the crisis probably did undermine the willingness and ability of major governments and multilateral institutions to invest other, non-military resources to address the challenges and instabilities that threaten societies and individuals around the world.

The conflicts in Iraq and Afghanistan continued. Some greater stability came to Iraq, and the United States announced the withdrawal of combat troops from Iraqi cities and villages in June 2009. Conditions worsened in Afghanistan. The USA more than doubled its troop levels in Afghanistan—from 32 000 at the end of 2008 to 68 000 at the end of 2009—with US President Barack Obama authorizing the deployment of an additional 30 000 troops in December 2009. Across the world, 17 major armed conflicts carried on in such places as Colombia, the Democratic Republic of the Congo, the Palestinian territories, Pakistan, the Philippines and Somalia. Major armed conflicts involving Rwanda and Uganda began anew in 2009. Fighting in Sri Lanka between government forces and the Liberation Tigers of Tamil Elam came to an end in 2009, but some 250 000 civilians were caught up in the fighting with significant losses of innocent life. Violence in Pakistan's Swat Valley region escalated in 2009, to include a major Pakistani military offensive against Taliban insurgents; hundreds of thousands of civilians were displaced and hundreds killed as a result of the fighting. Some of the greatest violence occurred not in traditionally defined, politically motivated conflict, but rather between Mexican authorities and criminal organizations involved in the drug trade, leaving thousands dead.

The year saw setbacks on the arms control and disarmament front as well. The Democratic People's Republic of Korea (DPRK, or North Korea) defied the expressed will of the United Nations as well as the concerns of neighbouring states by test-launching missiles in April, May and July and by carrying out a nuclear explosion in May. North Korea announced that it would permanently leave the Six Party Talks, informed the International Atomic Energy Agency (IAEA) that it would no longer cooperate with it, asked IAEA inspectors to leave the country and stated that it intends to reactivate the partially dismantled nuclear facility at Yongbyon. Concerns intensified throughout the year about Iran's nuclear intentions, especially in light of revelations in 2009 that the country was building a previously undeclared uranium enrichment plant, housed in an Islamic Revolutionary Guard Corps base near the city of Qom.

The past year saw some promising developments. In April President Obama's speech in Prague set forth a commitment to advance towards a world free of nuclear weapons. This set the tone for progress in Russian–US negotiations for further reductions in their strategic arsenals and helped lead to the landmark adoption by the UN Security Council, with 14 heads of state and government at the table, of Resolution 1887. The resolution reaffirmed the support of the Security Council for the goals of the 1968 Non-Proliferation Treaty (NPT), including nuclear disarmament and strengthening of the NPT regime, and urged action to reduce the threat of nuclear terrorism. Adoption of the resolution marked the first time since the mid-1990s that the Security Council put in place comprehensive and politically binding commitments on nuclear non-proliferation and disarmament. In part as a result of these milestones, Obama received the Nobel Peace Prize in 2009 for, in the words of the Chairman of the Norwegian Nobel Committee, his 'vision of and work for a world free from nuclear weapons'. In addition, during 2009 two nuclear weapon-free zone treaties entered into force: the Treaty of Semipalatinsk in Central Asia and the Treaty of Pelindaba in Africa. The Conference on Disarmament (CD) in Geneva was also able to agree, after a 12-year stalemate, on a draft programme of work, including the negotiation of a fissile material cut-off treaty. However, as of the end of 2009, the CD had failed to take the necessary procedural steps to actually begin substantive negotiations. In other positive developments, the peace process that was launched in Burundi in late 2008 held throughout 2009, free of major outbreaks of renewed violence.

Key themes of *SIPRI Yearbook 2010*

In this volume, the 41st edition of the SIPRI Yearbook, 34 leading experts from 16 countries examine and analyse these and other critical developments of the past year in such fields as international and regional security, armed conflict, multilateral peace operations, military spending, the arms industries, the conventional arms trade, non-proliferation, arms control, and confidence- and security-building measures. The core of the volume is 12 chapters organized in three main parts. Part I sets the scene by examining some of the key developments in international security related to conflict, conflict prevention and regional security relationships. Part II presents a broad range of information and analysis on global, regional and national trends in armaments, including on military expenditure, arms production, the arms trade and nuclear forces. Part III takes measure of developments on the disarmament scene over the past year, including assessments of nuclear non-proliferation and arms control, efforts to reduce chemical- and biological-related threats, conventional arms control, and controlling the transfer of other sensitive goods and technologies that may pose security concerns.

The chapters in this volume are supplemented by extensive appendices and annexes that provide further data and documentation on major armed conflict, multilateral peace operations, military spending, arms producers, the conventional arms trade, nuclear arsenals, international arms embargoes, arms control and non-proliferation agreements, multilateral security institutions and a chronology of major events related to international arms control, armaments and disarmament in 2009. As was the case for *SIPRI Yearbook 2009*, this year's edition again presents the Global Peace Index (GPI) developed by the Australia-based Institute for Economics and Peace in association with the Economist Intelligence Unit.

Three important themes emerge from the research and analysis in *SIPRI Yearbook 2010*.

1. The world's attention is increasingly drawn to the challenges and prospects for nuclear non-proliferation and disarmament. Both expectations and fears in relation to nuclear weapons were heightened by, among other important developments, the April 2009 Prague speech by President Obama, the detonation of a nuclear device by North Korea in May 2009, ongoing disarmament negotiations between Russia and the USA, and heightened concerns over Iran's nuclear activities. While there are hopes for continued nuclear disarmament in the future, nuclear weapons maintained their central place in the security planning of those states which possess them.

2. In the face of myriad security challenges, many of them arising from non-state actors and a continued diffusion of the means of violence, the multilateral institutions charged with mitigating these challenges continue their struggle to achieve mandates, realize reform and confront new realities. As discussed in this volume, this trend is starkly illustrated by the

challenges and choices facing multilateral peace operations, the trans-atlantic security alliance, the Common Security and Defence Policy of the European Union (EU), the international non-proliferation regime and dis-armament process, export control mechanisms and multilateral arms embargoes.

3. Despite the financial crisis and its aftershocks around the globe in 2008 and 2009, sustained upward trends in military spending, arms prod-uction and arms transfers continued essentially uninterrupted. The 'mili-tary burden'—the share of military spending within gross domestic prod-uct—likewise increased significantly.

II. *SIPRI Yearbook 2010*: highlights and findings

SIPRI Yearbook 2010 begins with a feature essay by one of the world's fore-most authorities on questions of arms control and disarmament, Ambas-sador James E. Goodby. In light of the increased attention now focused on these issues, his chapter provides a timely and insightful *tour d'horizon* of the many near- and longer-term challenges and opportunities for nuclear disarmament and non-proliferation and the vision of a world free of nuclear weapons. The chapter examines both procedural and political issues of nuclear disarmament, and reviews and analyses such important issues as Russian–US bilateral arms reductions; future multilateral dis-armament, global and regional agreements necessary to govern reductions and the elimination of nuclear weapons; and the role of deterrence in a world free of nuclear weapons. The chapter also provides a short history of US approaches to nuclear weapons and arms control to demonstrate how a country's views can change over time to be more favourably disposed towards disarmament and the elimination of nuclear weapons.

The chapter reaches some sober but hopeful conclusions. Recognizing that nuclear weapons 'have not lost their doomsday qualities', Goodby nevertheless sees a time of opportunity ahead. Importantly, in his view, world leaders are increasingly of the mind that, whatever advantages nuclear weapons may have, these are increasingly outweighed by their dis-advantages. He clearly makes the case that eliminating nuclear weapons will in no way be an easy task. Yet, because the question today is 'how can it be done?' rather than 'should it be done?', Goodby believes that the inter-national community is in a far better position than ever before in the nuclear age to take steps towards a world without nuclear weapons.

Security and conflicts

The three chapters of part I focus on important developments in inter-national security. This year these chapters examine the linkages between

crime and conflict, the civilian dimension of peace operations and Euro
Atlantic security institutions.

Focusing on the interrelationship of crime and conflict in many parts of
the world today, chapter 2 opens by making the point that crime and criminal violence can be as great a threat to stability as traditionally defined,
politically motivated armed conflict. To elaborate and examine the crime–
conflict linkage, and encourage further analysis of this relationship, the
chapter first provides an overview of the topic, outlines global trends in
crime and criminal violence, and discusses the nature and scale of links
between crime and armed conflict. In addition, it provides a number of case
studies to analyse the causes and impacts of organized crime within armed
conflicts (as in Afghanistan and Somalia) and to compare and contrast
armed conflict with intense criminal violence of a comparable scale (as in
Mexico).

In summarizing its principal findings, the author concludes with the
reminder that criminal violence is far more common than armed conflict or
one-sided violence against civilians. At the same time, it cannot be assumed
that close associations will develop between insurgent groups and organized criminals—in some cases that may be true, but not in all. In addition,
large-scale criminal activity in conflict and post-conflict areas may help
fund armed opposition groups, but they can also profit other political
actors including those loyal to recognized government authorities. In many
cases, state dysfunction, rather than criminal activity itself, may be the
more important factor in explaining violent instability, including criminal
violence. As such, combating organized crime in conflict and post-conflict
settings cannot be separated from overall efforts aimed at conflict resolution. At a minimum, far more study and resources should be devoted to
understanding and responding to the linkages between criminal activity
and traditionally defined armed conflict.

Chapter 2 is followed by two important appendices. One, prepared by the
Uppsala Conflict Data Program (UCDP), presents data and analysis on the
patterns in major armed conflict from 2000 to 2009. Two conflicts appear
in this appendix which did not appear in 2008: Rwanda and Uganda. The
other appendix is the Global Peace Index. First appearing in *SIPRI Yearbook 2009*, the GPI employs 23 indicators to rank 149 countries by their
relative state of peace. New Zealand stands at the top of the index as the
most peaceful country; Iraq is ranked as the least peaceful.

The authors of chapter 3 provide in-depth analysis and information
related to multilateral peace operations and peacebuilding activities. This
includes a highly informative appendix that presents extensive details on
the 54 multilateral peace missions in operation during 2009. This year the
chapter takes a close look at the increasingly important role that civilians
play as part of peace operations and peacebuilding worldwide. The authors

explain the drivers behind the expansion in the civilian dimension in peace operations and describe in particular the efforts undertaken in this regard by the United Nations, the European Union, the African Union and individual states to meet the growing 'civilian gap' in peace operations and peacebuilding around the world. The chapter uses the example of the United Nations Mission in Sudan (UNMIS) to highlight the systemic challenges for civilian operations, not least in terms of planning, recruit-ment, deployment and coherency of mission mandate.

The authors find that, 10 years after the seminal Brahimi Report pro-posed comprehensive reforms for the UN peacekeeping system—including an early call to strengthen civilian capacities in peace operations—the international community's record is decidedly mixed. The number of civil-ians mandated for roles in UN missions has increased, as has the number of civilian peace missions operated by regional organizations. However, these efforts still lack conceptual coherency and intra- and inter-organizational cooperation, and major operational challenges exist both at headquarters and in the field. Noting that the problem is far more than 'deploying the right experts in the right numbers', the chapter concludes cautiously: the emergent ambition to significantly reform and improve civilian operations is timely and much needed, but should not have over-expectations of suc-cess unless fundamental systemic, bureaucratic and operational challenges can be dealt with.

Chapter 4 examines the situation facing Euro-Atlantic security institu-tions at a time when they are undergoing considerable change, reflection and reassessment. The authors note that the current situation has its roots in longer-term trends, but that current rethinking about Euro-Atlantic security institutions has been hastened and made more urgent by the August 2008 Georgia–Russia conflict, the ongoing challenges of conflicts in Afghanistan and Iraq, and the impact of the global financial crisis in 2008 and 2009. In particular, the chapter delves into recent developments and difficulties for the North Atlantic Treaty Organization (NATO), the EU and the Organization for Security and Co-operation in Europe (OSCE).

Based on this analysis, the authors offer a number of findings and recom-mendations. Euro-Atlantic security institutions can justly claim credit for many successes, such as their role in the peaceful reunification of Europe and managing conflict in the Western Balkans. However, new challenges await, not least those associated with newly emerging global and trans-national security threats and relations with Russia and the other post-Soviet states. In the coming year, all three institutions will undertake important formal and informal reviews of their security strategies for the future. While the authors recognize that the current security-related chal-lenges to the Euro-Atlantic area—within that area, at its borders and in the wider global environment—argue for a new realism, that tendency should not lead to a lack of solidarity or, worse, to defeatism. At the same time, the authors note that a narrow geographic focus on Euro-Atlantic security cannot be sustained: transatlantic partners must recognize and act on the global diffusion of power and, accordingly, seek solutions to security challenges through cooperation with global institutions where other, non-Western interests are represented.

Military spending and armaments

The four chapters of part II provide some of the world's most in-depth and authoritative open-source analysis and information on military expenditure, arms production, conventional arms transfers and nuclear forces.

Chapter 5 documents and explains developments in military spending worldwide and region by region, with a special focus on these developments in 2009. More in-depth consideration is given this year to the effect of resource revenues on spending in Nigeria, Chile, Venezuela and Iraq and the impact of the conflict in Afghanistan on spending by the United Kingdom, the USA and Afghanistan itself. Detailed appendices for this chapter provide military expenditure figures for 165 countries for 2000–2009 and the reporting of military expenditure data to the United Nations and to SIPRI for 2001–2009.

Chapter 5 finds that global military spending rose to $1531 billion in 2009, 6 per cent higher in real terms than in 2008. Military spending worldwide was 49 per cent higher in 2009 than it was in 2000. In general, the global financial crisis has apparently not had an effect on military spending by major powers such as the USA (which accounted for 54 per cent of the increase in world military spending in 2009) and Russia, nor on the military spending of emerging regional powers, such as Brazil, China and India. Indeed, 14 of the top 15 military spenders increased their military expenditure in 2009 over 2008.

Developments within the world's arms-producing sector are described and analysed in chapter 6. Special focus is given to trends in mergers and acquisitions within the sector and to an extensive assessment of the impact of the global financial crisis and economic recession on the arms industry. This chapter also provides appendices cataloguing the 'SIPRI Top 100' arms-producing companies for 2008 and the major corporate acquisitions in the arms industries of member states of the Organisation for Economic Co-operation and Development (OECD) in 2009.

In step with the continuing increases in military spending noted in chapter 5, global arms production also continues to rise—suggesting no immediate impact from the financial crisis and recession. The world's largest weapon producers had arms sales of $385 billion in 2008, an increase of $39 billion over 2007. The top arms producers have seen annual increases in arms sales every year since 2002. For the first time since SIPRI began listing the world's top arms producers more than 20 years ago, a non-US firm—BAE Systems—tops the register. Russian arms companies had a strong showing in 2008, and firms delivering military-related services, armoured vehicles and unmanned aerial vehicles continued to prosper. With continued growth in military spending, ongoing major conflicts in Afghanistan and Iraq, and the monopsonistic nature of the arms industry, this sector looks likely to emerge relatively unscathed from the financial crisis and economic recession affecting much of the globe.

Chapter 7 presents the world's most comprehensive, open-source data set and in-depth analysis of the global trade in major conventional weapons. In addition to offering insights on the main trends in international arms transfers, the chapter also provides more specific analysis on major supplier states—the USA, Russia, Germany, France and the UK, which together accounted for 76 per cent of the world's arms exports—and gives special focus this year to arms transfers to North African states and to Iraq. The chapter's appendices include data and information on the suppliers and recipients of major conventional weapons worldwide, on the financial value of the international arms trade and on certain mechanisms—such as the UN Register of Conventional Arms and other multilateral and national reporting systems—that are intended to bring more transparency to the arms trade.

The chapter documents a continuing upward trajectory for the international arms trade: in 2005–2009 the volume of major conventional weapon transfers increased by 22 per cent in comparison with 2000–2004. China, India, the Republic of Korea (ROK, or South Korea), the United Arab Emirates and Greece were the top five recipients in 2005–2009, followed by Israel, Singapore, the USA, Algeria and Pakistan. The authors also find that the leading supplier positions of the USA and Russia are not likely to face a serious challenge in the foreseeable future. Nevertheless, their share of global arms exports is declining over time as a growing number of important second-tier suppliers find success in this marketplace. The chapter predicts that China, which has been the leading arms importer for much of the past decade, will fall from its top spot as its arms imports decline. The chapter also points to evidence of competitive behaviour in certain acquisitions by states in Latin America, the Middle East, North Africa and South East Asia, all regions that have seen significant growth in their arms imports in recent years.

Chapter 8 assesses developments in doctrine and deployments of the nuclear forces of the eight countries with nuclear weapons—the USA, Russia, China, the UK, France, India, Pakistan and Israel—and also provides detailed information on North Korea's military nuclear capabilities and gives special focus to the nuclear explosion it carried out in May 2009.

The chapter provides extensive analysis and numerous tables on the current nuclear arsenals and delivery systems of the eight nuclear-armed states, plus detailed appendices on global stocks of fissile materials and on nuclear explosions in 1945–2009.

The chapter notes that at the beginning of 2010 the eight nuclear weapon states possessed more than 7500 operational nuclear weapons, with almost 2000 of them maintained in a state of high operational alert. Counting all nuclear warheads, including those in operation, spares, those in storage and those intact warheads slated for dismantlement, these eight countries possess a total in excess of 22 000 warheads, more than 90 per cent of which are in the arsenals of Russia and the USA. A slight decline in the number of operational warheads results primarily from disarmament by Russia and the USA pursuant to the 2002 Strategic Offensive Reductions Treaty (SORT). On the other hand, the chapter concludes with the finding that, despite increased attention to global disarmament, the nuclear weapon states are committed to retaining their nuclear arsenals for many years to come and are taking steps to modernize these forces.

Non-proliferation, arms control and disarmament

Part III of this volume examines issues related to the control and diminution of weapons, weapon technologies, and other weapon-related materials and technologies. Specifically, these chapters consider nuclear non-proliferation and arms control, efforts to reduce chemical- and biological-related threats, conventional arms control, and controlling the transfer of other sensitive goods and technologies that may pose security concerns.

Chapter 9 provides a comprehensive overview and analysis of the developments in 2009 in nuclear arms control and non-proliferation. It describes and analyses a range of important developments: Russian–US arms control talks, the Iranian and North Korean nuclear programmes, suspected undeclared nuclear activities in Myanmar and Syria, and preparations for the 2010 Review Conference of the NPT.

In presenting its findings, the author flags the fact that there was some increased momentum for nuclear arms control in 2009—the beginning of formal negotiations on strategic weapon reductions between Russia and the USA and the entry into force of two new nuclear weapon-free zones. However, the year saw little to no progress in addressing concerns related to nuclear programmes in Iran and North Korea. Moreover, the CD in Geneva, which was able to agree to a draft programme of work for the first time in more than a decade, was unable to agree on the additional procedural steps necessary to actually begin substantive negotiations. Even Russian–US negotiations on the treaty to succeed the 1991 Treaty on the Reduction and Limitation of Strategic Offensive Arms (START Treaty) were not without complications. Sticking points included the monitoring mechanisms for verifying numerical limits and Russia's concerns related to the USA's advanced conventional weapon systems. The START Treaty expired in December 2009 and no follow-on was agreed until the New START Treaty was signed in April 2010. Overall, however, 2009 marked higher expectations about nuclear arms control, especially as top political leaders around the world began to give serious attention to further nuclear arms reductions and even the possibility of eliminating nuclear weapons in the long-term future. The key question for 2010 and beyond is how to put these expectations into action.

Chapter 10 focuses on international efforts to reduce threats from chemical and biological materials. The chapter first assesses the evolution of threat perceptions related to chemical and biological materials. The chapter also describes and analyses developments in 2009 related to the control and disarmament of chemical and biological weapons and to allegations of chemical and biological weapon development or use, such as in Afghanistan, Algeria, Israel, North Korea and Sri Lanka. The chapter also outlines efforts aimed at chemical and biological warfare prevention, response and remediation by such organizations as the United Nations, the European Union, the scientific and public health communities, and the private sector.

The authors reach a number of interesting conclusions. Threat perceptions related to chemical and biological materials are moving away from an overwhelming concern with the lethality of a given agent to a broader concern with not only loss of life, but also the effects of a chemical or biological attack on public order, critical infrastructure and the environment, with each type of threat requiring different approaches for prevention, remediation and response. In addition, the international community is moving away from its traditional focus on identifying and eliminating state military programmes for chemical and biological weapons, and placing greater emphasis on the control and oversight of the trade and use of sensitive chemical and biological materials. The chapter flags continuing efforts in this regard to develop licensing mechanisms to oversee activities in scientific research, as well as within the chemical industry and biotechnology sectors—such as work related to gene synthesis—which have potential security implications. The authors suggest caution not to exaggerate the potential damage to life and property that could result from biological and chemical attacks, and that more should be done by public authorities to promote a more balanced and realistic understanding of the threats posed by chemical and biological weapons.

Conventional arms control is the central focus of chapter 11. The chapter provides a detailed examination of important developments in the evolving architecture of arms control in Europe, such as the future of the 1990

Treaty on Conventional Armed Forces in Europe (CFE Treaty), developments in the 'Corfu process' on European security launched in 2009, and Russian proposals for a new European security pact. In addition, the chapter discusses developments within the OSCE, with a focus on confidence- and security-building measures and the reduction of surplus stockpiles of munitions, small arms and toxic rocket fuel. The chapter also offers an in-depth assessment of developments related to the control of anti-personnel mines (APMs), explosive remnants of war and cluster munitions.

The chapter finds that the prospects for conventional arms control in Europe are more hopeful than in past years, although the CFE Treaty remains in abeyance and its prospects uncertain. The Corfu process has given new momentum to the importance of conventional arms control within the OSCE. Also importantly, the appointment by the Obama Administration of a Special Envoy for Conventional Armed Forces in Europe signals renewed US commitment to conventional arms control in consultation with NATO, European partners and Russia. As for the control of inhumane, non-discriminating weapons such as APMs and cluster munitions, the chapter is likewise encouraging that intergovernmental bodies, national governments, and non-governmental and grassroots organizations are making progress in questioning the military utility of such weapons and in broadening global norms against their use.

Chapter 12 brings attention to controlling the transfer of goods, technologies and other items—mainly transfers of dual-use goods, but also items with purely military uses—which raise security-related concerns. The chapter outlines the controls put forward within the United Nations on proliferation-related items and also describes and analyses developments over the past year within the major supply-side export control regimes, with a special focus on their changing mission and on some of the common challenges they face, including dealing with 'intangible technology transfers'—such as know-how and software. It also examines how the EU and the EU member states have decided to address the challenges inherent in controlling cross-border, security-related transfers.

As the authors point out, while 'export controls' remains a commonly used term for the control of weapons and other non-weapon but nevertheless potentially sensitive security-related items, the term 'transfer controls'—which relates to such questions as transit, trans-shipment and brokering—is a more accurate and useful concept to employ. To put it another way, the authors make the key point that 'who is involved between supplier and recipient?' must now be a central aspect of any effort to understand and possibly stem the flows of security-related goods, technologies and know-how. An appendix includes data, information and analysis on the 29 mandatory multilateral arms embargoes in force during 2009.

III. Conclusions

The 12 chapters of *SIPRI Yearbook 2010* and their accompanying appendices and documentation provide the single most comprehensive and in-depth assessment of developments in international security, armaments and disarmament over the past year. As the analyses in this edition of the Yearbook suggest, the year began hopefully for many with the advent of a new US Administration. In addition, some positive momentum has been generated around the goals of arms control, disarmament and non-proliferation, resulting in important declarations and concrete actions in support of those goals.

However, the past year has also demonstrated just how difficult it is to make continued progress in meeting the many challenges that the world faces today. Taken as a whole, the contributions to this year's edition of the SIPRI Yearbook describe a world at a critical turning point. On questions of international security, the world faces continuing changes in the nature of armed conflict and instability towards greater diffusion of the means and actors involved in violence. Civilian contributions to peace operations are much needed, but the international community continues to struggle with how to best provide them. Meanwhile, the Euro-Atlantic security partnership also struggles to define new roles and relationships consistent with the threat environment for the coming decades. Many of these challenges are amply demonstrated in the ongoing difficulties in stabilizing Afghanistan.

Future directions in armaments and disarmament are likewise at a critical stage. Continued upward growth in military spending, arms production and arms transfers will depend on how the global financial situation changes in the year to come, as well as on developments in the conflicts in Afghanistan and Iraq. The year 2010 will be an important one for disarmament and non-proliferation as well, with the world watching for progress in bilateral disarmament between Russia and the USA: continuing differences between the two sides over US missile defence deployments may well derail further progress. The world will also look for progress on disarmament and tightened controls against would-be proliferators in the context of a successful NPT Review Conference. The CD in Geneva will need to begin substantive negotiations as called for in the draft programme of work adopted in 2009, such as on a fissile material cut-off treaty, but it is not clear that the body will be able to do so. The April 2010 summit of world leaders in Washington, DC, to address nuclear security will likewise attract great attention for what it says (or does not say) about the need to secure nuclear materials from falling in to the wrong hands. More broadly, new proliferation challenges have already begun to emerge in the area of dual-use technologies, requiring the international community to develop more effective mechanisms to prevent their misuse.

Looking ahead, SIPRI will continue to closely monitor, analyse and put forward recommendations on these and other emergent trends. In doing so, through the SIPRI Yearbook and other channels, SIPRI aims to fulfil its mandate to provide data, analysis and recommendations, based on open sources, to policymakers, researchers, media and the interested public.

1. A world without nuclear weapons: fantasy or necessity?

JAMES E. GOODBY

I. Introduction

The history of the nuclear era shows that from time to time states have changed their doctrinal approaches to nuclear deterrence and how to manage the 'ultimate weapon'. This suggests that the outlook for a world without nuclear weapons will be influenced as much by political thinking as by the military and technical considerations that will arise in the process of eliminating warheads and missiles. 'Thinking about the unthinkable' in Herman Kahn's day referred to the analysis of nuclear war.[1] The unthinkable today for some experts is a world without nuclear weapons, but thinking about this idea is now becoming a higher priority, and it is not a moment too soon.

Reluctance to change the status quo lessened after the publication of two articles by George Shultz, Henry Kissinger, William Perry and Sam Nunn, in January 2007 and January 2008.[2] They argued that the world was at a dangerous tipping point and that international responses to nuclear dangers had not risen to meet the threat. The articles challenged the states that possess nuclear weapons to adopt as a serious policy goal a world without nuclear weapons and to accept near-term steps that would make the world a safer place and create the conditions for achieving a world without nuclear weapons.[3]

How can this be done? Russia and the United States have sharply reduced their arsenals of nuclear weapons. The process began under Soviet leader Mikhail Gorbachev and US President Ronald Reagan in the 1980s. It continues under Russian President Dmitry Medvedev and US President Barack Obama in 2010. Will it proceed further, perhaps all the way to zero? Both presidents say they favour a world without nuclear weapons. Many analysts have shown how Russia and the USA could reduce nuclear warheads to a thousand or so apiece, while limiting the associated delivery

---

[1] Kahn, H., *Thinking about the Unthinkable* (Horizon Press: New York, 1962); and Kahn, H., *Thinking about the Unthinkable in the 1980s* (Simon & Schuster: New York, 1984).

[2] Shultz, G. P. et al., 'A world free of nuclear weapons', *Wall Street Journal*, 4 Jan. 2007; and Shultz, G. P. et al., 'Toward a nuclear-free world', *Wall Street Journal*, 15 Jan. 2008.

[3] The states that possess, or are widely believed to possess, nuclear weapons are China, France, India, Israel, Pakistan, Russia, the United Kingdom, the United States and possibly North Korea. See chapter 8 in this volume.

vehicles to a few hundred for each country. Several recent studies have gone still further by identifying steps that would include not only Russia and the USA but also all other states that currently possess nuclear weapons.[4] The end state that these studies envisage is zero nuclear weapons, or close to it.

These hypothetical models are useful for analytical purposes if for no other reason than to identify the practical problems that will have to be confronted in a global enterprise to eliminate all nuclear weapons. They show, among other things, that the process of eliminating nuclear weapons cannot stand alone. It must be accompanied by ancillary agreements that will limit other weapons.

Furthermore, a number of essentially political issues, quite separate and apart from what the late Sir Michael Quinlan called 'disarmament mechanisms', also need careful study.[5] These issues go to the heart of whether eliminating nuclear weapons from the world's arsenals is a practical proposition. Nuclear deterrence has become a seemingly indispensable component of relations between states. If all the world's nuclear-armed states believe that their interests will be served by eliminating nuclear weapons, then the process will gain traction. However, a single hold out could block the whole process.

In order to examine both the 'mechanical' and 'political' issues of nuclear disarmament in a new age of arms control, section II of this chapter discusses general approaches to medium-term Russian–US nuclear arms reductions. Other nuclear-armed states will have to join in making the elimination of nuclear weapons a truly global enterprise, and the content of multilateral negotiations is examined in section III. Programmes to eliminate nuclear weapons cannot be free standing: other military capabilities will also have to be constrained and those are identified in section IV. Nuclear deterrence will not disappear even if all nuclear weapons are eliminated but will take other forms; that concept is explored in section V. World government is not a requirement for achieving a world without nuclear weapons but governance issues at various levels must be addressed, and regional arrangements will be especially important. Both are assessed in section VI. It is important to understand that political and doctrinal changes, as much as or perhaps more than technical changes, have affected how governments view nuclear weapons and what they are willing to do to constrain them. The US experience in this regard is briefly

---

[4] In Sep. 2009 the 5 permanent members (P5) of the UN Security Council met in London for a wide-ranging discussion of confidence building, verification and compliance challenges associated with achieving further progress towards disarmament and non-proliferation. British Foreign and Commonwealth Office, 'P5 statement on disarmament and non-proliferation issues', 4 Sep. 2009, <http://www.fco.gov.uk/en/news/latest-news/?view=News&id=20804873#>.

[5] Quinlan, M., *Thinking about Nuclear Weapons: Principles, Problems, Prospects* (Oxford University Press: Oxford, 2009), pp. 161–63.

reviewed in section VII. Section VIII concludes by discussing the idea of a world without nuclear weapons as a necessary component of every responsible state's national security policy.

II. Staged reductions in Russian and US nuclear weapons

Russia and the United States together possess about 90 per cent of the world's inventory of nuclear weapons. Understandably, these states have taken the lead in reducing their nuclear arsenals. The next phase of Russian–US nuclear arms reductions would follow the implementation of the 2010 New START Treaty, the successor treaty to the 1991 Treaty on the Reduction and Limitation of Strategic Offensive Arms (START Treaty) and the 2002 Strategic Offensive Reductions Treaty (SORT).[6] This phase might be concluded in the medium-term but it is better to define this by a functional, rather than a time-bound measure. That construct is more meaningful than a guess about the time it would take to get there. The next phase of reductions will bring Russian and US nuclear forces to the lowest level that the two countries can accept in the absence of binding limitations on the nuclear forces of other states.

What that level might be is a rather subjective question but several private studies have coalesced around several hundred bombs and warheads for each side and delivery vehicles amounting to about half that number.[7] Much ambiguity must remain about future counting rules for warheads, bombs and missiles. Non-deployed bombs and warheads will be difficult to verifiably limit, and the limits may be less rigorously defined initially as a result. The increasing use of missiles and bombers for conventional weapons introduces additional complexities into the counting of delivery systems.

The New START Treaty defines a framework, including verification provisions, that will ease the future work of US and Russian negotiators, but the process will not be easy. Several difficult issues were set aside for future decision and an agreed framework for subsequent detailed negotiations would likely be the first step.

Several technical issues will have to be addressed in the next phase. In addition to the question of how to count and verify non-deployed bombs

---

[6] For a summary and other details of the START Treaty, SORT (also called the Moscow Treaty) and the New START Treaty see annex A in this volume.

[7] Global Zero Commission, 'Global Zero action plan', Feb. 2010, <http://static.globalzero.org/files/docs/GZAP_6.0.pdf>; Evans, G. and Kawaguchi, Y., *Eliminating Nuclear Threats: A Practical Agenda for Global Policymakers*, Report of the International Commission on Nuclear Non-proliferation and Disarmament (International Commission on Nuclear Non-proliferation and Disarmament: Canberra, 2009); Shultz, G. P. et al., *Reykjavik Revisited: Steps Toward a World Free of Nuclear Weapons* (Hoover Press: Stanford, CA, 2008); and Drell, S. D. and Goodby, J. E., *A World Without Nuclear Weapons: End-State Issues* (Hoover Press: Stanford, CA, 2009).

and warheads, they include: how to limit and reduce short-range (tactical) nuclear weapons; how to verify the dismantlement of nuclear warheads and ensure that this process is irreversible; and how to relate ballistic missile defence systems to further reductions in offensive systems.

These are not insurmountable issues. Solutions are readily available and under optimum conditions probably could be accepted by both sides. More difficult to assess is whether Russia and the USA will have the political will to proceed with deeper reductions of nuclear weapons. The outcome will depend primarily on two factors: (a) how the New START Treaty is implemented, and (b) whether other nuclear-armed states act in a way that encourages the process of Russian–US nuclear negotiations.

III. Broadening the circle: involving other nuclear-armed states in a campaign to eliminate nuclear weapons

One barrier to rapid, sustained Russian–US reductions in nuclear weaponry is the nuclear weapon programmes of other countries. These programmes are cited again and again in critical commentary on the goal of elimination. If other states that possess nuclear weapons were to join in a reduction and elimination programme, the effect on both Russia and the United States would be catalytic. It would energize their efforts to move towards deep reductions and, ultimately, to elimination of nuclear weapons.

The days when the interests of two superpowers dominated the world's strategic nuclear agenda are over. As Russian and US nuclear forces are reduced, other countries' nuclear arsenals will loom larger in security calculations. Regional conflicts also generate their own sets of impulses that affect nuclear decisions. Asia and Europe are rife with political dynamics that were suppressed or totally absent during the cold war. Eliminating the threat posed by nuclear weapons requires that many states actively participate in negotiations to reduce all nuclear weapon programmes anywhere in the world.

The level of nuclear forces that Russia and the USA may try to reach in the next phase could, in theory, be achieved without the participation of other nuclear-armed states. Russia and the USA will still have by far the greatest numbers of nuclear weapons in their arsenals even after additional reductions. In practice, however, unless there is a widely, and preferably universally, shared commitment to progressively eliminate all nuclear weapons, the momentum necessary to sustain further Russian–US negotiations will be lost.

Initial commitments by other nuclear-armed states

UN Security Council Resolution 1887 calls on all states to help create the conditions necessary for a world without nuclear weapons.[8] The resolution envisages concrete actions by many states. It was not intended that only Russia and the USA would act to reduce their nuclear arsenals while other states looked on.

A wide array of actions is available to other nuclear-armed states and many of these could be pursued without delay. Those states that possess nuclear weapons should adopt a verifiable and politically binding agreement in which they would declare that: 'fissile materials removed from nuclear weapons being eliminated and excess to national security requirements will not be used to manufacture nuclear weapons; no newly produced fissile materials will be used in nuclear weapons; and fissile materials from or within civil nuclear programmes will not be used to manufacture nuclear weapons'. This language appears in a declaration issued by Russian President Boris Yeltsin and US President Bill Clinton.[9] Early agreement on these points by all states that possess nuclear weapons would be a powerful signal that they are determined to create the conditions for a world without nuclear weapons. It would accelerate agreement by Russia and the USA on deeper cuts in their nuclear arsenals. The agreement would be open to all states that chose to join, although no special effort need be made to pressure them to join in. Not all the points would be relevant to states that had no nuclear weapons or fissile material production facilities. Discussions about a treaty with a similar intent that would be applicable even-handedly to all nations have been under way in the Geneva-based Conference on Disarmament, the UN forum for multilateral arms control negotiations, for several years. These talks should continue and a treaty should be negotiated as soon as possible. A less powerful agreement that would be binding on nuclear-armed states, as described above, would be one in which those states agree not to increase the number of nuclear weapons each may have and to offer greater transparency, in the form of data sharing. Measures to increase the length of time available for decision making before launching nuclear weapons would also be desirable.

Other near-term measures include: (*a*) establishing more nuclear weapon-free zones; (*b*) exchanging data on all nuclear programmes and holdings of fissile materials; (*c*) carrying out unilateral or parallel reductions in nuclear weapons; (*d*) making all uranium enrichment programmes

---

[8] UN Security Council Resolution 1887, 24 Sep. 2009.

[9] Woolley, J. T. and Peters, G., American Presidency Project, 'Joint statement on the transparency and irreversibility of the process of reducing nuclear weapons', 10 May 1995, <http://www.presidency.ucsb.edu/ws/index.php?pid=51341&st=&st1=>.

multilateral; (*e*) placing all spent nuclear fuel elements in internationally supervised interim storage sites; and (*f*) working to reduce regional tensions that drive nuclear weapon programmes.

Russian and US leadership will be required in measures such as these but initiatives in regional actions obviously must come from states in those regions. The three other permanent members of the UN Security Council—China, France and the United Kingdom—will have to assume leadership roles if the global enterprise is to become a reality. To varying degrees, their interests may encourage them to do so.

Longer-term multilateral nuclear arms reductions

Models of deep Russian–US reductions well below the 1000-warhead level have been developed and these are useful, but only for analytical purposes. The content of the actual stages might differ significantly from the models. The process of reductions will generate feedback that will provide a learning experience. All of the models of Russian–US reductions will be part of a multilateral framework. No longer will Russia and the USA proceed with nuclear reductions in the absence of limits on the nuclear forces of other countries.

One model, for analytical purposes, would proceed in three basic steps. First, Russia and the United States would reduce operationally deployed warheads and bombs of all types to low numbers (200–500); China, France and the UK would accept ceilings below 200; and India, Israel and Pakistan would freeze at then-current levels (assumed not to exceed 100). Second, each nuclear-armed state would reduce deployed warheads to zero and non-deployed warheads to no more than 200, after which each nuclear-armed state might reduce the latter category to an interim number of 50–100 apiece. A variant could have a mix of 50–100 operationally deployed or declared reserve warheads retained by each state while all other warheads would be eliminated. Finally, each nuclear-armed state would reduce warheads to zero while retaining monitored reconstitution capabilities within agreed parameters and for a period of agreed duration.

Although those numbers are hypothetical, they provide a framework for examining key security issues that the countries will face as they approach and enter the end state.

A pause for stocktaking would be in order when states had reduced to the level of 50–100 warheads apiece or less. The following conditions, among others, should have been met.

1. Procedures for challenge inspections to search for concealed warheads should have been established and satisfactorily exercised.

2. Warheads scheduled for elimination should be able to be dismantled under conditions that would assure their actual dismantling, with the nuclear components placed in secure and monitored storage pending final disposition.

3. Delivery vehicles scheduled for elimination should have been verifiably destroyed, and procedures should be in place to confirm that dual-use systems have not been armed with nuclear warheads.

4. Compliance mechanisms should have been established to enforce nuclear agreements.

5. Beyond the nuclear aspects, advances should have been made in creating and maintaining regional confidence-building regimes and restraints regarding conventional forces; progress should have been made in addressing and resolving regional disputes that threaten to trigger military actions; and international mechanisms to provide more effective compliance with nuclear agreements should have been put in place.

Verification is a major issue, but a less formidable obstacle than many think. Russia and the USA have had years of experience in successfully verifying numbers of operationally deployed nuclear warheads. The numbers and locations of the principal means of delivering warheads—bombers and missiles—can be monitored, which also provides insight into the status of non-deployed warheads.

The task of verification may become easier as progress towards zero is achieved. The rules of behaviour will be well established by then, which should make anomalies easier to spot and encourage whistle-blowers to speak out. Enforcement should be easier to obtain than under present circumstances. States that gave up their nuclear arsenals are not apt to be tolerant of those that defy a ban on acquiring nuclear weapons. A preventive attack would become a more realistic option than it is today.

During the time that it will take to negotiate and implement the steps towards the end state, a steady accumulation of vital information will occur. For example, the history of production of fissile materials will become better understood as time goes on. With that information, the upper limits of warhead production can be calculated more accurately. So, by the time the end state is reached, an accurate base of information about arsenals that have been built and about materials that will remain subject to restraints and elimination will be in hand.

All states that possess nuclear weapons would participate in some way in a verification process. It would not be a 'one size fits all' approach. Nuclear-free zones, with appropriate verification, might be more effective than a global approach in some cases. The standards of verification should be essentially equivalent, although the specific modes of verification might differ from zone to zone.

IV. Ancillary agreements necessary to support and sustain a world without nuclear weapons

There are two categories of supporting agreements that should be in force before and after the goal of eliminating nuclear weapons has been achieved. The first category consists of nuclear-related agreements that will form the essential building blocks of a world without nuclear weapons. The second category are those non-nuclear agreements necessary to forestall conflict and the resort to force by any means, such as confidence-building measures (CBMs) and constraints on conventional, biological and chemical weapons.

Nuclear-related agreements include the 1996 Comprehensive Nuclear-Test-Ban Treaty (CTBT), a fissile material cut-off treaty (FMCT) and measures to regulate uranium enrichment and plutonium separation.[10] Without such agreements nuclear weapon development programmes could continue, defeating the purpose of reductions in the world's nuclear stockpiles. Agreements that would strengthen the infrastructure of nuclear non-proliferation will also be necessary. These would include strengthening the International Atomic Energy Agency (IAEA), monitoring compliance with the 1968 Treaty on the Non-proliferation of Nuclear Weapons (Non-Proliferation Treaty, NPT) and enforcing measures to disrupt illicit trafficking in fissile materials.[11] Each of these nuclear-related agreements would make the world a safer place.

In the context of a world without nuclear weapons, confidence-building measures are necessary to sustain the basic contract to renounce nuclear weapons. CBMs generally provide for transparency, some types of constraint and means of rapid, secure communications regarding military activities. They are useful in defusing the regional conflicts that spur decisions to acquire nuclear weapons.

It is already clear that balanced restraints on conventional forces will be necessary if nuclear weapons are to be reduced significantly, let alone eliminated. The 1990 Treaty on Conventional Armed Forces in Europe (CFE Treaty) was concluded near the end of the cold war by states that were still adversaries at the time.[12] Soviet–US nuclear arms reduction treaties were concluded at about the same time. Europe will not be alone in requiring parallel actions of this type. Countries in the Middle East, South Asia and East Asia are almost certain to raise the issue of limiting con-

---

[10] For a summary and other details of the CTBT see annex A in this volume. On recent developments in the FMCT negotiations see chapter 12, section VI, in this volume.

[11] For a summary and other details of the NPT see annex A in this volume.

[12] For a summary and other details of the CFE Treaty see annex A in this volume. For recent developments in the CFE regime see also chapter 11, section II, in this volume.

vontional foroeo if nuolear weapono are to be eliminated. Limits on dual use delivery vehicles may also figure in these negotiations.

In a world without nuclear weapons, it will be more important than ever to ensure that the bans on the development, possession and use of chemical and, especially, biological weapons remain in force. Biological weapons have been called the 'poor state's atom bomb' because they are cheaper and easier to produce than their nuclear counterparts. States that agree to give up or forgo the nuclear option may be tempted to develop biological weapons as their ultimate deterrent. This would clearly undermine efforts to achieve a nuclear-free world. For this reason, high priority should be given to negotiating a verification protocol to the 1972 Biological and Toxin Weapons Convention (BTWC) at the earliest possible date to match the verification measures of the 1993 Chemical Weapons Convention.[13] Verification machinery should be in place on a global basis long before nuclear-armed countries enter the end state of a nuclear-reduction programme.

V. Deterrence in a world without nuclear weapons

Nuclear deterrence after zero

Deterrence in its original meaning existed long before nuclear weapons were invented. It has always relied on a variety of diplomatic, economic, and military skills and capabilities. These tools will continue to exist after nuclear weapons are eliminated. It is arguable that the imponderables, the non-quantifiable elements of the psychological condition that is called deterrence, are more potent than the physical presence of weapons, including nuclear weapons.

Nuclear deterrence will not disappear even if nuclear weapons are eliminated—a point which is too often overlooked. Nuclear deterrence will be manifested in a new form: the ability to reconstitute small nuclear arsenals. A quarter of a century ago Jonathan Schell, and later Michael Mazarr, pointed out that nuclear deterrence based on 'virtual' nuclear arsenals will exist even if nuclear weapons are eliminated.[14] Banning the existence of a ready-to-use arsenal does not eliminate the capability to build one. That capability would act to deter large-scale conventional war.

[13] For summaries and other details of the Convention on the Prohibition of the Development, Production and Stockpiling of Bacteriological (Biological) and Toxin Weapons and on Their Destruction and of the Convention on the Prohibition of the Development, Production, Stockpiling and Use of Chemical Weapons and on Their Destruction see annex A in this volume. See also chapter 10, sections III and IV, in this volume.

[14] Schell, J., *The Fate of the Earth* (Knopf: New York, 1982); Schell, J., *The Abolition* (Picador: London, 1984); and Mazarr, M. J. (ed.), *Nuclear Weapons in a Transformed World: The Challenge of Virtual Nuclear Arsenals* (St Martin's Press: New York, 1997).

This is not just a hypothetical model of nuclear deterrence. In 2008 the US secretaries of Defense and Energy issued a report in which they suggested that a 'responsive nuclear infrastructure' would make it possible, over time, for the USA to rely less on non-deployed nuclear warheads.[15] A responsive nuclear infrastructure means functioning nuclear laboratories and some capacity to produce nuclear weapons, if needed, in a timely way. This may be what nuclear deterrence will look like in the future. For the purists, it is not ideal, but it is a big improvement over what exists today.

Thus the question 'What takes the place of nuclear deterrence?' does not arise in the way the question is usually posed. The current two-tier system created by the NPT will be vastly changed but power imbalances of various types will remain, as they have throughout history. One example of this is that those countries that have built nuclear weapons will have advantages over those that have not, but inevitably disparities in nuclear capabilities will decrease over time.

Could conditions of stable deterrence be developed under such conditions? Would a world arms race take the form of a reconstitution race? New forms of arms control will have to be invented to deal with this risk. In order to minimize the risk of instability, agreement on five key questions will be necessary.

1. What are the elements of a responsive nuclear infrastructure, that is, one with a capacity for limited and timely reconstitution of a deterrent, and how might that be phased out over time?

2. What activities, facilities or weapon-related items should be limited or prohibited?

3. What can be done to assure early and reliable warning of a breakout attempt to develop nuclear weapons?

4. Can effective and plausible enforcement measures be devised and put in place?

5. How closely could a civil nuclear programme resemble a responsive nuclear infrastructure in the case of states that had not previously built nuclear weapons?

Extended deterrence in a world without nuclear weapons

The idea of eliminating nuclear weapons is frequently criticized on the grounds that without the protection of the US 'nuclear umbrella' some states that count on it for their security will find it necessary to acquire nuclear weapons of their own. Japan is the country usually mentioned in this context but other US allies are sometimes cited as well.

---

[15] US Department of Energy and US Department of Defence, 'National security and nuclear weapons in the 21st century', Sep. 2008, <http://www.defense.gov/pubs/>.

There are at least three problems with this theory. As pointed out above, nuclear deterrence will endure even if nuclear weapons are eliminated; second, deterrence and reassurance can and do exist in forms other than nuclear weapons; and third, there will be no 'nuclear deterrence gap' en route to zero: US nuclear weapons would continue to exist so long as the nuclear weapons of other states also existed.

These factors raise serious issues that will need to be examined and discussed between allies. One such issue is clarity regarding the maintenance of a 'virtual' nuclear arsenal. In a world without nuclear weapons, a robust nuclear infrastructure, civil as well as military, can give many countries the capacity to build, or reconstitute, a nuclear weapon arsenal. That capacity would be circumscribed by several factors: first, previous experience, or the lack of it, in building nuclear weapons; second, prohibitions on certain activities so that rapid breakout would not be possible; third, a deterrent against breakout in the form of a responsive nuclear infrastructure possessed by another state; and fourth, credible means of enforcement. Shultz, Kissinger, Perry and Nunn in another article in January 2010 spoke forcefully about the need for a robust US nuclear infrastructure and stated unequivocally that it could be maintained given adequate support.[16] This is consistent with their earlier articles appealing for an end to the threat posed by nuclear weapons. The Obama Administration proposed a significant increase in funding for nuclear infrastructure. If allies of the United States believed that reconstitutable US nuclear forces were an essential part of the US extended deterrent, they would want reassurance that reconstitution is possible in a timely way.

VI. Governance and institution building: how much must change?

Will the world have to become vastly different before the global climination of nuclear weapons can be achieved? Changes in some aspects of international relations would certainly be necessary. However, this probably does not require any form of world government or even the universal acceptance of democratic principles and institutions. There is room for interesting academic debate on those questions. After all, reaching the goal of a nuclear weapon-free world lies several years in the future, and the precise contours of the political and security arrangements do not have to be settled now. However, a brief discussion of political change is useful now, if only to demonstrate that a world without nuclear weapons is not a sheer fantasy.

---

[16] Shultz, G. P. et al., 'How to protect our nuclear deterrent', *Wall Street Journal*, 19 Jan. 2010.

Governance at the global level

Schell pointed out in his seminal work in the 1980s that nuclear deterrence based on the ability to reconstitute or create nuclear weapons is not a prescription for a world government. It is a prescription for nation states and for a system based on them as the main actors on the international stage.

Militarily, a world free of nuclear weapons means that the use of nuclear weapons would not be immediately available even to those who have the proven capacity to build them. Politically, a higher degree of cooperation among the permanent members of the UN Security Council than exists today would surely be necessary. Their role in a world without nuclear weapons would be to enforce compliance with the norms concerning non-production of nuclear weapons. If that role turns out to be beyond their capacity to fulfil, then getting to zero would have to wait for another day.

Clearly, as the process of making negotiations on nuclear arms reductions multilateral proceeds, there will be a greater need for management mechanisms. The Conference on Disarmament will not be capable of handling the multiple tasks involved in achieving a world without nuclear weapons. These include global nuclear negotiations dominated by a few big powers, regional negotiations in several different parts of the world, and developing and overseeing the variety of international mechanisms that are a part of the world's non-proliferation infrastructure (e.g. monitoring a comprehensive ban on nuclear testing).

A new system of nuclear governance is likely to be centred on the UN Security Council, relying on two important existing resolutions: 1540 and 1887.[17] The former was intended to improve national controls over sensitive nuclear, biological and chemical (NBC) materials. The apparatus set up to implement Resolution 1540 needs significant strengthening. Resolution 1887 was the product of the UN Security Council Summit meeting of 24 September 2009, chaired by President Obama. Resolution 1887 included a variety of ways to strengthen the international non-proliferation regime. Its call for conditions that would permit a nuclear-free world to be attained makes it a useful complement to Resolution 1540, and like that earlier resolution, it calls for strengthening controls over NBC materials. Together, the two resolutions have created a potential charter for a significant UN Security Council management role, which would give the countries of the world the tools they need to integrate their joint efforts to rid the world of nuclear weapons. Obviously, there will be tensions generated by this arrangement because states that are not members of the Security

---

[17] UN Security Council Resolution 1540, 28 Apr. 2004; and UN Security Council Resolution 1887 (note 8).

Council already have reacted against what they regard as big-power domination. If a better system can be invented it should be.

Impact on the United Nations Security Council

Reducing the world's inventories of nuclear weapons will be a wrenching experience for a number of countries, perhaps more so for the five permanent members of the UN Security Council than for the newer, de facto nuclear weapon states. The five did not become permanent members of the Security Council because they possessed nuclear weapons. However, the special status of these states has become almost as much associated with their being the only legally recognized nuclear weapon states, under the NPT, as with their permanent Security Council membership. Complicating this painful withdrawal from the ranks of 'legitimate' nuclear weapon states will be the expectation that, in return for surrendering its nuclear arms, India will also become a permanent member of the Security Council. If that happens, Japan would certainly demand entry, and so probably would Brazil. Both states, not coincidentally, have uranium enrichment facilities.

The politics of Security Council membership exemplify the ways in which a 'level playing field' in nuclear arms will have a levelling effect in other areas as well, a complex political–psychological challenge, requiring policies that will compensate for a sense of lost pride of place.

Regional arrangements

Although governance issues tend to focus on the UN Security Council, much of the process of eliminating nuclear weapons will in fact be based on regional arrangements, particularly in the Middle East, South Asia and North East Asia. In these cases, regional organizations will be important, and generally they will have to be created since they do not now exist.

Regional organizations would initially be limited to containing or resolving disputes and managing confidence-building measures. Eventually, such organizations should develop monitoring mechanisms in connection with nuclear weapon-free zone agreements. They would probably also develop links with the IAEA and the UN Security Council in order to cope with the task of supporting improved national control mechanisms to protect fissile material, as Security Council Resolution 1540 envisaged.

VII. How political and doctrinal changes pave the way for international agreements: the US case[18]

Nuclear disarmament

The prospects for reducing the threat of nuclear weapons are affected by doctrinal changes within states. In the years following the first nuclear explosions in 1945 the elimination of nuclear weapons was described by governments as necessary to the survival of the human race. Many of the atomic scientists of that day, Soviet as well as US, believed that, or came to believe it after the tests of hydrogen bombs. Political leaders at least went through the motions of trying to do something about it. UN resolutions endorsed the abolition of nuclear weapons and UN committees discussed methods and plans aimed at accomplishing that goal.

A nuclear arms race was a nightmare that must be avoided, it was thought, and proposals for eliminating nuclear weapons included plans for preventing the acquisition of national capabilities for manufacturing nuclear weapons. The best known of these was derived from a study launched in the USA at the end of World War II, led by Under Secretary of State Dean Acheson and the head of the Tennessee Valley Authority, David Lilienthal.[19] Their chief scientific advisor, Dr J. Robert Oppenheimer, had been scientific leader of the Manhattan Project to develop a US atomic bomb at Los Alamos, New Mexico. The onset of the Soviet–US cold war confrontation did not stop talks about eliminating nuclear weapons, but these became exercises in public posturing, not serious efforts to reach an accord.

The death of Joseph Stalin in 1953 and the rise of a more pragmatic Soviet leader, Nikita Khrushchev, coincided with the first term as US President (1953–57) of Dwight D. Eisenhower, who had been the Supreme Allied Commander in Europe in World War II. President Eisenhower saw nuclear weapons as apocalyptic devices that spelled the end of large-scale war as a rational instrument of policy. Yet he also saw them as key to reducing defence budgets and so adopted the doctrine of early use of nuclear weapons in the event of a war with the Soviet Union. 'Massive retaliation' was not his phrase, but it was an apt description of the strategy.

---

[18] US declaratory policies are sometimes expressed in the form of presidentially approved internal government documents. See e.g. 'A report to the National Security Council on basic national security policy', Washington, DC, 30 Oct. 1953, <http://www.fas.org/irp/offdocs/nsc-hst/nsc-162-2.pdf>. They may also be presented in presidential speeches. See e.g. 'Excerpts from major presidential speeches regarding missile defense', Missilethreat.com, <http://www.missilethreat.com/resources/pageID.264/default.asp>. President Obama's nuclear weapon policies are laid out in a US Department of Defense report. US Department of Defense (DOD), *Nuclear Posture Review Report* (DOD: Washington, DC, Apr. 2010).

[19] US Department of State, *Report on the International Control of Atomic Energy* (US Government Printing Office: Washington, DC, 16 Mar. 1946).

Limited nuclear war and 'partial measures'

By Eisenhower's second term, which began in 1957, he was convinced that a sterile propaganda exchange about nuclear weapons was not the right way to deal with the threat that they presented to life on earth. On the military side, experiments with low-yield 'tactical' nuclear weapons began. However, Eisenhower also authorized his chief disarmament advisor, Harold Stassen, to explore first steps towards controlling the arms race, so-called partial measures, with the Soviet Union. The Soviet leaders showed serious interest in this approach but little was accomplished. Some of the measures that are still being discussed or negotiated today in international forums come from that period. They include the CTBT, an FMCT and the idea of transparency in military activities as a confidence-building measure.

Prior to the transition from Eisenhower to President John F. Kennedy in January 1961, a Soviet–US agreement on a comprehensive test-ban treaty was almost within reach, with Khrushchev strongly supporting the effort. Unfortunately, the effort failed, but the groundwork had been laid for agreement on a multilateral limited test-ban treaty a few years later.[20]

Arms control

The nuclear disarmament paradigm, created in the immediate aftermath of World War II, had been seriously discredited by the late 1950s. It was seen as impractical. It had also become an 'all or nothing' approach that blocked any headway in controlling the threat posed by growing numbers of nuclear weapons. Eisenhower's partial measures responded to the need to make a beginning in the control of nuclear arms, but the idea lacked a unifying concept.

Another paradigm, that of 'arms control', was popularized by a summer study conducted by US scholars and published just as Kennedy was coming to power in the USA.[21] It advocated stability as the most important objective of Soviet–US negotiations and, indeed, of the nuclear postures of the two countries.

This paradigm was agnostic about the idea of reducing or eliminating nuclear weapons and instead focused on advising the Soviet and US governments on how to construct and operate their military equipment in a way that would minimize temptations to launch a nuclear attack. The idea was to ensure that retaliatory nuclear strikes would always be available, even after a first strike by an enemy. This would be a strong deterrent to any political or military leaders who might be considering a nuclear war.

---

[20] On the 1963 Partial-Test Ban Treaty see annex A in this volume.
[21] *Daedalus*, vol. 89, no. 4 (fall 1960).

During the 1960s, 1970s and much of the 1980s, the arms control paradigm was the prevailing doctrine influencing US and, to a lesser extent, Soviet negotiators. 'Stability', however, never became a useful formula by which to gauge the utility of Soviet–US agreements because each side had different ideas about that concept.

A return to the vision of a world free of nuclear weapons

Even at the height of classical arms control and its intellectual companion, 'assured destruction', there were those who questioned the morality and the logic of a doctrine based on a threat to commit mutual national suicide. US President Ronald Reagan, who came to power in 1981, was one of them. Reagan was an unusual politician, who brought to mind a favourite quotation of President Kennedy's brother Robert: 'Some people see things as they are and say why? I dream things that never were and say, why not?'[22]

Reagan was fortunate in having Gorbachev as his negotiating partner for the last few years of his administration, a man who was a revolutionary within his own system. Between them, they began the reversal of the more pernicious effects of the arms control and mutual assured destruction doctrines that had led to massive build-ups in nuclear weapons and what became, during the 1977–81 term of President Jimmy Carter, a concomitant preparation for 'protracted nuclear war'.[23]

The most notable of all the Soviet–US summit meetings of the cold war period was the summit meeting held in Reykjavik, Iceland, in October 1986, where Reagan and Gorbachev seriously contemplated and unreservedly endorsed the idea of eliminating all nuclear weapons. The US Secretary of State, George Shultz, strongly supported and encouraged Reagan's efforts to turn the page to a new era in Soviet–US nuclear relationships. In fact, a new chapter in the relationship really did begin at Reykjavik.

Two major treaties followed in the wake of that summit meeting. One of these, the 1987 Treaty on the Elimination of Intermediate-Range and Shorter-Range Missiles (INF Treaty), which eliminated an entire class of intermediate-range nuclear delivery system, was concluded before Reagan left office.[24] The other, the 1991 START Treaty, was largely fleshed out during Reagan's term of office and was concluded in the term of his successor, President George H. W. Bush. It has provided much of the

---

[22] Kennedy, R. F., Remarks, University of Kansas, 18 Mar. 1968, <http://www.jfklibrary.org/historical+resources/archives/reference+desk/speeches/rfk/rfkspeech68mar18ukansas.htm>.

[23] Presidential Directive/NSC-59, 'Nuclear weapons employment policy', 25 July 1980, <http://www.fas.org/irp/offdocs/pd/index.html>. For a discussion see Goodby, J. E., *At the Borderline of Armageddon: How American Presidents Managed the Atom Bomb* (Rowman & Littlefield: Lanham, MD, 2006), pp. 123–24.

[24] For a summary and other details of the INF Treaty see annex A in this volume.

conceptual framework for Russian–US nuclear negotiations down to the present day.

Retreat and renewal

From the end of the Reagan Administration in 1989 until late in 2006 the idea of eliminating nuclear weapons lay fallow, ignored as a negotiating objective by both Russia and the USA. Lack of interest at the top leadership levels in both countries accounted for most of this neglect. They were preoccupied with other issues, to be sure, but basically their perceptions of the peculiar, unique threat posed by nuclear weapons simply did not rise to the levels of concern shared by Gorbachev and Reagan.

Neither Russian nor US public opinion offered any evidence that the leaders of the two countries should do anything more about the nuclear threat than they were doing. The end of the cold war encouraged the view that nuclear war was yesterday's problem. The focus shifted to other issues. To add to the immobility, during the 2001–2009 Presidency of George W. Bush negotiations with Russia were seen as an unnecessary and unwelcome restraint on US policies and actions.

This situation changed after the publication of the two articles by Shultz, Kissinger, Perry and Nunn. The reactions to these articles surprised even their authors. Around the world, political and military leaders rallied to the idea. President Obama adopted the framework as his own. Chairing a meeting of the UN Security Council in September 2009, Obama presided over the unanimous adoption of Resolution 1887, which proclaimed that all states should work to create the conditions for a world without nuclear weapons.

VIII. Conclusions: looking ahead

Nuclear weapons still matter, in ways that defy the imagination. This is a time of danger. Nuclear weapons could be the cause of millions of deaths— on short notice and without any rational cause. Nuclear weapons have not lost their doomsday qualities. However, this may also be a time of opportunity: deep and irreversible reductions in the nuclear stockpiles of Russia and the United States may be possible and that would unlock the door to reductions in the nuclear holdings of other states that possess nuclear weapons.

Russia and the USA have been on a downward trajectory in their holdings of nuclear weapons since the late 1980s. The post-World War II discussions, in contrast, led only to a massive build-up. The Gorbachev–Reagan partnership produced real change and led to serious reductions. Their successors in office lacked the zeal, the opportunities or the interest to push ahead with the same vigour, but the downward trajectory continued nonetheless. This trend is likely to continue. One of the reasons for this is the radically changed political dynamic that exists between Russia and the USA. The change is like night and day if today is compared with the early cold war years. The course of history changed dramatically after 1986, the year of the Reykjavik Summit, to the point where 'things that never were' became possible.

More change lies ahead. New threats, terrorism among them, have come to preoccupy both Russia and the USA. The bipolar competition that drove the nuclear build-up still exists, but it is much attenuated. The technology of monitoring nuclear capabilities has moved far beyond where it was a quarter century ago, when the last serious effort to move towards elimination of nuclear weapons was launched.

The revival of interest in a world without nuclear weapons extends beyond Russia and the United States. There appears to be a growing conviction among opinion leaders in many countries that, whatever benefits nuclear weapons might have bestowed on those who controlled them during the dangerous years of the cold war, the disadvantages now outweigh any residual benefits. This assessment means that the basic bargain struck in the Non-Proliferation Treaty between the states that possess nuclear weapons and those that do not must be taken seriously; it must become the operational guide for future nuclear weapon policies. In this sense, the idea of a world without nuclear weapons is no longer a fantasy entertained by the dreamers of society but an operational reality, a necessary component of every responsible state's national security policy.

Recognizing that the task of eliminating nuclear weapons will be daunting, President Obama remarked in April 2009 that 'fatalism is a deadly adversary'.[25] The road to zero will not be an easy one: real and serious obstacles lie ahead. But without a genuine global commitment to that goal, preventing nuclear proliferation is a lost cause. The question must be 'How?' not 'Should we?'

---

[25] White House, 'Remarks by President Barack Obama, Hradcany Square, Prague, Czech Republic', 5 Apr. 2009, <http://www.whitehouse.gov/the_press_office/Remarks-By-President-Barack-Obama-In-Prague-As-Delivered/>.

Part 1. Security and conflicts, 2009

2. Armed conflict, crime and criminal violence

EKATERINA STEPANOVA

I. Introduction

Crime and criminal violence can pose as great a threat to national stability as armed conflict over government or territory.[1] Furthermore, in some areas of armed conflict, high-profile criminal business may have broader transnational implications and resonance than the conflict itself—but both are manifestations of the same weakness, dysfunction or absence of state structures. In many conflict and post-conflict contexts, a fragmentation of violence and diversification and proliferation of armed actors has been coupled with growing reliance by non-state actors on shadow—including criminal—economic activity as a source of funding. This process has contributed to the erosion of boundaries between political and criminal violence and between many ideologically driven actors and organized criminal groups.

This chapter aims to encourage a more active integration of the study of organized crime, especially transnational, and criminal violence into the broader analysis of collective organized armed violence. It also seeks to show that such integration should be broader than a narrow focus on crime–terrorism or crime–insurgency links in the context of armed conflicts.

Section II of this chapter explains the focus on criminal violence in and beyond conflict related contexts. It addresses the main data and methodological issues in the field; provides an outline of some global trends in crime and criminal violence; and examines the nature and scale of the links between armed conflict on the one hand and crime and criminal violence on the other. Section III analyses the causes and impacts of organized crime in 2009 in armed conflict settings. One case study examines the patterns and transnational implications of piracy based in Somalia. A second illustrates the dynamics of and interaction between the drug economy and armed conflict in Afghanistan. Section IV goes outside the classic conflict setting to examine the similarities and differences between armed conflict,

---

[1] 'Organized crime' is defined, for the purpose of this chapter, as self-perpetuating illegal activity carried out by a structured group over a period of time for material benefit. 'Criminal violence' refers to violence perpetrated by an organized criminal group in the pursuit of such a material benefit. On the definition of 'armed conflict' see appendix 2A.

as it is usually defined, and intense criminal violence of a comparable scale and intensity that undermines the security and stability of the affected states. A case study of Mexico is presented, where drug trade-related violence has become the main form of organized collective violence in recent years. Conclusions are presented in Section V. Appendix 2A presents the UCDP data on patterns of major armed conflicts in 2000–2009. Appendix 2B presents the 2010 Global Peace Index.

II. Crime and criminal violence: data, methodology and global trends

The relationship between political violence and organized crime or, more broadly, the illicit or informal economy is a vast subject. The focus here is on the comparative dynamics of armed conflict—one of the key forms of political violence—and criminal violence, exploring recent global trends in crime and criminal violence and presenting specific case studies of crime and criminal violence both in and beyond an armed conflict setting.

Data and methodology problems in studying global crime trends

Quantifying levels of crime, particularly organized crime, and comparing them across countries is difficult. Much less data is available on crime than on armed conflict. With all the limitations of conflict data, global trends in armed conflict are much better known than trends in global crime.[2]

The main source of data on global crime is the United Nations Survey of Crime Trends and Operation of Criminal Justice Systems (UNCJS), which are conducted by the UN Office on Drugs and Crime (UNODC).[3] This effort is supplemented by the International Crime Victims Survey (ICVS).[4] The use of other statistics, such as Interpol data sets comprising data reported directly from national police authorities, is restricted to governments.[5]

Making accurate quantitative and analytical cross-country comparisons of most categories of crime is problematic due to the varying (and generally insufficient) national reporting of crime and the divergence between data

[2] On the main trends in major armed conflicts in 2009 see appendix 2A.

[3] For the latest survey, including crime data provided by 86 countries, see UN Office on Drugs and Crime, 'The tenth United Nations Survey of Crime Trends and Operations of Criminal Justice Systems (Tenth CTS, 2005–2006)', <http://www.unodc.org/unodc/en/data-and-analysis/Tenth-United-Nations-Survey-on-Crime-Trends-and-the-Operations-of-Criminal-Justice-Systems.html>. Some of the latest UNODC data on criminal violence is published in Geneva Declaration, *Global Burden of Armed Violence* (Geneva Declaration Secretariat: Geneva, Sep. 2008), pp. 67–88.

[4] For a summary of the latest ICVS data see van Dijk, J., van Kesteren, J. and Smit, P., *Criminal Victimisation in International Perspective: Key Findings from the 2004–2005 ICVS and EU ICS* (Boom Legal Publishers: The Hague, 2008). Crime rates based on victim surveys tend to be higher than those derived from government data, but in both cases data mostly comes from developed countries.

[5] See Interpol, *Annual Report 2008* (Interpol: Lyon, 2009), pp. 15–17.

provided by different sources. Even fewer reliable statistics are available for most types of transnational crime.[6] Thus, the existing data does not reflect precise levels of crime and is only reliable enough for the purpose of identifying the main longer-term trends in crime rates at national, regional and international levels, some of which are presented below.

National homicide data is one of the few exceptions. National homicide rates are the least affected by under- or over-reporting; are the most reliable crime statistics available; and are one of the few indicators that are relatively comparable between countries.[7] In most countries, more accurate data is available on overall homicide levels than on many types of political violence—perhaps with the exception of terrorist attacks. Homicide rates are used as the main indicator of the incidence of criminal violence, which is of particular relevance for this chapter.

Some high-profile or heavily securitized categories of transnational crime are also relatively well represented with comparable data; for example, international piracy statistics and UN and national data on narcotics seizures or drug crop cultivation areas. Also, some countries maintain adequately detailed, well kept and accessible national crime statistics. The availability of reliable and comparable data has partly dictated the choice of case studies in this chapter.

The problems of crime data are much worse when it comes to assessing and measuring levels of criminal violence or the scale of organized criminal activity in the context of armed conflicts. This is a result not only of the inherent problems associated with reporting and gathering data in areas of armed conflict, but also of the difficulty of distinguishing between criminal and political violence. For example, large campaigns of both criminal and anti-criminal violence are sometimes integrated into data on one-sided violence against civilians.[8]

Broad trends in global crime

In contrast to armed conflicts, especially major armed conflicts, which have been in steady decline in recent decades, global levels of crime in general and levels of criminal violence in the developing world in particular have

---

[6] 'Transnational crime' is defined, for the purpose of this chapter, as criminal activity that is perpetrated by an organized criminal group that operates in more than 1 state; or that is substantially planned, prepared or controlled from or has direct or indirect effects in another state than that in which it is committed.

[7] Homicides are intentional killings of a purely criminal or semi-criminal type. Homicide data does not include either battle-related deaths or deaths from terrorism or most other types of one-sided violence.

[8] On the UCDP data set on one-sided violence see Harbom, L. and Wallensteen, P., 'Patterns of major armed conflicts, 1999–2008', *SIPRI Yearbook 2009*, pp. 75–77.

been slowly but steadily rising since at least the 1970s.[9] While official UN data on global crime levels in 2008–2009 will not be available for several years, the UNODC has indicated that there was a notable increase in many types of transnational crime in 2009, attributing it primarily to the impact of the global economic and financial crisis.[10]

The available data shows no simple correlation between socio-economic development and crime rates. Levels of recorded crime in some developed countries and regions for the 1980s and 1990s—the most recent complete decades for which UN data is available—were higher than the global average, although they had lower than average levels of violent crime.[11] Differences in recording practices only partly explain this. It is also a clear indication that higher levels of human and socio-economic development and integration into the global economy do not in and of themselves lead to reduced crime—and may even be accompanied by a rise in overall crime rates.

In contrast, those Arab Muslim countries that were not in a state of protracted armed conflict and collapse of governance generally had crime rates lower than the global average, sometimes much lower. Levels of socio-economic development are thus not the only—and not necessarily the main—factor behind crime rates but interact with other factors, including culture, religion and general state capacity. This is further illustrated by the fact that, according to the latest available UNODC data, homicide rates in South Asia are six times lower than homicide rates in Africa, even though the regions have comparable levels of gross domestic product.[12]

Based on the latest available complete global homicide data (for 2004) the three subregions most affected by violent crime are Southern Africa, Central America and South America, with homicide rates of between 25 and 35 per 100 000 people. The second most violent set of subregions, with homicide rates of 15–25 per 100 000, is comprised of the Caribbean and Eastern Europe. A third group includes North Africa, North America, and Central Asia and the South Causasus, with homicide rates in the range 5–10 per 100 000. The Middle East, Oceania, South Asia and South Eastern Europe all have lower homicide rates than North America, followed by East and South East Asia. Western and Central Europe have the lowest rates of homicide in the world.[13]

The global average of violent crime as a proportion of all crime does not exceed 10–15 per cent. Comparing the relatively static global trend in homi-

---

[9] UN Office for Drug Control and Crime Prevention, Centre for International Crime Prevention, *Global Report on Crime and Justice* (Oxford University Press: New York, 1999).

[10] UN News Service, 'UN anti-crime tsar warns of global reach of organized crime', 16 Apr. 2009, <http://www.un.org/apps/news/story.asp?NewsID=30490>.

[11] UN Office for Drug Control and Crime Prevention (note 9).

[12] Geneva Declaration (note 3), p. 73.

[13] Geneva Declaration (note 3), pp. 70–71.

cide rates since the early 1990s with the overall rise in global crime rates in the same period suggests that, overall, crime is actually becoming less violent.

Finally, comparison of global homicide totals with battle-related fatality data indicates that criminal violence is far more widespread than organized political violence. The best example is provided by sub-Saharan Africa in 2004, where there were 10 times more homicides, at 180 000, than conflict-related deaths.[14] In addition, the steady decline in numbers of armed conflicts since the early 1990s has not been matched by a global decline in homicide rates. Instead, most subregions have shown flat criminal homicide trends.[15]

Non-state combatants and organized crime groups: similarities and differences

The closest similarities between organized crime groups and politico-military non-state actors using proceeds from criminal activities as a 'war resource' are in their sources and methods of financing. Both may engage in criminal activities that are predatory (e.g. armed robberies, assaults etc.) or parasitical (e.g. collecting 'revolutionary' taxes or racketeering). Both are also interested in the general weakening of state control or of law and order, in maximum freedom of movement and so on, in order to allow them to operate.

Both politico-military groups and organized criminal groups are non-state actors. Although they display a wide range of organizational forms and patterns, both overall enjoy greater levels of structural and organizational flexibility than states do. While some more hierarchical structures can be found in both spheres—for example, large drug cartels or army-type guerrilla elements such as the Fuerzas Armadas Revolucionarias de Colombia (FARC, Revolutionary Armed Forces of Colombia) or the Maoist insurgents in Nepal until the late 2000s—there is a common trend towards hybrid and network structural elements joined by more horizontal and informal links.[16]

Despite these parallels, fundamental differences between politico-military groups and organized criminal groups persist. A politico-military group ultimately aims to bring about—or prevent—a change in the government of a state or territory in line with some political or ideological agenda. Violence and any criminal activities that yield material benefits or engage-

---

[14] Geneva Declaration (note 3), p. 72.

[15] Geneva Declaration (note 3), pp. 76–77.

[16] On the shift towards networks see Arquilla, J. and Ronfeldt, D. (eds), *Networks and Netwars: The Future of Terror, Crime, and Militancy* (RAND: Santa Monica, CA, 2001); and Stepanova, E., *Terrorism in Asymmetrical Conflict: Ideological and Structural Aspects*, SIPRI Research Report no. 23 (Oxford University Press: Oxford, 2008), pp. 100–50.

ment with criminal groups are means to achieve that aim. In contrast, organized criminal groups are essentially apolitical; illicit profit is their main motive and *raison d'être*. Penetration of state structures and confrontation with law enforcement agencies are only intended to support this goal. Thus, politico-military combatants in an armed conflict are contesting a declared incompatibility over territory or government, whereas criminal groups are not.

The political opportunism of organized criminal groups is reflected in the fact that such groups are as ready to engage in illicit cooperation with corrupt state officials or with government-aligned armed actors as they are to establish links with rebel groups. This partly explains why even in those conflict areas where close crime–insurgency links can be observed—such as in Afghanistan and parts of Africa and the Andean Belt—insurgents are not the only actors involved in organized crime or cooperating with organized criminal groups.[17] In fact, organized crime at its most advanced stages aims at forming a symbiosis with the state and with the legal economy.

Another difference between the two groups can be found in how they typically use their funds, even if the sources of funding are similar. Politico-military actors are more likely to use financial resources to maintain or enhance their military potential; meet the social needs of the population supporting the group and the administrative needs of 'governing' territory under their control; and otherwise advance their political and ideological agenda. Organized criminal groups are more likely to invest in business expansion or to use their profits for unproductive purposes, such as buying large estates or gambling.

These distinctions, however, do not preclude the possibility of the political or ideological degradation of politico-military actors into purely criminal groups or of their forming links with organized criminal groups that go beyond pragmatic or business-type relationships. The distinctions between politico-military and criminal actors may also be less relevant in conflict areas in dysfunctional or failed states with a high degree of fragmentation of armed violence, the spread of militias of different types and the emergence of 'warlords' (i.e. powerbrokers fighting for control of power and resources and exploiting opportunities offered by insecurity and a war economy). In such fragmented settings, it is often impossible to single out more politically oriented or more criminally dominated groups from the complex web of localized violence.[18]

---

[17] E.g. in Afghanistan, corrupt state officials and the government's regional allies may be no less involved in the illicit drug business than the armed Islamist opposition. See section III below.

[18] See e.g. Reno, W., *Warlord Politics and African States* (Lynne Rienner: Boulder, CO, 1999); and Mueller, J., 'The banality of "ethnic war"', *International Security*, vol. 25, no. 1 (summer 2000). On the integration of criminal violence in fragmented conflict-related contexts see Stepanova, E., 'Trends in armed conflicts', *SIPRI Yearbook 2008*, pp. 44–71.

Links between politico-military and criminal groups

Politico-military non-state actors in armed opposition to governments usually have limited possibilities to finance themselves from legal sources. Most of these groups by default operate primarily within an informal economy and must fund themselves mainly by engaging in various forms of shadow economic activity, including criminal activity.

During the cold war, major non-state armed actors often enjoyed substantial external financial support, particularly from the states of the two competing blocs. When armed groups engaged in criminal activity, they often acted through criminal intermediaries. As external support dried up, many insurgency movements and other non-state armed groups had to become partly or completely self-financed. They engaged more actively in shadow economic activity, stepped up their cooperation with organized criminal groups and, increasingly, cut out the criminal intermediaries in order to maximize financial gains from criminal activity. Although the phenomenon of external states supporting or sponsoring insurgents has not disappeared, most of the insurgent groups that have emerged since the cold war have had to develop closer relationships with organized criminal groups or directly engage in criminal activities in order to operate.

While these relationships and engagement may take different forms, the common stages can be identified.[19] Most of the examples cited are of groups that started with and have not publicly renounced a politico-military agenda and have become engaged in the drug economy. However, politico-military groups, including those aligned with the state, engage in a variety of criminal and other shadow economic activities.[20]

1. *'Activity appropriation' and limited cooperation.* This stage is passed by all militant groups engaged in criminal activity. Some predatory criminal activities require no special skills, structures or networks, making it possible for politico-military actors simply to carry them out independently of criminal actors. In the case of activities that cannot be 'appropriated' in this way—such as illicit trafficking in drugs or other commodities in order to generate funds or access arms—politico-military actors engage in limited and temporary cooperative relationships with criminal groups. Another

[19] On categorization of types of links between militancy and crime see e.g. Shelley, L. I. et al., *Methods and Motives: Exploring Links between Transnational Organized Crime & International Terrorism*, Report by Transnational Crime and Corruption Center (TRACC) (National Institute of Justice: Rockville, MD, 2005), pp. 34–39; and Stepanova, E., 'El negocio de las drogas ilícitas y los conflictos armados: alcance y límites de sus vínculos' [The illicit drug trade and armed conflict: the scope and limits of its links], ed. J. G. Tokatlian, *Drogas y prohibición* [Drugs and prohibition] (Libros de Zorzal: Buenos Aires, 2010), pp. 313–44.

[20] See e.g. De Koning, R., 'Resource–conflict links in Sierra Leone and the Democratic Republic of the Congo', SIPRI Insights on Peace and Security no. 2008/2, Oct. 2008, <http://books.sipri.org/product_info?c_product_id=364>.

example of limited cooperation would be organized criminal groups outsourcing functions such as providing security to traffickers or controlling local cultivation and trade to politico-military groups based in or controlling the area. Politico-military groups' limited role in the trade in illicit commodities, including drugs and arms, in consumer countries—as had was by the Irish Republican Army (IRA) and as practised by Euskadi Ta Askatasuna (ETA, Basque Homeland and Freedom)—would also fall under this category.[21]

2. *Deeper cooperation and symbiosis.* In this stage, the criminal and politico-military groups develop deeper, broader and virtually unlimited cooperation, sometimes on a national scale. FARC is often cited as an example in this regard. In Colombia, the relationship between FARC and criminal groups developed into a clear division of labour, with the rebels dominating control over coca cultivation, production and trade at the local level, while organized criminals dominating the trafficking of the drug to consumer countries. Another classic case is the Taliban in Afghanistan in the 1990s. Up until 2000, the Taliban collected regular tithes from much of the country's poppy cultivation and tried, with much less success, to tax the local drug trade, while the operation of drug laboratories and international trafficking largely remained out of their control.

3. *Merger.* In the next stage, the armed group becomes so heavily engaged in criminal and shadow economic activity that it is no longer possible to identify it as either predominantly politico-military or purely criminal. Examples include the Islamic Movement of Uzbekistan (IMU), some FARC elements and the Mong Thai Army that was active in Myanmar until the mid-1990s.[22]

4. *Complete criminalization and ideological degradation.* Some groups that originally emerged as genuine socio-political actors, or elements and breakaway factions of such groups, have effectively abandoned their ideological aims to focus primarily on criminal activities. Examples include the Abu Sayyaf group in the Philippines, which engages in predatory and other criminal activity to such a degree that its commitment to any genuine political goals is heavily disputed.[23] Other examples include some remnants of the Peruvian Sendero Luminoso (Shining Path) rebel movement that partake in controlling the distribution of the drug *paco* in the Argentinian

---

[21] See e.g. Federation of American Scientists, Intelligence Resource Program, 'Irish Republican Army', <http://www.fas.org/irp/world/para/ira.htm>; and Labrousse, A. and Laniel, L. (eds), *The World Geopolitics of Drugs, 1998/1999* (Kluwer Academic Publishers: Dordrecht, 2002), pp. 124–27.

[22] On the IMU see Naumkin, V. V., *Militant Islam in Central Asia: The Case of the Islamic Movement of Uzbekistan* (University of California, Berkeley, Institute of Slavic, East European and Eurasian Studies: Berkeley, CA, 2003). On the Mong Thai Army see Stepanova, E., 'Addressing drugs and conflict in Myanmar: who will support alternative development?', SIPRI Policy Brief, June 2009, <http://books.sipri.org/product_info?c_product_id=383>.

[23] See e.g. Abuza Z., 'The demise of the Abu Sayyaf group in the southern Philippines', *CTC Sentinel*, vol. 1, no. 7 (June 2008), pp. 10–12.

capital Buenos Aires.[24] This stage becomes more likely as an armed confrontation becomes protracted, its intensity stabilizes at a relatively low
level and the prospects of the politico-military group's political goals being
achieved in the foreseeable future fade away. While far from unavoidable,
the likelihood of a group's gradual criminalization reaching such a critical
point becomes greater in the wake of a military defeat, when some leftover
units may intensify their involvement in criminal activities. Similarly, even
in relatively effective and inclusive peace processes, more radical offshoots
of a politico-military group may remain outside the process, lose popular
support, become more isolated and, as a means of survival, become primarily criminal organizations.

This description does not imply that every politico-military non-state
actor will eventually develop extensive links with organized crime and
become criminalized. Nor does it imply that the same group, or parts of it,
cannot be related to organized crime in more than one way in different
spheres of illicit activity. Also, these are only rough descriptions of some
common types of link, and are not exhaustive or universal.

It is also important to note some specifics regarding the financing and
links to crime of many grassroots Islamist armed movements—ranging
from Hamas in the Palestinian territories to the Islamic Courts movement
in Somalia—that are in large part funded through the redistribution of
regular religious donations (*zakat*) and charitable donations from local
members and support groups and sources in other Muslim countries and
diasporas around the world. These funds are channelled through a chain of
Islamic charities, foundations and banking institutions. They are partly
used for the benign social, humanitarian and religious purposes for which
many of the donors believed they were to be used and partly redirected for
armed violence, sometimes including terrorism. Such a system could be
considered the reverse of money laundering. As well as not engaging in
predatory or violent crime, such groups actually attempt to enforce basic
law and order in areas under their control, albeit sometimes by extremely
harsh means. Furthermore, in their countries, communities and diasporas
these movements tend to enjoy a better reputation for financial efficiency
and probity in their operations than many secular or non-fundamentalist
Muslim authorities.[25] However, such groups—particularly when operating
in a context of weak or absent state control or of protracted conflict—frequently engage in parasitic activities such as taxing trade in all types of

---

[24] International Crisis Group (ICG), *Latin American Drugs I: Losing the Fight*, Latin America
Report no. 25 (ICG: Bogotá/Brussels, 14 Mar. 2008), p. 21.

[25] The IMU, which has evolved from a non-criminalized fundamentalist Islamist group to heavy
criminalization, including predatory criminal violence, is a rare exception to this general pattern.

commodities and resources—from consumer goods and fuel to precious metals, illicit drugs and arms.[26]

III. Transnational crime in armed conflict settings

Piracy and conflict in Somalia

In 2009 the frequency of pirate attacks continued to rise for the fourth successive year.[27] The global epicentre of piracy was the coastline of Somalia, the Gulf of Aden and the adjacent areas of the Indian Ocean. Somali pirates hijacked 47 out of 49 vessels hijacked worldwide during the year and took 867 of the total of 1052 hostages. They also carried out 53 per cent of all pirate attacks in 2009—217 out of 406.[28]

Somali pirates seized vessels and held crews hostage for ransom, usually without causing serious harm to the ships or hostages. Pirates controlled many small coastal villages and towns and were the main contributors to the relative prosperity of larger port towns such as Boosaso. Their speedboats and small vessels operated both from these strongholds and from larger 'mother ships'—often hijacked dhows or fishing boats—which allowed the pirates to operate far from the coast.[29] While in 2008 most Somali pirate attacks took place in the Gulf of Aden, in 2009 their geographic range expanded well into the Indian Ocean, as far as the Seychelles.[30] This was partly a result of international anti-piracy operations, which provided a relatively safe international transit corridor immediately off the Somali coast and the Horn of Africa.[31]

Pirates emerged as a force off the Somali coast with the collapse of the Somali state in the early 1990s. At first they largely performed a coping and resilience function, protecting Somalia's otherwise unprotected waters rich with tuna, shrimp and lobster from a surge of illegal commercial fishing (worth up to $300 million per year) and forcing foreign ships to pay a

---

[26] See Stepanova, E., 'Beyond "narcoterrorism": illicit drug business and terrorist tactics in armed conflicts', ed. J. Buxton, *The Politics of Narcotic Drugs: A Survey* (Routledge: London, 2010); and Stepanova, E., 'Illicit drug trafficking and Islamist terrorism as threats to Russia's security: the limits of the linkage', PONARS Policy Memo no. 393, Center for Strategic and International Studies, Dec. 2005, <http://csis.org/files/media/csis/pubs/pm_0393.pdf>.

[27] There were 239 piracy incidents in 2006, 263 in 2007, 293 in 2008 and 406 in 2009. International Maritime Bureau, Piracy Reporting Centre, '2009 worldwide piracy figures surpass 400', 14 Jan. 2010, <http://www.icc-ccs.org/index.php?option=com_content&id=385>.

[28] International Maritime Bureau (note 27). In 2009, 28 piracy incidents occurred off the coast of Nigeria, 15 in Indonesia and 13 in the South China Sea.

[29] Beckman, R. and Koh, T., 'Pirates and the law', *New York Times*, 21 Apr. 2009.

[30] International Maritime Bureau (note 27); and 'Somali pirates hit oil tanker in long-range attack', Associated Press, 9 Nov. 2009. At the time of writing, the longest-range Somali pirate attack took place on 9 Nov. 2009, 1852 kilometres east of the Somali capital, Mogadishu. EU NAVFOR Somalia, 'Longest range pirate attack on crude oil tanker in Indian Ocean', Press release, 9 Nov. 2009, <http://www.eunavfor.eu/2009/11/page/3/>.

[31] International Maritime Bureau (note 27).

'tax'.[32] Later on, piracy turned into a booming shadow economic industry and one of the few profitable—and cross-clan—activities for Somalis in coastal areas, with turnover in 2008 reaching $50–80 million, according to some estimates.[33] While a share of the ransoms extracted was set aside to buy arms, fuel and so on for further operations, the rest was divided among the pirates and their extended families and clan members, and often included a cut for 'bosses' and local officials.[34] More generally, Somali piracy in 2009 illustrated the elusive boundary between legal and illegal economies, and between elements of formal governance structures and organized crime in chronically weak or failed states torn by conflicts and instability. Somali pirates often described themselves as marines or coast-guards and were allegedly linked to elements in the regional authorities, senior national officials or even 'all significant political actors in Somalia'.[35]

While piracy benefited limited groups of people, as well as patronage systems connected to authorities in areas where they existed, it did not emerge as an effective coping strategy for the wider population, even in coastal areas.[36] Although high levels of insecurity and the use of informal money transfer systems made it difficult to trace where the cash from ransoms in Somalia went, the bulk of it was apparently put to unproductive uses such as building larger houses among huts, buying expensive cars or hosting opulent wedding parties. Piracy also scared off commercial cargo ships from Somali ports and may have been linked to the growth of kidnapping for ransom onshore.[37]

While pirate activity in Somalia was fragmented and scattered along the 3025 kilometre-long Somali coastline, its main hubs were in areas that were not the main hotbeds of the armed conflict in the country, such as the semi-autonomous Puntland, where it enjoyed a degree of patronage from the local authorities. Ironically, the most direct link between pirate activity and armed confrontation took the form of pirate attacks on ships that were carrying weapons for the Somali Government in violation of the UN arms embargo.[38] There is to date no credible evidence that piracy has directly fuelled armed conflict in Somalia, nor that pirates have any overt or systematic links to the Islamist insurgent groups, although some southern

---

[32] Hari, J., 'You are being lied to about pirates', *The Independent*, 5 Jan. 2009.
[33] Straziuso, J., 'US drones protecting ships from Somali pirates', Associated Press, 23 Oct. 2009; and Gettleman, J., 'Somalia's pirates flourish in a lawless nation', *New York Times*, 30 Oct. 2008.
[34] Gettleman, J., 'Somalia's pirates flourish in a lawless nation', *New York Times*, 31 Oct. 2008.
[35] Gettleman (note 34). See also Hari (note 32).
[36] While turnover from piracy reached $50–80 million in 2008 (see above), the total remittances from the Somali diaspora reportedly amounted to $1 billion. World Bank, 'Somalia: country brief', Aug. 2009, <http://go.worldbank.org/79I6OT35O0>.
[37] Gettleman (note 34).
[38] Guled, A., 'Somali pirates hijack two more ships', Reuters, 11 Nov. 2009, <http://www.reuters.com/article/idUSTRE5AA0VP20091111>.

pirate bases were in insurgent-held areas.[39] Pirates were viewed by both radical and the more moderate Islamists as un-Islamic forces and blamed for 'spoiling' devout Muslims and introducing alcohol, drugs and other 'evils'. The pirates appeared to be more wary of the Islamist forces onshore than of international naval patrols at sea.[40]

The main way in which the armed confrontation in turn affected the level of pirate activity was indirect, but perhaps more fundamental. This was the role of the ongoing armed confrontation between numerous groups and factions in undermining any governance arrangements at the national level and preventing the emergence of local or regional governance structures that are not dysfunctional, corrupt and partly financed by illicit transnational crime, such as the autonomous authorities of Puntland.[41] The conflict could be said to have been roughly between government forces—with formal backing from the UN and external military and intelligence support mainly from Ethiopia and the United States[42]—and the Islamist insurgents. However, the line of confrontation was not always clear, given the Islamist background of most government officials in 2009 and their former alliance with the radical Islamist al-Shabab insurgent group. In reality, none of the armed factions in 2009 was powerful, coherent or popular enough to prevail over others and end the violence. The African Union Mission in Somalia (AMISOM), a UN-mandated peacekeeping force, has compromised its local legitimacy by, among other things, its association with the Ethiopian forces that occupied Somalia from 2006 to January 2009 and were associated with some of the worst attacks against civilians in the country.[43]

While both ongoing armed violence of a more political, religious or clan-based nature onshore and piracy offshore can be seen as manifestations of the profound weakness or absence of state capacity in Somalia, the armed conflict can also be seen as a critical catalyst of that state weakness, even if its implications were less transnational and less publicized internationally than the threat posed by Somalia-based piracy to commercial navigation.

---

[39] Guled, A. and Sheikh, A., 'Somali pirates seize weapons ship, attack tanker', Reuters, 9 Nov. 2009, <http://www.reuters.com/article/idUSL9062439>.

[40] Gettleman, J., 'The pirate chronicles: for Somali pirates, worst enemy may be on shore', New York Times, 9 May 2009.

[41] The only exceptions from this general pattern are Somaliland in the north and areas controlled by the radical Islamists, including al-Shabab.

[42] In 2009 France started to train 500 Somali soldiers at its base in Djibouti and, in Jan. 2010, the EU decided to provide training to 2000 Somali troops. 'EU agrees to train Somali troops', BBC News, 25 Jan. 2010, <http://news.bbc.co.uk/2/hi/8479564.stm>.

[43] On the nature of the conflict in Somalia and on violence against civilians see Stepanova, E., 'Trends in armed conflicts: one-sided violence against civilians', SIPRI Yearbook 2009, pp. 46–52. The expansion of AMISOM is now opposed not only by anti-government Islamist insurgents but also by a group of clerics who back the Somali president. 'Somalia peacekeeping effort encounters country's resistance to foreign intervention', Voice of America, 23 Mar. 2009, <http://www1.voa news.com/english/news/a-13-2009-03-23-voa26-68824977.html>.

Ideally, efforts to address problems of internal state building and conflict resolution onshore in Somalia should be linked with the management of the piracy threat by external actors through enforcement and diplomatic means. However, they continued to develop as two separate tracks in 2009.

On 8 December 2008 the European Union (EU) deployed to the region its first naval operation under the European Security and Defence Policy, the EU Naval Force Somalia (EU NAVFOR Somalia, or Operation Atalanta) to escort ships, including vessels leased by the World Food Programme to deliver humanitarian relief to Somalia.[44] In 2009 the USA, the North Atlantic Treaty Organization (NATO) and several other states, including China, Russia, India, Japan and South Korea, deployed ships to patrol the area and combat piracy. One of Somalia's neighbours, Kenya, accepted pirates for trial from foreign forces and signed memoranda of understanding with the EU, the United Kingdom and the USA agreeing to try suspected pirates in return for assistance in upgrading its judicial system.[45]

Thus, the international response to Somali piracy developed in 2009, mounting more frequent and better-coordinated naval patrols and establishing procedures for the criminal prosecution of Somali pirates, including in cooperation with states in the region. However, there are limits to how much can be achieved with such an approach. While some progress was made by the international community in managing piracy, no visible progress was made regarding state building, including building or strengthening functional governance at the subnational level, or conflict resolution. The main condition for a long-term decline in piracy along the longest coastline in Africa can only be the revival of a semblance of functional government in Somalia, which requires a more representative Islamist government and an end to armed confrontation with the radical Islamists.

The present moderate Islamist government of Sheikh Sharif Sheikh Ahmed has international legitimacy and, unlike its recent predecessors, retains at least some domestic legitimacy. However, neither the government nor any other faction in Somalia is likely to prevail militarily, even with external support. The challenge of state building requires not only—and not even primarily—an internationally dictated solution, but a sustainable internal power-sharing arrangement. Such an arrangement could make use of any ties that some of the Islamists in the present government retain with parts of al-Shabab to sow further divisions among the radicals and integrate some of the rebel leaders, such as Abu Mansur and Sheikh

[44] EU NAVFOR Somalia, 'Mission: European Union naval operation against piracy', <http://www.eunavfor.eu/about-us/mission/>.

[45] Corder, M., 'Nations look to Kenya as venue for piracy trials', Associated Press, 17 Apr. 2009; and Marquand, R., 'Sticky legal battles await for captured Somali pirates', *Christian Science Monitor*, 14 Apr. 2009.

Hassan Dahir Aweys, into the government or, if that fails, even directly engage the key armed opposition actors. This kind of arrangement, however, is likely to be resisted by the USA, the key external actor in Somali affairs from outside the region, which has ruled out any political solution involving al-Shabab.

Illicit drugs and armed violence in Afghanistan

Afghanistan is the locus of one of the world's most intense major armed conflicts and of the great majority of global poppy cultivation and opiate production.[46] The opiate output of Afghanistan has grown exponentially since the toppling of the Taliban government by a US-led invasion in 2001. According to UNODC statistics, the area under poppy cultivation in 2007 was more than 25 times that in 2001, when the Taliban ban on opium poppy cultivation was in force.[47] While the area under poppy cultivation decreased in both 2008 and 2009, it remains more than 35 per cent greater than that in the pre-2001 peak year of 1999.[48]

In addition to the lack of functional state capacity in post-Taliban Afghanistan, other main factors behind the exponential growth of the opium economy have been its role as a socio-economic adaptation strategy for peasants in a country torn by decades of armed conflict and dominated by the shadow economy; the potential income from trafficking opiates, which make it the most lucrative illicit business for many smuggling networks overlapping with tribal and clan networks; and the role of the illicit drug business in financing the Taliban-dominated insurgency. This last factor has grown significantly in importance since the early years after the invasion, as the insurgency has gained strength and extended areas under its control. In 2006–2007 various insurgent groups and warlords collected $200–400 million a year in drug-related funds, according to UNODC estimates. This income came from levies on opium farmers; protection fees on laboratory processing of opiates; transit fees on drug convoys; and 'taxation' on imports of chemical precursors.[49] The UNODC is, however, careful to emphasize that those who profit from the opium business in Afghanistan include 'a broad range of profiteers, at home and abroad',

---

[46] In 2008 Afghanistan produced over 93% of opiates and accounted for 83% of poppy cultivation worldwide. UN Office on Drugs and Crime (UNODC), *World Drug Report 2009* (UNODC: Vienna, 2009), pp. 33–34.

[47] Poppy cultivation in Afghanistan reached its peak of 193 000 hectares in 2007, having risen from a low of 8000 ha in 2001. UN Office on Drugs and Crime (UNODC), *Afghanistan Opium Survey 2008* (UNODC: Vienna, Nov. 2008), p. 7.

[48] UN Office on Drugs and Crime (UNODC) and Afghan Ministry of Counter Narcotics, *Afghanistan Opium Survey 2009: Summary Findings* (UNODC: Vienna, Sep. 2009), p. 1.

[49] UN Office on Drugs and Crime (UNODC), *Addiction, Crime and Insurgency: The Transnational Threat of the Afghan Opium* (UNODC: Vienna, 2009), p. 2.

including purely criminal groups and even government officials.[50] Some field-based studies go further to suggest that there is a widespread perception in southern Afghanistan that 'corrupt officials are more involved in the drugs trade than anti-government elements', while the Taliban's involvement in the drug trade is seen by the local population as being limited to collecting an agricultural tithe (*ushr*), which is typically divided equally between the local mullah and the Taliban.[51]

The Afghan opium economy and its output have had dramatic transnational implications. According to the head of the UNODC, Antonio Maria Costa, Afghan opiates were in 2009 feeding a global trade in heroin that resulted in over 10 000 narcotics-related deaths in NATO member countries alone.[52] This not only underscores the scale of the impact of drugs of Afghan origin on the outside world but also calls into question the goals and relevance of the foreign military presence in Afghanistan. The implications of Afghanistan's booming opium economy for its neighbours, such as Iran, and the major transit and consumer states bordering the region, such as Russia, were even more serious.[53]

Despite the continued growth of the Afghan security forces, the USA and the NATO-led International Security Assistance Force (ISAF) were the most militarily powerful actors in Afghanistan during 2009, and the Taliban were the main insurgent force.[54] Annual US spending in Afghanistan now exceeds that in Iraq—$65 billion was proposed for Afghanistan, compared with $61 billion for Iraq in the financial year (FY) 2010 budget request, mostly for military- and security-related purposes.[55] The USA's overarching goal in Afghanistan—redefined in a December 2009 speech by US President Barack Obama—is 'to disrupt, dismantle, and defeat al Qaeda

[50] The UNODC also notes that Afghan farmers have annually gained up to $1 billion from opium production, whereas the global heroin market is worth around $65 billion per year. UN Office on Drugs and Crime (note 49), pp. 2–3.

[51] Mansfield, D., 'Responding to risk and uncertainty: understanding the nature of change in the rural livelihoods of opium poppy growing households in the 2007/2008 growing season', Report for the British Government's Afghan Drugs Inter-departmental Unit, July 2008, <http://www.davidmansfield.org/field_work.php>, p. 47.

[52] UNODC (note 49), p. 1; and Costa's presentation of this UNODC report quoted in MacFarquhar, N., 'Report shows Afghan drugs reach deep in the West', *New York Times*, 23 Oct. 2009.

[53] Iran reported the largest heroin seizures in 2007 (25% of the world total) and had one of the highest rates of opiate consumption (2.8% of its population). Russia quickly evolved from being primarily a transit point to become, by 2009, Europe's largest consumer market for opiates, with an addiction rate of 1.6% and, according to some estimates, the world's largest market for heroin of Afghan origin. UN Office on Drugs and Crime (note 46), pp. 42, 55; and Viktor Ivanov, head of the Russian Federal Drug Control Service, quoted in 'Russia is top heroin consumer, report finds', Reuters, 7 Mar. 2009.

[54] See Foxley, T., 'Security and politics in Afghanistan: progress, problems and prospects', *SIPRI Yearbook 2009*.

[55] Harrison, T., 'Analysis of the FY 2010 defense budget request', Presentation, Center for Strategic and Budgetary Assessments (CSBA), 12 Aug. 2009, <http://www.csbaonline.org/4Publications/PubLibrary/S.20090812.Press_Briefing_on_/S.20090812.Press_Briefing_on_.pdf>, p. 4. On military spending in and by Afghanistan see chapter 5 in this volume.

in Afghanistan and Pakistan, and to prevent its capacity to threaten America and our allies in the future'.[56] Anti-Taliban counterinsurgency in Afghanistan is seen as one of the main ways to achieve that goal. The US strategy envisages a surge of 30 000 additional US troops in Afghanistan and makes the transfer of security duties to Afghan forces a condition for US withdrawal.

Even though the Afghan opiates do not threaten the USA directly, from 2001 the USA was the largest contributor to counternarcotics efforts in Afghanistan, allocating about $2.9 billion in FYs 2001–2009. However, in March 2009 the US special representative for Afghanistan and Pakistan, Richard Holbrooke, called this 'the most wasteful and ineffective program I have seen in 40 years in and out of the government'.[57] In 2009 the Obama Administration called for a major review of US counternarcotics policy in Afghanistan.[58] The revised policy formally moved away from the USA's usual heavy reliance on forced eradication and prioritized a combination of interdiction—more effective drug seizures, targeting drug traders, cross-border traffickers and heroin laboratories—and alternative development measures, such as crop substitution.[59]

However, the stepped up counternarcotics efforts in Afghanistan were subordinated to the US counterinsurgency strategy, focusing on 'going after those targets where there is a strong nexus between the insurgency and the narcotics trade, to deny resources to the Taliban'.[60] While linking counternarcotics to anti-Taliban counterinsurgency was probably necessary to provide a 'national interest' justification for increasing counternarcotics assistance to Afghanistan—the USA is not directly threatened by Afghan-sourced opiates—it was also highly questionable, for reasons discussed below.

---

[56] White House, 'Remarks by the President in address to the nation on the way forward in Afghanistan and Pakistan', Press release, 1 Dec. 2009, <http://www.whitehouse.gov/the-press-office/remarks-president-address-nation-way-forward-afghanistan-and-pakistan>.

[57] Quoted in Blanchard, C. M., *Afghanistan: Narcotics and U.S. Policy*, Congressional Research Service (CRS) Report for Congress RL32686 (US Congress: Washington, DC, 21 Apr. 2009), p. i.

[58] The policy shift was first announced by Holbrooke during a G8 conference on stabilizing Afghanistan, Trieste, 27 June 2009. 'U.S. reverse Afghan drug policy', Reuters, 27 June 2009; Blanchard (note 57), pp. 7–8; and Presidential Determination on Major Illicit Drug Transit or Major Illicit Drug Producing Countries for Fiscal Year 2010, US Presidential Determination no. 2009-30 of 15 Sep. 2009, *Federal Register*, 23 Sep. 2009, pp. 48369–72.

[59] On the strengths and weaknesses of various counternarcotics measures and the counterproductive effects of forced eradication in Afghanistan see Rubin, B. R. and Sherman, J., *Counter-Narcotics to Stabilize Afghanistan: The False Promise of Crop Eradication* (New York University, Center on International Cooperation: New York, Feb. 2008); and Felbab-Brown, V., 'Afghanistan: when counternarcotics undermine counterterrorism', *Washington Quarterly*, vol 28, no. 4 (autumn 2005).

[60] Michael G. Vickers, Assistant Secretary of Defense for Special Operations/Low-Intensity Conflict and Interdependent Capabilities, quoted in Shanker, T. and Bumiller E., 'U.S. shifts Afghan narcotics strategy', *New York Times*, 23 July 2009.

NATO, for its part, struggled to execute a number of counternarcotics tasks in Afghanistan, mainly confined to assisting the Afghan authorities 'through training, intelligence and logistics, and *in-extremis* support', in 2009.[61] The guidance issued by the NATO defence ministers meeting in Budapest in October 2008 for the first time allowed ISAF to provide support in actions against drug laboratories and traffickers—but only those 'providing material support to the insurgents'.[62] NATO's transformation and its search for a new mission may have extended its purview beyond collective defence, but it did not, and probably could not, turn NATO into an effective police force or development agency—the types of actor better suited to counternarcotics. Although some NATO members, particularly those such as the UK whose own domestic markets were heavily affected by the trade in Afghan opiates, showed genuine interest in counternarcotics in Afghanistan, willingness to get involved varied from one member state to another.

Whether the renewed counternarcotics efforts of NATO and the USA can contribute to a significant and sustainable reduction in Afghanistan's opium output is doubtful. Their interests and capabilities in this field can have only limited impact on Afghanistan's deeply embedded opium economy. A more fundamental question, as in the case of anti-piracy efforts along the Somali coast, is whether counternarcotics can ever succeed in Afghanistan while the state is unable to establish even a minimally functional presence in much of the country.

Deeply embedded drug economies have never been—and cannot be—effectively undermined by external forces or actors. In the few cases where an opium economy has been reduced—for example, Maoist China, Myanmar since the mid-1990s and Thailand from the 1970s to the 2000s—it has primarily come as the result of actions by functional national authorities, usually with minimal foreign aid.[63] Afghanistan in 2000–2001 is another case in point. In 2001, the year of the US-led invasion, Afghan opium production had been reduced by 91 per cent in a year following a total religious ban (*haram*) imposed on 27 June 2000 by the Taliban regime.[64] The motivations behind the ban were multiple. When the Taliban came to power in 1996 Afghanistan was already the well-established hub of the regional shadow economy. The Taliban tried from the start to limit opium cultivation on religious grounds. They also taxed it, having established a form of rentier state taxing all sorts of formal and informal trade and agricultural

---

[61] NATO, *Afghanistan Report 2009* (NATO Public Diplomacy Division: Brussels, 2009), p. 29.

[62] NATO (note 61), p. 29.

[63] Stepanova, E. A., [The role of drug trafficking in the political economy of conflict and terrorism], (Ves Mir/IMEMO: Moscow, 2005) (in Russian); and Stepanova (note 22).

[64] UN International Drug Control Programme (UNDCP), *Afghanistan: Annual Opium Poppy Survey 2001* (UNDCP: Islamabad, 2001), p. ii.

production.[65] However, their revenues from taxing the smuggling of consumer goods were larger than those from opium cultivation; for example, in 1997 the Taliban collected $75 million in revenues from taxing the regional trade in consumer goods, and only $27 million from taxing poppy cultivation.[66] It may be that the 2000 opium cultivation ban was in part intended to avert further international sanctions that could have hurt the Taliban's income from taxing smuggling. Thus, market and political conditions coupled with a strong religious imperative favoured an opium cultivation ban.

Perhaps more importantly, by 2000 the Taliban had emerged as a functional de facto state controlling much of Afghanistan, with the exception of some regions in the north. They were able to impose basic (sharia) law and order and to ensure that their decisions were implemented at local level. No authority had managed to exercise effective governance in such a large part of the country since at least the 1970s, when a series of internationalized internal conflicts began, nor has any authority since the 2001 invasion.

Experience has shown that a major opium economy can be substantially weakened only if two basic, underlying conditions are in place: favourable global and regional market conditions and functioning state capacity, including some basically functioning governance in drug-producing areas. The precise combination of different types of counternarcotics strategies or the scale of foreign counternarcotics assistance has proved much less decisive.[67]

The drops in Afghan opium cultivation in 2008 and 2009 were largely the result of a positive market correction. Overproduction of opium in 2007 pushed opiate prices down. This combined with a sharp rise in wheat prices and food insecurity among Afghan peasant led to a discernible shift to wheat cultivation in Afghanistan, partly at the expense of poppy crops.[68]

However, the second condition—functioning state capacity—was missing in 2009, illustrated by significant poppy cultivation even in Kabul Province, close to the Afghan capital; a very low level of drug seizures; and the complicity of the government's powerbrokers in the regions and elements of the security services, especially the police, in the drug trade.[69] The armed confrontations with the insurgents that continued throughout 2009 and intensified around the presidential elections in August resulted in no

---

[65] For more detail see e.g. Rubin, B. R., 'The political economy of war and peace in Afghanistan', *World Development*, vol. 28, no. 10 (Oct. 2000).

[66] Naqvi, Z. F., *Afghanistan–Pakistan Trade Relations* (World Bank: Islamabad, 1999), pp. 15–16. At that time, the more profitable functions such as refinement of opium into heroin mostly took place outside Afghanistan.

[67] See e.g. Stepanova (note 19); Stepanova (note 22); Stepanova (note 26); and Stepanova (note 63).

[68] UN Office on Drugs and Crime and Afghan Ministry of Counter Narcotics (note 48), p. 25.

[69] UN Office on Drugs and Crime and Afghan Ministry of Counter Narcotics (note 48), p. 31. See also Mansfield (note 51).

apparent improvement and arguably a deterioration—in state function-ality. The controversy surrounding Hamid Karzai's re-election as president further damaged local and international perceptions of his government's legitimacy.

The prospects for a decisive military victory for either the insurgency or the Afghan Government and its international backers were bleak in 2009. Rather, the confrontation seems set to drag on for years. In these circumstances, no mix of counternarcotics measures, hard or soft, will succeed.

A sustainable reduction in Afghan opium production is completely dependent on the re-establishment of some form of functional governance that is able to restore some public services and provide minimal law and order and a non-confrontational relationship with the local population in areas that are out of stable control by the national government or foreign forces. This goal requires durable ceasefires; it is unlikely to be achieved in the midst of continuing armed confrontation with the Taliban. It is to be hoped that the increasingly vocal and high-profile calls for negotiation with at least parts of the insurgency heard at the beginning of 2010 will bear fruit.[70] Not only do they point to the best means of ending the conflict, but they also offer hopes of establishing more functional and locally legitimate authorities in the areas most affected by poppy cultivation and opium production. This is a *sine qua non* for a genuine and sustainable reduction in Afghanistan's opium economy.

IV. A new type of armed conflict?

Even in the absence of an armed conflict in the classic sense, violence committed by, between and against organized criminal groups may itself become comparable to that of an armed conflict in terms of its scale and intensity. Criminal violence in countries such as Brazil, Mexico and South Africa has acquired a chronic, systemic character and threatens to undermine social order at the national level and the governance system in several areas.

Such situations do not meet the classic definition of armed conflict for several reasons, even if they account for an equivalent number of fatalities. Perhaps the most important is that the definition of an armed conflict requires that the fighting be contesting a declared incompatibility over government or political control of territory. Most organized criminal groups engaged in fighting state security forces do not claim to be contesting such an incompatibility. Nevertheless, some of the more intense and lethal violent campaigns waged by criminal actors or the violence used by

---

[70] See e.g. Green, M., 'McChrystal sees Taliban role', *Financial Times*, 24 Jan. 2010; Tarling, S. and Reshad, F., 'Kabul seeks to reintegrate Taliban', *Financial Times*, 26 Jan. 2010; and Filkins, D., 'U.N. seeks to drop some Taliban from terror list', *New York Times*, 24 Jan. 2010.

governments as part of anti-criminal campaigns have already been included in data sets on one-sided violence against civilians—a type of violence distinct from armed conflict, even if it is often committed in conflict-related contexts.[71] In other cases, violence committed by criminal organizations is still categorized as purely criminal and is only reflected in national homicide statistics.

In cases of high homicide levels coupled with sustained patterns of widespread and intense armed confrontation between government security forces and violent organized criminal groups, it is worth exploring whether they actually herald the emergence of a new type of armed conflict, in terms of both actors and the type of incompatibility involved. One such case is drug trafficking-related violence in Mexico, which continued unabated in 2009.

Drug-related violence in Mexico

Unlike Afghanistan, a leading drug producer, Mexico primarily serves as a key transit point along a drug trafficking route. Mexico is a base for some of the most notorious violent drug trafficking organizations in the western hemisphere. Although it has not been the site of a classic armed conflict for more than a decade, Mexico is now experiencing the high-intensity, combat-style narcotics-related violence that could be compared with a major armed conflict.

The number of fatalities caused by organized crime, especially drug trafficking, has steadily increased in Mexico from 2100 in 2006 to 2600 in 2007 and at least 6200 in 2008—only 1 of the 16 major armed conflicts in 2008 caused more battle-related fatalities.[72] While Mexico has generally had high crime rates in the past, recent years have seen a sharp escalation of criminal and anti-criminal violence.

The role of Mexican organized criminal groups in trafficking illicit drugs has expanded intensively since 2001. Traditionally, Mexican groups controlled the trade in cannabis (which has long been produced in Mexico), but in recent years they have taken over the trafficking of cocaine, and its distribution in North America, from Colombian traffickers. This resulted from a combination of factors. Notably, Mexico's 'location curse' acquired special importance with the destruction of large Colombian cartels in the 1990s and the subsequent fragmentation of the Colombian drug business and 'outsourcing' of functions such as trafficking. By 2009 Mexican organized criminal groups had largely replaced criminal actors from

[71] On the UCDP one-sided violence data set see Harbom and Walensteen (note 8), pp. 75–77. On one-sided violence see Stepanova (note 43).

[72] Freedom House, 'Mexico', *Freedom in the World 2009* (Freedom House: Washington, DC, 16 July 2009); and Harbom and Wallensteen (note 8), pp. 81–83.

Colombia and elsewhere as the pre-eminent drug trafficking organizations in the Americas. The most recent stage of this process involved internal feuds over control of the groups and growing turf wars between them.

The most important and largest organized criminal groups in Mexico—including the Tijuana, Sinaloa, Gulf and Beltran Leyva cartels—have sought in recent years to establish their own quasi-states-within-a-state in areas under their control in order to maximize their profits and to contest the control of the most violence-prone cities, such as Ciudad Juárez and Tijuana.[73] Mexican organized criminal groups had diverse organizational structures, from more hierarchical and top-down to networks of semi-independent cells. All of the larger groups had paramilitary units or forces or, like the Gulf Cartel, which controlled territory along Mexico's eastern coastline, hired a paramilitary force, Las Zetas, to perform the same functions.[74] While most cartels smuggled cocaine, cannabis and, increasingly, opiates produced in the Andean Belt, a few groups specialized in trafficking methamphetamines to the USA. One of the latter, La Familia Michoacana, originally emerged as a vigilante anti-drug group. La Familia also stood out for its cult-like organization and pseudoreligious ideology, as well as its substantial recruitment of drug addicts. In Oct. 2009 the US Department of Justice targeted La Familia distribution networks in the USA in its largest operation ever undertaken against a Mexican drug cartel.[75]

After taking office in December 2006 Mexican President Felipe Calderón initiated a major crackdown on organized crime, with a 'zero tolerance' approach. The crackdown used military methods—and military forces—against the criminals. Calderón's campaign was intended to bolster his legitimacy after a very narrow victory in a heavily contested election by winning the support of a crime-weary population. By 2009 it had helped to create a cycle of violence, with gangs resorting to more intense and extreme violence in the hope that the population would pressure the authorities to seek a ceasefire with them. By some estimates there were over 6200 drug-related killings in Mexico in 2008, more than double the number in 2007, and over 1100 in the first half of 2009.[76] The majority of fatalities in 2007–2009 were among members of criminal groups and law

---

[73] Although the Mexican organized groups involved in drug trafficking are not strictly cartels in the economic sense of the word—organizations that cooperate to control prices and production—they are commonly referred to as such.

[74] Manwaring, M. G., A 'New' Dynamic in the Western Hemisphere Security Environment: The Mexican Zetas and Other Private Armies (US Army War College, Strategic Studies Institute: Carlisle, PA, Sep. 2009), p. 18.

[75] 'Mexico, U.S.: La Familia Michoacana's increasing woes', STRATFOR, 22 Oct. 2009, <http://www.stratfor.com/memberships/147679/>.

[76] Lacey, M., 'In drug war, Mexico fights cartel and itself', New York Times, 30 Mar. 2009. While these tallies are still lower than those of drug-trade related killings by Colombian cartels in the 1980s, the situation in Mexico has not been aggravated by a parallel major armed conflict, as it was in Colombia.

enforcement personnel (including the acting chief of federal police), although innocent civilians are often caught in crossfire and, in some cases, targeted directly with kidnappings and other abuses.[77] Drug-related and other criminal and anti-criminal violence were the prevailing forms of armed violence in Mexico in 2009, although they sometimes overlapped with other forms, for example agrarian violence over land rights in rural areas.[78]

The similarities of the Mexican Government's approach to the 'enforcement' component of the US-backed Colombian counternarcotics strategy were striking, especially in the large-scale use of armed forces to fight organized criminal groups. In 2009 the Mexican Government continued to deploy over 25 000 soldiers to the most insecure areas alongside the local police.[79] The troops confronted heavily armed paramilitary groups in urban settings, from the border town of Tijuana to the capital, Mexico City, using military-grade weapons that included anti-tank rockets and armour-piercing munitions. While this involvement of the military was partly motivated by the reputation of Mexico's armed forces as significantly less corrupt than the police, the military did not prove well suited for these essentially law enforcement tasks, especially in densely populated areas, and a growing number of soldiers and officers defected from the military to join the cartels.[80]

The United States also supported the Mexican crackdown, including through the supply of equipment and training to Mexican security forces under the Mérida Initiative (also known as Plan Mexico), similar to the support given to Colombia (Plan Colombia), but on a smaller scale. The Mérida Initiative was originally envisaged as a 2–3-year initiative providing counternarcotics assistance and funding of $1.4 billion to Central American countries, chiefly Mexico.[81] Criticisms have included that it fails to address root causes, such as poverty in Mexico and demand for drugs in the USA, and that human rights concerns linked to the Mexican Army's previous record in counternarcotics have been given too little attention.[82]

Yet another similarity between Mexico in the late 2000s and Colombia in the 1990s was the emergence and proliferation of vigilante self-defence groups that quickly transformed into major organized criminal actors themselves, such as La Familia Michoacana. While symmetrical means to confront an asymmetrical challenge—deploying cartel-style vigilante

---

[77] 'Mexico security memo: May 12, 2008', STRATFOR, 12 May 2008, <http://www.stratfor.com/memberships/116374/>.
[78] Malkin, E., 'Gunmen kill union leader in Mexico', *New York Times*, 1 Nov. 2009.
[79] Freedom House (note 72).
[80] Lacey (note 76).
[81] US Department of State, 'Merida Initiative', <http://www.state.gov/p/inl/merida/>.
[82] E.g. Witness for Peace, 'Merida Initiative "Plan Mexico" fact sheet', 2009, <http://www.witnessforpeace.org/article.php?id=698>.

groups to fight cartels—may actually be a more efficient strategy against
existing cartels than large-scale military deployments, it also guarantees
continuing turf wars and high levels of drug-related violence.

The ongoing large-scale police reform and the revamping of the entire
judicial system in Mexico are perhaps the more promising responses to the
ongoing violence in the long term. Measures undertaken so far include the
reorganization of the two federal police agencies under a single commander and the establishment of a new police training institute and of a
national database to share information and intelligence.[83] These measures
are especially urgent in view of both pervasive corruption, especially in the
police, which requires the rebuilding of entire forces across Mexico, and
the general inefficiency and limited functionality of the law enforcement
and judicial systems—illustrated by the fact that of the 50 000 arrests in
Mexico since the launch of the counternarcotics offensive in December
2006, only a small number were the result of thorough professional
investigations or ended in convictions.[84] In 2008 Mexico's chief organized-
crime prosecutor and the director of the national Interpol office were
arrested for accepting money from drug cartels.[85]

V. Conclusions

The main global trends in armed conflict and other forms of organized
political violence display different dynamics to those shown by global
trends in criminal violence. Criminal violence is incomparably more frequent and far more widespread than armed conflict or one-sided violence
against civilians. The decline and stabilization in the overall number of
armed conflicts contrasts with a slow but steady increase in overall global
crime levels in recent years, as well as a lack of any discernible decline in
global, regional and subregional levels of criminal violence. The distribution of criminal violence around the world also shows that the countries
and regions that display the highest rates of criminal violence are not
necessarily those most heavily affected by major armed conflicts, even
though the intensity and modes of armed violence in these areas approximate those typical of classic armed conflict. Protracted and intense armed
confrontation involving purely criminal organizations—whether the violence is aimed at the state, other non-state groups or civilians—and states
requires further empirical and theoretical research and deserves a category
of its own in crime and conflict analysis. Campaigns of criminal violence
are often matched—or even escalated—by high-intensity anti-criminal

---

[83] See Olson, E. L., *Police Reform and Modernization in Mexico, 2009* (Woodrow Wilson International Center for Scholars, Mexico Institute: Washington, DC, 2009).
[84] Lacey, M., 'In Mexican drug war, investigators are fearful', *New York Times*, 16 Oct. 2009.
[85] Ellingwood, K., 'Former anti-drug chief is arrested', *Los Angeles Times*, 22 Nov. 2008.

violence by police and other state security forces. Even in the most violence-prone regions, crime levels appear to be lower where the response goes beyond containment or harsh enforcement. This brings into question the attempts to apply military means to counter this type of armed violence.

As this chapter also shows, it cannot be taken for granted that close links will be forged between armed opposition groups and organized criminal actors, even in the midst of ongoing armed conflicts, especially where Islamist insurgents are concerned. There may be a high degree of collusion between transnational criminal and politico-military non-state actors in some conflict-affected regions but much less in others. Even where highly profitable and transnational forms of organized crime emerge in unstable, conflict-torn countries, such as piracy off the Somali coast, this may not have direct links with an armed insurgency.

The dominant illicit economic activities that form the basis of the large-scale and deeply embedded regional shadow economy—for example the opium economy centred in Afghanistan—play multifunctional roles in conflict or post-conflict environments: not only financing armed opposition groups, but yielding profits to most major local politico-military actors, including those loyal to the government, alongside criminal trafficking networks. Segments of weak or corrupt state systems may be no less closely involved in illegal business activity than armed opposition groups, while parts of the state security apparatus and government-affiliated actors (including former insurgents partly integrated into state security forces) may be heavily engaged in criminal violence.

In sum, the most important link between armed conflict and organized crime in conflict-affected areas may be more fundamental, even if less straightforward, than the role of revenues from criminal or informal economic activity in the financing of armed opposition groups. It may be more accurate to view both as key manifestations of general state dysfunction. At the same time, as shown by the cases of Afghanistan and Somalia, protracted armed conflicts with no decisive outcome in sight appear to pose more critical obstacles to rebuilding law, order and minimally functional governance at levels from national to local than even large-scale and transnational organized crime. The latter, in turn, can only be effectively addressed once the state has already regained some basic elements of functionality, such as the ability to provide minimal law and order. This explains why the fight against organized crime, including transnational crime, in such settings should not be divorced from genuine conflict resolution efforts. It also implies that finding political solutions to armed conflicts should take priority in the most complex and protracted conflict settings, as it is the *sine qua non* for rebuilding or extending functional state capacity and thus essential for effectively tackling organized crime.

Appendix 2A. Patterns of major armed conflicts, 2000–2009

LOTTA HARBOM AND PETER WALLENSTEEN*

I. Global patterns in major armed conflicts

In 2009, 17 major armed conflicts were active in 16 locations around the world (see tables 2A.1 and 2A.2). During the past decade, 30 major armed conflicts have been active in 29 locations worldwide.[1] There has been a slight overall reduction in the number of major armed conflicts over the past decade, but the trend has been uneven (see figure 2A.1). Starting at 19 in 2000, the number declined steadily until 2004, when the period's lowest figure was registered at 13; the following years saw an uneven increase.

For the sixth year running, no interstate conflict was recorded in 2009. During the decade 2000–2009 only three conflicts were fought between states: Eritrea–Ethiopia; India–Pakistan; and Iraq versus the United States and its allies. The first two of these conflicts concerned territory whereas the third was fought over governmental power. The remaining 27 conflicts recorded for this period were all fought within states, with seven concerning territorial issues and 20 governmental power. The dominance of governmental conflicts is also evident on an annual basis; in 9 of the 10 years of the period conflicts over government outnumbered those over territory. In 2009 there were 11 conflicts over government and only 6 over territory.

Six of the major armed conflicts active in 2009 were categorized as internationalized—that is, they included troops from a state that was not a primary party to the conflict but was aiding one of the conflict parties.[2] In all six cases

---

[1] The Uppsala Conflict Data Program (UCDP) defines a 'major armed conflict' as a contested incompatibility concerning government or territory over which the use of armed force between the military forces of 2 parties—of which at least 1 is the government of a state—has resulted in at least 1000 battle-related deaths in a single calendar year. After a conflict reaches this threshold, it reappears in the data set on major armed conflicts if it results in at least 25 battle-related deaths in a single year. Elsewhere, the UCDP uses the category 'war' rather than major armed conflict. War is defined by the same criteria except that the conflict must cause 1000 battle-related deaths every year. Thus, major armed conflicts listed in the SIPRI Yearbook may in some years be classified as minor armed conflicts in other UCDP lists, publications and databases.

[2] These 6 conflicts were those between the US Government and al-Qaeda; between the Afghan Government and the Taliban and Hezb-e-Islami; between the Iraqi Government and numerous

* Uppsala Conflict Data Program (UCDP), Department of Peace and Conflict Research, Uppsala University.

For table 2A.3 Marie Allansson was responsible for the conflict location Sri Lanka; Johan Brosché was responsible for Sudan; Helena Grusell for Colombia and Peru; Lotta Harbom for Uganda; Stina Högbladh for Rwanda; Emma Johansson for India; Joakim Kreutz for Iraq, Myanmar, Pakistan and the USA; Sara Lindberg for Somalia and the USA; Frida Möller for Israel; Therése Pettersson for the Philippines; Ralph Sundberg for Afghanistan and the USA; and Nina von Uexkull for Turkey

Table 2A.1. Number of major armed conflicts, by region and type, 2000–2009

The two types of incompatibility are over government (G) and territory (T).

Region	2000 G	2000 T	2001 G	2001 T	2002 G	2002 T	2003 G	2003 T	2004 G	2004 T	2005 G	2005 T	2006 G	2006 T	2007 G	2007 T	2008 G	2008 T	2009 G	2009 T
Africa	7	1	7	0	7	0	5	0	3	0	3	0	3	0	1	0	3	0	4	0
Americas	0	0	1	0	2	0	1	0	2	0	2	0	2	0	3	0	3	0	3	0
Asia	2	5	2	5	2	4	2	5	2	2	3	4	3	3	2	4	3	4	3	4
Europe	0	1	0	1	0	1	0	1	0	1	0	1	0	1	0	1	0	0	0	0
Middle East	1	2	1	2	0	2	1	2	1	2	1	2	1	2	1	2	1	2	1	2
Total	10	9	11	8	11	7	9	8	8	5	9	7	9	6	7	7	10	6	11	6
Total	19		19		18		17		13		16		15		14		16		17	

Table 2A.2. Number of locations of major armed conflict, by region, 2000–2009

Figures are numbers of locations with at least one major armed conflict.

	2000	2001	2002	2003	2004	2005	2006	2007	2008	2009
Africa	8	7	7	5	3	3	3	1	3	4
Americas	0	1	2	1	2	2	2	3	3	3
Asia	6	6	5	6	3	6	6	5	6	6
Europe	1	1	1	1	1	1	1	1	0	0
Middle East	3	3	2	3	3	3	3	3	3	3
Total	18	18	17	16	12	15	15	13	15	16

the external states contributed troops to the government side of the conflict.[3] Four of these six were more or less closely connected to the US-led 'global war on terrorism'. This pattern was even more evident in 2006–2008, when this was true of all internationalized conflicts.[4]

II. Regional patterns

In 2009 seven major armed conflicts were recorded for Asia, making it the region with the highest number for the seventh consecutive year. There were four major armed conflicts in Africa, three each in the Americas and the Middle East, and, for the second year running, none in Europe.

Africa was the region with the most conflicts in the 10-year period 2000–2009, with 12 major armed conflicts recorded (see figure 2A.2). During

insurgency groups; between the Somali Government and the al-Shabab militia and Hizbul-Islam; between the Rwandan Government and the Forces démocratiques de libération du Rwanda (FDLR, Democratic Liberation Forces of Rwanda); and between the Ugandan Government and Lord's Resistance Army (LRA).

[3] For the states contributing troops in these conflicts see table 2A.3.

[4] On the conflict between the US Government and al-Qaeda and the complex issues affecting its coding in the UCDP database see Eriksson, M., Sollenberg, M. and Wallensteen, P., 'Patterns of major armed conflicts, 1990–2001', *SIPRI Yearbook 2002*, pp. 67–68.

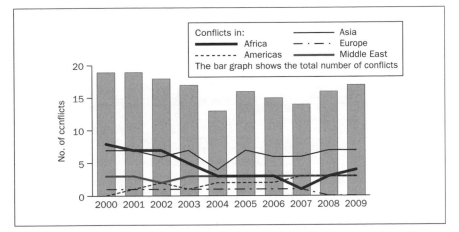

Figure 2A.1. Regional distribution and total number of major armed conflicts, 2000–2009

the first seven years of the 2000s there was a sharp decline in the number of major armed conflicts in the region, falling from eight to one. However, the figure increased in both 2008 and 2009 to reach four in the latter year. Only one of the 12 conflicts was fought between states: Eritrea–Ethiopia. Half of the intrastate conflicts were internationalized at some point, which distinguishes Africa from other regions: elsewhere, external involvement ranged from none (Europe) to 40 per cent (Middle East). All but 1 of the 12 major armed conflicts recorded in Africa were fought over governmental power.

The Americas has been the scene of three major armed conflicts during the decade 2000–2009. The number has slowly climbed from zero in 2000 and in 2009 it stood at three. All three conflicts were intrastate and concerned governmental power.

Nine major armed conflicts were recorded for Asia in 2000–2009. Apart from a dip in 2004, when four conflicts were active, the annual number of major armed conflicts has varied between six and seven throughout the period, with seven recorded in 2009. Two of the Asian conflicts—those between the Government of the Philippines and the rebel Communist Party of the Philippines and between the Government of India and Kashmir insurgents—were active in all years of the period. The region saw one interstate conflict fought over governmental power: India–Pakistan. The remaining eight intrastate conflicts were equally divided between the two types of incompatibility.

Only one of the 30 major armed conflicts active in the 2000–2009 period was fought in Europe: that between the Russian Government and the self-proclaimed Chechen Republic of Ichkeria. Since 2008 no major armed conflict has been recorded for Europe.[5]

---

[5] While fighting is continuing in and around Chechnya, this is viewed as taking place in the context of a new conflict, fought over a larger territory, termed the Caucasus Emirate by the rebels. Fighting in this conflict has not reached the threshold of 1000 battle-related deaths in a year, and so

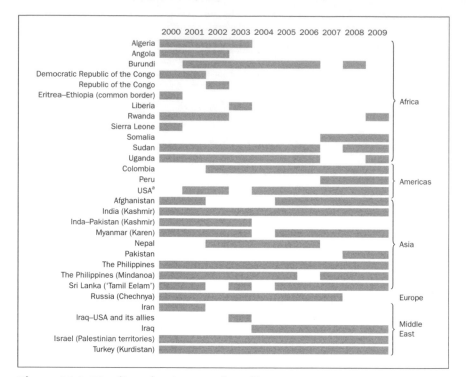

Figure 2A.2. Timeline of major armed conflicts, 2000–2009

When only the name of a country is given, this indicates a conflict over government. In the case of conflict over territory, the name of the contested territory appears in parentheses after the country name. The years given are those in the period 2000–2009 in which the major armed conflict was active (i.e. resulted in 25 or more battle-related deaths). Many of these conflicts were also active in years prior to 2000, and may be active again in future years.

[a] This is the conflict between the US Government and al-Qaeda.

The Middle East accounted for five major armed conflicts in 2000–2009. There have been three active conflicts in the region in each year apart from 2002, when two were active. The same three conflicts have been active since 2004: Iraq, Israel (Palestinian territories) and Turkey (Kurdistan). Turkey (Kurdistan) was active in all years of the period. The one interstate conflict recorded in the Middle East was that between Iraq and the USA and its allies. The remaining four were fought within states; two over government and two over territory.

it is not coded as a major armed conflict. See also Harbom, L. and Wallensteen, P., 'Patterns of major armed conflicts, 1999–2008', *SIPRI Yearbook 2009*, pp. 73–74.

III. Changes in the table of conflicts for 2009

Conflicts added to the table in 2009

Two conflicts appear in this year's table that were not active in 2008: Rwanda and Uganda.[6] In both cases the active rebel groups have over the years taken refuge outside their country of origin and the upsurge in fighting in 2009 was in both cases due to government offensives against rebel positions in neighbouring Democratic Republic of the Congo (DRC).[7]

On 20 January 2009 Rwandan Government troops crossed into the DRC and launched Operation Umoja Wetu ('our unity') alongside the Congolese Army. Aspiring to destroy the bases of the Forces démocratiques de libération du Rwanda (FDLR, Democratic Liberation Forces of Rwanda) in Nord- and Sud-Kivu as well as to generally weaken the hard core of the group, the operation was deemed a success when the Rwandan troops withdrew in late February. However, the FDLR recovered sooner than anticipated and in March the Congolese Army, assisted by the United Nations Organization Mission in the DRC (MONUC), launched Operation Kimia II against the rebels. Starting in Nord-Kivu, the operation moved south during the remains of the year. By the end of 2009 the rebels appeared to have been significantly weakened, but this came with a considerable cost for the civilian population in the area, who had become the target of attacks from both sides in the conflict.[8]

In the Ugandan case, government troops together with troops of the Government of South Sudan and from the DRC had launched a joint offensive, Operation Lightning Thunder, against the Lord's Resistance Army (LRA) in mid-December 2008. Information on what actually happened in eastern DRC during the last two weeks of 2008 is scarce. Based on publicly available documents and news reports, it was not possible to confirm that the number of battle-related deaths crossed the threshold of 25 during this period, and so the conflict was coded as inactive in 2008.[9] The joint offensive continued in 2009, amid mounting LRA atrocities against the civilian population. Operation Lightning Thunder ended on 15 March 2009, and the Ugandan troops officially left the DRC. The armed campaign continued through the rest of the year, however, albeit more covertly. Aside from the Congolese Army continuing to hunt for the scattered rebels, large contingents of the Ugandan Army remained in the neighbouring countries. During the year many of the rebels withdrew to the north and the north-east, entering southern Sudan and the Central African

[6] Fighting between the Government of Yemen and Shabab al-Mu'mineen caused over 1200 battle-related deaths in 2009. However, this fighting is not included as a major armed conflict because the group has never stated an incompatibility with the government concerning either government or territory, which is an integral part of the UCDP definition. While Shabab al-Mu'mineen has been critical of the government's foreign policy, it has never openly pronounced an aim of overthrowing the regime.

[7] The FDLR has been located in eastern DRC since the late 1990s and the LRA in southern Sudan throughout most of the 1990s and early 2000s and in north-eastern DRC since 2005.

[8] Human Rights Watch (HRW), 'You Will Be Punished': Attacks on Civilians in Eastern Congo (HRW: New York, Dec. 2009).

[9] A major armed conflict is considered to continue to be active only if it results in 25 or more battle-related deaths in a calendar year. See section V below.

Republic. By the end of the year it was difficult to determine whether the LRA was in fact, as the Ugandan Government claimed, a spent force, or if it was just in the midst of a tactical withdrawal.

Conflicts removed from the table in 2009

One of the major armed conflicts that appeared in the 2008 table was no longer active in 2009: Burundi. After having signed a peace agreement in December 2008, the Burundian rebel group Parti pour la liberation du people Hutu–Force nationale de liberation (Palipehutu–FNL, Party for the Liberation of the Hutu People–National Liberation Forces) did not take up arms again in 2009. Instead, as a first step to implement the new peace accord, the group was renamed FNL on 8 January—thus removing the controversial reference to ethnicity in its name—and started the process of registering as a political party. On 21 April the Ministry of the Interior approved the FNL's registration.[10]

Changes in intensity of conflict

Five of the 17 armed conflicts that were active in 2009 increased in intensity compared to 2008: Afghanistan, Colombia, Somalia, Pakistan and the conflict between the USA and its allies and al-Qaeda. The intensity of the latter two increased by more than 50 per cent.

The conflict between the Pakistani Government and the Tehrik-i-Taliban Pakistan (TTP, Movement of the Taliban in Pakistan) escalated in 2009. Despite some short-lived local truces with individual TTP commanders (most notably in the Swat Valley during March–May) and the death of the TTP leader, Baitullah Mehsud in a US missile strike in August, there was intense fighting throughout the year with five major government offensives as well as some attempts by the rebels to launch counteroffensives. Furthermore, during the year the hitherto rural rebels spread the conflict to urban areas, conducting a number of spectacular attacks in major cities. Nevertheless, by the end of 2009 the repeated government offensives had succeeded in forcing the TTP onto the defensive and in re-establishing government authority in areas previously under rebel control.

In 2009 the fighting in the conflict between the USA and its allies and al-Qaeda escalated dramatically. Since the conflict's start, the bulk of the fighting has taken place in Afghanistan. This changed in 2009, when the vast majority of fatalities were incurred in Pakistan as US forces, based in Afghanistan, carried out large numbers of aerial bombardments of al-Qaeda hideouts across the border. Al-Qaeda operatives responded by targeting civilians—often Afghans—accusing them of being US spies. Apart from events in Pakistan, fight-

---

[10] Human Rights Watch (HRW), *Pursuit of Power: Political Violence and Repression in Burundi* (HRW: New York, May 2009).

ing between the USA and its allies and al-Qaeda took place in Afghanistan and Somalia.[11]

Five major armed conflicts decreased in intensity between 2008 and 2009: India (Kashmir), Peru, Iraq, Sudan and Turkey (Kurdistan). The latter three decreased by more than 50 per cent.

In the Iraqi case, numerous developments contributed to the marked de-escalation of hostilities. In many of the previous years of conflict, a majority of fatalities were incurred in fighting between government or coalition troops and Jaish al-Mahdi (the Mahdi Army). However, in 2009 there was no fighting involving the latter group. Another factor influencing the situation was the withdrawal of international troops from the country; by August, all non-US coalition members had left Iraq. Since coalition troops have generally been a major target for the Iraqi insurgents, this also influenced the decline in the number of fatalities.

In the Darfur region of Sudan, the conflict between the Sudanese Government and the rebel Sudan Liberation Movement/Army (SLM/A) de-escalated markedly in 2009 compared to 2008. The SLM/A—already weakened by numerous splits—suffered from defections to the larger rebel group Justice and Equality Movement (JEM) during the year.[12] Also serving to dampen the conflict was the continued deployment of the African Union/United Nations Hybrid Operation in Darfur (UNAMID).

Fighting in the conflict between the Turkish Government and the Kurdistan Workers' Party (Partiya Karkerên Kurdistan, PKK)—ongoing since the 1980s—continued in 2009, albeit on a lower scale. Despite the fact that the government continued to refuse to negotiate with the rebels, some political moves were made that raised the hope for a solution. For the first time, talks were held with the pro-Kurdish Democratic Society Party (Demokratik Toplum Partisi, DTP) and in November a reform package aiming to grant Turkish Kurds more cultural and political rights was presented in the Turkish Parliament. The end of the year also saw some negative developments, as the Constitutional Court banned the DTP for cooperating with the PKK and the government started to launch cross-border attacks on rebel camps in Iraq.

The most violent conflicts in 2009

In six of the major armed conflicts active in 2009 there were more than 1000 battle-related deaths: Sri Lanka (c. 7500), Pakistan (more than 7000), Afghanistan (c. 5100), Iraq (c. 2000), Rwanda (c. 1800) and Somalia (c. 1500).

In Afghanistan both the Taliban and the Hezb-e-Islami continued fighting the government and the international forces present in the country. The clearest indications of the heightened intensity were the increase in the number of

[11] There was only 1 confirmed event in Somalia during 2009. On 14 Sep. US special forces in helicopters attacked a car in southern Somalia and killed Saleh Ali Saleh Nabhan, one of East Africa's most wanted al-Qaeda militants, together with 5 other people. 'Raid said to kill top al Qaeda militant in Somalia', Reuters, 14 Sep. 2009, <http://uk.reuters.com/article/idUKTRE58D3PW20090914>.

[12] Since fighting between government forces and JEM has never resulted in 1000 or more battle-related deaths, JEM is not included in the list of major armed conflicts in table 2A.3.

international soldiers killed and the relatively intense fighting that spread to previously almost untouched areas of Afghanistan. As in earlier years the Taliban mainly relied on roadside bombings, suicide bombings and ambushes as their main tactics. In 2009 the use of improvised explosive devices (IEDs) was higher than before. The Taliban also made frequent use of more brazen tactics; on several occasions they attacked and temporarily took over government buildings in provincial capitals throughout the country.

In January 2009, Somalia saw both the withdrawal of Ethiopian troops from the country and the swearing in of moderate Islamist leader, Sheikh Sharif Sheikh Ahmed, as its new president. Despite these developments, Sheikh Sharif did not succeed in winning the support of the more hard-line Islamists. The two main groupings opposing the new president were the al-Shabab militia and Hizbul-Islam, a new alliance.[13] In May al-Shabab and Hizbul-Islam began cooperating and subsequently launched a major offensive on Mogadishu that continued throughout June and came close to toppling the government. It was during this offensive that the vast majority of all battle-related deaths were incurred.[14]

In Sri Lanka, long-time rebels the Liberation Tigers of Tamil Eelam (LTTE) were completely defeated in 2009. Following major reverses in 2008, 2009 started off with yet another setback for the rebels, when the government succeeded in capturing the strategically important Elephant Pass, controlling access to the Jaffna Peninsula. A string of government advances followed in rapid succession as the rebels lost ground to the army. By early May the last remnants of the LTTE were trapped together with thousands of civilians in a small area, targeted by government forces with artillery fire. On 16 May Sri Lankan President Mahinda Rajapaksa declared victory over the rebels and the LTTE admitted defeat on the following day. Two days later, on 19 May, LTTE leader Velupillai Prabhakaran was killed by government forces.

IV. Definitions, sources and methods

Definitions

The UCDP defines a major armed conflict as a contested incompatibility concerning government or territory over which the use of armed force between the military forces of two parties, of which at least one is the government of a state, has resulted in at least 1000 battle-related deaths in at least one calendar year. The separate elements are defined as follows:

1. *Incompatibility that concerns government or territory.* This refers to the stated generally incompatible positions of the parties to the conflict. An *incompatibility that concerns government* refers to incompatible positions regarding the state's type of political system or the composition of the government. It may also involve an aim to replace the current government. An *incompatibility that*

---

[13] Fighting between Hizbul-Islam and the Somali Government did not exceed 1000 battle-related deaths in 2009, so this group is not included in the list of major armed conflicts in table 2A.3.

[14] On other developments in Somalia in 2009 see chapter 2, section III.

concerns territory refers to incompatible positions regarding the status of a territory and may involve demands for secession or autonomy (intrastate conflict) or the aim of changing the state in control of a certain territory (interstate conflict).

2. *Use of armed force.* This refers to the use of armed force by the military forces of the parties to the conflict in order to promote the parties' general position in the conflict. Arms are defined as any material means of combat, including anything from manufactured weapons to sticks, stones, fire or water.

3. *Party.* This refers to the government of a state, any of its allies, an opposition organization or an alliance of opposition organizations. The *government of a state* is the party that is generally regarded as being in central control, even by those organizations seeking to seize power. If this criterion is not applicable, the party controlling the capital of the state is regarded as the government. An *opposition organization* is any non-governmental group that has announced a name for itself, that has stated its political goals and that has used armed force to achieve them. A state or a multinational organization that supports one of the primary parties with regular troops and shares its position may also be listed as a party. A traditional peacekeeping operation is not considered to be a party to the conflict but is rather seen as an impartial part of a consensual peace process.

4. *State.* This refers to an internationally recognized sovereign government controlling a specific territory or an internationally non-recognized government controlling a specific territory whose sovereignty is not disputed by an internationally recognized sovereign state that previously controlled the territory in question.

5. *Battle-related deaths.* This refers to deaths caused by the warring parties that can be directly related to combat over the contested incompatibility. Once a conflict has reached the threshold of 1000 battle-related deaths in a calendar year, it reappears in the annual list of major armed conflicts in any year in which there are 25 or more battle-related deaths in fighting between the same parties and concerning the same incompatibility.[15] The focus is not on political violence per se but on incompatibilities that are contested by the use of armed force. Thus, only one major type of political violence is registered—battle-related deaths—which serves as a measure of the magnitude of a conflict. Other types of political violence are excluded, such as one-sided violence against civilians; unorganized or spontaneous public violence; and violence that is not directed at the state (e.g. rebel groups fighting each other).[16]

The period analysed in this appendix is 2000–2009, but the conflicts in table 2A.3 can have reached the required threshold of 1000 battle-related

[15] Since *SIPRI Yearbook 2008*, the threshold has been 25 battle-related deaths, bringing it in line with other UCDP data sets and ensuring that only major armed conflicts in which fighting took place during the year are included. In earlier editions of the SIPRI Yearbook the threshold was 1 battle-related death.

[16] The UCDP collects information on 2 of these types of violence: non-state conflicts and one-sided violence. Data on these additional categories can be found at the UCDP website, <http://www.ucdp.uu.se/>.

deaths in any calendar year since 1946 and need not have done so during the analysed period.

Sources

The data presented in this appendix is based on information taken from a wide selection of publicly available sources, both printed and electronic. The sources include news agencies, newspapers, academic journals, research reports, and documents from international and multinational organizations and non-governmental organizations (NGOs). In order to collect information on the aims and goals of the parties to the conflict, documents of the warring parties (governments, allies and opposition organizations) and, for example, the Internet sites of rebel groups are often consulted.

Independent news sources, carefully selected over a number of years, constitute the basis of the data collection. The Factiva news database is indispensable for the collection of general news reports. It contains more than 25 000 sources in 22 languages from 159 countries and provides sources from all three crucial levels of the news media: international (e.g. Agence France-Presse and Reuters), regional and local. However, the availability of the regional and national news sources varies, which means that for some countries several sources are consulted, whereas for other countries and regions only a few high-quality region- or country-specific sources are used.

The UCDP regularly scrutinizes and revises the selection and combination of sources in order to maintain a high level of reliability and comparability between regions and countries. One important priority is to arrive at a balanced combination of sources of different origin with a view to avoiding bias. The reliability of the sources is judged using the expertise of the UCDP together with advice from a global network of experts (academics and policymakers). Both the independence of the source and the transparency of its origins are crucial. The latter is important because most sources are secondary, which means that the primary source also needs to be analysed in order to establish the reliability of a report. Each source is judged in relation to the context in which it is published. The potential interest of either the primary or secondary source in misrepresenting an event is taken into account, as are the general climate and extent of media censorship. Reports from NGOs and international organizations are particularly useful in this context, complementing media reporting and facilitating cross-checking. The criterion that a source should be independent does not, of course, apply to sources that are consulted precisely because they are biased, such as government documents or rebel groups' Internet sites. The UCDP is aware of the high level of scrutiny required and makes great effort to ensure the authenticity of the material used.

Methods

The data on major armed conflicts is compiled by calendar year. It includes data on conflict locations, type of incompatibility, onset of the armed conflict, warring parties, total number of battle-related deaths, number of battle-related deaths in a given year and change in battle-related deaths from the previous year.[17]

The data on battle-related deaths is given the most attention in coding for the conflict database. Information on, for example, the date, news source, primary source, location and death toll is recorded for every event. Ideally, these individual events and figures are corroborated by two or more independent sources. The figures are then aggregated for the entire year of each conflict. The aggregated figures are compared to total figures given in official documents, in special reports and in the news media. Regional experts such as researchers, diplomats and journalists are often consulted during the data collection. Their role is mainly to clarify the contexts in which the events occur, thus facilitating proper interpretation of the published sources.

Because little precise information is publicly available on death figures in armed conflicts, the numbers presented by the UCDP are best viewed as estimates. Rather than always providing exact numbers, ranges are sometimes given. The UCDP is generally conservative when estimating the number of battle-related deaths. As more in-depth information on an armed conflict becomes available, the conservative, event-based estimates often prove more correct than others widely cited in the news media. If no figures are available or if the numbers given are unreliable, the UCDP does not provide a figure. Figures are revised retroactively each year as new information becomes available.

[17] See also the notes for table 2A.3.

Table 2A.3. Major armed conflicts in 2009

For the definitions, methods and sources used see section IV above and the notes below.

Location[a]	Incompatibility[b]	Year formed/year stated/ year joined/year entered[c]	Warring parties[d]	Total deaths (including 2009)[e]	Deaths in 2009[f]	Change from 2008[g]
Africa						
Rwanda*	Government	1990/1997/1997/1998	Government of Rwanda, Democratic Republic of the Congo			
			vs FDLR	<5000	>1800	n.a.

FDLR = Forces democratiques de liberation du Rwanda (Democratic Liberation Forces of Rwanda)

* Fighting took place in the Democratic Republic of the Congo.

Somalia	Government	1981/2006/2006/2008	Government of Somalia, Ethiopia			
			vs al-Shabab (The Youth)	. .	>1400	+
Sudan	Government	1983/2003/2003/2003	Government of Sudan			
			vs Sudan Liberation Movement/Army (SLM/A)	>4400	25–100	– –
Uganda*	Government	1971/1987/1988/1988	Government of Uganda, Democratic Republic of the Congo, Sudan			
			vs Lord's Resistance Army (LRA)	< 9550	> 200	n.a.

* Fighting took place in the Central African Republic, the Democratic Republic of the Congo and Sudan.

Americas						
Colombia	Government	1964/1964/1964/2002	Government of Colombia			
			vs FARC	<45 800	<400	+

FARC = Fuerzas Armadas Revolucionarias de Colombia (Revolutionary Armed Forces of Colombia)

				Total deaths	Deaths in 2009	Change from 2008
Peru	Government	1980/1980/1980/1981	Government of Peru vs Sendero Luminoso (Shining Path)	<28 100	25–100	–
USA*	Government	2001/2001/2001/2001	Government of USA, Multinational coalition** vs al-Qaeda	>3750	<550	+ +

* Fighting took place in Afghanistan, Pakistan and Somalia.
** In 2009 the US-led multinational coalition included troops from Canada, France, the Netherlands and Romania. Reliable information on states contributing troops is sensitive and hard to find, so this list should be seen as preliminary.

Asia

Afghanistan	Government	1978/1978/1980/1980 1978/1995/1995/2005	Government of Afghanistan, ISAF* vs Hezb-e Islami vs Taliban	.. ..	25–100 >5000	+ +

* The following countries contributed troops to the NATO-led International Security Assistance Force (ISAF) in 2009: Albania, Australia, Azerbaijan, Belgium, Bosnia and Herzegovina, Bulgaria, Canada, Croatia, Czech Republic, Denmark, Estonia, Finland, France, Georgia, Germany, Greece, Hungary, Iceland, Italy, Latvia, Lithuania, Luxembourg, Macedonia (Former Yugoslav Republic of), Netherlands, New Zealand, Norway, Pakistan, Poland, Portugal, Romania, Singapore, Slovakia, Slovenia, Spain, Sweden, Turkey, Ukraine, the UK and the USA.

India	Territory (Kashmir)	1977/1977/1984/1990	Government of India vs Kashmir insurgents	>30 150	>350	–
Myanmar	Territory (Karen State)	1948/1948/1948/1949	Government of Myanmar vs Karen National Union (KNU)	>15 400	25–100	0
Pakistan	Government	2007/2007/2008/2008	Government of Pakistan vs Tehrik-i-Taliban Pakistan (TTP, Movement of the Taliban in Pakistan)*	>10 000	>7000	+ +

* Some of the main leaders of the TTP used the name Ittehal-ul-Mujahideen (Union of Holy Warriors) during part of the year. Statements were also released under the name Fedayeen al-Islam (Islamic Patriots), another TTP subgroup.

Location[a]	Incompatibility[b]	Year formed/year stated/year joined/year entered[c]	Warring parties[d]	Total deaths (including 2009)[e]	Deaths in 2009[f]	Change from 2008[g]
Philippines	Government	1946/1968/1959/1982	Government of the Philippines vs Communist Party of the Philippines (CPP)	20 200–27 200	<200	0
Philippines	Territory (Mindanao)	1968/1981/1986/2000	Government of the Philippines vs Moro Islamic Liberation Front (MILF)	>38 200	>300	0
Sri Lanka	Territory ('Tamil Eelam')	1976/1976/1975/1987	Government of Sri Lanka vs Liberation Tigers of Tamil Eelam (LTTE)	>84 400	<7550	0
Middle East						
Iraq	Government	1963/2003/2003/2004	Government of Iraq, Multinational coalition* vs Iraqi insurgents**	<30 300	<2000	– –

* The US-led Multinational Force in Iraq included combat troops from Australia, El Salvador, Estonia, the UK and the USA. By the end of 2009, only US forces remained and on 1 Jan. 2010 the coalition was renamed the United States Forces–Iraq.
** These included primarily Dawlat al-'Iraq al-islamiyya (Islamic State of Iraq, ISI) and a multitude of smaller groups with unclear links to the ISI or the Baath Party.

Israel	Territory (Palestinian territories)	1964/1964/1965/1982	Government of Israel vs Palestinian organizations*	>16 700	>700	0

* These included Hamas (Islamic Resistance Movement) and Palestinian Islamic Jihad (PIJ).

Turkey*	Territory (Kurdistan)	1974/1974/1983/1992	Government of Turkey vs Partiya Karkerên Kurdistan (PKK, Kurdistan Workers' Party)	<31 750	<150	– –

* Fighting took place in Iraq and Turkey.

Notes: Although some countries are also the location of minor armed conflicts, the table lists only the major armed conflicts in those countries.

The conflicts in the table are listed by location, in alphabetical order, within 5 geographical regions: Africa, excluding Egypt; the Americas, including North, Central and South America and the Caribbean; Asia, including Oceania; Europe, including the Caucasus; and the Middle East—Egypt, Iran, Iraq, Israel, Jordan, Kuwait, Lebanon, Syria, Turkey and the states of the Arabian peninsula.

[a] 'Location' is the location of the government of the state that is being challenged by an opposition organization. If the geographical location of the fighting is different from the location of the government being challenged, these locations are given in a note.

[b] The stated general incompatible positions, 'government' and 'territory', refer to contested incompatibilities concerning, respectively, governmental power—type of political system or a change of central government or its composition—and territory—control of territory (interstate conflict), secession or autonomy. A location may have incompatibilities over several different territories, but only 1 incompatibility over government.

[c] 'Year formed' is the year in which a conflict party first stated the incompatibility. In conflicts where several parties have fought over the same incompatibility, the year that the incompatibility was first stated is given, even if the original stating party is no longer active in the conflict. 'Year stated' is the year in which 1 of the currently active opposition parties (see note d) first stated its incompatibility. 'Year joined' is the first year in which armed force was used in the conflict by at least 1 of the active opposition parties. 'Year entered' is the first year in which fighting between the government and 1 or more of the active opposition parties led to 1000 or more battle-related deaths in 1 calendar year and was therefore classified as a major armed conflict. Thus, 'Year formed' refers to the start of armed conflict in the conflict location, while 'Year stated', 'Year joined' and 'Year entered' refer to the involvement of at least 1 of the currently active opposition parties.

[d] The government party and its allies are listed first, followed by the opposition parties, which may be organizations or other states. Opposition parties are only listed in the table if fighting between them and the government over the declared incompatibility has passed the threshold of 1000 battle-related deaths in a calendar year. An opposition organization is any non-governmental group that has publicly announced a name for itself as well as its political goals and has used armed force to achieve its goals. Only those parties and alliances which were active during 2009 are listed in this column. A comma between 2 warring parties indicates an alliance. In cases where 2 governments have both stated incompatible positions, e.g. over a shared border, they are listed in alphabetical order.

[e] The figures for total battle-related deaths refer to those deaths caused by the warring parties since the start of the conflict that can be directly connected to the incompatibility. This figure thus relates to the 'Year formed' variable. In the case of intrastate conflicts, it should be noted that the figures include only battle-related deaths that can be attributed to fighting between the government and opposition parties that have at some point been listed in the table. Information that covers a calendar year is necessarily more tentative for the last months of the year. Experience has also shown that the reliability of figures improves over time; they are therefore revised each year.

[f] Numbers over 100 are, as far as possible, rounded to the nearest 100. Thus, figures ranging between 101 and 150 are presented as >100, while figures ranging between 151 and 199 are presented as <200. Figures between 25 and 100 are presented as 25–100.

[g] The 'Change from 2008' is measured as the increase or decrease in the number of battle-related deaths in 2009 compared with the number of battle-related deaths in 2008. Although the symbols are based on data that cannot be considered totally reliable, they represent the following changes:

++   increase in battle-related deaths of >50%
+   increase in battle-related deaths of >10 to 50%
0   stable rate of battle-related deaths (−10% to +10%)
−   decrease in battle-related deaths of >10 to 50%
− −   decrease in battle-related deaths of >50%
n.a. not applicable, since the major armed conflict is not recorded for 2008.

Appendix 2B. The Global Peace Index 2010

TIM MACINTYRE AND CAMILLA SCHIPPA*

I. Introduction

The concept of peace is notoriously difficult to define. The simplest way of approaching it is in terms of harmony achieved by the absence of war or conflict. Applied to states, this would suggest that those not involved in wars with neighbouring states or suffering internal violent conflicts have achieved a state of peace. This is what Johan Galtung defined as 'negative peace'—an absence of violence.[1] The concept of negative peace is immediately intuitive and empirically measurable and can be used as a starting point to elaborate its counterpart concept, 'positive peace': having established what constitutes an absence of violence, is it possible to identify which structures and institutions create and maintain peace?

The Global Peace Index (GPI) is a step in this direction. It is a measurement of peace that seeks to determine what cultural attributes and institutions are associated with states of peace. It is based on a scoring model that ranks 149 countries by their relative states of peace using 23 indicators. The indicators have been selected as being the best available data sets that reflect the incidence or absence of peace. They contain both quantitative data and qualitative scores from a range of trusted sources.

The GPI's principal aim is to investigate positive peace. It does this by identifying correlations with other indexes and databases and investigating the relative importance of a range of potential determinants or 'drivers' that may influence the creation and nurturing of peaceful societies, both internally and externally.

The Global Peace Index was founded by Steve Killelea, an Australian technology entrepreneur and philanthropist, and is published by the Institute for Economics and Peace (IEP), a think tank dedicated to research and education on the relationship between economic development, business and peace.[2] The GPI is developed by the Institute for Economics and Peace, supported by the Economist Intelligence Unit (EIU), which collates and calculates the data and rankings, and guided by an international advisory panel.[3]

---

[1] Galtung, J., 'Editorial', *Journal of Peace Research*, vol. 1, no. 1 (1964).

[2] More information on the IEP is available at <http://www.economicsandpeace.org/>.

[3] The choices of indicators and the weights assigned to them were agreed after extensive consultation with the GPI Advisory Panel, which included the following experts in 2009–10: Kevin Clements, Chairman (University of Otago), Ian Anthony (SIPRI), Sultan Barakat (University of York), Nick Grono (International Crisis Group), Ron Horvath (University of Sydney), Toshiya Hoshino (Osaka University), Linda Jamison (Center for Strategic and International Studies, Washington, DC), Manuela Mesa (Centro de Educación e Investigación para la Paz, Madrid), Dan Smith, Ekaterina Stepanova (IMEMO) and Paul van Tongeren (Global Partnership for the Prevention of Armed Conflict, The Hague).

* Institute for Economics and Peace

Table 2B.1. The Global Peace Index 2010

Rank	Country	Score	Rank	Country	Score
1	New Zealand	1.188	50	Bulgaria	1.785
2	Iceland	1.212	51	Zambia	1.813
3	Japan	1.247	51	Malawi	1.813
4	Austria	1.290	53	Sierra Leone	1.818
5	Norway	1.322	54	Latvia	1.827
6	Ireland	1.337	55	Tanzania	1.832
7	Denmark	1.341	56	Libya	1.839
7	Luxembourg	1.341	57	Burkina Faso	1.852
9	Finland	1.352	58	Morocco	1.861
10	Sweden	1.354	59	Namibia	1.864
11	Slovenia	1.358	60	Bosnia and Herzegovina	1.873
12	Czech Republic	1.360	61	Panama	1.878
13	Portugal	1.366	62	Greece	1.887
14	Canada	1.392	63	Gambia	1.890
15	Qatar	1.394	64	Nicaragua	1.924
16	Germany	1.398	65	Albania	1.925
17	Belgium	1.400	66	Moldova	1.938
18	Switzerland	1.424	67	Indonesia	1.946
19	Australia	1.467	68	Equatorial Guinea	1.948
20	Hungary	1.495	68	Jordan	1.948
21	Slovakia	1.536	70	Bahrain	1.956
22	Malaysia	1.539	71	Argentina	1.962
23	Oman	1.561	72	Cuba	1.964
24	Uruguay	1.568	73	Swaziland	1.966
25	Spain	1.588	74	Gabon	1.981
26	Costa Rica	1.590	75	Rwanda	2.012
27	Netherlands	1.610	76	Cyprus	2.013
28	Chile	1.616	77	Madagascar	2.019
29	Poland	1.618	77	Paraguay	2.019
30	Singapore	1.624	79	Senegal	2.031
31	United Kingdom	1.631	80	China	2.034
32	France	1.636	81	Bolivia	2.037
33	Botswana	1.641	82	Nepal	2.044
34	Laos	1.661	83	Brazil	2.048
35	Taiwan	1.664	83	Macedonia, FYR	2.048
36	Bhutan	1.665	85	United States	2.056
37	Tunisia	1.678	86	Angola	2.057
38	Viet Nam	1.691	87	Bangladesh	2.058
39	Kuwait	1.693	88	Montenegro	2.060
40	Italy	1.701	89	Peru	2.067
41	Croatia	1.707	90	Serbia	2.071
42	Lithuania	1.713	91	Guyana	2.095
43	South Korea	1.715	92	Mongolia	2.101
44	United Arab Emirates	1.739	93	Dominican Republic	2.103
45	Romania	1.749	94	Trinidad and Tobago	2.107
46	Estonia	1.751	95	Kazakhstan	2.113
47	Mozambique	1.779	95	Papua New Guinea	2.113
48	Ghana	1.781	97	Ukraine	2.115
49	Egypt	1.784	98	Jamaica	2.138

Rank	Country	Score	Rank	Country	Score
99	Liberia	2.148	125	Honduras	2.395
100	Uganda	2.165	126	Turkey	2.420
101	Ecuador	2.185	127	Ethiopia	2.444
102	Congo, Republic of the	2.192	128	India	2.516
103	El Salvador	2.195	129	Yemen	2.573
104	Iran	2.202	130	Philippines	2.574
105	Belarus	2.204	131	Burundi	2.577
106	Cameroon	2.210	132	Myanmar	2.580
107	Mexico	2.216	133	Sri Lanka	2.621
107	Saudi Arabia	2.216	134	Lebanon	2.639
109	Mali	2.240	135	Zimbabwe	2.678
110	Uzbekistan	2.242	136	Central African Republic	2.753
111	Cambodia	2.252	137	Nigeria	2.756
112	Guatemala	2.258	138	Colombia	2.787
113	Armenia	2.266	139	North Korea	2.855
114	Haiti	2.270	140	Congo, Dem. Republic of	2.925
115	Syria	2.274	141	Chad	2.964
116	Algeria	2.277	142	Georgia	2.970
117	Turkmenistan	2.295	143	Russia	3.013
118	Côte d'Ivoire	2.297	144	Israel	3.019
119	Azerbaijan	2.367	145	Pakistan	3.050
120	Kenya	2.369	146	Sudan	3.125
121	South Africa	2.380	147	Afghanistan	3.252
122	Venezuela	2.387	148	Somalia	3.390
123	Mauritania	2.389	149	Iraq	3.406
124	Thailand	2.393			

The Global Peace Index 2010 appears in table 2B.1. The results of the index are discussed in section II. The methodology of the GPI is explained in section III, while section IV investigates the potential determinants of peace that the GPI can help identify.

II. Highlights and changes

In the Global Peace Index 2010, New Zealand is ranked as the country most at peace for the second consecutive year, followed by Iceland and Japan. Small, stable and democratic countries are consistently ranked highly; 15 of the top 20 countries are Western or Central European countries. This is an increase from 14 last year, and reflects an improvement in Hungary's score. Qatar and Australia remain in the top 20, in 15th and 19th places, respectively. All five Scandinavian counties are in the top 10 of the 2010 GPI, although the scores and ranks of all but Iceland deteriorated slightly. Island nations generally fare well, with the notable exception of Sri Lanka.

For the fourth year running, the country ranked least at peace is Iraq. Somalia, Afghanistan and Sudan follow. All four countries are in a state of ongoing conflict and upheaval. Afghanistan's score improved slightly from last year and it rose by one position.

Table 2B.2. Countries with the greatest change in Global Peace Index score, 2009–10

Country	Score, 2010	Change in score, 2009–10	Rank, 2010	Change in rank, 2009–10[a]
Top 5 risers				
Ethiopia	2.444	−0.107	127	+1
Mauritania	2.389	−0.088	123	+1
Hungary	1.495	−0.080	20	+7
Lebanon	2.639	−0.078	134	−2
Haiti	2.270	−0.060	114	+2
Top 5 fallers				
Cyprus	2.013	+0.276	76	−28
Russia	3.013	+0.264	143	−7
Philippines	2.574	+0.247	130	−15
Georgia	2.970	+0.234	142	−8
Syria	2.274	+0.225	115	−23

[a] The Global Peace Index (GPI) 2009 included only 144 countries while the GPI 2010 includes 149 countries, which affects the change in rank between 2009 and 2010.

The average score for the 149 states surveyed in the 2010 GPI is 2.02 (based on a 1–5 scale), a slight rise (indicating a decline in peace) compared with 2009, when the average was 1.964. There is little variance between the overall scores of the top 20 countries (from 1.188 for New Zealand to 1.495 for Hungary, a difference of 0.307). The 20 lowest-ranked countries exhibit a far greater spread (from 2.574 for the Philippines to 3.406 for Iraq, a difference of 0.832).

The countries whose score has changed the most compared to the GPI for 2009 are listed in table 2B.2.[4]

III. Methodology and data sources

The indicators

The GPI advisory panel chose 23 indicators of the existence or absence of peace, divided into three thematic categories.[5]

1. *Measures of ongoing domestic and international conflict.* The GPI is intended to review the state of peace in countries over the past year, although many indicators are based on available data from the past two years. The advisory panel decided against including data reflecting a country's historical experience of domestic and international conflict on the grounds that the GPI uses authoritative statistics on ongoing intra- and interstate wars. These, combined with two indicators scored by the EIU's analysts, comprise 5 of the 23 indicators (see table 2B.3).

[4] For further analysis of why each of these countries has moved see Global Peace Index, *2010 Methodology, Results and Findings* (Institute for Economics and Peace: Sydney, 2010).

[5] For the precise definition of each indicator see Global Peace Index (note 4).

Table 2B.3. Measures of ongoing domestic and international conflict

Indicator	Weight	Source
Number of external and internal conflicts fought	5	UCDP/PRIO Armed Conflict Dataset
Estimated number of deaths from organized conflict (external)	5	UCDP
Number of deaths from organized conflict (internal)	5	IISS, Armed Conflict Database
Level of organized conflict (internal)	5	Economist Intelligence Unit
Relations with neighbouring countries	5	Economist Intelligence Unit

IISS = International Institute for Strategic Studies; PRIO = International Peace Research Institute, Oslo; UCDP = Uppsala Conflict Data Program.

Table 2B.4. Measures of societal safety and security

Indicator	Weight	Source
Perceptions of criminality in society	4	Economist Intelligence Unit
Number of displaced people as a percentage of the population	4	UNHCR Statistical Yearbook and IDMC
Political instability	4	Economist Intelligence Unit
Level of respect for human rights	4	Mark Gibney and Matthew Dalton, University of North Carolina/Amnesty International
Potential for terrorist acts	1	Economist Intelligence Unit
Number of homicides per 100 000 people	4	CTS
Level of violent crime	4	Economist Intelligence Unit
Likelihood of violent demonstrations	3	Economist Intelligence Unit
Number jailed per 100 000 people	3	International Centre for Prison Studies, King's College London, World Prison Population List
Number of internal security officers and police per 100 000 people	3	CTS

CTS = UN Office of Drugs and Crime, United Nations Surveys on Crime Trends and the Operations of Criminal Justice System; IDMC = Internal Displacement Monitoring Centre; UNHCR = UN High Commissioner for Refugees.

2. *Measures of societal safety and security.* Ten indicators assess the levels of safety and security in a country, ranging from perceptions of criminality in society to the level of respect for human rights and the rate of murders and violent crimes (see table 2B.4). The panel considered the difficulties of comparing international crime statistics. Five of these indicators have been scored by the EIU's team of country analysts. For the 2010 GPI, the measure of displaced people was revised to include the number of internally displaced people as a percentage of the population in addition to the number of refugees.

3. *Measures of militarization.* Eight of the indicators are related to a country's military build-up, reflecting the assertion that the level of militarization and

Table 2B.5. Measures of militarization

Indicator	Weight	Source
Military expenditure as a percentage of GDP	2	IISS, *The Military Balance*
Number of armed services personnel per 100 000 people	2	IISS, *The Military Balance*
Volume of transfers of major conventional weapons (imports) per 100 000 people	2	SIPRI Arms Transfers Database
Volume of transfers of major conventional weapons (exports) per 100 000 people	3	SIPRI Arms Transfers Database
Funding for UN peacekeeping missions	2	Institute for Economic and Peace
Aggregate weighted number of heavy weapons per 100 000 people	3	Institute for Economic and Peace
Ease of access to small arms and light weapons	3	Economist Intelligence Unit
Military capability/sophistication	2	Economist Intelligence Unit

IISS = International Institute for Strategic Studies.

access to weapons is directly linked to how at peace a country feels internationally (see table 2B.5). For the 2010 GPI, the measure of the aggregate number of heavy weapons, based on data from the Bonn International Center for Conversion (BICC), was replaced with a weighted rating of the destructive capability of heavy weapons.[6] In conjunction with SIPRI, data was sourced from the UN Register of Conventional Arms and *The Military Balance*.

All of the indicators are assigned a score ('banded') on a scale of 1–5. EIU country analysts score the qualitative indicators, and gaps in the quantitative data are filled by estimates.

Weighting the index

The advisory panel apportioned scores based on the relative importance of each of the indicators on a 1–5 scale. The consensus scores for each indicator are given in tables 2B.3–2B.5. Two sub-component weighted indices were then calculated from the GPI group of indicators: one that measures a country's level of internal peace and one that measures a country's level of external peace (its state of peace beyond its borders). The overall composite score and index were then calculated by applying a weight of 60 per cent to the measure of internal peace and 40 per cent for external peace. The advisory panel agreed to apply a heavier weight to internal peace on the assumption that a greater level of internal peace is likely to correlate with a lower level of external conflict.

IV. Investigating the set of potential determinants

The Global Peace Index can be used as a foundation on which to establish a measure of the incidence of peace. However, it cannot on its own explain why

---

[6] For the precise weighting categories see Global Peace Index (note 4)

the absence of violence occurs and whether groups ot countries exhibit sufficient similar deficiencies that result in an absence of peace.

In addition to the 23 indicators listed above, the GPI has identified a number of secondary indicators that measure: democracy, including government competence and efficacy; the strength of institutions and the political process; international openness; demographics; regional integration; religion and culture; education; and material well-being.[7] This list of potential drivers of peace is by no means exhaustive: it is limited to indicators for which data is both available from credible sources for all 149 countries and comparable and consistent in its measurement. Table 2B.6 lists each of these secondary indicators and the 23 primary GPI indicators. The correlation coefficients of the GPI scores and ranks and of the scores for the internal and external measures of peace are given for each indicator. The correlation coefficients are calculated across the 149 countries in the GPI.

Of the listed variables, the overall index continues to be strongly determined by the internal measure of peace, with a correlation coefficient of 0.96. The structural drivers of peace include good relations with neighbouring states, low levels of corruption, well functioning government, high levels of per capita income, a high rate of participation in primary and secondary education, freedom of the press, and a high degree of regional integration.

In addition, the social values and beliefs that are associated with peace have been analysed through correlating GPI results against global polling data.[8] The analysis provides insights into the social environment of peace. The most striking finding is the extremely high correlation (0.88) between a country's ranking in the Global Peace Index and how positively it is perceived by other countries. This implies that if a country wishes to improve its international standing, then a good way of doing it is to increase its peacefulness as measured by the GPI. Other societal attitudes that correlate with peace are tolerance, belief in the importance of freedom of expression, respect for human rights, not believing that one's own country is superior to others, and believing that the use of the military should be limited and internationally sanctioned. Such attitudinal differences between peaceful and less peaceful countries can help clarify the cultural mechanisms that may underpin the institutions and actions of countries that make them more or less peaceful.

When peace is viewed as consisting of the characteristics and attributes described above, the word 'peace' can be seen as a proxy for describing an interrelated set of structures. These structures create an environment where many activities can flourish, such as enhanced development, improved security, lower business risk, higher per capita income and improved human happiness. Additionally, peace creates resilience; it creates the ability for societies to absorb shocks more easily. Peace, when viewed through this lens, is a collection of activities that creates an optimal environment for human potential to flourish.

[7] For the sources and definitions of these secondary indicators see Global Peace Index (note 4).

[8] The analysis was conducted by the Institute for Economics and Peace in collaboration with the University of Maryland Program on International Policy Attitudes (PIPA), <http://www.pipa.org/>.

Table 2B.6. Correlation between the Global Peace Index 2010 and the indicators of peace and its possible determinants

Figures are correlation coefficients. Figures in bold are correlation coefficients greater than 0.5 or less than −0.5. Significance levels, which will be different for each indicator, have not been calculated.

	GPI score	GPI rank	Internal peace	External peace
Global Peace Index 2010 score	**1.00**	**0.96**	**0.96**	**0.59**
Global Peace Index 2010 rank	**0.96**	**1.00**	**0.94**	**0.50**
Internal peace	**0.96**	**0.94**	**1.00**	0.32
External peace	**0.59**	**0.50**	0.32	**1.00**
Global Peace Index indicators				
Number of external and internal conflicts fought	0.27	0.23	0.11	**0.57**
Estimated number of deaths from organized conflict (external)	0.17	0.12	0.05	0.40
Number of deaths from organized conflict (internal)	**0.66**	**0.56**	**0.63**	0.40
Level of organized conflict (internal)	**0.84**	**0.81**	**0.83**	0.43
Relations with neighbouring countries	**0.68**	**0.66**	**0.54**	**0.70**
Perceptions of criminality in society	**0.73**	**0.73**	**0.78**	0.22
Number of displaced people as a percentage of the population	0.47	0.35	0.37	0.47
Political instability	**0.73**	**0.76**	**0.75**	0.28
Level of respect for human rights	**0.85**	**0.83**	**0.84**	0.41
Potential for terrorist acts	**0.61**	**0.58**	**0.59**	0.35
Number of homicides per 100 000 people	**0.62**	**0.64**	**0.74**	−0.03
Level of violent crime	**0.63**	**0.67**	**0.76**	−0.04
Likelihood of violent demonstrations	**0.65**	**0.67**	**0.72**	0.13
Number jailed per 100 000 people	0.12	0.13	0.06	0.21
Number of internal security officers and police per 100 000 people	0.07	0.08	0.06	0.08
Military expenditure as a percentage of GDP	0.41	0.34	0.29	**0.51**
Number of armed services personnel per 100 000 people	0.25	0.20	0.10	**0.51**
Volume of transfers of major conventional weapons, (imports) per 100 000 people	−0.07	−0.12	−0.16	0.21
Volume of transfers of major conventional weapons (exports) per 100 000 people	−0.05	−0.09	−0.17	0.29
Funding for UN peacekeeping missions	0.20	0.22	0.22	0.04
Aggregate weighted number of heavy weapons per 100 000 people	−0.04	−0.05	−0.21	0.44
Ease of access to small arms and light weapons	**0.73**	**0.73**	**0.80**	0.17
Military capability/sophistication	−0.05	−0.06	−0.21	0.42
Potential determinants of peace				
Political Democracy Index	**−0.56**	**−0.56**	**−0.57**	−0.23
Electoral process	−0.38	−0.38	−0.38	−0.16
Functioning of government	**−0.64**	**−0.63**	**−0.64**	−0.29
Political participation	−0.46	−0.47	**−0.50**	−0.12
Political culture	**−0.63**	**−0.63**	**−0.67**	−0.19
Civil liberties	−0.49	−0.49	−0.48	−0.26
Corruption perceptions	**−0.70**	**−0.75**	**−0.78**	−0.12

	GPI score	GPI rank	Internal peace	External peace
Women in parliament (% of lower house)	−0.27	−0.29	−0.25	−0.17
Freedom of the press	**0.52**	**0.52**	**0.51**	0.27
Exports plus imports as % of GDP	−0.08	−0.10	−0.09	−0.01
Foreign direct investment (flow) as % of GDP	−0.13	−0.14	−0.11	−0.13
Number of visitors as % of domestic population	−0.43	−0.45	−0.48	−0.05
Net migration (% of total population)	−0.25	−0.32	−0.29	−0.01
15–34-year-old males as % of adult population	0.42	0.45	**0.53**	−0.09
Gender ratio of population: women : men	−0.10	−0.11	−0.10	−0.05
Gender inequality	−0.41	−0.41	−0.39	−0.21
Extent of regional integration	**0.62**	**0.62**	**0.62**	0.29
Current education spending (% of GDP)	−0.33	−0.34	−0.33	−0.16
Primary school enrolment ratio (% net)	−0.48	−0.43	**−0.53**	−0.10
Secondary school enrolment ratio (% net)	**−0.50**	−0.50	**−0.63**	0.10
Higher education enrolment (% gross)	−0.46	−0.48	**−0.57**	0.09
Mean years of schooling	**−0.58**	**−0.57**	**−0.66**	−0.04
Adult literacy rate (% of population over 15 years old)	−0.45	−0.41	**−0.51**	−0.04
Hostility to foreigners and private property	**0.59**	**0.58**	**0.61**	0.20
Importance of religion in national life	0.48	0.49	**0.51**	0.15
Willingness to fight	0.40	0.41	0.30	0.47
Nominal GDP ($ b., purchasing power parities)	−0.05	−0.04	−0.11	0.15
Nominal GDP ($ b., market exchange rates)	−0.11	−0.10	−0.17	0.13
GDP per capita	**−0.57**	**−0.61**	**−0.64**	−0.06
Gini index	0.32	0.36	0.45	−0.19
Economic Freedom of the World Index (Fraser Institute)	**−0.58**	**−0.59**	**−0.61**	−0.15
World Bank Ease of Doing Business Index	**0.52**	**0.54**	**0.62**	−0.07
WEF Global Competitiveness Index	−0.59	**−0.62**	**−0.72**	0.08
Unemployment (%)	0.18	0.15	0.18	0.10
Life expectancy	**−0.52**	**−0.52**	**−0.62**	0.04
Infant mortality per 1000 live births	**0.53**	**0.51**	**0.62**	0.02
Human Rights Index (HRIN)	**0.76**	**0.72**	**0.70**	**0.50**
Yale Environmental Performance Index	−0.48	−0.49	**−0.54**	−0.06
World Bank Worldwide Governance Indicators (WGI):				
WGI Voice and Accountability	**−0.61**	**−0.62**	**−0.62**	−0.25
WGI Political Stability and Absence of Violence	**−0.87**	**−0.85**	**−0.88**	−0.38
WGI Government Effectiveness	**−0.70**	**−0.73**	**−0.78**	−0.11'
WGI Regulatory Quality	**−0.66**	**−0.69**	**−0.72**	−0.16
WGI Rule of Law	**−0.76**	**−0.79**	**−0.84**	−0.13
WGI Control of Corruption	**−0.72**	**−0.76**	**−0.79**	−0.16
Cingranelli-Richards (CIRI) Human Rights Data Project:				
CIRI Physical Integrity Rights	**−0.77**	**−0.78**	**−0.74**	−0.40
CIRI Empowerment Rights	**−0.52**	**−0.51**	**−0.48**	−0.36

3. Civilian roles in peace operations

SHARON WIHARTA AND STEPHANIE BLAIR

I. Introduction

The year 2009 marked the 10th anniversary of the seminal Brahimi report, which proposed an overhaul of the United Nations peacekeeping system.[1] The report highlighted for the first time the centrality of the civilian contribution to the effectiveness of UN peace operations and called for a strengthened UN capacity in this area. A decade later, progress in the civilian dimension is mixed. The number of civilian tasks mandated in UN Security Council resolutions for UN peace operations and the number of civilian missions undertaken by regional organizations have increased dramatically in recent years. These increases are coupled with a near doubling of the number of civilians assigned to global multilateral peace operations: they currently exceed 6500 (see figure 3.1).[2]

The imperative for civilian personnel in peace operations came to the fore in 2009, most notably in Afghanistan. A new United States strategy for Afghanistan—announced in March—placed greater emphasis on security, governance and local development, while continuing to prioritize the rule of law and counternarcotics measures.[3] In order to realize the strategy, a 'civilian surge' would accompany the planned increased troop levels. The outgoing head of mission for the UN Assistance Mission in Afghanistan (UNAMA), Kai Ede, supported the change in strategy and cautioned against neglecting the political and civilian aspects of the peacebuilding process in Afghanistan.[4]

Given the strong need and continued demand for civilians, and the persistent challenges of deploying the appropriate people at the right time and in the appropriate numbers, significant attention has been paid to the 'civilian capacity gap'. This issue is thus at the top of the agenda of several governments and of multilateral organizations, including the UN, the European Union (EU), the North Atlantic Treaty Organization (NATO) and the African Union (AU). In 2009 the UN Secretary-General produced a report

---

[1] United Nations, Report of the Panel on United Nations Peacekeeping Operations (Brahimi Report), A/55/305–S/2000/809, 21 Aug. 2000.

[2] This figure does not include civilian police deployment. See also appendix 3A.

[3] DeYoung, K., 'Civilians to join Afghan buildup: "surge" is part of larger U.S. strategy studied by White House', *Washington Post*, 19 Mar. 2009.

[4] MacFarquhar, N., 'U.N. envoy to Afghanistan warns of peril of emphasizing security over social issues', *New York Times*, 7 Jan. 2010.

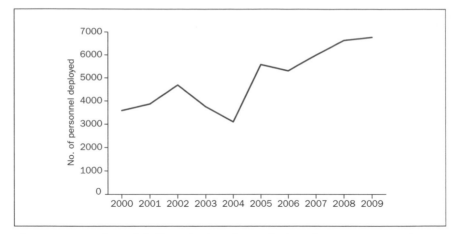

Figure 3.1. Number of civilians deployed to United Nations peace operations, 2000–2009

Source: SIPRI Multilateral Peace Operations Database, <http://www.sipri.org/databases/pko/>

on peacebuilding that underscores the need for increased civilian capacities and provides the impetus to critically review the UN's civilian capacity.[5] Although the civilian dimension of peace operations has been strengthened by a range of recent institutional innovations, such operations are still not appropriately configured and staffed for their roles. This chapter discusses how the civilian capacity gap should not be viewed or addressed simply as a recruitment or deployment issue, but should take into account, for example, the planning and financing of peace operations. Such an assessment highlights that the operational challenges in the civilian dimension are due to a lack of conceptual clarity.

Section II provides an overview of the state of play of the civilian dimension of peace operations and peacebuilding and surveys some of the ongoing institutional developments and reforms in multilateral organizations and national governments. Section III looks at the operational challenges plaguing the civilian component of the UN Mission in Sudan (UNMIS), as well as how the lack of conceptual clarity has affected the mission's efficacy. Section IV offers conclusions. Appendix 3A presents extensive data on the multilateral peace operations that were active for all or part of 2009.

---

[5] United Nations, Security Council, Report of the Secretary-General on peacebuilding in the immediate aftermath of conflict, S/2009/304, 11 June 2009.

11. Addressing the civilian capacity gap in peace operations

In the past decade peace operations have taken on a more multidimensional characteristic, integrating the political, humanitarian, development and military dimensions. Thus, a typical multidimensional peace operation is usually mandated to perform a variety of tasks to assist the host country's transition from conflict to sustainable peace. Peace operation mandates now routinely include basic civilian activities, such as demobilization, disarmament and reintegration (DDR); security sector reform (SSR); public information; rule of law; law and order; justice; human rights; humanitarian relief and rehabilitation; supporting the return of refugees and internally displaced persons; elections; constitutional support and institutional reform and capacity building. For many of these activities, the deployment of troops is neither appropriate nor relevant. Moreover, the functions require specific expertise that is predominantly found in the civilian sphere.

The sheer diversity of civilian functions and skills makes it difficult to address the question of capacity without first defining the term 'civilians'. Is the term restricted to the group that administers and manages the mission? Or is it broader? To what jobs does it refer? A number of 'toolkits' describe or seek to categorize the multitude of tasks and functions necessary in peacebuilding contexts. Most of them describe a basic core set of functions but illustrate the point that no common definition exists for the civilian roles and functions used by the AU, the EU and the UN, much less by individual countries[6] The monthly statistics produced by the UN's Department of Public Information on personnel deployment in UN peace operations include a broad category of civilian staff but do not disaggregate between civilians whose jobs range from information technology to the promotion of human rights. This diversity of definitions is further magnified by the difference in institutional mandates within which the civilians must operate. In this chapter, the term 'civilians' refers to non-uniformed personnel working in multilateral peace operations, but excludes 'humanitarian' non-governmental organizations (NGOs), such as the International Committee of the Red Cross (ICRC).

As mission mandates have grown increasingly complex, the requirement for qualified civilian expertise has grown apace, and with it a proliferation of civilian functions in peace operations, at least in the UN context. In fact, the recent UN Secretary-General report on peacebuilding identified two new core peacebuilding objectives: support for employment generation, in

---

[6] Chandran, R. et al., 'Recovering from war: gaps in early action', Report by the New York University (NYU) Center on International Cooperation for the British Department for International Development, NYU, New York, 1 July 2008, <http://www.cic.nyu.edu/peacebuilding/statebuilding.html>.

particular in agriculture and public works; and sustainable natural resource management.[7] The emergence of numerous peacebuilding objectives has led to the creation of multiple posts by various UN agencies and departments to address a single issue; this can lead to overlapping duties on the ground. Security sector reform is a good example. A dedicated unit in the UN Department of Peacekeeping Operations (DPKO) addresses SSR issues, but SSR is also dealt with by, among others, the UN Development Programme (UNDP), the Office of the High Commissioner for Human Rights (OHCHR) and the UN Development Fund for Women (UNIFEM).

While the proliferation of civilian functions may have led to greater awareness of and attention to typical peacebuilding priorities, reflecting the complexity and magnitude of peacebuilding, the purpose of some of the functions is less clear. For instance, civilian protection is one such ambiguous function. A recent study conducted for the DPKO and the UN Office for the Coordination of Humanitarian Affairs (OCHA) revealed that, despite a decade of including civilian protection in mandates, the UN still struggles with what it means, both definitionally and operationally, for a peace operation to protect civilians.[8] The lack of common understanding of what constitutes civilian protection, and therefore which agency or department within the UN should take the lead, has created inter-agency turf battles. In practice, this has led to a divisive debate on whether protection should be a cross-cutting or a separate civilian function in peace operations, and the division of labour between the military and civilian components has also been affected. A clearer definition of what constitutes 'expertise' and the requirements necessary for each civilian function would prevent duplicative efforts.

Common challenges and institutional responses

The dominance of the civilian agenda for many multilateral organizations and national governments parallels the process of enhancing international effectiveness in peacebuilding efforts. A multitude of institutional development processes that are intended to improve civilian capacity for stability operations, state building and crisis management efforts have been implemented across the spectrum of actors. As international and regional organizations as well as individual states have responded to the rising demand for civilian skills and expertise, a perceived 'civilian gap' has become apparent due to inadequate capabilities and capacities that have hampered

---

[7] United Nations (note 5), p. 18.

[8] Holt, V. and Taylor, G., with Kelly, M., *Protecting Civilians in the Context of UN Peacekeeping Operations: Successes, Setbacks and Remaining Challenges* (United Nations: New York, Nov. 2009).

implementation.[9] According to one analyst, 'the single most important limitation has been a lack of civilian capacity for such operations, which has led to an over reliance on military forces.' Although reform is an ongoing process, the reforms that have been made have been criticized as being 'marginally successful so far'.[10] However, institutional choices that are made concerning structures, policies and mechanisms will have direct impact on improved civilian capacity. Recruitment and deployment issues have been a top (if not the only) priority driving the civilian agenda. Nascent structures have also faced continuing upheaval because of structural reforms that aim to improve inter-agency processes in the desire to operationalize whole-of-government approaches. These organizations face a remarkably similar set of challenges and constraints—despite their differences in structure, purpose and even national context.

As multilateral organizations and national governments look to alternative solutions to expand and diversify the pool of civilian experts, a contentious issue, but one that deserves more attention, has arisen: the role of private sector actors. The emergence and growing role of these actors in the military dimension of peace operations through the provision of security, logistics and equipment to the EU, NATO and the UN and to some humanitarian NGOs has already received much attention in academic and policy discussions.[11] Critics argue against the use of private sector actors because of legitimacy, accountability and transparency concerns, which are exemplified by the US Government's recent experience of employing such contractors in Iraq. Concern also exists about a similar encroachment on the civilian sphere by private contractors. For example, the new NATO Training Mission in Afghanistan employs a significant number of private contractors.

Institutional developments in the civilian dimension of peace operations do not occur in isolation. Calls to strengthen civilian capacities raise the important question of financing. In the EU and the UN the planning and financing processes are separate and do not happen at the same pace. Missions are often hampered by slow and cumbersome budgeting cycles (as

---

[9] Blair, S. and Fitz-Gerald, A., 'The need for conceptual clarity: evaluating the current stabilisation debate', *Journal of Intervention and Statebuilding* (forthcoming 2010). See also Serafino, N. M., *Peacekeeping, Stabilization and Conflict Transitions: Background and Congressional Action on the Civilian Response/Reserve Corps and other Civilian Stabilization and Reconstruction Capabilities*, Congressional Research Service (CRS) Report for Congress RL32862 (US Congress: Washington, DC, 5 Feb. 2009).

[10] Bensahel, N., 'International perspectives on interagency reform: testimony presented before the House Armed Services Committee, Subcommittee on Oversight and Investigations on January 29, 2008', RAND Testimony series, Santa Monica, CA, <http://www.rand.org/pubs/testimonies/CT298/>, p. 1.

[11] For a discussion of the issue see Chesterman, S. and Lehnardt, C. (eds), *From Mercenaries to Market: The Rise and Regulation of Private Military Companies* (Oxford University Press: Oxford, 2007).

discussed in the context of UNMIS in section III below). At the national level, continued over-reliance on the military is arguably due to the fact that defence departments or ministries often have far larger budgets or discretionary spending authority than the civilian sector.[12] The civilian agenda must therefore take into account broader factors.

However, the issue of the civilian contribution to peace operations has been dominated by the West. Efforts behind the scene are under way to support multinational approaches through widening the debate to include actors from the 'Global South'.

The United Nations

As part of its ongoing broad 'Peace Operations 2010' reform agenda, the UN Secretariat issued two key documents in 2009: the Secretary-General's report on peacebuilding, and a DPKO–Department of Field Services (DFS) non-paper, 'A new partnership agenda: charting a new horizon for UN peacekeeping'.[13] Both aim to improve the efficacy of UN engagement in peacekeeping and peacebuilding and came about, in part, in response to the Security Council's 2008 request to the Secretary-General to provide advice and strategy for more effective UN support and assistance to countries that are in transition from conflict to peace.[14] Much of what was included in the two documents reinforced recurring lessons of the past decade. Their emphasis on better planning, achievable mandates, clarified roles for civilians, strengthened leadership teams in host countries and institutional harmonization within the UN system are recognition that much more needs to be done.

The Secretary-General's report on peacebuilding outlines what is needed in the civilian field and the gaps in the available capacity. It emphasizes the need to strengthen the leadership capacity of the political, peacekeeping, peacebuilding and development elements of any future UN presence in a host country. This approach is echoed in the 'New Horizons' paper; its emphasis on strong mission leadership capability is a shift to a peace operation 'that focuses on the skills, capacity and willingness of personnel, as well as material, to deliver required results'. Senior leaders are expected to possess substantial negotiation and mediation expertise, have in-depth regional knowledge with requisite language abilities, and possess vast

[12] Barton, F. and Unger, N., 'Civil–military relations, fostering development, and expanding civilian capacity', Brookings Institution and Center for Strategic and International Studies, Workshop Report, Apr. 2009, <http://www.brookings.edu/reports/2009/04_development_unger.aspx>.

[13] United Nations (note 5); and United Nations, Departments of Peacekeeping Operations and Field Support, *A New Partnership Agenda: Charting the New Horizon for UN Peacekeeping* (United Nations: New York, July 2009).

[14] United Nations, Security Council, Statement by the President of the Security Council, S/PRST/2008/16, 20 May 2008.

experience in strategic planning and the management of large, complex organizations. Recognizing that the number of individuals with such credentials is small, the UN proposed to focus on choosing a team of senior leaders. In order to improve the selection and retention process, in 2008 the DFS created a dedicated unit for senior leadership appointments. The 'New Horizons' paper also envisages a second-tier team of experts with similar expertise to support the management team.

However, no unified team of analytical, planning and coordination experts to support the executive team currently exists in the UN, and no structure or mechanism is in place in the UN Secretariat to assess the necessary support and expertise for in-country leadership teams. Instead, individual experts are deployed piecemeal by the respective agencies. Noting that civilian planning capacity is still weak, the DPKO was thus tasked to review the quality and efficacy of existing integrated task forces and the recently established integrated operational teams (IOTs) to determine if the task forces and IOTs could play a role to improve the current situation.[15]

The 'New Horizons' paper notes that considerable progress has been made in building up the reservoir of expertise in areas such as DDR, SSR and the rule of law. Other areas, such as public administration (i.e. public finance and basic monetary and fiscal policy expertise), have not come as far, in part perhaps because such expertise is not readily available in the UN system. The report recommends that, rather than building in-house capacity in these areas, strong partnerships should be developed with the World Bank and the International Monetary Fund to draw on their expertise.

Building on the lessons learned from previous and ongoing UN multidimensional peace operations (see section III), the 'New Horizons' paper articulates the importance of setting out clear operational standards for mission mandate tasks. Such standards would define the core tasks and operational requirements and serve as the basis for identifying the requisite personnel and resources. It appears, however, that the focus would be on uniformed personnel (military and police) instead of on the civilian component.[16] However, it is the latter that requires most, given their overlapping roles.

Both the Secretary-General's report on peacebuilding and the 'New Horizons' paper devote substantial attention to the issue of how to rapidly deploy civilian capacities to the field. Delaying such deployment can severely impede a mission's ability to implement its mandate. A recent

[15] United Nations, General Assembly, 'Implementation of the recommendations of the Special Committee on Peacekeeping Operations', Report of the Secretary-General, A/63/615, 17 Dec. 2008.
[16] Jovin, R., United Nations, Department of Peacekeeping Operations, Division of Policy Evaluation and Training, Interview with author, Jan. 2010.

study recommends that the UN abandon the current model of trying to deploy all civilian staff at once and instead adopt a three-phased approach: (*a*) deployment of a bare-bones team of up to 30 personnel in the start-up phase; (*b*) deployment of 'sector specialist teams' of 40–130 personnel in the 'ramp-up' phase; and (*c*) deployment of long-term personnel.[17] Another approach to the deployment challenge, which appears to be favoured not only by the UN but also by regional organizations and national governments, is the notion of a standing capacity or the creation of rosters (standby capacity).[18] A standing capacity refers to a group of staff that are employed full time with the express purpose of being available for rapid deployment when the need arises. A standby capacity consists of persons pre-identified to be deployed on demand. Staff can be pre-screened, pre-interviewed and even pre-contracted, depending on the level of investment. Another standby option, often referred to as a rostered capacity (i.e. a database of potential candidates), is to make use of people already employed who can be temporarily reassigned when emergency surge capacity is needed.

The UN intends to build on the early success of the DPKO's Standing Police Capacity and the mediation standby teams of the Department of Political Affairs (DPA). A standing capacity may be appropriate for police personnel, but less so for public administration experts. The two models are still in their infancy and, before rosters for each civilian function proliferate, existing models should be reviewed to assess their applicability to other civilian functions. Currently, no single point exists for national or multilateral actors to request or obtain information on available resources: who should administer a clearing house for the rosters, and where should it be located? The political will, or lack of it, to feed into and maintain the rosters should also be addressed or they may be in danger of becoming empty shells that are not used.

Interestingly, a 2006 proposal by the Secretary-General to introduce 2500 career positions for the development of 'a cadre of highly mobile, experienced, trained and multi-skilled civilian staff to meet the baseline human resources requirements of UN peace operations' has not been realized because the Advisory Committee on Administrative and Budgetary Questions (ACABQ) of the UN General Assembly's Fifth Committee did not

---

[17] Chandran, R. et al., *Rapid Deployment of Civilians for Peace Operations: Status, Gaps, and Options* (New York University, Center on International Cooperation: New York, Apr. 2009).

[18] See de Coning, C., 'Civilian expertise: partnership to match supply to demand', Paper presented at 'Cooperating for peace: the challenge and promise of partnerships in peace operations', Seminar co-hosted by Geneva Centre for Security Policy and International Peace Institute, Geneva, 10–11 Dec. 2009, <http://www.nupi.no/content/download/11498/112274/file/DeConing – Panel 4_ Civilian_Expertise.pdf>.

approve the proposal.[19] Under that proposal, career models would be developed, and selected staff would receive targeted training programmes and rotate between secretariat and field positions in order to gain a well-rounded experience of peace operations. However, the ACABQ argued that the human resource reform under way would address many of the concerns that gave rise to the proposal.[20]

Another initiative in the UN context is the move towards greater reliance on existing capacities in the host country. UN field missions and offices, particularly in developing countries, have been requested to identify qualified national staff, who will be placed on the rosters for potential selection for employment in post-conflict countries. This stems from an emerging consensus that neighbouring countries, countries with similar socio-economic and cultural backgrounds and countries that have previously undergone post-conflict transition can greatly contribute to the international community's peacebuilding efforts by sending civilian experts who may have a better understanding of the specific challenges of post-conflict countries.[21]

EU civilian capacity: an ongoing and ambitious transformation process

The EU's demanding agenda for reforming civilian crisis management operations deserves closer scrutiny. Civilian crisis management is an important tool under the EU's Common Security and Defence Policy (CSDP). The structures for civilian crisis management, as they are termed in the EU, have endured a year of sustained uncertainty because of the tumultuous upheavals associated with the approval of the 2007 Lisbon Treaty.[22] During the 10 years of its existence the CSDP (previously known as the European Security and Defence Policy, ESDP) has undergone profound institutional changes in intense periods of growing demand for civilian crisis management capabilities, including the conduct of 13 civilian operations since 2003.[23] However, 'the institutional structures that support

---

[19] For details of the Secretary-General's proposal for the 2500 civilian career peacekeepers see United Nations, General Assembly, 'Investing in people', Report of the Secretary-General, Addendum, 'Reforming the field service category: investing in meeting the human resources requirements of United Nations peace operations in the twenty-first century', A/61/255/Add.1, 22 Aug. 2006.

[20] United Nations, General Assembly, 'Fifth Committee takes up $300 million budget for 2008/09 peacekeeping support account', Press release, 6 June 2008, <http://www.un.org/News/Press/docs/2008/gaab3857.doc.htm>.

[21] United Nations (note 5).

[22] Treaty of Lisbon amending the Treaty on European Union and the Treaty establishing the European Community, signed 13 Dec. 2007, entered into force 1 Dec. 2009, <http://europa.eu/lisbon_treaty/>.

[23] The EU has conducted 13 civilian crisis management missions: 7 police (EUPM, EUPOL PROXIMA, EUPOL Kinshasa, EUPAT, EUPOL COPPS, EUPOL Afghanistan, and EUPOL RD Congo); 3 rule-of-law (EUJUST THEMIS, EUJUST LEX Iraq and EULEX Kosovo); 2 SSR (EUSEC

the planning and conduct of these operational activities are yet to come of age'.[24] The implementation of the Lisbon Treaty, which entered into force on 1 December 2009, will shape the EU's structural reform for years to come. It also highlights a sustained high level of ambition to be a global player in both foreign policy and operational terms through the creation of the European External Action Service (EEAS) and the merger of civilian and military planning functions. The creation of the Civilian Planning and Conduct Capability (CPCC) in 2007 and of the Crisis Management Planning Directorate (CMPD) in 2009 'mark a departure in ESDP institutional development'.[25] Finally, the ongoing Civilian Headline Goal (CHG) process (discussed below) has continued to undergo significant review and revision since 2004 with the adoption of CHG 2010 in 2007.

Civilian Headline Goals

At the June 2000 European Council, the EU set out its main tasks for civilian crisis management, known as the Civilian Headline Goals.[26] Initially comprising police, rule of law, civil administration and civil protection, these were extended in 2004 to include monitoring missions and support to EU special representatives by 2008.[27] Additionally, the EU indicated that it would also contribute to activities such as SSR and support DDR processes. Further demonstrating its high level of ambition, the EU indicated that it 'must be able to conduct concurrent civilian missions at different levels of engagement; to deploy civilian means simultaneously with military means at the outset of an operation and finally, civilian crisis management operations under the ESDP must be deployable autonomously, jointly or in close cooperation with military operations'.[28] Yet critical analysis suggests that the 'following process of civilian capability development by far exceeded general expectations in terms of both speed and quantitative success'.[29] According to one assessment, 'The so-called Civilian Headline Goal (CHG) process . . . was a rigorous attempt to get member states to commit civilians for potential deployment scenarios. Each member state pledged a

DR Congo and EU SSR Guinea Bissau); and 1 border control (EUBAM Rafah). For detailed information see the SIPRI Multilateral Peace Operations Database, <http://www.sipri.org/databases/pko/>; and appendix 3A. It is important to note that the EU classifies civilian police operations under the category of civilians. For details of all CSDP missions (including those excluded from the SIPRI database) see CSDP map, <http://www.csdpmap.eu>.

[24] Gebhard, C., 'The crisis management and planning directorate: recalibrating ESDP planning and conduct capacities', *CFSP Forum*, vol. 7, no. 4 (July 2009), pp. 8–14.

[25] Gebhard (note 24), p. 14.

[26] Council of the European Union, 'Strengthening the Common European Security and Defence Policy: Presidency Report to the Feira European Council', document 9149/00, Brussels, 15 June 2000.

[27] Council of the European Union, 'Civilian Headline Goal 2008', document 15863/04, Brussels, 17 Dec. 2004.

[28] Council of the European Union (note 27).

[29] Gebhard (note 24), p. 9.

certain number of civilians, and yet the CHG process does not appear to have helped the EU get boots on the ground.'[30]

In order to comply with its ambitious objectives, the EU adopted a step-by-step approach to the development of its civilian crisis management capabilities: 'it entails the definition of planning assumptions on the basis of scenarios, the elaboration of capability requirements lists, the assessment of national contributions and the identification of capability shortfalls'. In 2007, building on the results of the CHG 2008 and on the growing body of ESDP crisis management experience, the EU adopted CHG 2010 to 'help to ensure that the EU can conduct crisis management, in line with the European Security Strategy, by deploying civilian crisis management capabilities of high quality, with the support functions and equipment required in a short time-span and in sufficient quantity'.[31]

Recognizing the iterative nature of the CHG process, EU ministers set out an annual plan as part of CHG 2010, launched in 2007, to include the Report on Civilian Preparedness in October 2009 and the Civilian Capability Targets in November 2009. EU ministers agreed to hold 'a yearly conference to assess the state of play, monitor progress and guide future efforts in the field of civilian ESDP. Ministerial Guidelines will be issued at the end of the CHG 2010 process'.[32]

These initiatives highlight the inherently political nature of the EU's efforts in regard to its civilian agenda, with little attention paid to tangible results. Equally, this overly politicized process has overshadowed the challenges of the EU's decentralized approach to harnessing civilian capacity, which relies on seconded staff that have been selected and provided by member states. This leaves field missions overly reliant on member states' contributions and therefore often under-staffed. Finally, in 2009 implementing the Lisbon Treaty took centre stage and has become a significant focus for policymakers, taking scarce civilian capacity away from operations.

Structural reforms and implications of the Lisbon Treaty

The ratification of the Lisbon Treaty in 2009 provided the impetus for the reorganization of the EU's architecture. This included the creation of the post of the High Representative for Foreign Affairs and Security Policy, who is both a vice-president of the European Commission and a member of the Council, and the launch of the EEAS—the EU's new foreign service—to support her efforts. Unfortunately, the treaty provided little direction or

[30] Korski, D. and Gowan, R., *Can the EU Rebuild Failing States? A Review of Europe's Civilian Capacities* (European Council on Foreign Relations: London, Oct. 2009).

[31] Council of the European Union, 'Civilian Headline Goal 2010', document 14823/07, 19 Nov. 2007, para. 18.

[32] Council of the European Union (note 31).

guidance on the role of the EEAS and the necessary restructuring and merging of functions between the Council and the Commission with implications for civilian crisis management.[33] Recognition is growing that the implementation will be progressive, rather than a single launch, and it is likely to take until 2014.[34] Like reform processes elsewhere, the proposals in the Lisbon Treaty aim to improve the EU's ability to act in a more 'comprehensive' fashion on the international stage, not least in the area of civilian crisis management.

In June 2007 the EU created the Civilian Planning and Conduct Capability to oversee the operational level organization and control of missions, which became operational in May 2008. This provides the EU with a unified civilian commander and structural counterpart to the EU Military Staff (EUMS). In December 2008 the European Council agreed on the creation of the Crisis Management and Planning Directorate through the merger of former directorates VIII (defence aspects) and IX (civilian crisis management) of Directorate-General E (external and politico-military affairs) in the Council Secretariat, to integrate civilian and military planning at the strategic level, which became operational as of 16 December 2009.[35] However the transition and the modalities of relationships with other structures, in particular the CPCC, will take some time to function smoothly. At the time of writing much effort has been expended by officials on organizational restructuring, and in particular the relationship of the CMPD with the CPCC and how the EEAS will affect the planning of civilian missions.

---

[33] The Lisbon Treaty in matters relating to the Common Foreign and Security Policy offers only the following guidance: 'In fulfilling his mandate, the High Representative shall be assisted by a European External Action Service. This service shall work in cooperation with the diplomatic services of the Member States and shall comprise officials from relevant departments of the General Secretariat of the Council and of the Commission as well as staff seconded from national diplomatic services of the member states.' Treaty of Lisbon (note 22), Article 1(30), amending Article 13a of the Treaty on European Union. See also Avery, G., 'Europe's foreign service: from design to delivery', European Policy Centre Policy Brief, Nov. 2009, <http://www.epc.eu/TEWN/pdf/959676591_Europe's foreign service.pdf>, p. 1.

[34] Lieb, J. and Maurer, A., 'Creating the European External Action Service: preconditions for avoiding a rude awakening', SWP Comments no. 13, German Institute for International and Security Affairs (SWP), June 2008, <http://www.swp-berlin.org/en/produkte/swp_aktuell_detail.php?id=9162>, pp. 1–8. The authors note that the expiry of the EU budget for 2007–13 would generate a review of the EEAS's establishment in 2013. The period up to the Council's decision on the EEAS (expected in Apr. 2010) can be considered a first stage, to be followed by a second that will last years. A status report, to be produced in 2012, will review the function and organization of the EEAS; if necessary, the initial decision will be revised, possibly in 2014. Avery (note 33), p. 2; and Crowe, B., The European External Action Service: Roadmap for Success (Chatham House: London, May 2008), p. 8. For the political, legal and institutional reasons for the time needed to make the EEAS fully operational see Adebahr, C., 'The first will be the last: why the EU foreign service will remain embryonic for some time', CFSP Forum, vol. 6, no. 2 (Mar. 2008), pp. 5–9.

[35] Council of the European Union, Presidency Conclusions, Brussels, 11–12 Dec. 2008, Annex 2, Declaration by the European Council on the Enhancement of the European Security and Defence Policy (ESDP), Article 6.

One of the main concerns with the creation of the CMPD is the risk that the proposed integration of the civilian and military dimensions of EU crisis management strategic planning could lead in effect to the absorption of the civilian dimension into the military dimension. Merging of directorates VIII and IX could mean that the planning of civilian missions is not conducted by civilians with the relevant political, professional and operational expertise. The increased militarization of the CSDP could, in turn, have a negative impact on civilian crisis management.[36]

The African Union

The African Union has not yet deployed its own multidimensional peace operation or stand-alone civilian mission. However, its experience with the AU–UN Hybrid Mission in Darfur (UNAMID) and its own commitment to fully operationalize the African Standby Force (ASF), including the civilian component, by 2010—pushed the civilian aspects of peace operations to the top of the AU's agenda. Interestingly, developments in Africa differ from the European approach, which has focused on creating institutional structures and capacities in the public sector. In Africa, institutional developments do not consist of recalibrating individual governmental department or capacity because African governments often lack the capacity or resources to undertake such institutional changes. Instead, the civilian debate and the development of civilian expertise have been led by training institutions (often funded by external donors) working in support of the AU. This also reflects the militarization of peace operations within national governments and is made evident at the continent-wide level, where the structure of the ASF and the corresponding efforts to build its capacity have largely focused on military aspects.

The need to develop a civilian component in the ASF has also become apparent because it is the least developed or institutionalized of the ASF's three components. No civilian personnel serve on the AU ASF Planning Element or in a majority of the regional brigades. The development of the civilian policy framework has thus fallen to the training institutions. The absence of a civilian architecture in the AU has several implications: the civilian policy framework is not institutionalized and hence not properly integrated into the overall ASF framework.[37] It is hoped that the civilian dimension will be given greater attention by the UN's AU Peacekeeping

---

[36] European Peacebuilding Liaison Office, 'Statement on civilian–military integration in European security and defence policy', Brussels, 18 Feb. 2009, <http://www.eplo.org/documents/EPLO_Statement.pdf>. See also Gebhard (note 24).

[37] Dersso, S. A., 'The need for "civilianising" the African Standby Force', African Peace Support Trainers' Association, Peacekeeping This Month, 26 Mar. 2009, <http://www.apsta-africa.org/news/article260309.php>.

Support Team in the context of the Framework for the Ten-Year Capacity-Building Programme for the African Union.[38]

National efforts

Like the EU and the UN, individual states have struggled to close the gap between demand and supply of civilian capacity, while attempting to operationalize whole-of-government approaches through inter-agency integration. It is both a broad and narrow issue. Driven by the civilian deployment challenge, in 2004 three governments in particular—Canada, the United Kingdom and the USA, known as 'the trilaterals'—created inter-agency units to overcome these challenges. They have all adopted a similar, tiered approach to their deployment pools that combines the skills and experience of people across the public and private sector. However, these three countries face the common challenges of duty-of-care issues, retention and availability. Canada has created the Stabilisation and Reconstruction Task Force (START); the UK has established the Stabilisation Unit; and the USA has its Office of the Coordinator for Reconstruction and Stabilization (S/CRS). Yet a 'cultural gap' in all three countries impedes the integration necessary to realize a whole-of-government approach and deliver a 'unity of purpose towards a shared goal'.[39]

START was established in 2005 in the International Security Branch of the Department of Foreign Affairs and was 'created to enhance the Government of Canada's capacity for international crisis response through a coordinated, whole-of-government approach'.[40] As part of a reorganization of the Department of Foreign Affairs, the offices that dealt with humanitarian affairs, conflict prevention and peacebuilding, peacekeeping and peace operations, and mines and small arms were incorporated into START. Like its US counterpart, 'since it remains in a single ministry, it has not made much progress in achieving interdepartmental cooperation'.[41]

In 2004 the UK's Foreign and Commonwealth Office created a new Post Conflict Reconstruction Unit (PCRU) in order to facilitate government-wide planning, to build a deployable civilian capacity, and to serve as a source of expertise and lessons learned from previous operations. It is a joint office of the Ministry of Defence, the Foreign and Commonwealth Office and the Department for International Development. The PCRU changed its name to the Stabilisation Unit in December 2007. However, coordination has been hard to achieve in practice. It has been called 'an

[38] United Nations, General Assembly, Letter dated 11 December 2006 from the Secretary-General addressed to the President of the General Assembly, A/61/630, 12 Dec. 2006.
[39] Blair and Fitz-Gerald (note 9).
[40] For more information see Foreign Affairs and International Trade Canada, 'About START', <http://www.international.gc.ca/start-gtsr/start-definition-gtsr.aspx>.
[41] Bensahel (note 10).

orphan with three parents' and said to lack 'a single champion that is invested in its success and that has the power to promote its mission and force coordination among reluctant bureaucrats'.[42]

The S/CRS, created in July 2004, but only signed into law in September 2008, has a mission to 'lead, coordinate, and institutionalize' civilian capacities for post-conflict reconstruction and stabilization efforts.[43] Unfortunately, it was initially understaffed and, despite its mission to lead, the 'CRS has not yet been designated as the lead agency for any stabilization or reconstruction missions, and the planning frameworks it has established have not yet been fully utilized'.[44]

Other countries, notably in developed countries—including Australia, Denmark, Finland, Germany, Japan, the Netherlands, Norway and Sweden—have made attempts to contribute to the civilian agenda either through supporting multinational efforts in the EU and the UN or by training their own nationals, often including the creation of units in the relevant ministries or governmental agencies.[45] For example, the Japanese Ministry of Foreign Affairs has contributed to the budget of the Hiroshima Peacebuilders Centre at the University of Hiroshima, the German Government has created the Zentrum für Internationale Friedenseinsätze (ZIF, or Center for International Peace Operations), the Finnish Government has created the Centre for Civilian Crisis Management, and the Swedish Government created the Folke Bernadotte Academy. Denmark, the Netherlands and Norway have created stabilization units in their ministries of foreign affairs.

III. The UN Mission in Sudan

The various and ongoing efforts to create structures, mechanisms and policies in multilateral organizations and national governments to augment their civilian capabilities may not translate into concrete or workable solutions in the field. The UN Mission in Sudan illustrates the conceptual and operational challenges facing the civilian sphere in peacekeeping operations. UNMIS is not unique in its difficulty to fill and sustain its civilian component; other UN missions with sizeable civilian components face similar problems, as do EU stand-alone civilian missions. It is nevertheless

[42] Bensahel (note 10).

[43] Duncan Hunter National Defense Authorization Act for Fiscal Year 2009, US Public Law 110-417, signed into law 14 Oct. 2008, <http://thomas.loc.gov/cgi-bin/bdquery/z?d110:HR5658:>, title 16. In Dec. 2005 National Security Presidential Directive 44 designated the US State Department as the lead agency for such efforts, and directed the Coordinator to co-chair a new inter-agency Policy Coordinating Committee (PCC) for Reconstruction and Stabilization Operations. White House, National Security Presidential Directive/NSPD-44, Washington, DC, 7 Dec. 2005, <http://www.fas.org/irp/offdocs/nspd/nspd-44.html>.

[44] Bensahel (note 10).

[45] For an audit of countries' contributions to EU operations see Korski and Gowan (note 30).

useful to look at some of the issues facing the mission as examples of a more widespread set of challenges.

Established in March 2005, UNMIS currently has the second largest civilian component of a UN multidimensional peace operation, with 827 civilian staff deployed and an authorized ceiling of 1440.[47] As with other UN multidimensional operations, Security Council Resolution 1590 mandated the mission 'to support the implementation of the Comprehensive Peace Agreement' (CPA).[48] The implementation of the agreement entailed a comprehensive set of tasks and responsibilities for UNMIS: monitoring the ceasefire; establishing a DDR programme to promote political inclusiveness, including raising awareness and understanding of the ongoing peace process; promoting the rule of law, including the reform of state institutions (judiciary and police); monitoring and promoting human rights; offering electoral assistance; and facilitating the return of refugees and internally displaced persons. In addition, Resolution 1590 authorized the mission with Chapter VII powers to use force to protect civilians 'under imminent threat in its areas of deployment and as it deems within its capabilities'.[49]

In the run-up to the elections in 2010, 2009 proved to be a tense period of worsening insecurity in Southern Sudan, particularly in the Jonglei, Upper Nile and Lakes states. This added to the ongoing challenges that UNMIS faced in implementing its mandate. Since its inception, the mission has run into numerous difficulties with getting the necessary number and appropriately skilled personnel in almost every component—military, police and civilian—of the mission. This inevitably affected the mission's ability to implement its ambitious mandate.

Planning

UNMIS was preceded by an advance mission that was deployed to the field in June 2004. The UN Advance Mission in Sudan (UNAMIS), consisting of 164 civilian staff, was to facilitate the peace process and prepare the ground for an eventual fully fledged multidimensional mission on the signing of the Comprehensive Peace Agreement.[50] This was a novel step for the UN in its

[47] MONUC has the largest deployment of civilian personnel. See appendix 3A.

[48] UN Security Council Resolution 1590, 24 Mar. 2005. The text of the Comprehensive Peace Agreement is available at <http://www.usip.org/resources/peace-agreements-sudan>.

[49] Chapter VI of the UN Charter allows the UN Security Council to recommend measures for the peaceful settlement of international disputes, including the deployment of peacekeepers, to be taken with the consent of all parties concerned. Chapter VII empowers the Security Council to impose such measures on the parties as are needed to restore international peace and security, regardless of the parties' consent. Charter of the United Nations, 26 June 1945, <http://www.un.org/en/documents/charter/>.

[50] On UNAMIS see the SIPRI Multilateral Peace Operations Database (note 23); and Wiharta, S., 'Planning and deploying peace operations', *SIPRI Yearbook 2008*, pp. 97–112.

pre-mission planning process, and in theory it was to have resulted in the establishment of a needs-driven mission based on on-the-ground assessments and consultation with the parties to the CPA. However the escalation of the conflict in Darfur and the concomitant support provided by UNAMIS to the African Union Mission in Sudan (AMIS) diverted a considerable amount of UNAMIS resources. UNAMIS's political affairs, civil affairs and human rights components ended up focusing their attention on the political process in Darfur. For example, the first three Civil Affairs field offices were located in Darfur.[51] The unexpected responsibilities in Darfur resulted in a rushed final effort to start up UNMIS.

At the time of UNMIS's establishment, the UN's Integrated Mission Planning Process (IMPP) had not yet been formally constituted but was the framework for planning UNMIS.[52] UNAMIS received a concept of operations (objectives and priorities of the mission) and the basic elements of the mission plan (the mission structure, including the thematic and functional components) from the planning team headquarters in New York. UNAMIS and the existing UN Country Team (UNCT) thus had little influence on the shape of the mission. Essentially, UNAMIS's role was to come up with an organizational chart of the mission and an auditing exercise, specifying how many posts were necessary to implement each mandated task (e.g. human rights) for the comprehensive results-based framework that is submitted to the ACABAQ before the launch of a mission.

The incoming mission's lack of autonomy to recruit the appropriate individuals for the job was further impeded by the apparent politicization at UN headquarters in filling senior positions for UNMIS.[53] The results-based framework is designed to make UN peace operations more accountable—operations are measured against their key objectives, outputs and activities, with the view to adjust their resource requirements as necessary. While the missions have some input into the number of staff required for a particular function, they have little or no say in adjustments to the type of functions necessary, without an explicit change to the Security Council mandate. For instance, if it were deemed that an economic advisor was necessary for the mission, the head of mission would not be able to recruit such a person until the following budget cycle, and only if that were included in the Security Council mandate. Clearly, getting the right configuration for the complex civilian component of a UN peace operation is impeded by the UN's rather rigid bureaucratic architecture. However, the guidelines for the IMPP implementation were further improved in 2009 to ensure that

[51] Schumann, P., UNMIS, Director, Civil Affairs (Aug. 2004–Sep. 2005), Chief of Staff (Oct. 2005–Dec. 2006), Regional Representative and Coordinator in South Sudan (Jan.–Aug. 2007), Interview with the author, Jan. 2010.
[52] For more on the IMPP see Wiharta (note 50), pp. 97–112.
[53] Schumann (note 51).

field missions and the UNCTs play a greater role in designing the strategic framework by drawing up field-level guidelines.[54]

Recruitment and deployment challenges

UNMIS was slow to reach its authorized strength. By the end of 2005, nine months after it had been established, only half of the civilian staff were deployed. In September 2006 the vacancy rate of civilian personnel was reduced to 36.5 per cent but, reportedly, the number of personnel resigning was larger than the number of personnel hired.[55] More critically, it was the middle to senior management positions that were difficult to fill. Part of the problem had to do with the UN's recruitment procedure, which is a lengthy and cumbersome process. Senior mission leadership have indicated that filling all the civilian positions in the first year can be counterproductive and unnecessary. They favour a phased and flexible deployment during the start-up phase and have indicated that the usual recruitment cycle of 6–12 months should be waived so as to allow for more flexibility. For example, given the wide geographical spread of UNMIS field offices and the different priority areas for each of them, a specialist programme planner in the civil affairs section who is recruited for 3–9 months would have been preferable to several generalists for 6–12 months.[56]

Compounding the administrative difficulties is the physical and security environment in which UNMIS operates. UNMIS is considered to be one of the 'harsher' postings. The bulk of UNMIS civilian staff are deployed to the regional offices in Abeyi, Jonglei and Juba, remote parts of the country with harsh living conditions. At the same time, the government in Khartoum has imposed several restrictions on UNMIS personnel, thus limiting their movement and ability to carry out their tasks. These recruitment and deployment challenges refer only to the deployment of international (and to a large extent) Western civilian experts. Little effort has been made to identify qualified Sudanese staff to fill some of the civilian posts. UNMIS has the highest number of national professional officers compared to other UN missions, but such staff still represent less than 1 per cent of UNMIS's total civilian deployment.[57]

---

[54] Le Roy, A., UN Under Secretary-General for Peacekeeping Operations, Remarks made to the Special Committee on Peacekeeping Operations, 23 Feb. 2009, <http://www.un.org/en/peace keeping/articles/article230209.htm>.

[55] Center on International Cooperation, *Annual Review of Global Peace Operations 2007* (Lynne Reiner: Denver, CO, 2007), pp. 30–34.

[56] Schumann (note 51).

[57] United Nations, General Assembly, 'Financing arrangements for the United Nations Mission in the Sudan for the period from 1 July 2008 to 30 June 2009', Note by the Secretary-General, A/63/756, 11 Mar. 2009.

Clarity and coherence in mission mandates

The issue of coordination between different components of a peace operation is an important factor in ensuring that the civilian staff can effectively implement their programming activities. During the mission start-up phase the deployment of UNMIS's mission-support component, in particular the security unit, reportedly lagged behind the rest of the functional components. As a result, many functional components, such as the human rights, civil affairs and political affairs sections, were prevented from making field visits to undertake assessments that ultimately would inform the programming strategy.[58] Consequently, the initial programming priorities were general in nature, and UNMIS was perceived by the Sudanese population to be doing less. Better coordination between the various components could also lead to a more efficient use of mission resources. For instance, joint assessments between the military and civilian components in Juba meant that scarce resources, such as helicopters, were used more efficiently.

While systemic challenges are important in themselves, and need to be addressed to improve the efficacy of the civilian component, the fundamental question concerns the type of functions civilians should serve. In UNMIS, it was decided that civilian protection would be a stand-alone function. In Darfur, however, civilian protection was a cross-cutting function. A rape victim could thus be interviewed by several UN agencies, all with civilian protection as part of their remit. Whether or not this cross-cutting approach translates into tangible gains for the Sudanese population remains to be seen.[59] The lack of clarity of civilian functions also extends to the roles and responsibilities of different sections. For instance, the political and civil affairs sections often have overlapping duties. More importantly, the institutional reforms undertaken thus far by the UN do not adequately address the division of labour between the peace operation and the UN Country Team. Are they to work in parallel or should the UNCT's substantive work be subsumed by the peace operation? In Sudan, the UNCT was already working on issues such as rule of law, demining, DDR and refugee returns when UNMIS was established. This caused considerable confusion to the relevant Sudanese entities, which were already dealing with one UN partner and then had to work with another.

Interestingly, the Security Council resolution that established UNMIS was specific enough to ensure that it would have an adequately sized civilian component to implement the mandated tasks. However, it failed to ensure that the manpower was matched with much needed financial

[58] Schumann (note 51).
[59] McMurry, N., 'Protection in practice: the role of peacekeepers in Southern Sudan', Stimson Center, 7 Dec. 2009, <http://www.stimson.org/pub.cfm?ID=912>.

resources. Thus, despite having well-staffed sections, UNMIS was in a poor position to effectively implement its mandate because it did not have the requisite financial resources to carry out activities.

IV. Conclusions

Civilians play an ever more central role in peace operations and peace-building and, consequently, the growing demand for their expertise is unquestionable. The year 2009 was marked by sustained attention to the civilian dimension. In the past five years political commitment and insti-tutional efforts have expanded, creating structures to support the civilian contribution to peace operations and to overcome the deployment chal-lenges that have plagued past missions. These attempts to address the civil-ian gap reflect the resolve of the peacekeeping and peacebuilding com-munity to enhance the state of the civilian architecture.

Yet, despite the commitment to strengthening the civilian dimension and the range of institutional innovations described here, these nascent struc-tures are still neither appropriately configured nor provided with adequate resources. Enhancing the civilian dimension is a broader agenda and goes beyond expeditiously deploying the right experts in the numbers neces-sary. It requires revisiting the broader architecture and examining the link-ages between inter-related factors, such as financing peace operations and recruitment. It also necessitates critical analysis of the purpose and objec-tives of each civilian function in order to avoid duplication of tasks within the mission.

At the field level, UNMIS starkly illustrates that the challenges of civilian deployment cannot be resolved by reforms in the DPKO alone. An overhaul of other parts of the UN system, in particular the way in which missions are financed, is necessary if improved efficacy of peace operations is to be felt on the ground. 'Good institutional arrangements will not of themselves deliver the desired result, but their absence certainly makes this more difficult.'[60] More importantly, UNMIS highlights that peacebuilding calls for tailored approaches and, consequently, requires flexible approaches to mission design and staffing that can only be achieved through a more demand-driven and iterative planning process. The lessons learned from UNMIS and other missions have clearly fed into the recent multilateral and bilateral policy initiatives on civilian actors and underscore that, although an overhaul of the global civilian institutional architecture is necessary and timely, it is clearly highly ambitious.

---

[60] Crowe (note 34), p. 13.

Appendix 3A. Multilateral peace operations, 2009

KIRSTEN SODER AND KRISTER KARLSSON

I. Introduction

This appendix describes developments in peace operations in 2009 and draws on data collected in the SIPRI Multilateral Peace Operations Database to analyse trends in peace operations in the 10-year period 2000–2009.[1] The data presented here is a year-end snapshot for ongoing peace operations in 2009 and is meant to serve as a reference point to enable comparative analysis between 2009 and previous years.[2] Global trends are presented in section II and regional trends in section III. The sources and methods used when collecting the data are described in section IV, followed by details of all multilateral peace operations active during 2009.

II. Global trends

A total of 54 peace operations were conducted in 2009, taking place in 34 different locations. Six operations closed during 2008 and no new operation was launched in 2009, resulting in the first fall in the total number of operations since 2002 (see figure 3A.1). However, the upward trend in the number of deployed personnel continued into 2009: deployment totals increased by 16 per cent over 2008 to reach 219 278, 89 per cent of which were military personnel and 11 per cent were civilian staff (see figure 3A.2).[3] The known cost of peace operations reached a new record of $9.1 billion.

Over the decade 2000–2009, the annual number of peace operations first fell, to a low of 49 in 2002, then rose steadily, to reach 60 operations in 2008. This trend was reversed in 2009: with a total of 54 operations in 2009, the decade ended with the same number as it began in 2000 (see figure 3A.1). The number of deployed personnel initially followed a similar trend, as the 2000 level of 135 000 personnel decreased to the 10-year low of 102 525 in 2002. However, deployment levels then increased continually; in 2009 the total surpassed the 200 000 mark and was more than double the 2002 low (see figure 3A.2).[4]

---

[1] The SIPRI Multilateral Peace Operations Database can be accessed at <http://www.sipri.org/databases/pko/>.

[2] The figures for personnel deployments given in this appendix are generally estimates as of 31 Dec. 2009 or the date on which an operation terminated. They do not represent maximum numbers deployed or the total number of personnel deployed during the year.

[3] The number of civilians includes civilian observers, civilian police and civilian staff. See also chapter 3, figure 3.1.

[4] The Multinational Force in Iraq (MNF-I) is considered to have been a peace operation in 2003–2005. However, as a statistical outlier, the 154 000–183 000 personnel deployed with MNF-I are not included in the total personnel figures. Information on MNF-I from 2003 until 2008, when its UN mandate ended, can be found in the SIPRI Multilateral Peace Operations Database (note 1).

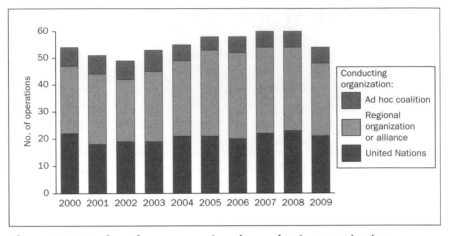

Figure 3A.1. Number of peace operations, by conducting organization, 2000–2009

Reflecting these trends, the number of operations with at least 5000 personnel has doubled since 2000, to reach 10 in 2009.

Principal conducting organizations

In 2009 the United Nations remained the main conductor of peace operations, conducting 21 operations with a total of 105 120 personnel. These accounted for 48 per cent of all personnel deployed. Although the North Atlantic Treaty Organization (NATO) conducted only 3 missions in 2009, it deployed 96 979 personnel, or 44 per cent of the total.[5] The European Union (EU), with 12 operations, and the African Union (AU), with 1 operation, each deployed just over 5000 personnel.

Seven of the UN's operations had more than 5000 personnel, including two—the UN Organization Mission in the Democratic Republic of the Congo (MONUC) and the AU/UN Hybrid Operation in Darfur (UNAMID)—with more than 20 000 personnel. These are the first UN operations with more than 20 000 personnel since the UN Protection Force (UNPROFOR) in the former Yugoslavia ended in 1995.

Despite additional deployments to operations carried out by the UN and the AU, disparities between authorized and actual personnel levels persisted in 2009. The UN missions MONUC, UNAMID and the UN Mission in the Central African Republic and Chad (MINURCAT) raised their deployment levels in

---

[5] Following a decision taken at the Apr. 2009 NATO Summit, the NATO Training Mission in Afghanistan (NTM-A) was launched in Nov. 2009 by integrating with the US-led police training programme Combined Security Transition Command Afghanistan (CSTC-A) to form NTM-A/CSTC-A. The combined command of NTM-A/CSTC, tasked to mentor and train Afghan security forces—police and military personnel—comprises 2700 personnel. In Dec. 2009, 220 were NATO personnel from Albania, Australia, Belgium, Canada, Denmark, Estonia, France, Germany, Italy, South Korea, Netherlands, Norway, Poland, Portugal, Spain, Turkey and the UK.

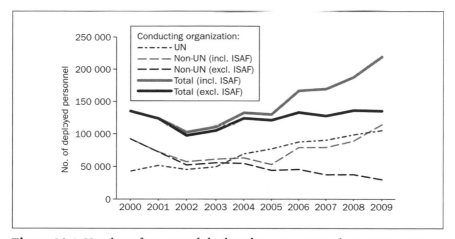

Figure 3A.2. Number of personnel deployed to peace operations, 2000–2009

ISAF = International Security Assistance Force.

2009, but still fell short of authorized numbers and contributed in large part to the UN's total shortfall of 15 700 personnel. However, the disparity between UN authorized and actual deployed personnel in 2009 was half the level of 2007. A similar pattern applied to the AU Mission in Somalia (AMISOM): even with the additional troops deployed in 2009, the mission's deployment level was still 3000 below its authorized strength.

Three peace operations ended during 2009—one conducted by the Organization for Security and Co-operation in Europe (OSCE), one conducted by the UN and one conducted by the EU (see section III).

Deployment levels

With no new operations in 2009, the increase in the number of personnel deployed was due to troop reinforcement for existing operations, most significantly for the NATO-led International Security Assistance Force (ISAF) in Afghanistan. For the fourth year running, ISAF was the largest operation, and during the year it became the largest ever NATO operation, as its troop level increased from 51 356 to 84 146—an increase of 64 per cent.[6] ISAF was nearly four times larger than the next largest operation, MONUC. In fact, the number of ISAF troops exceeded the total number deployed to the 12 UN peace operations with troops (83 089 troops, including UNAMID) and was also higher than the total number of troops deployed to the 11 operations carried out in Africa (69 757 troops).

The classification of ISAF as a peace operation is contentious and has potentially significant methodological consequences. In addition to the UN-mandated task of providing security, ISAF has taken on the tasks of helping Afghan

---

[6] The previous largest NATO operation was the Implementation Force (IFOR) in Bosnia and Herzegovina, which had 60 000 troops in 1995.

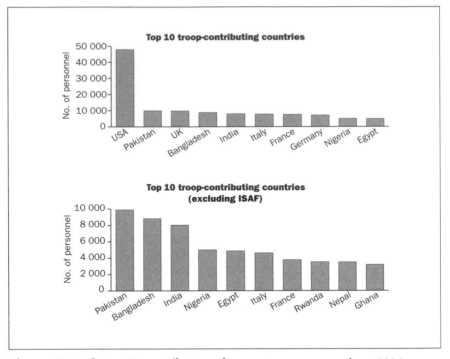

Figure 3A.3. The top 10 contributors of troops to peace operations, 2009

ISAF = International Security Assistance Force.

authorities to strengthen good governance and the rule of law and supporting reconstruction and development.[7] The latter tasks were a significant, although never dominant, part of ISAF's activities in the first years after its deployment in 2001. However, since 2006, when ISAF expanded its area of operation into the south and east of Afghanistan, it has become more and more engaged in the fight against insurgents alongside the US-led Operation Enduring Freedom–Afghanistan (OEF-A).[8] In 2009 nearly 33 000 additional troops were deployed to ISAF—almost 26 000 of them US troops—to 'stabilize the deteriorating situation in Afghanistan' and support the Afghan security forces in counter-insurgency efforts against the Taliban.[9] This shift to counterinsurgency argu-

[7] ISAF's mandate is defined in UN Security Council resolutions 1386, 20 Dec. 2001; 1510, 13 Oct. 2003; and 1890, 8 Oct. 2009. See also International Security Assistance Force, 'Our mission', <http://www.isaf.nato.int/en/our-mission/>. On the conflict in Afghanistan see also chapter 2, section III, chapter 4, section II, and chapter 5, sections V and VI, in this volume.

[8] OEF-A, which was launched to fight al-Qaeda and the Taliban regime following the terrorist attacks on the USA of 11 Sep. 2001, consisted of c. 36 000 troops as of Oct. 2009. 'Q&A: Isaf troops in Afghanistan', BBC News, 7 Oct. 2009, <http://news.bbc.co.uk/2/hi/7228649.stm>.

[9] White House, 'Statement by the President on Afghanistan', 17 Feb. 2009, <http://www.white house.gov/the_press_office/Statement-by-the-President-on-Afghanistan/>; and 'US warns of tough Afghan battle', Al Jazeera, 19 Feb. 2009, <http://english.aljazeera.net/news/americas/2009/02/2009218233411262319.html>. In Dec. 2009 US President Barack Obama authorized the deployment of 30 000 troops in addition to the extra troops deployed in 2009, following a request by Gen.

ably goes beyond the tactical use of force as employed by a robust peace operation—it is now a core part of ISAF's aims and activities.[10]

The function of peace operations has continuously evolved since they were
first deployed in the mid-20th century. Peace operations were originally tasked
with monitoring ceasefires and deploying interpositional forces to separate
warring parties. In response to the changing nature of conflict since the early
1990s, these tasks have given way to a 'complex model of many elements'.[11]
Several recent peace operations have become more involved in continuing
hostilities between governmental forces and insurgents; in some cases (e.g.
MONUC), peace operations have used force for reasons other than self-
defence. The activities of operations such as ISAF or the Multinational Force in
Iraq (MNF-I) may signal the onset of another phase in the evolution of peacekeeping in which the 'old walls that initially segregated peace operations from
war-fighting are crumbling'.[12]

Since ISAF accounted for 38 per cent of all personnel deployed to peace
operations in 2009, its classification as a peace operation has a significant
impact on the global trend in multilateral peace operations. Excluding ISAF
from the data set on multilateral peace operations paints a very different picture for 2009 and the past decade. Excluding ISAF, a total of 135 132 personnel
were deployed to 53 peace operations in 2009, and the upward trend in
deployed personnel over the decade is much less sharp (see figure 3A.2).
Excluding ISAF, there was a slight decrease in deployment numbers in 2009
compared to 2008, and between 2002 and 2009 the number of personnel
deployed increased by only 31 per cent (down from over 100 per cent when
including ISAF). Excluding ISAF, the UN is by far the largest conductor of
peace operations; it accounted for 78 per cent of all personnel deployed
(including UNAMID). While personnel deployment to UN operations has
increased almost continuously over the past 10 years, the number of personnel
deployed to non-UN peace operations other than ISAF has steadily decreased.

The large size of ISAF also influences the ranking of countries contributing
military personnel (including troops and military observers) as of December
2009 (see figure 3A.3). When including ISAF, the USA is by far the largest

---

Stanley McChrystal, Commander of ISAF and US Forces in Afghanistan. White House, 'Remarks by
the President in address to the nation on the way forward in Afghanistan and Pakistan', 1 Dec. 2009,
<http://www.whitehouse.gov/the-press-office/remarks-president-address-nation-way-forward-
afghanistan-and-pakistan>; and McChrystal, S. A. (Gen.), 'COMISAF's initial assessment', International Security Assistance Force, 30 Aug. 2009, <http://media.washingtonpost.com/wp-srv/
politics/documents/Assessment_Redacted_092109.pdf >.

[10] On robust peacekeeping see United Nations, Departments of Peacekeeping Operations and
Field Support, *United Nations Peacekeeping Operations: Principles and Guidelines* (United Nations:
New York, 2008), pp. 34–35.

[11] United Nations, Security Council, Report of the Panel on United Nations Peace Operations,
S/2000/809, 21 Aug. 2000, para. 18. See also Wiharta, S., 'Peacekeeping: keeping pace with changes
in conflict', *SIPRI Yearbook 2007*, pp. 110–12.

[12] Durch, W. J. and England, M. L., 'The purposes of peace operations', Center on International
Cooperation, *Annual Review of Global Peace Operations 2009* (Lynne Rienner: Boulder, CO, 2009),
p. 15; and Jones, B. with Cherif, F., *Evolving Models of Peacekeeping: Policy Implications & Responses*,
Report to the Department of Peacekeeping Operations (United Nations, Department of Peacekeeping Operations: New York, 2003), p. 1. On MNF-I see also note 4.

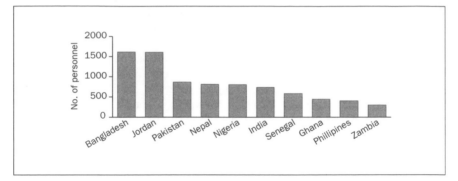

Figure 3A.4. The top 10 contributors of civilian police to peace operations, 2009

contributor of military personnel to peace operations: it provided 47 962 of the total of 194 862 military personnel deployed by 111 countries. Excluding ISAF, a total of 110 716 military personnel from 107 countries were deployed as of December 2009. Eight of the top 10 contributing countries came from either Africa or Asia and sent troops exclusively to UN operations; only Italy and France participated in non-UN missions.

As of December 2009 a total of 14 468 civilian police were deployed on peace operations by 108 countries. UN operations accounted for 88 per cent of deployed civilian police, roughly the same share as in 2008. All of the top 10 contributing countries are in Asia or Africa and these two regions account for 70 per cent of the civilian police deployed (see figure 3A.4). In contrast, countries in the Americas contributed only 3 per cent, the lowest regional share.

III. Regional trends

The increase in personnel deployments in 2009 was due to deployments to Africa and Asia. Asia replaced Africa as the region to which most personnel on peace operations were deployed. ISAF personnel accounted for 95 per cent of the personnel deployed to Asia.

In Africa, personnel deployed in 2009 increased by 8 per cent over 2008, while the number of operations fell by three (see table 3A.1). The vast majority of the personnel were sent to six operations conducted by the UN, the AU or jointly that had 5000 or more personnel.[13] While 84 per cent of personnel deployed to Africa are military, the relative increases in the numbers of civilian staff and civilian police were much higher: over the decade 2000–2009, the number of civilian staff increased nearly sixfold (from 821 to 4598) and the number of civilian police more than 140-fold (from 65 to 9201).[14] The EU Mili-

[13] These 6 missions were MONUC (21 515 personnel), UNAMID (21 042 personnel), the UN Mission in Liberia (UNMIL, 11399 personnel), the UN Mission in Sudan (UNMIS, 11099 personnel), the UN Operation in Côte d'Ivoire (UNOCI, 8935 personnel) and the AU Mission in Somalia (AMISOM, 5271 personnel).

[14] On the role of civilians in multilateral peace operations see chapter 3.

Table 3A.1. Number of peace operations and personnel deployed, by region and organization, 2009

Conducting organization	Africa	Americas Asia		Europe	Middle East	World
United Nations[a]	9	1	4	3	4	21
Regional organization or alliance[b]	6	1	2	14	4	27
Ad hoc coalition	1	0	3	0	2	6
Total operations[b]	16	2	9	17	10	54
Total personnel deployed[b]	85 562	9 571	88 270	19 750	16 125	219 278

[a] UN figures include peace operations led by the UN Department of Peacekeeping Operations, those led by the UN Department of Political Affairs and the AU/UN Hybrid Operation in Darfur (UNAMID).

[b] These figures include the International Security Assistance Force (ISAF) in Afghanistan.

Source: SIPRI Multilateral Peace Operations Database, <http://www.sipri.org/databases/pko/>.

tary Operation in Chad and the Central African Republic (EUFOR Tchad/RCA) closed in March 2009, as planned after one year of operation; the mission's mandate was transferred to MINURCAT.

With two operations fewer than in 2008, Europe was the only region in which there was a significant decrease in deployment numbers in 2009. Deployment numbers decreased by 26 per cent compared to 2008 and by 76 per cent over the decade 2000–2009. The latest reduction in the deployment numbers was due to the termination of the Commonwealth of Independent States (CIS) operations in Georgia in 2008, the restructuring and downsizing of the NATO Kosovo Force (KFOR), and the continued reduction of the UN presence in Europe.[15] The UN Administration Mission in Kosovo (UNMIK) decreased its deployment level by 87 per cent (from 1236 to 163 personnel) during 2009, and by the end of the year the UN stationed only 1362 personnel in Europe. This was the lowest number since the UN first deployed a peace operation to Europe, in 1964, and was also the lowest number of UN personnel deployed to any region in 2009.[16]

During 2009, two missions in Europe—one conducted by the UN and one by the OSCE—ended as a consequence of the August 2008 conflict between Georgia and Russia. The mandate of the UN Observer Mission in Georgia (UNOMIG) was not renewed by the UN Security Council, and the mission closed in June 2009. Russia, which recognizes Abkhazia and South Ossetia as independent states, vetoed the extension of the mission's mandate as the language used in draft resolutions referred to Georgia's territorial integrity.[17]

[15] The number of KFOR personnel fell from 14 411 in 2008 to 12 662 in Oct. 2009 and to c. 11 500 by Dec. 2009.

[16] The UN Peacekeeping Force in Cyprus (UNFICYP) was first deployed in Mar. 1964.

[17] 'Russia vetoes UN mission in Abkhazia', EurActiv, 16 June 2009, <http://www.euractiv.com/en/foreign-affairs/russia-vetoes-un-mission-abkhazia/article-183214>.

The OSCE Mission to Georgia finally ended in 2009. Russia had vetoed the extension of the operation in 2008, and the mandate of the unarmed military monitors deployed to the mission in August 2008 under a separate OSCE Permanent Council decision ended in June 2009. With the termination of the two CIS operations during 2008, the EU Monitoring Mission in Georgia (EUMM) is now the only multilateral peace operation in Georgia.[18]

The number of operations carried out in the Middle East remained stable at 10 in 2009. The number of personnel was slightly lower than in 2008 due to a reduction in the number of troops of the UN Interim Force in Lebanon (UNIFIL), which accounted for 76 per cent of the personnel deployed in the region.

No significant changes occurred in the Americas in 2009: the two existing operations in the region remained active and the number of deployment personnel was largely unchanged. All but 30 of the personnel in the region were deployed to the UN Stabilization Mission in Haiti (MINUSTAH). The mission's daily operations were disrupted by an earthquake in Haiti on 12 January 2010, which destroyed 50 per cent of the capital, Port-au-Prince, killed over 200 000 people and displaced up to 1 million more.[19] MINUSTAH's headquarters collapsed and 102 UN personnel were killed in what the UN Secretary-General, Ban Ki-moon, described as 'the single biggest loss in the history of [the UN]'.[20] MINUSTAH immediately responded with rescue teams, emergency relief and the coordination of international assistance.[21] Security Council Resolution 1908 increased the operation's military component by 2000 troops (to a total of 8940) and 1500 police (to a total of 3711).[22] As the lead organization for response and recovery in Haiti, the UN's efforts are scheduled to continue for at least 12 months and are likely to continue for far longer.[23] While MINUSTAH will focus on addressing problems of shelter and sanitation before the onset of the rainy season in May, the remainder of 2010 is likely to be dedicated to working towards the re-establishment of security, stability and state authority, as outlined in the benchmarks of the 2009 consolidation plan.[24]

---

[18] Soder, K., 'Multilateral peace operations, 2008', *SIPRI Yearbook 2009*, p. 125.

[19] United Nations, UN News Centre, 'Over 60,000 Haitians vaccinated as part of ongoing UN-backed campaign', 23 Feb. 2010, <http://www.un.org/apps/news/story.asp?NewsID=33863>.

[20] United Nations, Secretary-General, 'Secretary-General's press encounter on Haiti, following his briefing to the Security Council', New York, 18 Jan. 2010, <http://www.un.org/apps/sg/offthecuff.asp?nid=1371>.

[21] United Nations, Secretary-General, 'Secretary-General's press conference in Port-au-Prince', Port-au-Prince, 17 Jan. 2010, <http://www.un.org/apps/sg/offthecuff.asp?nid=1370>.

[22] UN Security Council Resolution 1908, 19 Jan. 2010.

[23] Holmes, J., UN Under-Secretary-General for Humanitarian Affairs and Emergency Relief Coordinator, Remarks, Ministerial Meeting on Haiti, Montreal, 25 Jan. 2010, <http://www.relief web.int/rw/rwb.nsf/db900sid/VDUX-822NR5>.

[24] United Nations, UN News Centre, 'Haiti: senior UN official stresses need for realistic goals before rainy season starts', 24 Feb. 2010, <http://www.un.org/apps/news/story.asp?NewsID=33887>; and United Nations, Security Council, Report of the Secretary-General on the United Nations Stabilization Mission in Haiti, S/2009/439, 1 Sep. 2009, annex 1, 'Consolidation plan: benchmarks and revised indicators of progress for the period 2009–2011'.

IV. Table of multilateral peace operations

Table 3A.2 provides data on the 54 multilateral peace operations that were conducted during 2009, including operations that were launched or terminated during the year. The table lists operations that were conducted under the authority of the UN and operations conducted by regional organizations and alliances or by ad hoc (non-standing) coalitions of states that were sanctioned by the UN or authorized by a UN Security Council resolution, with the stated intention to: (a) serve as an instrument to facilitate the implementation of peace agreements already in place, (b) support a peace process, or (c) assist conflict-prevention or peacebuilding efforts.

SIPRI follows the UN Department of Peacekeeping Operations (DPKO) description of peacekeeping as a mechanism to assist conflict-afflicted countries to create conditions for sustainable peace. Peacekeeping tasks may include monitoring and observing ceasefire agreements; serving as confidence-building measures; protecting the delivery of humanitarian assistance; assisting with the demobilization and reintegration processes; strengthening institutional capacities in the areas of judiciary and the rule of law (including penal institutions), policing, and human rights; electoral support; and economic and social development. Table 3A.2 thus covers a broad range of peace operations, reflecting the growing complexity of operation mandates and the potential for operations to change over time. The table does not include good offices, fact-finding or electoral assistance missions, nor does it include peace operations comprising non-resident individuals or teams of negotiators, or operations not sanctioned by the UN.

The operations are grouped in the table by the entity conducting them and listed chronologically within these groups. UN operations are divided into three subgroups: 15 observer and multidimensional peace operations run by the DPKO; 5 special political and peacebuilding missions; and the joint AU–UN mission in Darfur, UNAMID. The next seven groups include operations conducted or led by regional organizations or alliances: the AU (1 operation), the Communauté Économique des États de l'Afrique Centrale (CEEAC, the Economic Community of Central African States, 1 operation); the CIS (1 operation); the EU (12 operations); NATO (3 operations); the Organization of American States (OAS, 1 operation); and the OSCE (8 operations). The final group includes 6 UN-sanctioned operations led by ad hoc coalitions.

Operations that were launched in 2009 and new states joining an existing operation are shown in bold type. Operations and individual state participation that ended in 2009 are shown in italic type. Designated lead states (i.e. those that either have operational control or contribute the most personnel) are underlined for operations that have a police or military component. The legal instruments underlying the establishment of an operation—UN Security Council resolutions or formal decisions by regional organizations—and the date of first deployment of the operation are given in the first column.

The figures for approved personnel numbers listed are those most recently authorized for 2009. Numbers of locally recruited support staff and volunteers are not included in the table but, where available, are given in the notes. For EU operations, the approved total civilian personnel number is given in the civilian police row. Complete information on national contributions to the operations can be found in the SIPRI Multilateral Peace Operations Database.[25] The category 'observers' includes both military and civilian observers.

Personnel fatalities are recorded since the beginning of an operation and in 2009. Causes of death—whether accidental, by hostile act or through illness—are recorded for fatalities in 2009. As causes of death were not reported for all deaths in the year, these figures do not always add up to the total annual fatality figure. While the UN provides data on fatalities of locally recruited staff, other organizations or alliances do not.

Costs are reported in millions of US dollars at current prices. The budget figures are given for the calendar year rather than for financial years, in order to allow comparison of operations. Costs for the calendar year are calculated on the assumption of an even rate of spending throughout the financial year. Budgets set in currencies other than the US dollar are converted based on the International Monetary Fund's aggregated market exchange rates for 2009.[26] The costs recorded for UN and OSCE operations are the amounts budgeted. The figures provided for other operations represent actual spending.

The costs recorded for UN operations are core operational costs, which include the cost of deploying personnel, per diem payments for deployed personnel and direct non-field support costs (e.g. requirements for the support account for peacekeeping operations and the UN logistics base in Brindisi, Italy). The cost of UN peacekeeping operations is shared by all UN member states through a specially derived scale of assessed contributions that takes no account of their participation in the operations. Political and peacebuilding operations are funded through regular budget assessments. UN peacekeeping budgets do not cover programmatic costs, such as those for disarmament, demobilization and reintegration, which are financed by voluntary contributions. The costs recorded for operations conducted by NATO only represent common costs. These include mainly the running costs of the NATO headquarters (i.e. costs for civilian personnel and costs for operation and maintenance) and investments in the infrastructure necessary to support the operation. The costs of deploying personnel are borne by individual contributing states and are not reflected in the figures given here. Most EU operations are financed in one of two ways: civilian missions are funded through the Community budget, while military operations or operations with a military component are funded by contributions by the participating member states through the Athena mechanism.[27] For CIS operations no figures are provided as there is no

---

[25] SIPRI Multilateral Peace Operations Database (note 1). The database also gives full lists of mandated tasks, heads of missions and details of documentation relevant to individual missions.

[26] Details on the budgets of peace operations are available from the SIPRI Multilateral Peace Operations Database (note 1).

[27] The Athena mechanism is an instrument for the administration of common costs in EU operations with military or defense implications. The mechanism was agreed in Council Decision 2007/384/CFSP of 14 May 2007, *Official Journal of the European Union*, L152, 13 June 2007; and updated by Council Decision 2008/975/CFSP of 18 Dec. 2008 establishing a mechanism to administer the

designated common budget and countries participating in the missions bear the cost of troop deployments. In operations conducted or led by other organizations, such as by the OAS or ad hoc coalitions, budget figures may include resources for programme implementation.

For all these reasons, the budget figures presented in table 3A.2 are estimates and the budgets for different operations should not be compared.

Unless otherwise stated, all figures are as of 31 December 2009 or, in the case of operations that were terminated in 2009, the date of closure.

Data on multilateral peace operations are obtained from the following categories of open source: (a) official information provided by the secretariat of the organization concerned; (b) information provided by operations themselves, either in official publications or in written responses to annual SIPRI questionnaires; and (c) information from national governments contributing to the operation under consideration. In some instances, SIPRI researchers may gather additional information on an operation from the conducting organizations or governments of participating states by means of telephone interviews. These primary sources are supplemented with a wide selection of publicly available secondary sources consisting of specialist journals, research reports, news agencies, and international, regional and local newspapers.

financing of the common costs of European Union operations having military or defence implications (Athena), *Official Journal of the European Union*, L345, 23 Dec. 2008.

Table 3A.2. Multilateral peace operations, 2009

Legal instrument/ Deployment date/ Location	Countries contributing troops, observers (Obs.), civilian police (Civ. pol.) and civilian staff (Civ. staff) in 2009[a]	Troops/Obs./ Civ. pol./Civ. staff		Deaths: to date/ 2009/ (by cause[b])	Cost ($ m.): 2009/ unpaid
		Approved	Actual		
United Nations (UN)					
Total: 15 operations	**117 contributing countries***	74 456	67 754	1 128	5 590.2
		2 213	2 081	84	1 529.1
		8 918	8 220		
		6 039	4 826		

* This figure only includes countries deploying uniformed personnel to UN Department of Peacekeeping Operations (DPKO) operations during 2009.

UN Truce Supervision Organization (UNTSO)

UNTSO was established by SCR 50 (29 May 1948) and mandated to assist the Mediator and the Truce Commission in supervising the truce in Palestine after the 1948 Arab–Israeli War. In subsequent years it also assisted in observing the General Armistice Agreement of 1949 and the ceasefires in the aftermath of the 1967 Six-Day Arab–Israeli War. UNTSO cooperates with UNDOF and UNIFIL. A positive decision by the UN Security Council is required to terminate the operation.

SCR 50	Obs.: Argentina, Australia, Austria, Belgium, Canada, Chile, China, Denmark,	–	–	50	33.1
June 1948	Estonia, Finland, France, Ireland, Italy, Nepal, Netherlands, New Zealand,	141	151	1	–
Egypt, Israel,	Norway, Russia, Slovakia, Slovenia, Sweden, Switzerland, USA	–	–	(–, –, –)	
Lebanon, Syria		120	94*		

* The operation is supported by 128 locally recruited staff.

UN Military Observer Group in India and Pakistan (UNMOGIP)

UNMOGIP was established by SCR 91 (30 Mar. 1951) and mandated to supervise the ceasefire in Kashmir under the Karachi Agreement (July 1949). A positive decision by the UN Security Council is required to terminate the operation.

SCR 91	Obs.: Chile, Croatia, *Denmark*, Finland, Italy, Korea (South), **Philippines,**	–	–	11	8.5
Mar. 1951	Sweden, Uruguay	48	43	–	–
India, Pakistan		–	–		
(Jammu, Kashmir)		26	23*		

* The operation is supported by 47 locally recruited staff.

UN Peacekeeping Force in Cyprus (UNFICYP)

UNFICYP was established by SCR 186 (4 Mar. 1964) and mandated to prevent fighting between the Greek Cypriot and Turkish Cypriot communities and to contribute to the maintenance and restoration of law and order. Since the end of hostilities in 1974, the mandate has included monitoring the de facto ceasefire (Aug. 1974) and maintaining a buffer zone between the two sides. SCR 1898 (14 Dec. 2009) extended the mandate until 15 June 2010.

SCR 186	Troops: Argentina, Austria, **Brazil**, Canada, **Chile**, Croatia, Hungary, **Paraguay**, Peru, Slovakia, UK	860	855	180 55.9
Mar. 1964		69	66	1 24.7
Cyprus	Civ. pol.: *Argentina*, Australia, Bosnia and Herzegovina, Croatia, El Salvador, India, Ireland, Italy, **Montenegro**, Netherlands, **Ukraine**	41	39*	(–, 1, –)

* The operation is supported by 112 locally recruited staff.

UN Disengagement Observer Force (UNDOF)

UNDOF was established by SCR 350 (31 May 1974) and mandated to observe the ceasefire and the disengagement of Israeli and Syrian forces as well as to maintain an area of limitation and separation in accordance with the 1973 Agreement on Disengagement. SCR 1899 (25 Nov. 2009) extended the mandate until 30 June 2010.

SCR 350	Troops: *Austria*, Canada, Croatia, India, Japan, Poland	1 047	1 043	43 46.4
June 1974		–	–	– 19.9
Syria		–	–	
		49	40*	

* The operation is supported by 103 locally recruited staff.

UN Interim Force in Lebanon (UNIFIL)

UNIFIL was established by SCRs 425 and 426 (19 Mar. 1978) and mandated to confirm the withdrawal of Israeli forces from southern Lebanon and to assist the Lebanese Government in re-establishing authority in the area. In 2006, following the conflict between Israel and Hezbollah, The mission's mandate was altered by SCR 1701 (11 Aug. 2006) to encompass tasks related to establishing and monitoring a permanent ceasefire. SCR 1884 (26 Aug. 2009) extended the mandate until 31 Aug. 2010.

SCRs 425 and 426	Troops: Belgium, Brunei Darussalam, China, Croatia, Cyprus, **Denmark**, El Salvador, France, Germany, Ghana, Greece, Guatemala, Hungary, India, Indonesia, Ireland, _Italy_, Korea (South), FYROM, Malaysia, Nepal, **Niger**, *Norway*, *Poland*, Portugal, Qatar, Sierra Leone, Slovenia, Spain, Tanzania, Turkey	15 000	11 862	282 635.4
Mar. 1978		–	–	3 ..
Lebanon		–	–	(–, 1, 1)
		411	322*	

* The operation is supported by 660 locally recruited staff.

Legal instrument/ Deployment date/ Location	Countries contributing troops, observers (Obs.), civilian police (Civ. pol.) and civilian staff (Civ. staff) in 2009[a]	Troops/Obs./ Civ. pol./Civ. staff		Deaths: to date/ 2009 (by cause[b])	Cost ($ m.): 2009/ unpaid
		Approved	Actual		

UN Mission for the Referendum in Western Sahara (MINURSO)

MINURSO was established by SCR 690 (29 Apr. 1991) and mandated to monitor the ceasefire between the Polisario Front and the Moroccan Government; to observe the reduction of troops; and to prepare for an eventual referendum concerning the integration of Western Sahara into Morocco. SCR 1871 (30 Apr. 2009) extended the mandate until 30 Apr. 2010.

Legal instrument/ Deployment date/ Location	Countries contributing	Approved	Actual	Deaths	Cost
SCR 690	Troops: **Ghana**, Malaysia	27	27	15	50.6
Sep. 1991	Obs.: Argentina, Austria, Bangladesh, Brazil, China, Croatia, Djibouti, Egypt, El Salvador, France, Ghana, Greece, Guinea, Honduras, Hungary, Ireland, Italy,	203	199	–	54.2
Western Sahara	**Jordan**, *Kenya*, **Korea (South)**, Malaysia, Mongolia, Nigeria, Pakistan, Paraguay, Poland, <u>Russia</u>, Sri Lanka, Uruguay, Yemen	6	6		
	Civ. pol.: Egypt, El Salvador	108	97*		

* The operation is supported by 157 locally recruited staff and 18 UN volunteers.

UN Observer Mission in Georgia (UNOMIG)

UNOMIG was established by SCR 849 (9 July 1993) and SCR 858 (24 Aug. 1993) and mandated to verify the ceasefire between the Georgian Government and the Abkhazian authorities. In 1994, following renewed fighting and the signing of a second ceasefire agreement, its mandate was expanded to include monitoring and verification of the implementation of the agreement by SCR 937 (27 July 1994). In 2009 Russia, having recognized the independence of Abkhazia, rejected specific language regarding the territorial integrity of Georgia in UN Security Council draft resolutions and subsequently vetoed an extension of the UNOMIG mandate. The mission closed on 16 June 2009.

Legal instrument/ Deployment date/ Location	Countries contributing	Approved	Actual	Deaths	Cost
SCRs 849 and 858	Obs.: *Albania, Austria, Bangladesh, Croatia, Czech Republic, Denmark, Egypt, France, <u>Germany</u>, Ghana, Greece, Hungary, Indonesia, Jordan, Korea (South),*	–	–	12	36.1
Aug. 1993	*Lithuania, Moldova, Mongolia, Nepal, Nigeria, Pakistan, Poland, Romania,*	136	132	1	14.5
Georgia	*Russia, Sweden, Switzerland, Turkey, UK, Ukraine, Uruguay, USA, Yemen*	20	14	(–,–,–)	
	Civ. pol.: *Czech Republic, Germany, Ghana, Israel, Philippines, Poland, Russia, Sweden, Switzerland, Ukraine*	115	93*		

* The operation was supported by 201 locally recruited staff.

UN Interim Administration Mission in Kosovo (UNMIK)

UNMIK was established by SCR 1244 (10 June 1999) and mandated to promote the establishment of substantial autonomy and self-government in Kosovo; perform civilian administrative functions; maintain law and order; promote human rights; and ensure the safe return of refugees and displaced persons. Following Kosovo's declaration of independence and the deployment of EULEX Kosovo, UNMIK's mandate altered to monitoring and supporting local institutions. A positive decision by the UN Security Council is required to terminate the operation.

SCR 1244	Obs.: *Argentina, Bangladesh, Bolivia, Bulgaria, Chile,* **Czech Republic,** *Denmark, Ireland, Norway, Pakistan,* **Poland,** *Portugal, Romania, Russia, Spain,* **Turkey,** *Ukraine*	–	54	–	127.0
June 1999		8	9		..
Kosovo		8	8		
	Civ. pol.: *Argentina, Austria, Bangladesh, Brazil, Bulgaria, China, Croatia, Czech Republic, Denmark, Finland, France, Germany, Ghana, Greece, Hungary, India, Italy, Jordan, Kyrgyzstan, Lithuania, Malawi, Nigeria, Norway, Pakistan, Philippines, Poland, Romania, Russia, Slovenia, Spain, Sweden, Switzerland, Turkey, Uganda, UK, Ukraine, Zambia, Zimbabwe*	176	146*		

* The operation is supported by 285 locally recruited staff and 88 UN volunteers.

UN Organization Mission in the Democratic Republic of the Congo (MONUC)

MONUC was established by SCR 1279 (30 Nov. 1999) and mandated by SCR 1291 (24 Feb. 2000) to monitor the implementation of the ceasefire agreement between the Democratic Republic of the Congo (DRC), Angola, Namibia, Rwanda, Uganda and Zimbabwe; to supervise and verify the disengagement of forces; to monitor human rights violations; and to facilitate the provision of humanitarian assistance. The operation was given UN Charter Chapter VII powers by SCR 1493 (28 July 2003). By SCR 1856 (22 Dec. 2008) the mission was mandated to protect civilians, humanitarian personnel and UN personnel and facilities; to assist the disarmament, demobilization and reintegration (DDR) of foreign and Congolese armed groups; to assist security sector reform (SSR) and train and mentor Congolese armed forces; to contribute to the territorial security of the DRC; and to support the strengthening of democratic institutions and the rule of law. SCR 1906 (23 Dec. 2009) extended the mandate until 31 May 2010.

Legal instrument/ Deployment date/ Location	Countries contributing troops, observers (Obs.), civilian police (Civ. pol.) and civilian staff (Civ. staff) in 2009[a]	Troops/Obs./ Civ. pol./Civ. staff Approved	Actual	Deaths: to date/ 2009/ (by cause[b])	Cost ($ m.): 2009/ unpaid
MONUC continued					
SCR 1279	Troops: Bangladesh, **Belgium**, Benin, Bolivia, China, **Egypt**, Ghana, Guatemala,	19 815	18 646	155	1 294.7
Nov. 1999	India, Indonesia, Jordan, Malawi, Morocco, Nepal, Pakistan, Senegal, Serbia,	760	705	15	606.8
Democratic	South Africa, Tunisia, Uruguay	1 441	1 158	(–, 2, 9)	
Republic of the	Obs.: *Algeria*, Bangladesh, Belgium, Benin, Bolivia, Bosnia and Herzegovina,	1 234	1 006*		
Congo	Burkina Faso, **Cameroon**, Canada, China, Czech Republic, Denmark, Egypt,				
	France, Ghana, Guatemala, India, Indonesia, Ireland, Jordan, Kenya, Malawi,				
	Malaysia, Mali, **Mongolia**, Morocco, Mozambique, Nepal, Niger, Nigeria,				
	Norway, Pakistan, Paraguay, Peru, Poland, Romania, Russia, Senegal, South				
	Africa, Spain, Sri Lanka, Sweden, Switzerland, Tunisia, UK, Ukraine, Uruguay,				
	Yemen, Zambia				
	Civ. pol.: *Argentina*, Bangladesh, Benin, Burkina Faso, Cameroon, Central				
	African Republic, Chad, Côte d'Ivoire, **Egypt**, France, Guinea, India, Jordan,				
	Madagascar, Mali, Niger, Romania, Russia, Senegal, Sweden, Togo, Turkey,				
	Ukraine, Yemen				

* The operation is supported by 2636 locally recruited staff and 648 UN volunteers.

UN Mission in Liberia (UNMIL)

UNMIL was established by SCR 1509 (19 Sep. 2003) under UN Charter Chapter VII and mandated to support the implementation of the 2003 Comprehensive Peace Agreement; to assist in matters of humanitarian and human rights; to support SSR; and to protect civilians. UNMIL cooperates with UNOCI and UNIPSIL. SCR 1885 (15 Sep. 2009) extended the mandate until 30 Sep. 2010.

SCR 1509	Troops: Bangladesh, Benin, Bolivia, Brazil, China, Croatia, Ecuador, Ethiopia,	8 202	9 505	143	596.3
Oct. 2003	Finland, France, Ghana, Jordan, *Kenya*, Korea (South), Mongolia, Namibia,	133	118	20	68.4
Liberia	Nepal, Nigeria, Pakistan, Paraguay, Peru, Philippines, Senegal, Togo, *UK*,	1 343	1 324	(–, 6, 10)	
	Ukraine, USA, Yemen	546	452*		
	Obs.: Bangladesh, Benin, Bolivia, Bulgaria, China, Denmark, Ecuador, Egypt, El				
	Salvador, Ethiopia, Gambia, Ghana, Indonesia, Jordan, *Kenya*, Korea (South),				

Kyrgyzstan, Malaysia, Mali, Moldova, Montenegro, Namibia, Nepal, Niger, Nigeria, Pakistan, Paraguay, Peru, Philippines, Poland, Romania, Russia, Senegal, Serbia, Togo, Ukraine, USA, Zambia, Zimbabwe

Civ. pol.: Argentina, Bangladesh, Bosnia and Herzegovina, China, Czech Republic, Egypt, El Salvador, Fiji, Gambia, Germany, Ghana, Iceland, India, Jamaica, Jordan, Kenya, Kyrgyzstan, Malawi, Namibia, Nepal, Nigeria, Norway, Pakistan, Philippines, Poland, Russia, Rwanda, Serbia, Sri Lanka, Sweden, Turkey, Uganda, Ukraine, Uruguay, USA, Yemen, Zambia, Zimbabwe

* The operation is supported by 993 locally recruited staff and 228 UN volunteers.

UN Operation in Côte d'Ivoire (UNOCI)

UNOCI was established by SCR 1528 (27 Feb. 2004) under UN Charter Chapter VII and mandated to monitor the cessation of hostilities, movement of armed groups and the arms embargo; to support DDR and SSR; to assist with the creation of law and order, human rights and public information; to facilitate humanitarian assistance and rebuild state institutions; and to assist in the holding of free elections. In 2007 the mandate was expanded to support the full implementation of the Ouagadougou Political Agreement (4 Mar. 2007) and of the Supplementary Agreements (28 Nov. 2007). UNOCI cooperates with UNMIL and Operation Licorne. SCR 1911 (28 Jan. 2010) extended the mandate until 31 May 2010.

SCR 1528 / Apr. 2004 / Côte d'Ivoire				
Troops: Bangladesh, Benin, Brazil, Chad, Egypt, France, Ghana, Jordan, Morocco, Nepal, Niger, Pakistan, Paraguay, Philippines, Senegal, Tanzania, Togo, Tunisia, Uganda, Yemen	7 915	7 202	64	494.6
Obs.: Bangladesh, Benin, Bolivia, Brazil, Chad, China, Croatia, Ecuador, El Salvador, Ethiopia, France, Gambia, Ghana, Guatemala, Guinea, India, Ireland, Jordan, Korea (South), Moldova, Namibia, Nepal, Niger, Nigeria, Pakistan, Paraguay, Peru, Philippines, Poland, Romania, Russia, Senegal, Serbia, Tanzania, Togo, Tunisia, Uganda, Uruguay, Yemen, Zambia, Zimbabwe	200	189	10	132.2
Civ. pol.: Argentina, Bangladesh, Benin, Burundi, Cameroon, Canada, Central African Republic, Chad, Congo (Dem. Rep. of), Djibouti, France, Ghana, Jordan, Libya, Madagascar, Niger, Pakistan, Rwanda, Senegal, Switzerland, Togo, Turkey, Ukraine, Uruguay, Yemen	1 200	1 145	(-, 3, 5)	
	467	399*		

* The operation is supported by 692 locally recruited staff and 304 UN volunteers.

Legal instrument/ Deployment date/ Location	Countries contributing troops, observers (Obs.), civilian police (Civ. pol.) and civilian staff (Civ. staff) in 2009[a]	Troops/Obs./ Civ. pol./Civ. staff Approved	Actual	Deaths: to date/ 2009/ (by cause[b])	Cost ($ m.): 2009/ unpaid

UN Stabilization Mission in Haiti (MINUSTAH)

MINUSTAH was established by SCR 1542 (30 Apr. 2004) under UN Charter Chapter VII and mandated to maintain a secure and stable environment to ensure that the peace process is carried forward; to support SSR, including a comprehensive DDR programme, building the capacity of the national police and re-establishing the rule of law; to assist in the holding of free elections; to support humanitarian and human rights activities; and to protect civilians. SCR 1892 (13 Oct. 2009) extended the mandate to 15 Oct. 2010.

SCR 1542 June 2004 Haiti	Troops: Argentina, Bolivia, Brazil, Canada, Chile, *Croatia*, Ecuador, France, Guatemala, **India**, Jordan, **Korea (South)**, Nepal, Paraguay, Peru, Philippines, Sri Lanka, Uruguay, USA	6 940	7 032	59	606.7
		–	–	20	132.8
		2 211	2 025	(1, 13, 4)	
		552	484*		

Civ. pol.: Argentina, **Bangladesh**, Benin, Brazil, Burkina Faso, Cameroon, Canada, Central African Republic, Chad, Chile, China, Colombia, *Congo (Dem. Rep. of)*, Côte d'Ivoire, **Croatia**, Egypt, El Salvador, France, Grenada, Guinea, India, *Italy*, Jamaica, *Jordan*, Madagascar, Mali, Nepal, Niger, Nigeria, Pakistan, Philippines, Romania, Russia, Rwanda, Senegal, Serbia, Spain, Sri Lanka, Togo, Turkey, Uruguay, USA, Yemen

* The operation is supported by 1246 locally recruited staff and 215 UN volunteers.

UN Mission in Sudan (UNMIS)

UNMIS was established by SCR 1590 (24 Mar. 2005) under UN Charter Chapter VII, following the 2005 Comprehensive Peace Agreement, and mandated to monitor the implementation of the peace agreement; to protect and promote human rights; to facilitate the DDR process; and to protect civilians and UN personnel. SCR 1870 (20 May 2009) extended the mandate until 30 Apr. 2010.

SCR 1590 Mar. 2005 Sudan	Troops: Australia, Bangladesh, **Brazil**, Cambodia, Canada, China, Croatia, Denmark, Egypt, Finland, Germany, **Greece**, Guatemala, India, Japan, Jordan, Kenya, Korea (South), Malaysia, Nepal, Netherlands, New Zealand, **Nigeria**, Norway, Pakistan, **Romania**, Russia, Rwanda, Sierra Leone, Sweden, Turkey, UK, Yemen, Zambia	9 450	9 093	50	908.6
		525	476	8	397.9
		715	693	(1, 3, 3)	
		1 142	837*		

Obs.: Australia, Bangladesh, Belgium, Benin, Bolivia, *Botswana*, Brazil, Burkina Faso, Cambodia, Canada, China, Denmark, Ecuador, Egypt, El Salvador, Fiji,

Gabon, Germany, Greece, Guatemala, Guinea, India, Indonesia, **Iran**, Jordan, Kenya, Korea (South), Kyrgyzstan, *Malawi*, Malaysia, Mali, **Moldova**, Mongolia, Mozambique, Namibia, Nepal, Netherlands, New Zealand, Nigeria, Norway, Pakistan, Paraguay, Peru, Philippines, Poland, Romania, Russia, Rwanda, Sierra Leone, Sri Lanka, Sweden, Tanzania, Thailand, Uganda, Ukraine, *Uruguay*, Yemen, Zambia, Zimbabwe

Civ. pol.: *Argentina*, Australia, Bangladesh, Bosnia and Herzegovina, *Brazil*, Canada, China, *Denmark*, Egypt, El Salvador, Ethiopia, Fiji, Gambia, Germany, Ghana, India, Indonesia, **Jamaica**, Jordan, Kenya, Kyrgyzstan, Malaysia, Mali, Namibia, Nepal, Netherlands, Nigeria, Norway, Pakistan, Philippines, Russia, Rwanda, Samoa, Sri Lanka, Sweden, Turkey, Uganda, Ukraine, Uruguay, USA, Yemen, Zambia, Zimbabwe

* The operation is supported by 2626 locally recruited staff and 367 UN volunteers.

UN Integrated Mission in Timor-Leste (UNMIT)

UNMIT was established by SCR 1704 (25 Aug. 2006) and mandated to support the Government of Timor-Leste in post-conflict peacebuilding, capacity building and training of the East Timorese national police. SCR 1912 (26 Feb. 2010) extended the mandate until 26 Feb. 2011.

	Contributors					
SCR 1704	Obs.: Australia, Bangladesh, Brazil, China, Fiji, India, Malaysia, Nepal, New Zealand, Pakistan, Philippines, Portugal, Sierra Leone, Singapore	–			7	193.4
Aug. 2006		34	35		2	77.7
Timor-Leste	Civ. pol.: *Australia*, **Austria**, Bangladesh, Brazil, Canada, China, Croatia, Egypt, El Salvador, Gambia, India, **Jamaica**, *Japan*, **Jordan**, Korea (South), Kyrgyzstan, Malaysia, Namibia, Nepal, New Zealand, Nigeria, Pakistan, Philippines, Portugal, Romania, Russia, Samoa, Senegal, Singapore, Spain, Sri Lanka, Sweden, Thailand, Turkey, Uganda, Ukraine, Uruguay, Vanuatu, Yemen, Zambia, Zimbabwe	1 605 457	1 517 362*	(–, 1, –)		

* The operation is supported by 895 locally recruited staff and 198 UN volunteers.

UN Mission in the Central African Republic and Chad (MINURCAT)[a]

MINURCAT was established by SCR 1778 (25 Sep. 2007) and mandated to provide security and protection and monitor and promote human rights and the rule of law. In 2009 the mandate was expanded under UN Charter Chapter VII to deploy a military component to follow EUFOR Tchad/RCA; to contribute to the security and protection of civilians, UN personnel and UN facilities; and to contribute to regional peace. SCR 1861 (14 Jan. 2009) extended the mandate until 15 Mar. 2010.

Legal instrument/ Deployment date/ Location	Countries contributing troops, observers (Obs.), civilian police (Civ. pol.) and civilian staff (Civ. staff) in 2009[a]	Troops/Obs./ Civ. pol./Civ. staff		Deaths: to date/ 2009/ (by cause[b])	Cost ($ m.): 2009/ unpaid
		Approved	Actual		
SCR 1778 Sep. 2007 Central African Republic, Chad	Troops: Albania, Austria, Bangladesh, Burkina Faso, Cambodia, Congo (Rep. of), Croatia, Egypt, Ethiopia, Finland, France, Ghana, Ireland, Kenya, Malawi, Mongolia, Namibia, Nepal, Nigeria, Norway, Pakistan, Poland, Russia, Senegal, Serbia, Togo, Tunisia, USA	5 200	2 489	3	502.9
	Obs.: Bangladesh, Bolivia, Brazil, Ecuador, Egypt, Gabon, Gambia, Ghana, Jordan, Kyrgyzstan, Mali, Nepal, Nigeria, Pakistan, Poland, Portugal, Rwanda, Senegal, Spain, Tunisia, Uganda, Yemen, Zambia	25	24	3	..
		300	264	(1, 1, 1)	
	Civ. pol.: Benin, Burkina Faso, Burundi, Cameroon, Côte d'Ivoire, Egypt, Finland, France, Guinea, Jordan, Libya, Madagascar, Mali, Niger, Portugal, Rwanda, Senegal, Sweden, Togo, Turkey, Yemen	595	432*		

* The operation is supported by 474 locally recruited staff and 148 UN volunteers.

United Nations political and peacebuilding operations

Total: 5 operations	126 contributing countries	Approved	Actual	Deaths	Cost
		298	221	34	367.3
		113	105	6	–
		22	13		
		1 125	858		

UN Assistance Mission in Afghanistan (UNAMA)

UNAMA was established by SCR 1401 (28 Mar. 2002) and mandated to assist with the protection of human rights, the rule of law and gender issues; to support national reconciliation and rapprochement; and to manage humanitarian relief, recovery and reconstruction activities. Its mandate was expanded by SCR 1806 (20 Mar. 2008) to coordinate international assistance; to strengthen cooperation with ISAF; to manage all UN humanitarian relief, recovery and reconstruction activities in Afghanistan; to support efforts to improve governance and the rule of law and to combat corruption; and to promote human rights and provide technical assistance to the electoral process. SRC 1868 (23 Mar. 2009) extended the mandate until 23 Mar. 2010.

SCR 1401	Obs.: Australia, Bangladesh, Bolivia, **Canada**, Czech Republic, Denmark,	–	–	16	170.2
Mar. 2002	Germany, Korea (South), New Zealand, Norway, Paraguay, Portugal, Romania,	20	17	5	–
Afghanistan	**Sweden, UK**, Uruguay	8	3	(–, –, 4)	
	Civ. pol.: Bangladesh, Canada. Norway	425	339*		

Civ. staff: Albania, Angola, Argentina, Armenia, Australia, Austria, Azerbaijan, Bangladesh, Barbados, Belarus, Belgium, Bhutan, Bolivia, Bosnia and Herzegovina, Brazil, Bulgaria. Burundi, Cameroon, Canada, China, Colombia, Congo (Dem. Rep. of), Croatia, Cuba, Czech Republic, Denmark, Egypt, Estonia, Ethiopia, Fiji, Finland, France, Gambia, Germany, Ghana, Greece, Guatemala, Haiti, Iceland, India, Indonesia, Iran, Iraq, Ireland, Italy, Jamaica, Japan, Jordan, Kenya, Korea (South), Kyrgyzstan, Laos, Lebanon, Liberia, Lithuania, Malaysia, Mexico, Morocco, Myanmar, Nepal, Netherlands, New Zealand, Nigeria, Norway, Pakistan, Philippines, Poland, Portugal, Romania, Russia, Rwanda, Senegal, Serbia, Sierra Leone, South Africa, Spain, Sri Lanka, Sudan, Sweden, Syria, Tajikistan, Tanzania, Thailand, Trinidad and Tobago, Turkey, Uganda, UK, Ukraine, USA, Uzbekistan, Venezuela, Zimbabwe

* The operation is supported by 1328 locally recruited staff and 53 UN volunteers.

UN Assistance Mission in Iraq (UNAMI)

UNAMI was established by SCR 1500 (14 Aug. 2003) and mandated to support dialogue and national reconciliation; to facilitate humanitarian assistance and the safe return of refugees and displaced persons; to coordinate reconstruction and assistance programmes; to assist in capacity building and sustainable development; and to promote the protection of human rights, judicial and legal reform and strengthen the rule of law. UNAMI cooperates with US Forces–Iraq (formerly the Multinational Force in Iraq), NTM-I and EUJUST LEX. SCR 1883 (7 Aug. 2009) extended the mandate until 7 Aug. 2010.

Legal instrument/ Deployment date/ Location	Countries contributing troops, observers (Obs.), civilian police (Civ. pol.) and civilian staff (Civ. staff) in 2009[a]	Troops/Obs./ Civ. pol./Civ. staff		Deaths: to date/ 2009/ (by cause[b])	Cost ($ m.): 2009/ unpaid
		Approved	Actual		
UNAMI continued					
SCR 1500	Troops: Fiji	298	221	11	128.8
Aug. 2003	Obs.: Australia, Denmark, **Jordan**, **Nepal**, New Zealand, UK, **USA**	13	11	1	–
Iraq	Civ. staff: Algeria, Angola, Antigua and Barbuda, Argentina, Australia, Austria, Bangladesh, Barbados, Belgium, Bosnia and Herzegovina, Brazil, Bulgaria, Cambodia, Canada, Congo (Dem. Rep. of), Croatia, Czech Republic, Denmark, Ecuador, Egypt, Estonia, Ethiopia, Fiji, Finland, France, Georgia, Germany, Ghana, Greece, Hungary, India, Indonesia, Ireland, Israel, Italy, Jamaica, Japan, Jordan, Kenya, Korea (South), Lebanon, Liberia, Lithuania, FYROM, Malaysia, Morocco, Myanmar, Nepal, Netherlands, New Zealand, Nigeria, Norway, Pakistan, Palestinian territories, Philippines, Poland, Romania, Russia, Rwanda, Serbia, Sierra Leone, South Africa, Sudan, Sweden, Switzerland, Syria, Tajikistan, Tanzania, Thailand, Trinidad and Tobago, Uganda, UK, Ukraine, USA, Uzbekistan	459	321*	(–, –, –)	

* This operation is supported by 457 locally recruited staff.

UN Integrated Office in Burundi (BINUB)

BINUB was established by SCR 1719 (25 Oct. 2006) and mandated to assist the Burundian Government in consolidating peace and democratic governance, supporting the national DDR programme, promoting and protecting human rights, and coordinating donors and UN agencies. SCR 1902 (17 Dec. 2009) tasked the mission, working in close cooperation with the Government of Burundi, to support the electoral process, democratic governance, the consolidation of peace, sustainable reintegration and gender issues. In carrying out its mandate, BINUB cooperates with MONUC. SCR 1902 (17 Dec. 2009) extended the mandate to 31 Dec. 2010.

Legal instrument/ Deployment date/ Location	Countries contributing troops, observers (Obs.), civilian police (Civ. pol.) and civilian staff (Civ. staff) in 2009[a]	Approved	Actual	Deaths	Cost
SCR 1719	Obs.: *Bangladesh*, *Croatia*, *Egypt*, **Ghana**, *Netherlands*, Niger, Pakistan, **Senegal**,	–	–	–	37.9
Jan. 2007	Switzerland, *Tunisia*	7	5	–	–
Burundi	Civ. pol.: Benin, *Burkina Faso*, Cameroon, Côte d'Ivoire, *Madagascar*, Nigeria,	14	10		
	Turkey, Yemen	144	123*		

Civ. staff: Angola, Barbados, Belgium, Benin, Bosnia and Herzegovina, Burkina Faso, Cameroon, Canada, Congo (Rep. of), Côte d'Ivoire, Croatia, Djibouti, Dominican Republic, Ecuador, Egypt, El Salvador, Ethiopia, Fiji, Finland, Germany, Ghana, Guinea, Haiti, Honduras, India, Italy, Kenya, Korea (South), Lebanon, Liberia, FYROM, Mali, Mauritania, Mongolia, Morocco, Niger, Nigeria, Pakistan, Philippines, Russia, Rwanda, Sao Tome and Principe, Senegal, Sierra Leone, South Africa, Spain, Switzerland, Tanzania, Togo, Tunisia, UK, Ukraine, USA, Zambia, Zimbabwe

* The operation is supported by 240 locally recruited staff and 50 UN volunteers.

UN Mission in Nepal (UNMIN)

UNMIN was established by SCR 1740 (23 Jan. 2007) and mandated to assist monitoring the ceasefire arrangements; to implement and monitor the agreement on the management of arms and armed personnel; and to support the electoral process. SCR 1825 (23 July 2008) tasked the mission with monitoring arms and armed personnel and assisting the parties in the implementation of the agreement. SCR 1909 (21 Jan. 2010) extended the mandate to 15 May 2010.

SCR 1740	Obs.: **Austria**, Brazil, Egypt, Guatemala, Indonesia, Japan, Jordan, *Kazakhstan*,	–	–	6	18.6
Jan. 2007	**Korea (South)**, Malaysia, Nigeria, Paraguay, Romania, Sierra Leone, *South*	73	72	–	–
	Africa, Sweden, Switzerland, Uruguay, Zambia, Zimbabwe	–	–		
Nepal	Civ. staff: Afghanistan, Argentina, Australia, Bhutan, Bosnia and Herzegovina,	56	46*		
	Cambodia, China, Denmark, El Salvador, Fiji, Ghana, Guatemala, Guyana,				
	Iceland, India, Iraq, Ireland, Jamaica, Kenya, Palestinian territories,				
	Philippines, Russia, Serbia, Sierra Leone, South Africa, Sudan, Sweden, Syria,				
	Thailand, Uganda, UK, Uruguay, USA				

* The operation is supported by 120 locally recruited staff and 19 UN volunteers.

UN Integrated Peacebuilding Office in Sierra Leone (UNIPSIL)

UNIPSIL was established by SCR 1829 (4 Aug. 2008) and mandated to monitor and promote human rights, democratic institutions and the rule of law; and to support efforts to identify and resolve potential conflict threats. SCR 1886 (15 Sep. 2009) extended the mandate until 30 Sep. 2010.

SCR 1829	Civ. staff: Angola, Cameroon, Ethiopia, France, Germany, Ghana, India, Kenya,	–	–	1	11.8
Oct. 2008	Nepal, Nigeria, Philippines, Poland, Rwanda, Tanzania, Trinidad and Tobago,	–	–	–	–
Sierra Leone	Uganda, USA	–	–		
		41	29*		

* The operation is supported by 29 locally recruited staff.

Legal instrument/ Deployment date/ Location	Countries contributing troops, observers (Obs.), civilian police (Civ. pol.) and civilian staff (Civ. staff) in 2009[a]	Troops/Obs./ Civ. pol./Civ. staff		Deaths: to date/ 2009/ (by cause[b])	Cost ($ m.): 2009/ unpaid
		Approved	Actual		
African Union–United Nations					
Total: 1 operation	**59 contributing countries***	19 315	15 114	55	1 584.1
		240	260	26	200.0
		6 432	4 575		
		1 524	1 093		

* This figure only includes countries deploying uniformed personnel to UNAMID during 2009.

AU/UN Hybrid Operation in Darfur (UNAMID)
UNAMID was established by the AU PSC's 79th Communiqué on the Situation in Darfur (22 June 2007) and by SCR 1769 (31 July 2007) under UN Charter Chapter VII. The operation is mandated to contribute to the restoration of a secure environment, protect the civilian population, facilitate humanitarian assistance, monitor the implementation of related ceasefire agreements, and promote the rule of law and human rights. SCR 1891 (13 Oct. 2009) extended the mandate until 15 Oct. 2010.

Legal instrument/ Deployment date/ Location	Countries contributing troops, observers (Obs.), civilian police (Civ. pol.) and civilian staff (Civ. staff) in 2009[a]	Approved	Actual	Deaths	Cost
SCR 1769	Troops: *Australia*, Bangladesh, Bolivia, Burkina Faso, Burundi, *Canada*, China,	19 315	15 114	55	1 584.1
Oct. 2007	Egypt, Ethiopia, *France*, Gambia, Germany, Ghana, *Guatemala*, Indonesia, Italy,	240	260	26	200.0
Sudan	Jordan, Kenya, **Korea (South)**, Malawi, Malaysia, Mali, Namibia, Nepal,	6 432	4 575	(15, 1, 9)	
	Netherlands, Nigeria, Pakistan, Rwanda, Senegal, Sierra Leone, South Africa,	1 524	1 093*		
	Sweden, Tanzania, Thailand, *Togo*, Turkey, *UK*, Yemen, Zambia, Zimbabwe				
	Obs.: Bangladesh, Burkina Faso, Burundi, **Cameroon, China**, Egypt, Ethiopia,				
	Gambia, Ghana, **Guatemala**, Indonesia, Jordan, **Kenya**, Malawi, **Malaysia**, Mali,				
	Mozambique, Namibia, Nepal, Nigeria, Pakistan, Rwanda, <u>Senegal</u>, **Sierra Leone,**				
	South Africa, Tanzania, **Thailand**, Togo, Uganda, Yemen, Zambia, **Zimbabwe**				
	Civ. pol.: Bangladesh, *Botswana, Burkina Faso*, **Burundi, Cameroon**, Côte				
	d'Ivoire, Egypt, El Salvador, Fiji, Finland, *France*, Gambia, Germany, <u>Ghana</u>,				
	Indonesia, Jamaica, Jordan, **Kyrgyzstan**, Madagascar, Malawi, Malaysia, *Mali*,				
	Mauritania, **Namibia**, Namibia, Nepal, *Niger*, Nigeria, Norway, Pakistan, Palau,				
	Philippines, Rwanda, Samoa, Senegal, Sierra Leone, South Africa, *Sweden*,				
	Tajikistan, Tanzania, **Togo**, Turkey, Uganda, *UK*, **Vanuatu**, Yemen, Zambia				

* The operation is supported by 2517 locally recruited staff and 410 UN volunteers.

African Union (AU)

Total: 1 operation	2 contributing countries				
		8 000	5 221	..	200.0
		–	–		200
		270	6		
		–	44		

AU Mission in Somalia (AMISOM)

AMISOM was established by the AU PSC's 69th Communiqué (19 Jan. 2007) and endorsed by SCR 1744 (21 Feb. 2007) under UN Charter Chapter VII. It was mandated to support the peace process, humanitarian assistance and overall security in Somalia. In 2008 the mandate was expanded by SCR 1838 (Oct. 2008) to assist implementation of the Djibouti Agreement (19 Aug 2008), including training of Somali security forces in order to promote security in Mogadishu. SCR 1863 (16 Jan. 2009) expresses the UN's intent to establish a peacekeeping operation in Somalia as a follow-on force to AMISOM. The UN assists AMISOM in the planning and deployment process, provides a support package and has established a trust fund. Logistical, technical, financial and personnel support are provided by the EU, the Intergovernmental Authority on Development (IGAD), NATO, the League of Arab States, the UN and a number of individual countries. The AU PSC's 294th Communiqué on the Situation in Somalia (8 Jan. 2010) extended the mandate to 17 Jan. 2011. SCR 1910 (28 Jan. 2010) renewed UN endorsement for the operation until 31 Jan. 2011.

PSC 69th	Troops: Burundi, Uganda				
Communiqué and		8 000	5 221	..	200.0
SCR 1744		–	–		200
Mar. 2007		270**	6		(120, 5,
Somalia*		–	44		55)

* The mission's headquarters are in Nairobi, Kenya. The operation is currently deployed to secure the air and sea ports, Villa Somalia, the old university, the military academy and other strategic sites in Mogadishu.

** A police force of 270 officers is authorized. Due to the security situation in Mogadishu the deployment was delayed. AMISOM's Police Commissioner relocated to Mogadishu in Sep. 2009.

Legal instrument/ Deployment date/ Location	Countries contributing troops, observers (Obs.), civilian police (Civ. pol.) and civilian staff (Civ. staff) in 2009[a]	Troops/Obs./ Civ. pol./Civ. staff		Deaths: to date/ 2009/ (by cause[b])	Cost ($ m.): 2009
		Approved	Actual		
Communauté Économique des États de l'Afrique Centrale (CEEAC)					
Total: 1 operation	**7 contributing countries**	–	**500**	..	**40.6**
		–	30	..	
		–	..	..	
		–	..	..	

Mission for the Consolidation of Peace in the Central African Republic (MICOPAX)

MICOPAX was established by a decision of the 2002 Economic and Monetary Community of Central Africa (CEMAC) Libreville Summit (2 Oct. 2002) in order to secure the border between Chad and the Central African Republic (CAR). The mandate was expanded at the 2003 Libreville Summit (3 June 2003) to include contributing to the overall security environment, assisting in the restructuring of the CAR's armed forces and supporting the transition process. Coinciding with the transfer of authority on 12 July 2008 from CEMAC to CEEAC, the operation's mandate was expanded again to include promotion of political dialogue and human rights. The operation is mandated for 6-month periods, renewable until 2013.

Libreville Summit, 2 Oct. 2002	Troops: Cameroon, Chad, Congo (Dem. Rep. of), Congo (Rep. of), Gabon	–	500*	..	40.6**
	Obs.: Burundi, Cameroon, Chad, Congo (Rep. of), Equatorial Guinea, Gabon	–	30	..	
Dec. 2002	Civ. pol.: Equatorial Guinea	–	..	..	
Central African Republic		–	..		

* The operations is supported by and co-located with a detachment of c. 240 French soldiers (Opération Boali).
** This figure is approximate. The mission is financed by contributions from CEEAC, the EU (€14 625 000) and France.

Commonwealth of Independent States (CIS)					
Total: 1 operation	**3 contributing countries**	1 500	1 278	..	..
		–	10	..	..
		–	–		
		–	–		

Joint Control Commission Peacekeeping Force (JCC)

The JCC Peacekeeping Force was established pursuant to the Agreement on the Principles Governing the Peaceful Settlement of the Armed Conflict in the Trans-Dniester region, signed in Moscow by the presidents of Moldova and Russia (21 July 1992). The Joint Control Commission—a monitoring commission comprising representatives of Moldova, Russia and Trans-Dniester—was established to coordinate the activities of the joint force.

Bilateral agreement, 21 July 1992	Troops: Moldova, Russia, (Trans-Dniester)	1 500	1 278	..	..
July 1992	Obs.: Ukraine	–	10	..	..
Moldova (Trans-Dniester)		–	–		
		–	–		

European Union (EU)

Total: 12 operations	41 contributing countries	6 200	3 034	28	420.2
		323*	179	1	
		2 835**	1 422		
		–	893		

* The figure for total approved observers applies to EUMM only and includes civilian police and civilian staff.
** The figure for total approved civilian police includes civilian observers and civilian staff.

EU Police Mission in Bosnia and Herzegovina (EUPM)

The EUPM was established by CJA 2002/210/CFSP (11 Mar. 2002) and tasked with the establishment—through monitoring, mentoring and inspection—of a sustainable, professional and multi-ethnic police service in Bosnia and Herzegovina under Bosnian ownership. At the request of the Bosnian authorities, the mandate was modified to focus on the police reform process, strengthening of police accountability and efforts to fight organized crime. CJA 2009/906/CFSP (8 Dec. 2009), which further strengthened the mission's mandate to assist the fight organized crime and corruption within a broader rule-of-law approach in Bosnia and Herzegovina, extended the mandate to 31 Dec. 2011.

CJA 2002/210/CFSP	Civ. pol.: Austria, *Belgium, Bulgaria, Canada,* Cyprus, Czech Republic,	–	–	3	17.3
Jan. 2003	*Denmark, Estonia,* Finland, France, Germany, Greece, Hungary, *Iceland,*	–	–	–	
Bosnia and	Ireland, Italy, *Latvia,* Malta, Netherlands, *Norway,* Poland, *Portugal,* Romania,	205	82		
Herzegovina	Slovakia, Slovenia, Spain, Sweden, Switzerland, Turkey, UK, **Ukraine**	–	25*		
	Civ. staff: *Belgium,* Bulgaria, Canada, Finland, France, Germany, Ireland, Italy,				
	Norway, Portugal, Spain, Turkey, UK, Ukraine				

* The mission is supported by 152 locally recruited staff.

Legal instrument/ Deployment date/ Location	Countries contributing troops, observers (Obs.), civilian police (Civ. pol.) and civilian staff (Civ. staff) in 2009[a]	Troops/Obs./ Civ. pol./Civ. staff		Deaths: to date/ 2009/ (by cause[b])	Cost ($ m.): 2009
		Approved	Actual		

EU Military Operation in Bosnia and Herzegovina (EUFOR ALTHEA)

EUFOR ALTHEA was established by CJA 2004/570/CFSP (12 July 2004) and was endorsed and given UN Charter Chapter VII powers by SCR 1575 (22 Nov. 2004). It is mandated to maintain a secure environment for the implementation of the 1995 Dayton Agreement; to assist in the strengthening of local policing capacity; and to support Bosnia and Herzegovina's progress towards EU integration. By SCR 1895 (18 Nov. 2009) the mandate was extended for a further 12 months.

Legal instrument/ Deployment date/ Location	Countries contributing	Approved	Actual	Deaths	Cost
CJA 2004/570/CFSP and SCR 1575 Dec. 2004 Bosnia and Herzegovina*	Troops: Albania, Austria, Bulgaria, Chile, Estonia, Finland, France, Germany, Greece, Hungary, Ireland, Italy, *Latvia*, Lithuania, Luxembourg, FYROM, Netherlands, Poland, Portugal, Romania, Slovakia, Slovenia, Spain, Switzerland, Turkey, UK	2 500 – – –	2 024** – – 35	21 –	27.2 –

* A multinational manoeuvre battalion (made up of troops from Hungary, Poland, Spain and Turkey) is stationed in Sarajevo. Other elements of the mission are the integrated police unit (IPU) and the liaison and observer teams (LOTs), deployed to 5 regional coordination centres.
** The figure for actual troops deployed is as of Jan. 2010.

EU Advisory and Assistance Mission for Security Sector Reform in the Democratic Republic of the Congo (EUSEC RD Congo)

EUSEC RD Congo was established by CJA 2005/355/CFSP (2 May 2005). The mission's initial mandate was to advise and assist the authorities of the DRC, specifically the Ministry of Defence, on security matters, ensuring that their policies are congruent with international humanitarian law, principles of democratic governance and the rule of law. In 2009 the mission's mandate was broadened to include advising and assisting in SSR by facilitating the implementation of the guidelines adopted by the Congolese authorities in the revised plan for reform of the Congolese armed forces. In carrying out its activities, EUSEC operates in close coordination with MONUC and EUPOL RD Congo. CJA 2009/709/CFSP (15 Sep. 2009) extended the mandate until 30 Sep. 2010.

Legal instrument/ Deployment date/ Location	Countries contributing	Approved	Actual	Deaths	Cost
CJA 2005/355/CFSP June 2005 Democratic Republic of the Congo	Civ. staff: Austria, Belgium, France, Germany, Hungary, **Italy**, Luxembourg, Netherlands, Portugal, **Spain**, *Sweden*, UK	– – –	– – 43*	2 –	10.9 –

* The majority of the deployed personnel are military advisers. The mission is supported by 34 locally recruited staff.

EU Integrated Rule of Law Mission for Iraq (EUJUST LEX)

EUJUST LEX was established by CJA 2005/190/CFSP (7 Mar. 2005), in accordance with SCR 1546 (8 June 2004), to strengthen Iraq's criminal justice system through the training of magistrates, senior police officers and senior penitentiary staff. The operation cooperates with NTM-I and UNAMI. CJA 2009/475/CFSP (11 June 2009) extended the mandate to 30 June 2010.

CJA 2005/190/CFSP and SCR 1546	July 2005	Iraq/Europe*	Civ. staff: Belgium, Czech Republic, Denmark, Finland, France, Germany, Netherlands, Poland, Portugal, Romania, Spain, Sweden, UK				
			47**	50	–	–	12.4

* During 2009, for the first time EUJUST LEX carried out activities in Iraq, providing training, strategic advice and mentoring.
** The mission is supported by 2 locally recruited staff.

EU Border Assistance Mission for the Rafah Crossing Point (EU BAM Rafah)

EU BAM Rafah was established by CJA 2005/889/CFSP (12 Dec. 2005) on the basis of the Agreement on Movement and Access between Israel and the Palestinian Authority (15 Nov. 2005). It is mandated to monitor, verify and evaluate the performance of Palestinian Authority border control, security and customs officials at the Rafah Crossing Point with regard to the 2005 Agreed Principles for Rafah Crossing; and to support the Palestinian Authority's capacity building in the field of border control. Following riots in 2007, the Rafah Crossing Point was closed and only to be opened under exceptional circumstances. However, EU BAM Rafah retains full operational capabilities. CJA 2009/854/CFSP (20 Nov. 2009) extended the mandate until 24 May 2010.

CJA 2005/889/CFSP	Nov. 2005	Egypt, Palestinian territories (Rafah crossing point)	Civ. pol.: *Belgium, Finland, France,* **Germany,** *Hungary,* Italy, *Romania, Spain,* **Sweden**	Civ. staff: *Belgium,* **France,** Hungary, Italy, Spain, **Sweden,** *UK*			
			9*	10	96	–	3.5

* The mission is supported by 11 locally recruited staff.

Legal instrument/ Deployment date/ Location	Countries contributing troops, observers (Obs.), civilian police (Civ. pol.) and civilian staff (Civ. staff) in 2009[a]	Troops/Obs./ Civ. pol./Civ. staff		Deaths: to date/ 2009/ (by cause[b])	Cost ($ m.): 2009
		Approved	Actual		

EU Police Mission for the Palestinian Territories (EUPOL COPPS)

EUPOL COPPS was established by CJA 2005/797/CFSP (14 Nov. 2005). It is mandated to provide a framework for and advise Palestinian criminal justice and police officials and coordinate EU aid to the Palestinian Authority. CJA 2008/958/CFSP (16 Dec. 2008) extended the mandate until 31 Dec. 2010.

Legal instrument/ Deployment date/ Location	Countries contributing	Approved	Actual	Deaths	Cost
CJA 2005/797/CFSP	Civ. pol.: **Austria**, Belgium, Canada, Czech Republic, Denmark, Finland,	–	–	–	8.7
Jan. 2006	France, Germany, *Greece*, Italy, **Netherlands**, Norway, Sweden, UK	–	–	–	
Palestinian	Civ. staff: Austria, Estonia, Finland, Germany, Hungary, **Ireland**, Italy,	52	23		
territories	Netherlands, Spain, Sweden, UK	–	20*		

* The mission is supported by 23 locally recruited staff.

EU Police Mission in Afghanistan (EUPOL Afghanistan)

EUPOL Afghanistan was established by CJA 2007/369/CFSP (30 May 2007) at the invitation of the Afghan Government. The operation is tasked to strengthen the rule of law by contributing to the establishment of civil policing arrangements and law enforcement under Afghan ownership. The current mandate expires on 30 May 2010.

Legal instrument/ Deployment date/ Location	Countries contributing	Approved	Actual	Deaths	Cost
CJA	Civ. pol.: Canada, Croatia, Czech Republic, Denmark, Estonia, Finland, France,	–	–	–	100.8
2007/369/CFSP	Germany, Hungary, Italy, **Latvia**, Lithuania, Netherlands, **New Zealand**,	–	–	–**	
June 2007	Norway, Poland, Romania, Spain, Sweden, UK	400	163		
Afghanistan	Civ. staff: **Austria**, Belgium, **Canada**, Czech Republic, Denmark, Estonia,	–	104*		
	Finland, France, Germany, Greece, Hungary, Ireland, Italy, **Lithuania**,				
	Netherlands, **Norway**, *Poland*, Portugal, Romania, *Spain*, Sweden, UK				

* The operation is supported by 163 locally recruited staff.
** One locally recruited staff member died in an accident.

EU Police Mission in the Democratic Republic of the Congo (EUPOL RD Congo)

EUPOL RD Congo was established by CJA 2007/405/CFSP (12 June 2007). CJA 2009/769/CFSP (19 Oct. 2009) mandated the mission to assist the Congolese authorities in reforming and restructuring the Congolese Police; improving interaction between police and the criminal justice system; supporting efforts against sexual violence; and promoting gender, human rights and children aspects of the peace process. The mission cooperates with EUSEC RD Congo and MONUC. CJA 2009/466/CFSP (15 June 2009) extended the mandate until 30 June 2010.

CJA	Civ. pol.: Angola, Belgium, *Finland*, France, Italy, Portugal, *Romania, Spain*	–	–	7.8
2007/405/CFSP	Civ. staff: **Finland**, France, Germany, **Italy**, Portugal, Sweden, *Switzerland*	–	–	
July 2007		59	20	
Democratic Republic of the Congo*		–	12**	

* A permanent presence in eastern DRC (Goma and Bukavu) was established by CJA 2009/769/CFSP (19 Oct. 2009).
** The mission is supported by 15 locally recruited staff.

EU Military Operation in Chad and the Central African Republic (EUFOR Tchad/RCA)

EUFOR Tchad/RCA was established by CJA 2007/677/CFSP (15 Oct. 2007), with endorsement and UN Charter Chapter VII powers given by SCR 1778 (25 Sep. 2007). It was mandated to support MINURCAT, contribute to the protection of civilians and UN personnel, and facilitate humanitarian aid efforts. The mission closed on 15 Mar. 2009. MINURCAT took over, deploying a military component authorized by SCR 1861 (14 Jan. 2009).

CJA 2007/677/CFSP and SCR 1778	Troops: Albania, Austria, Belgium, Bulgaria, Croatia, Cyprus, Czech Republic, Finland, *France*, Germany, Greece, *Hungary*, Ireland, Italy, Lithuania, Luxembourg, Netherlands, Poland, Portugal, Romania, Russia, Slovakia, Slovenia, Spain, Sweden, UK	3 700	1 010**	1	33.7
Jan. 2008		–	–		
Central African Republic, Chad*		–	15		

* Operational headquarters were at Mont Valérien, France. Rear Force Headquarters were located at N'Djamena, force headquarters at Abéché, and 3 multinational battalions at Iriba, Forchana and Goz Beïda, all in Chad. The operation was supported by a detachment in Birao, CAR.
** The personnel figures include personnel assigned to the operation headquarters in Mont Valérien, France.

Legal instrument/ Deployment date/ Location	Countries contributing troops, observers (Obs.), civilian police (Civ. pol.) and civilian staff (Civ. staff) in 2009[a]	Troops/Obs./ Civ. pol./Civ. staff		Deaths: to date/ 2009/ (by cause[b])	Cost ($ m.): 2009
		Approved	Actual		

EU Rule of Law Mission in Kosovo (EULEX Kosovo)
EULEX Kosovo was established by CJA 2008/124/CFSP (4 Feb. 2008). With certain executive responsibilities, the operation is tasked to monitor, mentor and advise Kosovan institutions in the wider field of the rule of law. It cooperates with UNMIK and OMIK. The current mandate expires on 14 June 2010.

CJA 2008/124/CFSP	Civ. pol.: Austria, Belgium, Bulgaria, **Canada**, Croatia, Czech Republic,	–	–	1	158.7
Feb. 2008*	Denmark, Estonia, Finland, France, Germany, Greece, Hungary, Ireland, Italy,	–	–	1	
	Latvia, Lithuania, Luxembourg, **Malta**, Netherlands, Norway, Poland, Portugal,	1 951	1 124	(–, 1, –)	
Kosovo	Romania, Slovakia, Slovenia, Spain, Sweden, Switzerland, Turkey, UK, USA	–	443**		
	Civ. staff: Austria, Belgium, Bulgaria, **Canada**, Croatia, Czech Republic,				
	Denmark, Estonia, Finland, France, Germany, Greece, Hungary, Ireland, Italy,				
	Latvia, Lithuania, *Luxembourg, Malta,* Netherlands, Norway, Poland, Portugal,				
	Romania, Slovakia, Slovenia, Spain, Sweden, Switzerland, Turkey, UK, USA				

* EULEX Kosovo became operational by 9 Dec. 2008; the mission's full operational capability had been achieved by 6 Apr. 2009.
** The mission is supported by 1030 locally recruited staff.

EU Advisory Mission for Security Sector Reform in Guinea-Bissau (EU SSR Guinea-Bissau)
EU SSR Guinea-Bissau was established by CJA 2008/112/CFSP (12 Feb. 2008) and mandated to assist local authorities in planning the restructuring of the national security and armed forces and to advise in training and equipment procurement. CJA 2009/841/CFSP (17 Nov. 2009) extended the mandate to 31 May 2010.

CJA 2008/112/CFSP	Civ. staff: France, Germany, Italy, Portugal, Spain, **Sweden**	–	–	–	4.5
June 2008		–	–	–	
		–	–		
Guinea-Bissau		22	16*		

* Eight of the deployed personnel are military advisors. The operation is supported by 17 locally recruited staff.

EU Monitoring Mission in Georgia (EUMM)
The EUMM was established by CJA 2008/736/CFSP (15 Sep. 2008) in accordance with an EU–Russia agreement of 8 Sep. 2008, following the conflict in South Ossetia in Aug. 2008. The operation is tasked with monitoring and analysing progress in the stabilization process, focusing on compliance with the

6-point peace plan of 12 Aug. 2008, and in the normalization of civil governance; monitoring infrastructure security and the political and security aspects of the return of internally displaced persons and refugees; and supporting confidence-building measures. CJA 2009/572/CFSP (27 July 2009) extended the mandate to 14 Sep. 2010.

CJA	Obs.: Austria, **Belgium,** Bulgaria, Czech Republic, Denmark, **Estonia,** Finland,	–	–	34.6
2008/736/CFSP	France, Germany, Greece, Hungary, Ireland, Italy, Latvia, Lithuania,	323	179	
Oct. 2008	Luxembourg, Malta, Poland, Romania, Slovakia, **Slovenia,** Spain, Sweden, UK	–	–	
Georgia	Civ. staff: Austria, *Belgium,* Bulgaria, Czech Republic, Denmark, Estonia,	124*		
	Finland, **France,** Germany, Greece, *Hungary,* Ireland, Italy, Lithuania,			
	Netherlands, Poland, Portugal, Romania, Slovakia, Spain, Sweden, UK			

* The operation is supported by 74 locally recruited staff.

North Atlantic Treaty Organization (NATO) and NATO-led

Total: 3 operations	43 contributing countries	10 000	96 808	971	487.0
				310	
		–	–	–	
		300	171		

NATO Kosovo Force (KFOR)

KFOR was established by SCR 1244 (10 June 1999). Its mandated tasks include deterring renewed hostilities, establishing a secure environment, supporting UNMIK and monitoring borders. In 2008 NATO expanded the operation's tasks to include efforts to develop a professional, democratic and multi-ethnic security structure in Kosovo. A positive decision of the UN Security Council is required to terminate the operation.

SCR 1244	Troops: Armenia, Austria, Belgium, Bulgaria, Canada, **Croatia,** Czech Republic,	10 000**	12 662***	128	45.2
June 1999	Denmark, Estonia, Finland, France, Germany, Greece, Hungary, Ireland, Italy,	–	–	1	
Kosovo*	*Latvia,* Lithuania, Luxembourg, Morocco, Netherlands, Norway, Poland,	–	–	(–, –, –)	
	Portugal, Romania, Slovakia, Slovenia, *Spain,* Sweden, Switzerland, Turkey,	–	–		
	UK, Ukraine, USA				

* Along with KFOR headquarters in Pristina, KFOR contingents are grouped into several multinational task forces (MNTFs): MNTF Centre (Lipljan), led by Finland; MNTF North (Mitrovica), led by France; MNTF South (Prizren), led by Germany; MNTF West (Pec), led by Italy; and MNTF East (Urosevac), led by the USA. A Multinational Specialized Unit (Pristina) is led by Italy. A Tactical Reserve Manoeuvre Battalion (KTM) is also stationed in Pristina.

** At the end of 2009 KFOR continued to reduce its troop numbers in anticipation of a new authorization level of 10 000 personnel by early 2010.

*** Numbers are as of October 2009. Coinciding with the downsizing and restructuring of the operation at the end of Dec. 2009 approximately 11 500 troops were deployed. The restructuring of the operation was completed at the end of Jan. 2010.

Legal instrument/ Deployment date/ Location	Countries contributing troops, observers (Obs.), civilian police (Civ. pol.) and civilian staff (Civ. staff) in 2009[a]	Troops/Obs./ Civ. pol./Civ. staff		Deaths: to date/ 2009/ (by cause[b])	Cost ($ m.): 2009
		Approved	Actual		

International Security Assistance Force (ISAF)

ISAF was established by SCR 1386 (20 Dec. 2001) under UN Charter Chapter VII as a multinational force mandated to assist the Afghan Government to maintain security, as envisaged in Annex I of the 2001 Bonn Agreement. NATO took over command and control of ISAF in Aug. 2003. ISAF has had control of all 26 provincial reconstruction teams (PRTs) in Afghanistan since 2006. SCR 1890 (8 Oct. 2009) extended the mandate to 12 Oct. 2010.

SCR 1386	Troops: Albania, Australia, Austria, Azerbaijan, Belgium, **Bosnia and**	–	84 146	843	416.0
Dec. 2001	**Herzegovina**, Bulgaria, Canada, Croatia, Czech Republic, Denmark, Estonia,	–	–	309**	
Afghanistan*	Finland, France, Georgia, Germany, Greece, Hungary, Iceland, Ireland, Italy,	–	–	(287, –, –)	
	Latvia, Lithuania, Luxembourg, FYROM, Netherlands, New Zealand, Norway,	–	–	–	
	Poland, Portugal, Romania, **Singapore**, Slovakia, Slovenia, Spain, Sweden,				
	Turkey, UK, Ukraine, USA				

* The territory of Afghanistan is divided into 5 areas of responsibility: Regional Command (RC) Centre (Kabul), currently led by Turkey; RC North (Mazar-e Sharif), led by Germany; RC West (Herat), led by Italy; RC South (Kandahar), led by the UK; and RC East (Bagram), led by the USA.
** The number of fatalities is as of Sep. 2009.

NATO Training Mission in Iraq (NTM-I)

NTM-I was established pursuant to SCR 1546 (8 June 2004) and approved by the North Atlantic Council on 17 Nov. 2004. It is mandated to assist in the development of Iraq's security institutions through training and equipment of, in particular, middle- and senior-level personnel from the Iraqi security forces. In 2007 the mandate was revised to focus on mentoring and advising an Iraqi-led institutional training programme.

SCR 1546	Civ. staff: **Bulgaria**, *Czech Republic*, Denmark, Estonia, Hungary, Italy,	–	–	–	25.8
Aug. 2004	Lithuania, Netherlands, Poland, *Portugal*, Romania, *Slovenia*, Turkey, UK,	–	–	–	
Iraq*	Ukraine, USA	–	171	–	
		300			

* Activities of the NTM-I are carried out in Baghdad's secure 'green zone' and in undisclosed locations outside Iraq.

Organization of American States (OAS)

Total: 1 operation	20 contributing countries	–	–	–	–	7.0

Mission to Support the Peace Process in Colombia (MAPP/OEA)

MAPP/OEA was established by OAS Permanent Council (PC) Resolution CP/RES 859 (1397/04) of 6 Feb. 2004 to support the efforts of the Colombian Government to engage in a political dialogue with the National Liberation Army (ELN). It is also mandated to facilitate the DDR process.

CP/RES. 859	Civ. staff: Argentina, Belgium, Bolivia, Brazil, Chile, *Costa Rica*, Ecuador,	–	–	7.0
Feb. 2004	*Germany*, Guatemala, Italy, Mexico, Netherlands, Nicaragua, *Panama*, Peru,	–	–	
Colombia	Spain, Sweden, *Uruguay*, USA, Venezuela		30*	

* The operation is supported by 59 locally recruited staff.

Organization for Security and Co-operation in Europe (OSCE)

Total: 8 operations	48 contributing countries	–	–	–	243	402	10	98.7

OSCE Spillover Monitor Mission to Skopje

The OSCE Spillover Monitor Mission to Skopje was established at the 16th Committee of Senior Officials (CSO) meeting (18 Sep. 1992). It was authorized by the FYROM Government through articles of understanding agreed by an exchange of letters on 7 Nov. 1992. Its tasks include monitoring, police training, development and other activities related to the 2001 Ohrid Framework Agreement. PC.DEC/907 (24 Nov. 2009) extended the mandate to 31 Dec. 2010.

CSO 18 Sep. 1992	Civ. staff: Austria, *Azerbaijan*, Belarus, Bosnia and Herzegovina, Croatia, Czech	–	–	1	11.9
Sep. 1992	Republic, Estonia, France, Georgia, Germany, Hungary, **Iceland**, Ireland, Italy,	–	–		
Former Yugoslav Republic of Macedonia	*Japan*, Norway, **Portugal**, **Romania**, Russia, **Serbia**, Slovenia, Spain, Sweden, Turkey, *UK*, *Ukraine*, USA		58*		

* The mission is supported by 145 locally recruited staff.

Legal instrument/ Deployment date/ Location	Countries contributing troops, observers (Obs.), civilian police (Civ. pol.) and civilian staff (Civ. staff) in 2009[a]	Troops/Obs./ Civ. pol./Civ. staff		Deaths: to date/ 2009/ (by cause[b])	Cost ($ m.): 2009
		Approved	Actual		

OSCE Mission to Georgia

The OSCE Mission to Georgia was established at the 17th CSO meeting (6 Nov. 1992). It was authorized by the Georgian Government through an MOU on 23 Jan. 1993 and by South Ossetia's leaders through an exchange of letters on 1 Mar. 1993. Its initial mandate was to promote negotiations between the conflicting parties. The mandate was expanded at the 14th PC Meeting (29 Mar. 1994) to include monitoring the Joint Peacekeeping Forces in South Ossetia, ensuring liaison with UNOMIG in Abkhazia and promoting human rights and institutional development throughout Georgia. PC.DEC/450 (13 Dec. 1999) and PC.DEC/522 (19 Dec. 2002) expanded the mandate to include observing and reporting on cross-border movement between Georgia and the Russian republics of Ingushetia and Dagestan. In 2008 Russia vetoed the extension of the operation, asking for a separate mandate for the office in South Ossetia. PC.DEC/883 (12 Feb. 2009) extended the mandate of the additional unarmed military monitors who were authorized on 19 Aug. 2008 until 30 June 2009, when they withdrew.

CSO 6 Nov. 1992	*Civ. staff: Austria, Belarus, Bosnia and Herzegovina, Bulgaria, Czech Republic,*	–	–	–	8.3
Dec. 1992	*Denmark, Estonia, Finland, France, Germany, Greece, Hungary, Italy,*	–	–	–	
Georgia	*Kazakhstan, Latvia, Moldova, Norway, Poland, Romania, Serbia, Spain, Sweden,*	–	33*		
	Switzerland, Turkey, UK, Ukraine, USA				

* The mission was support by 34 locally recruited staff.

OSCE Mission to Moldova

The OSCE Mission to Moldova was established at the 19th CSO meeting (4 Feb. 1993) and authorized by the Moldovan Government through an MOU (7 May 1993). Its tasks include assisting the conflicting parties in pursuing negotiations on a lasting political settlement, and gathering and providing information on the situation. PC.DEC/909 (24 Nov. 2009) extended the mandate to 31 Dec. 2010.

CSO 4 Feb. 1993	*Civ. staff: Bulgaria, Estonia, Finland, France, Germany,* **Italy**, *Latvia, Poland,*	–	–	–	2.7
Apr. 1993	**Tajikistan**, UK, USA	–	–	–	
Moldova		13	13*		

* The mission is supported by 39 locally recruited staff.

Personal Representative of the Chairman-in-Office on the Conflict Dealt with by the OSCE Minsk Conference

A Personal Representative on the Conflict Dealt with by the OSCE Minsk Conference was appointed by the OSCE Chairman-in-Office (CIO) on 10 Aug. 1995. The Personal Representative's mandate consists of assisting the CIO in planning a possible peacekeeping operation, assisting the parties in confidence-building measures and in humanitarian matters, and monitoring the ceasefire between the parties. PC.DEC/925 (30 Nov. 2009) extended the mandate until 31 Dec. 2010.

CIO 10 Aug. 1995	Civ. staff: Bulgaria, Czech Republic, Hungary, **Kazakhstan**, Poland, UK	–	–	1.6
Aug. 1995		–	–	
Azerbaijan		–	–	
(Nagorno-Karabakh)		6	6*	

* The mission is supported by 11 locally recruited staff.

OSCE Mission to Bosnia and Herzegovina

The OSCE Mission to Bosnia and Herzegovina was established by decision MC(5).DEC/1 of the 5th meeting of the OSCE Ministerial Council (8 Dec. 1995), in accordance with Annex 6 of the 1995 Dayton Agreement. The operation is mandated to assist the parties in regional stabilization measures and democracy building. PC.DEC/918 (10 Dec. 2009) extended the mandate until 31 Dec. 2010.

MC(5).DEC/1	Civ. staff: Armenia, Austria, *Azerbaijan*, **Belarus, Belgium**, *Bulgaria*, Canada,	–	–	20.9
Dec. 1995	Croatia, *Czech Republic*, Finland, France, Germany, Greece, Hungary, Ireland,	–	–	
Bosnia and	Italy, Kyrgyzstan, Netherlands, **Portugal**, Romania, Russia, Slovakia, Slovenia,	–		
Herzegovina	Spain, Sweden, Tajikistan, **Turkey**, UK, USA		63*	

* The mission is supported by 443 locally recruited staff.

OSCE Presence in Albania

The OSCE Presence in Albania was established by PC/DEC/160 (27 Mar. 1997). In 2003 the operation's mandate was revised to include assisting in legislative, judicial and electoral reform; capacity building; anti-trafficking and anti-corruption activities; police assistance; and good governance. PC.DEC/910 (24 Nov. 2009) extended the mandate until 31 Dec. 2010.

PC/DEC 160	Civ. staff: Austria, Bulgaria, Czech Republic. Germany, *Italy*, Latvia, Lithuania,	–	–	4.8
Apr. 1997	**Montenegro**, Netherlands, *Portugal*, Romania, **Slovenia, Spain**, UK, USA	–	–	
Albania		–		
			25*	

* The mission is supported by 80 locally recruited staff.

Legal instrument/ Deployment date/ Location	Countries contributing troops, observers (Obs.), civilian police (Civ. pol.) and civilian staff (Civ. staff) in 2009[a]	Troops/Obs./ Civ. pol./Civ. staff		Deaths: to date/ 2009/ (by cause[b])	Cost ($ m.): 2009
		Approved	Actual		
OSCE Mission in Kosovo (OMIK)					
OMIK was established by PC.DEC/305 (1 July 1999). Its mandate includes training police, judicial personnel and civil administrators and monitoring and promoting human rights. The operation is a component of UNMIK. PC.DEC/835 (21 Dec. 2007) extended the mandate until 31 Jan. 2008, after which the mandate is renewed on a monthly basis unless one of the participating states objects.					
PC.DEC/305	Civ. staff: Armenia, Austria, Azerbaijan, Belarus, Bosnia and Herzegovina,	–	–	9	37.6
July 1999	Bulgaria, Canada, Croatia, Finland, France, Georgia, Germany, Greece,	–	–	–	
Kosovo	Hungary, Ireland, Italy, *Lithuania*, FYROM, Malta, Moldova, Montenegro,	–	–		
	Netherlands, Poland, Portugal, Romania, Russia, Slovakia, Spain, Sweden,	224	163*		
	Switzerland, Tajikistan, Turkey, UK, Ukraine, USA, Uzbekistan				

* The mission is supported by 586 locally recruited staff.

OSCE Mission to Serbia					
The OSCE Mission to Serbia was established by PC.DEC/401 (11 Jan. 2001). It is mandated to advise on the implementation of laws and to monitor the proper functioning and development of democratic institutions and processes in Serbia. It assists in the training and restructuring of law enforcement bodies and the judiciary. PC.DEC/912 (24 Nov. 2009) extended the mandate until 31 Dec. 2010.					
PC/DEC 401	Civ. staff: *Austria*, Bosnia and Herzegovina, Croatia, Estonia, France, Georgia,	–	–	–	11.0
Mar. 2001	Germany, **Greece**, Hungary, Ireland, Italy, Moldova, Netherlands, Norway,	–	–	–	
Serbia	Slovakia, Slovenia, Sweden, Turkey, UK, Ukraine, USA	–	41*		

* The mission is supported by 138 locally recruited staff.

Ad-hoc coalitions

Total: 6 operations	**32 contributing countries**	900	1 900	99	359.7
		2 180	1 710	6	
		–	246		
		–	274		

Neutral Nations Supervisory Commission (NNSC)

The NNSC was established by the agreement concerning a military armistice in Korea signed at Panmunjom (27 July 1953). It is mandated with the functions of supervision, observation, inspection and investigation of implementation of the armistice agreement.

Armistice Agreement / July 1953 / North Korea, South Korea	Obs.: Sweden, Switzerland	–	10	–	–	2.8*

* The yearly costs figure does not include unknown contributions from Poland and the USA.

Multinational Force and Observers (MFO)

MFO was established on 3 Aug. 1981 by the Protocol to the Treaty of Peace between Egypt and Israel, signed on 26 Mar. 1979. Deployment began on 20 Mar. 1982, following the withdrawal of Israeli forces from the Sinai but the mission did not become operational until 25 Apr. 1982, the day that Israel returned the Sinai to Egyptian sovereignty. The mission is mandated to observe the implementation of the peace treaty and to contribute to a secure environment.

Protocol to Treaty of Peace / Apr. 1982 / Egypt (Sinai)	Obs.: Australia, Canada, Colombia, **Czech Republic**, Fiji, France, Hungary, Italy, New Zealand, Norway, Uruguay, USA	2 000	1 678	66	4	(–, 1, 2)	38*	74.8
	Civ. staff: Australia, Canada, France, Norway, UK, USA							

* The mission is supported by 474 locally recruited staff.

Temporary International Presence in Hebron (TIPH 2)

TIPH 2 was established by the Protocol Concerning the Redeployment in Hebron (17 Jan. 1997) and the Agreement on the Temporary International Presence in Hebron (21 Jan. 1997). It is mandated to contribute to a secure and stable environment and to monitor and report breaches of international humanitarian law. The mandate is renewed every 6 months subject to approval from both the Israeli and Palestinian parties.

Hebron Protocol / Feb. 1997 / Palestinian territories (Hebron)	Obs.: Denmark, *Italy*, Norway, Turkey	180	22	–	2	42*	3.0
	Civ. staff: Denmark, Italy, Norway, Sweden, Switzerland, Turkey						

* The mission is supported by 8 locally recruited staff.

146 SECURITY AND CONFLICTS, 2009

Legal instrument/ Deployment date/ Location	Countries contributing troops, observers (Obs.), civilian police (Civ. pol.) and civilian staff (Civ. staff) in 2009[a]	Troops/Obs./ Civ. pol./Civ. staff		Deaths: to date/ 2009/ (by cause[b])	Cost ($ m.): 2009
		Approved	Actual		

Operation Licorne

Operation Licorne was deployed under the authority of SCR 1464 (4 Feb. 2003) and given UN Charter Chapter VII powers to support the ECOWAS mission (2003–2004)—in accordance with UN Charter Chapter VIII—in contributing to a secure environment and, in particular, to facilitate implementation of the 2003 Linas-Marcoussis Agreement. SCR 1528 (27 Feb. 2004) provides its current authorization and revised the mandate to working in support of UNOCI. SCR 1795 (15 Jan. 2008) expanded the mandate to support implementing the Ouagadougou Political Agreement (4 Mar. 2007) and the Supplementary Agreements (28 Nov. 2007), in particular to assist in the holding of free elections. SCR 1911 (28 Jan. 2010) extended the mandate to 31 May 2010.

Legal instrument/ Deployment date/ Location	Countries contributing troops	Approved	Actual	Deaths	Cost
SCR 1464	Troops: France	900	950*	24	97.8
Feb. 2003		–	–	–	–
Côte d'Ivoire		–	–	–	

* The mission is supported by a naval attachment in the Gulf of Guinea (Mission Corymbe, 300 personnel).

Regional Assistance Mission to Solomon Islands (RAMSI)

RAMSI was established under the framework of the 2000 Biketawa Declaration (28 Oct. 2000). It is mandated to assist the Solomon Islands Government in restoring law and order and in building up the capacity of the police force.

Legal instrument/ Deployment date/ Location	Countries contributing	Approved	Actual	Deaths	Cost
Biketawa	Troops: Australia, New Zealand, Papua New Guinea, Tonga	–	160	6	28.9**
Declaration	Civ. pol.: Australia, Cook Islands, Fiji, Kiribati, *Marshall Islands*, Micronesia,	–	–	2	
July 2003	Nauru, New Zealand, Niue, Palau, Papua New Guinea, Samoa, Tonga, Tuvalu,	–	246		(–, 1, 1)
Solomon Islands	Vanuatu	–	191*		
	Civ. staff: Australia, Canada, Fiji, **India**, New Zealand, Nigeria, Papua New				
	Guinea, **Samoa, Sri Lanka**, Tonga, UK				

* The operation is supported by a staff of 80 locally recruited professionals.
** This figure reflects only Australia's financial contribution to the operation.

International Security Forces (ISF)

ISF was deployed at the request of the Government of Timor-Leste to assist in stabilizing the security environment in the county and endorsed by SCR 1690 (20 June 2006). Its status is defined by an exchange of letters (25 May 2006) and status of forces agreement (26 May 2006) between Australia and Timor-Leste and an MOU between Australia, Timor-Leste and the UN (26 Jan. 2007). The operation cooperates with UNMIT.

Bilateral agreement,	Troops: Australia, New Zealand	–	790	1	152.4**
25 May 2006, and	Civ. staff: Australia	–	–	–	–
SCR 1690		–	–		
May 2006		–	3*		

Timor-Leste

* The mission is supported by approximately 350 local personnel.
** This figure reflects only Australia's financial contribution to the operation.

– = not applicable; . . = information not available; CJA = EU Council Joint Action; CP/RES = OAS Permanent Council Resolution; CSO = OSCE Senior Council (previously the Committee of Senior Officials); DDR = disarmament, demobilization and reintegration; FYROM = Former Yugoslav Republic of Macedonia; MC = OSCE Ministerial Council; MOU = Memorandum of Understanding; PC.DEC = OSCE Permanent Council Decision; PSC = AU Peace and Security Council; SCR = UN Security Council Resolution; SSR = security sector reform.

[a] Bold text = new in 2009; italic text = ended in 2009; underlined text = designated lead state.

[b] Where cause of death can be attributed, the 3 figures in parentheses are, respectively, deaths due to hostilities, accidents and illness in 2009. As causes of death were not reported for all deaths in the year, these figures do not always add up to the total annual fatality figure.

Source: SIPRI Multilateral Peace Operations Database, <http://www.sipri.org/databases/pko/>.

4. Euro-Atlantic security and institutions: rebalancing in the midst of global change

ALYSON J. K. BAILES AND ANDREW COTTEY

I. Introduction

The year 2009 was one of change, reflection and reassessment for the countries of North America and Europe. The reasons included the shock of armed conflict between Georgia and Russia in August 2008, the setbacks faced by Western interventions in Afghanistan and Iraq, and the impact of the global financial and economic crisis starting in the autumn of 2008. The inauguration of Barack Obama as president of the United States in January 2009 was both a result of, and a factor for, change. However, just as the difficulties exposed in 2008–2009 had built up over a longer period, finding remedies will be a tough and time-consuming challenge for the major security institutions involved—with no guarantee of success. It thus remains too early to judge whether a turning point has occurred in Euro-Atlantic security relations, let alone to map the new direction of advance.

This chapter examines the developments of 2009 and the trends they reflect with special reference to the North Atlantic Treaty Organization (NATO), the European Union (EU), and the Organization for Security and Co-operation in Europe (OSCE). Respectively, these organizations symbolize three different but interlocking approaches to security management in the Euro-Atlantic space: transatlantic cooperation, European integration and the pan-European approach. All of them are evolving in a global security environment where 'security' is increasingly interpreted in wide, multifunctional terms; where security interactions of all kinds (e.g. between regions and different categories of actors) are increasing; and hence, where institutions' success and standing increasingly depend on their outward-looking as well as inwardly directed roles. Behind this institutional picture lies the more fundamental set of power relations and power rankings among different 'poles' in the world system, where—at this stage in history—the clear trend is towards a reduced dominance by the West.

Against this background and not least in the light of the last point, 2009 was ushered in with hopes of improved Western unity. President Obama's interest in dialogue and non-coercive solutions and his openness to working with and strengthening institutions were as welcome to most Europeans as his specific policies on issues such as disarmament and climate change. However, 2009 failed to become one long celebration of renewed transatlantic closeness for numerous reasons, including the fact that the worst tensions of US President George W. Bush's first term in office had eased during his second term. Obama's very style dictated a gradual exploration of new solutions, many of which received a cool initial welcome from supposed beneficiaries (including Russia). Europe and the USA still had to share the daunting burden of NATO's operation in Afghanistan, and frictions persisted over Europe's limited military contributions there and elsewhere. Finally, the main new departures in European–US cooperation—including policy and institutional developments in response to the economic crisis—took place at the global level and in a multipolar rather than transatlantic setting. They did not necessarily strengthen the Europe-based institutions as such, and they underlined that the USA has many tasks and priorities that lie beyond—and potentially compete with—its engagement in Europe.

This chapter explores all these themes while documenting the major developments in each featured institution during 2009. Section II deals with NATO, section III with the EU and section IV with the OSCE and pan-European relations. Section V sums up the conclusions and revisits the general theme of European–US relations, present and future.

II. The North Atlantic Treaty Organization

NATO marked its 60th anniversary in 2009 with a summit meeting in April, jointly held in Strasbourg in France and Kehl in Germany, symbolizing peaceful cooperation and integration among Euro-Atlantic states since the end of World War II. In addition, in March French President Nicolas Sarkozy announced that France would rejoin NATO's integrated military command system; in April Albania and Croatia became the 27th and 28th members of NATO; and in August former Danish Prime Minister Anders Fogh Rasmussen took office as NATO's new secretary general. The year, however, was not one of celebration for NATO. Rather, it was marked by difficult debates over three issues in particular: NATO's ongoing operation in Afghanistan, NATO's troubled relationship with Russia and the development of a new strategic concept for the alliance.

Afghanistan

The ongoing conflict in Afghanistan, by far the largest and most challenging military operation NATO has faced to date, was the biggest issue confronting the alliance in 2009. The situation in Afghanistan in 2009 was an increasingly worrying one from the perspective of the international community: the central government remained weak, unable to exert control or implement policies across much of the country; violence against both

NATO forces and Afghan army, police and government personnel and facilities—primarily in the form of gun attacks, suicide bombings and improvised explosive devices (IEDs)—continued to escalate; and the Taliban were able to operate relatively freely in significant parts of southern and eastern Afghanistan and exercised de facto control over some areas. These issues, along with deep uncertainty about the long-term political direction of the country, severely limited efforts at economic reconstruction and development.

The number of troops under NATO command in Afghanistan, as part of the International Security Assistance Force (ISAF), rose from 55 100 in January 2009 to 89 400 troops by March 2010.[1] Given that the USA is by far the largest contributor of troops in Afghanistan, US policy inevitably drives wider NATO policy in the country. The Obama Administration came to power committed to withdrawing US troops from Iraq but equally to intensifying US efforts in Afghanistan, and it initiated a comprehensive review of Afghanistan policy. Even before the policy review was completed, President Obama took two decisions that indicated important elements of the new policy. First, on 22 January Richard Holbrooke—a highly experienced diplomat, known in particular for his role in ending the war in Bosnia and Herzegovina in the 1990s—was appointed as US special representative for Afghanistan and Pakistan and tasked with coordinating policy towards the two countries across the US Government. The decision indicated not only the belief that US policy needed to be better coordinated but more importantly the view that Afghanistan cannot be addressed separately from Pakistan.[2] Second, on 17 February Obama announced the deployment of an additional 17 000 troops to Afghanistan, stating that 'the situation in Afghanistan and Pakistan demands urgent attention and swift action . . . This increase is necessary to stabilize a deteriorating situation in Afghanistan'.[3]

The conclusions of the Obama Administration's policy review were announced on 27 March. The 'core goal' of US policy was defined as 'to disrupt, dismantle, and defeat al Qaeda and its safe havens in Pakistan, and to prevent their return to Pakistan or Afghanistan'.[4] Key elements of the

[1] North Atlantic Treaty Organization, 'International Security Assistance Force and Afghan National Army strength & laydown', 12 Jan. 2009 and 5 Mar. 2010, <http://www.isaf.nato.int/en/isaf-placemat-archives.html>. In addition, there are also significant numbers of US troops deployed in Afghanistan under US national, rather than NATO, command. See also appendix 3A, section II, in this volume.

[2] US Department of State, 'Special representative for Afghanistan and Pakistan', [n.d.], <http://www.state.gov/s/special_rep_afghanistan_pakistan/index.htm>.

[3] White House, 'Statement by the President on Afghanistan', 17 Feb. 2009, <http://www.whitehouse.gov/the-press-office/statement-president-afghanistan>.

[4] White House, 'Interagency Policy Group's report on US policy toward Afghanistan and Pakistan', White paper, 27 Mar. 2009, <http://www.whitehouse.gov/blog/09/03/27/A-New-Strategy-for-Afghanistan-and-Pakistan/>

policy were (*a*) an integrated Afghanistan–Pakistan policy, treating the two countries as 'one challenge' to be backed up by significantly increased US and international counterterrorism support to Pakistan; (*b*) increased international troop numbers in Afghanistan, with a particular emphasis on supporting the training of the Afghan National Army (ANA) and Afghan National Police Force (ANP), including 4000 more US troops in addition to the 17 000 announced in February for training Afghan security forces; and (*c*) increased civilian resources to support stabilization and reconstruction efforts in Afghanistan.[5]

NATO's leaders reaffirmed the alliance's ongoing engagement in Afghanistan at the Strasbourg–Kehl Summit in April 2009, stating that 'we remain committed for the long-run to supporting a democratic Afghanistan that does not become, once more, a base for terror attacks or a haven for violent extremism that destabilises the region and threatens the entire International Community. For this reason Afghanistan remains the alliance's key priority'.[6] In addition, NATO's leaders agreed to establish the NATO Training Mission-Afghanistan (NTM-A) to oversee the training of the ANA and ANP and to provide more trainers and mentors for the ANP, with the European member states agreeing to provide an additional 5000 troops (3000 for security relating to the September 2009 presidential elections and nearly 2000 for training the ANA).[7]

One central aspiration of the new NATO–US strategy was to reverse the Taliban's gains in southern Afghanistan—in particular in Helmand province, a major centre of Taliban influence—by using the increase in troops to not only defeat the Taliban in particular engagements, but also to hold territory gained and provide security for the local population. In June a British-led offensive, involving nearly 5000 NATO troops (700 British and 4000 US) and 650 ANA troops, was launched against Taliban forces.[8] This was followed in July by a US-led offensive, involving about 4000 US troops and 650 ANA and ANP troops.[9]

---

[5] White House (note 4); and White House, 'Remarks by the president on a new strategy for Afghanistan and Pakistan', 27 Mar. 2009, <http://www.whitehouse.gov/the_press_office/Remarks-by-the-President-on-a-New-Strategy-for-Afghanistan-and-Pakistan/>.

[6] NATO, Summit declaration on Afghanistan, Strasbourg–Kehl, 4 Apr. 2009, <http://www.nato.int/cps/en/natolive/news_52836.htm>.

[7] NATO (note 6); and International Institute for Strategic Studies (IISS), *Strategic Survey 2009: Annual Review of World Affairs* (Routledge: Abingdon, 2009), p. 307.

[8] On the operation, which was named Panchai Palang or Panther's Claw, see NATO, ISAF Public Affairs Office, '3 SCOTS launch massive air assault into Taliban stronghold', Press Release 2009-445, 22 June 2009, <http://www.nato.int/isaf/docu/pressreleases/2009/06/pr090623-445.html>; and 'UK forces launch Taliban assault', BBC News, 3 July 2009, <http://news.bbc.co.uk/2/hi/8131647.stm>.

[9] On the operation, which was named Khanjar or Strike of the Sword, see US Central Command, 'Marines, Afghan troops launch large operation in Helmand', 2 July 2009, <http://www.centcom.mil/en/press-releases/marines-afghan-troops-launch-large-operation-in-helmand.html>.

A second important objective of NATO–US strategy was to ensure that the Afghan presidential election would go ahead as planned in August 2009 and not be fundamentally disrupted by Taliban violence. In this basic objective NATO was successful: although insurgent attacks increased before the election, the election went ahead. Nevertheless, voter turnout was low, with some estimates putting it at only 35 per cent nationwide and less than 10 per cent in some districts of Helmand and Kandahar.[10] The election also appears to have been seriously marred by fraud in favour of the incumbent president, Hamid Karzai. Amid much controversy, Karzai was forced to accept a run-off election against his main challenger, Abdullah Abdullah, in November. Just before the run-off election, however, Abdullah withdrew, arguing that a transparent election was not possible. The run-off election was then cancelled and Karzai declared president. The presidential election was a significant setback for democratic development in Afghanistan and seriously damaged Karzai's standing.

In the wake of the August presidential election, President Obama ordered a further review of US policy towards Afghanistan. In December Obama announced the outcome of this review, arguing that 'the situation in Afghanistan has deteriorated ... Afghanistan is not lost, but for several years it has moved backwards ... The status quo is not sustainable'.[11] Specifically, he announced the deployment of an additional 30 000 US troops to join the roughly 70 000 troops already in Afghanistan and an initial withdrawal date of mid-2011. According to Obama, the US strategy was threefold: an intensified military effort to turn the tide against the Taliban but also to create the circumstances in which security could gradually be handed over to Afghan forces and NATO and US forces could leave; a parallel civilian surge to support reconstruction and development in Afghanistan; and a strengthened partnership with Pakistan to counter terrorism. Following Obama's announcement, foreign ministers from NATO members and other ISAF participating states announced that they would be 'investing more in training, equipping and sustaining' Afghan security forces, and non-US states agreed to supply an additional 7000 troops.[12] This was followed by an international donor conference in London in January 2010 that brought the Afghan Government together

[10] United Nations Development Programme (UNDP), *Afghanistan: Enhancing Legal and Electoral Capacity for Tomorrow (ELECT), Annual Progress Report* (UNDP: Kabul, 2009), p. 25; and Farmer, B., 'Afghanistan election: Hamid Karzai widens lead over Abdullah Abdullah', *Daily Telegraph*, 27 Aug. 2009.

[11] White House, 'Remarks by the president in address to the nation on the way forward in Afghanistan and Pakistan', West Point, 1 Dec. 2009, <http://www.whitehouse.gov/the-press-office/remarks-president-address-nation-way-forward-afghanistan-and-pakistan>.

[12] NATO, Statement on Afghanistan, 4 Dec. 2009, <http://www.nato.int/cps/en/natolive/news_59701.htm>; and NATO, 'Statement by NATO secretary general on force generation for Afghanistan', Press Release (2009) 193, 7 Dec. 2009, <http://www.nato.int/cps/en/natolive/news_60009.htm?mode=pressrelease>.

with the more than 70 countries and international organizations engaged in the country.[13] The conclusions from the conference called for a phased transition to an 'Afghan security lead' beginning in late 2010 or early 2011, an expansion of the ANA and ANP, an increase in international forces to train Afghan security forces and a parallel increase in international civilian personnel and resources in Afghanistan.[14]

As of early 2010, the outcome of NATO's intervention in Afghanistan remained deeply uncertain. The extent to which the US-led military surge would succeed in defeating the Taliban, enabling NATO forces to hold territory and thereby facilitate reconstruction, was unclear. Strengthening the Afghan security forces to the point where NATO can transfer responsibility for the country's security will be an extremely difficult task. Meanwhile, there is ongoing debate over how far it is desirable or possible to negotiate with the Taliban—or elements thereof—in order to bring them into Afghanistan's political process.[15] Although other NATO governments have formally supported the US-led strategy in Afghanistan, there is significant scepticism about the direction of that strategy.[16] This scepticism was reflected in decisions by the Canadian and Dutch governments to withdraw their troops from Afghanistan, discussions of similar withdrawals in other NATO countries and the reluctance of France and Germany to significantly increase their troop presences in Afghanistan.[17] Afghanistan appears likely to pose deeply troubling challenges for NATO in 2010 and beyond.

NATO and Russia

The August 2008 conflict in Georgia severely disrupted NATO–Russia relation. In response to Russia's military intervention in Georgia, NATO's foreign ministers decided that NATO 'cannot continue with business as usual' with Russia and put meetings of the NATO–Russia Council (NRC) on hold.[18] In 2009, however, political and institutional ties between NATO

[13] On the previous London Conference in Jan. 2006, which inaugurated a 5-year Afghan National Development Strategy, see Afghan Government, *Afghan National Development Strategy 1387–1391 (2008–2013)* (Afghanistan National Development Strategy Secretariat: Kabul, 2008).

[14] British Foreign and Commonwealth Office, 'Afghan leadership, regional cooperation, international partnership', 28 Jan. 2010, <http://afghanistan.hmg.gov.uk/en/conference/communique>.

[15] The UN special representative in Afghanistan, Kai Eide, reportedly met with representatives of the Taliban's leadership council in Jan. 2010 to explore the possibility of peace talks. Borger, J., 'UN in secret talks with Taliban', *The Guardian*, 28 Jan. 2010.

[16] Tisdall, S., 'Allies in disarray as Obama ponders Afghan plan', *The Guardian*, 5 Nov. 2009.

[17] In 2008 the Canadian Government announced its intention to withdrawal its 2500 troops by the end of 2011. In Feb. 2010 the Dutch Government stated its intention to begin pulling out its 2000 troops in Aug. 2010 and to be completely withdrawn by the end of the year. 'Canada to withdraw from Afghanistan South in 2011: PM', Agence France-Presse, 21 Feb. 2008; Traynor, I., 'NATO Afghanistan mission in doubt after Dutch withdrawal', *The Guardian*, 22 Feb 2010; and Schmitt, E. and Erlanger, S., 'U.S. seeks more allied troops for Afghanistan', *New York Times*, 25 Nov. 2009.

[18] NATO, Statement: meeting of the North Atlantic Council at the level of foreign ministers, Brussels, 19 Aug. 2008, <http://www.nato.int/cps/en/natolive/official_texts_29950.htm>; and NATO,

and Russia were gradually restored. The process began in December 2008 when NATO's foreign ministers agreed on 'a measured and phased approach' to re-establishing relations with Russia; 'mandated the Secretary General to re-engage with Russia at the political level; agreed to informal discussions in the NRC; and requested the Secretary General to report back to us prior to any decision to engage Russia formally in the NRC'.[19] Russia responded by stating that 'the alliance is returning to positions of realism. A majority of its countries did not tow behind attempts to reanimate the imaginary threat from the East in the Cold War spirit and are aware of the counterproductiveness of the absence of dialogue with Russia on key security issues'.[20] In March 2009 NATO's foreign ministers went further, agreeing to resume NRC meetings at the foreign ministerial level.[21] At the Strasbourg–Kehl Summit, NATO's leaders endorsed the decision to resume cooperation with Russia, stating that

Despite our current disagreements, Russia is of particular importance to us as a partner and neighbour. NATO and Russia share common security interests ... We are committed to using the NATO–Russia Council as a forum for political dialogue on all issues—where we agree and disagree—with a view towards resolving problems, addressing concerns and building practical cooperation.[22]

In June 2009 the first foreign ministerial–level meeting of the NRC since the conflict in Georgia took place. Summarizing the meeting, NATO's secretary general, Jaap de Hoop Scheffer, stated that 'the NRC, which has been in the neutral stand for almost a year, is now back in gear', the spirit of the meeting had been 'open and constructive' and that, while differences over Georgia and other issues had not been papered over, there was agreement 'not to let those disagreements bring the whole NRC train to a halt'.[23] NATO and Russia agreed to restart relations at the political level and to re-establish military-to-military contacts. They discussed specific areas for cooperation, including Afghanistan, counterterrorism, fighting piracy, weapons of mass destruction (WMD) proliferation and counternarcotics. After taking office as NATO's secretary general in August 2009, Anders

'NATO's foreign ministers reiterate their support for Georgia', 19 Aug. 2008, <http://www.nato.int/cps/en/natolive/news_43513.htm?mode=news>.

[19] NATO, Final communiqué: meeting of the North Atlantic Council at the level of foreign ministers, Brussels, 3 Dec. 2008, <http://www.nato.int/cps/en/natolive/official_texts_46247.htm>, paras 24–25.

[20] Russian Ministry of Foreign Affairs, Commentary regarding decisions adopted at NATO Council meeting in Brussels, 4 Dec. 2008, <http://www.ln.mid.ru/>.

[21] NATO, 'Allies agree to resume formal meetings of the NATO–Russia Council', 5 Mar. 2009, <http://www.nato.int/cps/en/natolive/news_51343.htm>.

[22] NATO, Strasbourg–Kehl Summit declaration, 4 Apr. 2009, para. 35, <http://www.nato.int/cps/en/natolive/news_52837.htm>.

[23] De Hoop Scheffer, J., NATO Secretary General, Press conference following the NATO–Russia Council meeting, Corfu, 27 June 2009, <http://www.nato.int/cps/en/natolive/opinions_55989.htm>.

Fogh Rasmussen signalled that building a more durable partnership with Russia would be one of his key aims. In his first major speech, Fogh Rasmussen called for a 'new beginning' in NATO–Russia relations and proposed three steps to accomplish that goal: reinforcing practical cooperation, rejuvenating the NRC and conducting a joint review of 21st century security challenges.[24] In December 2009 the NRC met at foreign ministerial level again, agreeing to launch a joint review of 21st century common security challenges, adopting an NRC work programme for 2010 and approving a set of measures aimed at improving the working methods of the NRC.[25] This was followed by a visit to Moscow by Fogh Rasmussen, during which he met with Russian President Dmitry Medvedev, Prime Minister Vladimir Putin, Foreign Minister Sergei Lavrov, parliamentary leaders and other Russian officials.[26] In January 2010 NATO and Russian chiefs of defence met—the first high-level NATO–Russia military contacts since the conflict in Georgia—and agreed on a framework for military-to-military cooperation.[27]

Developments in three other areas—NATO enlargement, missile defence and Afghanistan—had a significant bearing on NATO–Russia relations in 2009 and helped to facilitate improved ties. NATO's eastward enlargement has been a source of tension with Russia since the alliance's post-cold war enlargement process was launched in the mid-1990s. The issue of former Soviet republics, specifically Georgia and Ukraine, joining NATO is particularly sensitive, with Russia strongly opposing such a development and NATO divided on the issue. While stopping short of formally offering membership to Georgia and Ukraine, NATO's Bucharest Summit statement in April 2008 that these countries 'will become members of NATO' and that it had decided to 'begin a period of intensive engagement' with them in order to conclude membership action plans (MAPs) was an important part of the background to the August 2008 conflict in Georgia.[28]

In the wake of the conflict, however, the likelihood of Georgia or Ukraine joining NATO has diminished: NATO members appear reluctant to antagonize Russia by rapidly advancing either country's membership pros-

[24] Fogh Rasmussen, A., NATO Secretary General, 'NATO and Russia: a new beginning', Speech at the Carnegie Endowment, Brussels, 18 Sep. 2009, <http://www.nato.int/cps/en/natolive/opinions_57640.htm>.

[25] NATO, 'NATO and Russia agree to move partnership forward', News release, 4 Dec. 2009, <http://www.nato.int/cps/en/natolive/news_59970.htm?>.

[26] NATO, 'NATO secretary general holds talks with Russian leaders', News release, 16 Dec. 2009, <http://www.nato.int/cps/en/natolive/news_60203.htm?>; and NATO, 'NATO secretary general completes visit to Russia', News release, 17 Dec. 2009, <http://www.nato.int/cps/en/natolive/news_60224.htm>.

[27] NATO, International Military Staff, 'Chiefs of defence in NATO–Russia Council format agree on "NRC-MR framework for NATO–Russia military-to-military cooperation"', News release, 26 Jan. 2010, <http://www.nato.int/ims/news/2010/n100126a-e.html>.

[28] NATO, Bucharest Summit declaration, 3 Apr. 2008, <http://www.nato.int/cps/en/natolive/official_texts_8443.htm>, para. 23.

pects. In 2008–2009 NATO adopted the position of formally reaffirming its 2008 Bucharest decisions but not concluding MAPs with Georgia and Ukraine and instead supporting them through the NATO–Georgia Commission (NGC, established in 2008) and the NATO–Ukraine Commission (NUC, established in 1997) and annual national programmes (ANPs) of cooperation.[29] For the short-to-medium term, NATO membership for Georgia or Ukraine appears to be off the political agenda, and the issue has been at least partly neutralized as a source of tension between NATO and Russia. Nevertheless, differences of principle between NATO and Russia over the alliance's enlargement remain and could re-emerge in the future.

US missile defence plans were a further source of tension between NATO and Russia in the 2000s. In particular, the Bush Administration's plans to deploy missile defence interceptors in Poland and related radar systems in the Czech Republic, as part of larger plans for missile defence of US national territory, were strongly opposed by Russia. The Obama Administration came to power committed to reviewing US missile defence policy. In September 2009 President Obama announced the outcome of his administration's missile defence policy review: US policy was refocused on existing short- and medium-range missiles, rather than on long-range intercontinental ballistic missiles, which it argued posed a less immediate threat, and on existing available technologies, rather than on those under longer-term development. In effect, the Obama Administration's policy shifted US policy towards defending NATO territory from attack by short- and intermediate-range missiles and away from the longer-term goal of defence of US territory from long-range missiles, while not entirely abandoning the latter goal. Specifically, the new policy included shelving the plans for the deployments in Poland and the Czech Republic.[30] While reflecting a reassessment of threats and technology, it was clearly hoped that the review would also help to address Russia's concerns.

NATO and the USA also sought to strengthen cooperation with Russia on missile defence. At their July 2009 Moscow Summit, Obama and Medvedev agreed that their countries would undertake a joint assessment of the threat posed by ballistic missile proliferation and explore the spectrum of options for responding to missile threats; and, later in the year, Fogh Rasmussen argued that missile defence should be a central element of

[29] NATO (note 19); NATO (note 22), para. 29; and NATO, Final statement, Brussels, 4 Dec. 2009, <http://www.nato.int/cps/en/natolive/news_59699.htm>, para. 10.

[30] White House, 'Remarks by the president on strengthening missile defense in Europe', 17 Sep. 2009, <http://www.whitehouse.gov/the-press-office/remarks-president-strengthening-missile-defense-europe>. See also Rose, F. A., Deputy Assistant Secretary, US Bureau of Verification, Compliance, and Implementation, 'Challenges in Europe', Remarks at the 6th International Conference on Missile Defence, Lisbon, 10 Feb. 2010, <http://www.state.gov/t/vci/rls/137991.htm>.

NATO–Russia cooperation.[31] While these shifts contributed to the overall improvement in NATO–Russia relations in 2009, tensions remained over missile defences. At the end of 2009 Putin warned that US missile defence plans still posed a threat to Russia's nuclear deterrent; that Russia would, if necessary, enhance its offensive nuclear forces to counter US missile defences; and that progress in Russian–US strategic nuclear arms control was linked to the missile defence issue.[32]

Afghanistan was another factor in renewed NATO–Russia cooperation in 2009. NATO members and Russia share common concerns in relation to instability in Afghanistan, Islamic extremism and the drug trade. The most substantive area of NATO–Russia cooperation in relation to Afghanistan has been the transit across Russian airspace and territory of supplies and equipment for NATO forces in Afghanistan. In response to the increasing attacks on NATO's supply convoys in southern Afghanistan (coming via Pakistan, the main route for the transit of such supplies), from late 2008 Russia indicated willingness to expand its bilateral transit arrangements with NATO members that had been limited to air transit of non-lethal equipment.[33] In November 2008 Germany became the first NATO member to gain Russia's permission to use its railway system to transit military goods bound for Afghanistan.[34] In July 2009, during the Medvedev–Obama summit, Russia and the USA concluded an agreement that permits 4500 US flights per year through Russian airspace to Afghanistan, including those carrying lethal equipment.[35]

In 2009 NATO–Russia relations took on a new tone that was characterized by political will on both sides to rebuild and, if possible, deepen the relationship. There was a willingness to pursue cooperation despite significant disagreements and a desire to develop more substantive practical

[31] White House, 'Joint statement by Dmitry A. Medvedev, President of the Russian Federation, and Barack Obama, President of the United States of America, on missile defense issues', 6 July 2009, <http://www.whitehouse.gov/the_press_office/joint-statement-by-president-of-the-united-states-of-america-barack-obama-and-president-of-the-russian-federation-d-a-medvedev-concerning-afghanistan/>; and Fogh Rasmussen, A., NATO secretary general, 'NATO and Russia: partners for the future', Speech, Moscow, 17 Dec. 2009, <http://www.nato.int/cps/en/natolive/opinions_60223.htm>.

[32] Associated Press, 'Putin says Russia will build weapons to offset planned US missile defences', *The Guardian*, 29 Dec. 2009.

[33] Ganske, C., 'US Gen. Petraeus: Russia agrees to transit supplies for Afghanistan', Russia blog, 24 Jan. 2009, <http://www.russiablog.org/2009/01/us_gen_petreus_russia_agrees_t.php>; Reuters, 'NATO, Russia agree deal on Afghanistan', *Irish Times*, 6 Feb. 2009; and 'Moscow agrees to NATO transit to Afghanistan–source', rt.com, 12 Feb. 2009, <http://rt.com/Politics/2009-02-12/Moscow_agrees_to_NATO_transit_to_Afghanistan__source.html>.

[34] Lobjakas, A., 'Russia opens Afghan transit route for NATO's Germany', Radio Free Europe/Radio Liberty, 21 Nov. 2008, <http://www.rferl.org/content/Russia_Opens_Afghan_Transit_Route_For_NATOs_Germany/1351659.html>.

[35] White House, 'Fact sheet: United States–Russia military transit agreement', 6 June 2009, <http://www.whitehouse.gov/the_press_office/Fact-Sheet-United-States-Russia-Military-Transit-Agreement/>. It should be noted, however, that Russia and the USA continued to face problems in putting the agreement into practice.

cooperation. The relationship, however, is still a fragile one. Differences remain—over NATO enlargement, the 1990 Treaty on Conventional Armed Forces in Europe (CFE Treaty), missile defence, Georgia and Russia's policies in the former Soviet space.[36] Much of the Russian political and military elite still perceives NATO as a major threat. In NATO there is ongoing debate over the extent to which Russia poses a military threat, with some Central European member states calling for enhanced defence planning and preparations vis-à-vis Russia. The fragility of the relationship was indicated by other developments in 2009: the expulsion from NATO headquarters of Russian diplomats accused of spying and the retaliatory expulsion of diplomats from NATO's information office in Moscow, NATO military exercises in Georgia in May which Russia described as a 'provocation' and Belarusian–Russian military exercises in Belarus in September which Poland's defence minister, Bogdan Klich, described as 'a demonstration of strength'.[37] As illustrated by the 1999 conflict in Kosovo (when Russia broke off ties with NATO) and the 2008 conflict in Georgia (when NATO broke off ties with Russia), the NATO–Russia relationship can easily be disrupted by policy decisions on either side or by unexpected events. Building a more durable NATO–Russia partnership will remain a challenging, long-term task.

Towards a new strategic concept

At the Strasbourg–Kehl Summit, NATO leaders agreed to develop a new strategic concept for NATO. There was consensus that the alliance's existing 1999 strategic concept—coming before the 11 September 2001 terrorist attacks on the USA and NATO's intervention in Afghanistan—was now an outdated document and that NATO needed a redefined mission that could act as the basis for consensus among member states and sustain long-term public support.

The mandate from the Strasbourg–Kehl Summit tasked the secretary general 'to convene and lead a broad-based group of qualified experts, who in close consultation with all Allies will lay the ground for the Secretary General to develop a new Strategic Concept and submit proposals for its implementation for approval at our next summit'.[38] The new strategic concept will be developed in a three-phase process: (a) a reflection phase, which began in September 2009 and is to be completed in early 2010,

---

[36] For a summary and other details of the CFE Treaty see annex A in this volume. On developments in 2009 see chapter 11, section II, in this volume.

[37] Harding, L., 'Russia expels two diplomats as NATO begins military exercises in Georgia', *The Guardian*, 6 May 2009; and Day, M., 'Russia "simulates" nuclear attack on Poland', *Daily Telegraph*, 1 Nov. 2009. On military exercises in the Euro-Atlantic area see chapter 11 in this volume.

[38] NATO, Declaration on alliance security, Strasbourg–Kehl, 4 Apr. 2009, <http://www.nato.int/cps/en/natolive/news_52838.htm>.

involving a series of seminars to discuss the range of issues and challenges facing NATO; (b) a consultation phase, during which the group of experts will visit NATO member states to discuss their findings and proposals and which will conclude with the group of experts submitting their analysis and recommendations to the secretary general in April 2010; (c) and a drafting and negotiation phase from summer 2010, during which the secretary general will prepare a draft strategic concept, which will then be presented to heads of state and government for approval at a NATO summit to be held in Lisbon in late 2010.[39]

NATO's two post-cold war strategic concepts, of 1991 and 1999, were developed through standard processes of intergovernmental drafting and negotiation among NATO's member states. In contrast, the 2009–10 strategic concept process resembles that surrounding the 1967 Harmel Report, which involved a wide-ranging process of reflection in NATO in 1966–67 on NATO's purposes and strategy.[40] The Harmel Report was particularly significant because it crystallized a new NATO political strategy (the Harmel Doctrine) combining NATO's traditional roles of defence and deterrence with the parallel tasks of engagement and cooperation with the Eastern bloc—a strategy that provided the broad political consensus on which NATO operated for the next two decades. Clearly, it is hoped that the new strategic concept can provide a similar long-term basis for NATO.

The list of issues facing NATO in developing its new strategic concept is dauntingly long: the fundamental *raison d'être* of NATO; the balance between NATO's role in defending members' territory and its role elsewhere in the world; the nature and implications of the Article 5 security guarantee at the heart of the NATO treaty; the long-term direction of, and limits to, NATO enlargement; the nature and future development of NATO's various partnerships with non-members and other international organizations; the long-term character of NATO's relations with Russia; NATO's role in addressing 'new' security threats such as proliferation, terrorism, cybersecurity, energy security and climate change; the place of nuclear weapons in NATO strategy and NATO's roles in nuclear non-proliferation and disarmament; the long-term development of NATO's military infrastructure and member states' armed forces; and NATO's internal political and military decision-making structures. The difficulty of the policy challenges that these issues raise and the diversity of views in NATO—both on its overall future and on specific issues—suggest that

[39] The 12-member group of experts is chaired by Madeleine Albright, the former US secretary of State, with its members reflecting the geographic breadth of NATO's membership. On NATO's new strategic concept see the special section on NATO's website, <http://www.nato.int/strategic-concept/>.

[40] The report was named after Belgian Foreign Minister Pierre Harmel. NATO, 'The future tasks of the alliance (The Harmel Report)', Report of the Council, 13–14 Dec. 1967, <http://www.nato.int/cps/en/natolive/official_texts_26700.htm>.

achieving the kind of long-term consensus embodied in the Harmel Doctrine will be a difficult task indeed.

III. The European Union

In a report to the European Council in December 2008 about the implementation of the 2003 European Security Strategy, the EU High Representative for Common Foreign and Security Policy (CFSP), Javier Solana, wrote that 'The European Union carries greater responsibilities than at any time in its history.'[41] The three main factors he cited were the enlargement of the EU, which had 'spread democracy and prosperity across our continent'; the commitments enshrined in the European Neighbourhood Policy (ENP) towards non-member states in the east, south-east and south; and the EU's interventions in crises and conflicts abroad using the instrument of the Common Security and Defence Policy (CSDP, formerly known as the European Security and Defence Policy, ESDP), which celebrated its 10th anniversary in 2009.[42] If Solana had been speaking of the totality of EU activities, not just the sphere of CFSP, he could also have cited the EU's growing role in such non-military dimensions of security—at home and abroad—as financial and economic stability, energy, the management of climate change, public health, migration and border control, transport safety, and the combating of terrorism, crime, smuggling, human trafficking and proliferation as well as the promotion of human security through aid and good-governance policies.

Solana recognized, however, that the EU has struggled to cope with its expanding and increasingly explicit strategic role in its own continent's security and in the world. Like NATO, it faces the challenge of transforming its policies and its instruments in a testing environment, while trying to integrate and reconcile a much larger range of members. Solana himself, in the December 2008 report, called on the EU to be ready to 'shape events', to think strategically, to be 'effective and visible around the

---

[41] This and subsequent Solana quotations are from 'Report on the implementation of the European security strategy: providing security in a changing world', S407/08, Brussels, 11 Dec. 2008, <http://www.consilium.europa.eu/showPage.aspx?id=266&lang=en>. For the 2003 strategy see 'A secure Europe in a better world: European security strategy', Brussels, 12 Dec. 2003, <http://www.consilium.europa.eu/showPage.aspx?id=266&lang=en>.

[42] The ENP is based on European Commission strategy proposals dating from 2004; participants include Algeria, Armenia, Azerbaijan, Belarus, Egypt, Georgia, Israel, Jordan, Lebanon, Libya, Moldova, Morocco, Palestinian territories, Syria, Tunisia and Ukraine. The Commission's 'Eastern Partnership' includes Armenia, Azerbaijan, Belarus, Georgia, Moldova and Ukraine. See the ENP website, <http://ec.europa.eu/world/enp/>; and European Commission, External Relations, Eastern Partnership, 29 Mar. 2010, <http://ec.europa.eu/external_relations/eastern/>. The ESDP was launched by European Council decisions in Dec. 1999 in the framework of the CFSP dating from the 1992 Treaty of Maastricht. It allows military as well as civilian capabilities to be used under EU command for purposes of crisis management, and humanitarian and rescue missions. The first ESDP missions both inside and outside Europe were approved in 2003.

world' and to 'operate in a timely and coherent manner'. The whole aim of the redesign of EU governance enshrined in the Treaty of Lisbon was to overcome these weaknesses by deepening European unity to match the scale of geographical and functional widening.[43] The treaty finally entered into force on 1 December 2009—more than five years after the EU enlargement in 2004 whose concomitant and corrective it was meant to be.[44]

EU enlargement

Since the entry of Bulgaria and Romania in 2007 into the EU, the EU has had 21 members in common with NATO; and its challenges regarding further expansion lie primarily in the same areas, namely the Western Balkans and the nearer parts of the former Soviet Union.[45] Turkey has also been negotiating for EU membership since 2006 but has had some chapters of its talks frozen since October 2008 because of disputes arising from the lack of a reunification settlement on the divided island of Cyprus.[46] This problem was highlighted again in December 2009 when Turkey missed a deadline for opening its ports to vessels from the Republic of Cyprus, although some progress was made by the Turkish authorities during the year on other contentious fronts such as Turkey's relationship with Armenia. Some EU members, such as France and Germany, hold more general reservations about Turkish membership. An application for EU entry was also received from Iceland in July 2009 in the wake of the especially severe impact in that country of the economic crisis. A quick start to accession talks—perhaps in the spring of 2010—was expected at that time, although the outcome will be subject to a referendum in Iceland, and Icelandic public support for the EU declined steeply during 2009.

---

[43] The 2007 Treaty of Lisbon was an attempt to achieve the goals of the 2004 Treaty establishing a Constitution for Europe, which was doomed to failure by negative referendum results in France and the Netherlands in May and June 2005, respectively. Treaty of Lisbon, signed 19 Oct. 2007, entered into force 1 Dec. 2009, *Official Journal of the European Union*, C306, 17 Dec. 2007.

[44] In 2004, 10 countries joined the EU: Czech Republic, Estonia, Cyprus, Latvia, Lithuania, Hungary, Malta, Poland, Slovakia and Slovenia.

[45] EU membership candidates include Croatia, the former Yugoslav Republic of Macedonia and Turkey; potential EU membership candidates include Albania, Bosnia and Herzegovina, Iceland, Kosovo (under UN Security Council Resolution 1244), Montenegro and Serbia. Croatia, Turkey, Albania and Iceland are also members of NATO. 'Candidate country' status is granted to a state when its application to join the EU is officially accepted by the European Council; 'potential candidates' are those states that are pursuing membership application. On the framework for EU negotiations with the Western Balkan countries see European Commission, 'The stabilisation and association process', [n.d.], <http://ec.europa.eu/enlargement/enlargement_process/accession_process/how_does_a_country_join_the_eu/sap/index_en.htm>.

[46] The Republic of Cyprus is a member of the EU, although Turkey recognizes only the Turkish Republic of Northern Cyprus, and UN negotiations have yet to produce a peace settlement. One of Turkey's disputes with the Republic of Cyprus is regarding the non-implementation of promised EU benefits for Northern Cyprus.

EU public opinion has for some years reflected an enlargement fatigue linked with concerns on migration, employment and cultural dilution. The more general problem of overstretch was highlighted again in late 2008 and 2009 by the depth of the economic crisis in such new member states as Hungary and Latvia, requiring EU neighbours and banks to help sustain them and incidentally further deferring the prospect of most new members' adoption of the euro.[47] Only in the Western Balkans does the EU have such powerful motives to consolidate peace through integration that the enlargement process continues to move cautiously forward. Croatia has been in accession talks since 2005, and an obstacle regarding sea boundary disputes with Slovenia was overcome during 2009. Following the earlier examples of the Former Yugoslav Republic of Macedonia (FYROM) and Montenegro—which applied for entry in 2005 and 2008, respectively— Albania formally applied for EU entry in April and Serbia in December 2009. Bosnia and Herzegovina is a further potential candidate holding a Stabilization and Association Agreement. The feasibility of Kosovo's eventual entry is under consideration, although some EU members do not recognize its independence.

Eastern neighbours

Unlike NATO, the EU has not yet seriously contemplated membership for states like Georgia, Moldova and Ukraine but rather handles these—with Armenia, Azerbaijan and Belarus—in the ENP framework, where each partner may negotiate an action plan for cooperation and reform.[48] On 7 May 2009 a joint meeting of the EU and these states at Prague adopted a joint declaration on 'Eastern Partnership' designed to add new dynamism but also more rigorous standards for internal reform, following the lessons of the 2008 Georgia–Russia conflict when EU leaders were drawn in as mediators and the EU supplied a monitoring force.[49]

EU–Russia relations returned to near-normalcy in 2009 following the EU's postponement of negotiations on a new cooperation agreement in

[47] Slovakia adopted the euro on 1 Jan. 2009.

[48] While generally seen as an advance, the current ENP falls short of the Eastern partners' hopes regarding free trade and visa-free travel, since France, Germany and Italy rejected more generous provisions. On the ENP and Eastern Partnership see note 42.

[49] Council of the European Union, Joint Declaration of the Prague Eastern Partnership Summit, Prague, 7 May 2009, <http://europa.eu/rapid/pressReleasesAction.do?reference=PRES/09/78>. French President Sarkozy spearheaded an agreement on ceasefire plus withdrawal of Russian troops from undisputed Georgian territory. The EU Monitoring Mission in Georgia was provided under the CSDP. In Sep. 2009 a group of experts, commissioned by the EU Council, delivered a report on the Georgian crisis that blamed Georgia for opening hostilities, albeit under provocation. Council Decision 2008/901/CFSP of 2 Dec. 2008 concerning an independent international fact-finding mission on the conflict in Georgia, *Official Journal of the European Union*, L323, 3 Dec 2008; and Independent International Fact-Finding Mission on the Conflict in Georgia (IIFFMCG), *Report*, 3 vols (IIFFMCG: Sep. 2009).

Table 4.1. Selected European Union member states' personnel contributions to Common Security and Defence Policy missions

	France	Germany	Italy	UK	Spain	Poland	Netherlands	Sweden
Military missions, 2008	5 470	2 045	1 274	805	708	774	504	472
Civilian missions, 2009	275	259	282	125	64	158	62	143

Source: Grevi, G., Helly, D. and Keohane, D. (eds), *European Security and Defence Policy: The First Ten Years (1999–2009)* (European Union Institute of Security Studies: Paris, 2009).

mid-2008 because of the Georgia–Russia conflict. The EU sought to broker difficulties between Russia and Ukraine that might lead to further interruptions of Russian gas supplies to Ukraine, and in December 2009 Ukraine reached agreement with Russia on nuclear energy cooperation.[50] Also relevant to EU–Russia relations was the Council of the European Union's adoption on 8 December 2009 of guidelines for an EU policy in the Arctic that would prioritize the environment and seek to pre-empt conflict over resources by strengthening multilateral governance in the region.[51] What remains more elusive is a clear EU strategy for managing Europe's own energy dependence on Russia—or indeed, any other critical aspect of energy policy. Familiar issues include the differences between Germany and several smaller states over the security implications of such dependence, and reluctance in France and elsewhere to liberalize the internal energy market even for EU suppliers.

EU operations

The 10th anniversary of the CSDP in December 2009 stimulated many retrospectives on the 22 EU missions launched since 2003, of which just 6 were military and the others involved police, law-and-order, border-related or security sector reform tasks.[52] Following the launch of five missions in 2008, none were created in 2009.[53]

[50] On this and other details regarding EU–Russia developments see the Russian section of the European Commission's External Relations website, <http://ec.europa.eu/external_relations/russia/>.

[51] Council of the European Union, 'Conclusions on Arctic issues', Brussels, 8 Dec. 2009, <http://www.consilium.europa.eu/uedocs/cms_Data/docs/pressdata/EN/foraff/111814.pdf>.

[52] This is the official count. Some sources differ depending on whether follow-on operations are treated separately. The official review is in the 'European Security and Defence Policy: 1999–2009', *ESDP Newsletter*, Oct. 2009. See also Grevi, G., Helly, D. and Keohane, D. (eds), *European Security and Defence Policy: The First Ten Years (1999–2009)* (European Union Institute of Security Studies: Paris, 2009). For details of peace operations see the SIPRI Multilateral Peace Operations Database, <http://www.sipri.org/databases/pko/>.

[53] See appendix 3A in this volume.

The proliferation of small missions has caused concern given the administrative burdens involved and has been aggravated by lack of clear organizational models (among others for civil–military interaction), poor lesson learning and complicated funding systems.[54] Those who originally saw the CSDP as a way to harmonize member states' defence efforts at higher levels have also been disappointed, since great disparities remain in member states' total spending, in the effectiveness of that spending (including the share of equipment), and in what states will give for missions abroad (including the CSDP ones).[55] Countries do not necessarily contribute to CSDP actions in proportion to their ability, as some see reason to prioritize other NATO-led, United Nations-led or ad hoc operations—an obvious case being the United Kingdom's much larger troop contributions in Afghanistan and (formerly) Iraq (see table 4.1). The basic quandary is that CSDP efforts are doubly a matter of choice: the missions are not designed for member states' direct security needs, and the assignment of assets is left to states' own initiative in 'bottom-up' and ad hoc fashion. There are limits to what the tightening of common qualitative specifications—currently enshrined in the Headline Goal 2010—can achieve so long as nothing in the CSDP is legally binding, and the limited objectives of the CSDP prevent the EU, in effect, from addressing the total design of members' forces (including nuclear assets).[56]

Frustrations over deficient capabilities and limited impact have inspired much debate on the way forward in the CSDP, with prescriptions that range from concentrating on the few most capable states to finding a way around the remaining obstacles to EU–NATO cooperation. The need to accommodate a wide variety of national aims and attitudes has kept the basic aim of the CSDP somewhat vague and ambiguous from the start. The Helsinki decisions of 1999 spoke of 'conflict prevention and management' without specifying which conflicts particularly required EU intervention and with what desired outcomes.

In practice, the pattern of CSDP missions has followed opportunity more than design, falling roughly into three categories: major efforts in the Bal-

[54] For military missions, only limited 'common costs' are covered from EU funds under the 'Athena' financing mechanism, which was updated by the Council in Dec. 2008.

[55] Keohane, D. and Blommestijn, C., 'Strength in numbers? Comparing EU military capabilities in 2009 with 1999', European Union Institute of Security Studies, Policy Brief no. 5, Dec. 2009, <http://www.iss.europa.eu/uploads/media/PolicyBrief-05.pdf>. See also Giegerich, B. and Nicoll, A. (eds), *European Military Capabilities: Building Armed Forces for Modern Operations* (International Institute for Strategic Studies: London, July 2008).

[56] The Headline Goal 2010 sets out a timeline for assessing earmarked EU forces, upgrading their standards and developing the CSDP's central resources. The Headline Goal 2010 was approved by the Council of the European Union in May 2004 and endorsed by the European Council in June 2004. European Council, 'Headline Goal 2010', 17–18 June 2004, <http://www.consilium.europa.eu/uedocs/cmsUpload/2010 Headline Goal.pdf>. For official CSDP targets see also Council of the European Union, 'Ministerial declaration: ESDP ten years: challenges and opportunities', 17 Nov. 2009, <http://www.consilium.europa.eu/uedocs/cms_data/docs/pressdata/en/esdp/111262.pdf>.

kans, serving Europe's own security; moderately risky but transient missions in developing regions, often echoing former colonial responsibilities; and very small, specialized, low-risk deployments in neighbouring areas such as the Caucasus and the Middle East. The conservative approach to risk has, at least, avoided any serious scandals or disasters and the EU has not, as some feared in 1999, undergone a general militarization of its strategic character and image. In this light, the CSDP's limitations also reflect the overall balance of EU purposes and competences which are heavily slanted towards non-military, non-conflict dimensions of security. The longer-term question is, of course, whether NATO can indefinitely—and effectively—relieve the EU of the need to assume a heavier role in Europe's own defence.

The Treaty of Lisbon

When the EU's Treaty of Lisbon finally came into force on 1 December 2009, it created (among other things) the posts of a long-term president of the European Council and a high representative (HR) for Foreign Affairs and Security Policy, who will also (unlike Solana) be a vice-president of the European Commission. The European Council's decision in November 2009 to give these jobs to the little-known Herman van Rompuy (of Belgium) and Catherine Ashton (of the UK), respectively, disappointed those who sought strong central leadership and a clearer 'single address' for external partners. The choices may be explained by states' caution over transferring the initiative to Brussels too fast, but perhaps also by a focus on administrative competence. The HR in particular must negotiate with the Commission the creation of a single European External Action Service combining all previously separate EU staffs and funds for diplomacy, security and defence (as well as staff to be seconded from national foreign ministries).[57] It has been argued that the right time for bolder appointments will come the next time around, in 2013.[58]

Other security-related innovations of the treaty are more subtle and incremental, not least because several concrete ideas from the Constitutional Treaty of 2004 had been implemented earlier.[59] The principle of unanimity still prevails in the CFSP and the CSDP, and no joint, standing EU forces are foreseen. The powers of the Commission and the European Parliament in this sphere of policy remain limited. Four significant

[57] For a detailed study with organogram see Mauri, F. and Gya, G., 'The setting up of a European External Action Service (EEAS): laying the basis for a more coherent EU foreign policy', *European Security Review*, no. 47 (Dec. 2009).

[58] Missiroli, A., 'Two cheers and one lesson for the EU', European Policy Centre, Commentaries, 23 Nov. 2009, <http://www.epc.eu/en/pb.asp?TYP=TEWN&LV=187&see=y&t=32&PG=TEWN/EN/detailpub&l=12&AI=993>.

[59] On the Treaty establishing a Constitution for Europe see note 43.

novelties are (a) an expanded definition of the missions covered by the CSDP, to include military assistance and disarmament tasks among others; (b) the introduction of 'permanent structured cooperation' in defence, whereby a limited group of member states can adopt higher standards and specific goals for equipment cooperation and deployable forces—operational tasks may also be delegated to such groups; (c) a provision for mutual assistance in the case of armed aggression against a member state, qualified by references to the primacy of NATO for its members, and to the 'specific character' of non-allied countries' policies; and (d) the incorporation into the Lisbon Treaty of a 'solidarity' commitment based on a political declaration in March 2004 (after terrorist attacks in Madrid), whereby states will aid each other with military and other resources, on request, in response to terrorist attacks and natural or man-made disasters.[60]

While the treaty defines steps to elaborate items b and d, all four elements are essentially formulaic and permissive, their translation to action depending on each country's choice in specific cases. A more serious limitation is that all of these elements apply in the traditional 'second pillar' of Council-led external action and cannot solve the larger challenge of coordination between the CFSP, the CSDP and the EU's financial, economic and functional strengths, or indeed its internal security and border security policies. Yet such synergies are ultimately the key to EU effectiveness in specific crises and to the coherence of the EU's whole strategic personality. The next opportunity to review the EU's progress in these areas should be in June 2010 when the European Council is due to receive a report on future strategy from an independent 'reflection group', who were selected in 2008.[61] Most likely, however, as in the past, the power of events will determine the speed and success of Europe's strategic maturation.

IV. Renewing pan-European security cooperation?

Developments since 2008 have triggered an intense new round of debate on pan-European security structures. The 2008 conflict in Georgia was a dramatic failure for Europe's existing security institutions. In the wake of that conflict, concerns over a possible new cold war between Russia and

---

[60] A further change important for internal security is the introduction of qualified majority voting on police and judicial matters in the EU's area of Freedom, Security and Justice. Ireland and the UK have an opt-out from this clause but may opt in to new decisions on a case-by-case basis (as Denmark will also be able to do in the future). See Quille, G., *The Lisbon Treaty and its Implications for CFSP/ESDP*, Briefing Paper (European Parliament, Directorate-General for External Policies of the Union: Brussels, Feb. 2008).

[61] The international group consisting of 8 men and 4 women and led by former Spanish Prime Minister Felipe Gonzales was nominated by the European Council in Oct. 2008 and given its mandate 2 months later, following a French initiative. Council of the European Union, Presidency Conclusions, 14368/08, Brussels, 16 Oct. 2008; and the Reflection Group website, <http://www.reflectiongroup.eu/>.

the West intensified, triggering debate on what measures might be taken to avoid such a confrontation. In the USA, one of the first major foreign policy steps of the Obama Administration was its call to 'press the reset button' on relations with Russia. More concretely, since 2008 Russia has explicitly called for new pan-European security arrangements and in particular a new European security treaty. In response to these Russian proposals, the OSCE launched the 'Corfu process' to review and revive the OSCE's role.

Russia's proposed European security treaty

Russia's proposals for a European security treaty were first advanced by President Medvedev in a speech to German political, parliamentary and civic leaders in Berlin in June 2008.[62] Medvedev argued that 'we cannot resolve Europe's problems until we achieve a sense of identity and an organic unity between all of its integral components, including the Russian Federation . . . Atlanticism as a sole historical principle has already had its day. We need to talk today about unity between the whole Euro-Atlantic area from Vancouver to Vladivostok'.[63] As a concrete step towards these objectives, he called for 'a legally binding treaty on European security . . . a regional pact [which] could achieve a comprehensive resolution of the security indivisibility and arms control issues in Europe that are of such concern to us all'. Medvedev's proposals were further developed in October 2008 when he called for 'a new European security treaty' as the basis for 'an integrated and solid system of comprehensive security'.[64] These proposals have been a central theme of Russian diplomacy since 2008.[65]

In November 2009 Russia published a draft of its proposed European security treaty, arguing that the treaty would 'finally get rid of the legacy of the Cold War'.[66] Under the draft treaty, 'security measures' taken by states (individually or collectively, including by military alliances) will 'be imple-

---

[62] On the proposed European security treaty also see chapter 11 in this volume.

[63] Medvedev, D., President of Russia, Speech at meeting with German political, parliamentary and civic leaders, Berlin, 5 June 2008, <http://eng.kremlin.ru/speeches/2008/06/05/2203_type 82912type82914type84779_202153.shtml>.

[64] Medvedev, D., President of Russia, Speech at World Policy Conference, Evian, 8 Oct. 2008, <http://eng.kremlin.ru/speeches/2008/10/08/2159_type82912type82914_207457.shtml>.

[65] See e.g. Lavrov, S., Russian Minister of Foreign Affairs, 'Shake loose the cold war', *The Guardian*, 30 Jan. 2009; Permanent Mission of Russia to NATO, 'Dmitry Medvedev: "We must form the outline of the new security system"', Interview with the Spanish media, Gorky, 1 Mar. 2009, <http://www.natomission.ru/en/society/article/society/artnews/33/>; Rogozin, D., 'An end to cold peace', *The Guardian*, 30 Mar. 2009; Lavrov, S., Russian Minister of Foreign Affairs, Speech to the Carnegie Endowment for International Peace, Washington, DC, 7 May 2009, <http://www.carnegie endowment.org/events/?fa=eventDetail&id=1336>; and Medvedev, D., President of Russia, Address to the 64th Session of the UN General Assembly, New York, 24 Sep. 2009, <http://www.un.org/ga/64/generaldebate/RU.shtml>.

[66] 'European security treaty "to end cold war legacy": Medvedev', Agence France-Presse, 29 Nov. 2009.

mented with due regard to security interests' of all signatories.[67] States would agree (*a*) not to 'undertake, participate in or support any actions or activities affecting significantly [the] security' of other signatories; (*b*) not to allow decisions taken by 'military alliances, coalitions or organizations' of which they are members to 'affect significantly [the] security of any Party or Parties to the Treaty'; (*c*) and not to allow the use of their own or other states' territory for 'the purpose of preparing or carrying out an armed attack'.[68] If a signatory determines that 'a violation or a threat of violation' of the treaty exists, it may request 'consultations' with the relevant parties, which shall be held in an agreed number of days.[69] Any party to such consultations may propose the convening of a 'Conference of the Parties', which shall be held in a specified number of days and where decisions will be taken by consensus and be binding.[70] 'In case of an armed attack or a threat of such attack' against a signatory, an extraordinary conference of the parties will be convened 'immediately'; the decisions of such a conference would 'be taken by unanimous vote and shall be binding', but the state or states which have carried out the attack would be excluded from the decision.[71] In addition, 'every Party shall be entitled to consider an armed attack against any other Party an armed attack against itself. . . . it shall be entitled to render the attacked Party . . . the necessary assistance, including the military one'.[72] Clearly, the Russian proposal envisages something closely approximating to a pan-European collective security system in which all states commit to act if any signatory faces armed attack.

A number of motivations appear to lie behind the Russian proposal. The overarching objective is to establish a new European security architecture in which Russia is included as a full and equal partner. More concrete Russian motivations, however, relate to NATO—in particular the desire to prevent further enlargement, unilateral military action (such as NATO's intervention in Kosovo in 1999) and the eastward extension of NATO's military infrastructure. Medvedev has thus argued that the new European security architecture should be based on three 'nos': 'no ensuring one's security at the expense of others. No allowing acts (by military alliances or coalitions) that undermine the unity of the common security space. And finally, no development of military alliances that would threaten the security of other parties'.[73] Securing the right to take unilateral action if deemed necessary also seems a concern: hence, the reference in the draft treaty to the right of

[67] European security treaty, Unofficial translation, Draft, President of Russia, 29 Nov. 2009, <http://eng.kremlin.ru/text/docs/2009/11/223072.shtml>, Article 1.
[68] European security treaty (note 67), Article 2.
[69] European security treaty (note 67), Article 5.
[70] European security treaty (note 67), Article 6.
[71] European security treaty (note 67), articles 7 and 8.
[72] European security treaty (note 67), Article 7, para. 2.
[73] Medvedev (note 64).

a state to consider an armed attack on another state as an attack against itself and to provide assistance to any state so attacked.

The OSCE Corfu process

In response to Russia's proposals and the emerging debate on pan-European security, at the December 2008 OSCE Ministerial Council meeting in Helsinki, Finland's foreign minister Alexander Stubb, as OSCE chairman-in-office (CIO), organized an informal working lunch, attended by 52 OSCE ministers, to discuss the future of European security. As Stubb summarized the meeting, 'It was refreshing, it was frank, it was open, and it was analytical, and that in and of itself to me is part of the spirit of Helsinki.'[74] According to Stubb, there was 'a broad understanding' that the OSCE was 'the most suitable venue' for further discussions of European security.[75] Finland also included in the statements and decisions from the meeting a CIO perception paper that sought to reaffirm the role of the OSCE and the principles and commitments on which it is based and to place the OSCE as the primary venue for further discussions.[76]

The dialogue initiated at the December 2008 Helsinki Summit was continued at a series of meetings in Vienna—where the OSCE is based—in the first half of 2009. These discussions were followed by an informal meeting of OSCE foreign ministers, convened by the Greek CIO, on the island of Corfu. The Corfu meeting was attended by 51 foreign ministers and resulted in agreement on 'the need for an open, sustained, wide-ranging and inclusive dialogue on security' to be taken forward through a 'Corfu process'.[77] Following this, OSCE ambassadors met regularly in Vienna in the second half of 2009 to take the process forward.

In a document adopted at the December 2009 Ministerial Council meeting in Athens, OSCE foreign ministers reaffirmed 'the vision of a free, democratic and more integrated OSCE area, from Vancouver to Vladivostok, free of dividing lines and zones with different levels of security', declared it their 'highest priority ... to re-establish our trust and confidence, as well as to recapture the sense of common purpose that brought together our predecessors in Helsinki almost 35 years ago' and agreed 'to

[74] OSCE, 'OSCE "revitalized" at Helsinki Ministerial Council, high-level talks on European security to continue', Press release, 5 Dec. 2008, <http://www.osce.org/item/35566.html>.

[75] OSCE, 'Discussion on the future of security in Europe at OSCE Ministerial working lunch on 4 Dec. 2008', MC.DEL/92/08, 15 Dec. 2008, <http://www.osce.org/conferences/mc_2008.html?page=documents&session_id=353>.

[76] OSCE, 'Renewing the spirit of Helsinki', Perception Paper of the chairman-in-office, Annex to MC (16) Journal no. 2 (5 Dec. 2008), 16th Meeting of the Ministerial Council, Helsinki, 4–5 Dec. 2008, <http://www.osce.org/conferences/mc_2008.html?page=documents&session_id=346>, pp. 40–41.

[77] OSCE, '"Corfu process" launched to take European security dialogue forward, says OSCE Chairperson', Press release, Corfu, 28 June 2009, <http://www.osce.org/cio/item_1_38493.html>.

continue and further develop' the Corfu process.[78] The Corfu process should 'build on three basic guidelines': 'adherence to the concept of comprehensive, cooperative and indivisible security', 'compliance with OSCE norms, principles and commitments in all three OSCE dimensions' and 'determination to strengthen partnership and cooperation in the OSCE area'.

OSCE foreign ministers also tasked the OSCE chairmanship in 2010 (held by Kazakhstan) to continue to develop the Corfu process through 'regular informal meetings, at the level of permanent representatives', with the chairmanship to provide, by the end of June 2010, an interim report summarizing the proposals put forward.[79] The dialogue is to focus on eight areas: (a) implementation of all OSCE norms, principles and commitments; (b) the OSCE's role in early warning, conflict prevention and resolution, crisis management and post-conflict rehabilitation; (c) arms control and confidence- and security-building regimes; (d) transnational and multidimensional threats and challenges; (e) economic and environmental challenges; (f) human rights and fundamental freedoms, as well as democracy and the rule of law; (g) enhancing the OSCE's effectiveness; and (h) interaction with other organizations and institutions.[80]

Prospects

What are the prospects for a new deal on pan-European security? There are good reasons to doubt that a European security treaty will be adopted in anything like the form proposed by Russia and that, even if it were, it would change pan-European security dynamics in the ways hoped for by Russia. From a theoretical perspective, all-encompassing collective security systems of the type proposed by Russia face severe and probably insuperable obstacles. In particular, they presume that states, especially the major powers, will be able to agree on what constitutes a threat, an act of aggression or a situation warranting the use of military force and on how to respond in such circumstances. Such agreement is rarely, if ever, the case— as the two defining European crises of the post-cold war era, in Kosovo in 1999 and in Georgia in 2008, starkly illustrated.[81] To the extent that Russia's goal is to constrain NATO, NATO member states are unlikely to

[78] OSCE, Ministerial Declaration on the OSCE Corfu process, 'Reconfirm-review-reinvigorate security and co-operation from Vancouver to Vladivostok', MC.DOC/1/09, Athens, 2 Dec. 2009, <http://www.osce.org/cio/42119.html>.

[79] OSCE, 'The Corfu process', <http://www.osce.org/cio/42119.html>.

[80] OSCE, 'Furthering the Corfu process', Decision no. 1/09, MC.DEC/1/09, Athens, 2 Dec. 2009, <http://www.osce.org/cio/42119.html>.

[81] Joffe, J., 'Collective security and the future of Europe: failed dreams and dead ends', Survival, vol. 34, no. 1 (spring 1992), pp. 36–50; and Mearsheimer, J. J., 'The false promise of international institutions', International Security, vol. 19, no. 3 (winter 1994/95), pp. 26–37.

accept any agreement which formally limits NATO's decision making or the right, in principle, to extend membership to other European states. Western governments are also sceptical of approaches that emphasize legally binding constraints, arguing that such treaties are unenforceable and cannot resolve what are essentially political differences between states. In addition, legally binding treaties require ratification by relevant national procedures, creating an additional obstacle to their conclusion and implementation (in particular in the USA, where the Senate zealously guards its right to ratify treaties).

The proposal raises an additional sensitive issue: how far to reopen the existing OSCE *acquis*, in particular in the area of democracy and human rights. Here, Russia and some of the other former Soviet states favour a 'Helsinki II' approach that would involve reopening OSCE commitments on democracy and human rights or downgrading existing OSCE processes and institutions for the monitoring and promotion of these commitments. In contrast, the 'Helsinki plus' approach, favoured by Western states, emphasizes maintaining the existing OSCE *acquis* in this area and exploring how it and mechanisms for implementing and supporting it may be strengthened. Behind this issue are deep—perhaps even fundamental— differences between the Western democracies and Russia and some of the former Soviet states. Nevertheless, the inclusion in the December 2009 Ministerial Council document of a commitment to develop the Corfu process on the basis of 'compliance with OSCE norms, principles and commitments *in all three OSCE dimensions, in full and in good faith, and in a consistent manner by all*' suggests the basis of an approach on this issue to which all OSCE states may be able to agree.[82]

In summary, the development of the Corfu process suggests that there is a new level of political commitment among all OSCE states to reform and strengthen pan-European security structures, but there also remain important substantive differences between OSCE member states. In particular, there is a real gap between Russia's interest in a legally binding European security treaty constraining NATO and Western states' views of how best to proceed. It is uncertain whether this gap can be bridged at all; but any hope of doing so, and thereby giving real new substance to pan-European security cooperation, will demand sustained high-level political attention and more creative diplomatic thinking than Europe has seen for a while.

[82] OSCE (note 78), (emphasis added).

V. Conclusions

The 20th anniversary in 2009 of the fall of the Berlin Wall offered a chance to review how far European security has come since the cold war, where the transition remains incomplete and what new challenges demand solution. The EU, NATO and the OSCE can all claim credit for allowing much of Europe to be reunified through enlargement without East–West violence, for damping down conflict in the Western Balkans, and for starting to seriously tackle new functional and global aspects of security. As this chapter illustrates, however, the unresolved aspects of coexistence with Russia, the future of the post-Soviet space generally, and European action in the wider world are the focus of serious self-examination in the EU, NATO and the OSCE which began in 2009 but will continue in 2010 and beyond.

Experiences from September 2001 to 2009 will lend these reviews a tone of sober realism. Scars remain from divisions provoked by the USA's 'global war on terrorism' and by the application of military force to proliferation issues, while both sides of the Atlantic have digested hard lessons about the limitations of Western power. In addition to the wars in Afghanistan and Iraq, setbacks and violent outbreaks in the Middle East and in western former Soviet Union states have underlined that 'integrated Europe' is surrounded by less stable zones which it seems singularly powerless to influence or control. The vulnerability of both large and small Western economies to the global financial crisis has added new reasons for concern and created new difficulties over spending for defence and security. Early responses to the crisis often revealed nationalistic, beggar-my-neighbour instincts not far below the surface, even in heavily integrated EU states.

Europe's institutions should not, however, let the new realism of diminishing Western power translate into defeatism. Scaling down ambitions too far would leave them, at best, managing rather than resolving their problems—including problems of internal consensus. None of the institutions reviewed will help its survival by standing still or slipping backwards, even if all could benefit from revisiting certain past wisdoms and adapting them to the present. In the last resort, the goals of security, democracy and Atlantic partnership are the primary concern, and the region's institutions in their present form are secondary instruments. From the evidence presented in this chapter, the longer-term viability of the EU instrument may seem better guaranteed than that of NATO and the OSCE—and the strength of will shown by EU leaders in finally pushing through the Lisbon Treaty, for avowed purposes of self-renewal, could be the latest proof.

Any review of Euro-Atlantic security in 2009 that is limited to Europe and North America must, however, give an incomplete and slanted impression. The larger lessons of the year have all been about shifts of power at global level, including the increased readiness of non-European players to parlay their strength into institutional representation and policy influence. The decisive role played by China in economic, financial and climate matters, and its increasing strategic stake in Africa and South America, are obvious examples. India and Brazil have also survived the global crisis as 'rising powers', contrasting with Russia which has seen some of the vulnerabilities behind its recent more 'assertive' stance exposed. The replacement of the Group of Eight industrialized nations (G8) by the G20 has given leverage also to smaller countries and poorer regions. Similar shifts can be seen in the functional composition of security priorities, where some issues—proliferation, terrorism, energy, climate change, food security, population and migration—can only be mastered through complete global cooperation, while the pattern of active conflict is dominated by non-Euro-Atlantic regions (Africa, Asia and the Middle East). In combination, these changes do not necessarily neutralize the still considerable military and economic strengths of the West, or the relevance of its political models and expertise. However, they do require the Euro-Atlantic partners to seek solutions increasingly through global institutions, frameworks and agreements, where other power centres are represented at the table, and non-Western voices are more often decisive.

In such a world, it is not practical for the European–US partnership to retain the same meaning and content, or limit itself to the same methods, as 60 years ago when NATO was created. The relative importance of what Europe and the USA do together in NATO, or even along the bilateral EU–US axis, is bound to be reduced, but there are new openings, too, for them to work jointly or share burdens at global level. It was not easy for the two sides of the Atlantic to maximize these chances while the Bush Administration propounded a vision of global confrontation and unilateral US leadership that most Europeans could not share. President Obama's recognition of US limitations and interest in peaceful accommodation with other powers could correct that or, conversely, could lead to the USA seeking solutions with China (as the 'G2'), with Russia, or with other states that leave the EU on the sidelines. Europe might even see advantage, on some issues including the 'harder' security ones, in being left aside to pursue its own (as yet) more limited interests and ambitions.

These are the basic reasons why this chapter cannot end by celebrating a new dawn in Euro-Atlantic relations. The relationship seems certain to stay less fraught, for some while, than it was during the previous two US presidential terms. Whether it will be closer and more productive depends less on the institutions discussed here, and more on whether, in a multipolar future, the two parties will see more benefit in togetherness or in freedom to play the field.

Part II. Military spending and armaments, 2009

Chapter 5. Military expenditure

Chapter 6. Arms production

Chapter 7. International arms transfers

Chapter 8. World nuclear forces

5. Military expenditure

SAM PERLO-FREEMAN, OLAWALE ISMAIL AND CARINA SOLMIRANO

I. Introduction

World military expenditure rose in 2009, reaching an estimated $1531 billion, an increase of 5.9 per cent in real terms compared with 2008, and 49 per cent higher than in 2000.[1] This represents approximately 2.7 per cent of global gross domestic product (GDP)—the 'military burden'—or $224 per person.[2] The sharp increase in the military burden—from 2.4 per cent of GDP in 2008—is due to the increase in real military spending, the fall in global GDP and an increase in the value of the US dollar, which magnifies the impact of the high US military burden on the global figure.[3]

Almost all regions and subregions shared in the global increase (see figure 5.1). Over half of the real-terms increase came from the United States, but such major spenders as Brazil, China and India also made large increases, reflecting their continued economic growth and aspirations for global and regional influence.

The global financial crisis and economic recession have not led to a general fall in military spending, despite the resulting falls in government revenues and increases in deficits. While military spending has not been a major component of the one-off economic stimulus packages that most developed countries and other large economies have used to counteract the effects of the recession, it has not usually been cut either.[4] Of the 120 countries for which data is available, 65 per cent increased military spending in 2009, including 16 of the Group of 20 (G20) leading developed and developing economies.[5] However, some smaller economies that are less able to sustain high deficits have cut military spending.

---

[1] Except where otherwise stated, all US dollar figures for 2009 are at current (2009) prices and exchange rates, while all percentage changes are in real terms, calculated using constant 2008 prices and exchange rates. The change of base year for constant dollar calculations to 2008 from 2005 (as used in *SIPRI Yearbook 2009*) has led to substantial changes in the constant dollar figures, due to both inflation and the change of the value of the dollar against other currencies.

[2] See appendix 5A.

[3] The International Monetary Fund forecasts a fall in global output of 1.1% in 2009. International Monetary Fund, World Economic Outlook database, Oct. 2009, <http://www.imf.org/external/ns/cs.aspx?id=28>.

[4] For a survey of these stimulus packages see chapter 6, section IV, in this volume.

[5] The G20 is made up of representatives of 19 states—Argentina, Australia, Brazil, Canada, China, France, Germany, India, Indonesia, Italy, Japan, South Korea, Mexico, Russia, Saudi Arabia, South Africa, Turkey, the UK and the USA—and the European Union. Of the 19 states, only Argentina, Indonesia and Italy did not increase their military spending.

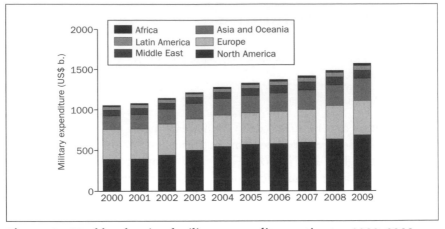

Figure 5.1. World and regional military expenditure estimates, 2000–2009

Figures are in US$ b., at constant (2008) prices and exchange rates.

Source: Appendix 5A, table 5A.1.

Sections II–VII of this chapter survey regional trends in military spending in Africa, Latin America, the Middle East, Asia and Oceania, Europe, and North America, respectively. In the first three of these regions, natural resource revenues have played an important role in determining both the levels and the dynamics of military spending in many countries. Although these revenues have often contributed to rapid rises in spending in recent years, in 2009 falls in commodity prices linked to the economic crisis have slowed this trend in some cases. The conflict in Afghanistan has created increasing costs for the European and North American countries with a major troop presence there. Meanwhile both Afghanistan and Iraq illustrate the difficulties of rebuilding and sustaining a country's armed forces from scratch following invasion, in particular when external military aid is reduced. Section VIII concludes.

Appendix 5A contains comprehensive data on military spending in 2000–2009, including information on world and regional trends, the major spenders, and tables of data for 165 countries, along with the sources and methods used to produce this data. Appendix 5B presents statistics on the reporting by governments of their military spending to SIPRI and the United Nations.

II. Africa

Military expenditure in Africa is estimated to have been $27.4 billion in 2009, an increase of 6.5 per cent in real terms compared to 2008. The increase, continuing the trend of the past decade, has been underpinned by a combination of ongoing military modernization programmes, counter-terrorism measures, internal security challenges and economic growth, fuelled especially by increased oil and gas production and prices. Many established major spenders in Africa (e.g. Algeria, Angola, Nigeria, Libya and Sudan) and emerging mid-level spenders (e.g. Chad) have huge endowments of energy resources.

Over the past decade, the expansion in the global economy has sustained high demand and high prices for oil and gas, providing increased income and investment for energy-rich countries in Africa, which have helped to shape the level and dynamics of their military expenditure. Oil extraction can also be a source of conflict, and the need to secure production often becomes a rationale for military spending.[6] High oil demand has also heightened the strategic importance of African countries to countries and corporations outside the region, with whom most African energy producers have reached military accords that have facilitated major procurement programmes. The examples of Angola, Chad and Nigeria show how revenues from oil are influencing military spending in all corners of Africa.

Angola's military spending reached 251 billion kwanzas ($3.2 billion) in 2009, an increase of 19 per cent in real terms since 2008 and of 40 per cent since 2000. Increased oil production and prices have contributed to this rise, coupled with the modernization and reform of Angola's armed forces following the end of the civil war in 2002. Oil production increased from 750 000 barrels per day in 1999 to around 2 million in 2009, and income from oil sales accounted for 83 per cent of government current receipts in 2007.[7]

Chad's military expenditure totalled 206 billion CFA francs (436 million) in 2009. While this is 33 per cent lower in real terms than in 2008, it is almost six times higher than spending in 2005. The changes in military spending can be explained by a burgeoning rebellion—with successive rebel incursions into the capital city of N'Djamena in 2006 and 2008[8]—and fluctuations in state oil revenues—specifically from increased oil output from 2005.[9] Under a 2001 agreement, the Chadian Government agreed to devote a substantial proportion of its oil revenue to poverty reduction in return for the World Bank part-financing construction of the 1070-

---

[6] See e.g. Kaldor, M., Karl, T. L. and Said, Y. (eds), *Oil Wars* (Pluto Press: London, 2007); and Ross, M. L., 'What do we know about natural resources and civil war?' *Journal of Peace Economics*, vol. 41 (2004), <http://dx.doi.org/10.1177/0022343304043773>; and Pronińska, K., 'Energy and security: regional and global dimensions', *SIPRI Yearbook 2007*.

[7] Angolan Ministry of Finance (MOF), *Orçamento Geral do Estado 2007: Balanço Geral da Execução* [State budget 2007: general balance of execution] (MOF: Luanda, Apr. 2007), p. 23.

[8] 'Battle for control of Chad palace', BBC News, 3 Feb. 2008, <http://news.bbc.co.uk/2/hi/7223760.stm>.

[9] Esso Exploration and Production Chad Inc., *Chad/Cameroon Development Project Annual Report 2009*, Project Update no. 27 (Exxon Mobil: [2010]), p. 70.

kilometre Chad–Cameroon oil pipeline.[10] However, Chad failed to comply with key requirements of the agreement, with revenues used to fund military expenditure.[11] In 2008 the World Bank pulled out of the agreement and recalled its loans.[12]

Nigeria

Nigeria in many ways encapsulates the complex relationship between—on the one hand—military expenditure and—on the other—corruption, off-budget spending, armed conflict, revenues from oil and other commodities, and military ties with external powers that may be seen in several other African countries (e.g. Chad and Sudan).[13] In 2008 it was the largest exporter of crude oil in Africa and the 13th largest worldwide, and oil and gas sales accounted for 81 per cent of government revenues.[14] Oil revenues have fuelled high economic growth, which averaged 7.7 per cent annually in 2000–2008, and has contributed to increased military expenditure.[15] Official military spending totalled 224 billion naira ($1.5 billion) in 2009, an increase of 4.0 per cent in real terms since 2008 and of 101 per cent since 2000.

Nigeria's military spending figures are uncertain and are probably significantly underestimated, due to weak budgetary systems and substantial extra-budgetary spending.[16] In particular, the management of Nigeria's oil revenues are surrounded by severe accountability and transparency issues, including several off-budget practices used to finance additional military spending. These practices include the use of proceeds from 'excess crude accounts'—in which any oil revenues above budgeted projections are deposited[17]—and 'security votes' by state governments to provide financial

[10] World Bank, 'The Chad–Cameroon Petroleum Development and Pipeline Project', <http://go. worldbank.org/WBTHSIE6S0>.

[11] International Monetary Fund (IMF), *Chad: Staff Monitored Program*, IMF Country Report no. 09/206 (IMF: Washington, DC, July 2009). Between the beginning of the project and the end of 2009, the government had received $5 billion in royalties and tax from oil exports. Esso Exploration and Production Chad Inc. (note 9), p. 70.

[12] World Bank, 'World Bank statement on Chad–Cameroon Pipeline', Press Release 2009/073/ AFR, 9 Sep. 2008, <http://go.worldbank.org/2XPFIDG260>.

[13] Oyefusi, A., 'Oil-dependence and civil conflict in Nigeria', Working Paper WPS/2007-09, Oxford University, Centre for the Study of African Economies, June 2007, <http://www.csae.ox.ac. uk/workingpapers/wps-list.html>.

[14] World Bank, 'Nigeria: country brief', Sep. 2009, <http://go.worldbank.org/FIIOT240K0>.

[15] International Monetary Fund (IMF), International Finance Statistics, <http://www.imf statistics.org/>.

[16] Omitoogun, W. and Oduntan, T., 'Nigeria', eds W. Omitoogun and E. Hutchful, SIPRI, *Budgeting for the Military Sector in Africa: The Processes and Mechanisms of Control* (Oxford University Press: Oxford, 2006), pp. 169–78.

[17] In particular, the Excess Domestic Crude Account is managed by the state-owned Nigerian National Petroleum Corporation (NNPC) on behalf of the president. See e.g. Shekarau, A. I., 'Israeli arms contract: govt paid 107.5 million euros from crude account', *Daily Trust*, 1 Aug. 2006.

and material support to the military when conducting internal security operations.[18] The latter practice is most common in oil-producing states, which are guaranteed 13 per cent of the revenue from locally produced oil; for example, the governments of Delta, Akwa Ibom and River states are reported to have contributed 15 billion naira ($100 million) to finance the military operations in Gbaramatu, Delta State, on 13 May 2009.[19] The funds provided by these state 'security votes' are neither audited nor transparently disbursed as they are used at the discretion of the state governor and are rarely routed through the national Ministry of Defence (MOD).

Military operations to protect oil production in the Niger Delta have directly driven increases in federal military expenditure. While there has been an upsurge in internal security challenges across Nigeria since 1999, they have been most acute in the oil-rich Niger Delta region, where an insurgency has disrupted oil production. The situation worsened in 2009, with attacks reported to have cut production by 1 million barrels per day in mid-2009.[20]

The high demand for oil and gas has also affected military expenditure through recent and planned arms acquisitions. Increased oil income has funded successive supplementary budgets that have tended to include substantial extra funding for the military.[21] This is due to the strong influence of the military in politics, the insurgency in the Niger Delta region, opportunities for financial corruption and reduced pressure (in response to transnational terrorism) from international aid donors to lower military spending. Since 2000 the Nigerian Government has invested heavily in aerial surveillance systems, attack helicopters and fighter aircraft for the air force; new amphibious craft, including 193 Cobra armoured vehicles for the army; and new patrol boats and forward operating bases for the navy.[22] Some acquisitions have been made using off-budget funds, including direct payments by the presidency or through the state-owned Nigerian National Petroleum Corporation (NNPC), thereby bypassing the MOD, the parliament and the government's own Due Process Office. For example, in 2006 the government made a €107.5 million ($135 million) payment from the

[18] Under Nigeria's constitution, funding and control of the military are the exclusive preserve of the federal government, but state governors also have a role in security provision. Constitution of the Federal Republic of Nigeria 1999, 29 May 1999, <http://www.nigeria-law.org/ConstitutionOfThe FederalRepublicOfNigeria.htm>, Article 4.

[19] Ganagana, M., 'Governors, JTF may scuttle amnesty', *Sunday Sun*, 19 July 2009; Abbah, T., 'FG sinks N3.2 trillion into Niger Delta', *Sunday Trust*, 9 Aug. 2009; and Constitution of the Federal Republic of Nigeria 1999 (note 18), Article 162.

[20] E.g. Oredein, O, 'Attacks cripple Shell's Niger Delta operations', *Wall Street Journal*, 19 July 2009.

[21] E.g. Folasade-Koyi, A., 'Senate approves N102.2bn supplementary budget', *Daily Independent*, 31 July 2009.

[22] Bergen Risk Solutions, *Niger Delta Maritime Security*, Quarterly Review vol. 1, no. 1 (Bergen Risk Solutions: Bergen, July 2007); and SIPRI Arms Transfers Database, <http://www.sipri.org/ databases/armstransfers/>.

Domestic Crude Account to the Israeli company Aeronautics for the supply of air surveillance weapons.[23] The high price of oil has also led to an increase in the trade in stolen crude oil in the Niger Delta region, with illegal armed groups using proceeds to acquire arms.[24]

Oil also appears to be shaping Nigeria's military relationships with other countries; interest in Nigeria's resources seems to have led to strengthened military ties and enhanced military cooperation packages with China in particular. China has bid for up to 6 billion barrels of Nigerian oil and has sought oil licensing concessions in exchange for infrastructural developments, while simultaneously emerging as a major supplier of Nigeria's military acquisitions, including F-7NI combat aircraft and munitions.[25] The emergence of China in the military expenditure–oil nexus in Nigeria may reflect its speedier responses to demand and their lower emphasis on human rights concerns when making arms sales.[26]

Nigeria's increased oil income has generated economic growth, but has also created a vicious cycle of increased revenues lacking in transparency, increased strategic importance of oil infrastructure, increased grievances and insurgency, and increased military spending to secure production.

III. Latin America

The effects of the global economic crisis on military spending in Latin America were varied in 2009. The crisis slowed previously high economic growth rates and reduced exports—the region's GDP was projected to fall by 1.8 per cent and exports by 23 per cent in 2009[27]—which affected state revenues, in particular in countries reliant on commodity exports. However, Latin America was less affected by the crisis than had been expected, largely due to a combination of current account surpluses, remittances from outside the region and expansionary fiscal policies.[28]

In Central America and the Caribbean, military spending rose by 9.7 per cent in real terms to reach $5.6 billion in 2009. In Mexico, the militarization of the response to drug-related violence led to an increase of military expenditure of 11 per cent in real terms compared to 2008.[29] The budget of

---

[23] Shekarau (note 17).

[24] Davis, S., *The Potential for Peace and Reconciliation in the Niger Delta* (Coventry Cathedral: Coventry, Feb. 2009), pp. 151–70.

[25] 'Nigeria spends $251m for Chinese F-7 fighters after oil deals', *Defense Industry Daily*, 30 Sep. 2005, <http://www.defenseindustrydaily.com/nigeria-spends-251m-for-chinese-f7-fighters-after-oil-deals-01269/>.

[26] Mahtani, D., 'Nigeria shifts to China arms', *Financial Times*, 28 Feb. 2006.

[27] Economic Commission for Latin America and the Caribbean (ECLAC), *Preliminary Overview of the Economies of Latin America and the Caribbean*, Briefing Paper (ECLAC: Santiago, Dec. 2009), pp. 7, 15.

[28] Economic Commission for Latin America and the Caribbean (note 27), p. 14.

[29] On the drug-related criminal violence in Mexico see chapter 2, section IV, in this volume.

the Mexican Navy, which has been key in intercepting drugs and arms shipments to the USA, was increased by 20 per cent to cover the costs of personnel increases and equipment acquisitions.[30]

The recent trend of increasing military expenditure in South America continued in 2009: military spending in the region reached $51.8 billion, an increase of 7.6 per cent in real terms compared to 2008. Brazil and Colombia, the biggest spenders in the region, increased their military spending by 16 per cent and 11 per cent in real terms, respectively. However, Chile and Venezuela, two other big spenders that both have a high dependence on commodity exports, cut their military budgets.

Chile

Largely because of a fall in copper prices, Chile's military spending decreased by 5 per cent in 2009 compared to 2008, following an increase of 56 per cent in the period 2000–2008. Under the 1958 Restricted Law on Copper, the Chilean armed forces automatically receive 10 per cent of copper revenues to help finance arms acquisitions.[31] Between 1990 and 2007, the state-owned copper company Corporacion Nacional del Cobre (CODELCO, National Copper Corporation) is reported to have transferred $7.4 billion to the military, amounting to 21 per cent of the country's military budget.[32] However, in the first nine months of 2009, CODELCO transferred $650 million to the military, 37 per cent less than in the same period in 2008.[33]

Funding the Chilean military with off-budget revenues from a state-owned company is controversial. The off-budget nature of the funds has raised concerns in recent years, including accusations that military officers have received illegal commissions from arms deals.[34] In September 2009 President Michelle Bachelet announced a proposal to repeal the 1958 law. Under the proposal, allocations for arms procurement will be made on a yearly basis as part of the national budget; there will be a 12-year strategic plan for long-term procurement, revisable every four years by the president; and the unspent funds received under the 1958 law will be used to

[30] 'El presupuesto de la Armada mexicana aumentará un 20% en 2008 [*sic*]' [The Mexican Navy's budget will increase by 20% in 2008], Infodefensa.com, 27 Dec. 2008, <http://infodefensa.com/lamerica/noticias/noticias.asp?cod=994>.

[31] Ley Reservada del Cobre [Restricted Law on Copper], Law no. 13.196 of 29 Oct. 1958 (most recently modified in 1987), unpublished.

[32] Gastine, A., 'CODELCO CEO questions Copper Law', *Santiago Times*, 25 June 2008.

[33] CODELCO, 'Profits through September: Codelco earned more than US$2 billion thanks to record production', 30 Oct. 2009, <http://www.codelco.cl/english/prensa/archivo/fr_prensa_archivo2009.html>; and CODELCO, 'Codelco obtains pre-tax profit of US$4.864 billion through 30 September 2008', 3 Nov. 2008, <http://www.codelco.cl/english/prensa/archivo/fr_prensa_archivo2008.html>.

[34] Bonnefoy, P., 'Chile reconsiders military expenditure provision', *Global Post*, 21 Mar. 2009.

create a contingency fund for the replacement or refurbishment of equipment.[35]

The aim of the proposed funding system is to match future military acquisitions to the security priorities of Chile. Under the current system, arms may be acquired in part because of the availability of funds rather than for clear security needs. Ending automatic military funding from copper revenues would improve transparency in Ministry of Defence finances and ensure that the whole military budget falls within parliamentary oversight, thus allowing proper scrutiny of defence issues.[36] By early 2010 the proposed law was in discussion in the Defence Committee of the Chilean Chamber of Deputies.

Venezuela

Venezuela's actual military expenditure has consistently exceeded the initial budget in recent years.[37] Thus, although the country's budgeted military spending of 9.0 billion bolívares ($4.2 billion) in 2009 would represent a decrease of 25 per cent over 2008—the largest fall in Latin America—the drop may not be realized.

As oil revenues make up almost 50 per cent of Venezuela's revenue, high oil prices have allowed the Venezuelan Government to increase its financial reserves, undertake large-scale social programmes and cushion the impact of the global economic crisis on the country.[38] Oil revenues and economic growth have permitted Venezuela to increase military expenditure by 136 per cent in real terms between 2003 and 2008.

This long-term increase in Venezuela's military spending is connected to a far-reaching modernization and restructuring of the country's armed forces. In 2009 the government continued implementation of a 2005 military doctrine which aims to modernize military equipment, improve civil–military links and increase civilian participation in the defence of the country.[39] In March 2009 the Ministry of Defence was restructured, including the appointment of a vice-minister of defence education, responsible for training military personnel, and a vice-minister of services, in charge of providing logistical support to the armed forces.[40] In July a new River

[35] Higuera, J., 'Chile submits draft for procurement funding reform', *Jane's Defence Weekly*, 7 Oct. 2009, p. 11.

[36] 'Chile derogaría ley de cobre que financia compra de armas' [Chile would eliminate copper law that funds arms imports], *El Comercio* (Lima), 9 Sep. 2009.

[37] Actual spending in 2008 was 9.3 billion bolívares ($4.3 billion), 30% more than the approved budget of 7.1 billion bolívares ($3.3 billion).

[38] By 2008 Venezuela is reported to have accumulated more than $40 billion in foreign reserves. 'Venezuela: oil prices increases sustainability fears', *New York Times*, 2 Feb. 2009.

[39] Stålenheim, P. et al., 'Military expenditure', *SIPRI Yearbook 2006*, pp. 314–15.

[40] 'Chávez modifica la estructura de su Ministerio de Defensa' [Chávez modifies the structure of the Ministry of Defence], Infodefensa.com, 20 Mar. 2009, <http://infodefensa.com/lamerica/

Squadron was activated and reserve units were upgraded to combat battalions. The government also decided to double the number of armoured
battalions and secured a $2.2 billion loan from Russia to buy tanks and anti-
aircraft systems.[41] Although Venezuela's use of a loan to purchase arms
may seem strange given its large oil reserve funds, the terms of the loan are
obscure and the advantages to Venezuela are therefore unclear.

Two new laws were passed in 2009 aimed at increasing civilian involvement in the military, one of the pillars of Venezuela's defence strategy. The
first, on the military draft and recruitment, made military service compulsory for Venezuelan men and women between the ages of 18 and 60.[42]
The second established the Bolivarian National Militia as a full component
of Venezuela's military. The militia, whose main mission is to assist with
territorial defence, will contain civilians, or 'citizen-soldiers', who register
to receive military training.[43] It will be under the operational command of
the president but the administrative responsibility of the MOD.[44]

Although the decision to create the militia dates back to 2005, it is not
coincidental that the announcement came shortly after Colombia and the
USA approved an agreement on military bases in October 2009.[45] Venezuela has denounced the agreement—which grants the USA access to seven
military bases in Colombia—as US interference in regional affairs, height-
ening the tensions that have prevailed between Colombia and Venezuela
since 2008.[46] Given the current relationship with Colombia, Venezuela's

noticias/noticias.asp?cod–1262>; and Decreto no. 6.628 mediante el cual se dicta el Reglamento
Orgánico del Ministerio del Poder Popular para la Defensa [Decree no. 6628 dictating the Organic
Regulations of the Ministry of People's Power for Defence], 12 Mar. 2009, *Gaceta Oficial de la Repub-
lica Bolivariana de Venezuela*, no. 39,137, 12 Mar. 2009.

[41] Guevara, I., 'Venezuela announces latest reorganisation programme', *Jane's Defence Weekly*,
5 Aug. 2009, p. 8; Dickerson, L., 'Venezuelan Army to strengthen tank force', Forecast International,
27 July 2009; and 'Chávez gets USD 2.2 billion loan to buy Russian weapons', *El Universal* (Caracas),
14 Sep. 2009. See also chapter 7, section II, in this volume.

[42] Ley de conscripcion y alistamiento militar [Law on conscription and military recruitment],
Gaceta Oficial de la Republica Bolivariana de Venezuela, extraordinary no. 5933, 21 Oct. 2009, p. 24.

[43] The militia will be composed of 2 units: the 'territorial militia' of general citizens and 'combat-
ant troops' from 'public and private institutions'. Ley de reforma parcial del Decreto no. 6.239 con
rango valor y fuerza de ley orgánica de la Fuerza Armada Nacional Bolivariana [Law for the partial
reform of Decree no. 6239 with the rank value and force of organic law of the Bolivarian National
Armed Forces], *Gaceta Oficial de la Republica Bolivariana de Venezuela*, extraordinary no. 5933,
21 Oct. 2009.

[44] 'Chávez reforma las Fuerzas Armadas y crea la Milicia Bolivariana' [Chávez reforms the Armed
Forces and creates the Bolivarian Militia], Infodefensa.com, 23 Oct. 2009, <http://infodefensa.com/
lamerica/noticias/noticias.asp?cod=1997>.

[45] On the initial militia plans see Stålenheim et al. (note 39); and 'Venezuela: Chávez plans for
"integral defence"', *Latin American Security & Strategic Review*, Feb. 2005.

[46] See e.g. 'UNASUR and the Colombian bases issue', *Latin American Security & Strategic Review*,
Aug. 2009; 'As US–Colombia bases deal is signed, Lula calls for all-round transparency', *Latin
American Security & Strategic Review*, Oct. 2009; and 'Colombia: revelado el texto final del acuerdo
con EE.UU. sobre bases militares', [Colombia: final text of the agreement with the US on military
bases is revealed], Infolatam, 22 Oct. 2009, <http://www.infolatam.com/entrada/colombia_
revelado_el_texto_final_del_acu-16802.html>.

own restructuring of its military and an expected economic recovery, more increases in military expenditure are likely in coming years.

IV. The Middle East

The continuous increase in Middle East military spending since 2002 has levelled off from 2008, with the regional total estimated at $103 billion in 2009. While the global economic crisis may be one factor behind this change, through its effect on the price of oil, the impact on the region has been mixed.

The crisis certainly affected revenues of oil-producing countries in the Middle East, as oil prices first rose from an average of $92 per barrel in January 2008 to $141 in July before falling to $33 in December; members of the Gulf Cooperation Council (GCC) suffered the most.[47] Some governments were able to mitigate the effects by implementing countercyclical measures, such as the use of international reserves and increased spending.[48] As oil prices have stabilized at around $70 per barrel since August 2009, it is expected that the incomes of oil exporting countries in the region will grow once more in 2010.[49]

The 2009 military budgets of some of the biggest oil-producing countries declined sharply as they were based on the lower oil prices of 2008. For example, Iraq's military spending fell by 28 per cent in real terms (see below) and Oman's by 13 per cent. In contrast, Saudi Arabia—the world's second-largest oil producer—increased its military expenditure by 2.7 per cent in real terms, to 155 billion riyals ($41.3 billion) in 2009 or 33 per cent of its total national budget. Despite a decline of 9 per cent in estimated government revenues in 2009, the Saudi Government increased total expenditure by 16 per cent, creating an estimated budget deficit of 65 billion riyals ($17.3 billion), its first such deficit since 2004.[50]

Iraq[51]

As a result of the fall in oil prices, Iraq's 2009 budget for the Ministry of Defence decreased by 28 per cent in 2009 in real terms to 4863 billion

[47] Organization of the Petroleum Exporting Countries (OPEC), *World Oil Outlook 2009* (OPEC Secretariat: Vienna, 2009), p. 23; and International Monetary Fund (IMF), *Regional Economic Outlook: Middle East and Central Asia* (IMF: Washington, DC, Oct. 2009), p. 6. The GCC members are Bahrain, Kuwait, Oman, Qatar, Saudi Arabia and the United Arab Emirates.

[48] International Monetary Fund (note 47), p. 6.

[49] International Monetary Fund (note 47), pp. 12, 14.

[50] Saudi Arabian Monetary Authority (SAMA), *Forty Fifth Annual Report: The Latest Economic Developments* (SAMA: Riyadh, July 2009), p. 127; and 'Saudi Arabia's 2009 budget', Jadwa Investment, 23 Dec. 2008, <http://www.jadwa.com/research/pages/economic-research.aspx>.

[51] All conversions of Iraqi dinars to US dollars in this subsection are made at the average exchange rate of the year to which they refer.

dinars ($4.2 billion). The total security budget was 11 332 billion dinars ($9.7 billion) in 2009, including the Ministry of Interior budget of 6469 billion dinars ($5.5 billion), down from 13 196 billion dinars ($11.1 billion) in 2008.[52] The total national budget for 2009 was cut from an originally proposed 89.4 trillion dinars ($79 billion) to 66.3 trillion dinars ($58.6 billion) due to a one-third reduction in oil export prices compared with the original expectations.[53]

According to one report, the MOD had originally estimated that it required a budget of $15 billion; it then requested $9 billion, but it only received $4.2 billion.[54] Paradoxically this budget reduction has come at a time when Iraq is slowly taking over responsibility for its own security. The Ministry of Defence had to cut its hiring quota and limit or cancel some of its planned arms procurement programmes, which may cause further delays in training and equipping the Iraqi security forces (ISF) before the complete withdrawal of US military forces in 2011.[55] The budget cut may also have further implications for the integration of the Sons of Iraq (SOI) local Sunni militias into the ISF, which ground to a halt in 2009. The Iraqi Government is committed to funding the salaries of SOI members, as their integration is widely seen as important to promoting Sunni–Shia reconciliation, but the future extent of the integration programme, and its effect on the budget, remains uncertain.[56]

The USA has also sharply reduced its funding to the Iraqi Government. US contributions to the Iraqi Security Forces Fund (ISFF), which supports the Iraqi defence and interior ministries, totalled $18 billion between 2003 and 2009.[57] However, funding for the ISFF for 2009 was reduced to $1 billion from an initial request of $2.8 billion, itself reduced from an original planned request of $5.1 billion. This reduction was based on the assumption that Iraq would spend $8 billion in 2008 and $11 billion in 2009.[58] More reductions are likely as the USA reduces its presence in Iraq and

---

[52] Federal General Budget Law 2009, approved by the Presidency Council on 2 Apr. 2009, *Official Gazette of the Republic of Iraq*, no. 4117, 13 Apr. 2009 (in Arabic); and US Department of Defense (DOD), *Measuring Stability and Security in Iraq*, Report to Congress (DOD: Washington, DC, Sep. 2009), pp. 11–12. The 2008 figure includes the original and supplementary budgets assigned to the ministries of Defence and Interior. See Perlo-Freeman, S. et al., 'Military expenditure', *SIPRI Yearbook 2009*, p. 206.

[53] International Monetary Fund (IMF), *Iraq: Second Review Under the Stand-by Arrangement and Financing Assurances Review*, IMF Country Report no. 08/383 (IMF: Washington, DC, 3 Dec. 2008), p. 9.

[54] Cordesman, A. H. and Mausner, A., *Withdrawal from Iraq: Assessing the Readiness of Iraqi Security Forces* (Center for Strategic and International Studies: Washington, DC, Aug. 2009), p. 97.

[55] 'Budget of Iraqi security forces strained, PM says', *USA Today*, 10 July 2009; and 'U.S.: Iraq budget shortfall poses security challenge', *USA Today*, 30 Sep. 2009.

[56] US Department of Defense (note 52), p. 24.

[57] US Special Inspector General for Iraq Reconstruction (SIGIR), *Quarterly Report and Semi-annual Report to the United States Congress* (SIGIR: Arlington, VA, 30 Jan. 2010), pp. 20–22.

[58] Cordesman and Mausner (note 54), p. 96.

refocuses its attention on Afghanistan, where it continues to fund the expansion of the Afghan National Army (ANA; see section V below).

Iraq's budget reduction—as well as structural and organizational issues such as budget execution problems, deficiencies in funding plans and inadequate decision-making processes[59]—is likely to have an impact on the ability of the ISF to maintain security in the country. While violence has decreased and security incidents are at their lowest levels in more than five years, sectarian violence and insurgent attacks have continued to cause heavy casualties.[60] In June 2009 Iraqi security forces assumed responsibility for the security of Iraqi cities, villages and localities. They will assume further responsibility at the end of August 2010, when the mission of the United States Force–Iraq will change from combat to providing training and support to the ISF, in line with the 2008 Status of Forces Agreement between Iraq and the USA.[61]

Although Iraq has been updating its military equipment in recent years, the planned improvements of its land and air capabilities are far from completed. The cuts in military expenditure may affect future orders of military equipment for the ISF and plans to create a 6000-strong air force. An outdated and under-equipped ISF could have negative consequences for the country's future stability, and may hamper the country's ability to take full responsibility for its security following the scheduled withdrawal of US troops.[62] Given the resources and time needed to equip and train a new air force, these problems will be particularly acute for the Iraqi Air Force, which is expected to take over control of Iraqi air space from 2012.

The decrease in Iraq's military budget could be reversed in 2010, depending on oil production levels and prices. Even so, with oil revenues contributing 99 per cent of Iraq's total central government revenues, this creates difficulty in assuring a predictable level of long-term funding. A further problem is the poor levels of budget execution which affect all areas of government expenditure.[63] The challenges ahead for Iraq illustrate the difficulties of rebuilding the military after conflict as well as those of sustaining post-conflict security over the longer term.

[59] US Department of Defense (note 52), p. 53. See also Cordesman and Mausner (note 54).

[60] US Department of Defense (note 52), p. 22.

[61] US Government Accountability Office (GAO), *Operation Iraqi Freedom: Preliminary Observations on DOD Planning for the Drawdown of U.S. Forces from Iraq*, GAO-10-179 (GAO: Washington, DC, 2 Nov. 2009), p. 1; and Iraq–USA Agreement on the withdrawal of United States forces from Iraq and the organization of their activities during their temporary presence in Iraq, signed 17 Nov. 2008, entered into force 1 Jan. 2009, <http://georgewbush-whitehouse.archives.gov/news/releases/2008/11/20081127-2.html>. Until 1 Jan. 2010 the United States Force–Iraq was known as the Multi-National Force–Iraq.

[62] Gelfand, L. and D. Wasserbly, 'US accelerates Iraq withdrawal', *Jane's Defence Weekly*, 7 Oct. 2009, p. 18; and Darling, D., 'Iraqi budgetary issues hinder equipment outfitting of security forces', Forecast International, 2 Oct. 2009. On Iraq's recent and upcoming arms acquisitions see chapter 7, section V, in this volume.

[63] Cordesman and Mausner (note 54), pp. 98–102.

V. Asia and Oceania

Military expenditure in Asia and Oceania increased by 8.9 per cent in real terms in 2009, to reach $276 billion, with increases in all subregions.

China is the biggest military spender in the region: its expenditure of 686 billion yuan ($100 billion) in 2009 was 15 per cent higher in real terms than in 2008. China's absolute real-terms increase was almost equal to the total regional increase.[64] The Chinese Government's official budget report describes the purposes of increased spending as being to improve the living conditions and benefits of troops; to continue to develop the use of information and communications technology within the armed forces (what is usually called 'network-centric warfare' in the West and 'informationized warfare' in China); to improve equipment and support facilities; to improve disaster-relief capabilities; and to rebuild infrastructure following the 2008 Sichuan earthquake.[65]

India's military expenditure totalled 1851 billion rupees ($36.3 billion) in 2009, an increase of 13 per cent in real terms over 2008. India's military spending has risen by 67 per cent since 2000. This increase has been pushed by the country's economic growth and rise as a regional power but also by the growth of China—its main regional competitor[66]—the continuing conflict with Pakistan and, increasingly in recent years, the rising threat of terrorism. India plans to spend at least $30 billion by 2012 on military modernization, although this may be affected by continuing delays in procurement processes.[67]

Kazakhstan was the only country in Central Asia for which 2009 military expenditure data is available. Although its spending was unchanged in real terms in 2009, at 199 billion tenge ($1.3 billion), since 2000 it has increased by 360 per cent—enabled by rapid economic growth due in part to oil and gas revenues—as the country has sought to modernize its armed forces. Kazakhstan is seeking to create a 'mobile, professional [military] force' able to undertake a range of missions, focused on what the country's 2007 military doctrine identifies as cross-border threats of terrorism, arms and drugs smuggling, and illegal migration.[68]

---

[64] The official defence budget does not cover the whole of Chinese military expenditure. The figures given here for China are SIPRI estimates, which are c. 45% higher than the official budget. For the basis of SIPRI's estimates, which have been revised in 2010, see appendix 5A, section II.

[65] Chinese Ministry of Finance, 'Report on the implementation of the central and local budgets for 2008 and on the draft central and local budgets for 2009', 5 Mar. 2009, <http://www.gov.cn/english/2009-03/15/content_1259811.htm>.

[66] Indian Ministry of Defence (MOD), *Annual Report 2008–09* (MOD: New Delhi, 2009), pp. 5–6.

[67] Matthews, N., 'Acquisition plans aimed at raising India's capabilities', *Defense Technology International*, Jan. 2009, p. 40.

[68] Hodge, N., 'Kazakhstan identifies modernisation plans', *Jane's Defence Weekly*, 25 Apr. 2007, p. 31.

Military expenditure in Australia increased by 8.5 per cent in real terms in 2009, to reach 25.7 billion Australian dollars ($19.0 billion). Following a major restructuring of its defence policy, as reflected in its 2009 defence white paper, Australia plans to increase its military spending by 3 per cent annually up to 2018, and then by 2.2 per cent each year until 2030.[69] The white paper also sets out plans to acquire military equipment worth $52 billion over 20 years.[70] These acquisitions reflect an expected change in the military situation in the Asia–Pacific region, in which the USA would decrease its current engagements and China would continue to grow in power.[71]

Afghanistan

Military expenditure in Afghanistan cannot be separated from the ongoing conflict in the country, the role played by the USA and other international forces, and military aid from the USA.[72] Like Iraq, Afghanistan faces challenges to rebuild its army from scratch and to sustain, over the long term, a military capable of securing the state. Unlike Iraq, Afghanistan has no oil revenues, and so has a much smaller budget than Iraq. Although this means that the budget is not subject to fluctuations in oil prices, Afghanistan's revenues cannot pay for the country's reconstruction, including the army.

Afghanistan's military spending has increased steadily, at an average annual rate of 7.5 per cent since 2003, when the Afghan National Army started to increase its size. In 2009 military expenditure totalled 12.8 billion afghanis ($250 million), an increase of 19 per cent in real terms over 2008 and of 55 per cent since 2003. The 2009 increase is driven by the decision in 2008—encouraged by the USA and the North Atlantic Treaty Organization (NATO)—to further increase the size of the ANA from 80 000 to 134 000 troops by 2011.[73] This major increase also reflects the fragile security situation in Afghanistan, which has deteriorated since 2005: the number of attacks by insurgent groups increased from 2388 in 2005 to

[69] Australian Department of Defence (DOD), *Defending Australia in the Asia Pacific Century: Force 2030, Defence White Paper 2009* (DOD: Canberra, 2009), p. 137.

[70] Grevatt, J., 'Australia reveals 20-year Defence White Paper', *Jane's Defence Weekly*, 13 May 2009, p. 5; and Australian Department of Defence (note 69), chapter 9.

[71] 'Australia outlines military plans', BBC News, 2 May 2009, <http://news.bbc.co.uk/2/hi/8030 292.stm>.

[72] On developments in Afghanistan see also chapter 2, section III, and chapter 4, section II, in this volume.

[73] In 2008 the US Administration of President George W. Bush had proposed to increase the ANA to 134 000 personnel by 2010, at a cost of $12 billion. A proposal was also discussed in 2009 by the new US Administration of President Barack Obama to double that number, but a decision has not been taken on this. See Shanker, T. and Schmitt, E., 'US plans vastly expanded Afghan security force', *New York Times*, 18 Mar. 2009.

10 889 in 2008.[74] Between January and August 2009, almost 13 000 attacks were reported, over 2.5 times the number during the same period in 2008.[75]

In 2009 the government reported that security spending—that is, spending by the Defence and Interior ministries—absorbed 47 per cent of Afghanistan's core operating budget. The domestic funding of Afghanistan's military is dwarfed by external military aid: 94 per cent of ANA funding in 2009 came from military aid.[76] Between 2002 and 2009 the USA provided $21 billion to the ANA and the Afghan National Police (ANP)—$14.2 billion for the ANA and $7 billion for the ANP. In 2009 alone it provided $4 billion for the ANA and $1.5 billion for the ANP—almost double the total given in 2008.[77] Funding has been mainly directed at equipping and sustaining the ANA, upgrading garrisons and support facilities, enhancing ANA intelligence capabilities, and expanding education and training.[78] The Afghan Government is committed to funding only the core costs—salary and food—of 70 000 military personnel.[79] Thus, the Afghan Government will remain dependent on external aid for the continued build-up of the ANA.[80]

The attempt to increase the size of the ANA has met some challenges including high illiteracy rates, a low proportion of Pashtun recruits and reluctance by some soldiers to fight fellow Afghans.[81] After months of recruiting objectives being missed, a salary increase in 2009 helped to raise the number of ANA and ANP recruits. The new salary—$240 per month—is intended to compete with the payments offered by the Taliban.[82] In Afghanistan, even more so than in Iraq, if recruitment targets are met, a major concern around the growth of the army is that funding still depends on external donors, especially the USA. Self-reliance for the Afghan military would require expenditure far higher than current national budgetary

[74] US Government Accountability Office (GAO), *Afghanistan: Key Issues for Congressional Oversight*, GAO-09-473SP (GAO: Washington, DC, Apr. 2009), p. 15.

[75] US Government Accountability Office (GAO), *Afghanistan's Security Environment*, GAO-10-178R (GAO: Washington, DC, Nov. 2009), p. 2. On the violence in Afghanistan see chapter 2, section III, in this volume.

[76] Afghan Ministry of Finance (MOF), *1388 National Budget* (MOF: Kabul, 2009), p. 5. Afghanistan's national budget consists of a core operating budget and a core development budget. External donors funded almost all of the development budget and 39–50% of the operating budget over the period 2005–2009.

[77] US Government Accountability Office (note 74), p. 4.

[78] US Department of Defense (DOD), *United States Plan for Sustaining the Afghanistan National Security Forces* (DOD: Washington, DC, June 2008), p. 7.

[79] Afghan Ministry of Finance (note 76), p. 17.

[80] Afghan Ministry of Finance (note 76), p. 28.

[81] Constable, P., 'You have to learn this now', *Washington Post*, 2 Aug. 2009; 'What to watch in the Afghanistan war: training the Afghan Army', *Christian Science Monitor*, 11 Dec. 2009; and Sellin, L., 'Outside view: training the Afghan Army', 5 Jan. 2010, United Press International, <http://www.upi.com/Top_News/2010/01/05/UPI-83911262709907/>.

[82] Kessler, G., 'Pay increase for Afghan troops boosts interest', *Washington Post*, 10 Dec. 2009.

resources allow; Afghan President Hamid Karzai has acknowledged that achieving self-reliance could take 15 years.[83]

VI. Europe

Military expenditure in Europe was $386 billion in 2009, an increase of 2.7 per cent in real terms over 2008. The effect of the global economic crisis on military expenditure in Europe varied. In Western Europe, the recent trend of flat or slightly rising spending was largely unchanged, as governments chose to sustain public spending to boost the economy.[84] However, in Central and Eastern Europe—where in may cases the crisis has struck economies harder and where governments' had insufficient reserves and levels of credit-worthiness to maintain large deficits—a number of countries made significant cuts to military spending as a direct result of the crisis, including Bulgaria, Croatia, Estonia, Lithuania, Romania, Serbia, Slovakia and Ukraine.[85] Some of the richer Central European countries—the Czech Republic, Hungary and Poland—increased spending.

Meanwhile, Russia was forced to produce a revised budget in mid-2009 with substantial cuts to initial spending plans, leading to its smallest real-terms rise in military spending in a decade.[86] Nonetheless, President Dmitry Medvedev and Prime Minister Vladimir Putin emphasized that, because of the high priority given by the government to modernizing the Russian arms industry and military, the State Defence Order—which covers all equipment and supplies procured for the security forces—would be maintained.[87]

---

[83] 'Afghanistan "unable to pay for troops for 15 years"', BBC News, 8 Dec. 2009, <http://news.bbc.co.uk/2/hi/8400806.stm>; and Byrd, W., 'Financing, oversight critical for Afghanistan army, police', End Poverty in South Asia blog, World Bank, 2 Apr. 2009, <http://blogs.worldbank.org/endpoverty insouthasia/financing-oversight-critical-afghanistans-army-police>.

[84] France and Germany even included modest amount of military spending in their stimulus packages. See chapter 6, section IV, in this volume.

[85] 'Economic woes hurt SE Europe defense budgets', Agence France-Presse, 21 Oct. 2009, <http://www.defensenews.com/story.php?i=4335014>; Višnar, F., 'I vojska mora štedjeti' [The army also has to economize], Vjesnik, 5 Mar. 2009; Cowan, G., 'Estonia cuts defence budget in economic downturn', Jane's Defence Industry, 17 Feb. 2009; Holdanowicz, G., 'Lithuania slashes defence budget', Jane's Defence Industry, 10 Feb. 2009; 'Serbian Defence Ministry to cut spending, minister says', Radio B92, 7 Apr. 2009, Transcript, World News Connection; Kominek, J., 'Slovakia faces hard choices after 10% budget cut', Jane's Defence Weekly, 8 Apr. 2009, p. 12; and Petrov, V., 'Defence budget shortfall will lead to cuts, says Ukrainian MoD', Jane's Defence Industry, 24 Feb. 2009.

[86] Cooper, J., 'Military expenditure in the Russian Federation, 2007–2009: a research note', n.d., <http://www.sipri.org/research/armaments/milex/publications/unpubl_milex>.

[87] Cooper (note 86); and 'Volume of the State Defense Order in 2009 will remain on preplanned level of 1.3 trillion rubles', ARMS-TASS, 2 June 2009, Translation from Russian, World News Connection.

Spending on the conflict in Afghanistan

One factor in the military expenditure decisions of numerous European countries is their participation in NATO's International Security Assistance Force (ISAF) in Afghanistan.[88] This creates direct operational costs and raises strategic questions about procurement priorities, a dilemma sharpened by the strain on budgets caused by the global economic crisis. This is most acute for the United Kingdom, which has the largest European force in Afghanistan and which is most directly involved in combat operations (see below), but similar debates have arisen in other countries.[89] In particular, the UK's present focus on major naval and air platforms and systems—aimed at maintaining or increasing global power-projection capabilities—has been called into question. Some commentators, including senior military figures, have argued that more emphasis should be placed on equipment designed to support large numbers of troops engaged in the type of low-intensity, asymmetric warfare seen in Afghanistan. This includes military vehicles, body armour, unmanned aerial vehicles (UAVs), helicopters, and equipment for communications, intelligence, surveillance and reconnaissance.[90]

At the end of 2009 the UK had 9500 troops in Afghanistan, followed by Germany (4280), France (3750) and Italy (3150).[91] For most countries, the cost of these deployments represents a relatively small share of their overall military spending. Germany budgeted €570 million ($792 million) for operations in Afghanistan in 2009, and France €330 million ($458 million), while Italy budgeted €242 million ($336 million) for the first 6 months of 2009.[92] For Germany this represents 1.7 per cent of total military spending and for France less than 1 per cent, while for Italy the implied annual cost is

---

[88] European countries covered by the SIPRI Military Expenditure Database that did not participate in ISAF are Belarus, Cyprus, Malta, Moldova, Montenegro, Russia, Serbia and Switzerland. For a list of countries that contributed troops to ISAF in 2009 see appendix 3A, table 3A.2, in this volume. See also North Atlantic Treaty Organization, 'International Security Assistance Force and Afghan National Army strength & laydown', 22 Dec. 2009, <http://www.isaf.nato.int/en/isaf-place mat-archives.html>.

[89] E.g. on the debate in France see Withington, T., 'France's Afghan dilemmas', ISN Security Watch, 9 Feb. 2009, <http://www.isn.ethz.ch/isn/Current-Affairs/Security-Watch/Detail/?lng=en& id=96200>.

[90] E.g. Richards, D. (Gen.), Chief of the General Staff, 'Future conflict and its prevention: people and the information age', Speech, International Institute For Strategic Studies, London, 18 Jan. 2010, <http://www.iiss.org/recent-key-addresses/general-sir-david-richards-address/>.

[91] North Atlantic Treaty Organization (note 88). The USA had 45 780 troops in Afghanistan.

[92] 'Bundeswehr-Einsatz verteuert sich massiv' [Bundeswehr use expands massively], Der Spiegel, 25 Nov. 2009; French Senate, Avis présenté au nom de la commission des affaires étrangères, de la défense et des forces armées (1) sur le projet de loi de finances pour 2010, adopté par l'Assemblée Nationale [Notices submitted on behalf of the Committee on Foreign Affairs, Defence and Armed Forces (1) on the budget bill for 2010 passed by the National Assembly], vol. 4, Défense: Préparation et emploi des forces [Defence: preparation and use of forces] (French Senate: Paris, 19 Nov. 2009), p. 31; and Valpolini, P. and Pape, A., 'The Italian balancing job', Jane's Defence Weekly, 1 July 2009, pp. 22–27.

Table 5.1. British expenditure and troop numbers in Afghanistan, 2003–2009

Year	2003	2004	2005	2006	2007	2008	2009	Total, 2003–2009
Expenditure on Afghanistan (£ m.)[a]	46	67	199	738	1 504	2 623	3 495	8 672
Total military expenditure (£ m.)[a]	29 338	29 524	30 603	31 454	33 486	36 431	37 784	
Troops deployed in Afghanistan[b]	267	580	461	5 200	7 753	8 750	9 500	

[a] Expenditure figures are for the financial year from April of the given year to March of the following year.

[b] Troops deployed figures are the numbers deployed at the end of the calendar year.

Sources: UK Defence Statistics <http://www.dasa.mod.uk/>; British House of Commons, Defence Committee, *Ministry of Defence Main Estimates 2009–10*, 9th Report of Session 2008–09, HC 773 (The Stationery Office: London, 2 July 2009); SIPRI Multilateral Peace Operations Database, <http://www.sipri.org/databases/pko/>; North Atlantic Treaty Organization, 'International Security Assistance Force and Afghan National Army strength & laydown', 22 Dec. 2009, <http://www.isaf.nato.int/en/isaf-placemat-archives.html>.

1.8 per cent of total military spending. The costs are much more significant for the UK, which budgeted £3.5 billion ($5.4 billion) for Afghanistan operations for the 2009/10 financial year, 9.2 per cent of total military spending. British spending on Afghanistan has increased exponentially from just £46 million ($75 million) in 2003/2004, especially since the deployment of forces in the Taliban stronghold of Helmand in 2006 (see table 5.1).

The United Kingdom

The cost of the conflict in Afghanistan is one of several factors putting heavy strain on the British military budget. While some war-related purchases are funded from the Treasury's contingency fund, new equipment purchases for use in Afghanistan, such as the 22 Chinook helicopters ordered in 2009, come from the main Ministry of Defence budget and are expected to lead to cuts in personnel and equipment elsewhere.[93] Moreover, the British Government has faced criticism—including, tacitly, from the military—that British forces in Afghanistan are under-equipped, which has created pressure to devote more resources there.[94]

In addition to the financial pressure caused by the ongoing conflict in Afghanistan, military spending is likely to be cut in coming years, along

[93] 'Cuts made to boost UK Afghan mission', BBC News, 15 Dec. 2009, <http://news.bbc.co.uk/2/hi/8413135.stm>.

[94] Ritchie, A., 'British MPs set to challenge Brown on Afghanistan', Agence France-Presse, 16 July 2009, <http://www.defensenews.com/story.php?i=4190239>.

with other areas of spending, in order to reduce the UK's soaring budget deficit caused by the economic crisis. The deficit for 2009/10 is estimated at £178 billion ($277 billion).[95] This will be true whoever takes power after the May 2010 general election—both the Labour and Conservative parties have promised to hold a strategic defence review.[96]

Furthermore, two major reports have exposed a 'black hole' in the UK's military finances caused by an equipment programme whose cost over the coming decade exceeds even high-end projections of military spending. This programme includes aircraft carriers, a replacement for the Trident nuclear weapon system, nuclear-powered submarines, a new generation of surface combatants, F-35 (Joint Strike Fighter) combat aircraft, A400M transport aircraft, a third tranche of Typhoon combat aircraft, military vehicles, UAVs and communications systems. A review of acquisition for the MOD (the Gray Review), published in October 2009, found that the MOD had 'a substantially overheated equipment programme, with too many types of equipment being ordered for too large a range of tasks' and that the programme 'is unaffordable on any likely projection of future budgets'.[97] The National Audit Office Major Projects Report for 2009 agreed. It found that, if the military budget were to increase by 2.7 per cent (in absolute terms) from 2011, the gap between the cost of the equipment programme and available resources would be £6 billion ($9.3 billion) over the subsequent 10 years, while with a constant budget (and a real-terms decrease), the gap would rise to £36 billion ($56 billion).[98]

The Gray Review identified a range of systemic failings in the equipment planning and acquisition system. It concluded that no clear responsibility exists to ensure that plans match available resources. Individual services have an incentive to bid as high as possible for themselves and to underestimate likely costs in order to maximize the chance of their programme being approved. This tendency is reinforced by the government's extreme reluctance to cancel programmes once initiated. Instead, budgetary shortfalls have been dealt with by extending programme schedules, which saves money in the short term but costs more in the long term.

---

[95] British Treasury, *Securing the Recovery: Growth and Opportunity—Pre-Budget Report 2009*, Cm 7747 (Her Majesty's Stationery Office: London, 9 Dec. 2009).

[96] British Ministry of Defence, 'Strategic Defence Review outlines', Press release, 7 July 2009, <http://www.mod.uk/DefenceInternet/DefenceNews/DefencePolicyAndBusiness/StrategicDefence ReviewOutlined.htm>; and 'Tories plan early defence review', BBC News, 16 Sep. 2009, <http://news.bbc.co.uk/2/hi/8258719.stm>.

[97] Gray, B., *Review of Acquisition for the Secretary of State for Defence*, Independent report (Bernard Gray: Oct. 2009), p. 6.

[98] British National Audit Office, *Ministry of Defence: The Major Projects Report 2009*, HC85-I, Session 2009–2010 (The Stationery Office: London, 15 Dec. 2009), p. 22.

VII. North America

The conflict in Afghanistan has also been causing a growth in costs in both Canada and the USA.

Canada's military expenditure reached 22.3 billion Canadian dollars ($19.2 billion) in 2009, an increase of 6.6 per cent in real terms over 2008, and of 49 per cent compared to 2000. Afghanistan accounted for a significant share of this increase. Canada had 2830 troops stationed in Afghanistan as of the end of 2009.[99] Unlike the USA, Canada does not make specific war appropriations; however, information on war costs is available in annual Department of National Defence (DOND) performance reports.[100] The Canadian Government has estimated that the total 'incremental costs' (i.e. costs that would not have been incurred were it not for the conflict) of the Afghanistan mission would total 11.3 billion Canadian dollars ($9.9 billion) by the time when Canadian forces are due to leave in 2011; 9 billion Canadian dollars ($7.9 billion) of this is for the DOND.[101] Incremental costs include equipment destroyed and capital equipment procured specifically for Afghanistan and not returned to Canada, but it has been argued that some purchases are not accounted for, including tanks, artillery and armoured vehicles worth over 2 billion Canadian dollars ($1.75 billion), which, while having uses beyond Afghanistan, were bought primarily for use there.[102] The long-term costs of veteran care are also not included (as in the USA).

The United States

The US Administration of President Barack Obama made its first defence budget request in 2009, for financial year (FY) 2010, representing a refocusing of US military spending, albeit not a major strategic shift.[103] The economic crisis has not been a significant factor in US military spending—like other major Western economies, the US Government has sought to provide a fiscal stimulus to the economy and postpone reducing the budget deficit. The $787 billion stimulus package included only $7 billion of extra military expenditure, perhaps reflecting the view that military spending is not the most effective way to create jobs: according to one study, each $1 billion of US military expenditure created 8900 jobs, compared to 12 200

[99] North Atlantic Treaty Organization (note 88).

[100] E.g. Canadian Ministry of National Defence, *National Defence 2008–09 Estimates*, part III, *Departmental Performance Report* (DOND: Ottawa, 2009).

[101] Canadian Government, 'Cost of the Afghanistan mission 2001–2011', Backgrounder, 25 Nov. 2009, <http://www.afghanistan.gc.ca/canada-afghanistan/news-nouvelles/2009/2009_02_25a.aspx>.

[102] Perry, D., 'Canada's seven billion dollar war: the cost of Canadian forces operations in Afghanistan', *International Journal*, vol. 63, no. 3 (summer 2008), pp. 703–25.

[103] US financial years start on 1 Oct. of the year before the named year.

jobs for spending on clean energy, 14 000 jobs for health spending and 20 800 jobs for education.[104] However, President Obama has excluded 'national security' spending from a planned future spending freeze aimed at reducing the deficit.[105]

US military expenditure (outlays for 'National Defense') increased in FY 2009 by 7.7 per cent to reach $661 billion. This was mostly the result of budget decisions of the previous administration of President George W. Bush, but includes $79.9 billion from a war supplemental appropriation passed by the US Congress in 2009, and $7 billion from the stimulus package.[106]

The Obama budget for 2010

President Obama presented his first budget request—for FY 2010—to the Congress in May 2009. The proposed budget included $534 billion for the 'base' Department of Defense (DOD) budget, which covers the regular expenditure of the DOD not directly related to the conflicts in Afghanistan and Iraq. The proposed budget also included a separate request for $130 billion for 'Overseas Contingency Operations' (OCO), which covers the costs of these conflicts. By making a separate request for funding for war costs as part of the main budget request, the Obama Administration hoped to replace the Bush Administration's much-criticized use of 'emergency' war supplemental appropriations.[107] This change in practice involved moving $13 billion of items formerly funded by supplementals into the base budget. After this change, the total budgetary authority requested ($693 billion) was almost identical to the amount authorized in 2009 ($694 billion).[108]

The FY 2010 budget presented in May 2009 did not take account of President Obama's decision in November 2009 to send an additional 30 000 troops to Afghanistan, which will take the US force in Afghanistan

[104] Pollen, R. and Garrett-Peltier, H., *The U.S. Employment Effects of Military and Domestic Spending Priorities: An Updated Analysis* (University of Massachusetts, Political Economy Research Institute: Amherst, MA, 9 Oct. 2009).

[105] White House, 'Remarks by the President in State of the Union Address', 27 Jan. 2010, <http://www.whitehouse.gov/the-press-office/remarks-president-state-union-address>.

[106] The large increase comes despite a levelling-off of the budgetary authority passed by Congress for FY2009. A *budgetary authority* authorizes government spending; however the actual expenditure itself—or *outlays*—may take place in both the current and in subsequent financial years. The years 2006–2008 saw substantial excesses of authority over outlays, with outlays catching up in 2009 as previously authorized funds were spent. US Office of Management and Budget, *Budget of the United States Government, Fiscal Year 2011: Historical Tables* (Government Printing Office: Washington, DC, 2010), pp. 56–62, 90–94; and US Congressional Budget Office, *The Budget and Economic Outlook: Fiscal Years 2008 to 2018* (US Congress: Washington, DC, Jan. 2008), pp. 165–81.

[107] For a discussion of the issues surrounding US war funding see Perlo-Freeman et al. (note 52), pp. 185–89.

[108] As well as the base budget and the OCO budget, the total includes a small amount of mandatory defence spending, Department of Energy spending on the US nuclear weapon programme and some military spending in other departments.

Table 5.2. US outlays for the Department of Defense and total national defence, financial years 2001, 2003, 2006–2010

Figures are in US$ b. Years are financial years (starting 1 Oct. of the year before the named year).

	2001	2003	2006	2007	2008	2009	2010[a]
Outlays at current prices							
DOD, military	290.2	387.2	499.3	528.6	594.6	636.7	692.0
Military personnel	74.0	106.7	127.5	127.5	138.9	147.3	155.0
O&M	112.0	151.4	203.8	216.6	244.8	259.2	279.4
Procurement	55.0	67.9	89.8	99.6	117.4	129.2	147.2
RDT&E	40.5	53.1	68.6	73.1	75.1	79.0	79.3
Military construction	5.0	5.9	6.2	7.9	11.6	17.6	23.8
Family housing	3.5	3.8	3.7	3.5	3.6	2.7	4.0
Other[b]	0.3	−1.6	−0.4	0.2	3.2	1.5	3.3
DOE, military	12.9	16.0	17.5	17.1	17.1	17.6	20.0
Other, military	1.6	1.6	5.1	5.7	4.3	6.8	7.2
Total national defence	**304.8**	**404.8**	**521.8**	**551.3**	**616.1**	**661.0**	**719.2**
Outlays at constant (FY 2005) prices							
Total national defence	363.1	444.6	499.3	509.2	548.6	580.2	626.2
Outlays as a share of gross domestic product (%)							
Total national defence	*3.0*	*3.7*	*4.0*	*4.0*	*4.3*	*4.6*	*4.9*

DOD = Department of Defense; DOE = Department of Energy; FY = financial year; O&M = operations and maintenance; RDT&E = research, development, test and evaluation.

[a] Figures for 2010 are estimates.

[b] A negative number in this category is the result of difficulties in classifying budget activities according to function rather than to spending agency or organization.

Source: US Office of Management and Budget, *Budget of the United States Government, Fiscal Year 2011: Historical Tables* (Government Printing Office: Washington, DC, 2010), pp. 61–62, 131–32.

to 98 000—treble the level at the end of 2008.[109] As a result, the administration presented a $33 billion supplemental request for FY 2010 to the Congress in February 2010, despite Obama's intention to abandon the practice.[110] This figure—which equates to $1.1 million for each extra soldier—is in line with an analysis by the Centre for Strategic and Budgetary Assessments (CSBA) in December 2009, which found that, while the cost per troop deployed varied according to composition of forces, mission and the

[109] White House, 'Remarks by the President in address to the nation on the way forward in Afghanistan and Pakistan', 1 Dec. 2009, <http://www.whitehouse.gov/the-press-office/remarks-president-address-nation-way-forward-afghanistan-and-pakistan>; and US Department of Defense, 'Active duty military personnel strengths by regional area and by country (309A)', 31 Dec. 2008, <http://siadapp.dmdc.osd.mil/personnel/MILITARY/miltop.htm>.

[110] The supplemental request for FY 2010 was included with the FY 2011 budget request. US Office of Management and Budget, *Budget of the U.S. Government, Fiscal Year 2011* (Government Printing Office: Washington, DC, 2010), pp. 55–59.

actions of opposing forces, overall operational costs in both Afghanistan and Iraq depended closely on troop numbers.[111]

The Obama budget request for FY 2010 called for the termination of a number of major weapon programmes, in particular the F-22 stealth combat aircraft, the C-17 transport aircraft, an alternative engine for the F-35 (Joint Strike Fighter) combat aircraft and the VH-71 presidential helicopter, and also included cuts to missile defence funding and some major land and naval systems. In contrast, additional funding was included for increases in US Army and US Marine Corps troop strengths; an increase in DOD contracting personnel; increased funding for UAVs, intelligence, surveillance and reconnaissance (ISR) equipment, and cyberwarfare; and an increased purchase of F-35 aircraft. Supporting the budget proposal, US Defense Secretary Robert Gates argued that it was more important to spend money on areas related to current US conflicts than to increase the USA's lead in capabilities where it is already dominant.[112] Nonetheless, the bulk of procurement spending in the budget is still devoted to traditional major weapon platforms and systems. However, while the 2010 DOD Appropriations Act, passed by the Congress in December 2009, accepted the termination of the F-22 programme, it restored the C-17 and F-35 alternative engine programmes. Overall, the $636.3 billion of spending approved in the act was around $3 billion less than the president requested.[113]

The original modest real-terms increase in 2010 outlays proposed by the FY 2010 budget has now been further increased by the supplemental appropriation. US military expenditure in 2010 is now forecast to reach $720 billion, or 4.9 per cent of GDP (see table 5.2).

VIII. Conclusions

The long-term rise in global military expenditure continued—indeed, accelerated—in 2009. The global financial crisis and economic recession have not slowed this rise, even though spending on the military has not been widely included in government's economic stimulus packages. However, in the near future governments will have to reduce their public sector deficits. When the cuts take place will depend on governments' overall economic strategies—the balance between reducing deficits and the fear of

---

[111] Harrison, T., 'Estimating funding for Afghanistan', Center for Strategic and Budgetary assessments (CSBA) Update, 1 Dec. 2009, <http://www.csbaonline.org/2006-1/3.Publications/Publications_List.shtml?>.

[112] Gates, R., US Secretary of Defense, 'Defense budget recommendation statement', 6 Apr. 2009, <http://www.defense.gov/Speeches/Speech.aspx?SpeechID=1341>.

[113] The act covers only spending on personnel, operations and maintenance, procurement. and research and development. Department of Defense Appropriations Act 2010, US Public Law 111-118, signed into law 19 Dec. 2009, <http://www.govtrack.us/congress/bill.xpd?bill=h111-3326>.

jeopardizing economic recovery by cutting too quickly; whether the resulting spending cuts affect military expenditure will depend on the degree of
priority given to the military. A number of smaller economies, less able to
sustain high deficits, have already cut military spending as a result of the
crisis.

One impact of the crisis on military spending in some countries has been
through the fall in the price of oil and other commodities. In the Middle
East, the link between commodity exports and military spending and arms
imports has for a long time been a feature almost too obvious to be
remarked on. However, in recent years this link has become an increasingly
significant factor in other developing regions, including Africa and South
America. In many countries in both regions, exploitation of recently discovered reserves combined with rising oil prices in particular have fuelled
rapid growth in military spending over the past five years or so. The fall in
oil prices in 2009 contributed to reductions in spending in some countries,
including Chad, Chile and Iraq, and smaller rises than in recent years in
others, including Nigeria, Saudi Arabia and Russia. However, while falling
oil prices may have slowed the rising trend in military expenditure, it has
not been halted.

The escalating conflict in Afghanistan is having a growing impact on the
military spending of both Afghanistan itself and the foreign countries with
forces there. By far the largest costs are incurred by the United States,
which accounts for the majority of foreign troops, but the costs are also
high in relative terms for Canada and the United Kingdom. This is one of a
number of factors putting pressure on the British military budget at present.

The inauguration of the Obama Administration has not halted the growth
in US military spending. While the US presence in Iraq is starting to wind
down, that in Afghanistan is escalating; meanwhile, while there has been
some refocusing of priorities in regular 'peacetime' spending, the overall
goal of retaining global military dominance has not changed. Other emerging powers, such as Brazil, China and India, have also continued to increase
spending. While local conflicts drive spending in some cases, it is in general
hard to link the rising trend to any increase in major global security threats;
rather, it appears to reflect the long-term strategies of the world's major
global and regional powers.

Appendix 5A. Military expenditure data, 2000–2009

SAM PERLO-FREEMAN, OLAWALE ISMAIL, NOEL KELLY AND
CARINA SOLMIRANO*

I. Introduction

This appendix presents the latest SIPRI military expenditure data for the years
2000–2009. The principal regional trends and trends among major spenders
are described in section II, along with a discussion of how China's military
spending can best be estimated. Section III explains SIPRI's sources and
methods, and contains tables with the complete data series for 2000–2009.

II. Regional trends and major spenders

Boxes 5A.1–5A.6 highlight the significant trends in regional military spending
and the world's top 15 military spenders in 2009 are listed in table 5A.1. These
15 countries accounted for 82 per cent of world military spending, with the
top 5 accounting for 61 per cent, slightly higher shares than in 2008. The
United States accounted for by far the largest share, 43 per cent—far ahead of
China, which cemented its position as the second largest spender, with France,
the United Kingdom and Russia some way behind. The small increase in the US
share (from 41 per cent in 2008) is due to the appreciation of the US dollar in
2009. The identities of the top 15 spenders have remained the same since 2007,
although the rankings below the top 5 changed somewhat in 2009, with European countries slipping down the rankings—due to a combination of currency
changes and relative changes in actual spending levels (indeed in some cases
despite increases in currency values against the dollar).

It is striking that 14 of the top 15 countries—the exception being Italy—
increased their spending in 2009. For Japan and Germany, this represents a
reversal—at least temporary—of a generally falling trend over the decade.

* Contribution of military expenditure data, estimates and advice are gratefully acknow-
ledged from Julian Cooper (Centre for Russian and East European Studies, University of
Birmingham), David Darchiashvili (Center for Civil–Military Relations and Security
Studies, Tbilisi), Dimitar Dimitrov (University of National and World Economy, Sofia),
Paul Dunne (University of the West of England, Bristol), Iñigo Guevara y Moyano
(Colectivo de Análisis de la Seguridad con Democracia, Querétaro), Iduvina Hernández
(Asociación para el estudio y la promoción de la seguridad en democracia, Guatemala
City), Nazir Kamal (United Nations, New York), Pavan Nair (Jagruti Seva Sanstha,
Pune), Elina Noor (Institute of Strategic and International Studies Malaysia, Kuala
Lumpur), Pere Ortega (Centre d'Estudis per la Pau J. M. Delàs, Barcelona), Tamara
Pataraia (Caucasus Institute for Peace, Democracy and Development, Tbilisi), Thomas
Scheetz (Lincoln University College, Buenos Aires), Ron Smith (Birkbeck College,
London) and Ozren Zunec (University of Zagreb).

Box 5A.1. World trends in military expenditure

- Estimated total world military expenditure in 2009 was $1531 billion (at current prices).
- Spending increased by 5.9 per cent in real terms over 2008 and by 49 per cent compared to 2000.
- The USA's real-terms increase of $47 billion accounts for 54 per cent of the world increase.
- Spending increased in all regions and subregions except the Middle East.
- The region with fastest real-terms increase in 2009 was Asia and Oceania, at 8.9 per cent.
- The subregion with fastest real-terms increase in 2009 was South Asia, at 10.9 per cent.
- The global financial crisis and economic recession have had little impact on world military expenditure.

While the majority of countries worldwide also increased their spending, the proportion of countries with falling spending is much higher outside the top spenders. This may mainly reflect the fact that these larger economies are better able to withstand the effects of the economic crisis, as they are more able than smaller economies to sustain very high deficits to stimulate the economy; another factor may be the desire of many of the major spenders to maintain their quest for global and regional influence. China and India continued their rapid increase of recent years, the USA increased at its fastest rate since 2004, and Australia, Brazil and the UK also accelerated their growth in military spending. Russia however increased its spending by just 4.7 per cent, much more slowly than in recent years, mostly due to the financial crisis. Saudi Arabia's growth rate also slowed, most likely due to the fall in oil prices in 2009. The growth rates of France, Japan, Germany and Spain were small, in line with previous trends. Canada and South Korea's increases were also in line with recent trends.

The shares of gross domestic product (GDP) devoted to military spending (the military burden) on the part of the major spenders varies considerably, from just 0.9 per cent in the case of Japan to 8.2 per cent for Saudi Arabia. However, only 4 of the top 15 spenders—Saudi Arabia, the USA, Russia and South Korea—have military burdens above the global average of 2.7 per cent.

The ranking of the top military spenders depends on the exchange rate used to convert national military expenditure figures into US dollars. SIPRI uses market exchange rates (MERs). These rates are determined by the supply of and demand for currencies used in international transactions and do not always accurately reflect differences in price levels between countries. An alternative would be to use GDP-based purchasing power parity (PPP) exchange rates, which seek to control for differences in price levels in order to provide a measure of the real purchasing power of the GDP of each country. Using PPP rates would give a very different picture of the top 15 spenders.[1] While the USA and

---

[1] The conversion to PPP is based on the relative PPP to MER exchange rates for 2008 implicit in World Bank, *World Development Report 2010: Development and Climate Change* (World Bank: Washington, DC, 2009).

Table 5A.1. The 15 countries with the highest military expenditure in 2009

Spending figures are in US$, at current prices and exchange rates.

Rank	Country	Spending ($ b.)	Change, 2000–2009 (%)	Spending per capita ($)	Share of GDP, 2008 (%)[a]	World share (%)
1	USA	661	75.8	2 100	4.3	43
2	China	[100]	217	[74.6]	[2.0]	[6.6]
3	France	63.9	7.4	1 026	2.3	4.2
4	UK	58.3	28.1	946	2.5	3.8
5	Russia	[53.3]	105	[378]	[3.5]	[3.5]
Sub-total top 5		**937**				**61**
6	Japan	51.0	–1.3	401	0.9	3.3
7	Germany	45.6	–6.7	555	1.3	3.0
8	Saudi Arabia[b]	41.3	66.9	1 603	8.2	2.7
9	India	36.3	67.3	30.4	2.6	2.4
10	Italy	35.8	–13.3	598	1.7	2.3
Sub-total top 10		**1 147**				**75**
11	Brazil	26.1	38.7	135	1.5	1.7
12	South Korea	24.1	48.2	499	2.8	1.6
13	Canada	19.2	48.8	568	1.3	1.3
14	Australia	19.0	50.2	892	1.8	1.2
15	Spain	18.3	34.4	408	1.2	1.2
Sub-total top 15		**1 254**				**82**
World		**1 531**	**49.2**	**224**	**2.7**	**100**

[ ] = estimated figure; GDP = gross domestic product.

   [a] The figures for national military expenditure as a share of GDP are for 2008, the most recent year for which GDP data is available.

   [b] The figures for Saudi Arabia include expenditure for public order and safety and might be slight overestimates.

Sources: SIPRI Military Expenditure Database, <http://www.sipri.org/databases/milex/>; and United Nations Population Fund (UNFPA), *State of World Population 2009: Facing a Changing World—Women, Climate and Population* (UNFPA: New York, 2009), p. 91.

China would remain very clearly the top 2, the ratio between US and Chinese military spending would decrease from 6.6 : 1 to 3.2 : 1. The next three biggest spenders would be India, Russia and Saudi Arabia. Turkey and Colombia would enter the top 15, replacing Australia and Canada.[2]

In general, the effect of using PPP rates is to increase the relative size of expenditure figures of developing and transition economies. For those such countries for which data was available for 2008, the median increase in military expenditure figures from using PPP rates instead of MERs was around a factor of 2. Three-quarters of these countries would see their relative figures increase by at least two-thirds. Meanwhile, using PPP rates would cause the GDP and military expenditure figures of most 'developed' countries to fall

---

   [2] Iran should almost certainly be in the top 15 measured by PPP, in place of Colombia, but data for Iran's military spending in 2009 was unavailable.

Box 5A.2. Trends in military spending in Africa

- Estimated total military expenditure in Africa in 2009 was $27.4 billion ($10.0 billion in North Africa and $17.4 billion in sub-Saharan Africa).
- Spending increased by 6.5 per cent in real terms over 2008 (7.7 per cent in North Africa and 5.1 per cent in sub-Saharan Africa) and by 62 per cent compared to 2000 (107 per cent in North Africa and 42 per cent in sub-Saharan Africa).
- The regional increase was partially offset by a substantial fall in Chad, from an unprecedented high level in 2008, due to oil revenues.
- The trend in Africa is overwhelmingly determined by five major-spending countries: Algeria, Angola, Morocco, Nigeria and South Africa.
- Increases in 2009 by these major spenders continue longer-term trends: over the decade 2000–2009 military spending rose in real terms by 127 per cent in Morocco, 105 per cent in Algeria, 101 per cent in Nigeria, 53 per cent in South Africa and 40 per cent in Angola.
- Oil and gas revenues are a significant factor behind the spending in many countries.

Note: Estimates for Africa and its subregions in 2009 are uncertain due to missing data for some countries.

Box 5A.3. Trends in military spending in the Americas

- Estimated total military expenditure in the Americas in 2009 was $738 billion ($5.6 billion in Central America and the Caribbean, $680 billion in North America and $51.8 billion in South America).
- Spending increased by 7.6 per cent in real terms over 2008 (9.7 per cent in Central America and the Caribbean, 7.6 per cent in North America and 7.6 per cent in South America), and by 72 per cent compared to 2000 (28 per cent in Central America and the Caribbean, 75 per cent in North America and 48 per cent in South America).
- In North America, the USA spent $661 billion (an increase of 7.7 per cent) and Canada $19.2 billion (an increase of 6.6 per cent).
- Almost all of the increase in Central America and the Caribbean was due to the 11 per cent rise by Mexico, the result of increasing drug-related violence.
- Expenditure in South America increased despite a fall in GDP due to the economic crisis.
- The largest absolute real-terms increase in South America was in Brazil ($3.8 billion), and the largest relative increases in Uruguay (24 per cent), Ecuador (18 per cent), Brazil (16 per cent) and Colombia (11 per cent).
- The largest percentage decrease was made by Venezuela, where spending fell by 25 per cent.

relative to the USA, by a median rate of 17 per cent—reflecting the low value of the US dollar at market exchange rates in 2008.

PPP rates better represent the volume of goods and services that can be purchased with a given sum of money in each country than do MERs. GDP-based PPP exchange rates are estimates based on statistical surveys of price data for a basket of goods and services that are major components of the GDP, including both traded and non-traded items. While they measure the volume of goods and services purchasable in the general economy of each country, this does not mean that they are a better measure than MERs of the volume of military goods

Box 5A.4. Trends in military spending in Asia and Oceania

- Estimated total military expenditure in Asia and Oceania in 2009 was $276 billion ($210 billion in East Asia, $44.0 billion in South Asia and $20.4 billion in Oceania).
- Spending increased by 8.9 per cent in real terms over 2008 (8.6 per cent in East Asia, 11 per cent in South Asia and 8.2 per cent in Oceania) and by 67 per cent compared to 2000 (71 per cent in East Asia, 57 per cent in South Asia and 47 per cent in Oceania).
- China accounted for most of the Asian and East Asian increases in 2009, with an increase of 15 per cent.
- The largest relative real increases in East Asia in 2009 were in Taiwan (19 per cent), Thailand (19 per cent) and Timor-Leste (54 per cent).
- The increase in Oceania in 2009 was almost all due to Australia.
- Most of the increase in South Asia was due to India (13 per cent), but Afghanistan also had a big increase (19 per cent).

Box 5A.5. Trends in military spending in Europe

- Estimated total military expenditure in Europe in 2009 was $386 billion ($60 billion in Eastern Europe and $326 billion in Western and Central Europe).
- Spending increased by 2.7 per cent in real terms over 2008 (2.6 per cent in Eastern Europe and 2.8 per cent in Western and Central Europe), and by 16 per cent compared to 2000 (108 per cent in Eastern Europe and 6.6 per cent in Western and Central Europe).
- The increase in Eastern Europe was much smaller than in previous years, largely due to the economic crisis.
- The largest absolute increases (in constant 2008 prices) were in the UK ($3.7 billion), Turkey ($2.9 billion) and Russia ($2.7 billion).
- The largest relative increases in real terms were in Cyprus (21 per cent), Turkey (18 per cent), the Former Yugoslav Republic of Macedonia (18 per cent) and Belarus (17 per cent).
- The largest relative real decrease was in Georgia (39 per cent), from exceptionally high levels in 2008 due to the conflict with Russia in South Ossetia. There were also large falls in Moldova (25 per cent) and Montenegro (19 per cent).

and services that may be obtained. In particular, PPP rates are unlikely to reflect the relative costs of advanced weapons technology and systems in each country. In addition, as PPP rates are estimates, they are less reliable than MERs. Thus, SIPRI uses market exchange rates to convert military expenditure data into US dollars, despite their limitations.[3]

Estimating China's military spending

In its estimates of Chinese military expenditure, SIPRI seeks to take into account a number of sources of military expenditure outside the official defence budget. Such sources of military expenditure include funding from other central government ministries (some of which is publicly available, some

---

[3] On the issues involved in international comparison and currency conversion and the use of PPP rates see Ward, M., 'International comparisons of military expenditures: issues and challenges of using purchasing power parities', *SIPRI Yearbook 2006*.

Box 5A.6. Trends in military spending in the Middle East

- Estimated total military expenditure in the Middle East in 2009 was $103 billion.
- The lack of data for some countries makes the figures for Middle East highly uncertain; it is not possible to conclude with certainty if total spending increased or decreased in 2009.
- Between 2000 and 2009 spending increased by 40 per cent in real terms.
- The largest relative real increases in 2009 were in Lebanon (20 per cent), Bahrain (11 per cent), Jordan (11 per cent) and Syria (8.7 per cent).
- The largest relative decreases were in Iraq (28 per cent) and Oman (13 per cent).
- The fall in oil prices in 2009 severely affected the revenues of regional oil producers.

---

of which is not), funding from local government and funding from internal People's Liberation Army (PLA) sources—the latter probably represents a much smaller share of the total than in the past. SIPRI's estimate of China's military spending is based on a methodology used in a study published in *SIPRI Yearbook 1999*, which provides estimates of Chinese military spending from 1989 to 1998, based on both the official defence budget and data and estimates for a number of items outside the budget (see below).[4] Since then, SIPRI has produced estimates for Chinese military spending assuming, in most cases, a rate of change in these additional items equal to that of the official budget, with two exceptions. First, the earnings of the PLA from its commercial activities are assumed to have declined steadily since 1999, as a policy of divestment from such activities has been followed. Second, the rate of change in spending on arms imports and in PLA earnings from arms exports are assumed to have followed the rate of change of China's arms imports and exports as measured by the SIPRI Trend Indicator Value (TIV).[5]

For the current edition of the SIPRI Yearbook and in the SIPRI Military Expenditure Database, SIPRI has updated its estimates for China for the years 1997–2009 using additional data from various editions of the China Public Finance Yearbook and the China Statistical Yearbook. This has allowed previous estimates of some elements of the total figure for Chinese military spending to be replaced with actual expenditure data and some other estimates to be improved. However, the previous methodology, in terms of the items included in the total and the approach to estimating those items for which actual expenditure data is not available, remains unchanged.

This exercise has resulted in surprisingly small changes in the total estimate for Chinese military spending; for each year, the change is less than 1 per cent of the total, in most years much less. This reflects increases in figures for some items compared to previous estimates, but decreases in others.

The items outside the official defence budget that are included in the estimate are: (*a*) central and local government spending on the paramilitary People's Armed Police (PAP); (*b*) soldiers' demobilization and retirement payments from the Ministry of Civil Affairs; (*c*) subsidies to the arms industry; (*d*) additional military research and development (R&D) funding by civilian

---

[4] Wang, S., 'The military expenditure of China, 1989–98', *SIPRI Yearbook 1999*.
[5] For the definition of the TIV see appendix 7A in this volume.

government ministries; (*e*) additional military construction expenses; (*f*) Chinese arms imports; (*g*) a share of revenue from Chinese arms exports; and (*h*) residual military-owned enterprises. Estimates for items *d, f, g* and *h* are unchanged; estimates for items *a* and *b* have been updated with actual expenditure figures (with estimates for recent years based on the rate of change of the official budget); estimates for item *c*—subsidies to the arms industry—have been updated based on a share of the total budget for industrial subsidies (with further estimates for 2007–2009 based on the average rate of decline of this figure in previous years); and estimates for item *e*—additional military construction—have been updated based on a share of the government's capital infrastructure budget (with further estimates for 2007–2009 based on the rate of change of the official defence budget).

The resulting SIPRI estimates for Chinese military spending come to roughly 1.4–1.5 times the official defence budget for most years. SIPRI's current estimate for R&D spending is quite high, suggesting a share of R&D in overall military spending close to that of the USA, and considerably higher than for major European arms producers. In contrast, SIPRI estimates do not at present include estimates for local government funding of the PLA.

A 2006 report by the US–China Policy Foundation, based on a analysis of available Chinese-language sources, broadly concurs with the list of items included by SIPRI, but also adds various forms of funding to the PLA from local government, as well as some higher education expenses for PLA officers and compensation for disaster relief activities.[6] The report concludes, however, that there is not at present enough information to make a reasonable estimate of total Chinese defence-related spending.

While details of some elements of Chinese military spending outside the official defence budget are publicly available (such as the PAP budget) others—most importantly R&D spending—are not, and can at present only be the subject of educated guesswork. Further research based on publicly available Chinese-language sources could provide improved estimates, but without greater transparency on the part of the Chinese Government, a completely accurate figure is not currently possible.

III. Tables of military expenditure

Table 5A.2 presents military expenditure by region, by certain international organizations and by income group for the period 2000–2009 in US dollars at constant (2008) prices and exchange rates, and also for 2009 in current US dollars. Military expenditure by individual countries is presented in table 5A.3 in local currency at current prices for the period 2000–2009 and in table 5A.4 in US dollars at constant (2008) prices and exchange rates for the period 2000–2009 and for 2009 in current US dollars. Table 5A.5 presents military expenditure for the period 2000–2008 as a percentage of countries' gross domestic

---

[6] Blasko, D. J. et al., 'Defense-related spending in China: a preliminary analysis and comparison with American equivalents', United States–China Policy Foundation, Nov. 2006, <http://www.uscpf. org/v2/defensestudies.html>.

product. Notes and explanations of the conventions used appear below table 5A.5.

Conversion to constant US dollars has been made using market exchange rates for all countries. As the base year for conversion to constant US dollars has been changed to 2008, the figures in table 5A.4 are substantially different from those in *SIPRI Yearbook 2009*, where the base year 2005 was used. The effects of the change of base year are twofold. First, as is usually the case, adopting a later base year tends to increase most figures due to the effects of inflation between 2005 and 2008. Second, there were significant exchange rate changes between 2005 and 2008, with the US dollar falling against a majority of world currencies, including a significant fall against the euro, the Chinese yuan and the Japanese yen (but not the British pound). This has increased the relative size of the constant dollar figures of those countries whose currency has risen against the dollar. Conversely, the rise of the dollar against most currencies in 2009 means that, unusually, the current dollar figures for 2009 shown in the last column of tables 5A.2 and 5A.4 are generally lower than the constant (2008) dollar figures for the same year. This includes the figure for the world total in table 5A.2. Caution should therefore be exercised in comparing the current and constant dollar figures for 2009.

The data in local currency at current prices is presented on a financial year basis, while all other data is presented on a calendar year basis. Those countries with financial years that do not coincide with calendar years are indicated in table 5A.3. In all but one such case, the current price local currency figure shown for a given year is for the financial year *beginning* in that calendar year. For example, the local currency figure for a financial year running from 1 July 2008 to 30 June 2009 is shown in the table as being for 2008. The exception is the USA, where each figure is for the financial year beginning on 1 October of the year previous to that indicated. Thus, the figure for the financial year 1 October 2008–30 September 2009 is listed under 2009. A few countries have changed their financial year during the period 2000–2009. These cases are indicated in footnotes.

Military expenditure data from different editions of the SIPRI Yearbook should not be combined because the data series are continuously revised and updated. This is true in particular for the most recent years as figures for budget allocations are replaced by figures for actual expenditure. In some cases entire series are revised as new and better data becomes available. Revisions in constant dollar series can also be caused by significant revisions in the economic statistics of the International Monetary Fund (IMF) that are used for these calculations. Changes in base years and method of currency conversion also hinder comparison between editions. The SIPRI Military Expenditure Database, accessible at <http://www.sipri.org/databases/milex/>, includes consistent series dating back to 1988 for most countries. Data for the years 1950–87—published in previous editions of the SIPRI Yearbook—cannot always be combined with the post-1987 data since SIPRI conducted a major review of the data for many countries for the period beginning in 1988.

The purpose of the data

The main purpose of the data on military expenditure is to provide an easily identifiable measure of the scale of resources absorbed by the military. Military expenditure is an 'input' measure, which is not directly related to the 'output' of military activities, such as military capability or military security. Long- and short-term changes in military spending may be signs of a change in military output, but interpretations of this type should be made with caution.

The purpose of the specific tables are as follows. The country data on military expenditure in local currency at current prices (table 5A.3) is the original data for all the other tables. This is provided to contribute to transparency and to enable comparison with data reported in government sources and elsewhere. Data in constant dollars is provided to allow for comparison over time for individual countries (table 5A.4) and for regions, organizations and income groups, as well as for the world total (table 5A.2). Data in current dollars for the most recent year (here 2009) is provided for the purpose of international comparison across countries (table 5A.4) and across regions (table 5A.2). The current dollar figures also facilitate comparison with other economic indicators, which are often expressed in current dollar terms. Data on military expenditure as a share of GDP is provided (in table 5A.5) as an indicator of the proportion of a country's resources used for military activities, that is, as an indicator of the economic burden of military expenditure, also called the 'defence burden' or the 'military burden'.

The coverage of the data

The military expenditure data in tables 5A.2–5A.5 covers 164 countries for the 10-year period 2000–2009. Total military expenditure figures are calculated for three types of country groupings—geographical region, international organization and country income group (categorized by gross national income per capita). The coverage of each of these groupings is provided in the notes to table 5A.2.

The definition of military expenditure

The guideline definition of military expenditure used by SIPRI includes expenditure on the following actors and activities: (*a*) the armed forces, including peacekeeping forces; (*b*) defence ministries and other government agencies engaged in defence projects; (*c*) paramilitary forces, when judged to be trained and equipped for military operations; and (*d*) military space activities. It includes all current and capital expenditure on: (*a*) military and civil personnel, including retirement pensions of military personnel and social services for personnel; (*b*) operations and maintenance; (*c*) procurement; (*d*) military research and development; and (*e*) military aid (in the military expenditure of the donor country). It does not include civil defence and current expenditure for past military activities, such as for veterans' benefits, demobilization, conversion and weapon destruction. While this definition serves as a guideline, in practice it is often difficult to adhere to due to data limitations.

The limitations of the data

There are three main types of limitations of the data: reliability, validity and comparability.

The main problems of reliability are due to the less than comprehensive coverage of official military expenditure data, the lack of detailed information on military expenditure and the lack of data on actual, rather than budgeted, military expenditure. In many countries the official data covers only a part of total military expenditure. Important items can be hidden under non-military budget headings or can even be financed entirely outside the government budget. Many such extra-budgetary and off-budget mechanisms are employed in practice.[7]

The validity of expenditure data depends on the purpose for which it is used. Since expenditure data is a measure of monetary input, its most valid use is as an indicator of the economic resources consumed for military purposes. For the same reason, its utility as an indicator of military strength or capability is limited. While military expenditure does have an impact on military capability, so do many other factors such as the balance between personnel and equipment, the technological level of military equipment, and the state of maintenance and repair, as well as the overall security environment in which the armed forces are to be employed.

The comparability of the data is limited by two different types of factor: the varying coverage (or definition) of the data and the method of currency conversion. The coverage of official data on military expenditure varies significantly between countries and over time for the same country. For the conversion into a common currency, the choice of exchange rate makes a great difference in cross-country comparisons (as discussed in section II). This is a general problem in international comparisons of economic data and is not specific to military expenditure. However, since international comparison of military expenditure is often a sensitive issue, it is important to bear in mind that the interpretation of cross-country comparisons of military expenditure is greatly influenced by the choice of exchange rate.[8]

---

[7] For an overview of such mechanisms see Hendrickson, D. and Ball, N., *Off-budget Military Expenditure and Revenue: Issues and Policy Perspectives for Donors*, Conflict, Security and Development Group (CSDG) Occasional Papers no. 1 (King's College: London, Jan. 2002).

[8] For comprehensive overviews of the conceptual problems and sources of uncertainty involved in military expenditure data sets see e.g. Brzoska, M., 'World military expenditures', eds K. Hartley and T. Sandler, *Handbook of Defense Economics*, vol. 1 (North-Holland: Amsterdam, 1995); and Ball, N., 'Measuring third world security expenditure: a research note', *World Development*, vol. 12, no. 2 (Feb. 1984). On African countries see Omitoogun, W., *Military Expenditure Data in Africa: A Survey of Cameroon, Ethiopia, Ghana, Kenya, Nigeria and Uganda*, SIPRI Research Report no. 17 (Oxford University Press: Oxford, 2003).

Methods

SIPRI data is based on open sources and reflects the official data reported by governments. However, the official data does not always conform to the SIPRI definition of military expenditure. Nor is it always possible to recalculate data according to the definition, since this would require detailed information about what is included in the official defence budgets and about extra-budgetary and off-budget military expenditure items. In many cases SIPRI is confined to using the data provided by governments, regardless of definition. If several data series are available, which is often the case, SIPRI chooses the data series that corresponds most closely to the SIPRI definition of military expenditure. Nevertheless, priority is given to choosing a uniform time series for each country, in order to achieve consistency over time, rather than to adjusting the figures for individual years according to a common definition. In addition, estimates have to be made in specific cases.

Estimation

Estimates of military expenditure are predominantly made when the coverage of official data diverges significantly from the SIPRI definition or when no complete consistent time series is available. In the first case, estimates are made on the basis of an analysis of primarily official government budget and expenditure accounts. The most comprehensive estimates of this type are for China and Russia, which have been presented in detail in previous editions of the SIPRI Yearbook.[9] In the second case, when only incomplete times series are available, the figures from the data series which corresponds most closely to the SIPRI definition are used for the years covered by that series. Figures for the missing years are then estimated by applying the percentage change between years in an alternative series to the data in the first series, in order to achieve consistency over time.

All estimates are based on official government data or other empirical evidence from open sources. Thus, no estimates are made for countries that do not release any official data, and no figures are displayed for these countries.

SIPRI estimates are presented in square brackets in the tables. Round brackets are used when data is uncertain for reasons beyond SIPRI's control, for example, when the data is based on a source of uncertain reliability and in cases when data expressed in constant dollars or as shares of GDP is uncertain due to uncertain economic data.

The data for the most recent years includes two types of estimate, which apply to all countries. First, figures for the most recent years are for adopted budget, budget estimates or revised estimates, the majority of which will be revised in subsequent years. Second, in table 5A.4 the deflator used for the final year in the series is an estimate based on part of a year or as provided by the IMF. Unless exceptional uncertainty is involved, these estimates are not bracketed.

[9] Cooper, J., 'The military expenditure of the USSR and the Russian Federation, 1987–97', *SIPRI Yearbook 1998*; and Wang (note 4). On China see also section II above.

The totals for the world, regions, organizations and income groups in table 5A.2 are estimates because data is not available for all countries in all years. In cases where data for a country is missing at the beginning or end of the series, these estimates are made on the assumption that the rate of change for that country is the same as the average for the region to which it belongs. In cases where data is missing in the middle of the series, the estimates are made on the assumption of an even trend between the end values. When no estimate can be made, countries are excluded from all totals.

Calculations

The original country data is provided in local currency at current prices (table 5A.3). This is shown on a financial year basis, in contrast to previous editions of the SIPRI Yearbook, when these figures were shown on a calendar year basis. This change has been made to allow a direct comparison between SIPRI data and primary source documents, such as national budgets.

Figures in constant US dollars and as a share of GDP (tables 5A.4 and 5A.5) are displayed on a calendar year basis, which makes it necessary to convert financial year figures to calendar year figures for those countries where there financial and calendar years differ. These calculations are made on the assumption of an even rate of expenditure throughout the financial year. Local currency data is then converted to US dollars at constant prices and exchange rates (table 5A.3) using the national consumer prices index (CPI) for the respective country and the annual average market exchange rate. The use of CPIs as deflators means that the trend in the SIPRI military expenditure for each country (in constant dollars) reflects the real change in its purchasing power for country-typical baskets of civilian consumer goods.[10]

Sources

The sources for military expenditure data are, in order of priority: (*a*) primary sources, that is, official data provided by national governments, either in their official publications or in response to questionnaires; (*b*) secondary sources which quote primary data; and (*c*) other secondary sources.

The first category consists of national budget documents, defence white papers and public finance statistics as well as responses to a SIPRI questionnaire that is sent out annually to the finance and defence ministries, central banks, and national statistical offices of the countries in the SIPRI Military Expenditure Database (see appendix 5B). It also includes government responses to questionnaires about military expenditure sent out by the United Nations and, if made available by the countries themselves, the Organization for Security and Co-operation in Europe (OSCE).

---

[10] A military-specific deflator is a more appropriate choice for the purpose of measuring purchasing power in terms of the amount of military personnel, goods and services that could be bought for the military expenditure. However, military-specific deflators are not available for most countries.

The second category includes international statistics, such as those of the North Atlantic Treaty Organization (NATO) and the IMF. The data for the 16 pre-1999 NATO member states has traditionally been taken from military expenditure statistics published in a number of NATO sources. The introduction by NATO of a new definition of military expenditure in 2005 has made it necessary to rely on other sources for some NATO countries for the most recent years. The data for many developing countries is taken from the IMF's *Government Finance Statistics Yearbook*, which provides a defence heading for most IMF member countries, and from country reports by IMF staff. This category also includes publications of other organizations that provide references to the primary sources used, such as the Country Reports of the Economist Intelligence Unit.

The third category of sources consists of specialist journals and newspapers.

The main sources for economic data are the publications of the IMF: *International Financial Statistics, World Economic Outlook* and country reports by IMF staff.

Table 5A.2. Military expenditure by region, by international organization and by income group, 2000–2009

Figures are in US $b. at constant 2008 prices and exchange rates for 2000–2009 and, in the right-most column, marked *, in current US$ b. for 2009. Figures do not always add up to totals because of the conventions of rounding.

	2000	2001	2002	2003	2004	2005	2006	2007	2008	2009	2009*
World total	**1 053**	**1 078**	**1 142**	**1 213**	**1 279**	**1 329**	**1 371**	**1 418**	**1 484**	**1 572**	**1 531**
Geographical regions											
Africa	17.1	17.6	18.6	18.5	20.8	21.6	22.6	(23.6)	(26.0)	(27.7)	(27.4)
North Africa	5.1	6.5	6.5	6.8	7.4	7.7	7.7	8.3	9.8	(10.5)	(10.0)
Sub-Saharan Africa	12.0	11.1	12.1	11.7	13.4	14.0	14.9	(15.3)	(16.3)	(17.1)	(17.4)
Americas	432	439	485	541	587	617	630	649	690	743	738
Central American and the Caribbean	4.9	5.0	4.8	4.7	4.4	4.7	5.1	5.7	5.8	6.3	5.6
North America	391	394	441	500	545	571	580	596	635	684	680
South America	35.6	39.1	39.1	35.7	37.9	41.4	45.2	46.8	49.2	53.0	51.8
Asia and Oceania	166	177	185	193	204	214	226	241	254	277	276
Central Asia	0.8	0.9	1.0	1.1	1.2	1.4	1.6	2.2	2.2	..	..
East Asia	122	131	139	146	152	159	170	183	192	209	210
Oceania	14.7	15.3	15.8	16.3	16.9	17.5	18.5	19.5	20.0	21.6	20.4
South Asia	28.3	29.1	29.2	29.9	33.9	35.6	36.0	36.8	40.0	44.4	44.0
Europe	367	368	381	385	387	389	397	403	413	424	386
Eastern Europe	33.1	36.1	40.0	42.8	44.8	49.6	55.3	61.0	67.1	68.8	60.0
Western and Central Europe	333	332	341	342	342	339	342	342	346	355	326
Middle East	71.3	77.2	73.4	75.4	80.2	87.9	95.5	101	(101)	(100)	(103)
Organizations											
ASEAN	18.7	19.5	20.5	22.7	22.9	23.6	24.3	26.9	27.1	27.9	25.1
CIS	33.9	37.0	40.9	43.9	46.0	51.0	56.9	63.2	69.3	70.4	61.4
European Union	280	279	285	289	308	306	308	314	316	323	297
NATO	694	697	752	813	864	887	900	916	958	1 018	987
NATO Europe	303	302	311	313	320	317	320	320	323	334	306

OECD	800	803	860	923	968	993	1006	1025	1068	1130	1098
OPEC	57.0	62.3	56.7	59.3	66.6	74.0	82.0	89.4	92.3	86.3	90.3
OSCE	758	764	823	887	933	951	979	1002	1050	1110	1068
Income group											
Low	6.2	5.9	6.1	6.2	6.3	6.4	6.7	7.4	7.6	7.4	7.5
Lower middle	91.7	103	105	117	129	140	154	166	181	197	198
Upper middle	114	121	127	124	128	135	146	153	164	174	159
High	841	848	901	966	1016	1047	1065	1092	1133	1194	1167

World military spending per capita

119	121	128	145	161	172	183	200	220	224	

World military burden (world military spending as a share (%) of world gross domestic product, in current prices)

2.3	2.3	2.4	2.5	2.5	2.5	2.4	2.4	2.4	2.7	

( ) = total based on country data accounting for less than 90% of the regional total; .. = available data account for less than 60% of the regional total.

Notes: The world total and the totals for regions, organizations and income groups in table 5A.2 are estimates, based on data in table 5A.4. Totals for regions and income groups cover the same groups of countries for all years. Totals for organizations cover only the member countries in the year given. When military expenditure data for a country is missing for a few years, estimates are made, most often on the assumption that the rate of change in that country's military expenditure is the same as that for the region to which it belongs. When no estimates can be made, countries are excluded from the totals. The countries excluded from all totals in table 5A.2 are Benin, Cuba, Equatorial Guinea, Guyana, North Korea, Myanmar, Qatar, Somalia and Viet Nam.

Geographical regions

Africa includes the 50 countries of the following subregions: North Africa: Algeria, Libya, Morocco, Tunisia. *Sub-Saharan Africa*: Angola, Benin, Botswana, Burkina Faso, Burundi, Cameroon, Cape Verde, Central African Republic, Chad, Congo (Republic of the), Congo (Democratic Republic of the, DRC), Côte d'Ivoire, Djibouti, Equatorial Guinea, Eritrea, Ethiopia, Gabon, Gambia, Ghana, Guinea, Guinea-Bissau, Kenya, Lesotho, Liberia, Madagascar, Malawi, Mali, Mauritania, Mauritius, Mozambique, Namibia, Niger, Nigeria, Rwanda, Senegal, Seychelles, Sierra Leone, Somalia, South Africa, Sudan, Swaziland, Tanzania, Togo, Uganda, Zambia, Zimbabwe.

The Americas includes the 25 countries of the following subregions: Central America and the Caribbean: Belize, Costa Rica, Cuba, Dominican Republic, El Salvador, Guatemala, Haiti, Honduras, Jamaica, Mexico, Nicaragua, Panama. *North America*: Canada, USA. *South America*: Argentina, Bolivia, Brazil, Chile, Colombia, Ecuador, Guyana, Paraguay, Peru, Uruguay, Venezuela.

Asia and Oceania includes the 32 countries of the following subregions: Central Asia: Kazakhstan, Kyrgyzstan, Tajikistan, Turkmenistan, Uzbekistan. *East Asia*: Brunei Darussalam, Cambodia, China, Indonesia, Japan, North Korea, South Korea, Laos, Malaysia, Mongolia, Myanmar, Philippines, Singapore,

Taiwan, Thailand, Timor-Leste, Viet Nam. *Oceania*: Australia, Fiji, New Zealand, Papua New Guinea. *South Asia*: Afghanistan, Bangladesh, India, Nepal, Pakistan, Sri Lanka.

Europe includes the 44 countries of the following subregions: Central and Western Europe: Albania, Austria, Belgium, Bosnia and Herzegovina, Bulgaria, Croatia, Cyprus, Czech Republic, Denmark, Estonia, Finland, France, Germany, Greece, Hungary, Iceland, Ireland, Italy, Latvia, Lithuania, Luxembourg, Macedonia (Former Yugoslav Republic of, FYROM), Malta, Montenegro, Netherlands, Norway, Poland, Portugal, Romania, Serbia, Slovakia, Slovenia, Spain, Sweden, Switzerland, Turkey, UK. *Eastern Europe*: Armenia, Azerbaijan, Belarus, Georgia, Moldova, Russia, Ukraine.

The Middle East includes the 14 countries Bahrain, Egypt, Iran, Iraq, Israel, Jordan, Kuwait, Lebanon, Oman, Qatar, Saudi Arabia, Syria, United Arab Emirates (UAE), Yemen.

Organizations

Association of Southeast Asian Nations (ASEAN): Brunei Darussalam, Cambodia, Indonesia, Laos, Malaysia, Myanmar, Philippines, Singapore, Thailand, Viet Nam.

Commonwealth of Independent States (CIS): Armenia, Azerbaijan, Belarus, Georgia (–2008), Kazakhstan, Kyrgyzstan, Moldova, Russia, Tajikistan, Turkmenistan, Ukraine, Uzbekistan.

European Union: Austria, Belgium, Bulgaria (2007–), Cyprus (2004–), Czech Republic (2004–), Denmark, Estonia (2004–), Finland, France, Germany, Greece, Hungary (2004–), Ireland, Italy, Latvia (2004–), Lithuania (2004–), Luxembourg, Malta (2004–), Netherlands, Poland (2004–), Portugal, Romania (2007–), Slovakia (2004–), Slovenia (2004–), Spain, Sweden, UK.

North Atlantic Treaty Organization (NATO): Albania (2009–), Belgium, Bulgaria (2004–), Canada, Croatia (2009–), Czech Republic, Denmark, Estonia (2004–), France, Germany, Greece, Hungary, Iceland, Italy, Latvia (2004–), Lithuania (2004–), Luxembourg, Netherlands, Norway, Poland, Portugal, Romania (2004–), Slovakia (2004–), Slovenia (2004–), Spain, Turkey, UK, USA. *NATO Europe* excludes Canada and the USA.

Organisation for Economic Co-operation and Development (OECD): Australia, Austria, Belgium, Canada, Czech Republic, Denmark, Finland, France, Germany, Greece, Hungary, Iceland, Ireland, Italy, Japan, South Korea, Luxembourg, Mexico, Netherlands, New Zealand, Norway, Poland, Portugal, Slovakia, Spain, Sweden, Switzerland, Turkey, UK, USA.

Organization of the Petroleum Exporting Countries (OPEC): Algeria, Angola (2007–), Indonesia (–2008), Iran, Iraq, Kuwait, Libya, Nigeria, Qatar, Saudi Arabia, United Arab Emirates, Venezuela.

Organization for Security and Co-operation in Europe (OSCE): Albania, Armenia, Austria, Azerbaijan, Belarus, Belgium, Bosnia and Herzegovina, Bulgaria, Canada, Croatia, Cyprus, Czech Republic, Denmark, Estonia, Finland, France, Georgia, Germany, Greece, Hungary, Iceland, Ireland, Italy, Kazakhstan, Kyrgyzstan, Latvia, Lithuania, Luxembourg, Macedonia (Former Yugoslav Republic of, FYROM), Malta, Moldova, Montenegro (2006–), Netherlands, Norway, Poland, Portugal, Romania, Russia, Serbia, Slovakia, Slovenia, Spain, Sweden, Switzerland, Tajikistan, Turkey, Turkmenistan, UK, Ukraine, USA, Uzbekistan.

Income group

The country coverage of income groups is based on figures of 2008 gross national income (GNI) per capita as calculated in World Bank, *World Development Report 2010: Development and Climate Change* (World Bank: Washington, DC, 2009).

Low-income countries (GNI per capita ≤$975 in 2008): Afghanistan, Bangladesh, Benin, Burkina Faso, Burundi, Cambodia, Central African Republic, Chad, Congo (Democratic Republic of the, DRC), Eritrea, Ethiopia, Gambia, Ghana, Guinea, Guinea-Bissau, Haiti, Kenya, North Korea, Kyrgyzstan, Laos, Liberia, Madagascar, Malawi, Mali, Mauritania, Mongolia, Mozambique, Nepal, Niger, Rwanda, Senegal, Sierra Leone, Somalia, Tajikistan, Tanzania, Togo, Uganda, Uzbekistan, Yemen, Zambia, Zimbabwe.

Lower-middle-income countries (GNI per capita $976–$3855 in 2008): Albania, Angola, Armenia, Azerbaijan, Belize, Bolivia, Cameroon, Cape Verde, China, Congo (Republic of the), Côte d'Ivoire, Djibouti, Ecuador, Egypt, El Salvador, Georgia, Guatemala, Guyana, Honduras, India, Indonesia, Iran, Iraq, Jordan, Lesotho, Moldova, Morocco, Nicaragua, Nigeria, Pakistan, Papua New Guinea, Paraguay, Philippines, Sri Lanka, Sudan, Swaziland, Syria, Thailand, Timor-Leste, Tunisia, Turkmenistan, Ukraine, Viet Nam.

Upper-middle-income countries (GNI per capita $3856–$11 905 in 2008): Algeria, Argentina, Belarus, Bosnia and Herzegovina, Botswana, Brazil, Bulgaria, Chile, Colombia, Costa Rica, Cuba, Dominican Republic, Fiji, Gabon, Jamaica, Kazakhstan, Latvia, Lebanon, Libya, Lithuania, Macedonia (Former Yugoslav Republic of, FYROM), Malaysia, Mauritius, Mexico, Montenegro, Myanmar, Namibia, Panama, Peru, Poland, Romania, Russia, Serbia, Seychelles, South Africa, Turkey, Uruguay, Venezuela.

High-income countries (GNI per capita ≥$11 906 in 2008): Australia, Austria, Bahrain, Belgium, Brunei Darussalam, Canada, Croatia, Cyprus, Czech Republic, Denmark, Equatorial Guinea, Estonia, Finland, France, Germany, Greece, Hungary, Iceland, Ireland, Israel, Italy, Japan, South Korea, Kuwait, Luxembourg, Malta, Netherlands, New Zealand, Norway, Oman, Portugal, Qatar, Saudi Arabia, Singapore, Slovakia, Slovenia, Spain, Sweden, Switzerland, Taiwan, United Arab Emirates, UK, USA.

Military spending per capita and military burden

The spending per capita figures are based on estimated world population figures from United Nations Population Fund (UNFPA), *State of World Population* various editions (UNFPA: New York, 2000–2009).

The military burden figures are based on world GDP figures from the International Monetary Fund's World Economic Outlook database, Oct. 2009, <http://www.imf.org/external/ns/cs.aspx?id=28>. The figure for world GDP in 2009 is a projection.

Table 5A.3. Military expenditure by country, in local currency, 2000–2009

Figures are in local currency at current prices and are for Jan.–Dec. financial years unless otherwise indicated. Countries are grouped by region and subregion.

State	Currency	2000	2001	2002	2003	2004	2005	2006	2007	2008	2009
Africa											
North Africa											
Algeria[1]	m. dinars	141 576	161 505	167 380	170 764	201 930	214 320	224 767	273 415	334 044	383 621
Libya	m. dinars	556	496	575	700	894	904	807	807	1 347	..
Morocco[2]	m. dirhams	13 694 /	16 619	16 254	17 418	17 182	18 006	18 775	19 730	22 824	24 615
Tunisia	m. dinars	456	483	491	525	554	608	662	629	657	731
Sub-Saharan Africa											
Angola[‖,3]	b. kwanzas	5.9	8.9	19.1	50.0	68.3	119	158	156	182	251
Benin	m. CFA francs	10 321	9 612	18 122	20 077	22 072	[24 677]	[25 601]	..	[30 330]	..
Botswana[†]	m. pula	998	1 305	1 451	1 503	1 464	1 556	1 686	[2 031]	[2 380]	[2 673]
Burkina Faso[†]	m. CFA francs	21 500	22 259	24 666	25 571	30 289	33 649	37 081	45 448	54 884	51 740
Burundi	b. francs	30.5	44.2	41.8	47.0	49.4	53.6	46.0	50.1	52.0	..
Cameroon[§]	m. CFA francs	83 236	99 000	52 000	109 556	116 808	117 670	134 345	142 198	155 203	162 085
Cape Verde	m. escudos	814	572	530	565	573	614	614	635	663	..
Central African Republic[‡,4]	m. CFA francs	..	..	7 445	8 729	7 979	8 121	..	9 160	14 111	16 995
Chad[5]	b. CFA francs	18.8	22.5	23.9	23.8	26.7	29.3	..	187	274	206
Congo, Republic of[§]	m. CFA francs	..	28 374	35 035	38 728	40 050	41 954	44 070	50 849	63 420	..
Congo, DRC[6]	m. francs	2 901	..	..	31 908	54 983	78 292	96 045	106 046	89 486	99 100
Côte d'Ivoire[7]	b. CFA francs	..	..	..	124	133	132	140	155	165	..
Djibouti	m. francs	4 625	4 629	5 909	7 422	6 639	7 970	[8 800]	6 135	6 447	..
Equatorial Guinea	m. CFA francs	..	..	..	2 520	..	..	..	..	..	..
Eritrea	m. nakfa	2 220	1 884	2 104	2 452	..	..	..	..	..	4 788
Ethiopia[b]	m. birr	3 307	2 610	2 341	2 452	2 920	3 009	3 005	3 453	4 000	..
Gabon[8]	b. CFA francs	65.0	66.0	66.0	63.0	65.0	60.0	58.0	(59.0)	..	..
Gambia[‡]	m. dalasis	42.5	38.5	45.0	57.0	58.0	85.3	78.2	113	..	..

Ghana[||9]	m. cedis	27.7	23.2	29.3	46.2	50.7	58.2	69.4	118	120	159
Guinea[10]	b. francs	80.3	171	194	167	182	..	..	..	..	..
Guinea-Bissau[||11]	m. CFA francs	6 786	4 533	4 435	4 362	..	6 391	..	..	..	..
Kenya[b]	m. shillings	14 439	16 258	17 430	19 921	21 219	26 652	27 540	39 062	41 209	44 820
Lesotho[a]	m. maloti	208	199	209	207	202	218	245	292	190	452
Liberia[b]	m. dollars	..	..	..	43.4	175	458	228	214	400	569
Madagascar[||12]	b. ariary	63.9	85.7	78.9	89.8	102	108	116	154	176	..
Malawi[a]	m. kwacha	698	988	1 186	1 309	2 752	4 452	[5 525]	[5 923]	..	..
Mali[13]	b. CFA francs	41.4	43.8	45.8	51.6	54.5	63.2	68.9	75.6	77.3	83.3
Mauritania[14]	b. ouguiyas	9.1	13.3	9.9	16.4	18.6	17.7	22.0	..	29.4	30.1
Mauritius[b]	m. rupees	253	270	299	308	293	349	337	392	481	..
Mozambique[||]	m. meticais	843	1 048	1 267	1 422	1 753	1 436	1 459	1 773	2 034	2 320
Namibia[a 15]	m. dollars	617	905	935	994	1 107	1 260	1 375	1 683	2 372	2 598
Niger	b. CFA francs	14.3	18.2	14.4	14.3	16.7	17.3	..	..	..	..
Nigeria	b. naira	37.5	63.5	108	75.9	85.0	88.5	99.9	122	192	224
Rwanda[16]	b. francs	23.9	25.2	24.3	24.3	23.8	25.1	30.1	30.4	37.0 /	64.1
Senegal[§¶]	m. CFA francs	44 400	50 500	51 829	56 293	56 819	65 619	77 678	92 407	97 116	..
Seychelles	m. rupees	59.0	64.3	64.1	66.1	87.6	81.0	79.3	102	80.9	82.3
Sierra Leone	m. leones	48 769	59 408	56 955	66 841	62 026	68 056	[83 686]	[87 998]	[133 080]	..
Somalia	shillings	..	..	..	..	..	..	..	..	..	..
South Africa[a]	m. rand	15 351	17 577	20 788	22 576	22 652	26 190	26 561	[28 302]	[31 259]	[35 894]
Sudan[‡]	m. pounds	1 510	1 034	1 276	1 039	3 200	2 838	3 338	..	..	..
Swaziland[‡ a]	m. emalangeni	173	168	202	255	233	410	392	451	..	..
Tanzania[b]	b. shillings	117	147	125	135	143	172	197	217	247	326
Togo	m. CFA francs	..	..	..	16 757	15 757	17 532	..	..	25 529	..
Uganda[b]	b. shillings	234	244	267	331	379	393	407	549	[732]	[593]
Zambia	b. kwacha	..	..	..	490	626	747	596	1 120	1 068	
Zimbabwe[||17]	m. dollars	15.4	15.3	37.3	136	1 300	2 942	26 604	22 700	..	..

Americas
Central America and the Caribbean

Belize[a]	th. dollars	13 600	15 300	15 800	17 600	19 400	22 100	25 100	27 400	32 400	..

State	Currency	2000	2001	2002	2003	2004	2005	2006	2007	2008	2009
Costa Rica[18]	m. colones	–	–	–	1 259	1 303	1 640	1 695	1 876	2 016	–
Cuba[19]	m. pesos	..	–	..	–	–	–	–	–	[9 667]	[9 537]
Dominican Republic	m. pesos	2 872	3 742	4 440	3 578	4 093	6 687	6 339	7 609	..	..
El Salvador[20]	m. US dollar	112	109	109	106	106	109	116	122	117	135
Guatemala	m. quetzales	1 225	1 546	1 239	1 245	813	768	993	1 043	1 259	1 351
Haiti[a]	th. gourdes	–	–	–	–	–	–	–	–	–	–
Honduras†[21]	m. lempiras	516	646	898	919	928	1 004	1 041	1 598	2 199	2 101
Jamaica[a]	m. dollars	1 896	2 212	2 936	3 244	3 368	3 804	5 100	6 005	5 792	..
Mexico[a]	m. pesos	[31 422]	[33 074]	[33 578]	[35 014]	35 314	39 467	44 496	52 235	54 977	64 348
Nicaragua[22]	m. córdobas	390	389	460	537	527	568	614	717	809	838
Panama	m. balboas	–	–	–	–	–	–	–	–	–	–
North America											
Canada[a]	m. dollars	12 314	13 191	13 379	14 143	14 951	16 001	17 066	19 255	21 026	[22 273]
United States[23]	m. dollars	301 697	312 743	356 720	415 223	464 676	503 353	527 660	556 961	616 073	661 049
South America											
Argentina	m. pesos	3 265	3 182	3 413	3 988	4 285	4 935	5 643	7 109	8 771	[8 715]
Bolivia[24]	m. bolivianos	999	1 213	1 243	1 373	1 388	[1 412]	[1 490]	[1 774]	[1 806]	[2 008]
Brazil	m. reais	20 753	25 557	28 224	25 829	28 608	33 080	35 686	39 887	42 730	52 153
Chile§[25]	b. pesos	1 502	1 615	1 765	1 843	2 159	2 388	2 892	2 939	3 125	3 013
Colombia[26]	b. pesos	5 818	6 932	7 833	9 778	10 209	11 099	13 125	14 238	17 858	20 614
Ecuador	m. US dollars	266	384	505	739	710	954	950	1 310	1 548	1 915
Guyana	m. dollars	..	..	..	..	..	..	..	..	..	..
Paraguay†[27]	b. guaraníes	277	270	288	294	364	347	431	476	577	626
Peru[28]	m. nuevos soles	3 638	3 187	2 982	3 092	3 397	3 820	4 011	3 918	4 057	4 520
Uruguay	m. pesos	[3 663]	4 384	4 333	4 967	5 261	5 696	6 168	6 812	8 397	11 126
Venezuela‖[29]	m. bolívares	1 216	1 383	1 244	1 588	2 740	4 292	6 436	6 377	9 286	8 978

Asia and Oceania

Central Asia

Country	Currency										
Kazakhstan	b. tenge	[199]	185	167	100	78.7	58.0	47.5	37.7	32.5	20.4
Kyrgyzstan[30]	m. som	:	6 755	4 222	3 606	3 100	2 688	2 408	2 055	1 734	1 864
Tajikistan	m. somoni	:	:	:	:	:	134	107	70.7	29.6	21.5
Turkmenistan	b. manat	:	:	:	:	:	:	:	:	:	:
Uzbekistan[31]	b. sum	:	:	:	:	:	:	53.0	44.5	41.1	37.5

East Asia

Country	Currency										
Brunei Darussalam[32]	m. dollars	[482]	[482]	492	472	449	308	530 /	405 /	390	421
Cambodia	b. riel	:	[498]	[388]	328	289	272	270	265	280	309
China[33]	b. yuan	[686]	[599]	[511]	[432]	[364]	[322]	[283]	[256]	[223]	[180]
Indonesia[34]	b. rupiah	[49 777]	[48 599]	[48 257]	[41 736]	[34 658]	32 100	27 446	19 291	16 416	11 449 /
Japan[a § † 35]	b. yen	4 774	4 780	4 801	4 814	4 856	4 903	4 953	4 956	4 955	4 936
Korea, North	b. won	:	:	:	:	:	:	:	:	:	:
Korea, South	b. won	30 721	28 733	25 765	24 039	22 694	[20 421]	[18 884]	[17 643]	[16 708]	[15 609]
Laos	b. kip	:	(185)	(157)	(135)	(125)	(121)	(115)	(115)	(112)	(107)
Malaysia	m. ringgit	13 679	14 717	13 649	11 981	11 817	10 728	10 950	8 504	7 351	5 826
Mongolia	m. tugriks	:	:	66 200	46 232	35 914	32 891	27 899	28 071	25 384	26 126
Myanmar[a 36]	b. kyats	:	:	:	:	:	:	76.1	76.1	64.0	63.5
Philippines	m. pesos	64 992	61 965	62 188	51 527	47 634	43 847	44 440	38 907	35 977	36 208
Singapore[a]	m. dollars	11 447	10 803	10 009	9 628	9 252	8 620	8 238	8 204	7 820	7 423
Taiwan	b. dollars	[308]	[262]	[256]	[235]	[248]	253	238	225	248	243
Thailand	m. baht	[162 135]	[137 135]	[110 540]	[86 706]	[79 519]	[75 498]	77 027	76 724	75 413	71 268
Timor-Leste[37]	m. US dollar	38.0	23.7	[11.5]	24.4 /	9.8	6.6	:	:	:	:
Viet Nam	b. dong	36 180	34 848	28 735	20 577	16 278	14 409	13 058	:	:	:

Oceania

Country	Currency										
Australia[b]	m. dollars	25 703	23 027	21 179	20 156	18 111	16 699	16 006	14 739	14 397	12 608
Fiji[† 38]	m. dollars	:	77.2	75.9	71.6	72.9	81.1	70.7	67.6	74.7	68.2
New Zealand[b]	m. dollars	2 134	2 046	1 875	1 807	1 645	1 528	1 518	1 419	1 403	1 453
Papua New Guinea[39]	m. kina	109	95.0	112	93.7	94.2	78.7	68.8	66.3	85.5	85.0

State	Currency	2000	2001	2002	2003	2004	2005	2006	2007	2008	2009
South Asia											
Afghanistan[40]	m. afghanis	..	..	..	5 622	5 404	5 544	6 358	11 506	11 471	12 783
Bangladesh[b]	m. takas	34 020	34 020	34 190	38 110	41 150	44 860	53 980	59 510	68 850	70 150
India[a 41]	b. rupees	647	703	722	774	964	1 025	1 091	1 182	1 482	1 851
Nepal[b q]	m. rupees	3 817	5 882	7 420	8 255	10 996	11 745	11 136	11 389	14 521	15 597
Pakistan[‡]	b. rupees	157	182	195	220	244	281	292	325	361	410
Sri Lanka[42]	b. rupees	[63.3]	[60.3]	[54.7]	[52.3]	62.7	64.7	82.2	117	157	171
Europe											
Eastern Europe											
Armenia[† 43]	b. drams	36.7	36.8	36.8	44.3	52.3	64.4	78.3	95.8	121	[128]
Azerbaijan[‖]	m. manats	[107]	[123]	[136]	[173]	[224]	288	641	812	1 344	1 206
Belarus	b. roubles	[123]	247	366	475	679	975	1 355	1 603	1 887	2 501
Georgia[† 44]	m. lari	[37.2]	[49.4]	74.6	91.5	135	388	720	1 556	1 625	1 009
Moldova[† q 45]	m. lei	63.3	76.7	94.7	115	116	151	216	276	383	285
Russia[46]	b. roubles	[271]	[365]	[470]	[568]	[656]	[806]	[967]	[1 144]	[1 448]	[1 693]
Ukraine[§]	m. hryvnias	6 184	5 848	6 266	7 615	8 963	12 328	15 082	20 685	25 341	[26 077]
Western and Central Europe											
Albania[§ q 47]	m. leks	6 519	7 638	8 220	9 279	10 373	11 000	13 831	17 619	21 450	23 633
Austria	m. euros	[2 090]	[1 999]	1 999	2 111	2 158	2 160	2 105	2 566	2 560	2 504
Belgium	m. euros	3 463	3 393	3 344	3 434	3 433	3 400	3 434	3 773	4 036	3 872
Bosnia–Herzegovina[† 48]	m. marka	..	..	501	351	315	273	278	281	325	371
Bulgaria[† 49]	m. leva	[746]	[887]	[947]	[986]	1 025	1 101	1 171	1 475	1 631	1 548
Croatia[50]	m. kunas	[5 461]	[5 251]	[5 775]	[4 757]	4 250	4 323	4 959	5 277	6 412	6 021
Cyprus[† ‖]	m. euros	[299]	[360]	[253]	[255]	271	302	304	295	310	378
Czech Republic[51]	m. koruny	44 670	44 978	48 924	53 194	52 481	58 445	55 358	53 261	48 360	55 984
Denmark	m. kroner	19 339	21 017	21 269	21 075	21 441	20 800	23 173	22 731	24 410	23 124
Estonia	m. krooni	1 329	1 640	2 028	2 376	2 581	3 346	3 928	5 079	5 409	4 917
Finland	m. euros	1 691	1 653	1 712	2 006	2 131	2 206	2 281	2 203	2 468	2 580

Country	Currency										
France[52]	m. euros	36 702	37 187	38 681	40 684	42 690	42 545	43 457	44 273	45 063	45 991
Germany	m. euros	30 554	30 648	31 168	31 060	30 610	30 600	30 365	31 090	31 921	[32 861]
Greece	m. euros	5 921	5 986	6 085	[5 355]	[6 028]	[6 818]	[7 321]	[7 496]	[8 620]	[9 474]
Hungary	m. forint	226 041	272 426	279 569	314 380	310 731	318 552	296 665	326 205	321 486	[340 798]
Iceland[†][53]	m. krónur	–	–	–	–	–	–	–	–	688	1 227
Ireland	m. euros	[754]	858	862	855	887	921	949	1 003	1 081	1 032
Italy[54]	m. euros	24 325	24 592	25 887	26 795	27 476	26 959	26 631	[26 275]	[26 560]	[25 744]
Latvia	m. lats	42.4	54.6	91.0	108	124	154	206	251	305	344
Lithuania	m. litai	796	860	908	1 077	1 139	[1 150]	[1 292]	[1 516]	[1 711]	[1 596]
Luxembourg	m. euros	139	179	192	205	[213]	[238]	[263]	[268]	..	..
Macedonia, FYR[55]	m. denars	4 602	15 397	6 841	6 292	6 683	6 259	6 149	7 272	7 229	8 531
Malta[†‖]	m. euros	25.9	28.4	28.7	30.0	32.5	34.3	35.3	35.8	38.3	36.1
Montenegro[56]	m. euros	..	..	..	..	..	41.6	42.3	39.9	48.6	40.9
Netherlands	m. euros	6 482	6 929	7 149	7 404	7 552	7 693	8 145	8 387	8 348	8 738
Norway	m. kroner	25 722	26 669	32 461	31 985	32 945	31 471	32 142	34 439	33 102	[35 115]
Poland	m. zlotys	13 763	14 864	15 401	16 249	17 793	19 023	19 959	[22 768]	[25 596]	[27 169]
Portugal	m. euros	2 393	2 598	2 765	2 755	2 996	3 248	3 242	3 190	3 285	[3 307]
Romania‖	m. lei	2 031	2 864	3 491	4 151	4 994	5 757	6 324	6 358	7 558	6 960
Serbia[57]	m. dinars	21 292	33 060	43 695	42 070	43 154	41 996	47 342	56 792	63 295	64 291
Slovakia[†‖]	m. euros	523	632	662	762	762	848	898	934	[1 000]	[948]
Slovenia‖	m. euros	207	275	328	360	396	413	485	506	566	612
Spain	m. euros	7 599	7 972	8 414	8 587	9 132	9 508	11 506	12 219	13 105	[13 199]
Sweden[58]	m. kronor	44 542	42 639	42 401	42 903	40 527	41 240	41 150	43 163	39 710	[40 314]
Switzerland[†¶][59]	m. francs	4 503	4 476	4 461	4 437	4 381	4 344	3 972	4 120	4 389	[4 465]
Turkey‖	m. liras	6 248	8 844	13 641	15 426	15 568	16 232	19 260	18 333	21 014	[26 314]
United Kingdom[a][60]	m. pounds	23 552	24 874	26 991	29 338	29 524	30 603	31 454	33 486	36 431	37 784

Middle East

Country	Currency										
Bahrain[61]	m. dinars	121	126	150	175	180	183	203	222	245	[279]
Egypt[b]	m. pounds	11 569	12 148	13 333	14 563	14 804	15 933	17 922	19 350	21 718	22 831
Iran[a¶][62]	b. rials	24 443	27 847	21 665	34 955	49 628	69 664	81 283	74 616	90 464	..
Iraq[§][63]	b. dinars	..	..	..	..	(892)	(1 649)	(2 117)	(2 437)	(6 352)	(4 863)

State	Currency	2000	2001	2002	2003	2004	2005	2006	2007	2008	2009
Israel[64]	m. shekels	39 587	41 788	48 957	46 351	44 060	45 739	49 690	49 390	50 504	53 064
Jordan	m. dinars	375	375	370	434	416	428	497	732	886	981
Kuwait[a]	m. dinars	707	784	882	950	1 039	1 020	1 059	1 304	1 237	1 310
Lebanon	b. pounds	1 402	1 445	1 368	1 392	1 439	[1 451]	[1 521]	[1 737]	1 763	2 150
Oman[‡ 65]	m. rials	809	933	958	1 010	1 144	1 404	1 550	1 663	1 775	1 545
Qatar[66]	m. riyals	..	..	3 324	3 428	3 374	3 901	4 610	6 391	..	..
Saudi Arabia[§ 67]	m. riyals	74 866	78 850	69 382	70 303	78 414	95 146	110 779	132 922	143 336	154 772
Syria[68]	b. pounds	49.3	53.4	55.3	67.1	70.2	75.7	74.9	82.7	86.8	101
United Arab Emirates[69]	m. dirhams	[24 240]	[24 062]	[22 775]	[24 645]	[27 951]	[27 626]	[35 619]	[42 697]	..	..
Yemen	b. riyals	76.6	91.1	130	148	136	156	162	209	239	..

Notes: See below table 5A.5.

Table 5A.4. Military expenditure by country, in constant US dollars for 2000–2009 and current US dollars for 2009

Figures are in US $m. at constant 2008 prices and exchange rates for 2000–2009 and, in the right-most column, marked *, in current US$ m. for 2009. Figures are for calendar years except for the USA, for which the figures are for financial years. Countries are grouped by region and subregion.

State	2000	2001	2002	2003	2004	2005	2006	2007	2008	2009	2009*
Africa											
North Africa											
Algeria[1]	2 774	3 036	3 102	3 085	3 523	3 679	3 763	4 422	5 172	5 677	5 283
Libya	437	427	549	683	892	879	773	728	1 100	..	..
Morocco[2]	1 382	2 500	2 379	2 520	2 449	2 541	2 566	2 642	2 945	3 143	3 055
Tunisia	476	494	489	509	519	558	581	536	533	571	541
Sub-Saharan Africa											
Angola‖[3]	2 062	1 243	1 274	1 632	1 601	2 268	2 664	2 337	2 424	2 893	3 164
Benin	30.1	26.9	49.5	54.1	58.9	[62.5]	[62.5]	..	[67.7]	..	..
Botswana	271	332	354	341	316	302	292	[321]	[336]	[353]	[362]
Burkina Faso†	62.9	62.1	67.3	68.4	81.3	84.9	91.4	112	123	112	110
Burundi	52.0	68.9	66.1	68.9	65.4	62.5	52.2	52.4	43.9	..	..
Cameroon§	241	241	261	280	297	294	319	334	347	352	343
Cape Verde	13.3	9.1	8.2	8.7	9.0	9.6	9.1	9.0	8.8	..	..
Central African Republic‡[4]	..	..	20.5	23.1	21.6	21.3	..	22.4	31.5	36.7	36.0
Chad[5]	54.0	57.5	58.1	58.9	69.8	70.9	..	459	611	412	436
Congo, Republic of§	..	81.5	96.4	107	108	110	108	122	142	..	..
Congo, DRC[6]	65.4	..	..	112	185	217	236	222	160	127	128
Côte d'Ivoire[7]	..	..	..	323	341	327	338	368	369	..	..
Djibouti	35.1	34.6	43.8	54.0	46.8	54.5	[58.2]	38.6	36.3	..	..
Equatorial Guinea	..	..	..	..	..	..	..	..	..	..	..
Eritrea	473	350	335	327	327	..	..	..	..	..	..
Ethiopia	1 272	808	665	547	594	587	530	486	388	422	373
Gabon[8]	168	167	167	156	160	146	143	(139)	..	..	..
Gambia‡	3.4	3.0	3.2	3.5	3.1	4.3	3.9	5.3	..	..	..

State	2000	2001	2002	2003	2004	2005	2006	2007	2008	2009	2009*
Ghana[||9]	94.0	59.1	65.1	80.9	78.9	78.7	84.6	130	114	127	114
Guinea[10]	62.3	126	139	108	99.8	..	..	..	..	..	..
Guinea-Bissau[||11]	19.2	12.4	11.7	12.0	..	16.8	..	..	..	..	..
Kenya	422	485	522	527	520	549	543	608	580	518	556
Lesotho	45.6	47.9	36.7	34.5	32.2	32.8	34.5	37.6	26.1	43.6	45.6
Liberia	..	..	..	..	4.2	10.4	4.8	4.0	4.9	7.1	7.1
Madagascar[||12]	82.4	103	82.1	94.6	94.2	84.5	81.4	98.2	103	..	..
Malawi	13.2	14.1	15.2	15.6	26.3	38.3	[43.9]	[45.1]	..	..	..
Mali[13]	117	117	117	134	146	159	170	184	173	182	176
Mauritania[14]	64.9	90.7	65.0	103	106	89.6	105	..	122	122	115
Mauritius	14.4	14.5	14.9	15.3	14.4	14.7	14.4	14.0	15.3	..	..
Mozambique[||]	81.8	93.2	96.5	95.4	104	79.8	71.6	80.5	83.7	92.5	84.6
Namibia[15]	134	159	159	156	165	183	192	215	266	283	300
Niger	40.4	49.4	38.1	38.5	44.8	43.0	..	..	..	..	..
Nigeria	835	1 189	1 795	1 105	1 076	950	990	1 150	1 616	1 681	1 501
Rwanda[16]	82.7	84.7	79.9	74.6	65.1	62.9	69.3	64.2	67.7	72.7	75.2
Senegal[§¶]	122	135	135	147	148	168	194	218	217	..	..
Seychelles	10.3	10.7	10.6	10.5	13.4	12.3	12.1	14.7	8.6	6.6	6.1
Sierra Leone	31.9	38.1	37.7	41.2	33.4	32.8	[36.8]	[34.7]	[44.6]	..	..
Somalia	..	..	..	..	..	..	..	..	..	..	..
South Africa	2 573	2 893	3 111	3 263	3 367	3 686	3 736	[3 708]	[3 694]	[3 926]	[4 100]
Sudan[‡]	1 390	873	1 011	773	2 198	1 797	1 971	..	..	..	..
Swaziland[‡]	36.9	34.7	35.3	41.2	45.4	59.5	59.2	60.0	..	..	..
Tanzania	147	171	167	151	154	167	182	191	194	216	217
Togo	..	..	..	45.0	44.8	43.9	..	..	57.0	..	..
Uganda	214	216	232	250	286	286	277	311	[372]	[341]	[326]
Zambia	..	..	..	..	210	227	248	179	299	251	212
Zimbabwe[||17]	..	..	..	..	..	..	..	..	..	..	..

Americas

Central America and the Caribbean

Belize	9.2	9.5	9.7	10.4	11.2	12.2	13.2	14.3	15.6	..	..
Costa Rica[18]	–	–	–	–	–	–	–	–	–	–	–
Cuba[19]	..	..	..	(1 259)	(1 303)	(1 734)	(1 830)	(2 026)	(2 177)	..	..
Dominican Republic	241	289	326	206	156	244	215	243	[279]	[272]	[265]
El Salvador[20]	153	144	141	135	129	126	130	130	117	134	135
Guatemala	295	346	257	245	149	130	157	155	166	175	166
Haiti	–	–	–	–	–	–	–	–	–	–	–
Honduras†[21]	51.4	58.7	75.7	72.0	67.2	66.8	65.6	94.2	116	105	111
Jamaica	61.7	65.7	79.2	82.6	76.6	73.6	87.5	96.9	80.3	..	..
Mexico	[4 066]	[4 024]	[3 889]	[3 879]	3 737	4 016	4 370	4 934	4 940	5 490	4 762
Nicaragua[22]	40.3	37.9	43.2	47.9	43.3	42.6	42.2	44.4	41.8	41.7	41.2
Panama	0	0	0	0	0	0	0	0	0	0	0
North America											
Canada	13 823	14 183	14 258	14 519	15 069	15 731	16 463	17 948	19 290	[20 564]	[19 238]
United States[23]	377 228	380 271	426 982	485 975	529 673	554 930	563 549	578 340	616 073	663 255	661 049
South America											
Argentina	2 201	2 168	1 848	1 903	1 958	2 057	2 121	2 455	2 790	[2 608]	[2 349]
Bolivia[24]	208	249	252	270	261	[252]	[255]	[279]	[250]	[268]	[286]
Brazil	19 550	22 531	22 947	18 306	19 021	20 581	21 310	22 983	23 302	27 124	26 077
Chile§[25]	3 835	3 981	4 246	4 310	4 998	5 364	6 282	6 116	5 982	5 683	5 372
Colombia[26]	4 766	5 259	5 588	6 511	6 419	6 643	7 533	7 742	9 076	10 055	9 512
Ecuador	534	560	655	888	831	1 090	1 053	1 420	1 548	1 821	1 915
Guyana	..	..	..	..	..	..	..	..	..	..	..
Paraguay†[27]	125	114	110	98.0	116	104	118	120	132	140	126
Peru[28]	1 504	1 292	1 206	1 223	1 296	1 434	1 477	1 417	1 387	1 502	1 501
Uruguay	[352]	404	350	336	326	337	343	351	401	496	493
Venezuela‖[29]	2 563	2 591	1 903	1 853	2 627	3 548	4 681	3 908	4 329	3 254	4 186

State	2000	2001	2002	2003	2004	2005	2006	2007	2008	2009	2009*
Asia and Oceania											
Central Asia											
Kazakhstan	335	493	540	640	731	921	1 079	1 623	1 541	[1 540]	[1 348]
Kyrgyzstan[30]	90.2	78.4	91.0	104	111	123	135	144	185	:	:
Tajikistan	19.7	19.6	41.7	54.1	63.4	:	:	:	:	:	:
Turkmenistan	:	:	:	:	:	:	:	:	:	:	:
Uzbekistan[31]	68.2	58.7	49.9	53.8	:	:	:	:	:	:	:
East Asia											
Brunei Darussalam[32]	308	284	302	315	248	301	339	353	[342]	[336]	[331]
Cambodia	125	114	104	105	102	102	109	[120]	[123]	:	:
China[33]	[31 200]	[38 400]	[44 400]	[48 500]	[53 100]	[59 000]	[68 800]	[77 900]	[86 200]	[98 800]	[100 400]
Indonesia[34]	2 970	3 136	3 294	4 397	4 840	[4 731]	[5 037]	[5 478]	[5 011]	[4 908]	[4 791]
Japan[§][35]	47 496	48 009	48 496	48 596	48 225	47 888	47 347	47 124	46 296	46 859	51 029
Korea, North	:	:	:	:	:	:	:	:	:	:	:
Korea, South	[18 306]	[18 835]	[19 354]	[20 012]	[20 891]	22 595	23 419	24 477	26 072	27 130	24 059
Laos	(24.0)	(23.2)	(21.6)	(18.7)	(17.8)	(17.2)	(17.4)	(19.3)	(21.2)	:	:
Malaysia	2 122	2 640	2 999	3 824	3 691	3 948	3 864	4 314	4 412	4 078	3 881
Mongolia	44.2	40.4	44.3	41.8	45.6	44.2	54.1	71.0	:	:	:
Myanmar[36]	:	:	:	:	:	:	:	:	:	:	:
Philippines	1 270	1 181	1 240	1 369	1 275	1 287	1 310	1 538	1 402	1 424	1 365
Singapore	5 997	6 141	6 474	6 538	6 661	7 076	7 136	7 412	7 513	7 966	7 762
Taiwan	8 448	8 618	7 851	8 317	8 715	8 325	7 848	8 406	8 319	9 866	9 324
Thailand	2 702	2 813	2 842	2 803	[2 673]	[2 693]	[2 807]	[3 500]	[4 117]	[4 908]	[4 729]
Timor-Leste[37]	:	:	:	:	:	10.3	20.6	[25.9]	23.7	36.6	38.0
Viet Nam	:	:	:	1 338	1 370	1 430	1 683	2 170	2 138	2 073	2 120
Oceania											
Australia	13 389	13 929	14 589	14 980	15 570	16 142	17 138	18 090	18 540	20 109	19 005
Fiji[†][38]	57.0	59.9	53.8	54.0	60.3	52.9	50.7	51.3	48.4	:	:

New Zealand	1 242	1 215	1 170	1 196	1 213	1 227	1 291	1 352	1 378	1 447	1 306
Papua New Guinea[39]	52.5	48.3	33.5	30.3	34.0	39.9	38.8	46.0	35.2	37.2	39.5
South Asia											
Afghanistan[40]	..	..	..	176	180	163	178	260	228	272	250
Bangladesh	803	803	779	781	785	795	856	901	936	938	1 007
India[41]	21 874	22 636	22 566	23 070	26 773	28 295	28 465	28 866	32 334	36 600	36 341
Nepal[¶]	81.4	105	140	156	187	206	193	179	186	194	194
Pakistan[‡]	3 920	4 195	4 508	4 814	5 015	5 210	5 269	5 275	4 877	4 823	4 716
Sri Lanka[42]	[1 458]	[1 217]	[1 007]	[905]	1 009	934	1 078	1 320	1 450	1 525	1 485
Europe											
Eastern Europe											
Armenia[†][43]	165	160	159	183	201	246	291	341	396	[405]	[352]
Azerbaijan[‖]	[251]	[284]	[306]	[382]	[463]	542	1 112	1 210	1 635	1 434	1 500
Belarus	[296]	369	383	388	469	611	793	865	883	1 036	896
Georgia[†][44]	[43.4]	[55.0]	78.7	92.2	129	341	580	1 148	1 090	665	604
Moldova[†][¶][45]	14.2	15.6	18.3	19.9	17.8	20.7	26.3	29.9	36.8	27.5	25.6
Russia[46]	[29 700]	[33 000]	[36 600]	[39 000]	[40 600]	[44 200]	[48 400]	[52 500]	[58 300]	[61 000]	[53 300]
Ukraine[§]	2 658	2 245	2 387	2 758	2 977	3 606	4 045	4 917	4 811	[4 258]	[3 351]
Western and Central Europe											
Albania[§][¶][47]	98.9	112	112	126	138	143	175	217	256	276	249
Austria	[3 623]	[3 376]	3 317	3 454	3 460	3 385	3 252	3 879	3 750	3 650	3 478
Belgium	6 101	5 832	5 655	5 717	5 598	5 394	5 352	5 775	5 912	5 674	5 377
Bosnia and Herzegovina[†][¶][48]	..	..	453	315	283	236	227	226	243	276	264
Bulgaria[†][49]	[945]	[1 046]	[1 056]	[1 076]	1 052	1 076	1 067	1 239	1 220	1 127	1 100
Croatia[50]	[1 411]	[1 307]	[1 414]	[1 144]	1 002	987	1 096	1 134	1 299	1 191	1 139
Cyprus[†][‖]	[551]	[651]	[445]	[430]	447	486	477	452	454	550	524
Czech Republic[51]	3 280	3 155	3 371	3 663	3 514	3 842	3 549	3 318	2 833	3 246	2 937
Denmark	4 481	4 759	4 702	4 562	4 588	4 372	4 781	4 610	4 788	4 476	4 313
Estonia	182	212	253	293	309	384	432	524	506	460	437
Finland	2 850	2 716	2 770	3 217	3 411	3 501	3 564	3 358	3 615	3 768	3 583

State	2000	2001	2002	2003	2004	2005	2006	2007	2008	2009	2009*
France[52]	62 707	62 496	63 779	65 716	67 520	66 096	66 449	66 673	66 009	67 316	63 876
Germany	51 487	50 646	50 790	50 095	48 557	47 798	46 695	46 740	46 759	[48 022]	[45 640]
Greece	11 335	11 085	10 874	[9 243]	[10 112]	[11 045]	[11 493]	[11 437]	[12 627]	[13 917]	[13 158]
Hungary	2 078	2 292	2 235	2 402	2 223	2 201	1 973	2 010	1 868	[1 900]	[1 684]
Iceland[†][53]	–	–	–	–	–	–	–	–	7.8	12.5	9.9
Ireland	[1 489]	1 616	1 552	1 487	1 510	1 530	1 517	1 528	1 583	1 581	1 433
Italy[54]	43 150	42 443	43 602	43 956	44 100	42 428	41 053	[39 777]	[38 906]	[37 427]	[35 756]
Latvia	146	183	299	345	372	433	545	602	634	692	682
Lithuania	429	457	481	577	603	[594]	[643]	[714]	[726]	[648]	[643]
Luxembourg	248	311	327	341	[347]	[379]	[408]	[406]	..	..	..
Macedonia, FYR[55]	139	441	192	174	183	172	163	186	173	204	193
Malta[†][||]	46.4	49.5	48.9	50.5	53.3	54.5	54.6	54.6	56.0	51.6	50.1
Montenegro[56]	..	..	..	..	..	..	69.9	63.7	71.2	57.9	56.8
Netherlands	11 311	11 606	11 593	11 758	11 848	11 868	12 424	12 589	12 228	12 642	12 136
Norway	5 322	5 356	6 435	6 187	6 343	5 968	5 957	6 336	5 869	[6 098]	[5 584]
Poland	7 072	7 240	7 362	7 707	8 148	8 532	8 852	[9 863]	[10 626]	[10 860]	[8 705]
Portugal	4 439	4 616	4 746	4 579	4 864	5 156	5 008	4 794	4 812	[4 884]	[4 593]
Romania[||]	2 250	2 360	2 348	2 422	2 604	2 754	2 839	2 722	3 000	2 616	2 282
Serbia[57]	1 692	1 347	1 490	1 306	1 207	1 011	1 020	1 150	1 136	1 070	951
Slovakia[†][||]	1 102	1 241	1 257	1 334	1 239	1 343	1 362	1 377	[1 410]	[1 316]	[1 317]
Slovenia[||]	443	544	604	628	667	679	778	783	829	888	850
Spain	14 443	14 627	14 978	14 835	15 313	15 423	18 030	18 627	19 196	[19 409]	[18 332]
Sweden[58]	7 787	7 278	7 085	7 033	6 619	6 706	6 601	6 774	6 025	[6 135]	[5 267]
Switzerland[†][¶][59]	4 522	4 451	4 408	4 356	4 267	4 182	3 784	3 896	4 052	[4 141]	[4 104]
Turkey[||]	21 758	19 946	21 223	19 155	17 481	16 549	17 768	15 551	16 140	[19 009]	[16 977]
United Kingdom[60]	54 055	55 909	59 310	62 618	62 352	62 397	622 74	63 042	65 615	69 271	58 327
Middle East											
Bahrain[61]	368	387	462	531	535	529	576	609	651	[721]	[742]
Egypt	3 562	3 807	3 982	4 171	3 946	3 938	4 030	4 058	3 780	3 665	4 013

Iran¶62	7 409	8 175	6 148	7 195	9 109	11 296	12 233	10 158	9 174	. .	. .
Iraq§63	. .	. .			. .	(2 845)	(2 383)	(2 097)	(5 324)	(3 814)	(4 156)
Israel64	12 856	13 423	14 888	13 993	13 357	13 685	14 559	14 397	14 076	14 309	13 495
Jordan	768	754	730	842	781	777	850	1 187	1 250	1 392	1 383
Kuwait	4 023	3 954	4 080	4 396	4 732	4 580	4 550	5 109	4 660	4 589	4 485
Lebanon	1 173	1 214	1 129	1 134	1 153	[1 171]	[1 163]	[1 276]	1 169	1 408	1 426
Oman‡65	2 621	3 049	3 140	3 303	3 713	4 476	4 786	4 849	4 617	4 003	4 018
Qatar66			1 588	1 602	1 476	1 569	1 657	2 020	. .	. .	. .
Saudi Arabia§67	23 523	25 053	21 995	22 157	24 632	29 680	33 809	38 946	38 223	39 257	41 273
Syria68	1 586	1 668	1 731	1 985	1 988	1 999	1 798	1 911	1 732	1 883	2 144
United Arab Emirates69	[10 940]	[10 575]	[9 725]	[10 201]	[11 016]	[10 254]	[12 098]	[13 052]	. .	. .	. .
Yemen	956	1 016	1 286	1 327	1 082	1 113	1 041	1 245	1 196	. .	. .

Notes: See below table 5A.5.

Table 5A.5. Military expenditure by country as percentage of gross domestic product, 2000–2008

Countries are grouped by region and subregion.

State	2000	2001	2002	2003	2004	2005	2006	2007	2008
Africa									
North Africa									
Algeria[1]	3.4	3.8	3.7	3.3	3.3	2.8	2.6	2.9	3.0
Libya	3.1	2.7	2.2	2.2	2.2	1.6	1.2	1.0	1.3
Morocco[2]	2.3	3.9	3.6	3.7	3.4	3.4	3.3	3.2	3.4
Tunisia	1.7	1.7	1.6	1.6	1.6	1.6	1.6	1.4	1.3
Sub-Saharan Africa									
Angola‖[3]	6.4	4.5	4.5	4.8	4.0	4.7	4.6	3.6	3.0
Benin	0.6	0.5	0.9	1.0	1.0	[1.1]	[1.0]	. .	[1.1]
Botswana	3.6	3.8	3.8	3.8	3.4	3.1	2.8	[2.8]	[2.7]
Burkina Faso†	1.2	1.1	1.1	1.0	1.1	1.1	1.2	1.3	1.4
Burundi	6.0	8.0	7.2	7.3	6.6	6.2	4.7	4.9	4.0
Cameroon§	1.3	1.3	1.3	1.4	1.4	1.3	1.4	1.5	1.5
Cape Verde	1.3	0.8	0.7	0.7	0.7	0.7	0.6	0.5	0.5
Central African Republic‡[4]	. .	. .	1.1	1.3	1.2	1.1	. .	1.1	1.6
Chad[5]	1.9	1.8	1.7	1.5	1.1	0.9	. .	5.0	6.6
Congo, Republic of§	. .	1.4	1.7	1.9	1.7	1.3	1.1	1.4	1.1
Congo, DRC[6]	1.0	. .	. .	1.4	2.1	2.3	2.3	2.1	1.4
Côte d'Ivoire[7]	. .	. .	. .	1.5	1.5	1.4	1.5	1.5	1.5
Djibouti	4.7	4.5	5.6	6.7	5.6	6.3	[6.4]	4.1	3.7
Equatorial Guinea	. .	. .	. .	. .	. .	. .	. .	. .	. .
Eritrea	32.7	22.1	20.7	20.9	. .	. .	. .	. .	. .
Ethiopia	9.6	4.7	3.6	2.9	2.8	2.5	2.1	1.7	1.4
Gabon[8]	1.8	1.9	2.0	1.8	1.7	1.3	1.1	(1.0)	. .
Gambia‡	1.0	0.9	1.0	1.1	0.4	0.5	0.4	0.5	. .
Ghana‖[9]	1.0	0.6	0.6	0.7	0.6	0.6	0.6	0.8	0.7

Guinea[10]	1.5	2.9	3.1	2.4	2.2	..	..	..	..
Guinea-Bissau‖ [11]	4.4	3.1	3.2	2.9	..	3.8	..	..	..
Kenya	1.3	1.5	1.6	1.6	1.6	1.7	1.6	1.8	1.9
Lesotho	3.9	3.3	2.9	2.8	2.4	2.4	2.3	2.4	1.6
Liberia	..	..	..	..	0.7	1.5	0.6	0.5	0.6
Madagascar‖ [12]	1.2	1.4	1.3	1.3	1.2	1.1	1.0	1.1	1.1
Malawi	0.7	0.7	0.8	0.7	1.2	1.6	[1.6]	[1.5]	..
Mali[13]	2.2	2.0	1.9	2.0	1.9	2.0	2.1	2.1	1.9
Mauritania[14]	3.5	4.6	3.2	4.9	4.7	3.6	3.0	..	3.7
Mauritius	0.2	0.2	0.2	0.2	0.2	0.2	0.2	0.2	0.2
Mozambique‖	1.3	1.2	1.3	1.3	1.4	0.9	0.8	0.8	0.8
Namibia[15]	2.7	2.2	2.8	2.9	2.9	3.1	2.9	3.0	3.5
Niger	1.2	1.4	0.9	0.9	1.0	0.9	0.5	..	..
Nigeria	0.8	1.3	1.5	0.9	0.7	0.6	1.9	0.6	0.8
Rwanda[16]	3.4	3.4	3.1	2.5	2.1	1.9	1.5	1.6	1.5
Senegal§¶	1.3	1.4	1.4	1.3	1.2	1.4	1.9	1.6	1.6
Seychelles	1.7	1.8	1.7	1.7	2.3	2.1	1.9	2.1	1.3
Sierra Leone	3.7	3.7	2.9	2.9	2.1	2.0	[2.1]	[1.9]	[2.4]
Somalia	..	..	..	..	..	..	..	..	..
South Africa‡	1.6	1.7	1.7	1.8	1.6	1.6	1.5	[1.4]	[1.3]
Sudan‡	4.8	2.9	3.2	2.3	5.8	4.4	4.4	..	..
Swaziland‡	1.6	1.4	1.5	1.7	1.7	2.1	2.0	1.9	..
Tanzania	1.5	1.6	1.4	1.2	1.1	1.1	1.2	1.1	1.1
Togo	..	..	..	1.6	1.5	1.5	..	..	1.9
Uganda	2.5	2.4	2.4	2.3	2.3	2.2	2.0	2.0	[2.3]
Zambia	..	..	..	..	1.9	2.0	1.9	1.3	2.0
Zimbabwe‖ [17]	4.7	2.2	2.2	2.5	5.5	2.3	1.9	..	..
Americas									
Central America and the Caribbean									
Belize	0.9	0.9	0.8	0.9	0.9	1.0	1.0	1.1	1.1
Costa Rica[18]	–	–	–	–	–	–	–	–	–

State	2000	2001	2002	2003	2004	2005	2006	2007	2008
Cuba[19]	..	..	..	..	..	..	..	..	..
Dominican Republic	0.7	0.9	1.0	0.6	0.5	0.7	0.5	0.6	[0.6]
El Salvador[20]	0.9	0.8	0.8	0.7	0.7	0.6	0.6	0.6	0.5
Guatemala	0.8	0.9	0.8	0.7	0.4	0.4	0.4	0.4	0.4
Haiti	–	–	–	–	–	–	–	–	–
Honduras[†21]	0.5	0.5	0.7	0.6	0.6	0.5	0.5	0.7	0.8
Jamaica	0.5	0.5	0.6	0.6	0.5	0.5	0.6	0.6	0.6
Mexico	[0.6]	[0.6]	[0.5]	[0.5]	0.4	0.4	0.4	0.5	0.5
Nicaragua[22]	0.8	0.7	0.8	0.9	0.7	0.7	0.7	0.7	0.7
Panama	–	–	–	–	–	–	–	–	–
North America									
Canada	1.1	1.2	1.2	1.1	1.1	1.1	1.2	1.2	1.3
United States[23]	3.1	3.1	3.4	3.8	4.0	4.0	3.9	4.0	4.3
South America									
Argentina	1.1	1.2	1.1	1.1	1.0	0.9	0.9	0.9	0.8
Bolivia[24]	1.9	2.3	2.2	2.2	2.0	[1.8]	[1.6]	[1.7]	[1.5]
Brazil	1.8	2.0	1.9	1.5	1.5	1.5	1.5	1.5	1.5
Chile[§25]	3.7	3.7	3.8	3.6	3.7	3.6	3.7	3.4	3.5
Colombia[26]	3.0	3.2	3.4	3.7	3.4	3.3	3.4	3.3	3.7
Ecuador	1.7	1.8	2.0	2.6	2.2	2.6	2.3	2.9	2.8
Guyana	..	..	..	..	..	..	..	..	..
Paraguay[†27]	1.1	1.0	1.0	0.8	0.9	0.8	0.8	0.8	0.8
Peru[28]	2.0	1.7	1.5	1.5	1.4	1.5	1.3	1.2	1.1
Uruguay	[1.5]	1.8	1.7	1.6	1.4	1.4	1.3	1.3	1.3
Venezuela[‖29]	1.5	1.6	1.2	1.2	1.3	1.4	1.6	1.3	1.4
Asia and Oceania									
Central Asia									
Kazakhstan	0.8	1.0	1.1	1.1	1.0	1.0	1.0	1.3	1.2

Kyrgyzstan[30]	2.9	2.3	2.7	2.9	2.8	3.1	3.2	3.0	3.7
Tajikistan	1.2	1.2	2.1	2.2	2.2	. .	. .	. .	. .
Turkmenistan	. .	. .	. .	. .	. .	. .	. .	. .	. .
Uzbekistan[31]	1.2	0.8	0.6	0.5	. .	. .	. .	. .	. .
East Asia									
Brunei Darussalam[32]	5.7	5.2	5.3	5.1	3.6	3.9	3.8	3.9	[3.9]
Cambodia	2.2	1.8	1.6	1.5	1.3	1.1	1.1	[1.1]	[1.1]
China[33]	[1.8]	[2.0]	[2.1]	[2.1]	[2.0]	[2.0]	[2.0]	[2.0]	[2.0]
Indonesia[34]	1.0	1.0	1.1	1.4	1.4	[1.2]	[1.2]	[1.2]	[1.0]
Japan[§][†][35]	1.0	1.0	1.0	1.0	1.0	1.0	1.0	0.9	0.9
Korea, North	. .	. .	. .	. .	. .	. .	. .	. .	. .
Korea, South	[2.6]	[2.6]	[2.4]	[2.5]	[2.5]	2.6	2.6	2.6	2.8
Laos	(0.8)	(0.7)	(0.6)	(0.6)	(0.5)	(0.4)	(0.4)	(0.4)	(0.4)
Malaysia	1.6	2.1	2.2	2.6	2.3	2.3	2.1	2.1	2.0
Mongolia	2.1	1.9	1.9	1.6	1.5	1.3	1.2	1.4	. .
Myanmar[36]	2.3	1.8	1.3	. .	. .	. .	. .	. .	. .
Philippines	1.1	1.0	1.0	1.0	0.9	0.9	0.9	0.9	0.8
Singapore	4.7	5.0	5.1	5.1	4.6	4.5	4.2	3.9	4.1
Taiwan	2.4	2.5	2.2	2.3	2.3	2.2	2.0	2.0	2.1
Thailand	1.4	1.5	1.4	1.3	[1.2]	[1.1]	[1.1]	[1.3]	[1.5]
Timor-Leste[37]	. .	. .	. .	. .	. .	2.5	5.2	[6.0]	4.7
Viet Nam	. .	. .	. .	2.1	2.0	1.9	2.1	2.5	2.4
Oceania									
Australia	1.8	1.8	1.9	1.8	1.8	1.8	1.8	1.8	1.8
Fiji[†][38]	1.9	2.0	1.7	1.6	1.7	1.4	1.3	1.4	1.3
New Zealand	1.3	1.2	1.1	1.1	1.1	1.0	1.1	1.1	1.1
Papua New Guinea[39]	0.9	0.8	0.6	0.5	0.6	0.6	0.5	0.5	0.4
South Asia									
Afghanistan[40]	. .	. .	. .	2.2	2.1	1.7	1.6	2.2	1.9
Bangladesh	1.3	1.2	1.1	1.1	1.1	1.0	1.0	1.0	1.0

State	2000	2001	2002	2003	2004	2005	2006	2007	2008
India[41]	3.1	3.0	2.9	2.8	2.9	2.8	2.6	2.5	2.6
Nepal[¶]	0.8	1.1	1.4	1.6	1.9	2.2	2.2	1.9	2.0
Pakistan[‡]	3.7	3.8	3.9	3.7	3.6	3.4	3.3	2.9	2.6
Sri Lanka[42]	[5.0]	[4.3]	[3.3]	[2.9]	3.0	2.6	2.8	3.3	3.6
Europe									
Eastern Europe									
Armenia[†43]	3.6	3.1	2.7	2.7	2.7	2.9	2.9	3.0	3.3
Azerbaijan[||]	[2.3]	[2.3]	[2.2]	[2.4]	[2.6]	2.3	3.4	3.2	3.8
Belarus	[1.3]	1.4	1.4	1.3	1.4	1.5	1.7	1.6	1.5
Georgia[†44]	[0.6]	[0.7]	1.0	1.1	1.4	3.3	5.2	9.2	8.5
Moldova[†¶45]	0.4	0.4	0.4	0.4	0.4	0.4	0.5	0.5	0.6
Russia[46]	[3.7]	[4.1]	[4.4]	[4.3]	[3.8]	[3.7]	[3.6]	[3.5]	[3.5]
Ukraine[§]	3.6	2.9	2.8	2.8	2.6	2.8	2.8	2.9	2.7
Western and Central Europe									
Albania[§¶47]	1.2	1.3	1.3	1.3	1.4	1.4	1.6	1.8	2.0
Austria	[1.0]	[0.9]	0.9	0.9	0.9	0.9	0.8	0.9	0.9
Belgium	1.4	1.3	1.2	1.2	1.2	1.1	1.1	1.1	1.2
Bosnia and Herzegovina[†¶48]	..	..	3.9	2.4	2.0	1.6	1.5	1.3	1.4
Bulgaria[†49]	[2.8]	[3.0]	[2.9]	[2.8]	2.6	2.6	2.4	2.6	2.4
Croatia[50]	[3.1]	[2.8]	[2.8]	[2.1]	1.7	1.6	1.7	1.7	1.9
Cyprus[†||]	[3.0]	[3.4]	[2.3]	[2.2]	2.1	2.2	2.1	1.9	1.8
Czech Republic[51]	2.0	1.9	2.0	2.1	1.9	2.0	1.7	1.5	1.3
Denmark	1.5	1.6	1.5	1.5	1.5	1.3	1.4	1.3	1.4
Estonia	1.4	1.5	1.7	1.7	1.7	1.9	1.9	2.1	2.2
Finland	1.3	1.2	1.2	1.4	1.4	1.4	1.4	1.2	1.3
France[52]	2.5	2.5	2.5	2.6	2.6	2.5	2.4	2.3	2.3
Germany	1.5	1.5	1.5	1.4	1.4	1.4	1.3	1.3	1.3
Greece	4.3	4.1	3.9	[3.1]	[3.2]	[3.5]	[3.5]	[3.3]	[3.6]

Hungary	1.7	1.8	1.6	1.7	1.5	1.4	1.2	1.3	1.2
Iceland†[53]	-	-	-	-	-	-	-	-	-
Ireland	[0.7]	0.7	0.7	0.6	0.6	0.6	0.5	0.5	0.6
Italy[54]	2.0	2.0	2.0	2.0	2.0	1.9	1.8	[1.7]	[1.7]
Latvia	0.9	1.0	1.6	1.7	1.7	1.7	1.8	1.7	1.9
Lithuania	1.7	1.8	1.7	1.9	1.8	[1.6]	[1.6]	[1.5]	[1.5]
Luxembourg	0.6	0.8	0.8	0.8	[0.8]	[0.8]	[0.8]	[0.7]	:
Macedonia, FYR[55]	1.9	6.6	2.8	2.5	2.5	2.2	2.0	2.1	1.8
Malta†‖	0.7	0.7	0.7	0.7	0.7	0.7	0.7	0.7	0.7
Montenegro[56]	:	:	1.5	1.6	:	:	2.1	1.8	1.8
Netherlands	1.6	1.5	1.5	1.6	1.5	1.5	1.5	1.5	1.4
Norway	1.7	1.7	2.1	2.0	1.9	1.6	1.5	1.5	1.3
Poland	1.8	1.9	1.9	1.9	1.9	1.9	1.9	[1.9]	[2.0]
Portugal	2.0	2.0	2.0	2.0	2.1	2.2	2.1	2.0	2.0
Romania‖	2.5	2.5	2.3	2.1	2.0	2.0	1.8	1.6	1.5
Serbia[57]	6.0	4.7	4.8	3.8	3.3	2.6	2.5	2.6	2.4
Slovakia†‖	1.7	1.9	1.8	1.9	1.7	1.7	1.6	1.5	[1.5]
Slovenia‖	1.1	1.3	1.4	1.4	1.5	1.4	1.6	1.5	1.5
Spain	1.2	1.2	1.2	1.1	1.1	1.0	1.2	1.2	1.2
Sweden[58]	2.0	1.8	1.8	1.7	1.5	1.5	1.4	1.4	1.3
Switzerland†¶[59]	1.1	1.0	1.0	1.0	1.0	0.9	0.8	0.8	0.8
Turkey‖	3.7	3.7	3.9	3.4	2.8	2.5	2.5	2.2	2.2
United Kingdom[60]	2.4	2.4	2.5	2.5	2.5	2.4	2.4	2.4	2.5
Ukraine§	3.6	2.9	2.8	2.8	2.6	2.8	2.8	2.9	2.7
Middle East									
Bahrain[61]	4.0	4.2	4.7	4.8	4.3	3.6	3.4	3.2	3.0
Egypt	3.2	3.3	3.4	3.3	3.0	2.9	2.7	2.5	2.3
Iran¶[62]	3.8	4.0	2.5	2.9	3.3	3.8	3.8	2.9	2.7
Iraq§[63]	:	:	:	:	(1.9)	(2.6)	(2.7)	(2.9)	(5.4)
Israel[64]	7.8	8.1	9.1	8.6	7.8	7.6	7.6	7.2	7.0
Jordan	6.3	5.9	5.4	6.0	5.1	4.8	4.8	6.1	5.9

State	2000	2001	2002	2003	2004	2005	2006	2007	2008
Kuwait	7.2	7.7	7.4	6.5	5.8	4.3	3.6	3.8	3.2
Lebanon	5.4	5.4	4.7	4.6	4.4	[4.4]	[4.5]	[4.6]	3.9
Oman‡65	10.8	12.5	12.4	12.2	12.1	11.8	11.0	10.4	7.7
Qatar66	..	..	4.7	4.0	2.9	2.5	2.2	2.5	..
Saudi Arabia§67	10.6	11.5	9.8	8.7	8.4	8.0	8.3	9.2	8.2
Syria68	5.5	5.5	5.4	6.3	5.6	5.1	4.4	4.1	3.4
United Arab Emirates69	[9.4]	[9.8]	[8.6]	[7.9]	[7.4]	[5.6]	[5.9]	5.9	..
Yemen	4.7	5.3	6.6	6.6	5.1	4.6	3.9	4.4	4.2

.. = not available or not applicable; – = nil or a negligible value; ( ) = uncertain figure; [ ] = SIPRI estimate; | = change of multiple of currency; / = change of financial year (FY).

[a] The FY runs from April of the year indicated to March of the following year.

[b] The FY runs from July of the year indicated to June of the following year.

[†] All figures exclude military pensions.

[‡] All figures are for current spending only (i.e. exclude capital spending).

[§] All figures are for the adopted budget, rather than actual expenditure.

[¶] All figures exclude spending on paramilitary forces.

[||] This country changed or redenominated its currency during the period; all figures have been converted to the latest currency.

[1] The figures for Algeria for more recent years are budget figures. In July 2006 the Algerian Government issued supplementary budgets increasing the total expenditure by 35%. It is not clear if any of these extra funds were allocated to the military.

[2] Morocco changed its FY in 2000. Previously it had operated a July–June FY, which changed to Jan.–Dec. from 2001. The local currency figure for 2000 is the sum of the figure for FY 1999/2000 (5754 million dirhams) and the figure for a special 6-month FY from July–Dec. 2000 (7940 million dirhams).

[3] The rate of implementation of Angola's budget can vary considerably. Military expenditure for Angola should be seen in the context of highly uncertain economic statistics due to the impact of war on the Angolan economy.

[4] Investment expenditure for the Central African Republic for 2005 totalled 775 000 CFA francs.

[5] Chad's military expenditure increased sharply after 2005 due to conflict in the east of the country, with exceptional military expenditure financed by oil revenues. Figures for 2006 are not available, but available information suggests a large increase over 2005 and a smaller increase from 2006 to 2007.

[6] The figures for the Democratic Republic of the Congo do not include profits from extensive military-run mining operations.

[7] The figures for Côte d'Ivoire for 2003 are for budgeted spending rather than actual expenditure.

[8] The figures for Gabon exclude off-budget spending financed by the Provisions pour Investissements Hydrocarbures (PIH), an investment fund based on tax revenues from foreign oil companies active in Gabon.

[9] The figures for Ghana for 2001 are for the adopted budget rather than actual spending.

[10] The figures for Guinea might be an underestimate as the IMF reports large extra-budgetary spending for the military.

[11] An armed conflict broke out in Guinea-Bissau in 1998, which led to a substantial increase in defence expenditure, especially in 2000 and 2001. According to the IMF, the increase was financed by a credit from the banking system and by promissory notes.

[12] The figures for Madagascar include expenditure for the gendarmerie and the National Police.

[13] The figures for Mali are for defence and security.

[14] The figures for Mauritania are for operating expenditure only.

[15] The figures Namibia for 2002 include a supplementary allocation of 78.5 million Namibian dollars.

[16] Rwanda changed its FY in 2009 from Jan.–Dec. to July–June. The local currency figure for Rwanda for 2009 is the sum of a special 6-month budget for Jan.–June 2009 (20.6 billion Rwandan francs) and the first full July–June FY of 2009–2010 (43.6 billion Rwandan francs). The figures for 2005 and 2006 include allocations for African Union (AU) peacekeeping missions.

[17] The figures for Zimbabwe should be used with caution because of extremely high inflation.

[18] Costa Rica has no armed forces. Expenditure for paramilitary forces, border guards, and maritime and air surveillance is less than 0.05% of GDP.

[19] Figures for Cuba are for Defence and Internal Order. The figures shown in table 5A.4 are for current US dollars, converted at the official exchange rate for each year, instead of constant (2008) US dollars, due to the lack of reliable inflation data for Cuba. Data for military expenditure as a share of GDP is not given due to the lack of reliable GDP data for Cuba.

[20] The figures for El Salvador do not include local government spending on the Armed Forces Pensions Fund or the Pharmaceutical Centre for the Armed Forces. If included, total military spending for 2007 would be $205.7 million.

[21] The figures for Honduras do not include military pensions or arms imports. For the years 2005, 2006 and 2007, spending on military pensions was budgeted at an additional 58.9, 73.6 and 107.4 million lempiras, respectively.

[22] The figures for Nicaragua include military aid from USA and Taiwan for the years 2002–2009 of 12.5, 16.9, 13.6, 11.1, 7.3, 28.8, 12.2 and 11.6 million cordobas, respectively.

[23] All figures for the USA are for FY (1 Oct. of the previous year to 30 Sep. of the stated year), rather than calendar year.

[24] The figures for Bolivia include some expenditure for civil defence.

[25] The figures for Chile are for the adopted budget. They include direct transfers from the state-owned copper company Corporacion Nacional del Cobre (CODELCO) for military purchases. These transfers increased rapidly between 2005 and 2008 owing to rising copper prices, then fell in 2009, also along with copper prices.

[26] The figures for Colombia for 2002–2007 include special allocations totalling 2.5 billion pesos from a war tax decree of 12 Aug. 2002. Most of these allocations were spent between 2002 and 2004.

[27] The figures for Paraguay for 2003 are for the modified budget, rather than actual expenditure. Spending on military pensions is not included; for the years 2007, 2008 and 2009 it amounted to 208, 239.3 and 271.7 billion guaranies, respectively.

[28] The figures for Peru for 2005 do not include the transfer of 20% of gas production revenues from the state-owned company CAMISEA for the armed forces and national police.

[29] The figures for Venezuela for 2009 are for the initial budget. In recent years, Venezuela's actual military spending has consistently been significantly higher than the initial budget, by 44% in 2006, 15% in 2007 and 30% in 2008. The figures for Venezuela do not include substantial extra-budgetary expenditure on arms imports.

[30] The figures for Kyrgyzstan include spending on internal security, which accounts for a substantial part of total military spending.

[31] The figures for Uzbekistan expressed in constant US dollars should be seen in the light of considerable difference between the official and the unofficial exchange rates.

[32] The local currency figure for Brunei Darussalam for 2003 is for a special 15-month FY from Jan. 2003 to Mar. 2004. FYs up to 2002 are Jan.–Dec., those from 2004 onwards are Apr.–Mar.

[33] The figures for China are for estimated total military expenditure, including estimates for items not included in the official defence budget. They are based on publicly available figures for official military expenditure and for certain other items, and estimates for other items where there is no publicly available data. These estimates are based on the percentage change in official military expenditure and on the assumption of a gradual decrease in the commercial earnings of the People's Liberation Army (PLA). See section II above; and Wang, S., The military expenditure of China, 1989–98', *SIPRI Yearbook 1999*.

[34] The local currency figure for Indonesia for 2000 is for a special 9-month FY April–Dec. 2000. Prior to this, FYs ran from Apr. to Mar.; all subsequent FYs are Jan.–Dec.

[35] The figures for Japan include spending on the activities of the Special Action Committee on Okinawa (SACO).

[36] The figures for Myanmar are not presented in US dollar terms owing to the extreme variation in stated exchange rate between the kyat and the US dollar.

[37] The local currency figure for Timor-Leste for 2007 is for a special 6-month FY July–Dec. 2007. Previous FYs, up to 2006/2007, are July–Dec.; subsequent FYs, from 2008, are Jan.–Dec.. The figures for military expenditure as a share of GDP for Timor-Leste are based on GDP data that excludes oil and gas revenues, which in recent years have been several times higher than Timor-Leste's GDP itself.

[38] Fiji's spending on military pensions for the years 1998–2002 amounted to roughly 3.5% of annual military spending.

[39] The figures for Papua New Guinea are for the 'recurrent' part of the budget. For the years 2006–2008, 'development' spending amounted to 2, 3 and 6 million kina, respectively. Both the recurrent and development budgets include current and capital spending.

[40] The figures for Afghanistan are for core budget expenditure on the Afghan National Army. Military aid from foreign donors—which in 2009 included $4 billion from the USA, 16 times Afghanistan's domestic military expenditure—is not included.

[41] The figures for India include expenditure on the paramilitary forces of the Border Security Force, the Central Reserve Police Force, the Assam Rifles, the Indo-Tibetan Border Police and, from 2007, the Sashastra Seema Bal, but do not include spending on military nuclear activities.

42 The figures for Sri Lanka for 2000 do not fully reflect the special allocation of 28 billion rupees for war-related expenditure. The figures for 2009 include a 33 billion rupees supplementary allocation following the end of the civil war.

43 If the figures for Armenia were to include military pensions they would be 15–20% higher.

44 The budget figures for Georgia for 2003 are believed to be an underestimation of actual spending because of the political turmoil during the year.

45 Adding all military items in Moldova's budget, including expenditure on military pensions and paramilitary forces, would give total military expenditure for 2005, 2006 and 2007 of 343, 457 and 530 million lei, respectively.

46 For the sources and methods of the military expenditure figures for Russia see Cooper, J., 'The military expenditure of the USSR and the Russian Federation, 1987–97', SIPRI Yearbook 1998.

47 The figures for Albania prior to 2006 do not fully include pensions.

48 The figures for Bosnia and Herzegovina from 2005 onwards are for the armed forces of Bosnia and Herzegovina, which was formed in 2005 from the Croat–Bosniak Army of the Federation of Bosnia and Herzegovina and the Bosnian Serb Army of Republika Srpska. The figures prior to 2005 include expenditure for the Army of the Federation of Bosnia and Herzegovina and the Army of Republika Srpska. The figures for Bosnia and Herzegovina do not include spending on arms imports.

49 According to NATO figures, Bulgaria's total spending, including pensions, was 1393, 1712 and 1749 million leva in 2006, 2007 and 2008, respectively.

50 The figures for Croatia for 2006–2009 include sums allocated from central government expenditure for repayments on a loan for a military radar system. The sums allocated were 147.8, 117.4, 69.8 and 51.9 million kunas in 2006, 2007, 2008 and 2009, respectively.

51 The figures for the Czech Republic do not include military aid to Afghanistan or Iraq. Aid to Afghanistan was 18.7 million koruny in 2004 and 612.6 million koruny in 2007. Aid to Iraq was 1.1 million koruny in 2005.

52 The figures for France from 2006 are calculated with a new methodology due to a change in the French budgetary system and financial law.

53 Iceland does not have an army or other military and, until the establishment of the Icelandic Defence Agency in June 2008, had no budget for defence or military affairs. The Icelandic Defence Agency is responsible for maintaining defence installations such as the Icelandic Air Defence System, intelligence gathering and military exercises.

54 The figures for Italy include spending on civil defence, which typically amounts to about 4.5% of the total.

55 The definition of military expenditure for FYROM changed from 2006. Border troops were transferred from the Ministry of Defence to the Ministry of Interior Affairs and part of the military pensions, previously entirely excluded, are now included.

56 Montenegro declared its independence from the State Union of Serbia and Montenegro on 3 June 2006.

57 Montenegro seceded from the State Union of Serbia and Montenegro on 3 June 2006. The figures for Serbia up to 2005 are for the State Union of Serbia and Montenegro (known as the Federal Republic of Yugoslavia until Feb. 2003) and for 2006 onwards for Serbia alone.

58 Sweden changed its accounting system in 2001, giving rise to a series break between 2000 and 2001. This break means that the decrease in military expenditure between 2000 and 2001 is overestimated by 1.4 percentage points.

59 Because of a change in Switzerland's accounting system, the decrease in spending between 2005 and 2006 might be overestimated. Figures for Switzerland do not include expenditure on military pensions or paramilitary forces.

[60] From 2001 the UK moved from a cash-based accounting system to a resource-based system. The figures for the UK from 2001 are based on the 'Net Cash Requirement' figures given in the annual UK Defence Statistics, which are closest to the old cash definition. The Net Cash Requirement definition differs slightly from the cash definition used up to 2000. The effect on the figures for British military expenditure is unknown.

[61] The figures for Bahrain do not include extra-budgetary spending on defence procurement.

[62] The figures for Iran do not include spending on paramilitary forces such as the Islamic Revolutionary Guards Corps.

[63] The figures for Iraq are uncertain because of the high rate of inflation and since they are budget figures that may be subject to revision due to variations in the price of oil.

[64] The figures for Israel include military aid from the USA, which in 2009 was $2.55 billion.

[65] The figures for Oman are for expenditure on defence and national security.

[66] The figures for Qatar are for expenditure on defence and security.

[67] The figures for Saudi Arabia are for expenditure on defence and security.

[68] The figures for Syria in US dollars have been converted from local currency using the market exchange rate for the base year of 2008 of 1 dollar = 46.5 Syrian pounds. Previously, Syria operated an official exchange rate of 1 dollar = 11.225 Syrian pounds, which was used in previous editions of the SIPRI Yearbook. Syria abolished the official rate in 2007, moving to the parallel market rate that had previously operated unofficially.

[69] The military expenditure of the United Arab Emirates is uncertain and lacking in transparency. The only available sources of data are IMF Staff Country Reports and the IMF's *Government Finance Statistics*. The Country Reports include two lines relating to military expenditure: the Goods and Services expenditure of the Defence and Interior ministries (which does not include military wages, salaries and pensions), and Abu Dhabi Federal Services, which the reports say are mainly defence and security expenditure. *Government Finance Statistics* give only the Goods and Services figures. The SIPRI figures are estimated as 80% of the Abu Dhabi Federal Services item, plus 100% of the Goods and Services figures. The latter item is estimated for 2006–2007 assuming a constant real value.

Source: SIPRI Military Expenditure Database, <http://www.sipri.org/databases/milex/>.

Appendix 5B. The reporting of military expenditure data

NOEL KELLY

I. Introduction

The public availability of information on military expenditure has increased significantly in recent years. This is due in part to the increasing levels of transparency in many countries that is associated with an increase of democratic governance and civilian control of the military as well as with the development of the Internet: increasing numbers of governments make budgetary information—including military budgets—available online. These national systems of reporting vary considerably in terms of both the level of coverage of the data provided (e.g. what items are included in a national defence budget) and the level of disaggregation.

This appendix focuses on international systems of reporting military expenditure data that seek to create a common reporting standard for such information. A number of systems exist at a regional level: the Organization for Security and Co-operation in Europe (OSCE) requires its participating states to annually report their military budgets and expenditure of the previous year, although this information is not publicly available. The North Atlantic Treaty Organization (NATO) also annually reports the military expenditure of its member states according to a common definition.

However, a significant source of official data on military expenditure, and the only official global reporting system, remains the annual government reporting within the framework of the United Nations Standardized Instrument for Reporting Military Expenditures. In addition, governments also have an opportunity to report military expenditure data to SIPRI in response to SIPRI's annual requests. For comparative purposes, this appendix provides information on the reporting of military expenditure data to the UN and SIPRI. The systems of reporting are described in section II. The trends in reporting for the period 2001–2009 are presented in section III and the levels of reporting in 2009 in section IV.

II. The reporting systems

The United Nations reporting system

Each year the UN Secretary-General invites all member states through a *note verbale* to report their military expenditure for the most recent financial year. The basis for this request is a 1980 UN General Assembly resolution.[1] Suc-

---

[1] UN General Assembly Resolution A/RES/35/142 B, 12 Dec. 1980. The texts of UN General Assembly resolutions are available at <http://www.un.org/documents/resga.htm>.

cessive biennial General Assembly resolutions have called for the continued reporting of military expenditure by member states.[2]

The justification for this request has evolved over the years. The initial purpose was to use the reporting system as a step toward gradual reductions in military budgets.[3] The justification stated in the latest resolution is that the General Assembly is convinced 'that transparency in military matters is an essential element for building a climate of trust and confidence between States worldwide and that a better flow of objective information on military matters can help to relieve international tension and is therefore an important contribution to conflict prevention'.[4]

Countries are requested to report annually (by 30 April) their military expenditure for the most recent financial year for which data is available. Preferably and to the extent possible, they are asked to use the reporting instrument developed for this purpose—the UN Standardized Instrument for Reporting Military Expenditures—but they can use any other format for reporting military expenditure developed by other international or regional organizations, and can submit nil reports, if appropriate.[5] The standardized instrument is in the form of a matrix with fields for the reporting of disaggregated data by function (e.g. personnel, operations and maintenance, procurement, construction, and research and development (R&D), each broken down into subcategories) and by military service (e.g. air force, army and navy) and to give aggregated totals.[6] In the belief that some countries found this matrix too complicated and in order to encourage reporting by more countries, in 2002 the UN introduced an alternative, simplified reporting form that requests only aggregate data by service on personnel, operations and procurement.

The UN Office for Disarmament Affairs (ODA, formerly the Department for Disarmament Affairs) manages the system. The reported data is included in an annual report by the UN Secretary-General to the General Assembly and is published in appropriate UN media.[7] In addition, the ODA periodically publishes documents analysing the reporting trends to the UN.[8]

[2] The most recent such resolution is UN General Assembly Resolution A/RES/64/22, 2 Dec. 2009.

[3] See Omitoogun, W. and Sköns, E., 'Military expenditure data: a 40-year overview', *SIPRI Yearbook 2006*, pp. 276–77, 286, 291.

[4] UN General Assembly Resolution A/RES/64/22 (note 2).

[5] UN General Assembly Resolution A/RES/64/22 (note 2), para. 1.

[6] The standardized instrument is reproduced in United Nations, Department for Disarmament Affairs, *Transparency in Armaments: United Nations Standardized Instrument for Reporting Military Expenditures—Guidelines* (United Nations: New York, [n.d.]), pp. 7–8.

[7] The most recent report is United Nations, General Assembly, 'Objective information on military matters, including transparency of military expenditures', Report of the Secretary-General, A/64/113, 24 June 2009; and addenda A/64/113/Add.1, 14 Sep. 2009, and A/64/113/Add.2, 30 Oct. 2009.

[8] The most recent example is United Nations, Office for Disarmament Affairs, *United Nations Standardized Instrument for Reporting Military Expenditures: Pattern of Global and Regional Participation by States 1996–2007* (United Nations: New York, [n.d.]).

The SIPRI reporting system

SIPRI has sent requests for data on military expenditure to governments via various national government offices and embassies on an annual basis since 1993. Such requests are sent to most of the 174 countries that are included in the SIPRI Military Expenditure Database.[9] The SIPRI questionnaire is a simplified version of the UN instrument, with fields for data on spending on military and civilian personnel, operations and maintenance, procurement, military construction, military R&D, paramilitary forces, and military aid provided and received. Data is requested for the five most recent years in order to ensure consistency over time. The reported data is one source of information used in preparing SIPRI's tables of military expenditure.[10]

III. Trends in reporting military expenditure, 2001–2009

Table 5B.1 presents the number of countries reporting their military spending to the UN and SIPRI for the period 2001–2009. The figures exclude reporting by very small states and the submission of nil reports.[11]

There has been an evident decrease in the reporting in recent years: while 85 countries reported to either the UN or SIPRI in 2006, only 68 did so in 2009.[12] This decrease in total reporting reflects a drop in the response rate to both SIPRI and the UN.

While SIPRI has increased the number of requests sent to countries, the number of responses has been dropping, particularly since 2005. Since 2001 the rate of response to the SIPRI request has varied between a high of 41 per cent (in 2003) and a low of 32 per cent (in 2008).

In total since the introduction of the UN's standardized instrument, over 120 member states have submitted a report at least once.[13] In 2009 the UN response rate decreased significantly, to 27 per cent, the lowest response rate to date. Since 2001 the rate of response to the UN reporting system has never exceeded 37 per cent (in 2002). This low level of reporting limits the effectiveness of the instrument as a means of making consistent international comparisons of global military expenditure.

---

[9] SIPRI does not send requests to 2 countries in the database: Costa Rica and Somalia. In addition, the database includes data on a number of states that no longer exist, including Czechoslovakia, the German Democratic Republic (East Germany), the Yemen Arab Republic (North Yemen), the People's Democratic Republic of Yemen (South Yemen) and Yugoslavia. The SIPRI Military Expenditure Database is available at <http://www.sipri.org/databases/milex/>.

[10] See appendix 5A.

[11] The UN receives reports with no data (nil reports) usually from countries that do not maintain regular armed forces. These countries are often very small states, with the exception of Costa Rica and Tunisia in 2009; while Costa Rica has no regular military forces, Tunisia does and reports military spending in government publications.

[12] It has not been possible to calculate the total reporting of military expenditure to the UN or SIPRI before 2006.

[13] United Nations (note 8), adjusted for submissions in 2008 and 2009.

Table 5B.1. Number of countries reporting their military expenditure to the United Nations and SIPRI, 2001–2009

	2001	2002	2003	2004	2005	2006	2007	2008	2009
UN reporting system[a]									
Number of UN member states	189	191	191	191	191	192	192	192	192
Number of reports to the UN[b]	56	70	64	68	62	69	66	68	51
Standardized reports	56	70	54	54	55	54	48	53	42
Simplified reports[c]	..	..	10	14	7	15	18	15	9
Nil reports[d]	5	11	11	10	12	11	12	8	6
SIPRI reporting system									
States in the SIPRI Military Expenditure Database[e]	165	167	167	167	167	168	168	168	169
Number of SIPRI requests	158	158	158	159	167	165	165	165	167
Number of reports to SIPRI	63	61	64	62	67	60	55	53	58
Total number of reports to the UN or SIPRI[f]	..	..	..	..	..	85	78	78	68

[a] The UN data for 2009 includes late submissions up to 30 Oct. 2009, but some countries may report after this date.

[b] These figures exclude nil reports.

[c] The totals for UN simplified reports exclude one small state (Suriname) that reported with this format for 2006, 2008, and 2009. Countries reporting to the UN with both the standardized and simplified reports are listed as standardized reports to avoid double-counting.

[d] A nil report is a questionnaire returned to the UN with no data entered, usually submitted by a country that does not maintain regular armed forces. Totals include those from states not in the SIPRI Military Expenditure Database.

[e] The SIPRI Military Expenditure Database excludes many small states with populations under 1 million.

[f] Totals may be smaller than the sums of reports to the UN and SIPRI because the same country may report to both organizations. Totals before 2006 are not available because of changes in the way responses to the UN and SIPRI are counted.

Sources: United Nations, 'Objective information on military matters, including transparency of military expenditures', Reports of the Secretary-General, various dates, 2001–2009; and submitted SIPRI questionnaires.

The reasons for the general low level of reporting and for the fall in 2009 are unclear. A comparison of participation in the UN instrument with other sources of data used by SIPRI suggests that a majority of those countries that never or rarely respond to the UN instrument also make only limited or no information on military expenditure available online; however, a significant minority do make detailed information available, raising the question of why they do not also report this information to the UN. In 2010–11, a Group of Governmental Experts (GGE) is due to review the UN instrument. The GGE's report should give further analysis of why responses from states are inconsistent and decreasing over time.

IV. The reporting of military expenditure data in 2009

Reporting by countries to the UN and SIPRI in 2009 is presented in table 5B.2. In order to facilitate comparison between the reporting to the UN and SIPRI, the table excludes reporting by very small states—which are excluded from the SIPRI database—and the submission of nil reports.

A total of 68 countries answered the UN and SIPRI requests for reporting on military expenditure information in 2009. Of the 168 UN member states (other than very small states), 30 per cent submitted standardized or simplified responses to the UN (excluding nil reports). Of the 167 states to which SIPRI sent requests, 35 per cent responded with information.

The region with the highest reporting rate was Europe, with 91 per cent of countries submitting responses to the UN or SIPRI in 2009 (95 per cent in Western and Central Europe and 71 per cent in Eastern Europe). The response rates in the Americas and Asia were both 36 per cent (100 per cent in North America, 45 per cent in South America, and 20 per cent in Central American and the Caribbean; and 41 per cent in East Asia, 40 per cent in Oceania, 17 per cent in South Asia and 0 per cent in Central Asia). The lowest rates of reporting military expenditure were in the Middle East (21 per cent) and Africa (10 per cent).

Table 5B.2. Reporting of military expenditure data to the United Nations and SIPRI, by region, 2009

Figures are numbers of countries. Nil reports to the UN and reports by countries not included in the SIPRI Military Expenditure Database are not included.

Region/subregion[a]	Reporting to the UN			Reporting to SIPRI			Total SIPRI and UN reports[b]
	Requests	Countries reporting data	Total	Requests	Countries reporting data	Total	
Africa							
North Africa	4	–	0	4	–	0	0
Sub-Saharan Africa	46	Burkina Faso[c]	1	45[d]	Burkina Faso, Mauritius[e], Namibia, Seychelles, South Africa	5	5
Americas							
Central America and the Caribbean	15	Mexico[f]	1	14[g]	Guatemala, Honduras, Mexico	3	3
North America	2	USA	1	2	Canada, USA	2	2
South America	11	Argentina, Brazil, Colombia, Peru	4	11	Brazil, Bolivia	2	5
Asia and Oceania							
Central Asia	5	–	0	5	–	0	0
East Asia[i]	16	China[c], Japan, South Korea[c], Philippines[c], Thailand[c]	5	17[h]	China[e], Indonesia, Japan, South Korea, Philippines, Taiwan	6	7
Oceania	5	Australia, New Zealand	2	5	Australia	1	2
South Asia	6	Nepal[f]	1	6	–	0	1
Europe							
Eastern Europe	7	Armenia[c], Belarus, Moldova, Russia, Ukraine	5	7	Armenia, Belarus, Moldova, Russia, Ukraine	5	5

Region		Countries A			Countries B		
Western and Central Europe	37	Austria, Belgium, Bosnia and Herzegovina[f], Bulgaria, Croatia[f], Cyprus[f], Czech Republic, Estonia, Finland, France, Germany, Ireland, Italy, Latvia, Lithuania, FYROM, Malta, Montenegro[f], Norway, Poland, Portugal, Romania[f], Serbia[f], Slovakia, Slovenia[e], Spain[f], Sweden, Switzerland, Turkey[f]	29	37	Austria, Belgium, Bulgaria, Croatia, Cyprus[f], Czech Republic, Denmark, Estonia, Finland, Germany, Greece, Hungary, Iceland, Ireland, Italy, Latvia, Lithuania, FYROM, Malta, Montenegro, Netherlands, Norway, Poland[e], Portugal, Sweden, Romania, Serbia, Slovakia, Slovenia, Switzerland, Turkey, UK	42	35
Middle East	14	Israel[c], Lebanon[c]	2	14	Jordan[e], Lebanon	2	3
Total	168[i]		51[j]	167		58	68

FYROM = Former Yugoslav Republic of Macedonia.

[a] Countries are grouped in the geographical regions used in the SIPRI Military Expenditure Database. See appendix 5A.

[b] Totals may be smaller than the sums of reports to the UN and SIPRI because the same country may report to both organizations.

[c] These 9 countries used the simplified form when reporting to the UN.

[d] There are 46 sub-Saharan African countries in the SIPRI Military Expenditure Database, but SIPRI is unable to send requests to Somalia because of a lack of contact details.

[e] These 4 countries did not use the SIPRI questionnaire in their report to SIPRI.

[f] These 10 countries used both the simplified and standardized forms when reporting to the UN.

[g] There are 15 Central American and Caribbean countries in the SIPRI Military Expenditure Database, but SIPRI did not send a request to Costa Rica in 2009.

[h] The SIPRI Military Expenditure Database includes the non-UN member state Taiwan.

[i] In addition, the UN sent requests to 24 states not in the SIPRI Military Expenditure Database.

[j] In addition, 6 UN member states—Andorra, Costa Rica, Monaco, Nauru, Samoa and Tunisia—submitted nil reports to the UN and 1 state that is not included in the SIPRI Military Expenditure Database—Suriname—submitted a simplified report.

Sources: Submitted SIPRI questionnaires; and United Nations, General Assembly, 'Objective information on military matters, including transparency of military expenditures', Report of the Secretary-General, A/64/113, 24 June 2009; and addenda A/64/113/Add.1, 14 Sep. 2009; and A/64/113/Add.2, 30 Oct. 2009.

6. Arms production

SUSAN T. JACKSON

I. Introduction

In 2008 the world's 100 largest arms-producing companies—the SIPRI Top 100—maintained the upward trend in their arms sales, which reached $385 billion.[1] While companies headquartered in the United States again dominated the Top 100, for the first time a non-US headquartered company registered the highest level of arms sales—BAE Systems of the United Kingdom.[2] The conflicts in Afghanistan and Iraq continued to heavily influence sales of military equipment such as armoured vehicles, unmanned aerial vehicles (UAVs) and helicopters in 2008. At the same time, sales registered by military services companies continued to grow, as did the arms sales of Russian companies to both domestic and foreign customers.

Following peak levels earlier in the decade, the number of large transnational mergers and acquisitions fell again in 2009. There was, however, more consolidation in the Israeli, Russian and US industries as well as a continued pattern of arms-producing companies diversifying into the security industry. Even though more than a year has passed since the onset of the global financial crisis and economic recession, many arms-producing companies continued to increase arms sales in 2009.

Section II of this chapter presents and analyses the main trends in the SIPRI Top 100 arms-producing companies for 2008. Section III covers major merger and acquisition activity among arms-producing companies in 2009. Drawing on a sample of company financial reports from 2009 and government strategies, section IV discusses the impact of the financial crisis and the ensuing economic downturn on the arms industry. Section V concludes the chapter. Appendix 6A lists the SIPRI Top 100 arms-producing companies in 2008, and appendix 6B lists the major acquisitions within Organization for Economic Co-operation and Development (OECD) arms industries in 2009.

---

[1] The delay in publication of the accounts of many of the companies discussed here means that 2008 is the most recent year for which arms sales figures are available. Discussion of merger and acquisition activity in this chapter refers to developments during 2009.

[2] The internationalization of the arms-producing industry means that companies based in one country often belong to a company or group with headquarters in another country. In this chapter, a country designation refers to the location of a company's headquarters.

Table 6.1. Trends in arms sales of companies in the SIPRI Top 100 arms-producing companies, 2002–2008

	2002	2003	2004	2005	2006	2007	2008	2002–2008
Arms sales at current prices and exchange rates								
Total ($ b.)	195	235	274	289	312	346	385	
Change (%)		20	17	5	8	11	11	97
Arms sales at constant (2008) prices and exchange rates								
Total ($ b.)	209	249	283	299	331	362	385	
Change (%)		19	14	6	11	9	6	84

Note: The figures in this table refer to the companies in the SIPRI Top 100 in each year, which means that they refer to a different set of companies each year, as ranked from a consistent set of data. E.g. the figures shown above for 2007 differ from those in table 6.2.

Source: Appendix 6A; and the SIPRI Arms Industry Database.

II. The SIPRI Top 100 arms-producing companies, 2008[3]

The total arms sales of the SIPRI Top 100 arms-producing companies in 2008 (outside China) increased by $39 billion to reach $385 billion. The total arms sales of the Top 100 have increased each year since 2002 and by a total of 84 per cent in real terms (see table 6.1).

As in previous years, US companies led in both the number of companies in the Top 100 and the share of total arms sales for 2008, followed by West European companies (see table 6.2). However, the country-based composition of the Top 100 has changed in some significant ways. For the first time since the initial SIPRI Top 100, for 1988, a non-US company heads the list: BAE Systems of the UK.[4] In addition, a Russian company—Almaz-Antei—is among the 20 largest arms-producing companies for the first time.[5] No Australian-owned company appears in the SIPRI Top 100 for 2008 follow-

[3] The companies in the SIPRI Top 100 account for the majority of the global financial value of military goods and services—in particular, high-technology systems and services. Because of a lack of comparable financial data, the SIPRI Top 100 does not cover all arms-producing countries. However, with a few exceptions, the volume of arms production in omitted countries is believed to be relatively small. Chinese companies would almost certainly appear in the Top 100 (and probably in the top 50) if satisfactory data were available. Apart from the omission of China, analysis of the companies in the Top 100 is sufficient to capture the major trends in the global arms industry.

SIPRI data on arms-producing companies is revised on an on-going basis when improved data is available. For this reason, it is not possible to make a strict comparison between editions of the SIPRI Yearbook. In addition, coverage may differ due to problems of obtaining data to make satisfactory estimates for all companies every year. As a result the data used here on the SIPRI Top 100 for 2007 may differ from that published in *SIPRI Yearbook 2009*, even though the data set used for each edition of the Yearbook is consistent as far as is possible across countries and over time.

[4] For the 1988 SIPRI Top 100 see Anthony, I. et al., 'Arms production', *SIPRI Yearbook 1990*, pp. 325–31.

[5] SIPRI has only collected data on Russian arms-producing companies since 2002. Given the state of the Russian arms industry following the end of the cold war, it is unlikely that a Russian company would have reached the top 20 in arms sales prior to 2002.

ing BAE Systems' acquisition of Tenix Defence Systems in early 2008.[6] Hewlett-Packard entered the Top 100 following its acquisition of EDS, a former Top 100 arms-producing company. Some other new entrants at the bottom of the Top 100—such as Shaw Group of the USA and Uralvagonzavod of Russia—had arms sales close to the lower-tier Top 100 arms-producing companies in previous years.

BAE Systems

BAE Systems' move to first place in the Top 100 is notable for a variety of reasons. It is a UK-based company, but its arms sales rely on production that takes place in a number of locations outside the UK, including the USA.[7] In 2008 it generated £9.4 billion ($17.3 billion) in sales in the USA, compared with £3.4 billion ($6.25 billion) in the UK and £5.7 billion ($10.5 billion) elsewhere; indeed, BAE's British revenues fell between 2007 and 2008, while its US revenues increased.[8] Its two largest operating groups (Electronics, Intelligence & Support and Land & Armaments) are headquartered in the USA. In 2008 these two groups contributed 59 per cent of the company's total sales—up from 47 per cent in 2007—and they had 55 200 employees worldwide, with 46 900 in the USA. In the UK, BAE had a total of 32 800 employees.[9] In 2008 BAE Systems ranked fourth in the list of largest US Department of Defense (DOD) contractors, up from sixth in 2007; approximately 43 per cent of the company's consolidated revenues from DOD contracts was generated by the two US-based operating groups in 2008.[10] Recent acquisitions elsewhere have also contributed to BAE's revenue growth, demonstrating the importance of the company's other home markets. For example, the Tenix acquisition made BAE Systems the largest arms producer in Australia.

Despite this growth, the past few years have been turbulent for BAE Systems, which has been facing allegations of bribery and corruption in

---

[6] Two international subsidiaries located in Australia—BAE Systems Australia and Thales Australia—would rank in the Top 100 if they were independent companies. See Appendix 6A. The 5 largest arms producers in Australia are now foreign owned.

[7] BAE Systems refers to those countries in which it has a significant manufacturing capability as 'home markets'. With the addition of India in 2009, BAE has 7 home markets: Australia, India, Saudi Arabia, South Africa, Sweden, the UK and the USA. BAE Systems, *Annual Report 2008: Leveraging Global Capability* (BAE Systems: London, [2009]), p. 16; and BAE Systems, 'BAE Systems establishes India advisory board confirming India as key strategic focus', Press release, 8 Sep. 2009, <http://www.baesystems.com/Newsroom/NewsReleases/autoGen_1098991439.html>.

[8] BAE Systems, *Annual Report 2008* (note 7), p. 118. BAE attributes 95% of its 2008 total sales to arms sales.

[9] BAE Systems, *Annual Report 2008* (note 7), pp. 16, 35, 36, 38, 40, 118. Of these, 30 200 are employed by the UK-based operating group Programmes & Support.

[10] 'Contracts from Dept. of Defense (FY 2008)', USAspending.gov, <http://www.usaspending.gov/fpds/fpds.php?maj_agency_cat=97&fiscal_year=2008>; and BAE Systems, *Annual Report 2008* (note 7), p. 118.

Table 6.2. Regional and national shares of arms sales for the SIPRI Top 100 arms-producing companies, 2008 compared to 2007

Arms sales figures are in US$ b., at current prices and exchange rates. Figures do not always add up to totals because of the conventions of rounding. Chinese companies are not included due to a lack of comparable and sufficiently accurate data.

Number of companies	Region/ country[a]	Arms sales ($ b.)		Change in arms sales, 2007–08 (%)		Share of total Top 100 arms sales, 2008 (%)
		2008	2007[b]	Nominal[c]	Real[d]	
45	**North America**	**230.6**	**206.2**	*12*	*8*	*60.0*
44	USA	229.9	205.7	*12*	*8*	*59.8*
1	Canada	0.7	0.6	*19*	*16*	*0.2*
34	**Western Europe**	**122.1**	**108.6**	*12*	*8*	*31.7*
11	United Kingdom	49.7	45.8	*8*	*13*	*12.9*
7	France	23.2	23.9	*–3*	*–12*	*6.0*
1	Trans-European[e]	17.9	13.1	*37*	*24*	*4.7*
4	Italy	15.2	11.6	*31*	*18*	*4.0*
5	Germany	8.0	7.4	*9*	*–1*	*2.1*
1	Sweden	3.0	2.8	*8*	*2*	*0.8*
2	Spain	2.9	2.3	*27*	*14*	*0.7*
1	Switzerland	0.8	0.6	*31*	*15*	*0.2*
1	Norway	0.7	0.5	*37*	*27*	*0.2*
1	Finland	0.7	0.6	*5*	*–6*	*0.2*
7	**Eastern Europe**	**10.8**	**8.1**	*34*	*14*	*2.8*
7	Russia	10.8	8.1	*34*	*14*	*2.8*
14	**Other**	**21.1**	**16.9**	*25*	*13*	*5.5*
4	Japan[f]	7.0	4.8	*46*	*26*	*1.8*
4	Israel	6.9	5.5	*25*	*5*	*1.8*
3	India[g]	4.2	3.7	*12*	*9*	*1.1*
2	South Korea	1.8	1.7	*3*	*17*	*0.5*
1	Singapore	1.3	1.1	*16*	*6*	*0.3*
100	**Total**	**384.6**	**339.7**	*13*	*8*	*100.0*

[a] Figures for a country or region refer to the arms sales of the Top 100 companies headquartered in that country or region, including those in its foreign subsidiaries. They do not reflect the sales of arms actually produced in that country or region.

[b] Arms sales figures from 2007 refer to companies in the SIPRI Top 100 for 2008 and not to the companies in the Top 100 from 2007.

[c] This column gives the change in arms sales 2007–2008 in current US dollars.

[d] This column gives the change in arms sales 2007–2008 in constant (2008) US dollars.

[e] The company classified as trans-European is EADS. See appendix 6A.

[f] Figures for Japanese companies are based on contracts with the Japanese Ministry of Defence.

[g] Figures for India include a rough estimate for Ordnance Factories.

Source: Appendix 6A.

connection with arms contracts in Africa, the Middle East, and Central and Eastern Europe. Both the British Serious Fraud Office (SFO) and the US Department of Justice (DOJ) have investigated these deals.[11] In February 2010 the company reached a 'ground breaking global agreement' with the SFO and the DOJ: it pleaded guilty in the UK to a charge of 'breach of duty to keep accounting records in relation to payments made to a former marketing adviser in Tanzania' and in the USA to a charge of 'conspiring to make false statements . . . in connection with certain regulatory filings and undertakings', avoiding charges related to bribery and corruption.[12] The company agreed to pay fines totalling £30 million ($55 million) in the UK and $400 million in the USA. Through these settlements, BAE Systems reduced the risk that it will be barred from bidding on military contracts in the UK and the USA. However, while the US State Department determined the impact of the DOJ deal on export controls, it placed a temporary administrative hold on most export licence applications from BAE.[13] While BAE has denied the allegations of bribery and corruption, advocacy groups in the UK challenged the settlements.

Companies whose arms sales increased most in 2008

Thirteen companies increased their arms sales by more than $1 billion in 2008 (compared with 12 in 2007) and 23 increased these sales by more than 30 per cent (compared with 25 in 2007), reflecting overall trends in military expenditure and procurement (see table 6.3).[14] In contrast, only six companies in the SIPRI Top 100 had decreased arms sales in 2008. Two of these companies—SAFRAN of France and Boeing of the USA—experienced decreases of more than $1 billion.

Year-on-year changes measured in current dollars (as shown in table 6.3) are often significantly distorted by currency fluctuations. The discrepancy between the nominal and real-terms changes in tables 6.1 and 6.2 illustrates this effect. In 2008, in particular, a strong euro and yen against a weakened dollar led to an exaggeration of the nominal increase in the arms sales of

[11] On these and similar allegations see 'The BAE files', *The Guardian*, <http://www.guardian.co.uk/world/bae>; and Raphael, M., 'Investigating and prosecuting fraud & corruption in the international business environment', Peters & Peters, 3rd Annual Fraud and Corruption Summit 2009, Brussels, 18–20 Mar. 2009, <http://www.petersandpeters.com/news/articles.php>.

[12] British Serious Fraud Office, 'BAE Systems plc', Press release, 5 Feb. 2010, <http://www.sfo.gov.uk/press-room/latest-press-releases/press-releases-2010/bae-systems-plc.aspx>; and BAE Systems, 'BAE Systems plc announces global settlement with United States Department of Justice and United Kingdom Serious Fraud Office', Press release, 5 Feb. 2010, <http://www.baesystems.com/Newsroom/NewsReleases/autoGen_1101517013.html>.

[13] Pfeifer, S. and Kirchgaessner, S., 'US grounds BAE export applications', *Financial Times*, 8 Mar. 2010.

[14] Six companies—EADS, Navistar, Finmeccanica, Almaz-Antei, AM General and ITT—experienced both types of increase. On military expenditure and procurement see also chapters 5 and 7 in this volume.

Table 6.3. Companies in the SIPRI Top 100 with the largest increases in arms sales in 2008

Figures are in US$ m., at current prices and exchange rates. The percentage change measures the nominal change in arms sales.

Rank, 2008	Company	Country	Sector	Arms sales ($ m.)		Change, 2007–2008	
				2008	2007	$ m.	%
Companies with the largest absolute increase in arms sales (by more than $1 b.)							
7	EADS	Trans-Eur.	Ac El Mi Sp	17 900	13 100	4 800	*36.6*
20	Navistar	USA	MV	3 900	370	3 530	*954.1*
8	Finmeccanica[a]	Italy	A Ac El MV Mi SA/A	13 240	9 850	3 390	*34.4*
1	BAE Systems	UK	A Ac El MV Mi SA/A Sh	32 420	29 860	2 560	*8.6*
18	Almaz-Antei	Russia	Mi	4 340	2 780	1 560	*56.1*
4	Northrop Grumman	USA	Ac El Mi Ser Sh Sp	26 090	24 600	1 490	*6.1*
6	Raytheon	USA	El Mi	21 030	19 540	1 490	*7.6*
10	Thales	France	A El MV Mi SA/A Sh	10 760	9 350	1 420	*15.1*
19	AM General	USA	MV	4 040	2 670	1 370	*51.3*
16	ITT Corporation	USA	El	5 170	3 850	1 320	*34.3*
5	General Dynamics	USA	A El MV SA/A Sh	22 780	21 520	1 260	*5.9*
11	United Technologies	USA	Ac El Eng	9 980	8 760	1 220	*13.9*
12	SAIC	USA	Ser Comp(MV)	7 350	6 250	1 100	*17.6*
Companies with the largest relative increase in arms sales (by more than 30%)							
20	Navistar	USA	MV	3 900	370	3 530	*954.1*
53	Kawasaki Heavy Industries	Japan	Ac Eng Mi Sh	1 480	580	896	*155.2*
46	DynCorp	USA	Ser	1 860	900	962	*106.7*
52	Mitsubishi Electric	Japan	El Mi	1 510	820	689	*84.1*
72	Shaw Group	USA	Ser	800	450	351	*77.8*
43	Cobham	UK	Comp(Ac El)	1 910	1 220	690	*56.6*
18	Almaz-Antei	Russia	Mi	4 340	2 780	1 560	*56.1*
63	NEC	Japan	El	950	610	341	*56.0*
70	VSE Corp.	USA	Ser	830	540	294	*54.6*
19	AM General	USA	MV	4 040	2 670	1 370	*51.3*
55	Force Protection	USA	MV	1 330	890	440	*49.4*
90	Uralvagonzavod	Russia	MV	640	460	180	*38.8*
76	Kongsberg Gruppen	Norway	El Mi SA/A	740	540	200	*37.0*
7	EADS	Trans-Eur.	Ac El Mi Sp	17 900	13 100	4 800	*36.6*
23	Textron	USA	Ac El Eng MV	3 420	2 510	910	*36.3*
45	Navantia	Spain	Sh	1 880	1 390	490	*35.3*
41	Serco	UK	Ser	1 950	1 440	510	*35.4*
16	ITT Corp.	USA	El	5 170	3 850	1 320	*34.3*
51	Rafael	Israel	Ac Mi SA/A Oth	1 530	1 140	390	*34.2*
8	Finmeccanica[a]	Italy	A Ac El MV Mi SA/A	13 240	9 850	3 390	*34.4*

Rank, 2008	Company	Country	Sector	Arms sales ($ m.)		Change, 2007–2008	
				2008	2007	$ m.	%
36	Oshkosh Corp.	USA	MV	2 070	1 570	500	31.8
31	Elbit Systems	Israel	El	2 520	1 910	610	31.9
74	RUAG	Switzerl.	A Ac Eng SA/A	760	580	180	31.0

A = artillery; Ac = aircraft; El = electronics; Eng = engines; Mi = missiles; MV = military vehicles; SA/A = small arms/ammunition; Sh = ships; Sp = space; Ser = services; Oth = other; Comp( ) = components, services or anything else less than final systems in the sectors within the parentheses—used only for companies that do not produce final systems.

a Finmeccanica's figures are based on pro forma results for the acquisition of DRS Technologies as if DRS had been acquired on 1 Jan. 2008.

Source: Appendix 6A.

some companies, such as Cobham and EADS. The effect is particularly noticeable in the cases of Italian and Japanese companies in the Top 100 (see table 6.2).

However, much of the growth shown in table 6.3 reflects actual increases in arms sales. There are several factors behind these increases. First, and most significantly, was military equipment procurement for the conflicts in Afghanistan and Iraq. Second, the sales of companies providing military services continued to increase, also partly in relation to the conflicts in Afghanistan and Iraq. Third, Russian companies benefited from government support of the arms industry and force modernization and from increased arms sales abroad.

Separately from these trends, other notable increases in arms sales include the $5 billion increase by the trans-European company EADS, in large part due to higher tanker sales and revenues related to the delayed A400M transport aircraft programme.[15]

Military equipment companies: armoured vehicles and unmanned aerial vehicles[16]

Armoured vehicle and UAV sales and contracts maintained their strength in 2008. For the fourth consecutive year, many of the companies that produce armoured vehicles saw high growth rates in their revenues. Of the 23 companies with arms sales increases of 30 per cent or more, 5 primarily produce armoured vehicles.

---

[15] EADS applied accounting methods to the A400M programme that benefited its revenue line. EADS, *EADS Annual Review 2008: We Have What It Takes* (EADS: Leiden, [2009]), p. 44.

[16] UAVs are also referred to as unmanned aircraft systems (UASs), a term that encompasses the entire system, not just the aircraft.

Four of these five companies are headquartered in the USA, and the growth in their sales reflects the impact of the Afghanistan and Iraq conflicts on armoured vehicle purchases by that country. The largest cause of hostile deaths and injuries of US and other foreign armed forces in Afghanistan and Iraq is explosive devices, which can be countered by the use of armoured vehicles.[17] The US armed forces are upgrading and replacing armoured vehicles due to wear and tear and loss in the conflicts. Most of the armoured vehicles that the USA has ordered are mine-resistant ambush-protected (MRAP) vehicles, Joint Light Tactical Vehicles (JLTVs) and High Mobility Multipurpose Wheeled Vehicles (HMMWVs).[18]

Another factor contributing to the increase in sales of armoured vehicles is a more general replacement of national fleets. For example, Russia has started purchasing armoured vehicles in an effort to modernize its inventories.[19]

Two companies that manufacture armoured vehicles moved into the top 20 arms producers: Navistar and AM General Corporation. Due to $4 billion in sales of MRAP all-terrain vehicles (M-ATV) to the US DOD, Navistar had by far the largest relative increase in arms sales in 2008—954 per cent—and it jumped into the Top 100 at 20th place. Another armoured vehicle manufacturer, Force Protection, had a near 50 per cent increase in sales, although the increase was less than $500 million.[20]

Other companies in the Top 100 with broader ranges of products also increased their arms sales as a result of growth in armoured vehicle sales. For example, partly because of armoured vehicle contracts, the arms sales of BAE Systems, General Dynamics, SAIC and Thales each increased by over $1 billion and those of Textron by 36 per cent.[21] In addition, suppliers

[17] According to US DOD figures, 61% of the deaths and 65% of the injuries of US military personnel in Afghanistan and Iraq caused by hostile actors were due to explosive devices. US Department of Defense, Statistical Information Analysis Division, 'Global war on terrorism by reason October 7, 2001 through January 2, 2010: weaponry, explosive devices', <http://siadapp.dmdc.osd.mil/personnel/CASUALTY/castop.htm>.

[18] Total funding for US Overseas Contingency Operations was set at $23.9 billion, including funds allocated to MRAPs and UAVs. National Defense Authorization Act for Fiscal Year 2010, US Public Law no. 111-84, signed into law on 28 Oct. 2009, <http://thomas.loc.gov/cgi-bin/query/z?c111:H.R.2647:>.

[19] Kupriyanova, A. and Irtegova, I., 'Defended with state orders: focus on helicopters', URALSIB Capital, Moscow, 6 July 2009, <http://www.uralsibcap.ru/products/download/090706_Defense_Sector_Update.pdf;?docid=7936&lang=en>. See also section IV below.

[20] Force Protection first entered the Top 100 in 2007 as a result of armoured vehicle sales.

[21] BAE Systems attributes like-for-like growth to the USA's demand for armoured vehicles. General Dynamics' increase in arms sales stemmed from refurbishment of armoured vehicles worn out in the war zones as well as the production of new vehicles, particularly M-1 Abrams tanks and MRAPs. SAIC integration of communication systems into MRAPs is a leading contributor to its growth. Increased sales in electronic and warfare systems, in part in relation to those integrated into the Bushmaster armoured vehicle, contributed to Thales' arms sales growth. Textron produces an average of 50 armoured vehicles a month. BAE Systems, *Annual Report 2008* (note 7), p. 29; General Dynamics, *Annual Report 2008* (General Dynamics: Falls Church, VA, [2009]), p. 5; SAIC, *Form 10-K Annual Report under Section 13 or 15(d) of the Securities and Exchange Act of 1934 for the Fiscal Year*

of components for land systems increased their sales. For example, sales by Cobham and SAIC of radios and electronic warfare systems—products that are integrated into MRAPs and explosive device detection equipment used in Afghanistan and Iraq—were particularly strong.[22]

Competitions for contracts for armoured and logistical vehicles remain crowded by bidding companies because these contracts are large but few in number. This can contribute to tension in the bidding process. For example, in 2008 the US Army chose the US company Oshkosh for a contract potentially worth $3.5 billion for the supply of medium technical vehicles (known as the family of medium tactical vehicles, FMTV). However, BAE Systems and Navistar protested and subsequently secured a recommendation from the US Government Accountability Office (GAO) that the US Army reconsider its choice based on these two companies' past performances and capabilities.[23] In another example, Hägglunds, a Swedish subsidiary of BAE Systems, appealed against the award to Patria of Finland of a Swedish order for armoured vehicles worth $340 million. The bidding process was found to be unfair and non-transparent and as a result the international tender was relaunched.[24] The level of competition is likely to remain high as long as the conflicts in Afghanistan and Iraq continue because armoured vehicles are critical to the fighting there. The US Army's plans to implement a troop surge in Afghanistan will only heighten demand for armoured vehicles.[25]

The UAV market remained strong in 2008. Major UAV producers include Northrop Grumman and Textron of the USA and Elbit Systems and Israel Aerospace Industries of Israel. It is often unclear how much of a company's UAV sales are to the military market specifically, especially since UAV equipment can have both military and civilian use. For example, Textron reported that a key factor in its higher arms sales in 2008 was its 2007 acquisition of AAI, one of the primary suppliers of UAVs to the US military.[26] The company also reported that AAI was the primary contrib-

Ended January 31, 2009 (US Securities and Exchange Commission: Washington, DC, 27 Mar. 2009), p. 28; Thales, *Annual Report 2008* (Thales: Neuilly-sur-Seine, 2009), p. 11; and Textron, *Annual Report 2008* (Textron: Providence, RI, 2009), p. 4.

[22] Cobham, *Annual Report and Accounts 2008* (Cobham: Wimborne, 2009), p. 5; and SAIC (note 21), p. 28.

[23] US Government Accountability Office (GAO), 'Decision on bid protest by Navistar Defense and BAE Systems regarding army truck award to Oshkosh', Press statement, 14 Dec. 2009, <http://www.gao.gov/press/navistar_2009dec14.html>.

[24] O'Dwyer, G., 'FMV re-runs AMV tender', *Defense News*, 7 Jan. 2010.

[25] 'FMTV 2010–2015: Oshkosh wins the re-compete', *Defense Industry Daily*, 14 Dec. 2009, <http://www.defenseindustrydaily.com/FMTV-2010-2015-Oshkosh-Wins-The-Re-Compete-05744/>; and Roosevelt, A., 'FMTV contract awards top $3 billion to date in 2008', *Defense Daily*, 25 Nov. 2008, <http://www.defensedaily.com/publications/dd/FMTV-Contract-Awards-Top-$3-Billion-To-Date-In-2008_4844.html>.

[26] Textron, *Form 10-K Annual Report under Section 13 or 15(d) of the Securities and Exchange Act of 1934 for the Fiscal Year Ended January 3, 2009* (US Securities and Exchange Commission: Washington, DC, 26 Feb. 2009), p. 17.

utor to the increase of $820 million in its revenue that resulted from acquisitions of new business. However, it is not certain how much of this revenue contribution came from AAI's UAV military sales because AAI has civilian government and commercial customers in addition to the US military.

One measure of activity in this segment is government contracts for UAVs for their armed forces. Contracts for UAVs from the US DOD, the largest UAV customer, were worth $1.1 billion in 2008, up from $690 million in 2007.[27] Israeli and US UAV producers dominate the market, although other countries are eager for their UAV producers to grow for both domestic consumption and export.[28] The UAV market is expected to continue growing in the near-to-medium term.[29]

Military services companies

Eighteen companies in the 2008 Top 100 are categorized as military services companies.[30] These companies provide military services as a result of governments' outsourcing of traditional military roles to private companies.[31] The recent increase in these companies' revenues continued in 2008: three increased their arms sales by more than 30 per cent—DynCorp International, VSE Corporation and Serco—and another three by close to 30 per cent—ManTech International Corporation, Jacobs Engineering Group and CACI International. DynCorp generated 54 per cent of its military-related revenue from business related to the Afghanistan and Iraq conflicts, while CACI International's sales to the US DOD rose by nearly 41 per cent in 2008 as a result of acquisitions of services companies.[32]

A number of companies that are not primarily service companies generate a significant amount of their arms sales through their services divisions. For example, ITT Corporation reported a 50 per cent increase in sales by its Defense Electronics & Services segment in 2008. This was mostly because of the full integration of EDO Corporation—which ITT purchased

[27] 'Contracts search results (FY 2008)', USAspending.gov, <http://www.usaspending.gov/fpds/fpds.php?psc_cat=15&psc_sub=1550&maj_agency_cat=97&fiscal_year=2008>.

[28] Wezeman, S., *UAVs and UCAVs: Developments in the European Union*, Briefing paper (European Parliament: Brussels, Oct. 2007). E.g. Pakistan is set to domestically produce some of the parts for the Italian Falco UAV in order to decrease its reliance on imports and to build its internal surveillance capabilities. Bokhari, F., 'Pakistan formally launches new domestic UAV', *Jane's Defence Weekly*, 26 Aug. 2009, p. 8.

[29] 'Interview: Marion Blakely, President and CEO, AIA', *Defense News*, 14 Dec. 2009, p. 30. AIA is the US Aerospace Industries Association.

[30] In addition, VT Group became a services company in Oct. 2009 when it sold its BVT Surface Fleet subsidiary to BAE Systems.

[31] Perlo-Freeman, S. and Sköns, E., 'The private military services industry', SIPRI Insights on Peace and Security no. 2008/1, Sep. 2008, <http://books.sipri.org/product_info?c_product_id=361>.

[32] DynCorp International, *Annual Report 2009* (DynCorp International: Falls Church, VA, 2009), p. 1; and CACI International, *Form 10-K Annual Report under Section 13 or 15(d) of the Securities and Exchange Act of 1934 for the Fiscal Year Ended June 30, 2008* (US Securities and Exchange Commission: Washington, DC, 27 Aug. 2008), p. 8.

in late 2007—that resulted in ITT's overall arms sales increase of $1.3 billion (34 per cent).[33] Hewlett-Packard's entry into the Top 100 stemmed from its purchase of EDS in 2008. EDS—now known as HP Enterprise Services—provides information technology (IT) services to the US and other armed forces.

Russian companies

The increase in the arms sales of the Russian companies in the Top 100 (14 per cent in real terms) was as a result of the Russian Government's continued spending on arms procurement and arms industry development, the consolidation of the Russian arms industry and the continued growth of exports.[34] Almaz-Antei, producer of the S-300 and S-400 series of air defence systems, headed the Russian companies in 2008.[35] It has tripled its arms sales from $960 million in 2003 to $4.3 billion in 2008. TRV Corporation, another aerospace company, also maintained its rapid rates of growth. TRV's arms sales more than quadrupled from $220 million in 2004 to $1.2 billion in 2008. Uralvagonzavod delivered more tanks to the Russian armed forces and for export than any Russian company has since 1993, increasing its armoured vehicle sales in 2008 by 39 per cent to reach $640 million.[36]

Despite the growth in its arms sales, the state of Russia's arms industry remains in question.[37] Russia has begun importing advanced technologies for incorporation into its newly produced weapon platforms for both export and domestic recipients. It has indicated that it intends to import UAVs and advanced naval platforms to meet the demands of the Russian military and also to contribute to the modernization of its arms industry.[38] Following plant and city tours, President Dmitry Medvedev, Prime Minister Vladimir Putin and other Russian officials have criticized the state of the arms industry, especially in terms of technology and quality.[39] Furthermore, Russian arms producers face challenges from a number of its major

[33] ITT Corporation, 'ITT reports solid 2008 fourth quarter and full-year results', Press release, 4 Feb. 2009, <http://www.itt.com/news/2009/0204-4q08-earnings.asp>.

[34] See chapter 7, section II, in this volume; and section IV below.

[35] The S-300 and S-400 are also known by their US/NATO designations of SA-10 and SA-21. See also chapter 8, section III, in this volume.

[36] Uralvagonzavod produced 62 tanks for the Russian Ministry of Defence and 113 for export to Algeria and India. Barabanov, M., 'Russian tank production sets a new record', *Moscow Defense Brief*, no. 2, 2009, pp. 8–9.

[37] On the Russian arms industry up to 2006 see Cooper, J., 'Developments in the Russian arms industry', *SIPRI Yearbook 2006*.

[38] Russia has purchased UAVs from Israel and is in talks to purchase the French Mistral. Barabanov, M. 'The Mistral problem', *Moscow Defense Brief*, no. 3, 2009, pp. 2–4. See also chapter 7, section II, in this volume.

[39] President of Russia, 'Excerpts from transcript of meeting on defence industry's development', 26 Oct. 2009, <http://eng.kremlin.ru/text/speeches/2009/10/26/2110_type82913type82917_222368. shtml>; and Russian Government, 'Prime Minister Vladimir Putin addressed the 11th Congress of the United Russia party', 21 Nov. 2009, <http://www.premier.gov.ru/eng/visits/ru/8327/events/8323/>.

Table 6.4. The largest acquisitions within OECD arms industries, 2009

Figures are in US $m., at current prices. Companies are US-based unless stated otherwise.

Buyer company	Acquired company	Seller company	Deal value ($ m.)
Precision Castparts Corp.	Carlton Forge Works	Privately owned	850
General Dynamics	Axsys Technologies	Publicly listed	643
BAE Systems (UK)	BVT Surface Fleet (UK)	VT Group (UK)	558
Goodrich Corp.	Atlantic Inertial Systems	J. F. Lehman & Co.	375
Woodward Governor	HR Textron	Textron	365
ManTech International	Sensor Technologies	Privately owned	242
Jacobs Engineering Group	AWE Management Ltd (UK)	British Nuclear Fuels Ltd (UK)	195
Chemring Group (UK)	Hi-Shear Technology	Publicly listed	132

Source: Appendix 6B.

recipients (including China) that are seeking to develop and increase their own production for domestic consumption and could also become rivals in established Russian export markets.[40]

III. Mergers and acquisitions, 2009

In general, the pace and size of mergers and acquisitions have dropped noticeably since the peak levels a few years ago. The mega-deals of the past were non-existent in 2009 (see table 6.4 and appendix 6B).[41] The acquisition of US companies by British companies slowed, while US domestic acquisitions continued.[42] Consolidation within the Russian aerospace industry continued apace under the United Aircraft Corporation (UAC) umbrella and, in Israel, Elbit Systems further consolidated its domination of the domestic market.

Mergers and acquisitions in OECD arms industries

In 2009 all arms industry transactions within the OECD with a value known to be over $100 million involved British or US companies; the majority of these were US national acquisitions (see table 6.4 and appendix 6B). However, more than half of the known-value acquisitions in 2009

---

[40] See chapter 7, section II, in this volume.

[41] The most recent acquisition worth over $1 billion was Dassault's purchase of Alcatel-Lucent's shares in Thales for €1.57 billion ($2.14 billion), which was announced in 2008 and finalized in May 2009. Dassault Aviation, 'Dassault Aviation completes the acquisition of Alcatel-Lucent's stakes in Thales', Press release, 20 May 2009, <http://www.dassault-aviation.com/en/aviation/press/press-kits/2009.html?L=1>.

[42] On British acquisitions of US companies in earlier years see Perlo-Freeman, S., 'Arms production', *SIPRI Yearbook 2009*, pp. 277–79.

had a value below $100 million, ranging from $13 million to $90 million.[43] Almost half of these smaller acquisitions were of companies in the USA, which marks the continued trend for US and foreign companies to expand in the lucrative US market.[44] Three of the companies that were acquired in 2009 were subsidiaries of companies in the Top 100 for 2008.[45]

Non-OECD consolidation and acquisitions

Outside the OECD member countries, consolidation and acquisitions in Russia and Israel are of particular note. Russia has been working for some time to consolidate and streamline its aerospace industry and, to accomplish this task, formed the United Aircraft Corporation in 2006. Although the consolidation has been slow, four companies (including military and civil aircraft companies) were further integrated into UAC in 2009: MiG Aircraft, KAPO, Aviastar and Sokol.[46] UAC also holds interests in military aircraft producers Sukhoi, Irkut and Iluyshin, among others. In April 2009 Russia completed the process of establishing a state-owned shipbuilding management company, the United Shipbuilding Corporation, which encompasses large-scale shipbuilding enterprises as well as design and construction bureaus.[47]

Elbit Systems—the largest privately owned company in Israel's arms industry—completed six acquisitions in 2009: one in the USA and five in Israel, reflecting further consolidation of the Israeli market.[48] By some accounts Elbit now owns over 90 per cent of Israel's non-state-owned arms-producing companies.[49] As a result of earlier acquisitions bearing fruit, Elbit's earnings doubled in 2008.[50]

[43] There were also at least 10 deals for which the financial data was not disclosed. The majority of these involved acquisitions by large companies of smaller, privately owned companies that are expected to fill product line gaps, provide access to desired markets, etc. For details of all the deals discussed here see appendix 6B.

[44] On this phenomenon see Perlo-Freeman (note 42), pp. 275–79.

[45] VT Group sold its stake in BVT Surface Fleet to BAE Systems; Textron sold HR Textron to Woodward Governor; and QinetiQ sold its Underwater Systems to Atlas Electronik's UK business.

[46] 'KAPO joins United Aircraft Corporation', Interfax, 26 Oct. 2009; [UAC increased its share in the Ulyanovsk aviation plant 'Aviastar-SP' to 26.25% of shares], RIA Novosti, 27 Oct. 2009, <http://volga.rian.ru/economy/20091027/81796201.html> (in Russian); and 'United Aircraft Corp buys 100% stake in MiG aircraft maker', RIA Novosti, 23 Oct. 2009, <http://en.rian.ru/russia/20091023/156570250.html>.

[47] Loskutova, O., 'JSC "United Shipbuilding Corporation": looking into the future (Interview with corporation president Vladimir Pakhomov)', Maritime Market, no. 3(29), 2009.

[48] Wagstaff-Smith, K., 'Elbit completes purchase of BVR Systems', Jane's Defence Industry, 19 Nov. 2009.

[49] Pettibone, R., 'Growth continues apace at Elbit Systems', Forecast International, 8 Oct. 2009.

[50] Anderson, G., 'Elbit doubles earnings in 2008 fuelled by acquisitions', Jane's Defence Industry, 11 Mar. 2009.

Acquisitions in the security industry[51]

In 2009 several of the arms-producing companies in the SIPRI Top 100 acquired companies in the security industry. While the term 'security industry' lacks a well-formed and universally accepted definition, the broadest sense of the term encompasses products and services as diverse as alarm systems, electronic access control and biometrics, and surveillance and security consulting.[52] The security industry companies that were acquired in 2009 supply security-related goods and services in fields such as cybersecurity (e.g. encryption technologies), surveillance (e.g. border control integrated systems), identification (e.g. biometric technologies), detection (e.g. explosives detection) and public safety (e.g. crisis management services). While detailed financial data is lacking for many of these transactions, it seems reasonable to note that there is an emerging pattern of acquisitions of these types of companies.

Cybersecurity and intelligence were key sectors for security industry acquisitions. Boeing, DynCorp International, Harris, QinetiQ, Raytheon, SAIC and Ultra Electronics all made purchases of smaller companies that specialize in these areas.[53] Many of the acquired companies are located in the USA, which provides foreign purchasers with potential access to the US military market.[54] For example, both QinetiQ and Ultra Electronics of the UK purchased US cybersecurity firms to employ this strategy.[55] Other transatlantic purchases were SAFRAN's takeover of Motorola's biometric unit (to gain access to the US identification market) and of GE Security's Homeland Protection division (to benefit from the US stimulus package for security-related expenditure).[56] These acquisitions are in line with increased government demand and shifting focus to international terrorism, organized crime, illegal immigration and piracy.

These acquisition strategies build on similar activities in recent years. SAFRAN worked on reforming itself into an aerospace, defence and secur-

---

[51] Vincent Boulanin, a guest researcher at SIPRI from École des Hautes Études de Science Sociales (EHESS), Paris, contributed to this subsection.

[52] On the ambiguity of what comprises the security industry and the growing debate about how to measure security-related expenditure see Stevens, B. et al., *The Security Economy* (Organisation for Economic Co-operation and Development: Paris, 2004).

[53] Boeing purchased eXMeritus; DynCorp bought Kroll Government Services and Phoenix Consulting Group; Harris acquired Crucial Security; QinetiQ bought Cyveillance; Raytheon bought BBN Technologies; SAIC acquired Atlan; and Ultra Electronics bought Scytale.

[54] Jean-Paul Hebert of EHESS cited in Tran, P., 'European firms see growth in civil defense', *Defense News*, 4 Apr. 2008, p. 8.

[55] QinetiQ, 'QinetiQ strengthens presence in US cyber security market through acquisition of Cyveillance, Inc', Press release, 6 May 2009, <http://www.qinetiq.com/home/newsroom/news_releases_homepage/2009/2nd_quarter/cyveillance.html>; and Ultra Electronics, 'Ultra acquires US communication security business', Press release, 19 Oct. 2009, <http://www.ultra-electronics.com/press_releases.php?year=2009>.

[56] Tran (note 54).

ity company by selling off its commercial mobile phone business in 2008. Also in 2008, BAE Systems acquired Detica as a major part of its strategy to develop security sales in its various home markets. The Detica acquisition will help BAE Systems to benefit from the British Government's growing focus on intelligence and security.[57]

IV. The limited impact of the financial crisis on the arms industry

The fallout from the 2008 financial crisis and the ensuing recession has been less immediate and has had a less direct impact on arms sales than experienced in other industries. While both industrial production and global trade in merchandise declined sharply in late 2008 and in 2009, and business and consumer confidence collapsed, the sales of arms-producing companies were still strong.[58] Company strategies remained broadly the same as before the crisis. The few government stimulus packages that were directed at the arms industry were relatively small compared to the overall total stimulus. Several factors insulated the arms industry from the full force of the crisis and recession, including high levels of military spending, the monopsonistic character of the arms market, and the ongoing conflicts in Afghanistan and Iraq.[59]

The performance of the arms industry

It is clear from the survey in section II that the financial crisis had no negative impact on arms sales in 2008. These sales increased at roughly the same rate as in the previous year despite the global downturn in gross domestic product and in other types of industry. Overall country and regional arms shares in the SIPRI Top 100 were relatively stable year-on-year (see table 6.2), indicating that the financial crisis did not have a meaningful impact on 2008 arms sales in any particular region. Furthermore, a sample of data for 2009 indicates that arms sales continued to increase steadily around the world even in the midst of the crisis. Order books for weapons and military-related services remained largely intact. The fact that military expenditure continued to increase significantly in 2009 also indicates that demand for the goods and services of the arms industry remains largely unaffected.[60]

[57] BAE Systems, *Annual Report 2008* (note 7), p. 40.
[58] On the crisis see International Monetary Fund (IMF), *World Economic Outlook: Crisis and Recovery* (IMF: Washington, DC, Apr. 2009).
[59] A monoponistic market is one in which many suppliers compete for orders from a single buyer. In the case of a national arms industry, the single buyer in the domestic market is the national government.
[60] See chapter 5 in this volume.

There are many examples of companies with both military and non-military activities that experienced drops in their overall revenues due to cuts in commercial sales in 2009 and that are relying on the military side of their business as a stable source of income.[61] These include companies in sectors such as engines, automobiles, semiconductors and construction machinery, in which companies around the globe have seen a drop in demand and, in many cases, prices also.[62]

As expected, contracts for the Afghanistan and Iraq conflicts meant that US companies had another strong year in military sales. For example, Lockheed Martin's sales continued to rise during 2009 in such areas as mission and combat systems, tactical missile programmes, simulation and training activities, and the F-35 and C-130J aircraft programmes for both deliveries and support activities.[63] DynCorp International reported increases in revenues and back orders in the second half of 2009 due in particular to a ramp up of the US Army's Logistics Civilian Augmentation Program IV (LOGCAP IV) in Afghanistan and Kuwait.[64] In 2009 Oshkosh Corporation claimed significant growth in its military segment, although not enough to offset declines in its commercial segment. This increase came from military demand for new trucks and for parts and services.[65] Honeywell's early financial results for 2009 showed decreases in its aerospace sales. The company attributed the decreases to lower commercial sales which were only partially offset by strong military sales: the company continues to win large contracts from the US DOD and the British Ministry of Defence.[66]

[61] This finding is based on a sample of company annual reports and related news articles from the USA, Western Europe, Israel and Japan. Companies surveyed include Pratt & Whitney, Rockwell Collins, Meggitt, QinetiQ, Rolls-Royce, Thales, Rheinmetall, RUAG, Indras, Israel Aerospace Industries, Toshiba, Itochu and Japan Steelworks. The majority of examples cited here are US or West European companies because at the time of writing they were the companies that had released preliminary results for 2009. There are reports that Russian arms-producing companies are sharing the experiences described here. See e.g. 'Russian aviation industry focused on warplanes in 2009—UAC', Interfax, 28 Dec. 2009. On the case of Turkey see Sariibrahimoglu, L., 'Undeterred by financial crisis, Turkish defense companies plan to increase domestic arms production', *Eurasia Daily Monitor*, 27 Feb. 2009.

[62] E.g. companies in Japan were hit by a sharp decline in semiconductor prices. See e.g. Toshiba, *Annual Report 2009* (Toshiba: Tokyo, 2009), p. 3.

[63] Lockheed Martin did note lower volume in other areas (e.g. the F-22 and F-16 combat aircraft programmes) although sales did not fall. Lockheed Martin, 'Lockheed Martin announces third quarter 2009 results', Press release, 20 Oct. 2009, <http://www.lockheedmartin.com/news/press_releases/2009/1020hq-3q-2009-earnings.html>.

[64] DynCorp International, *Form 10-Q Pursuant to Section 13 or 15(d) of the Securities and Exchange Act of 1934 for Quarterly Period Ended Oct. 2, 2009* (US Securities and Exchange Commission: Washington, DC, 27 Nov. 2009), p. 34.

[65] Oshkosh Corporation, *2009 Annual Report: When Experience Counts* (Oshkosh Corporation: Oshkosh, WI), p. 1. On the contested award to Oshkosh of a contract to produce medium tactical vehicles for the US Army see section II above.

[66] Honeywell, Quarterly sales reports, 1st–3rd quarters 2009, <http://investor.honeywell.com/phoenix.zhtml?c=94774&p=irol-news>.

In the UK, half-year results for BAE Systems showed a continued increase in the company's revenues and order book.[67] Meggitt's half-year results in 2009 showed that its military sales increased by 31 per cent while its civilian orders remained flat. The company's military sales were based on the high demand for combat systems and a new extended contract for combat training in the UK.[68] Finmeccanica of Italy registered a 30 per cent jump in revenues for the first three quarters of 2009, driven by military aeronautics and electronics, in part because DRS Technologies (which it acquired in 2008) had already beaten whole-year new order expectations for 2009.[69] SAFRAN of France had revenue and net income increases in part because of sales of military engines by its Aerospace Propulsion business.[70] Rheinmetall of Germany relied on its military segment to compensate for drops in its automotive segment.[71] In addition, Krauss-Maffei Wegmann benefited through a joint venture with Rheinmetall from a €3.1 billion ($4.6 billion) German Government contract for Puma armoured vehicles.[72]

For other countries it is more difficult to find timely information on individual companies but, even with the poor global economic climate, national arms industries seem to be doing well overall. The Russian Government announced that, despite the financial crisis, the output of the Russian arms industry grew by 3.7 per cent in 2009.[73] In Australia, the aerospace sector in particular has been shielded from the crisis by military work.[74]

Company strategies

By and large, arms-producing companies have not adopted any new strategies in response to the financial crisis. Rather, they have maintained the strategies developed over the past decade or so: international arms sales, business reform and diversification into other sectors. Because the USA has been by far the largest military spender and is anticipated to remain so, many of these companies have been trying to establish or expand partnerships in the USA or to complete acquisitions there in order to deal with the

---

[67] BAE Systems, *Half-yearly Report: Leveraging Global Capability* (BAE Systems: London, July 2009).

[68] Meggitt, 'Interim presentation for the 6 months ended 30 June 2009', 4 Aug. 2009, <http://www.meggitt.com/?OBH=290>.

[69] 'Strong showing', *Aviation Week & Space Technology*, 9 Nov. 2009, p. 26.

[70] SAFRAN, 'Safran reports nine-month revenue 2009', Press release, 16 Oct. 2009, <http://www.safran-group.com/site-safran-en/finance-397/financial-publications/financial-press-releases/2009-658/article/safran-reports-nine-month-revenue?10091>.

[71] Pettibone, R., 'Rheinmetall buoyed by defense', Forecast International, 15 Oct. 2009.

[72] Rheinmetall, 'Billion plus order for Rheinmetall', Press release, 6 July 2009, <http://www.rheinmetall.de/index.php?lang=3&fid=2160>.

[73] 'Russia does not need to buy arms abroad—Putin', Interfax, 3 Dec. 2009.

[74] Brown, M., 'Aerospace industry weathers global crisis', ABC News, 29 Nov. 2009, <http://www.abc.net.au/news/stories/2009/11/29/2756484.htm>.

economic downturn.[75] At the same time, companies have still been considering other markets such as Latin America, East Asia and the Middle East as having growth potential.

Arms-producing companies often have some leeway when developing response strategies to deal with potential financial stress such as the global financial crisis and recession. Legal budgetary processes mean that military budgets, including procurement budgets, tend to be shielded from immediate reductions. Furthermore, the arms industry generally operates on long-term contracts, which mitigate the impact of recessions and give companies time to adjust their business strategies.

Government policies

The economic rescue and stimulus packages that several governments implemented in response to the financial crisis have had varying degrees of implications for the arms industry. The arms industry has not been excluded from receiving funds from these packages and in some cases has received special treatment.[76]

Russia pledged not to cut military purchases and has been trying to increase procurement even though its oil revenues fell significantly in 2009.[77] However, even without the crisis, support for the arms industry has been a longer-term pursuit of the Russian Government as it has attempted to modernize its forces. According to official reports, Russia allocated approximately 970 billion roubles ($33 billion) to the arms industry in 2009 with more promised for 2010.[78] To meet the challenges posed by the financial crisis and recession while simultaneously encouraging the country's military modernization, the Russian Government has provided credit rate subsidies, made direct contributions to authorized capital and issued the right for companies to use state guarantees on bank credits.[79] For example,

---

[75] Among others, MBDA, Rheinmetall, Thales, Dassault, Honeywell, Rafael, Toshiba, Fuji Heavy Industries and Fincantieri are considering this strategy. E.g. Kongsberg (Norway) opened a US factory to assemble weapon control systems for the US market, gaining in sales and market access. Kongsberg, *Annual Report and Sustainability Report 2008* (Kongsberg Gruppen: Kongsberg, [2009]), pp. 5, 22.

[76] Poland is one example of direct economic stimulus to the arms industry, although the amounts were relatively low. 'Polish arms industry to receive crisis funds', Polish Press Agency (PAP), 22 July 2009.

[77] Gavrilov, Yu., [Instead of 'Topol'], *Rossiyskaya Gazeta*, 10 Dec. 2009 (in Russian); and Abdullaev, N., 'Russia pushes industry support through recession', *Defense News*, 7 Sep. 2009.

[78] 'Some 33bn dollars allocated for Russian defence industry in 2009—Putin', Interfax, 18 Nov. 2009; and Chuter, A. and P. Tran, 'Financial crises creates bleak spending outlook', *Defense News*, 7 Sep. 2009.

[79] 'Some 33bn dollars allocated for Russian defence industry in 2009' (note 78). Although subsidies have been provided for some of the smaller supplier companies in order to prevent bankruptcies, the majority of assistance is to the larger producers on the Russian state list of those companies eligible to receive crisis aid. 'Russia's Putin signs orders granting subsidies to struggling

Russian officials have pledged state backing of loans to arms-producing companies with export financing supported by at least Vneshekonombank and Vneshtorgbank, two Russian banks critical to the industry.[80] Early in 2009 the Russian Government proposed implementing emergency aid measures that would allow companies to negotiate longer-term raw materials contracts in order to support companies' need for flexibility in the face of price fluctuations.[81] In addition, military exports are considered a key means for obtaining hard foreign currency, which is another reason why these exports receive government support.[82]

Similarly, French leaders have been supportive of maintaining military spending and procurement. In response to the financial crisis, France committed stimulus money directly to the arms industry. The government allocated 10 per cent of its economic stimulus package to the Ministry of Defence, amounting to approximately €2.3 billion ($3.4 billion).[83] Of this amount, at least €1.4 billion ($2 billion) was designated for arms producers. However, French companies are wary that the eventual necessity of the government balancing budgets and repaying debt could jeopardize political commitments to procurement spending in the long run.[84]

Germany implemented a small stimulus package in 2008 and in early 2009 a larger package worth over €50 billion ($63 billion) with €500 million ($634 million) for the military. Half of this amount was for construction projects while the other half was for procuring high-tech military equipment including vehicles and other equipment needed by German personnel deployed in Afghanistan, making this portion of the stimulus spending more like supplementary military spending.[85]

Italy made funding cuts to all its ministries. However, part of the cuts at the Ministry of Defence is expected to be eliminated by using funds dedicated to other ministries.[86]

defence enterprises', Interfax, 16 Nov. 2009; and 'List of enterprises where state will get stake is ready—minister', ITAR-TASS, 23 Mar. 2009.

[80] Makienko, K., 'Economic crisis and Russia's defense industry', *Moscow Defence Brief*, no. 1, 2009; and ['VTB Severo-Zapad' provided a loan to JSC 'Machine Building Plant Arsenal'], RIA Novosti, 9 Nov. 2009, <http://nw.rian.ru/economy/20091109/81803119.html> (in Russian).

[81] McDermott, R., 'Russia feels pinch over arms plans', *Asia Times*, 16 Jan. 2009.

[82] Kislov, A. and Frilov, A., 'Issues and prospects of Russian military exports', *International Affairs* (Moscow), no. 5, 2009.

[83] French Ministry of Defence. 'Contribution significative de la Defense au plan de relance de l'economie fracaise' [Defence's significant contribution to the plan to relaunch the French economy], <http://www.defense.gouv.fr/ministre/actualite_et_dossiers/archives_a_la_une/contribution_signifi cative_de_la_defense_au_plan_de_relance_de_l_economie_francaise>.

[84] Chuter and Tran (note 78).

[85] 'German defense to benefit from state stimulus package', Translation from German Radio, Defence Talk, 4 Mar. 2009, <http://www.defencetalk.com/german-defense-to-benefit-from-state-stimulus-package-16466/>; and Schulte, S., 'Coming together', *Jane's Defence Weekly*, 4 Nov. 2009, pp. 44–47.

[86] Chuter and Tran (note 78).

The US Government passed an $800 billion economic stimulus package in early 2009. The portion of the funding allocated to the Department of Defense included projects on facilities operation and maintenance, medical facility modernization, environmental clean-up, and research, development, testing and evaluation. Procurement of weapons and military services was not included in the package.[87]

Australia included a military-related component in its stimulus package; for example, it provided 246 million Australian dollars ($206 million) to build housing for military personnel and their families, although this money goes to construction firms, not arms producers.[88] Separate from the stimulus package, the government issued a Defence White Paper which some believe could act as an economic stimulus package for the arms industry because it allows for more than 100 billion Australian dollars ($83.9 billion) to be spent over the next decade on procurement for the armed forces.[89]

China's overall stimulus package is estimated at 4 trillion yuan ($585 billion).[90] Specific details on the package's funds for the arms industry were not provided. However, China reportedly has provided state loans totalling at least $75 billion to companies that also produce weapons, such as the aircraft producer AVIC and the shipbuilders CSSC and CSIC.[91] These loans are intended to be used by the companies to improve infrastructure and for research and development.[92] In addition to loans, the government offered tax rebates on value added taxes to some industries, including shipbuilding.[93] Shipbuilding also received other types of support, such as technology upgrades and support for mergers and acquisitions within the industry.[94]

---

[87] American Recovery and Reinvestment Act of 2009, US Public Law no. 111-5, signed into law on 17 Feb. 2009, <http://thomas.loc.gov/cgi-bin/query/z?c111:h1:>. See also chapter 5, section VII, in this volume.

[88] Australian Government, 'Nation building: economic stimulus plan, defence housing', 2009, <http://www.economicstimulusplan.gov.au/housing/>.

[89] Australian Department of Defence, *Defending Australia in the Asia Pacific Century: Force 2030—Defence White Paper 2009* (Australian Government: Canberra, 2009); and 'Industry welcomes Defence White Paper', *Manufacturers' Monthly*, May 2009, <http://www.manmonthly.com.au/Article/Industry-welcomes-Defence-White-Paper/479544.aspx>.

[90] US Library of Congress, 'Financial stimulus plans: recent developments in selected countries', 17 Apr. 2009, <http://www.loc.gov/law/help/financial_stimulus_plan.php#China>.

[91] Grevatt, J., 'China's defence industry bucks wider market downturn', *Jane's Defence Industry*, 2 Sep. 2009. In early 2009, AVIC was reported as the largest borrower of these loans, but it is not known what proportion of the loans was dedicated to the arms side of AVIC's business. See Lagerkranser, P., 'China banks surge to world's biggest may be too good to be true', Bloomberg.com, 30 Apr. 2009, <http://www.bloomberg.com/apps/news?pid=20601109&sid=aueh06DOY37A>.

[92] Grevatt, J., 'China's defence industry bucks wider market downturn', *Jane's Defence Industry*, 2 Sep. 2009.

[93] Wallis, K., 'China stimulus package to benefit larger yards', *Lloyds List*, 26 Feb. 2009.

[94] Hao, T., 'Shipbuilders in consolidation mode', *China Daily*, 16 Feb. 2009.

V. Conclusions: continuity despite the crisis

The financial crisis and recession have not had a significant negative impact on the arms industry. Arms sales in 2008 continued their upward trend and an initial assessment of 2009 company statements shows strong results for their military segments for that year also. Furthermore, regional shares remained stable in 2008, indicating that no particular region experienced a negative impact from the early effects of the crisis. There are several factors that contribute to the continuity despite a global financial crisis and recession, including high levels of military expenditure, the inherent characteristics of the arms industry and the ongoing conflicts in Afghanistan and Iraq.

As the largest military spender and arms procurer, the policy of the USA regarding the financial crisis and recession has a potentially strong impact on the global arms industry. Cuts have not materialized in either the USA's overall military expenditure or its procurement. On the contrary, US military expenditure increased in 2009.[95] While the industry will continue to watch closely to see if the USA shifts its spending away from procurement of large weapon systems, for now many of these programmes either remain intact or have been postponed but not cancelled outright.[96] Spending on armoured vehicles and UAVs for the conflicts in Afghanistan and Iraq will continue and, at least in the short term, the USA is expected to continue to hire contractors and outsource military-related services.

The monopsonistic structure of the arms industry, the consequent strong relationships between arms producers and governments, and the industry's perceived importance to national security also shield it from the immediate impact of severe economic downturns.[97] This status is reflected in the continued high levels of arms sales, high profits, large backlogs and strong cash flows generated by arms production even as other industries verge on faltering and need more government economic assistance.

With the conflicts in Afghanistan and Iraq continuing and with the industry likely to emerge relatively unscathed after the recession, the expectation is that the current trends in the arms industry will continue.

[95] See chapter 5 in this volume.
[96] Hartley, K. and Solomon, B., 'NATO and the economic and financial crisis', NATO Research Paper no. 52, Oct. 2009, <http://www.ndc.nato.int/research/series.php?icode=1>.
[97] See e.g. Sköns, E. and Dunne, J. P., 'Economics of arms production', ed. L. Kurtz, *Encyclopedia of Violence, Peace, and Conflict*, 2nd edn, vol. 1 (Elsevier: Oxford, 2008); and Dunne, J. P., 'The defense industrial base', eds K. Hartley and T. Sandler, *Handbook of Defense Economics*, vol. 1 (North-Holland: Amsterdam, 1995).

Appendix 6A. The SIPRI Top 100 arms-producing companies, 2008

SUSAN T. JACKSON AND THE SIPRI ARMS INDUSTRY NETWORK*

I. Selection criteria and sources of data

Table 6A.1 lists the world's 100 largest arms-producing companies (excluding Chinese companies), ranked by their arms sales in 2008—the SIPRI Top 100 for 2008. The table contains information on each company's arms sales in 2007 and 2008 and its total sales, profit and employment in 2008. It includes public and private companies but excludes manufacturing or maintenance units of the armed services. Only companies with operational activities in the field of military goods and services are listed, not holding or investment companies. Chinese companies are excluded because of the lack of readily available data. Companies from other countries might also have been included at the lower end of the list had sufficient data been available.

Publicly available information on arms sales and other financial and employment data on the arms industry worldwide are limited. The sources of data for table 6A.1 include company annual reports and websites, a SIPRI questionnaire, and news published in the business sections of newspapers, in military journals and by Internet news services specializing in military matters. Press releases, marketing reports, government publications of contract awards and country surveys are also consulted. Where no data is available from these sources, estimates have been made by SIPRI. The scope of the data and the geographical coverage are largely determined by the availability of information. All the data is continuously revised and updated and may change between different editions of the SIPRI Yearbook.

II. Definitions

Arms sales are defined by SIPRI as sales of military goods and services to military customers, including both sales for domestic procurement and sales for export. Military goods and services are those which are designed specifically for military purposes and the technologies related to such goods and services. Military goods are military-specific equipment, and do not include general purpose goods, such as oil, electricity, office computers, uniforms and boots. Military services are also military-specific. They include technical services such as

---

* Participants in the network for 2008 were Gülay Günlük-Şenesen (Istanbul University), Jean-Paul Hébert (Centre Interdisciplinaire de Recherches sur la Paix et d'Etudes Stratégiques, Paris), Shinichi Kohno (Mitsubishi Research Institute, Tokyo), Valerie Miranda (Istituto Affari Internazionali, Rome), Pere Ortega (Centre d'Estudis per la Pau J. M. Delàs, Barcelona) and Paek Jae Ok (Korea Institute for Defense Analyses, Seoul).

information technology, maintenance, repair and overhaul, and operational support; services related to the operation of the armed forces, such as intelligence, training, logistics and facilities management; and armed security in conflict zones. They do not include the peacetime provision of purely civilian services, such as health care, cleaning, catering, and transportation, but supply services to operationally deployed forces are included.[1]

This definition of arms sales serves as a guideline; in practice it is difficult to apply. Nor is there any good alternative, since no generally agreed standard definition exists. The data on arms sales in table 6A.1 often reflects only what each company considers to be the defence share of its total sales. The comparability of the company arms sales figures given in table 6A.1 is therefore limited.

Data on total sales, profit and employment is for entire companies, not for arms-producing divisions alone. All data is for consolidated sales, including those of national and foreign subsidiaries. The data on profit represents profit after taxes. Employment data is year-end figures, except for those companies that publish only a yearly average. All data is presented on the financial year basis reported by the company in its annual report.

III. Calculations

Arms sales are sometimes estimated by SIPRI. In some cases SIPRI uses the figure for the total sales of a 'defence' division, although the division may also have some, unspecified, civil sales. When the company does not report a sales figure for a defence division or similar entity, estimates can sometimes be made based on data on contract awards, information on the company's current arms production programmes and figures provided by company officials in media or other reports.

The data for arms sales is used as an approximation of the annual value of arms production. For most companies this is realistic. The main exception is shipbuilding companies. For these companies there is a significant discrepancy between the value of annual production and annual sales because of the long lead (production) time of ships and the low production run (number). Some shipbuilding companies provide estimates of the value of their annual production. This data is then used by SIPRI for those companies.

All data is collected in local currency and at current prices. For conversion from local currencies to US dollars, SIPRI uses the International Monetary Fund (IMF) annual average of market exchange rates (as provided in *International Financial Statistics*). The data in table 6A.1 is provided in current dollars. Changes between years in this data are difficult to interpret because the change in dollar values is made up of several components: the change in arms sales, the rate of inflation and, for sales conducted in local currency, fluctuations in the exchange rate. Sales on the international arms market are

---

[1] For a more detailed list of the types of activities classified as 'military services' see Perlo-Freeman, S. and Sköns, E., 'The private military services industry', SIPRI Insights on Peace and Security no. 2008/1, Sep. 2008, <http://books.sipri.org/product_info?c_product_id=361>.

often conducted in dollars. Fluctuations in exchange rates thus do not have an impact on the dollar values but affect instead the value in local currency. If the value of the dollar declines, then the company's revenue in local currency falls and, if its production inputs are paid for in local currency—which most often is the case—this has a negative impact on the company's profit margins. Calculations in constant dollar terms are difficult to interpret for the same reasons. Without knowing the relative shares of arms sales derived from domestic procurement and from arms exports, it is impossible to interpret the exact meaning and implications of the arms sales data. This data should therefore be used with caution. This is particularly true for countries with strongly fluctuating exchange rates.

Table 6A.1. The SIPRI Top 100 arms-producing companies in the world excluding China, 2008[a]

Figures for arms sales, total sales and profit are in US$ m.

Rank[b] 2008	2007	Company[d]	Country	Sector[e]	Arms sales[c] 2008	2007	Total sales, 2008	Arms sales as % of total sales, 2008	Total profit, 2008	Total employment, 2008
1	2	BAE Systems	UK	A Ac El MV Mi SA/A Sh	32 420	29 860	34 086	95	3 250	106 400
2	3	Lockheed Martin	USA	Ac El Mi Sp	29 880	29 400	42 731	70	3 217	146 000
3	1	Boeing	USA	Ac El Mi Sp	29 200	30 480	60 909	48	2 672	162 200
4	4	Northrop Grumman	USA	Ac El Mi Ser Sh Sp	26 090	24 600	33 887	77	−1 262	123 600
5	5	General Dynamics	USA	A El MV SA/A Sh	22 780	21 520	29 300	78	2 459	92 300
6	6	Raytheon	USA	El Mi	21 030	19 540	23 174	91	1 672	73 000
S	S	BAE Systems Inc. (BAE Systems, UK)	USA	A El MV SA/A	19 970	14 910	19 974	100	1 971	55 200
7	7	EADS	Trans-Eur.	Ac El Mi Sp	17 900	13 100	63 346	28	2 302	118 350
8	9	Finmeccanica[f]	Italy	A Ac El MV Mi SA/A	13 240	9 850	25 037	53	996	73 400
9	8	L-3 Communications	USA	El Ser	12 160	11 240	14 901	82	949	65 000
10	10	Thales	France	A El MV Mi SA/A Sh	10 760	9 350	18 543	58	952	63 250
11	11	United Technologies	USA	Ac El Eng	9 980	8 760	58 681	17	4 689	220 000
12	12	SAIC	USA	Ser Comp(MV)	7 350	6 250	10 070	73	452	45 400
13	16	KBR[g]	USA	Ser	5 730	5 000	11 581	50	319	57 000
14	13	Computer Sciences Corp.	USA	Ser	5 710	5 420	16 740	34	1 115	92 000
15	15	Honeywell	USA	El	5 310	5 020	36 556	15	2 792	128 000
16	19	ITT Corp.	USA	El	5 170	3 850	11 695	44	795	40 800
17	17	Rolls-Royce[h]	UK	Eng	4 720	4 580	16 695	28	−2 472	38 900
18	23	Almaz-Antei[i]	Russia	Mi	4 340	2 780	4 624	94	100	89 870
19	25	AM General[j]	USA	MV	4 040	2 670				..
S	S	MBDA (BAE Systems, UK/ EADS, trans-European/ Finmeccanica, Italy)	Trans-Eur.	Mi	3 950	4 110	3 953	100	206	..
20	–	Navistar[k]	USA	MV	3 900	370	14 724	26	134	17 800

Rank[b] 2008	2007	Company[d]	Country	Sector[e]	Arms sales[c] 2008	2007	Total sales, 2008	Arms sales as % of total sales, 2008	Total profit, 2008	Total employment, 2008
S	S	DRS Technologies (Finmeccanica)	Italy	El	3 870	3 230	3 870	100	110	..
21	18	DCNS	France	Sh	3 660	3 860	3 660	100	192	12 240
22	20	General Electric	USA	Eng El	3 650	3 460	182 515	2	17 410	323 000
S	S	Eurocopter (EADS, trans-European)	France	Ac	3 610	2 800	6 568	55	..	..
S	S	Pratt & Whitney (United Technologies)	USA	Eng	3 550	3 580	12 695	28	..	37 990
23	27	Textron	USA	Ac El Eng MV	3 420	2 510	14 246	24	486	43 000
S	S	Sikorsky (United Technologies)	USA	Ac	3 060	2 770	5 368	57	..	16 940
24	22	Mitsubishi Heavy Industries[l]	Japan	Ac MV Mi Sh	3 040	2 780	32 660	9	234	67 420
25	14	SAFRAN	France	El	3 020	5 230	15 123	20	375	54 490
26	24	Saab	Sweden	Ac El Mi	3 000	2 770	3 610	83	-37	13 290
27	31	URS Corp.	USA	El	2 680	2 290	10 086	27	220	50 000
28	28	Alliant Techsystems	USA	SA/A	2 680	2 460	4 583	58	155	19 000
29	29	Rheinmetall	Germany	A El MV SA/A	2 660	2 400	5 665	47	198	21 020
30	–	Hewlett-Packard[m]	USA	Ser	2 540	0	136 022	2	7 828	321 000
31	36	Elbit Systems	Israel	El	2 520	1 910	2 638	95	204	10 880
S	S	CASA (EADS, trans-European)	Spain	Ac	2 510	1 150	2 824	89	99	5 730
32	32	Rockwell Collins	USA	El	2 370	2 230	4 769	50	678	20 300
33	34	Israel Aerospace Industries	Israel	Ac El Mi	2 230	1 960	3 600	62	91	16 000
S	S	EADS Astrium (EADS, trans-Eur.)	France	Sp	2 200	1 700	6 280	35	..	15 000
34	33	QinetiQ	UK	Ser	2 170	2 160	2 972	73	173	14 060
S	S	MBDA France (MBDA, trans-Eur.)	France	Mi	2 100	2 050	2 130	100	247	4 290
35	30	Groupe Dassault	France	Ac	2 100	2 380	5 488	38	546	12 440
36	45	Oshkosh Corp.	USA	MV	2 070	1 570	7 138	29	79	14 000
37	41	Sukhoi (UAC)[i]	Russia	Ac	2 040	1 710	2 173	94	-107	29 980
38	35	Babcock International Group	UK	Ser	2 020	1 920	3 496	58	136	16 390
39	38	CEA	France	Oth	2 010	1 760	5 136	39	-479	15 580
40	40	Harris	USA	El	1 980	1 720	5 311	37	444	16 500

41	46	Serco	UK	Ser	1950	1440	5 743	34	183	42 680
42	42	Krauss-Maffei Wegmann[n]	Germany	MV	1950	1690	2 050	95	..	3 400
43	51	Cobham	UK	Comp(Ac El)	1910	1220	2 697	71	176	12 040
44	43	Hindustan Aeronautics[o]	India	Ac Mi	1910	1670	2 384	80	400	30 000
45	48	Navantia	Spain	Sh	1880	1390	2 139	88	−82	5 540
46	58	DynCorp International[p]	USA	Ser	1860	900	3 101	60	70	22 500
S	S	Alenia Aeronautica (Finmeccanica)	Italy	Ac	1820	1780	1 820	100	136	9 200
47	47	CACI International	USA	Ser	1810	1390	2 421	75	83	12 000
48	44	Goodrich	USA	Comp(Ac)	1770	1600	7 062	25	681	15 300
49	39	ThyssenKrupp	Germany	Sh	1760	1740	78 223	2	3 332	199 370
50	49	ManTech International Corp.	USA	Ser	1760	1350	1 871	94	90	7 900
51	52	Rafael	Israel	Ac Mi SA/A Oth	1530	1140	1 530	100	46	6 000
52	63	Mitsubishi Electric[l]	Japan	El Mi	1510	820	35 460	4	118	..
53	83	Kawasaki Heavy Industries[l]	Japan	Ac Eng Mi Sh	1480	580	12 951	11	113	32 270
54	50	Indian Ordnance Factories[q]	India	A SA/A	1380	1230	1 679	82	..	112 000
55	60	Force Protection	USA	MV	1330	890	1 330	100	47	1 170
56	53	ST Engineering (Temasek)	Singapore	Ac El MV SA/A Sh	1280	1100	3 777	34	335	19 000
57	37	VT Group	UK	Ser Sh	1210	1870	2 015	60	200	13 000
S	S	Thales Air Defence (Thales, France)	UK	Mi	1200	..	1 200	100	138	..
58	54	TRV Corp.[i]	Russia	Mi	1170	1050	1 212	96	111	21 200
59	59	Irkut Corp. (UAC)[i]	Russia	Ac	1150	900	1 248	92	−41	12 140
S	S	BAE Systems Australia (BAE Systems, UK)	Australia	El SA/A Sh	1090	470	1 090	100	..	5 500
60	56	GKN	UK	Comp(Ac)	1070	950	8 044	13	−197	40 000
61	55	Samsung	S. Korea	A El MV Sh	1010	1030	173 439	1	10 684	276 000
62	61	Indra	Spain	El	1000	870	3 484	29	266	24 810
63	78	NEC[l]	Japan	El	950	610	40 786	2	−2 870	143 330
64	57	Diehl	Germany	Mi SA/A	940	900	3 117	30	21	11 390
S	S	AgustaWestland (Finmeccanica)	Italy	Ac	930	930	2 981	31	232	5 750
S	S	Selex Communications (Finmeccanica)	Italy	Comp(El Oth)	900	890	1 105	82	−95	4 400
65	62	Bharat Electronics	India	El	900	840	1 063	85	171	11 960

Rank[b]		Company[d]	Country	Sector[e]	Arms sales[c]		Total sales, 2008	Arms sales as % of total sales, 2008	Total profit, 2008	Total employment, 2008
2008	2007				2008	2007				
66	–	Precision Castparts Corp.	USA	Comp(Ac)	890	..	6 828	13	1 045	20 300
67	64	Nexter	France	A MV SA/A	850	800	850	100	145	2 720
68	66	Vertolety Rossii (OPK Oboronprom)[i]	Russia	Ac	850	690	1 660	51	115	..
69	69	Meggitt	UK	Comp(Ac)	830	670	2 137	39	182	8 140
70	93	VSE Corp.	USA	Ser	830	540	1 044	80	19	1 920
71	–	SIAE	France	Comp(Ac)	810	470	810	100	..	4 000
72	–	Shaw Group[r]	USA	Ser	800	450	6 998	11	141	26 000
73	67	LIG Nex1	S. Korea	El	770	690	770	100	38	2 440
S	S	Thales Nederland (Thales, France)	Netherl.	El	770	..	770	100	35	..
74	85	RUAG	Switzerl.	A Ac Eng SA/A	760	580	1 419	54	47	6 310
75	77	SRA International	USA	El	750	610	1 507	50	73	6 500
S	S	Samsung Techwin (Samsung)	S. Korea	A El Eng MV	750	770	2 123	35	133	4 190
76	94	Kongsberg Gruppen	Norway	El Mi SA/A	740	540	1 960	38	104	5 240
77	65	Aerospace Corp.	USA	Ser	740	700	839	88	..	4 000
S	S	Galileo Avionica (Finmeccanica)	Italy	El	730	670	837	87	44	2 790
78	76	Ultra Electronics	UK	El	730	620	947	77	3	3 580
79	68	MTU Aero Engines	Germany	Eng	730	680	3 989	18	263	7 540
80	80	Moog	USA	Comp(El Mi)	720	590	1 903	38	119	8 840
81	90	ARINC (Carlyle Group)[s]	USA	Ser	700	550	1 163	60	..	3 100
82	75	Teledyne Technologies	USA	El	680	620	1 893	36	111	8 800
83	86	CAE	Canada	El	680	570	1 558	44	187	7 000
84	91	Fiat[t]	Italy	Eng MV	680	550	86 940	1	2 520	198 140
S	S	Iveco (Fiat)	Italy	MV	680	550	15 950	4	832	27 110
85	96	Jacobs Engineering Group[u]	USA	Ser	670	520	11 252	6	421	57 100
86	74	Patria	Finland	Ac MV SA/A	670	640	783	86	3	2 800
87	70	Fincantieri	Italy	Sh	670	660	4 299	15	15	9 190
S	S	BAE Systems Hägglunds (BAE Systems, UK)	Sweden	MV	670	460	675	99	..	1 040

		Company	Country	Sector						
88	79	Curtiss-Wright Corp.	USA	Comp(Ac Sh)	660	610	1 830	36	109	7 970
89	81	MITRE[v]	USA	Ser	650	590	1 235	53	:	7 010
S	S	Santa Bárbara Sistemas (General Dynamics, USA)	Spain	A MV SA/A	650	620	650	100	26	1 870
90	–	Uralvagonzavod[i]	Russia	MV	640	460	1 851	35	-241	33 140
91	71	Alion Science and Technology	USA	Ser	640	660	740	86	-25	3 270
S	S	Thales Australia (Thales, France)	Australia	A El MV Mi SA/A Sh	630	630	935	68	:	3 510
92	87	Avio (Cinven, UK)	Italy	Eng	630	570	2 426	26	-122	5 090
93	99	Chemring Group	UK	SA/A	620	500	651	96	76	3 000
94	–	Israel Military Industries	Israel	A MV SA/A	620	490	650	95	:	3 200
95	73	Cubic Corp.	USA	Ser	610	640	881	69	37	6 000
96	100	KBP[i]	Russia	SA/A	610	490	611	99	:	7 130
97	95	Vought Aircraft Industries (Carlyle Group)	USA	Ac	610	530	1 797	34	94	6 500
98	98	Esterline Technologies	USA	Comp(Ac SA/A)	590	510	1 483	40	121	9 700
99	89	Chugach Alaska Corp.[w]	USA	Ser	570	560	:	:	:	..
100	–	Day & Zimmermann[x]	USA	SA/A Oth	550	490	2 400	23	:	24 000

[a] Although several Chinese arms-producing enterprises are large enough to rank among the SIPRI Top 100, it has not been possible to include them because of lack of comparable and sufficiently accurate data. In addition, there are companies in other countries, such as Kazakhstan and Ukraine, that could also be large enough to appear in the SIPRI Top 100 list if data were available, but this is less certain.

[b] Companies are ranked according to the value of their arms sales in 2008. An S denotes a subsidiary company. A dash (–) indicates that the company did not rank among the SIPRI Top 100 for 2007. Company names and structures are listed as they were on 31 Dec. 2008. Information about subsequent changes is provided in these notes. The 2007 ranks may differ from those published in SIPRI Yearbook 2009 owing to continual revision of data, most often because of changes reported by the company itself and sometimes because of improved estimations. Major revisions are explained in these notes.

[c] Dots (. .) indicate that data is not available.

[d] For subsidiaries and operational companies owned by a holding or investment company, the name of the parent company is given in parentheses along with its country, where it differs.

[e] Key to abbreviations: A = artillery; Ac = aircraft; El = electronics; Eng = engines; Mi = missiles; MV = military vehicles; SA/A = small arms/ammunition; Ser = services; Sh = ships; Sp = space; Oth = other; Comp(.) = components, services or anything else less than final systems in the sectors within the parentheses—used only for companies that do not produce final systems.

[f] Finmeccanica acquired DRS Technologies in Oct. 2008. The figures presented here treat the acquisition as if it had occurred on 1 Jan. 2008.

[g] The arms sales figures for KBR are an estimate based on LOGCAP III payments and payments by the British Ministry of Defence (MOD).

[h] The arms sales figures for Rolls-Royce are estimates, as the company does not publish information on the civil–military breakdown of its Marine Division's sales and has not responded to requests for this information.

[i] This is the 7th year in which Russian companies have been covered by the SIPRI Top 100. There may be other Russian companies that should be in the list but for which insufficient data is available. Figures for Russian companies' total sales and profits are from Expert RA, the Russian rating agency; the figures for arms sales shares estimates and employment are from the Centre for Analysis of Strategies and Technologies (CAST), Moscow.

Many Russian arms-producing companies are being consolidated into 4 large state-owned conglomerates: United Aircraft Corporation (UAC), OPK Oboronprom, United Shipbuilding Corporation (USC) and Rostekhnologii. However, comparable data on these conglomerates is not available. Thus, even though Sukhoi and Irkut are part of UAC and Vertolety Rossii is a subsidiary of OPK Oboronprom, these 3 companies are reported as parent companies in the Top 100. For more detail on Russian arms-producing industry consolidation, see section II of chapter 6; and Perlo-Freeman, S. et al., 'The SIPRI Top 100 arms-producing companies, 2007', *SIPRI Yearbook 2009*, pp. 286–87.

[j] Limited financial data is available for AM General. The SIPRI estimate of arms sales is based on a 2-year average of US Department of Defense (DOD) prime contract awards.

[k] In previous years, Navistar's arms sales figures were calculated using an average of DOD contracts. The figures for 2008 and 2007 reported here are based on information on arms sales for those years released by the company. This change revised Navistar's sales downward, and so altered the company's ranking for 2007.

[l] Arms sales figures for Japanese companies represent new military contracts rather than arms sales.

[m] Hewlett-Packard (HP) acquired EDS in HP's fourth quarter of 2008. The total sales figure presented here is pro forma as if EDS had been part of HP for the company's entire financial year. Prior to the acquisition, HP was not considered an arms-producing company according to the SIPRI definition. Because HP does not report EDS's civil and military sales separately, the arms sales estimate for 2008 is based on EDS's arms sales from 2007.

[n] The arms sales figures for Krauss-Maffei Wegmann are based on a small estimate of the company's non-military sales.

[o] The arms sales share of total sales for Hindustan Aeronautics is taken from the *Defense News* Top 100 for 2008.

[p] The arms sales figure for DynCorp is revenues from the US DOD. This is probably an underestimate, as some security contracts with the US State Department should probably be classified as military business, and are thus 'arms sales' according to the SIPRI definition.

[q] All figures for Indian Ordnance Factories are estimates.

[r] Limited financial data is available for Shaw Group. The SIPRI estimate of arms sales is based on a 2-year average of US DOD prime contract awards.

[s] The arms sales share of total sales for ARINC is taken from the *Defense News* Top 100 for 2008.

[t] The arms sales of Fiat are those of its Iveco trucks and commercial vehicles division, which sells some military vehicles.

[u] The arms sales figures for Jacobs Engineering Group are based on US DOD prime contract awards.

[v] The arms sales figures for MITRE are based on US DOD prime contract awards.

[w] The arms sales figures for Chugach Alaska Corporation are based on US DOD prime contract awards.

[x] The arms sales figures for Day & Zimmerman are based on US DOD prime contract awards.

Appendix 6B. Major arms industry acquisitions, 2009

SUSAN T. JACKSON

Table 6B.1 lists major acquisitions in the arms industries of member states of the Organisation for Economic Co-operation and Development (OECD) that were announced or completed between 1 January and 31 December 2009. It is not an exhaustive list of all acquisition activity but gives a general overview of strategically significant and financially noteworthy transactions.

Table 6B.1. Major acquisitions in the OECD arms industries, 2009

Figures are in US $m., at current prices.

Buyer company (country)/ Subsidiary (country)[a]	Acquired company (country)	Seller company (country)[b]	Deal value ($ m.)[c]	Revenue or employees[d]
Within North America (Companies are US-based unless indicated otherwise)				
Precision Castparts Corp.	Carlton Forge Works	Privately owned	850	..
General Dynamics	Axsys Technologies	Publicly listed	643	$253 m.
Goodrich	Atlantic Inertial Systems	J. F. Lehman & Co.*	375	$180 m.
Woodward Governor	HR Textron	Textron	365	$260 m.
ManTech International Corp.	Sensor Technologies Inc.	Privately owned	242	..
Moog	GE Aviation Systems' Flight Control Actuation business	GE Aviation Systems	90	$100 m.
Rackable Systems[e]	Silicon Graphics Inc.	Publicly listed	43	$354 m.
FLIR Systems	OmniTech Partners	Privately owned	42	$22 m.
Curtiss-Wright Corp.	EST Group	Privately owned	40	$20 m.
Danaher Corp./Tektronix	Sypris Test & Measurement	Sypris Solutions	39	..
Microsemi	Endwave's defence electronics and security business unit	Endwave Corp.	28	..
CAE (Canada)	xwave (Canada)	Bell Alliant	22	200 employees

Buyer company (country)/ Subsidiary (country)[a]	Acquired company (country)	Seller company (country)[b]	Deal value ($ m.)[c]	Revenue/ employees[d]
FLIR Systems	Directed Perception Inc.	Privately owned	20	..
Teledyne Technologies/ Teledyne Instruments	Ocean Design	Privately owned	20	..
Applied Signal Technology	Pyxis Engineering	Privately owned	16	$12 m.
FLIR Systems	Salvador Imaging	Privately owned	13	35 employees
Alliant Techsystems	Eagle Industries	Privately owned	..	2300 employees
Ranger Aerospace*	US Logistics	Privately owned	..	600 employees
Lockheed Martin	Universal Systems & Technologies	Privately owned	..	400 employees
Arrow Electronics	A. E. Petsche Co.	Privately owned	..	$220 million
Lockheed Martin	Gyrocam Systems	Privately owned	..	138 employees
OCC	Applied Optical Systems	Privately owned	..	$7 m.
Goodrich	Cloud Cap Technologies	Privately owned	..	30 employees
Transatlantic: West European acquisitions of companies based in North America				
Chemring Group (UK)	Hi-Shear Technology Corp. (USA)	Publicly listed	132	$26 m.
Finmeccanica (Italy)/ DRS Technologies (USA)	Soneticom (USA)	Privately owned	..	$9 m.
Transatlantic: North American acquisitions of companies based in Western Europe				
Jacobs Engineering Group (USA)	AWE Management Ltd (UK)	British Nuclear Fuels Ltd (UK)	195	..
Lockheed Martin (USA)/ Lockheed Martin UK (UK)	Imes Strategic Support Ltd (UK)	Imes Group (UK)	..	$37 m.
Within Western Europe				
BAE Systems (UK)	45% of BVT Surface Fleet (UK)	VT Group (UK)	558	7000 employees[f]
ThyssenKrupp (Germany)	25% of ThyssenKrupp Marine Systems (Germany)[g]	One Equity (USA)*	..	$2 b.
ThyssenKrupp (Germany) and EADS (trans-European)/ Atlas Elektronik UK (UK)[h]	Underwater Systems (UK)	QinetiQ (UK)	36	220 employees

Saab (Sweden)	60% of TietoSaab Systems (Finland)[i]	Tieto (Finland)	..	$13 m.
RUAG (Switzerland)	GEKE Schutztechnik (Germany)	GEKE (Germany)	..	..
Other				
Electro Optical Systems (Australia)/ EOS Defense Systems (USA)	Recon Optical's remote weapon system business unit (USA)	Goodrich (USA)	..	..
EADS (trans-European)/ Eurocopter (France)	Euroheli (Japan)	Itochu Corp. (Japan)	..	60 employees
Ultra Electronics (UK)	Avalon Systems (Australia)	Privately owned	13	22 employees

* = Investment company.

[a] In cases where the acquisition was completed by a subsidiary, rather than directly by the parent company, the name of the subsidiary is also given.

[b] 'Publicly listed' means that the company's shares were publicly traded on a stock exchange of its home country, with no single majority shareholder. 'Privately owned' means the company was owned by one or more private shareholders, with its shares not traded on any stock exchange.

[c] In cases where the deal value is not available in US dollars, currency conversion has been made using the International Monetary Fund average exchange rate for the calendar month in which the transaction was made. Companies do not always disclose the values of transactions.

[d] The acquired company's annual revenue is listed where known (either actual revenue for 2008 or expected revenue for 2009 or 2010). Where revenue is not available in US dollars, currency conversion has been made using the International Monetary Fund average exchange rate for the appropriate year. Where information is not available for the acquired company's revenue, the acquired company's number of employees is shown, where known. Within each regional category, acquisitions are listed first in order of deal size where known, then in order of the acquired company's revenue where known. Where only employee numbers are known, the acquisitions are listed according to a conservative estimate of the likely range of revenues of the acquired company.

[e] After the acquisition, Rackable Systems changed its name to that of the acquired company, Silicon Graphics Inc. (SGI).

[f] BAE Systems now owns 100% of the former joint venture BVT Surface Fleet. The number of employees is the reported number for BAE Systems Surface Ships, the successor company of BVT Surface Fleet.

[g] ThyssenKrupp now owns 100% of ThyssenKrupp Marine Systems.

[h] Atlas Elektronik, the German-based parent company of Atlas Elektronik UK, is a joint subsidiary of ThyssenKrupp and EADS.

[i] Saab now owns 100% of TietoSaab.

Sources: SIPRI arms industry files on mergers and acquisitions.

7. International arms transfers

PAUL HOLTOM, MARK BROMLEY, PIETER D. WEZEMAN AND
SIEMON T. WEZEMAN

I. Introduction

The volume of international transfers of major conventional weapons continues to increase. The upward trend in the volume of deliveries that began in 2005 continued in 2009, and the average annual level for the period 2005–2009 was 22 per cent higher than the annual average for 2000–2004 (see figure 7.1).[1]

The five largest suppliers for 2005–2009—the United States, Russia, Germany, France and the United Kingdom—accounted for 76 per cent of the volume of exports of major conventional weapons, down from 80 per cent in 2000–2004 (see table 7.1). Although the dominant position of the USA and Russia as by far the largest suppliers of arms is unlikely to be challenged in the near future, the number of second-tier arms suppliers is growing. Several governments in major arms-exporting states are making high-level political visits to potential recipients and establishing or reorganizing arms export promotion agencies to assist their domestic arms industries in securing export contracts.[2] Section II of this chapter details significant developments among the main supplier states in 2009.

The major recipient region for the period 2005–2009 was Asia and Oceania (41 per cent of all imports), followed by Europe (24 per cent), the Middle East (17 per cent), the Americas (11 per cent) and Africa (7 per cent). The major recipient countries for 2005–2009 were China (9 per cent), India (7 per cent), South Korea (6 per cent), the United Arab Emirates (UAE, 6 per cent) and Greece (4 per cent). In the period 2005–2009 the volume of arms transferred to China was 20 per cent lower than in 2000–2004 and to India was 7 per cent lower.

Recent acquisitions by certain states in Latin America, the Middle East, North Africa and South East Asia suggest that a pattern of reactive arms

---

[1] SIPRI data on arms transfers refers to actual deliveries of major conventional weapons. SIPRI uses a trend-indicator value (TIV) to compare the data on deliveries of different weapons and to identify general trends. TIVs give an indication only of the volume of international arms transfers and not of the actual financial values of such transfers. Since year-on-year deliveries can fluctuate, a 5-year moving average is employed to provide a more stable measure of trends. For a description of the TIV and its calculation see appendix 7A and the SIPRI Arms Transfers Programme website at <http://www.sipri.org/databases/armstransfers/background>.

[2] On developments in arms production see chapter 6 in this volume.

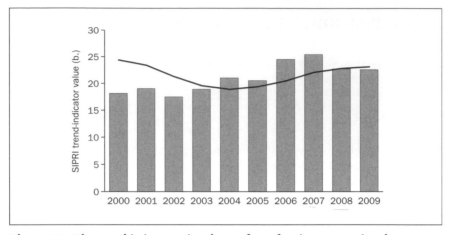

Figure 7.1. The trend in international transfers of major conventional weapons, 2000–2009

Note: The bar graph shows annual totals and the line graph shows the five-year moving average. Five-year averages are plotted at the last year of each five-year period. See appendix 7A for an explanation of the SIPRI trend-indicator value.

Source: SIPRI Arms Transfers Database, as of 12 Feb. 2010, <http://www.sipri.org/databases/armstransfers/>.

acquisitions is emerging, that could develop into regional arms races. There have been significant increases in the volume of arms imported by Israel (102 per cent), Singapore (147 per cent) and Algeria (102 per cent). While these three states were not among the 10 largest arms importers for the period 2000–2004, they ranked sixth, seventh and ninth for 2005–2009, respectively. To illustrate the concerns raised by these trends, section III of this chapter examines arms transfers to North Africa.

Iraqi armed forces are re-equipping themselves following the 2003 invasion and subsequent conflict. The United Nations arms embargo on the Iraqi Government was lifted in 2004, and in 2005–2009 Iraq was the 24th largest recipient of major conventional arms.[3] As the country prepares for the final withdrawal of foreign armed forces, section IV discusses international transfers to the Iraqi armed forces.

Section V presents conclusions.

Appendix 7A explains the methodology behind SIPRI's data collection and the trend-indicator value used to measure the volume of arms transfers. It provides trend-indicator value (TIV) data on all recipients and suppliers of major conventional weapons for the period 2005–2009.[4] Although an estimate of the total financial value of the global arms trade in 2008

---

[3] On developments in multilateral arms embargoes see appendix 12A in the volume.
[4] On TIV see note 1.

Table 7.1. The five largest suppliers of major conventional weapons and their main recipients, 2005–2009

Supplier	Share of global arms exports (%)	Main recipients (share of supplier's transfers, %)		
		1st	2nd	3rd
USA	30	South Korea (14)	UAE (11)	Israel (11)
Russia	23	China (35)	India (24)	Algeria (11)
Germany	11	Turkey (14)	Greece (13)	South Africa (12)
France	8	UAE (25)	Singapore (21)	Greece (12)
UK	4	USA (23)	India (15)	Saudi Arabia (10)

UAE = United Arab Emirates.

Source: SIPRI Arms Transfers Database, <http://www.sipri.org/databases/armstransfers/>.

cannot be given, appendix 7B presents official data on the financial value of orders, export licences and arms exports for 1999–2008. Appendix 7C describes the current status of existing mechanisms for international public transparency in arms transfers. Except where indicated, the information on deliveries and contracts referred to in this chapter is taken from the SIPRI Arms Transfers Database.[5]

II. Major supplier developments, 2009

The United States

In August 2009 US President Barack Obama initiated a comprehensive review of the US export control system.[6] It remains unclear when this review will be completed or what impact it will have on US transfers of arms, military equipment and related technologies. In its first year in office, the Obama Administration showed little sign of departing from the preceding Administration of President George W. Bush regarding the supply of arms to states long-regarded as allies in regions of tension or involved in efforts to combat international terrorism. The USA continues to restrict transfers of technology to key allies (e.g. technology associated with the F-35 Joint Strike Fighter, JSF, combat aircraft programme). By early 2010

---

[5] The SIPRI Arms Transfers Database, available at <http://www.sipri.org/databases/arms transfers/>, contains data on all transfers of major conventional weapons between 1950 and 2009. The data for 2005–2009 and for 2009 on which most of this chapter is based is given in the 'Register of major conventional weapon transfers, 2009' and the 'Register of major conventional weapons, 2005–2009', which are available at <http://www.sipri.org/databases/armstransfers/recent_trends>. The data on which this chapter is based is valid as of 12 Feb. 2010. The figures in this chapter may differ from those in previous editions of the SIPRI Yearbook because the SIPRI Arms Transfers Database is updated annually.

[6] White House, Statement of the press secretary, 13 Aug. 2009, <http://www.whitehouse.gov/the_press_office/Statement-of-the-Press-Secretary/>.

the US Congress had still not ratified defence cooperation treaties agreed in 2007 with the UK and Australia.

For 2005–2009, Asia and Oceania accounted for 39 per cent of US deliveries of major conventional weapons, followed by the Middle East (36 per cent) and Europe (18 per cent).[7] South Korea was the largest recipient of US exports of major conventional weapons for 2005–2009 (see table 7.1). The USA delivered 40 F-15K combat aircraft and advanced air-to-air and air-to-surface missiles to South Korea in this period, with 21 more F-15Ks on order. In addition, it continues to provide equipment for South Korea's indigenously built destroyers and frigates.

Pakistan accounted for around 3 per cent of US exports for 2005–2009. Most of these deliveries were provided as aid for use in counterterrorism efforts. US military (and economic) aid to Pakistan was secured with the Enhanced Partnership with Pakistan Act in October 2009.[8] This act makes the provision of aid conditional on Pakistan increasing its cooperation with the USA in combating al-Qaeda and the Taliban. This conditionality has drawn criticism from the Pakistani military leadership and media, which have expressed concern that it infringes on Pakistan's sovereignty.[9] Although the USA accounted for 35 per cent of Pakistan's arms imports for 2005–2009, China was Pakistan's largest supplier for this period, accounting for 37 per cent of imports. China's share is likely to grow in the future. In 2009, for example, while the USA delivered the first of 18 F-16C combat aircraft, China delivered the first of 42 JF-17 combat aircraft, with Pakistan planning to acquire up to a total of 300 JF-17 and 36 J-10 combat aircraft from China.

The Obama Administration approved upgrades for Taiwan's Patriot surface-to-air missile (SAM) systems and the delivery of associated Patriot Advanced Capability-3 (PAC-3) missiles, which have an anti-ballistic missile (ABM) capability.[10] These sales were agreed by the Bush Administration in 2008 and are part of a package of deals that have been under discussion since 2001.[11] The USA has not yet decided on a further Taiwan-

---

[7] See table 7A.4 in appendix 7A.

[8] Enhanced Partnership with Pakistan Act, US Public Law 111-73, signed into law 15 Oct. 2009. US aid is either in the form of donations of surplus equipment or as financing of Pakistani orders for new equipment from the USA. For the latter, the USA budgeted in 2005–2009 c. $1.5 billion in aid. Lum, T., *U.S. Foreign Aid to East and South Asia: Selected Recipients*, Congressional Research Service (CRS) Report for Congress RL31362 (US Congress, CRS: Washington, DC, 8 Oct. 2008).

[9] Bokhari, F., 'Pakistan generals voice concern over US accord', *Jane's Defence Weekly*, 21 Oct. 2009, p. 7; and Rizvi, H.-A., 'Limited options', *Daily Times* (Lahore), 4 Oct. 2009.

[10] White, A., 'US, Taiwan agree $3.2bn Patriot deal', *Jane's Defence Weekly*, 26 Aug. 2009, p. 15.

[11] See Wezeman, S. T., Bromley, M. and Wezeman, P. D., 'International arms transfers', *SIPRI Yearbook 2009*, p. 303.

ese request for 66 F-16C combat aircraft. As in previous cases of US arms sales to Taiwan, China has strongly protested.[12]

Israel and the UAE were the main destinations of US arms exports to the Middle East, each accounting for 11 per cent of US deliveries for 2005–2009. The last of 102 F-16I combat aircraft ordered by Israel in 1999 and 2001 was delivered in 2009. Although Israel currently has no outstanding orders of comparable size, negotiations are ongoing for an order for up to 100 F-35 combat aircraft. Israel will remain a major recipient of US arms and military equipment because it receives substantial financial aid to buy US military equipment.[13]

In 2009 the USA delivered 18 AH-64D combat helicopters to the UAE. The UAE also placed preliminary orders for 12 C-130J and 6 C-17 transport aircraft that could be used to support coalition troops in Afghanistan.[14] In 2008 it ordered Patriot SAM systems with PAC-3 missiles and is close to signing an order for the more advanced Terminal High-Altitude Area Defence (THAAD) ABM SAM system—acquisitions that have been made in response to a perceived threat from Iranian ballistic missiles. Several other Middle Eastern countries have recently ordered or announced plans to buy ABM SAM systems from the USA. Kuwait has ordered a modernization of its Patriot SAM systems and requested PAC-3 missiles. The Patriot SAM systems with PAC-3 missiles are among the systems being offered for Turkey's long-range air and missile defence systems (T-LORAMIDS) programme.[15]

Aircraft accounted for around 70 per cent of US exports of major conventional weapons in the period 2005–2009. The USA delivered 292 F-16 and 48 F-15 combat aircraft to 11 countries in 2005–2009.[16] The USA is currently the only country offering a fifth-generation combat aircraft already

[12] Phipps, G., 'US to outline Taiwan defence package'; and Grevatt, J., '. . . as China raises spectre of embargo over Patriot sale', *Jane's Defence Weekly*, 13 Jan. 2010, p. 5.

[13] US President Obama requested $2.775 billion in foreign military financing (FMF) aid for Israel for US FY 2010, in line with an agreement made by the Bush Administration in 2007 to increase FMF aid annually to reach $3 billion in 2012. Sharp, J. M., *U.S. Foreign Aid to Israel*, Congressional Research Service (CRS) Report for Congress RL33222 (US Congress, CRS: Washington, DC, 4 Dec. 2009). See also Stålenheim, P., Perdomo, C. and Sköns, E., 'Military expenditure', *SIPRI Yearbook 2008*, pp. 202–205.

[14] US Defense Security Cooperation Agency, 'United Arab Emirates: logistics support for C-17 Globemaster Aircraft', Transmittal no. 09-61, News release, 18 Dec. 2009; and US Defense Security Cooperation Agency, 'United Arab Emirates: logistics support and training for 12 C-130J-30 Aircraft', Transmittal no. 09-67, News release, 28 Dec. 2009, <http://www.dsca.mil/PressReleases/36-b/36b_index.htm>.

[15] There have been conflicting reports over whether or not China and Russia would participate in this project. France is reportedly interested. Kemal, L., 'China, Russia decline to bid for Turkey's missile project', *Today's Zaman*, 8 Dec. 2009; and 'European manufacturer to enter Turkish missile tender', *Today's Zaman*, 6 Feb. 2010.

[16] The recipients were Chile, Greece, Israel, Jordan, South Korea, Oman, Pakistan, Poland, Portugal, Singapore and the UAE.

in production for export—the F-35 combat aircraft.[17] In 2009 the Nether-lands and the UK ordered their first F-35s as part of the final development phase, while Australia selected the F-35 as its future combat aircraft.[18]

Access to US technology remains a problem in the USA's relations with close allies. Several partners in the F-35 programme have been informed that they would not be granted access to software to maintain or modify their F-35s.[19] Despite these restrictions, both the Dutch and Norwegian defence ministries continue to support the purchase of the F-35 over other combat aircraft.[20] The USA's refusal to share technology gives other sup-pliers an edge over the USA in competitions for combat aircraft. For example, in the ongoing competitions for new combat aircraft in Brazil and India, competitors from Western Europe and Russia are willing to offer extensive technology transfers and access to software codes.[21] Suppliers that are able to offer combat aircraft without any US components may win orders from countries interested in developing an indigenous aircraft industry with export potential.[22]

Russia

Asia and Oceania accounted for 69 per cent of the volume of major conven-tional weapons exported from Russia for the period 2005–2009, followed by Africa (14 per cent), the Americas (8 per cent) and the Middle East (6 per cent). Combat aircraft accounted for 40 per cent of the volume of Russian exports during this period. It is expected that deliveries of major

[17] Although there is no agreed definition for '5th generation' combat aircraft, it is generally agreed that its key attributes are a high level of stealth (including weapons carried internally), advanced sensors integrated into a wider network and a 'super cruise' ability (i.e. the ability to fly a prolonged period faster than the speed of sound). Currently, the only aircraft in service meeting those requirements is the US F-22, which is not available for export. The Russian Sukhoi PAK FA, to be produced in cooperation with India, made its first flight in late 2009. For a brief discussion of the scope of the F-35 programme see Wezeman, S. T. et al., 'International arms transfers', *SIPRI Yearbook 2007*, pp. 390–91.

[18] Australian Department of Defence (DOD), *Defending Australia in the Asia Pacific Century: Force 2030, Defence White Paper 2009* (DOD: Canberra, 2009), p. 78.

[19] Kerr, J., 'Australia orders first batch of F-35As', *Jane's Defence Weekly*, 2 Dec. 2009, p. 5. Coun-tries that have contributed funding to the programme include Australia, Canada, Denmark, Italy, the Netherlands, Norway, Turkey and the UK.

[20] Norwegian Ministry of Defence, 'The Joint Strike Fighter recommended to replace the F-16', Press Release no. 80/2009, 20 Nov. 2008, <http://www.regjeringen.no/en/dep/smk/press-center/Press-releases/2008/the-joint-strike-fighter-recommended-to-.html?id=537010>; and 'Minister says not buying JSF could cost millions', *Radio Netherlands*, <http://www.defpro.com/news/details/6843/>, 16 Apr. 2009,

[21] Anderson, G. and Caffrey, C., 'Final offers submitted for Brazil's F-X2', *Jane's Defence Weekly*, 14 Oct. 2009, p. 10; and Leclerq, M., 'Brazil to assemble French fighters for Latin market', Agence France-Presse, 7 Sep. 2009.

[22] E.g. the fact that the Swedish Gripen-NG offered to Brazil has a US engine was brought up as a liability in the Brazilian combat aircraft competition. In 2005 the USA prevented Brazil from selling 24 Super Tucano light combat aircraft to Venezuela because they contained US-made components. 'Brazil won't buy off-the-shelf arms like Venezuela: minister', Agence France-Presse, 16 Sep. 2009.

conventional weapons to China will continue to decline as its domestic arms industries are increasingly able to meet domestic procurement needs. In addition, Russia faces increased competition for Indian orders from Israel, the USA and European suppliers. Russian President Dmitry Medvedev has announced his support for the joint development and production of military products with other countries to help 'strengthen our ties with these states'.[23] Russia has also attempted to increase its competitiveness in Latin America, the Middle East and North Africa by offering payments through barter, Russian participation in economic projects, credit and exchanges of debt for arms.[24]

Despite decreasing arms sales to China, Rosoboronexport—the Russian state arms export agency—announced in 2009 that China remains interested in Russian military transport and tanker aircraft, aircraft engines, and air-defence and naval systems.[25] Yet the November 2009 meeting of the Russian–Chinese Joint Commission on Military-Technical Cooperation concluded with no significant new deals.[26] In contrast, Ukraine signed a contract worth an estimated $350 million to supply four Zubr air-cushion landing craft to China.[27] Earlier reports had suggested that China planned to order up to 10 of these craft from Russia.[28]

Russia accounted for 77 per cent of India's arms imports for 2005–2009, followed by the UK (8 per cent) and Israel (5 per cent). In March 2010 it was announced that the Indian Government had agreed to pay $2.3 billion for the modernized *Gorshkov* aircraft carrier, with delivery rescheduled for 2012.[29] Russia will also deliver an Akula-II nuclear submarine on a lease to the Indian Navy in the second half of 2010.[30] In October 2009 India and Russia concluded a 10-year bilateral agreement on military-technical cooperation (for 2011–20) under which commitments were made for the joint development of helicopters, infantry fighting vehicles and a fifth-

---

[23] 'Medvedev backs co-production of Russian arms with other countries', RIA Novosti, 11 June 2009, <http://en15.rian.ru/russia/20090611/121955938.html>; and 'Russian arms exports to grow by up to $800 mln in 2009', RIA Novosti, 27 May 2009, <http://en.rian.ru/russia/20090527/155102926.html>.

[24] Chernyak, I., [Kalashnikov series: the general director of Rosoboronexport, Anatoly Isaikin: despite the crisis, our arms exports set records], *Rossiiskaya gazeta*, 10 Apr. 2009.

[25] Solovev, V., [Rosoboroneksport strengthens its position], *Nezavisimoe Voennoe Obozrenie*, 6 Feb. 2009.

[26] Mukhin, V., [Russian–Chinese arms embargo], *Nezavisimaya gazeta*, 30 Nov. 2008.

[27] Two will be built in Ukraine and two in China. ['FSC More' to build Zubr amphibious hovercraft for PRC: minister of industrial policy], Interfax, 7 Aug. 2009.

[28] Minnick, W., 'China to buy armed hovercraft', *Defense News*, 11 Sep. 2006, p. 48.

[29] The sum had reportedly been agreed in Dec. 2009. 'Aircraft carrier Admiral *Gorshkov*', Press Information Bureau of India, 15 Mar. 2010, <http://www.pib.nic.in/release/release.asp?relid=59626&kwd=[/fn>; and Luthra, G. R., '*Gorshkov* price is settled with Russia at $2.3 billion', Thaindian News, 17 Dec. 2009 <http://www.thaindian.com/newsportal/business/gorshkov-price-is-settled-with-russia-at-23-billion_100290643.html>.

[30] Solovyov, D., 'Russia to lease nuclear submarine to India—report', Reuters, 12 Jan. 2010.

generation combat aircraft.[31] At the same time, the USA's efforts to increase its share of the Indian defence market were rewarded in 2009 when India and the USA overcame disagreements over end-use monitoring provisions for contracts for six C-130J transport aircraft and eight P-8A maritime patrol aircraft agreed in 2008. This demonstrated that India and the USA can accommodate each other's requirements to facilitate arms transfers, increasing competition for Indian defence orders.

Russia secured deals with Viet Nam in 2009 for eight Su-30MK combat aircraft and six Type-636 (Kilo Class) submarines. Viet Nam exercised an option to purchase 12 more Su-30MKs in February 2010.[32] The arrangement for securing orders from Viet Nam is believed to be comparable to that used to secure a major deal with Algeria in 2006.[33] In this case, Russia is cancelling Viet Nam's debt and helping the country to modernize its shipbuilding industry; in exchange, Viet Nam will purchase Russian arms and provide Russia with access to oil.[34]

Venezuela accounted for 7 per cent of Russian arms exports for 2005–2009 and was Russia's fourth largest recipient. In September 2009 Venezuela received a $2.2 billion credit for arms purchases after officially recognizing the independence of Abkhazia and South Ossetia. While most reports mention a firm deal for 92 T-72M1M tanks, it is not clear what the remainder of the credit will be used to purchase. Much attention has been paid to statements by Venezuelan President Hugo Chávez that suggest that air-defence systems are a priority, while other armoured vehicles and various artillery systems are also rumoured to be covered by the credit arrangement.[35]

Russia has targeted the Middle East as a potential market for air defence equipment, armoured vehicles and aircraft. In 2009 it announced high hopes for a deal worth at least $2 billion to supply helicopters, tanks, armoured vehicles and air-defence systems to Saudi Arabia.[36] Saudi Arabia is reportedly tying the deal to a Russian guarantee not to deliver five S-300

---

[31] The 10-year agreement was signed by Indian Prime Minister Manmohan Singh and President Medvedev in Dec. 2009. 'Defence pact with Russia to boost defence capability: India', *Hindustan Times*, 8 Dec. 2009; Majumdar, B., 'India, Russia agree arms pact likely worth $5 bln', Reuters, 15 Oct. 2009; and 'Russia, India to jointly develop 5th-generation fighter', RIA Novosti, 15 Oct. 2009, <http://en.rian.ru/russia/20091015/156475971.html>.

[32] 'Russia, Vietnam sign fighter jet deal—report', Agence France-Presse, 10 Feb. 2010.

[33] Wezeman et al. (note 18), p. 395.

[34] Grevatt, J., 'Oil, debt underpin Russian submarine sale to Vietnam', *Jane's Defence Weekly*, 6 May 2009, p. 19.

[35] 'Chavez announces Russian missile purchase', Agence France-Presse, 11 Sep. 2009; Toothtaker, C., 'Venezuela gets $2.2B in credit for Russian arms', Associated Press, 13 Sep. 2009; Daniel, F. J. and Rondon, P., 'Venezuela buys powerful missiles with Russian loan', Reuters, 13 Sep. 2009; 'Venezuela to build strong air defenses with Russian aid', RIA Novosti, 14 Sep. 2009, <http://en.rian.ru/mlitary_news/20090914/156118402.html>; and Nikol'skii, A., [Smerch to shield Venezuela], *Vedomosti*, 15 Sep. 2009. See also chapter 5, section III, in this volume.

[36] 'Russia, Saudi Arabia "set to finalise arms deal"', Agence France-Presse, 30 Aug. 2009.

(SA-20) long-range SAM systems to Iran—with French, Israeli and US leaders also publicly appealing to the Russian Government to stop the delivery.[37] Russia and Israel have reportedly discussed the impact of each other's arms exports on their respective security, with Russia highlighting concerns about Israeli exports of military equipment to Georgia and Israel highlighting Russian arms sales to Iran.[38] Apart from international pressure, other factors that have been given to explain the delay in Russian deliveries of S-300s to Iran include the lack of payment and technical problems.[39] However, reports in early 2010 indicated that Russia intends to press ahead with the deliveries to Iran.[40]

Germany, France and the United Kingdom

Germany, France and the UK have traditionally formed a second tier of suppliers after the USA and Russia. They collectively accounted for 23 per cent per cent of global arms exports for the period 2005–2009. As a group, their largest recipient regions for the period 2005–2009 were Europe (36 per cent), Asia (29 per cent) and the Middle East (12 per cent). In recent years there have been ongoing efforts at the European Union (EU) level to both harmonize member states' arms export policies and integrate the activities of its arms manufacturers.[41] However, states continue to maintain final control on all aspects of export licensing and promote the products of their indigenous arms producers abroad. This continues to lead to differences between EU member states regarding the acceptability of certain destinations and the amount of technology transfer attached to individual deals.[42]

---

[37] Clover, C. and England, A., 'Saudis seek Russian pledge on missiles', *Financial Times*, 29 Sep. 2009; [Barack Obama grabs Russia's arms], *Kommersant*, 23 Sep. 2009; 'Russia to review air defence sale to Iran: Peres', Agence France-Presse, 19 Aug. 2009; and Ravid, B., 'France implores Moscow to cancel sale of missiles to Iran', *Ha'aretz*, 11 Sep. 2009.

[38] Keinon, H., 'Russia unlikely to sell S-300s to Iran', *Jerusalem Post*, 17 Feb. 2009. In Jan. 2009 Russia imposed a unilateral arms embargo on Georgia, prohibiting transfers from Russia and threatening sanctions against foreign entities that contribute to a 'destabilizing build-up' of arms and military equipment in Georgia. [Decree of the President of the Russian Federation on measures to prohibit deliveries to Georgia of military and dual-use goods], Russian Presidential Decree no. 64s, 16 Jan. 2009, <http://graph.document.kremlin.ru/doc.asp?ID=50420>.

[39] Similar reasons have been given to explain the delay in Russia's delivery of 8 MiG-31E combat aircraft to Syria. At the same time, Russia has begun deliveries of Pantsyr-S1 short- to medium-range air-defence systems. 'Iran "has not paid Russia" in "frozen" missile deal', Agence France-Presse, 21 Oct. 2009.

[40] [Vladimir Nazarov: military strike against Iran would be a huge mistake], *Kommersant*, 15 Feb. 2010; and 'Russia "fixing" technical issues delaying S-300 deliveries to Iran', RIA Novosti, 15 Feb. 2010, <http://en.rian.ru/world/20100215/157891672.html>.

[41] Bromley, M., *The Impact on Domestic Policy of the EU Code of Conduct on Arms Exports: The Czech Republic, the Netherlands and Spain*, SIPRI Policy Paper no. 21 (SIPRI: Stockholm, May 2008).

[42] On EU transfer controls and technology transfers see chapter 12 in this volume.

The volume of Germany's arms exports for 2005–2009 was more than twice the volume for 2000–2004. Armoured vehicles and ships accounted for 71 per cent of Germany's exports in this period. A significant proportion of German exports of armoured vehicles were transfers of surplus German equipment. In the period 2005–2009, Germany exported 1116 second-hand armoured vehicles, compared to 636 newly built armoured vehicles.[43]

During the period 2005–2009 Germany delivered three Type-209 submarines to South Africa and an additional ten submarines were built under licence in Brazil, Italy, South Korea and Turkey. During 2009, Turkey signed a €2 billion ($2.8 billion) deal with Germany for the licensed production of six Type-214 submarines, but there was no reported progress on the contract for the transfer of Type-214 submarines to Pakistan.[44] A contract for four Type-214 submarines for Greece was cancelled because of Greece's outstanding €545 million ($758 million) debt to the supplier.[45] However, later reports indicated that Greece was willing to accept three Type-214 submarines in an effort to resolve the dispute.[46]

The volume of France's arms exports was 30 per cent higher in 2005–2009 than in 2000–2004. French exports have been boosted by deliveries of 25 Mirage-2000 combat aircraft to Greece and 34 to the UAE and of 6 La Fayette frigates to Singapore.[47] Aircraft accounted for about 37 per cent of France's arms exports for the period 2005–2009. During 2009 French companies signed a €1 billion ($1.4 billion) deal with India for the modernization of around 51 Mirage-2000 combat aircraft, a €360 million ($500 million) deal with Iraq for 24 EC-135 light helicopters, a €212 million ($294 million) deal with Mexico for 6 EC-225 helicopters and a deal with Saudi Arabia for 3 A-330 multi-role tanker transport (MRTT) aircraft in addition to the 3 ordered in 2008.

There are indications that French arms exports are being boosted by two interlinked factors: strong political support for arms exports and a willingness to engage in far-reaching technology transfer agreements. In September 2009, during French President Nicolas Sarkozy's visit to Brazil, France reached final agreement with Brazil on the transfer of 4 conventionally

---

[43] Countries that either received German armoured vehicles or had them on order during 2005–2009 include Australia, Austria, Belgium, Brazil, Canada, Chile, the Czech Republic, Denmark, Greece, Lithuania, Luxembourg, Netherlands, Pakistan, Romania, Singapore, Spain, Sweden, Switzerland, Turkey and the UAE.

[44] Bokhari, F., 'Pakistan displays naval offensive capabilities', *Jane's Defence Weekly*, 17 Mar. 2010, p. 32.

[45] 'ThyssenKrupp cancels Greek submarine order', Reuters, 21 Sep. 2009.

[46] Fish, T. and Valmas, T. L., 'Hellenic Navy accepts Greek-built submarines', *Jane's Defence Weekly*, 25 Nov. 2009, p. 6.

[47] Transfers to Greece, Singapore and the UAE accounted for 58% of France's arms exports during 2005–2009. The UAE is reportedly interested in selling its fleet of 60 Mirage-2000 combat aircraft, recently supplied by France, in order to help finance the acquisition of new combat aircraft, with French Rafale and US F-35 combat aircraft in the running. Trimble, S., 'Dubai 09: UAE reveals fifth-generation fighter ambitions', *Flightglobal*, 15 Nov. 2009.

powered submarines and technology to assist in the development of Brazil's first nuclear-powered submarine, valued at almost €7 billion ($9.7 billion), and 50 EC-725 helicopters, worth around €2 billion ($2.8 billion). In both deals, French offers of technology transfer appear to have been a major influence on Brazil's decision, with the conventional submarines and helicopters to be manufactured in Brazil.[48] Brazil's national defence strategy of December 2008 stresses the development of an 'autonomous technological capacity', and Brazil is seeking to leverage advantages for its domestic arms industry via extensive technology transfer agreements in arms import deals.[49] In December 2009 Brazil signed a €2.5 billion ($3.5 billion) deal with Italy's Iveco Defence Vehicles for 2044 armoured personnel carriers, with production also due to take place in Brazil.[50]

The volume of British arms exports was 13 per cent lower in 2005–2009 than in 2000–2004. During 2009 British companies signed several agreements, including a deal with Norway for 200 Sting Ray anti-submarine torpedoes, a deal with Canada for 25 UFH/M-777 155-mm towed guns and a £500 million ($775 million) contract with Saudi Arabia to service the Saudi fleet of Eurofighter Typhoon combat aircraft.[51] Transfers of aircraft accounted for 44 per cent of British arms exports for the period 2005–2009. The 24th and final British-built Hawk trainer aircraft for India was delivered in 2009. The first 5 of 42 Hawk trainer aircraft to be built under licence in India were also produced.[52] Also during 2009, the first 8 of 72 Eurofighter Typhoons were delivered to Saudi Arabia.[53] Sales of additional Eurofighter Typhoons from the UK to Saudi Arabia were discussed in 2009, although Saudi Arabia was also said to be considering purchases of F-15 combat aircraft from the USA.[54]

There are calls in the UK for the government to play a more active role in promoting British arms exports, similar to the role the French Government has played in arms sales since 2007. In 2008 the British Government made the Department for Business, Innovation and Skills responsible for pro-

---

[48] Zibechi, R., 'Brazil emerges as a military power', *Americas Program Special Report* (Washington, DC: Center for International Policy, 14 Oct. 2009), <http://americas.irc-online.org/am/6494>.

[49] Brazilian Ministry of Defence (MOD), *National Strategy of Defence* (MOD: Brasília, 8 Dec. 2008).

[50] Kington, T., 'Brazil inks deal for Iveco personnel carriers', *Defence News*, 21 Dec. 2009.

[51] Jennings, G. and Gelfand, L., 'Saudi Arabia and UK agree RSAF Typhoon support deal', *Jane's Defence Weekly*, 21 Oct. 2009, p. 17.

[52] BAE Systems, 'BAE Systems completes Indian Hawk aircraft deliveries', Press Release no. 209/2009, 5 Nov. 2009, <http://www.baesystems.com/Newsroom/NewsReleases/autoGen_1091051 14126.html>.

[53] 'Britain delivers first Eurofighter jets to Saudi', Agence France-Presse, 12 June 2009. On BAE Systems see chapter 6, section II, in this volume.

[54] Hepher, T. and Shalal-Esa, A., 'Saudi weighs Eurofighter, F-15 for new fighter deal', Reuters, 18 June 2009.

moting arms exports abroad.[55] Although the main opposition party called for this responsibility to be returned to the Ministry of Defence, senior executives within the British defence industry have stated that the current system is working well for them and may not need to be changed.[56] Sweden is also exploring the possibility of better coordinating the government's role in promoting arms exports and in late 2009 announced plans to create a new arms export authority.[57]

III. Arms transfers to North Africa

In recent years concerns have been expressed that regional rivals Algeria and Morocco are engaged in an 'arms race', which is also influencing Libya's arms acquisition plans.[58] Although Algeria, Libya, Morocco and Tunisia accounted for only 3 per cent of global arms imports for the period 2005–2009, their total imports were 62 per cent higher than 2000–2004.[59] Algeria accounted for 89 per cent of transfers to North Africa during 2005–2009, but Morocco, which accounted for less than 6 per cent of the volume for the same period, has placed significant orders in 2008 and 2009, lending weight to arms race fears. The likelihood of interstate conflict between Algeria and Morocco is low. However, these reactive acquisitions do not contribute to an improvement in Algerian–Moroccan relations or improve the chances of an acceptable political settlement being reached in the UN-

[55] Holtom, P., Bromley, M. and Wezeman, P. D., 'International arms transfers', *SIPRI Yearbook 2008*, p. 302.

[56] Chuter, A., 'U.K Tories aim to boost arms exports', *Defence News*, 13 Sep. 2009.

[57] Tolgfors, S., Swedish minister for Defence, 'Ny myndighet ska driva på den svenska vapen-exporten' [New authority should run Swedish weapons exports], *Dagens Industri*, 25 June 2009.

[58] The classic arms race model defines an arms race as a situation in which a state's build-up of weaponry is positively related to the amount of weaponry its rival has and to the grievance felt towards the rival and negatively related to the amount of arms it has already. Richardson, L. F., *Arms and Insecurity: A Mathematical Study of Causes and Origins of War* (Boxwood Press: Pittsburgh, Pa., 1960). However, this model is designed for situations in which 20–30 years of time series data are available. For situations that are developing as the analysis is undertaken, the only approach is to analyse the motivations behind specific arms acquisitions and look for evidence of competitive behaviour. 'North African arms race', Al-Jazeera, 15–16 Apr. 2008, <http://english.aljazeera.net/pro grammes/insidestory/2008/04/20086150573511579.html>; 'L'Algérie et le Maroc augmentent leur budget défense. Maghreb: les dessous d'une course à l'armement' [Algeria and Morocco increased their defence budget. Maghreb: an arms race revealed], *El Watan*, 12 May 2009; 'Libya fuels North African "arms race"', United Press International, 20 Oct. 2009; 'Morocco doubles military budget', Afrol News, 9 Dec. 2009, <http://www.afrol.com/articles/31948>; Sorenson, D. S., 'Civil–military relations in North Africa', *Middle East Policy*, vol. 14, no. 4 (2007), p. 108; Tran, P., 'North Africa emerging as hungry defense market', *Defense News*, 11 Sep. 2006; and Vatanka, A. and Weitz, R., 'Russian roulette: Moscow seeks influence through arms exports', *Jane's Intelligence Review*, Jan. 2007, p. 39.

[59] These 4 countries comprise North Africa. Egypt is considered to be in the Middle East and Mauritania to be in sub-Saharan Africa. Tunisia was not a significant importer of major conventional weapons for the period 2005–2009 and has not announced plans to procure significant quantities of major conventional weapons.

backed talks on the future status of Western Sahara.[60] This section provides an overview of recent and upcoming international transfers of arms and military equipment to Algeria, Morocco and Libya to help assess arms race claims. It considers a number of the factors driving these acquisitions and the concerns regarding them. It also highlights the competition between major suppliers to secure contracts in the region.

Recent orders for arms by Algeria, Libya and Morocco are influenced by a perceived need to carry out extensive modernization of their armed and security forces. Various political and security reasons—such as national prestige, regional rivalry, internal security and counterterrorism—are also at play.[61] It is also assumed that these acquisitions and procurement plans reflect the continued influence of the armed forces in these states.[62] In the cases of Algeria and Libya, increased oil and gas revenues have been cited as providing the means to upgrade existing holdings and acquire new weapons, which has attracted the attention of a number of major arms suppliers.[63] The correlation between increased resource revenues and spending on arms imports raises questions about whether windfall revenues from natural resources would deliver more security in these countries if invested in development, education and health programmes.[64]

In addition to receiving financial rewards and gaining access to natural resources, European states and the USA supply arms to North Africa in order to maintain political influence with and the stability of favourable regimes, as well as to support counterterrorism operations and assist with improving border security capabilities to prevent illicit trafficking of arms and drugs and irregular migration.

Algeria

Military spending has increased dramatically in Algeria over the past decade, and it is estimated to have had the highest military expenditure in

[60] Western Sahara is a largely Moroccan-controlled territory in North Africa. A Spanish colony until 1976, it is a disputed territory claimed by Morocco and the Polisario Front, a nationalist independence group supported by Algeria. Its legal status remains unresolved.

[61] Cordesman, A. H. and Nerguizian, A., *The North African Military Balance: Force Developments in the Maghreb* (Center for Strategic and International Studies: Washington, DC, Jan. 2009), pp. 2–3; and Wezeman, P. D., 'Arms transfers to Central, North and West Africa', SIPRI Background Paper, Apr. 2009, <http://books.sipri.org/product_info?c_product_id=377 >, pp. 3–4.

[62] Cook, S. A., *Ruling but not Governing: The Military and Political Development in Egypt, Algeria, and Turkey* (Johns Hopkins University Press: Baltimore, MD, 2007); Gelfand, L., 'Spending to thrive', *Jane's Defence Weekly*, 28 Jan. 2009, pp. 22–27; Joffé, G., 'Political dynamics in North Africa', *International Affairs*, vol. 85, no. 5 (2009), pp. 931–49; and Sorenson (note 58).

[63] On the relationship between resource revenues and military expenditure see chapter 5 in this volume.

[64] 'Challenges to economic security', *Arab Human Development Report 2009: Challenges to Human Security in the Arab Countries* (United Nations Development Programme, Regional Bureau for Arab States: New York, 2009), pp. 99–119; and Spencer, C., 'North Africa: the hidden risks to regional stability', Chatham House Middle East and North Africa Briefing Paper 2009/01, Apr. 2009.

Africa in 2009.[65] The increase in military spending has accompanied strong economic growth, based on increased oil and gas production and prices. The volume of Algerian imports of major conventional weapons for the period 2005–2009 increased by 102 per cent in comparison with 2000–2004, with Algeria rising from the 18th to the 9th largest recipient of major conventional weapons globally. During the period 2005–2009, Russia accounted for an estimated 92 per cent of these transfers. Other suppliers included China, France, South Africa, Spain, Ukraine and the UK.

In March 2006 Algeria and Russia concluded an arms deal reported to be worth $6.5 billion. Under the deal, Russia agreed to cancel $4.5 billion of Algeria's Soviet-era debt, much of which was due to arms imports, in exchange for orders for arms.[66] Russia has delivered to Algeria an estimated 15 of 38 Pantsyr mobile air-defence systems and 28 Su-30MKA combat aircraft in 2008–2009, 185 T-90S tanks in 2006–2008, and missiles for these platforms. Delivery of 16 Yak-130 trainer aircraft and 2 Type-636E (Kilo Class) submarines are expected in 2010–11.

Algeria is seeking to acquire helicopters and naval equipment from France, Germany, Italy or the UK. Reports in 2009 suggested that Algeria will follow up its 2007 order for six EH-101-400 helicopters and four Super Lynx-300 helicopters from AgustaWestland with an order for up to 100 helicopters for Algerian border security forces.[67] Algeria's major naval procurement plans relate to the acquisition of four frigates, two of which are to be built in Algeria. British, French, German and Italian shipbuilders are competing for the order.[68]

This military modernization programme marks a shift in Algeria's procurement priorities, as it focuses on the upgrading and replacement of major conventional platforms acquired in the 1970s and 1980s rather than the acquisition of equipment for counterinsurgency operations.[69] The continuing influence of the military in Algerian politics has played a role in the acquisition of new weapons.[70]

Morocco

Unlike neighbouring Algeria, Morocco does not have significant oil and gas fields and has therefore not benefited from the high prices for these commodities. Nevertheless, military spending in Morocco increased by 127 per

[65] See appendix 5A in this volume.

[66] Vatanka and Weitz (note 58), p. 39.

[67] Ghimrassa, B., 'Algeria and Italy in major arms deal', *Asharq Alawsat*, 17 Sep. 2009; and O'Connell, D. and Ripley, T., '$5 billion Algerian helicopter deal for UK plant', *Sunday Times*, 27 Sep. 2009.

[68] 'Algeria seeks European stealth frigates', United Press International, 2 Oct. 2009.

[69] Gelfand (note 62), p. 24.

[70] Gelfand (note 62), pp. 22–27; and Sorenson (note 58).

cent during the period 2000–2009, in contrast to an increase of 105 per cent for Algeria.[71] The volume of transfers to Morocco for the period 2005–2009 declined by around 25 per cent in comparison with 2000–2004, ranking it the 64th largest arms importer in the world. During 2005–2009, 78 per cent of Moroccan imports came from Russia, followed by Belgium (8 per cent), Switzerland (7 per cent) and the USA (7 per cent). Transfers to Morocco in 2005–2009 included 12 Tunguska mobile air-defence systems from Russia, and surplus artillery and armoured personnel carriers from Belgium, Switzerland and the USA.

In recent years, a number of significant orders for the Moroccan armed forces have been announced. France is modernizing 27 Moroccan Mirage F-1 combat aircraft with RC400 radar and MICA air-to-air missiles. Although Morocco was expected to be the first export customer for France's Rafale combat aircraft, it instead opted for 24 F-16C combat aircraft and missiles from the USA. In 2009 Morocco also ordered 24 PC-9 trainer aircraft and 3 CH-47D helicopters from the USA. Particular attention has been paid to whether Moroccan orders for advanced combat aircraft are in direct response to Algerian combat aircraft received from Russia.[72]

Despite losing its first export order for Rafale, France secured a €470 million ($653 million) deal with Morocco in 2008 for the first export of the FREMM frigate, with delivery scheduled for 2013. Also in 2008, Morocco ordered three SIGMA frigates from the Netherlands in a €510 million ($709 million) deal, to be delivered in 2012–14.

Factors behind Morocco's acquisitions are its regional rivalry with Algeria, the placating of the armed forces with the procurement of new equipment and the dormant conflict in Western Sahara.[73] Mohamed Abdelaziz, the president of the Polisario Front, has stated that he is concerned that Moroccan arms acquisitions could have a negative impact on UN-backed talks to resolve the Western Sahara issue.[74] In early 2009 the UN Mission for the Referendum in Western Sahara (MINURSO) reported an improved situation on the ground with regard to Moroccan and Polisario forces in Western Sahara.[75] Although talks continued in 2009, there was

---

[71] See appendix 5A in this volume.

[72] Sorenson (note 58), p. 108.

[73] Cordesman and Nerguizian (note 61), p. 24; and Sorenson (note 58), p. 108.

[74] 'Morocco arms move may hit Sahara talks: Polisario', Reuters, 2 Mar. 2008. On background to the conflict and Polisario Front see note 60.

[75] United Nations, Security Council, Report of the Secretary-General on the situation concerning Western Sahara, S/2009/200, 13 Apr. 2009, paras 13–26. On MINURSO see also appendix 3A, table 3A.2, in this volume.

little change in positions from the main protagonists (Algeria, Morocco and the Polisario Front).[76]

Libya

Following the lifting of the UN arms embargo in 2003, it was expected that Libya would seek to modernize, upgrade and replace a significant quantity of the major conventional weapons that it had acquired in the 1970s and 1980s.[77] Libya, like Algeria, has both the desire to modernize its armed forces and the means to pay for it; thus, Libya has come to be regarded as a promising market for a number of major arms suppliers.[78] The heads of government of France, Italy, Russia and the UK have visited Libyan leader Muammar Qadhafi in recent years, accompanied by arms company representatives and rumours of multi-billion dollar arms deals.[79] To date these efforts have not resulted in significant orders. For the period 2005–2009, Libya was ranked as the 110th largest arms importer in the world, and its only imports of major conventional weapons in 2005–2009 were the first 6 of 10 A-109K helicopters from Italy for border patrols and the first consignment of MILAN-3 anti-tank missiles from France.

In August 2008 Italy and Libya signed a Treaty of Friendship, Partnership and Cooperation, under which Italian companies will assist Libya in the strengthening of its border controls to combat terrorism, organized crime, drug trafficking and irregular migration.[80] Italy has concluded a number of deals with Libya in recent years to assist with the development of Libyan border security capabilities, and in January 2008 Libya signed a contract for an ATR-42MP maritime patrol aircraft for border control purposes.[81] By equipping Libyan border security agencies, Italian companies

---

[76] Moroccan Embassy, 'Moroccan initiative for negotiating an autonomy statute for the Sahara Region', Washington, DC, [n.d.], <http://dcusa.themoroccanembassy.com/moroccan_embassy_moroccan_sahara_initiative.aspx>; and United Nations (note 68), para. 12.

[77] See Hart, J. and Kile, S. N., 'Libya's renunciation of nuclear, biological and chemical weapons and ballistic missiles', SIPRI Yearbook 2005.

[78] Cowan, G. and Smith, M., 'Suitors eye Libyan market', Jane's Defence Weekly, 2 Jan. 2008, p. 19.

[79] Holtom, Bromley and Wezeman (note 55), pp. 303–304; and Wezeman, Bromley and Wezeman (note 11), pp. 305–306.

[80] Human Rights Watch (HRW), Pushed Back, Pushed Around: Italy's Forced Return of Boat Migrants and Asylum Seekers, Libya's Mistreatment of Migrants and Asylum Seekers (HRW: New York, 2009).

[81] 'Italian customs service delivers three FPB to Libyan Coast Guard', Al Defaiya, 20 June 2009; Finmeccanica, 'Finmeccanica and AgustaWestland JV in Libya in the aeronautics and security systems sector EUR 80 million contract signed for ten A109 Power helicopters', Press release, 17 Jan. 2006, <http://www.finmeccanica.it/Holding/EN/Corporate/Sala_stampa/Comunicati_stampa/Anno_2006/>; Finmeccanica, 'Agreement signed with the Libyan Government to create a joint venture in the sector of electronics for defence and security', Press release, 2 Apr. 2007, <http://www.finmeccanica.com/Holding/EN/Corporate/Sala_stampa/Comunicati_stampa/Anno_2007/>; Finmeccanica, 'SELEX Sistemi Integrati signed an agreement with Libya, worth EUR 300 million, for border security and control', Press release, 7 Oct. 2009, <http://www.finmeccanica.it/Holding/EN/Corporate/Sala_stampa/Comunicati_stampa/Anno_2009/>; and Alenia Aeronautica, 'Libya signs

appear to hope that they will benefit from the prospective modernization of the Libyan armed forces.[82]

In November 2006 Libya signed a contract with France worth €140 million ($195 million) to refurbish Libyan Mirage F-1 combat aircraft.[83] Reports appeared in 2007 that Libya and France were negotiating a €4.5 billion ($6.3 billion) arms deal for Rafale combat aircraft, helicopters, Gowind corvettes and patrol vessels.[84] However, the only order placed with France since 2007 has been for an undisclosed number of MILAN-3 anti-tank missiles, although contradictory reports on the planned sale of 14 Rafales appeared in 2009.[85]

Vladimir Putin failed to replicate Russia's 2006 Algerian 'arms-for-debt cancellation' arrangement in Libya during a presidential visit in April 2008.[86] Russian hopes for the conclusion of a deal for $2 billion worth of arms faded in October–November 2008 as Qadhafi stressed during his visits to Russia, Ukraine and Belarus that Libya was being presented with a lot of offers for military equipment. However, in 2009 the Russian media claimed that Russia had concluded deals with Libya for 3 BPS-500 (Project-12418) fast attack craft and the overhaul of 145 Libyan T-72 tanks.[87] In January 2010, during the visit of Libyan Defence Minister Younis Jaber to Moscow, there were premature reports that Libya had ordered 12–15 Su-35 combat aircraft, 4 Su-30 combat aircraft, 6 Yak-130 trainer aircraft and air-defence systems.[88] Negotiations continue on a package of arms worth an estimated $2 billion.[89]

As demonstrated by its courting by major suppliers and a potential loosening of restrictions on arms exports to Libya by the USA, Libya is no longer considered a threat to international peace and security but rather a potentially lucrative market.[90] Libya does not face significant external threats to its national security that would justify large-scale acquisitions

---

order for ATR-42MP maritime patrol aircraft', Press release, 17 Jan. 2008, <http://www.alenia-aeronautica.it/Eng/Media/Pages/PressReleases.aspx?btnPagX=6&anno=2008&tip=&tst=>.

[82] Gething, M. J., 'Aermacchi wins overhaul work on Libyan trainers', *Jane's Defence Weekly*, 15 Aug. 2007, p. 18.

[83] Lewis, J. A. C., 'France to refurbish Libyan Mirages', *Jane's Defence Weekly*, 29 Nov. 2006, p. 19.

[84] 'Libya, France sign MOU for purchase of 14 Rafale fighters', Agence France-Presse, 10 Dec. 2007; and Lewis, J. A. C., 'Libyan–French accord offers promise of major acquisitions', *Jane's Defence Weekly*, 19 Dec. 2007, p. 5.

[85] 'Deal near on Libya Rafale buy', *Defense News*, 23 Mar. 2009, p. 3; and Johnson, R. F., 'Dassault denies sale of Rafale to Libya is imminent', *Jane's Defence Weekly*, 1 Apr. 2009, p. 21.

[86] Wezeman, Bromley and Wezeman (note 11), pp. 305–306.

[87] 'Russia, Libya sign warship contract worth up to $200 mln', RIA Novosti, 10 Mar. 2009, <http://en.rian.ru/russia/20090310/120495201.html>; and 'Russia set to modernize Libya's Soviet-era tanks', RIA Novosti, 17 Aug. 2009, <http://en.rian.ru/mlitary_news/20090817/155830388.html>.

[88] Nikol'skii, A., [Qadhafi did not disappoint], *Vedomosti*, 26 Jan. 2010.

[89] 'Russia says talk of $2 bln arms contract with Libya premature', RIA Novosti, 30 Jan. 2010, <http://en.rian.ru/russia/20100130/157722762.html>.

[90] Wolf, J., 'U.S. eyes arms sales to Libya', Reuters, 6 Mar. 2009; and Seetharaman, D. and Wolf, J., 'U.S. eyes Vietnam, Libya arms sales', Reuters, 14 Dec. 2009.

and has therefore not been under pressure to buy, but has rather been able to play suppliers against each other. However, it has been suggested that Qadhafi and Libya's influential armed and security forces are unlikely to accept lagging behind their North African neighbours and new orders for major conventional weapons will be placed soon.[91]

IV. Arms transfers to Iraq

Arms supplies have played a significant role in the conflict in Iraq and have the potential to further destabilize the country's fragile political situation. This section discusses arms flows—including both major conventional weapons and small arms and light weapons (SALW)—to Iraq during the past five years, with a particular focus on Iraq's efforts in 2009 to rebuild its armed forces and exert greater control over arms acquisitions and limit its dependence on the USA for its security needs and arrangement of arms supplies.

Since 2003 Iraqi and US officials have alleged that armed non-state groups in Iraq have received arms and training from sources in Iran and Syria.[92] In mid-2009 US intelligence sources suggested that it had become increasingly difficult to smuggle weapons from Iran to Iraq, but that those weapons entering Iraq tended to be more sophisticated than before.[93] However, an analysis of the weapons captured from these armed groups suggests that a large proportion of their holdings have been taken from Iraqi stockpiles.[94] The US Government has established new accountability procedures for SALW supplies to Iraq to prevent diversion to these groups.[95] Nonetheless, concerns remain that non-state actors continue to steal or buy weapons from Iraqi armed forces personnel and therefore the risk of post-shipment diversion remains and with it the potential for increased armed violence in Iraq in the future.[96] The instability that these armed groups could cause has not only affected acquisitions by the Iraqi armed forces and US troops in Iraq, but also influenced Saudi Arabia's decision to invest in an advanced border security system along its border with Iraq.[97]

[91] Lutterbeck, D., 'Arming Libya: transfers of conventional weapons past and present', *Journal of Contemporary Security Policy*, vol. 30, no. 3 (Dec. 2009).

[92] Felter, J. and Fishman, B., *Iranian Strategy in Iraq, Politics and 'Other Means'*, Occasional Paper Series (Combating Terrorism Center: West Point, NY, 13 Oct. 2008), pp. 71–82; and Muir, J., 'All quiet on Iraq's western front', BBC News, 18 Nov. 2009, <http://news.bbc.co.uk/2/hi/8363899.stm>.

[93] US Department of Defense (DOD), *Measuring Stability and Security in Iraq*, Report to Congress (US DOD: Washington, DC, Sep. 2009), pp. 26–27.

[94] Felter and Fishman (note 92), appendix C.

[95] US DOD (note 93), p. 59; and Williams, P., *Criminals, Militias, and Insurgents: Organized Crime in Iraq* (Strategic Studies Institute: Carlisle, PA, June 2009), p. 183.

[96] US DOD (note 93), p. 59; and Williams (note 95).

[97] Irish, J., 'EADS near $1 billion Saudi–Iraq border deal: executives', Reuters, 24 June 2008; and Taverna, M. A., 'Saudi win will help EADS lessen dependence on commercial aircraft', *Aviation Week & Space Technology*, 13 July 2009, p. 27.

Iraq was subject to a UN arms embargo during the 1990s, which was lifted in June 2004 for transfers to the Iraqi Government.[98] Iraq ranked as the 24th largest arms importer for the period 2005–2009, with more than 11 000 light armoured personnel carriers (APCs) accounting for the majority of its major conventional weapon imports. The USA was the largest supplier of major conventional weapons to Iraq during this period, accounting for 52 per cent of the volume of deliveries, followed by Russia (14 per cent), Ukraine (7 per cent), Hungary (6 per cent), Italy (5 percent), Poland (4 per cent) and Turkey (4 per cent).[99] Large numbers of SALW were also delivered during 2005–2009, including over 600 000 SALW from several European countries arranged by the USA and significant numbers supplied directly from China, Serbia and the USA.[100] The Iraqi armed forces have been increasingly able to pursue a military campaign to defeat a range of armed non-state groups but have remained dependent on foreign forces, mainly US, for support from combat aircraft and other major conventional weapons.[101]

Developments in 2009 and the future

The level of violence in Iraq in 2009 showed a marked drop in comparison to 2007–2008.[102] However, with the withdrawal of US combat forces from Iraqi cities in June 2009, the planned withdrawal of US troops from Iraq by 2011 and the risk that violence could flare up again, the Iraqi Government has focused attention on rebuilding its armed forces and acquiring more major conventional weapons.[103] By the end of 2009, Iraq had placed orders for 280 M-1A1 tanks, 24 Bell-407 helicopters and 6 C-130J transport aircraft from the USA; over 400 BTR-4 APCs and 6 An-32 transport aircraft from Ukraine; 24 EC-135 helicopters from France; and 22 Mi-17 helicopters

[98] On the embargo see appendix 12A in this volume.

[99] As of 30 Sep. 2009 the US had provided $20.72 billion to develop the Iraqi security forces since 2003, but only part of this money was used to fund weapons. US Special Inspector General for Iraq Reconstruction (SIGIR), *Quarterly Report to the United States Congress* (SIGIR: Arlington, VA, 30 Oct. 2009), p. 45. See also chapter 5, section IV, in this volume.

[100] 'Probing the grey area: irresponsible small arms transfers', *Small Arms Survey 2007: Guns and the City* (Cambridge University Press: Cambridge, 2007) pp. 81–85; 'Serbia, Iraq agree on $100 m weapons deal', Agence France-Presse, 28 Aug. 2009; and Wright, R. and Tyson, A. S., 'Iraqis to pay China $100 million for weapons for police', *Washington Post*, 4 Oct. 2007.

[101] E.g. when Iraqi troops launched a major offensive against opposition forces in Mar. 2008, aircraft from Multinational Force–Iraq provided air support. Cordesman, A. H. and Mausner, A., *Withdrawal from Iraq: Assessing the Readiness of Iraqi Security Forces* (Center for Strategic and International Studies: Washington, DC, Aug. 2009), pp. 21–22.

[102] SIGIR (note 99), pp. 44–45. See also appendix 2A, section III, in this volume.

[103] The extent of the Iraqi plans was reflected in Iraqi discussions with the USA about possible arms purchases, details of which can be found in US notifications to Congress about possible FMS contracts. These are published on the website of the US Defense Security Cooperation Agency (DSCA), <http://www.dsca.osd.mil/>. See also Perlo-Freeman, S. et al., 'Military expenditure', *SIPRI Yearbook 2009*, pp. 208–209.

bought from Russia via the USA and upgraded by a US company. While these weapons can play a role in internal military operations, they are also a major step in rebuilding Iraq's military capabilities for responding to external threats.

A major and costly next step will be to re-establish an air force and air-defence system. In 2007 Iraq revealed long-term plans to build an air force with 38 squadrons.[104] However, in 2009 the air force was still small and equipped with only a few light aircraft and helicopters suitable for attacking ground targets. Iraq still lacks combat aircraft and land-based air-defence systems to defend its air space, although in late 2009 Iraq received an air surveillance radar from the USA to enable it to begin to monitor its air space. During 2009 discussions about the possible procurement of combat aircraft continued, although no orders have been placed.[105] In preparation for the acquisition of combat aircraft, Iraq ordered 15 T-6A trainer aircraft from the USA in 2009 and has received the first 4.

It remains to be seen when, and to what extent, Iraq's significant arms procurement plans will be fulfilled. The economic crisis and drop in oil prices have drastically curtailed Iraq's ability to finance its own arms procurement plans, and as a result of a lower security budget, the level of US military assistance has also been cut.[106] Based on what is known about current orders and procurement plans, it seems reasonable to assume that the USA will remain the main supplier of arms to Iraq for the coming years. According to the US Government, during the period September 2006 to August 2008 Iraq ordered $3.6 billion worth of goods and services via the US Government Foreign Military Sales (FMS) programme, and in 2009 it was reported that FMS contracts with Iraq valued at $5.5 billion were being executed.[107] However, Iraq is experiencing problems fulfilling the specific financial requirements and procedures for using this programme. Iraq's poor credit rating and inability to pay for military equipment and services in advance in 2009 has held up the signing and implementation of contracts for weapons from or via the USA.[108]

To avoid the problems associated with the FMS programme and to decrease dependence on the USA, Iraq continues to seek other suppliers. Other advantages for buying from non-US suppliers include lower prices and quicker deliveries of weapons. For example, in 2009 Iraq was discuss-

[104] US Department of Defense (DOD), *Measuring Stability and Security in Iraq*, Report to Congress (US DOD: Washington, DC, Dec. 2007), p. 49.

[105] Wall, R., 'Iraqi Air Force advisers pressed to complete their work', *Aviation Week & Space Technology*, 5 Oct. 2009, p. 39; and Al-Nidawi, O. F. and Bay, A., 'Iraq needs a real air force', *Wall Street Journal*, 11 Sep. 2009, p. 17.

[106] See chapter 5, section IV, in this volume.

[107] Financial Policy and Internal Operations Business Operations, US Defense Security Cooperation Agency, 'Historical facts book', 30 Sep. 2008, <http://www.dsca.mil/programs/biz-ops/facts book/default.htm>, p. 3; and SIGIR (note 99), p. 49.

[108] Chon, G., 'Iraq is struggling to buy equipment', *Wall Street Journal*, 30 Sep. 2009.

ing the procurement of light and medium combat aircraft not only with the USA but also with France, the Czech Republic and South Korea, as well as exploring possible arms deals with Brazil, Russia, Serbia and Ukraine.[109]

V. Conclusions

Since the end of the cold war, the five largest suppliers of major conventional weapons have remained the same: the USA, Russia, Germany, France and the UK. However, their share of global arms exports is slowly declining as a number of states are challenging the established second tier of arms suppliers. It has become increasingly difficult to compare the official data on export orders and actual arms exports published by the major arms suppliers, demonstrating the continued utility of SIPRI data for monitoring and measuring international arms transfers. It is expected that in the coming years SIPRI data will show a change with regard to the largest importer, as China will drop from the top spot. Asian and Middle Eastern countries are expected to remain among the world's largest importers.

SIPRI data shows that the overwhelming majority of arms transfers to North Africa for the period 2005–2009 were destined for Algeria. However, Morocco has placed significant orders for combat aircraft, missiles and naval vessels that will lead to a significant increase in its volume of arms imports. The timing of the conclusion of deals for major conventional weapons by regional rivals Algeria and Morocco is worrying for a region that lacks security- and confidence-building transparency mechanisms. Although it is unlikely that these acquisitions in themselves will lead to conflict, they do not help to improve relations between the two countries. Furthermore, their acquisitions are likely to influence Libyan plans.

Despite problems accessing US military assistance for arms procurement, Iraq continues to rely on the USA for the provision of arms and military equipment to rebuild its armed forces. It has made arrangements for the acquisition of arms and military equipment from other suppliers using its own funds, but its ambitious procurement plans have been hit by the economic crisis and declining oil prices. Nevertheless, the timetable for the withdrawal of US forces from Iraq lends a sense of urgency to international efforts to provide Iraq with the arms and military equipment it seeks to meet its perceived internal and external security needs.

---

[109] Kim, J. K., 'Iraq Asks for Korea's T-50 trainer jets', *Korea Times*, 15 Mar. 2009; Cody, E., 'France hopes to jump start its arms sales with new Iraqi Government', *Washington Post*, 4 July 2009; Rolfsen, B., 'Iraq may get used U.S. F-16s', *Defense News*, 7 Sep. 2009; Kominek, J., 'Czech Republic courts Iraq with L-159 trainers', *Jane's Defence Weekly*, 11 Nov. 2009; 'Iraq signs weapons deals with foreign countries to improve security', 15 Apr. 2009, BBC Monitoring Middle East, Text of report by Iraqi Media Network weekly newspaper *Al-Sabah* on 15 Apr. 2009; and Interfax, 'Ukraine signs first of set of contracts for supplying arms worth $550 m to Iraq', *Kyiv Post*, 11 Dec. 2009.

Appendix 7A. The suppliers and recipients of major conventional weapons, 2005–2009

THE SIPRI ARMS TRANSFERS PROGRAMME

I. Introduction

The SIPRI Arms Transfers Programme maintains the SIPRI Arms Transfers Database, which contains information on deliveries of major conventional weapons to states, international organizations and non-state armed groups since 1950.[1] SIPRI ascribes a trend-indicator value (TIV) to each weapon or subsystem included in the database. SIPRI then calculates the volume of transfers to, from and between all of the above-listed entities using the TIV and the number of weapon systems or subsystems delivered in a given year. TIV figures do not represent financial values for weapon transfers; they are an indicator of the volume of transfers. Therefore, TIV figures should not be cited directly. They are best used as the raw data for calculating trends in international arms transfers over periods of time, global percentages for suppliers and recipients, and percentages for the volume of transfers to or from particular states.

The database covers the period from 1950 to the most recent full calendar year. Data collection and analysis are continuous processes. As new data becomes available, the database is updated for all years included in the database.[2]

Section II outlines the sources and methods for arms transfers data. Tables 7A.1 and 7A.2 present, respectively, the SIPRI TIV for all recipients and suppliers of major conventional weapons for the period 2005–2009. Table 7A.3 presents the sources of the weapons transferred to the 10 largest recipients of major conventional weapons in the period 2005–2009. Table 7A.4 shows the regional distribution of the exports of the 10 largest suppliers of major conventional weapons for the period 2005–2009.

II. Sources and methods for arms transfers data

Sources

Data on arms transfers are collected from a wide variety of sources: newspapers and other periodicals; annual reference books; monographs; official national and international documents; information from industry; and blogs and other Internet publications. The common criterion for all these sources is that they are open, that is, published and available to the public.

---

[1] SIPRI Arms Transfers Database, <http://www.sipri.org/databases/armstransfers/>.

[2] Thus, data from several editions of the SIPRI Yearbook or other SIPRI publications cannot be combined or compared. Readers who require time-series TIV data for periods before the years prior to 2005 should contact the SIPRI Arms Transfers Programme via <http://www.sipri.org/>.

Such open information cannot, however, provide a comprehensive picture of world arms transfers. Published reports often provide only partial information, and substantial disagreement between them is common. Since publicly available information is inadequate for the tracking of all weapons and other military equipment, SIPRI covers only what it terms major conventional weapons. Order and delivery dates and exact numbers (or even types) of weapons ordered and delivered, or the identity of suppliers or recipients, may not always be clear. Exercising judgement and making informed estimates are therefore important elements in compiling the SIPRI Arms Transfers Database. All sources of data as well as calculations of estimates are documented in the SIPRI Arms Transfers Database. Estimates are conservative and may very well be underestimates.

Selection criteria

SIPRI uses the term 'arms transfer' rather than 'arms trade' or 'arms sale'. SIPRI covers not only sales of weapons, including manufacturing licences, but also other forms of weapon supply, such as aid and gifts.

The weapons transferred must be destined for the armed forces, paramilitary forces or intelligence agencies of another country. Weapons supplied to or from an armed non-state actor in an armed conflict are included as deliveries to or from the individual armed non-state actor, identified under separate 'recipient' or 'supplier' headings. Supplies to or from international organizations are also included and categorized in the same fashion. In cases where deliveries are identified but it is not possible to identify either the supplier or the recipient with an acceptable degree of certainty, transfers are registered as coming from 'unknown' suppliers or going to 'unknown' recipients. Suppliers are termed 'multiple' only if there is a transfer agreement for weapons produced by two or more cooperating countries and if it is not clear which country will make the delivery.

To qualify for inclusion in the database, weapons must be transferred voluntarily by the supplier. This includes weapons delivered illegally—without proper authorization by the government of the supplier or the recipient country—but excludes captured weapons and weapons obtained from defectors. Finally, the weapons must have a military purpose. Systems such as aircraft used mainly for other branches of government but registered with and operated by the armed forces are excluded. Weapons supplied for technical or arms procurement evaluation purposes only are not included.

The coverage: major conventional weapons

SIPRI covers only what it terms major conventional weapons, defined as:

1. *Aircraft*: all fixed-wing aircraft and helicopters, including unmanned reconnaissance/surveillance aircraft, with the exception of microlight aircraft, powered and unpowered gliders and target drones.

2. *Armoured vehicles*: all vehicles with integral armour protection, including all types of tank, tank destroyer, armoured car, armoured personnel carrier, armoured support vehicle and infantry fighting vehicle. Only vehicles with very light armour protection (such as trucks with an integral but lightly armoured cabin) are excluded.

3. *Artillery*: naval, fixed, self-propelled and towed guns, howitzers, multiple rocket launchers and mortars, with a calibre equal to or above 100 millimetres.

4. *Sensors*: (*a*) all land-, aircraft- and ship-based active (radar) and passive (e.g. electro-optical) surveillance systems with a range of at least 25 kilometres, with the exception of navigation and weather radars, (*b*) all fire-control radars, with the exception of range-only radars, and (*c*) anti-submarine warfare and anti-ship sonar systems for ships and helicopters. In cases where the system is fitted on a platform (vehicle, aircraft or ship), the register only notes those systems that come from a different supplier from that of the platform.

5. *Air defence systems*: (*a*) all land-based surface-to-air missile (SAM) systems, and (*b*) all anti-aircraft guns with a calibre of more than 40 mm. This includes self-propelled systems on armoured or unarmoured chassis.

6. *Missiles*: (*a*) all powered, guided missiles and torpedoes with conventional warheads, and (*b*) all unpowered but guided bombs and shells. Unguided rockets, free-fall aerial munitions, anti-submarine rockets and target drones are excluded.

7. *Ships*: (*a*) all ships with a standard tonnage of 100 tonnes or more, and (*b*) all ships armed with artillery of 100-mm calibre or more, torpedoes or guided missiles, with the exception of most survey ships, tugs and some transport ships.

8. *Engines*: (*a*) engines for military aircraft, for example, combat-capable aircraft, larger military transport and support aircraft, including helicopters; (*b*) engines for combat ships, such as fast attack craft, corvettes, frigates, destroyers, cruisers, aircraft carriers and submarines; (*c*) engines for most armoured vehicles—generally engines of more than 200 horsepower output. In cases where the system is fitted on a platform (vehicle, aircraft or ship), the register only notes those systems that come from a different supplier from the supplier of the platform.

9. *Other*: (*a*) all turrets for armoured vehicles fitted with a gun of at least 20-mm calibre or with guided anti-tank missiles, (*b*) all turrets for ships fitted with a gun of at least 57-mm calibre, and (*c*) all turrets for ships fitted with multiple guns with a combined calibre of at least 57 mm. In cases where the system is fitted on a platform (vehicle or ship), the register only notes those systems that come from a different supplier from the supplier of the platform.

The statistics presented refer to transfers of weapons in these nine categories only. Transfers of other military equipment—such as small arms and light weapons, trucks, artillery under 100-mm calibre, ammunition, support equipment and components, as well as services or technology transfers—are not included.

The SIPRI trend indicator

The SIPRI system for the valuation of arms transfers is designed as a trend-measuring device. It allows the measurement of changes in the total flow of major weapons and its geographical pattern. The trends presented in the tables of SIPRI trend-indicator values are based only on actual deliveries during the year or years covered in the relevant tables and figures, not on orders signed in a year.

The TIV system, in which similar weapons have similar values, shows both the quantity and quality of the weapons transferred—in other words, it describes the transfer of military resources. It does not reflect the financial value of (or payments for) weapons transferred. This is impossible for three reasons. First, in many cases no reliable data on the value of a transfer is available. Second, even if the value of a transfer is known, in almost every case it is the total value of a deal, which may include not only the weapons themselves but also other items related to these weapons (e.g. spare parts, armament or ammunition) as well as support systems (e.g. specialized vehicles) and items related to the integration of the weapon in the armed forces (e.g. training, or software changes to existing systems). Third, even if the value of a transfer is known, important details about the financial arrangements of the transfer (e.g. credit or loan conditions and discounts) are often unavailable.[3]

Measuring the military implications of transfers would require a concentration on the value of the weapons as a military resource. Again, this could be done from the actual money values of the weapons transferred, assuming that these values generally reflect the military capability of the weapon. However, the problems listed above would still apply (e.g. a very expensive weapon may be transferred as aid at a 'zero' price, and therefore not show up in financial statistics, but still be a significant transfer of military resources). The SIPRI solution is a system in which military resources are measured by including an evaluation of the technical parameters of weapons. The purpose and performance of a weapon are evaluated, and it is assigned a value in an index that reflects its value as a military resource in relation to other weapons. This can be done under the condition that a number of benchmarks or reference points are established by assigning some weapons a fixed place in the index, thus forming its core. All other weapons are compared to these core weapons.

In short, the process of calculating the SIPRI TIV for individual weapons is as follows. For a number of weapon types it is possible to find the average unit acquisition price in open sources. It is assumed that such real prices roughly reflect the military resource value of a system. For example, a combat aircraft bought for $10 million may be assumed to be a resource twice as great as one bought for $5 million, and a submarine bought for $100 million may be assumed to be 10 times the resource a $10 million combat aircraft would repre-

---

[3] It is possible to present a very rough idea of the economic factors from the financial statistics now available from most arms-exporting countries. However, most of these statistics lack sufficient detail. Such data is available from the SIPRI Arms Transfers Programme via <http://www.sipri.org/contents/armstrad/>.

sent. Weapons with a real price are used as the core weapons of the valuation. Weapons for which a price is not known are compared with core weapons in the following steps.

1. The description of a weapon is compared with the description of the core weapon. In cases where no core weapon exactly matches the description of the weapon for which a price is to be found, the closest match is sought.

2. Standard characteristics of size and performance (weight, speed, range and payload) are compared with those of a core weapon of a similar description. For example, a 15 000-kilogram combat aircraft would be compared with a combat aircraft of similar size.

3. Other characteristics, such as the type of electronics, loading or unloading arrangements, engine, tracks or wheels, armament and materials, are compared.

4. Weapons are compared with a core weapon from the same period.

Weapons in a 'used' condition are given a value 40 per cent of that of a new weapon. Used weapons that have been significantly refurbished or modified by the supplier before delivery (and have thereby become a greater military resource) are given a value of 66 per cent of the value when new. In reality there may be huge differences in the military resource value of a used weapon depending on its condition and the modifications during the years of use.

The SIPRI trend indicator does not take into account the conditions under which a weapon is operated (e.g. an F-16 combat aircraft operated by well-balanced, well-trained and well-integrated armed forces has a much greater military value than the same aircraft operated by a developing country; the resource is the same but the effect is very different). The trend indicator also accepts the prices of the core weapons as genuine rather than reflecting costs that, even if officially part of the programme, are not exclusively related to the weapon itself. For example, funds that appear to be allocated to a particular weapon programme could be related to optional add-ons and armament or to the development of basic technology that will be included (free of cost) in other programmes. Such funds could also act, in effect, as government subsidies to keep industry in business by paying more than the weapon is worth.

In cases were subsystems, such as sensors and engines, are produced and delivered by suppliers other than the supplier of the platform on which the subsystems are fitted, the TIV calculation of the value of the platform would be reduced by the value of components. The TIV of the components would be listed as coming from a supplier different to the supplier of the platform.

Table 7A.1. The recipients of major conventional weapons, 2005–2009

The table includes all countries and non-state actors that imported major conventional weapons in the five-year period 2005–2009. Ranking is according to 2005–2009 total imports. Figures are SIPRI trend-indicator values (TIV). Figures and percentages may not add up because of the conventions of rounding. The right-hand column shows the recipient state's share of global arms imports for 2005–2009.

Rank 2005–2009	Rank 2004–2008[a]	Recipient	Volume of imports (TIV)						% share, 2005–2009
			2005	2006	2007	2008	2009	2005–09	2005–2009
1	1	China	3 511	3 831	1 474	1 481	595	10 892	9
2	2	India	1 036	1 257	2 179	1 810	2 116	8 398	7
3	4	South Korea	686	1 650	1 758	1 821	1 172	7 087	6
4	3	UAE	2 198	2 026	938	748	604	6 514	6
5	5	Greece	389	598	1 796	563	1 269	4 615	4
6	6	Israel	1 113	1 117	859	665	158	3 912	3
7	14	Singapore	543	52	368	1 123	1 729	3 816	3
8	7	United States	501	581	731	808	831	3 453	3
9	11	Algeria	156	308	471	1 518	942	3 394	3
10	13	Pakistan	332	262	613	939	1 146	3 292	3
11	10	Turkey	1 005	422	585	578	675	3 264	3
12	23	Malaysia	51	410	546	541	1 494	3 041	3
13	9	Chile	400	1 041	723	577	231	2 972	3
14	12	Australia	470	682	629	380	757	2 919	3
15	8	Egypt	628	777	676	214	217	2 513	2
16	15	Poland	97	459	1 006	623	94	2 279	2
17	17	Venezuela	23	442	805	764	172	2 206	2
18	16	Japan	301	459	469	584	391	2 203	2
19	18	South Africa	181	689	768	387	139	2 164	2
20	24	Norway	14	469	494	536	576	2 090	2
21	19	United Kingdom	27	333	702	506	288	1 855	2
22	25	Spain	307	287	323	361	430	1 708	1
23	20	Taiwan	763	625	12	12	102	1 514	1
24	28	Iraq	165	253	268	351	365	1 401	1
25	31	Indonesia	31	58	577	241	452	1 359	1
26	21	Italy	148	420	488	189	112	1 357	1
27	26	Canada	106	102	427	427	80	1 143	1
28	22	Saudi Arabia	148	185	64	115	626	1 138	1
29	27	Iran	78	470	344	91	91	1 075	1
30	33	Brazil	192	193	207	212	210	1 014	1
31	38	Portugal	131	218	60	159	431	999	1
32	30	Germany	195	401	76	95	137	905	1
33	41	Austria	22	2	305	220	330	879	1
34	29	Romania	494	69	90	70	56	778	1
35	35	Peru	368	193	172	2	33	767	1
36	39	Netherlands	76	57	215	132	243	723	1
37	36	Czech Republic	622	51	15	20	5	712	1
38	32	Viet Nam	333	42	1	250	44	670	1
39	42	Jordan	35	81	182	136	195	629	1
40	45	Oman	164	281	4	66	93	607	1
41	62	Afghanistan	31	3	41	152	344	571	0
42	34	Yemen	306	60	160	45	–	571	0

Rank 2005–2009	Rank 2004–2008[a]	Recipient	Volume of imports (TIV)						% share, 2005–2009
			2005	2006	2007	2008	2009	2005–09	2009
43	56	Colombia	15	48	144	92	250	549	0
44	46	Finland	91	118	114	152	70	544	0
45	51	Syria	7	70	–	292	175	543	0
46	78	NATO	–	116	–	–	420	536	0
47	37	Denmark	92	102	191	90	47	523	0
48	48	Georgia	74	100	174	77	81	506	0
49	54	Bulgaria	149	20	45	123	153	489	0
50	47	Hungary	13	265	205	5	2	488	0
51	50	Azerbaijan	45	148	210	21	49	473	0
52	53	Belgium	0	5	157	177	84	423	0
53	44	Switzerland	164	82	114	14	31	405	0
54	52	Sweden	82	124	62	64	46	378	0
55	40	Sudan	96	68	33	128	39	364	0
56	57	Kuwait	16	–	276	5	17	314	0
57	55	Bangladesh	9	214	75	12	–	310	0
58	61	France	–	60	69	7	149	286	0
59	43	Eritrea	281	–	4	–	–	285	0
60	150	Qatar	–	–	–	–	285	285	0
61	58	Belarus	6	254	–	–	–	260	0
62	65	Ecuador	48	15	2	140	46	251	0
63	60	Kazakhstan	42	41	82	25	49	240	0
64	63	Morocco	90	48	32	49	–	220	0
65	69	Tunisia	168	2	–	7	8	186	0
66	49	Mexico	47	69	11	–	57	185	0
67	68	Bahrain	63	63	26	19	7	178	0
68	67	Sri Lanka	25	42	30	64	–	161	0
69	82	Nigeria	–	14	57	17	73	161	0
70	79	Estonia	17	6	30	50	56	158	0
71	59	Thailand	61	44	8	12	34	158	0
72	70	Namibia	–	72	6	66	10	154	0
73	77	Chad	–	9	18	89	23	139	0
74	74	New Zealand	8	5	71	2	48	134	0
75	84	Uruguay	20	7	3	65	37	132	0
76	85	Kenya	–	–	89	–	35	124	0
77	71	Lithuania	15	45	4	26	26	116	0
78	76	Croatia	–	–	14	99	3	116	0
79	75	Latvia	7	11	51	44	0	113	0
80	72	Myanmar	79	29	3	–	–	110	0
81	80	Russia	–	5	100	–	1	106	0
82	83	Angola	40	7	20	20	11	98	0
83	90	Albania	42	–	5	13	25	85	0
84	86	Equatorial Guinea	–	–	33	41	6	79	0
85	64	Argentina	3	9	24	21	11	69	0
86	81	Philippines	14	20	16	10	4	65	0
87	88	Gabon	–	22	21	21	–	64	0
88	89	African Union	51	8	–	4	–	63	0
89	92	Cambodia	–	14	40	–	4	58	0
90	91	Cyprus	20	26	12	–	–	58	0
91	87	Ireland	4	11	18	21	1	53	0

Rank 2005–2009	Rank 2004–2008[a]	Recipient	Volume of imports (TIV)						% share, 2005–2009
			2005	2006	2007	2008	2009	2005–09	
92	135	Lebanon	1	–	3	–	47	50	0
93	101	Turkmenistan	–	–	–	–	47	47	0
94	95	Senegal	14	8	19	1	3	45	0
95	94	Jamaica	13	13	15	2	–	43	0
96	96	Zimbabwe	20	20	–	–	–	40	0
97	104	Barbados	–	–	13	13	13	38	0
98	107	Mali	13	–	8	2	7	30	0
99	98	Uganda	17	5	–	3	1	26	0
100	114	Mongolia	–	–	–	14	12	26	0
101	103	Zambia	0	23	3	–	–	26	0
102	106	Burkina Faso	19	1	4	–	1	24	0
103	105	Rwanda	–	3	15	6	–	24	0
104	102	North Korea	5	5	5	5	5	23	0
105	109	Tanzania	9	11	0	–	0	21	0
106	110	Tajikistan	–	13	7	–	–	20	0
107	113	Bolivia	1	8	2	3	5	18	0
108	111	Malta	18	–	–	–	–	18	0
109	100	DRC	–	17	–	–	–	17	0
110	130	Libya	–	3	3	–	11	17	0
111	140	Palestinian Authority	–	–	2	–	14	15	0
112	93	Ghana	0	0	13	–	–	14	0
113	108	Slovenia	2	2	2	–	6	13	0
114	123	Botswana	–	–	–	–	10	10	0
115	117	Sierra Leone	–	10	–	–	–	10	0
116	118	Laos	4	–	–	7	–	10	0
117	120	Seychelles	10	–	–	–	–	10	0
118	121	Maldives	–	10	–	–	–	10	0
119	116	Hezbollah (Lebanon)[b]	0	9	–	–	–	10	0
120	122	Central African Rep.	–	9	–	–	–	9	0
121	99	Dominican Republic	2	–	–	–	6	8	0
122	115	Djibouti	8	–	–	–	–	8	0
123	125	Niger	–	–	–	7	0	7	0
124	127	Trinidad & Tobago	–	–	6	–	–	6	0
125	128	Cameroon	5	0	–	1	–	6	0
126	129	Comoros	–	–	–	5	–	5	0
127	131	Slovakia	4	–	1	–	–	5	0
128	136	Benin	–	–	3	–	2	5	0
129	97	Nepal	5	–	–	–	–	5	0
130	132	Congo	4	0	0	–	–	4	0
131	119	Kyrgyzstan	3	2	–	–	–	4	0
132	134	El Salvador	–	–	–	4	–	4	0
133	151	Luxembourg	–	–	–	–	4	4	0
134	138	Brunei	1	2	–	–	–	2	0
135	137	United Nations	1	1	–	–	–	2	0
136	73	Armenia	–	–	1	–	–	1	0
137	141	Guinea	1	–	0	–	–	1	0
138	152	Bahamas	–	–	–	–	1	1	0
139	139	Lesotho	–	1	–	–	–	1	0
140	142	Haiti	–	–	1	–	–	1	0

Rank 2005– 2009	Rank 2004– 2008[a]	Recipient	Volume of imports (TIV)						% share, 2005– 2009
			2005	2006	2007	2008	2009	2005–09	2009
141	133	Paraguay	1	–	–	–	–	1	0
142	143	Honduras	–	–	–	0	–	0	0
143	144	Guatemala	–	–	–	0	–	0	0
144	145	Guyana	–	–	–	0	–	0	0
145	146	UIC (Somalia)[b]	–	0	–	–	–	0	0
146	147	Macedonia	–	0	–	–	–	0	0
147	148	LTTE (Sri Lanka)[b]	0	–	–	–	–	0	0
Total			**20 557**	**24 528**	**25 443**	**22 768**	**22 640**	**115 936**	*100*

0 = <0.5; DRC = Democratic Republic of the Congo; NATO = North Atlantic Treaty Organization; UAE = United Arab Emirates.

Note: The SIPRI data on arms transfers relates to actual deliveries of major conventional weapons. To permit comparison between the data on such deliveries of different weapons and to identify general trends, SIPRI uses a trend-indicator value. This value is only an indicator of the volume of international arms transfers and not of the financial values of such transfers. Thus, it is not comparable to economic statistics such as gross domestic product or export/import figures. The method for calculating the trend-indicator value is described in section II of this appendix.

[a] The rank order for recipients in 2004–2008 differs from that published in *SIPRI Yearbook 2009* because of subsequent revision of figures for these years.

[b] These are deliveries to a non-state actor or rebel group: LTTE = Liberation Tigers of Tamil Eelam; UIC = Union of Islamic Courts.

Source: SIPRI Arms Transfers Database, <http://www.sipri.org/databases/armstransfers/>.

Table 7A.2. The suppliers of major conventional weapons, 2005–2009

The table includes all countries and non-state actors that exported major conventional weapons in the five-year period 2005–2009. Ranking is according to 2005–2009 total exports. Figures are SIPRI trend-indicator values (TIV). Figures and percentages may not add up because of the conventions of rounding. The right-hand column shows the supplier state's share of global arms exports for 2005–2009.

Rank 2005 2009	Rank 2004– 2008[a]	Supplier	Volume of exports (TIV) 2005	2006	2007	2008	2009	2005–09	% share, 2005– 2009
1	1	United States	6 600	7 394	7 658	6 093	6 795	34 539	30
2	2	Russia	5 321	6 156	5 243	6 026	4 469	27 216	23
3	3	Germany	1 875	2 510	3 002	2 499	2 473	12 359	11
4	4	France	1 633	1 577	2 342	1 831	1 851	9 234	8
5	5	United Kingdom	915	808	987	1 027	1 024	4 762	4
6	6	Netherlands	583	1 221	1 322	554	608	4 288	4
7	7	Italy	743	525	706	424	588	2 986	3
8	10	Spain	108	757	565	603	925	2 958	3
9	8	China	306	599	412	544	870	2 731	2
10	11	Sweden	537	417	367	457	353	2 130	2
11	9	Ukraine	281	557	799	269	214	2 120	2
12	12	Israel	315	282	379	271	760	2 007	2
13	13	Switzerland	267	306	324	467	270	1 634	1
14	14	Canada	235	231	343	236	177	1 222	1
15	17	Belgium	161	58	19	228	217	684	1
16	15	South Africa	24	129	148	161	154	616	1
17	18	South Korea	48	94	228	80	163	612	1
18	16	Poland	17	236	148	76	93	570	0
19	19	Belarus	24	35	6	292	–	356	0
20	20	Finland	27	97	24	67	40	254	0
21	21	Turkey	46	61	35	43	36	220	0
22	25	Austria	3	61	93	16	33	206	0
23	24	Czech Republic	68	45	31	33	19	196	0
24	23	Montenegro[b]	..	71	109	–	–	180	0
25	27	Brazil	1	28	26	72	49	176	0
26	28	Chile	–	–	–	133	–	133	0
27	38	Singapore	3	–	–	1	124	128	0
28	37	Portugal	–	–	–	87	40	127	0
29	40	Australia	50	5	1	6	51	113	0
30	33	Jordan	17	–	13	28	44	101	0
31	35	Iran	1	91	–	2	5	99	0
32	32	Bulgaria	66	5	9	8	7	94	0
33	26	Uzbekistan	4	–	–	–	90	94	0
34	34	India	13	28	21	11	22	94	0
35	36	Hungary	82	–	6	–	–	88	0
36	29	Libya	45	12	–	9	12	78	0
37	41	Moldova	18	3	15	20	11	68	0
38	30	Norway	12	14	1	2	17	45	0
39	42	Romania	2	8	32	–	3	45	0
40	22	Denmark	1	5	3	15	12	36	0
41	39	Greece	13	23	–	–	–	36	0
42	31	Slovakia	–	7	18	8	–	33	0

Rank 2005– 2009	Rank 2004– 2008[a]	Supplier	Volume of exports (TIV)						% share, 2005– 2009
			2005	2006	2007	2008	2009	2005–09	2009
43	52	Venezuela	–	6	–	3	17	27	0
44	47	UAE	11	9	3	–	–	23	0
45	45	Pakistan	20	–	–	–	–	20	0
46	43	Indonesia	8	8	–	–	–	16	0
47	49	Kyrgyzstan	–	–	–	16	–	16	0
48	50	Viet Nam	–	14	–	–	–	14	0
49	48	Kazakhstan	–	12	–	–	–	12	0
50	54	Serbia[b]	–	6	–	–	–	6	0
51	55	Qatar	–	6	–	–	–	6	0
52	61	Ireland	–	–	–	1	4	5	0
53	58	Philippines	–	–	4	–	–	4	0
54	59	Syria	–	3	–	–	–	3	0
55	60	Argentina	–	2	–	–	–	2	0
56	63	Oman	1	–	–	–	–	1	0
57	64	Costa Rica	–	–	–	0	–	0	0
58	65	Luxembourg	–	–	0	–	–	0	0
–	–	Unknown supplier[c]	53	8	2	50	0	113	0
Total			**20 557**	**24 528**	**25 443**	**22 768**	**22 640**	**115 936**	**100**

0 = <0.5; UAE = United Arab Emirates.

Note: The SIPRI data on arms transfers relates to actual deliveries of major conventional weapons. To permit comparison between the data on such deliveries of different weapons and to identify general trends, SIPRI uses a trend-indicator value. This value is only an indicator of the volume of international arms transfers and not of the financial values of such transfers. Thus, it is not comparable to economic statistics such as gross domestic product or export/import figures. The method for calculating the trend-indicator value is described in section II of this appendix.

[a] The rank order for suppliers in 2004–2008 differs from that published in *SIPRI Yearbook 2009* because of subsequent revision of figures for these years.

[b] The figure for 2005 for Serbia is for the State Union of Serbia and Montenegro. From 2006 onwards Serbia and Montenegro are separate states.

[c] One or more unknown supplier(s).

Source: SIPRI Arms Transfers Database, <http://www.sipri.org/databases/armstransfers/>.

Table 7A.3. The 10 largest recipients of major conventional weapons and their suppliers, 2005–2009

Figures are the supplier's share, as a percentage, of the total volume of imports per recipient. Only suppliers with a share of 1 per cent or more of total imports of any of the 10 largest recipients are included in the table. Smaller suppliers are grouped together under 'Other'. Figures may not add up because of the conventions of rounding.

Supplier	China	India	South Korea	UAE	Greece	Israel	Singapore	USA	Algeria	Pakistan
Brazil	–	–	–	–	1	–	–	–	–	–
Canada	–	–	<0.5	–	<0.5	<0.5	<0.5	21	<0.5	–
China	..	–	–	–	–	–	–	–	2	37
France	3	2	10	35	23	–	51	4	2	9
Germany	<0.5	1	20	1	35	2	6	7	–	4
Israel	–	5	–	–	<0.5	..	3	3	–	–
Italy	–	<0.5	<0.5	<0.5	4	–	1	1	–	1
Libya	–	–	–	<0.5	–	–	–	–	–	1
Netherlands	–	<0.5	1	–	4	–	–	–	–	–
Poland	–	3	–	–	–	–	–	<0.5	–	–
Romania	–	–	–	1	–	–	–	–	–	–
Russia	89	77	3	–	1	–	–	–	92	1
South Africa	–	–	–	<0.5	–	–	–	9	1	–
Spain	–	–	–	–	–	–	–	4	2	–
Sweden	3	–	–	–	–	–	–	<0.5	–	3
Switzerland	–	–	<0.5	<0.5	3	–	2	18	–	5
Turkey	–	–	–	<0.5	–	–	–	–	–	1
Ukraine	3	–	–	–	2	–	–	1	1	2
United Kingdom	1	8	–	–	26	98	–	31	1	–
United States	–	2	66	60	–	–	37	..	–	35
Uzbekistan	–	1	–	–	–	–	–	–	–	–
Other	–	–	–	<0.5	–	–	<0.5	<0.5	–	–

Table 7A.4. The 10 largest suppliers of major conventional weapons and their destinations, by region, 2005–2009

Figures are the supplier's share, as a percentage, of the total volume of exports per recipient region. Figures may not add up because of the conventions of rounding. For the states in each region and subregion see page xxiv.

Recipient region	Supplier									
	USA	Russia	Germany	France	UK	Netherlands	Italy	Spain	China	Sweden
Africa	<0.5	14	13	2	6	<0.5	6	3	12	12
North Africa	<0.5	12	1	1	<0.5	–	1	–	2	<0.5
Sub-Saharan Africa	<0.5	2	12	1	6	<0.5	6	3	9	12
America	5	8	7	7	33	24	33	26	5	1
South America	2	8	5	5	11	21	31	20	5	–
Asia and Oceania	39	69	25	47	24	19	12	9	63	7
Central Asia	<0.5	1	–	–	–	–	–	–	–	<0.5
East Asia	28	44	19	38	9	17	9	9	6	1
Oceania	5	–	4	4	<0.5	2	<0.5	–	–	1
South Asia	5	24	2	5	15	1	3	–	57	5
Europe	18	3	40	18	24	49	38	62	–	80
European Union	17	1	39	17	18	48	37	8	–	77
Middle East	36	6	15	27	13	8	11	<0.5	21	–
Other	1	<0.5	–	–	–	–	–	–	–	–

Notes for tables 7A.3 and 7A.4: – = nil; <0.5 = between 0 and 0.5; UAE = United Arab Emirates.

Source for tables 7A.3 and 7A.4: SIPRI Arms Transfers Database, <http://www.sipri.org/databases/armstransfers/>.

Appendix 7B. The financial value of the arms trade, 1999–2008

MARK BROMLEY

Table 7B.1 presents official data on the financial value of the arms trade in 1999–2008. The countries included in the table are those that provide official data on the financial value of 'arms exports', 'licences for arms exports' or 'arms export agreements' for at least 6 of the 10 years covered and for which the average of the values given exceeds $10 million. In all cases, the 'Stated data coverage' follows the language used in the official publication from which the data has been extracted. National practices in this area vary, but 'arms exports' generally refers to the financial value of arms actually exported, 'licences for arms exports' generally refers to the financial value of licences for arms exports issued by the national export licensing authority, and 'arms export agreements' refers to the financial value of agreements signed for arms exports. The arms export data for the different states in the table are not necessarily comparable and may be based on significantly different definitions and methodologies.

In previous years SIPRI presented an estimate of the total financial value of the global arms trade. However, in 2009 only three of the established five largest arms exporters in terms of officially reported financial values—France, Russia and the United States—released data on the financial value of their actual arms exports for 2008; the other two—Israel and the United Kingdom—did not. For this reason, no estimate of the total financial value of the global arms trade are given.

In previous years Israel released a figure for the value of actual arms exports, but it did not do so for 2007 and 2008. Official data from the Israeli Government refers only to 'contracts signed'.[1] The UK previously released data on the value of its actual arms exports, but it did not do so for 2008. Official data from the British Government refers only to 'export orders placed'. In November 2008 the British Government announced that it was ceasing production of data on actual arms exports due to 'the technical difficulty of continuing to produce reliable statistics'.[2]

---

[1] Opall-Rome, B., 'Israel 3rd among world arms suppliers: MoD', *Defense News*, 5 Oct. 2009, p. 6.
[2] British Ministry of Defence, 'Cessation of defence export delivery and defence employment statistics in UK defence statistics', 14 Nov. 2008, <http://www.mod.uk/DefenceInternet/DefenceNews/DefencePolicyAndBusiness/CessationOfDefenceExportDeliveryAndDefenceEmploymentStatisticsInUkDefenceStatistics.htm>

Table 7B.1. The financial value of global arms exports according to national government and industry sources, 1999–2008

Figures are in US$ m. at constant (2008) prices. Conversion to constant (2008) US dollars is made using the market exchange rates of the reporting year and the US consumer price index (CPI). Years are calendar years, unless otherwise stated.

State	1999	2000	2001	2002	2003	2004	2005	2006	2007	2008	Stated data coverage
Australia	430	27	62	295	450[a]	..	..	..	..	..	Arms exports
Austria	..	..	..	50	153	6	155	194	176	308	Arms exports
Belgium	544	649	420	264	325	23	351	410	1 960	1 386	Licences for arms exports
Brazil	857	897	924	1 291	880	770	351	1 178	1 279	1 956	Licences for arms exports
Canada	516	224	353	200	57	325	314	376	166	379	Arms exports
Czech Republic	378	402	465	517	605	564	293	339	..	..	Arms exports[b]
	124	100	65	87	110	127	121	125	247	278	Arms exports
Denmark	..	..	..	..	140	176	166	244	678	311	Licences for arms exports
	..	..	83	128	106	144	120	175	279	239	Licences for arms exports
Finland	55	27	44	61	65	59	141	71	107	136	Arms exports
	..	28	40	66	135	464	60	115	81	494	Licences for arms exports
France	5 354	3 155	3 445	4 990	5 673	10 080	5 229	5 402	6 452	4 648	Arms exports
	6 503	8 056	4 398	4 230	5 573	4 785	5 640	7 699	8 044	9 644	Licences for arms exports
Germany	2 002	783	399	358	1 761	1 598	2 235	1 841	1 582	2 089	Arms exports[c]
	4 167	3 275	4 010	3 670	6 425	5 388	5 780	5 613	5 213	8 478	Licences for arms exports
Greece	62	24	55	59	148	21	40	118	46	70	Licences for arms exports
Hungary	..	21	11	8	15	13	16	21	24	22	Arms exports
	..	..	..	..	65	57	44	83	136	174	Licences for arms exports
India	28	..	..	27	90	87	67	91	89	160[d]	Arms exports
Ireland	83	36	59	41	46	38	41	62	47	45	Licences for arms exports
Israel	2 076	2 206	2 432	2 394	2 750	2 964	2 866	3 204	..	..	Arms exports
	2 820	3 115	3 063	4 817	3 511	4 218	3 859	5 233	5 815	6 326	Arms export agreements
Italy	1 220	696	603	549	832	679	1 139	1 300	1 801	2 603	Arms exports
	1 846	986	939	1 036	1 693	2 109	1 866	2 937	6 742	8 292	Licences for arms exports
Korea, South	255	69	243	168	281	479	287	267	876	1 030	Arms exports

Netherlands	504	480	708	507	1 520	883	1 611	1 507	1 242	1 843	Licences for arms exports
Norway	203	151	217	344	500	341	420	486	567	690	Arms exports
Poland	..	50	61	96	242	372	398	368	408	539	Licences for arms exports
Portugal	15	25	21	7	41	24	16	1	38	111	Licences for arms export
Romania	87	48	30	53	81	48	51	107	87	122	Arms exports
Russia	4 382	4 601	4 505	5 769	6 554	6 589	6 754	6 942	7 684	8 350	Arms exports
	..	..	..	..	..	..	..	..	11 422	9 400	Arms export agreements
Slovakia	72	55	113	37	50	92	69	86	105	104	Licences for arms exports
South Africa	232	250	245	291	479	483	..	457	590	714	Licences for arms exports
Spain	194	159	251	310	506	575	574	1 132	1 326	1 368	Arms exports
	..	..	371	638	353	623	1 686	1 736	2 787	3 700	Licences for arms exports
Sweden	572	597	360	423	938	1 131	1 273	1 501	1 475	1 927	Arms exports
	1 119	633	2 813	723	1 306	1 007	2 235	2 176	1 050	1 457	Licences for arms exports
Switzerland	200	158	186	213	329	369	228	339	402	667	Arms exports
Turkey	109	154	163	297	387	223	372	376	436	576	Arms exports
Ukraine	..	625	608	598	585	..	..	..	727	800	Arms exports
United Kingdom	2 052	3 256	2 683	1 690	1 896	2 903	2 788	2 669	4 301	..	Arms exports
	..	..	3 382	3 601	5 930	4 211	4 135	3 194	1 865	3 612	Licences for arms exports
	10 549	8 961	7 282	9 043	9 329	9 488	7 996	10 861	20 052	8 010	Arms export agreements
United States	21 641	16 086	11 111	11 785	12 998	13 402	13 196	13 299	12 941	12 232	Arms exports
	18 387	21 849	13 789	15 549	16 944	14 455	14 115	17 116	25 667	37 796	Arms export agreements

.. = data not available.

[a] This figure is for the period 1 July 2003–30 June 2004.

[b] These figures exclude exports to the USA.

[c] These figures cover only exports of 'war weapons' as defined by German national legislation.

[d] This figure is for the period 1 Apr. 2008–31 Mar. 2009.

Sources: Published information or direct communication with governments or official industry bodies. For a full list of sources and all available financial data on arms exports see <http://www.sipri.org/research/armaments/transfers/measuring/financial_values>.

Appendix 7C. Transparency in arms transfers

MARK BROMLEY AND PAUL HOLTOM

I. Introduction

Official and publicly accessible data on arms transfers is important for assessing states' arms export and arms procurement policies. However, publishing data on arms sales and acquisitions is a sensitive issue for nearly all states. This appendix analyses recent developments in official international, regional and national reporting mechanisms which aim, in whole or in part, to increase the quality and quantity of publicly available information on international arms transfers.

Section II describes trends in reporting to the United Nations Register of Conventional Arms (UNROCA), while section III considers reporting on arms exports by individual states and by the European Union (EU). Section IV considers the available information on the brokers who arrange and facilitate arms sales. Confidential intergovernmental exchanges of information on arms transfers, such as those that occur within the Organization for Security and Co-operation in Europe (OSCE), the Organization of American States (OAS) and the Wassenaar Arrangement, are not addressed here.[1]

II. The United Nations Register of Conventional Arms

UNROCA is the key international mechanism of official transparency on arms transfers. Established in 1991, it requests all UN member states to report information about the export and import of seven categories of conventional weapons.[2] While UNROCA has made a significant contribution to greater public transparency in this area, a number of factors limit its utility, including incomplete submissions or non-submissions by certain states, discrepancies between different states' reports and the limited coverage of the reporting categories.[3]

---

[1] See also chapter 12 in this volume. Another source of information on the international arms trade is the customs data of the UN Commodity Trade Statistics Database (Comtrade). The Norwegian Initiative on Small Arms Transfers (NISAT) collects and collates customs data from Comtrade in order to produce an annual register of small arms exports. See the NISAT Small Arms Trade Database at <http://www.prio.no/NISAT/Small-Arms-Trade-Database/>. Comtrade data is not discussed in this appendix because it is neither intended nor designed to be a tool for increasing the amount of publicly available information on international arms transfers.

[2] The categories are battle tanks, armoured combat vehicles, large-calibre artillery systems, combat aircraft, attack helicopters, warships, and missiles or missile launchers. States are also invited to submit information on their holdings and procurement from domestic production of major conventional weapons as well as international transfers of small arms and light weapons.

[3] See Holtom, P., 'Nothing to report: the lost promise of the UN Register of Conventional Arms', *Contemporary Security Policy*, vol. 31, no. 1 (Apr. 2010), pp.61–87.

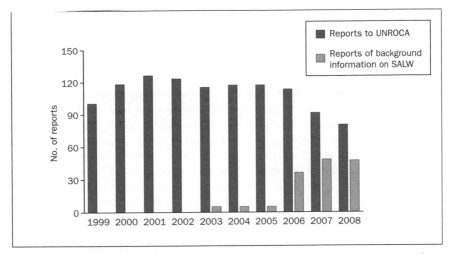

Figure 7C.1. Number of reports submitted to the United Nations Register of Conventional Arms (UNROCA), 1999–2008

SALW = small arms and light weapons.

Source: UNROCA database, <http://disarmament.un.org/un_register.nsf>.

The recent downward trend in states' participation in UNROCA continued during 2009 (see figure 7C.1). As of 31 December 2009, only 79 states had submitted reports on their arms transfers during 2008.[4] This is even fewer than the previous low of 85, in 1998. The drop reflects a fall in the number of states submitting 'nil reports'—a report that simply declares that the country neither imported nor exported arms—as 34 of the states that submitted a nil report for 2005 and 2006 did not report for 2007 or 2008. In 2009 a group of governmental experts (GGE) appointed by the UN Secretary-General to review the continuing operation and development of UNROCA reported that it 'was unable to make judgements about States' reasons for not submitting "nil" returns'.[5] However, it noted that 'outreach, updating national points of contact and follow-up by the Office for Disarmament Affairs' are essential for making states aware of this option.

There may be other reasons for a decline in reporting. Kenya submitted nil reports to UNROCA for 2005–2007, but as of December 2009 had not submitted a report for 2008. Kenya's nil report for 2007 was contradicted by sub-

---

[4] Indonesia submitted its report on 5 Jan. 2010, bringing the total number of submissions on arms transfers during 2008 to 80. In comparison, 90 states had reported to the Register by 31 Dec. 2008, 112 by 31 Dec. 2007 and 113 by 31 Dec. 2006. UNROCA database, <http://disarmament.un.org/un_register.nsf>.

[5] United Nations, General Assembly, 'Continuing operation of the United Nations Register of Conventional Arms and its further development', Note by the Secretary-General, A/64/296, 14 Aug. 2009, para. 19. GGE reviews take place every 3 years. One of the main tasks of each GGE is to consider ways to increase levels of reporting to UNROCA towards universal participation. The GGE reports of 1994, 1997, 2000, 2003 and 2006 are available at <http://www.un.org/disarmament/conv arms/Register/HTML/Register_GGE_Reports.html>.

missions by China and Ukraine that detailed exports to Kenya during 2007.[6] The discrepancy in reports, and allegations that Ukrainian exports to Kenya were actually transferred to the Government of Southern Sudan, led to negative publicity, which may have led Kenya to suspend its participation in UNROCA.

The conflict in South Ossetia in 2008 also appears to have had an impact on Georgia's participation in UNROCA. Georgia consistently submitted reports on its arms imports and exports for 1998–2007 but has not submitted a report for 2008. Since the Rose Revolution of November 2003, and the election of Mikheil Saakashvili as president, Russian officials have called for limits on 'destabilizing' arms transfers to Georgia. These calls have had a mixed impact. The Czech Republic, Turkey and Ukraine continued to supply arms to Georgia. However, it appears that bilateral pressure on Israel and states in the western Balkans led to some deals being cancelled.[7] Georgia's decision not to submit a report to UNROCA for 2008 may be an attempt to limit Russia's ability to monitor its arms imports.

Following limited but positive recommendations on expanding the scope of UNROCA by the 2003 and 2006 GGEs, it was hoped that the 2009 GGE would recommend further expansions, and thereby increase its relevance for UN members. Proposals to expand the existing categories were discussed, including several which have been discussed by previous GGEs: to include force-projection and force-multiplier systems, to amend the parameters of weapons covered by existing categories, and to include information on unmanned aerial vehicles (UAVs).[8] Following on from the positive response to the *invitation* to report background information on international transfers of small arms and light weapons (SALW), the GGE considered the case for *requesting* states to submit information on SALW transfers to a new, eighth category of UNROCA.[9]

The 2009 GGE did not recommend expansion of UNROCA and so there will be no changes to the scope of UNROCA before the next GGE in 2012. The 2009 GGE recognized that a new category for SALW would 'assist in monitoring and highlighting destabilizing accumulations of SALW' and noted the possibility of UNROCA losing relevance if it did not include SALW. However, the GGE failed to reach consensus on the creation of such a category.[10] The 2009 GGE report contained only one substantive recommendation: that the UN Secretary-General seek the views of member states on whether the absence of SALW as a full category in UNROCA has limited the relevance of the register and directly affected decisions on participation.[11]

---

[6] Bromley, M. and Kelly, N., 'Transparency in arms transfers', *SIPRI Yearbook 2009*, pp. 337–38.

[7] Holtom, P., 'Arms transfers to Georgia', Presentation at the Conference on Caucasus Studies: Migration–Society–Language, Malmö University, 28–30 Nov. 2008, <http://195.178.225.22/CSmsl/program.html>.

[8] United Nations, A/64/296 (note 5), para. 43-8.

[9] Forty-seven states reported on international transfers of SALW for 2008, representing more than half of the states that submitted reports to UNROCA. Sixty-five states have reported to UNROCA on international transfers of SALW at least once for 2005–2008.

[10] United Nations, A/64/296 (note 5) para. 51.

[11] United Nations, A/64/296 (note 5), para. 75.

III. National and regional reports on arms exports

Since the early 1990s an increasing number of governments have published national reports on arms exports.[12] As of January 2010, 32 states had published at least one national report on arms exports since 1990, and 28 have done so since 2006 (see table 7C.2 below).

Albania published its first national report on arms exports in December 2009, providing information on export and import licences granted during 2007 and 2008, broken down by the destination or origin of the goods.[13]

South Africa's National Conventional Arms Control Committee (NCACC), which oversees the implementation of the country's arms export policy, is legally obliged to provide the parliament and the public with annual reports on arms exports.[14] Despite this obligation, prior to 2009 the most recent public report, released in 2007, detailed arms transfers during 2003 and 2004.[15] Reports detailing transfers in 2005 and 2006 were presented to the parliament but were blocked from public release.[16] In August 2009 the opposition Democratic Alliance (DA) party attacked the NCACC's record on arms export controls, alleging that the NCACC had recently authorized—or was considering—transfers to Iran, Libya, Syria, Venezuela, Zimbabwe and North Korea.[17] In response, the ruling African National Congress (ANC) stated that the DA was potentially guilty of releasing classified information and the individuals involved could face up to 20 years in jail, although no action was taken.[18] Following the controversy, the NCACC gave its first briefing to parliament since August 2005 and released a public report detailing arms exports from South Africa in 2008.[19]

Under the European Union's Common Rules governing the control of exports of military technology and equipment (Common Rules), EU member states exchange data on the financial value of their export licence approvals and actual exports along with information on their denials of arms export licences. The data on licences and exports, along with aggregated data on denials, is compiled in a publicly available annual report. The EU published its

[12] A list of the published reports is maintained on the SIPRI website at <http://www.sipri.org/research/armaments/transfers/transparency/national_reports>.

[13] Albanian State Export Control Authority, *Annual Report on Export Control for 2007 and 2008* (Albanian Ministry of Defence: Tirana, 2009).

[14] National Conventional Arms Control Act, Act no. 41 of 2002, Assented to 12 Feb. 2003, *Government Gazette* (Cape Town), 20 Feb. 2003.

[15] South African National Conventional Arms Control Committee (NCACC), 2003 and 2004 annual reports, 2007, available on the SIPRI website (note 12).

[16] Democratic Alliance (DA), 'Arming dictators all over the world: National Conventional Arms Control Committee in crisis', 2 Aug. 2009, <http://www.da.org.za/newsroom.htm?action=view-news-item&id=7065>.

[17] Democratic Alliance (note 16).

[18] Ncana, N., 'ANC wants Maynier off arms panel', *The Times* (Johannesburg), 2 Sep. 2009.

[19] South African National Conventional Arms Control Committee (NCACC), 2008 annual reports, 27 Aug. 2009, available on the SIPRI website (note 12). See also Parliamentary Monitoring Group, 'National Conventional Arms Control Committee (NACC) Introductory & Annual Report 2008 briefing', 2 Sep. 2009, <http://www.pmg.org.za/print/18065>.

Table 7C.1. Numbers of EU member states submitting a complete data set to the EU annual report, 2004–2009[a]

Annual report	Year covered	No. of states making submissions	No. of states making full submissions	Proportion of states making full submissions (%)
11th	2009	27	19	70
10th	2008	27	17	63
9th	2007	25	15	60
8th	2006	25	17	68
7th	2005	25	13	52
6th	2004	22[b]	6	26

[a] A 'complete data set' is taken to be data on the financial value of both arms export licences issued and actual exports, broken down by both destination and EU Common Military List category.

[b] Because the 6th annual report covers export licences issued and actual exports in 2003, the 10 member states that joined the EU in May 2004 were not obliged to submit data. Instead, they were invited to submit figures for 2003 if they were available, which 7 of them did.

Source: Council of the European Union, EU annual reports, <http://www.consilium.europa. eu/showPage.aspx?id=1484>.

11th annual report in November 2009, covering transfers during 2008.[20] The level of detail on export licences and actual exports in the EU annual report has increased substantially since publication of the sixth annual report in 2004, when states were asked to submit data on the financial value of both arms export licences and actual arms exports, broken down by both destination and EU Common Military List category.

All 27 EU member states supplied information to the 11th annual report and 19 provided data for all requested categories. This is the highest proportion of states that have submitted a complete data set to the EU annual report since the enlargement of the EU in 2004 (see table 7C.1). However, the three largest arms exporters in the EU—France, Germany and the United Kingdom—all failed to make full submissions, thereby diluting the overall value of the report as a transparency instrument. Germany and the UK have long had technical difficulties with collecting and submitting data on actual arms exports disaggregated by EU Common Military List categories. The fact that the UK has decided to cease collecting data on actual arms exports is likely to further limit its ability to make full submissions to the EU annual report.[21]

In 2009 five states in South Eastern Europe—Albania, Bosnia and Herzegovina, the Former Yugoslav Republic of Macedonia (FYROM), Montenegro and Serbia—produced a regional report on arms exports, containing infor-

[20] Council of the European Union, Eleventh annual report according to Article 8(2) of Council Common Position 2008/944/CFSP defining common rules governing control of exports of military technology and equipment, *Official Journal of the European Union*, C265, 6 Nov. 2009. All 11 annual reports are available at <http://www.consilium.europa.eu/showPage.aspx?id=1484>.

[21] See appendix 7B.

mation on arms export licences granted during 2007.[22] The structure and format of the report are modelled on the EU annual report.[23] All of the participating states have already published national arms export reports, many of which contain more detailed information than the regional report. However, the publication of the regional report provides the first instance of the EU model of regional reporting being used by non-EU states.

IV. Publishing information on brokering licences

Governments and arms manufactures often rely on arms brokers to arrange and facilitate sales.[24] However, arms brokers have been implicated in facilitating the supply of arms to states subject to UN or regional arms embargoes along with terrorist, insurgent and organized crime groups and other 'undesirable' end-users. Effective controls on arms brokering are therefore widely seen as necessary for limiting illicit arms transfers. Information on the activities of arms brokers, and on states' interpretation of their brokering controls, remains largely outside the public domain. In recent years a number of states have started to provide some information on the individuals and companies that have been licensed to act as brokers or on approvals and denials of particular licences for brokering activities.

Since 2004 Estonia has published online information on companies or individuals that are registered to act as arms brokers, including the names of the individuals registered to act as brokers, the countries between which they can arrange transactions and the date of entry into the register.[25] Information on brokering authorizations and licences issued or denied is published in Estonia's Strategic Goods Commission activity reports.[26] Since 2005 the UK has included information on approvals and denials of licences for brokering activities by country of destination in its annual and quarterly arms export reports, giving information on the exporter country, the number of licences

---

[22] States reached agreement on producing the report in June 2009 and it was published by the South Eastern and Eastern Europe Clearinghouse for the Control of Small Arms and Light Weapons (SEESAC) in Dec. 2009. SEESAC, *Regional Report on Arms Exports in 2007* (SEESAC: Belgrade, 2009).

[23] The possibility of producing a regional version of the EU annual report for South Eastern Europe was discussed during an EU-sponsored outreach event in Slovenia in May 2008. Council of the European Union, Tenth Annual Report according to Operative Provision 8 of the European Code of Conduct on Arms Exports', *Official Journal of the European Union*, C300, 22 Nov. 2008, p. 2.

[24] One definition of a broker (in this case, of SALW) is 'a person or entity acting as an intermediary that brings together relevant parties and arranges or facilitates a potential transaction of small arms and light weapons in return for some form of benefit, whether financial or otherwise.' United Nations, General Assembly, Report of the Group of Governmental Experts established pursuant to General Assembly resolution 60/81 to consider further steps to enhance international cooperation in preventing, combating and eradicating illicit brokering in small arms and light weapons, A/62/163, 30 Aug. 2007, Para. 8.

[25] Estonian Ministry of Foreign Affairs, 'Registered brokers of military goods', <http://www.vm.ee/?q=en/node/5035>.

[26] The activity reports of the Estonian Strategic Goods Commission are available at <http://www.vm.ee/?q=en/node/5039>.

issued or denied, and a description of the goods.[27] Since 2006, Romania's annual and quarterly arms export reports have included perhaps the most detailed information released by any state on approvals and denials of brokering licences and actual transfers covered by brokering licences.[28] Information is sorted by the country of destination and military list category and includes the exporter country, the number of licences issued or denied, the criteria under which any licences were refused, and a description of the goods concerned.

In June 2003 the Council of the European Union adopted Common Position 2003/468/CFSP, aimed at setting agreed minimum standards in the control of arms brokering across all EU member states. The common position requires member states to establish a system for exchanging information on brokering activities including denials of brokering licence applications.[29] In April 2008 member states agreed to share information on approvals of brokering licences and to publish information on approvals and denials of brokering licences in the EU annual report.[30] The 11th annual report contains a table providing information on brokering licences granted and denied by the EU member states during 2008.[31] The table presents information broken down by either destination or individual licence—depending on the reporting state—and includes details of the destination of the goods, the origin of the goods, their financial value, their EU Common Military List category and the quantity of items involved. Although in several cases not all categories of information have been provided, the table is a notable boost to transparency in this area. It provides details of brokering licences issued by 11 EU member states, the majority of which have not previously published such detailed information.[32]

---

[27] The reports are available on the website of the British Department for Business, Innovation and Skills, <http://www.exportcontroldb.bis.gov.uk/>.

[28] The reports are available on the SIPRI website (note 12).

[29] Council of the European Union, Council Common Position 2003/468/CFSP of 23 June 2003 on the control of arms brokering, *Official Journal of the European Union*, L159, 25 June 2003, Article 5.

[30] Council of the European Union (note 23), p. 3.

[31] Council of the European Union (note 20).

[32] The states are Austria, Bulgaria, the Czech Republic, Germany, Lithuania, the Netherlands, Poland, Romania, Spain, Sweden and the UK.

Table 7C.2. States participating in international, regional, and national reporting mechanisms which aim, in whole or in part, to increase the quality of publicly available information on international arms transfers, 2007–2009

An x denotes that the state reported at least once in the period 2007–2009.

State	UNROCA Exports or imports	UNROCA Background information on SALW	National report Exports	National report Licence denials[a]	European Union annual report Exports	European Union annual report Complete data set[b]
Albania	x (nil)	x	x			
Andorra	x (nil)					
Antigua and Barbuda	x (nil)	x				
Argentina	x	x (nil)				
Armenia	x (nil)	x				
Australia	x	x				
Austria	x		x		x	x
Azerbaijan	x					
Bahamas	x (nil)					
Bangladesh	x	x				
Belarus	x		x			
Belgium	x	x	x[c]		x	
Belize	x (nil)					
Bhutan	x (nil)					
Bolivia	x (nil)	x				
Bosnia and Herzegovina	x	x	x	x		
Brazil	x					
Brunei Darussalam	x (nil)	x				
Bulgaria	x	x	x		x	x
Burkina Faso	x					
Burundi	x (nil)					
Canada	x	x	x			
Chile	x	x				
China	x					
Colombia	x	x				
Comoros	x (nil)					
Cook Islands	x (nil)					
Costa Rica	x (nil)					
Croatia	x	x				
Cuba	x (nil)					
Cyprus	x	x			x	x
Czech Republic	x	x	x	x	x	x
Denmark	x	x	x	x	x	
Djibouti	x (nil)					
El Salvador	x (nil)	x (nil)				
Estonia	x		x		x	x
Fiji	x (nil)	x (nil)				
Finland	x		x		x	x
France	x	x	x		x	

State	UNROCA		National report		European Union annual report	
	Exports or imports	Background information on SALW	Exports	Licence denials[a]	Exports	Complete data set[b]
Gabon	x (nil)					
Gambia	x (nil)					
Georgia	x	x				
Germany	x	x	x	x	x	
Ghana	x (nil)	x (nil)				
Greece	x	x			x	x
Grenada	x (nil)					
Guatemala	x (nil)					
Haiti	x (nil)	x				
Hungary	x	x			x	x
Iceland	x (nil)					
India	x					
Indonesia	x	x				
Ireland	x	x			x	x
Israel	x					
Italy	x	x	x		x	
Jamaica		x (nil)				
Japan[d]	x (nil)					
Jordan	x					
Kazakhstan	x	x				
Kenya	x (nil)					
Kiribati	x (nil)					
South Korea	x	x				
Kyrgyzstan	x (nil)					
Latvia	x	x			x	x
Lebanon	x (nil)	x (nil)				
Liechtenstein	x (nil)	x				
Lithuania	x	x			x	x
Luxembourg	x (nil)	x			x (nil)	x (nil)
Malaysia	x					
Maldives	x (nil)					
FYROM	x (nil)		x			
Mali	x (nil)	x (nil)				
Malta	x (nil)	x (nil)			x	x
Mauritius	x (nil)					
Mexico	x	x				
Micronesia	x (nil)					
Moldova	x (nil)	x				
Monaco	x (nil)					
Mongolia	x (nil)					
Montenegro	x	x	x	x		
Mozambique	x (nil)					
Namibia	x (nil)					
Nauru	x (nil)					
Netherlands	x	x	x	x	x	x
New Zealand	x	x				
Nicaragua	x (nil)					

| State | UNROCA | | National report | | European Union annual report | |
	Exports or imports	Background information on SALW	Exports	Licence denials[a]	Exports	Complete data set[b]
Norway	x	x	x	x		
Pakistan	x					
Palau	x (nil)					
Panama	x (nil)	x				
Paraguay	x (nil)					
Peru	x	x				
Philippines	x	x				
Poland	x	x			x	
Portugal	x	x	x		x	x
Romania	x	x	x	x	x	x
Russia	x					
Saint Lucia	x (nil)	x (nil)				
Saint Vincent and the Grenadines	x (nil)	x				
Samoa	x (nil)					
San Marino	x (nil)					
Senegal	x	x				
Serbia	x (nil)		x	x		
Seychelles	x (nil)					
Sierra Leone	x (nil)					
Singapore	x					
Slovakia	x	x	x		x	x
Slovenia	x	x	x		x	x
Solomon Islands	x (nil)					
South Africa	x					
Spain	x		x		x	x
Suriname	x (nil)					
Swaziland	x (nil)	x (nil)				
Sweden	x	x[e]	x		x	
Switzerland	x	x	x			
Tajikistan	x (nil)					
Togo	x (nil)	x (nil)				
Tonga	x (nil)					
Trinidad and Tobago		x				
Turkey	x	x				
Tuvalu	x (nil)					
Ukraine	x	x	x			
United Kingdom	x	x	x	x	x	
United States	x		x			
Viet Nam	x (nil)					
Zambia	x (nil)					
126 states	**124 (63 nil)**	**65 (11 nil)**	**29**	**10**	**27**	**19**

FYROM = Former Yugoslav Republic of Macedonia; SALW = small arms and light weapons.

Note: The European Union Annual Report is the annual report according to Article 8(2) of Council Common Position 2008/944/CFSP defining Common Rules governing control of exports of military technology and equipment and, until 2008, the annual report according to Operative Provision 8 of the European Union Code of Conduct on Arms Exports.

[a] A country is marked as providing information about export licence denials if it identify the countries for which export licences have been denied.

[b] A country is marked as providing information on all categories submitted if it provided data on the financial value of both arms export licences and actual arms exports, broken down by both destination and EU Military List category.

[c] Since early 2003 the 3 regional governments of Belgium (Brussels, Flanders and Wallonia) have been responsible for reporting on export licences and exports.

[d] Japan submitted background information to UNROCA on the procurement of SALW through national production in 2006, 2007 and 2008.

[e] Sweden did not submit information on the number of SALW imported and exported, only the categories of weapon systems, and the origin or destination.

Sources: UNROCA database, <http://disarmament.un.org/un_register.nsf>; national reports, <http://www.sipri.org/research/armaments/transfers/transparency/national_reports/>; and Council of the European Union, EU annual reports, <http://consilium.europa.eu/cms3_fo/showPage.asp?id=1484>.

8. World nuclear forces

SHANNON N. KILE, VITALY FEDCHENKO, BHARATH GOPALASWAMY AND
HANS M. KRISTENSEN

I. Introduction

At the start of 2010 eight nuclear weapon states possessed more than 7500
operational nuclear weapons (see table 8.1). Almost 2000 of these are kept
in a state of high operational alert. If all nuclear warheads are counted—
operational warheads, spares, those in both active and inactive storage, and
intact warheads scheduled for dismantlement—the United States, the Russian Federation, the United Kingdom, France, China, India, Pakistan and
Israel together possess a total of more than 22 000 warheads.

All five legally recognized nuclear weapon states, as defined by the 1968
Treaty on the Non-Proliferation of Nuclear Weapons (Non-Proliferation
Treaty, NPT)—China, France, Russia, the UK and the USA—appear determined to remain nuclear powers and are either modernizing or about to
modernize their nuclear forces.[1] At the same time, Russia and the USA are
in the process of reducing their operational nuclear forces from cold war
levels as a result of two bilateral treaties—the 1991 Treaty on the Reduction
and Limitation of Strategic Offensive Arms (START Treaty) and the 2002
Treaty on Strategic Offensive Reductions (SORT).[2] Sections II and III of
this chapter discuss the composition of the deployed nuclear forces of the
USA and Russia, respectively. The nuclear arsenals of the other three
nuclear weapon states are considerably smaller, but all three states are
either deploying new weapons or have announced their intention to do so.
Sections IV–VI present data on the delivery vehicles and warhead stockpiles of the UK, France and China, respectively.

Reliable information on the operational status of the nuclear arsenals and
capabilities of the three states that have never been party to the NPT—
India, Israel and Pakistan—is difficult to find. In the absence of official
declarations, the available information is often contradictory or incorrect.
India and Pakistan are expanding their nuclear strike capabilities, while
Israel appears to be waiting to see how the situation in Iran develops. Sections VII–IX provide information about the Indian, Pakistani and Israeli

---

[1] According to the NPT, only states that manufactured and exploded a nuclear device prior to
1 Jan. 1967 are recognized as nuclear weapon states. For a summary and other details of the NPT see
annex A in this volume.

[2] For summaries and other details of the START and SORT treaties see annex A in this volume.

Table 8.1. World nuclear forces, January 2010

All figures are approximate.

Country[a]	Year of first nuclear test	Deployed warheads[b]	Other warheads[c]	Total
United States	1945	2 468	~7 100[d]	~9 600
Russia	1949	4 630	7 300[e]	~12 000
United Kingdom	1952	160	65	225
France	1960	300	–	300
China	1964	..	200[f]	240
India	1974	..	60–80[g]	60–80
Pakistan	1998	..	70–90[g]	70–90
Israel	..	..	80[g]	80
Total		~7 560	~14 900	~22 600

[a] North Korea conducted nuclear test explosions in 2006 and 2009, but there is no public information to verify that it has operational nuclear weapons.

[b] 'Deployed' means on missiles or bases with operational forces.

[c] These are warheads in reserve, awaiting dismantlement or that require some preparation (e.g. assembly or loading on launchers) before they become fully operationally available.

[d] This figure includes 2600 in reserve in the US Department of Defense stockpile (for a total stockpile of c. 5100 warheads). A further 3500–4500 are scheduled to be dismantled by 2022.

[e] This figure includes warheads in reserve or awaiting dismantlement.

[f] China's warheads are not thought to be deployed on launchers.

[g] The stockpiles of India, Pakistan and Israel are thought to be only partly deployed.

nuclear arsenals, respectively. The nuclear capabilities of the Democratic People's Republic of Korea (DPRK, or North Korea) are discussed in section X. Brief conclusions are given in section XI.

Appendix 8A contains tables of global stocks of fissile materials—highly enriched uranium (HEU) and separated plutonium, the raw material for nuclear weapons. Appendix 8B gives details of nuclear explosions since 1945, with details of the May 2009 explosion in North Korea, which took the total number of explosions to 2054.

The figures presented here are estimates based on public information and contain some uncertainties, as reflected in the notes to the tables.

II. US nuclear forces

As of January 2010 the USA maintained an estimated arsenal of approximately 2468 operational nuclear warheads, consisting of roughly 1968 strategic and 500 non-strategic warheads (see table 8.2). In addition to this operational arsenal, approximately 2600 warheads are held in reserve, for a total stockpile of approximately 5100 warheads. Several thousand more retired warheads are awaiting dismantlement.

This force level is a slight change compared with the estimate presented in *SIPRI Yearbook 2009*.[3] The change reflects the limited additional withdrawal from deployment of warheads on strategic nuclear delivery vehicles (intercontinental ballistic missiles, ICBMs; submarine-launched ballistic missiles, SLBMs; and long-range bombers), which has allowed the USA to go below the limit of 2200 operationally deployed strategic warheads three-and-a-half-years before the deadline set under SORT.[4]

The 2010 START Treaty, signed by US President Barack Obama and Russian President Dmitry Medvedev on 8 April 2010, will set a force level of 700 deployed strategic delivery vehicles and 1550 for their associated warheads to be reached seven years after ratification.[5] This represents a modest reduction in the level of 1700–2200 operationally deployed strategic warheads set by SORT and 1600 strategic delivery vehicles set by the 1991 START treaty.

The Nuclear Posture Review (NPR) published in April 2010 will set the US nuclear posture for the next 5–10 years.[6] Previous US Government proposals—as formulated in the 2001 NPR[7]—to build a new nuclear weapon production facility with a capacity to produce hundreds of nuclear weapons per year (later scaled back to 50–80 per year) were reformulated in December 2008 to a proposal to build a Chemistry and Metallurgy Research Replacement–Nuclear Facility (CMRR–NF) at Los Alamos National Laboratory (LANL) that would have a limited capacity to produce 20 pits (plutonium cores) per year and an emergency capacity of 80 pits.[8] The shift limits the vision presented by the 2001 NPR to create a 'responsive infrastructure' capable of quickly producing large numbers of warheads in response to unexpected developments.

A study completed in 2009 by the JASON panel of the Mitre Corporation rejects claims that it was necessary to build replacement warheads because of difficulties with certifying the reliability of existing warheads.[9] Even so, a

---

[3] Kile, S. N., Fedchenko, V. and Kristensen, H. M., 'World nuclear forces', *SIPRI Yearbook 2009*.

[4] Norris, R. S. and Kristensen, H. M., 'Nuclear notebook: U.S. nuclear forces, 2009', *Bulletin of the Atomic Scientists*, vol. 65, no. 2 (Mar. 2009). Under SORT, Russia and the USA are obligated to reduce their aggregate number of operationally deployed strategic nuclear warheads to no more than 1700–2200 each by 31 Dec. 2012.

[5] For a summary and other details of the New START Treaty see annex A in this volume.

[6] US Department of Defense (DOD), *Nuclear Posture Review Report* (DOD: Washington, DC, Apr. 2010).

[7] US Department of Defense, 'Special briefing on the Nuclear Posture Review', Transcript, 9 Jan. 2002, <http://www.defense.gov/transcripts/transcript.aspx?transcriptid=1108>. See also Kristensen, H. M. and Handler, J., 'World nuclear forces', *SIPRI Yearbook 2002*, pp. 527–28.

[8] US Department of Energy, National Nuclear Security Administration, 'Record of decision for the complex transformation supplemental programmatic environmental impact statement—operations involving plutonium, uranium, and the assembly and disassembly of nuclear weapons', *Federal Register*, vol. 73, no. 245 (19 Dec. 2008), pp. 77 644–56.

[9] JASON Program Office, *Life Extension Program (LEP)*, Executive Summary, Mitre Corporation, 9 Sep. 2009. The JASON panel is a group of independent scientists that advises the US Government on matters of science and technology.

Table 8.2. US nuclear forces, January 2010

Type	Designation	No. deployed	Year first deployed	Range (km)[a]	Warheads x yield	No. of warheads
Strategic forces						**1 968**
Bombers[b]		*113/60*				*316*
B-52H	Stratofortress	93/44	1961	16 000	ALCM 5–150 kt	216[c]
B-2	Spirit	20/16	1994	11 000	B61-7, -11, B83-1 bombs	100[d]
ICBMs		*450*				*500*
LGM-30G	Minuteman III					
	Mk-12[e]	(0)	1970	13 000	1–3 x 170 kt	(0)[e]
	Mk-12A	250	1979	13 000	1–3 x 335 kt	250
	Mk-21 SERV	200	2006	13 000	1 x 300 kt	250
SSBNs/SLBMs		*228*				*1 152*
UGM-133A	Trident II (D5)[f]					
	Mk-4	..	1992	>7 400	4 x 100 kt	568
	Mk-4A	..	2008	>7 400	4 x 100 kt	200
	Mk-5	..	1990	>7 400	4 x 475 kt	384
Non-strategic forces						**500**
B61-3, -4 bombs[g]		..	1979	..	0.3–170 kt	400
Tomahawk SLCM		..	1984	2 500	1 x 5–150 kt	(100)[h]
Total						**2 468[i]**

.. = not available or not applicable; ( ) = uncertain figure; ALCM = air-launched cruise missile; ICBM = intercontinental ballistic missile; kt = kiloton; SERV = security-enhanced re-entry vehicle; SLBM = submarine-launched ballistic missile; SLCM = sea-launched cruise missile; SSBN = nuclear-powered ballistic missile submarine.

[a] Aircraft range is for illustrative purposes only; actual mission range will vary according to flight profile and weapon loading.

[b] For bombers, the first figure in the 'No. deployed' column is the total number in the inventory, including those for training, test and reserve. The second figure is for the primary mission inventory aircraft (i.e. the number of operational aircraft assigned for nuclear and conventional wartime missions).

[c] All advanced cruise missiles (ACMs) have been retired and the total ALCM inventory has been reduced to 528, of which an estimated 216 are deployed on two bases. Under the 2010 New START Treaty, each nuclear bomber is attributed only 1 weapon.

[d] Operational gravity bombs are only included for the B-2A bomber. The B-52H can also deliver bombs, but its nuclear mission is thought to be focused on ALCM since the bomber is not capable of penetrating modern air defence systems.

[e] The Department of Defense missed the Sep. 2009 deadline for fully retiring the W62 warhead (which is loaded in the Mk-12 re-entry vehicle), although all have probably been removed from operational missiles.

[f] Although D5 missiles are counted under START as carrying 8 warheads each, the US Navy is estimated to have downloaded each missile to an average of 4 warheads to meet the SORT-mandated warhead ceiling. Delivery of the W76-1 warhead began in Oct. 2008.

[g] The number of B61 bombs deployed in Europe was reduced by half between 2005 and 2006, to roughly 200.

[h] Another 190 W80-0 warheads are in inactive storage; the life-extension programme for the warhead has been deferred. The TLAM/N is being retired.

^{i} Including the additional *c.* 2600 warheads in reserve, the total stockpile is *c.* 5100 warheads. There are another 3500–4500 additional warheads awaiting dismantlement and a further *c.* 14 000 plutonium pits are stored at the Pantex Plant in Texas.

Sources: US Department of Defense, various budget reports and press releases; US Department of Energy, various budget reports and plans; US Department of State, START I Treaty Memoranda of Understanding, 1990–July 2009; US Department of Defense, various documents obtained under the Freedom of Information Act; US Air Force, US Navy and US Department of Energy, personal communication; 'Nuclear notebook', *Bulletin of the Atomic Scientists*, various issues; and authors' estimates.

debate is expected in 2010 on how much life extension programmes can change the designs of existing warheads.

In parallel with efforts to reduce the nuclear stockpile, the US Department of Defense (DOD) has revised its nuclear-strike plans to reflect new presidential guidance and a transition in war planning from the Single Integrated Operational Plan (SIOP) of the cold war to a set of smaller and more flexible strike plans. An updated strategic war plan—OPLAN (Operations Plan) 8010-08 Strategic Deterrence and Global Strike—was put into effect in December 2008, with an update published in February 2009. It focuses on Russia and China but also includes a series of strike options against four other adversaries. The plan is predominantly nuclear but also includes conventional strike options.[10]

To exercise OPLAN 8010, the US Strategic Command (STRATCOM) conducted the Global Thunder 09 nuclear exercise in September 2009 to test the readiness of ballistic missiles and long-range bombers. Shortly after the exercise, Russia requested an 'open display' of B-2 bombers at Whiteman Air Force Base (AFB), Missouri, and an ICBM re-entry vehicle on-site inspection at Warren AFB, Wyoming, in accordance with START.[11] These were the last Russian inspections in the USA under the treaty before it expired on 5 December 2009.

In an effort to increase the readiness and proficiency of its nuclear mission, the US Air Force (USAF) reorganized its nuclear command structure. The Air Force Global Strike Command (AFGSC) was formally activated at Barksdale AFB, Louisiana, on 7 August 2009. The new command took control of the USAF's ICBMs on 1 December 2009 and of its long-range bombers on 1 February 2010; this consolidated all strategic USAF wings

---

[10] Kristensen, H. M., 'Obama and the nuclear war plan', Federation of American Scientists (FAS) Strategic Security Blog, Feb. 2010, <http://www.fas.org/blog/ssp/2010/02/warplan.php>; and Kristensen, H. M., Norris, R. S. and Oelich, I., *From Counterforce to Minimal Deterrence* (Federation of American Scientists/Natural Resources Defense Council: Washington, DC, Apr. 2009). See also Kile, Fedchenko and Kristensen (note 3), p. 349.

[11] Knee, D., 'Russians make history as START draws to end', *Air Force Print News Today*, 15 Sep. 2009, <http://www.warren.af.mil/news/story.asp?id=123181490>.

under one command.[12] When fully operational, AFGSC will consist of more than 23 000 people. In addition, the standardization and training of nuclear inspection teams have been changed to improve the quality of the 10–14 nuclear surety inspections that are performed across the major commands each year.[13]

Strategic bombers

The US Air Force has 20 B-2 and 93 B-52H bombers, of which 16 and 44, respectively, are thought to have nuclear missions. The USAF is studying options for a new nuclear-capable long-range strike aircraft to begin replacing the current bomber force from 2018.[14]

Approximately 316 nuclear warheads are estimated to be deployed with the bombers, including the aircraft-delivered B61-7, B61-11 (on the B-2 only) and B83-1 gravity bombs and the W80-1 warhead carried on air-launched cruise missiles (ALCMs, on the B-52H only). Most of USAF ALCMs and bombs have been withdrawn from service due to the accelerated implementation of the 2004 Nuclear Weapons Stockpile Plan and to meet the SORT limit.

Land-based ballistic missiles

The US ICBM force is changing significantly as part of the implementation of SORT. Approximately 500 warheads were deployed on 450 ICBMs as of January 2010, a reduction of 50 warheads compared with 2009. All W62 warheads have probably been removed from operational missiles, although the DOD missed its September 2009 deadline for retiring the weapon completely. As the 170-kiloton W62 is removed from the missiles, the modern 300-kt W87/Mk-21 security enhanced re-entry vehicle (SERV) is being installed. The increased power of the W87 warhead broadens the range of targets of the Minuteman III ICBM force. All missiles will carry only one warhead each, but several hundred additional warheads will be kept in storage for future upload if necessary.

The multi-year $7 billion upgrade of the Minuteman III force is nearly complete. The service life of the Minuteman III missile has been extended to 2030, delaying plans to deploy a replacement ICBM in 2018. Develop-

[12] US Air Force, Air Force Global Strike Command, 'Air Force Global Strike Command officials assume B-52, B-2 mission', News release, 1 Feb. 2010, <http://www.afgsc.af.mil/news/story.asp?id=123188329>.
[13] US Air Force Inspection Agency, 'Air Force officials establish core team for nuclear surety inspections', 31 Aug. 2009, <http://www.af.mil/news/story.asp?id=123159500>.
[14] US Department of Defense, 'Aircraft investment plan, fiscal years (FY) 2011–2040', Submitted with the FY 2011 budget, Feb. 2010, <http://www.militarytimes.com/static/projects/pages/30year aviation.pdf>.

ment work on a follow-on missile continues, to replace the Minuteman III in 2030–40.

There were two Minuteman III flight tests in 2009, compared to four in 2008. A missile taken from Minot AFB, North Dakota, was launched from Vandenberg AFB, California, on 29 June. The three unarmed W78/Mk-12A re-entry vehicles landed near Kwajalein Atoll, Marshall Islands, approximately 6740 kilometres away.[15] On 23 August a Minuteman III, probably taken from Malmstrom AFB, Montana, was test-launched with a single re-entry vehicle to the same range.[16]

In addition to test launches, the ICBM wings conducted several nuclear exercises during 2009. In June, 11 national agencies and 1300 personnel conducted Nuclear Weapons Accident/Incident Exercise 2009 at Warren AFB in a simulated terrorist attack against the base. This was the largest and most complex exercise ever conducted at an ICBM base.[17]

Ballistic missile submarines

On 27 March 2009 the USS *Alaska* nuclear-powered ballistic missile submarine (SSBN) arrived at Kings Bay Naval Submarine Base, Georgia, after completing a 26-month refuelling overhaul at Norfolk Naval Shipyard, Virginia. The submarine was previously based at Bangor Naval Submarine Base, Washington. The transfer to the Atlantic Ocean increases the number of SSBNs based at Kings Bay from five to six. The remaining eight SSBNs are based at Kitsap Naval Base near Bangor, Washington. Similarly to the USAF command reorganization, the US Navy decided in 2009 to split command of its Trident submarine groups into two, one overseeing Submarine Group 10 at Kings Bay and the other overseeing Submarine Group 9 at Kitsap. Submarine Group 10 will be further subdivided, with one commodore for the SSBNs of Submarine Squadron 20 and another for the nuclear-powered cruise missile submarines (SSGNs) of Submarine Squadron 16.[18]

All 14 US Navy Ohio Class SSBNs carry Trident II (D5) missiles. Twelve operational SSBNs carry a total of 288 D5 SLBMs, which are estimated to carry an average of 4 warheads each, for a total of about 1152 warheads. (Two additional SSBNs are undergoing overhaul at any given time, and

[15] US Air Force, Vandenberg Air Force Base, 'Vandenberg successfully launches Minuteman III', News release, 29 June 2009, <http://www.vandenberg.af.mil/news/story.asp?id=123156457>.

[16] US Air Force, Vandenberg Air Force Base, 'Vandenberg launches Minuteman III', News release, 23 Aug. 2009, <http://www.vandenberg.af.mil/news/story.asp?id=123164556>.

[17] US Air Force, Warren Air Force Base, 'Warren hosts national-level exercise', News release, 26 June 2009, <http://www.warren.af.mil/news/story.asp?id=123156188>.

[18] US Navy, Submarine Group 10 Public Affairs, 'Navy's only combined submarine squadron splits to enhance warfighting readiness', 30 Mar. 2009, <http://www.navy.mil/search/display.asp?story_id=43845>.

their 48 missiles and 192 warheads are not included in the total.) With eight SSBNs based in the Pacific Ocean and six in the Atlantic Ocean, and a patrol rate comparable to that during the cold war, more than 60 per cent of US SSBN patrols now take place in the Pacific (compared to an average of only 15 per cent during the 1980s). This change reflects a shift in focus of the USA's post-cold war planners to China and other potential adversaries in the Pacific region.

The rate of production of the D5LE SLBM, a modified version of the D5, which began in 2008, doubled to 24 missiles in 2009. A total of 108 missiles will be purchased by 2012, at a cost of more than $4 billion.[19] The first D5LE will be deployed in 2010. The modified D5 will arm the Ohio Class SSBNs for the rest of their service lives, which have been extended from 30 to 44 years.

The oldest SSBN is scheduled to retire in 2027 followed by the next boat in 2030, reducing the SSBN force to 12. To offset subsequent retirements, the US Navy plans to begin construction of the first of a new SSBN class in 2019, the second in 2022, and one each year in 2024–33.[20] The first SSBN(X), as the new class is currently called, is scheduled to become operational in 2029. It is likely to carry fewer missiles than the current Ohio Class—probably 16—to permit more boats under future arms control agreements and provide greater operational flexibility. The new SSBN programme is projected to cost at least $80 billion.[21]

Delivery of the W76-1/Mk-4A warhead, a modernized version of the existing W76/Mk-4, began in 2008. The W76-1/Mk-4A warhead is equipped with a new fuse that allows more flexibility in setting the height of burst to 'enable W76 to take advantage of [the] higher accuracy of [the] D5 missile' and bring more targets, including hard targets, within range.[22] The first warhead was delivered to the US Navy in late October 2008, and entered the stockpile in late-February 2009. Production of approximately 2000 W76-1 warheads is planned up to 2017, four years earlier than previously planned.[23]

During 2009, US SSBNs test-launched four D5 missiles: one from the USS *Alabama* in the Pacific on 13 February; two from the USS *West Virginia* in the Atlantic on 3–4 September; and one from the USS *Alaska* in the

[19] US Department of the Navy, *Fiscal Year (FY) 2010 Budget Estimates, Justification of Estimates: Weapons Procurement (P-1)* (Department of the Navy: Washington, DC, May 2009), pp. 1–5.

[20] O'Rourke, R., *Navy Force Structure and Shipbuilding Plans: Background and Issues for Congress*, Congressional Research Service (CRS) Report for Congress RL32665 (US Congress, CRS: Washington, DC, 22 Dec. 2009), pp. 7, 11.

[21] O'Rourke (note 20), p. 29.

[22] US Department of Energy (DOE), Office of Defense Programs, *Stockpile Stewardship and Management Plan: First Annual Update*, partially declassified and released under the US Freedom of Information Act (DOE: Washington, DC, Oct. 1997), p. 1-14.

[23] Norris, R. S. and Kristensen, H. M., 'Nuclear notebook: U.S. nuclear forces, 2010', *Bulletin of the Atomic Scientists*, vol. 66, no. 3 (May/June 2010).

Atlantic on 19 December, marking the 130th consecutive successful flight test of the D5 since 1989.

Non-strategic nuclear weapons[24]

As of January 2010 the USA retained approximately 500 active non-strategic nuclear warheads. These consisted of approximately 400 B61 gravity bombs and 100 W80-0 warheads for the sea-launched Tomahawk cruise missiles (TLAM/Ns, from Tomahawk land-attack missile, nuclear). Another 800 non-strategic warheads, including 190 W80-0 warheads, are in inactive storage.

Approximately 200 B61 bombs are deployed in Europe at six airbases in five European members of the North Atlantic Treaty Organization (NATO): Belgium, Germany, Italy, the Netherlands and Turkey.[25] The aircraft of non-nuclear weapon NATO countries that are assigned nuclear strike missions with US nuclear weapons include Belgian and Dutch F-16 aircraft and German and Italian Tornado combat aircraft. The US arsenal in Europe may include inactive bombs. A portion of the new Joint Strike Fighter (F-35 Block IV) force may eventually be nuclear-capable.

TLAM/Ns are earmarked for deployment on selected Los Angeles, Improved Los Angeles and Virginia Class nuclear-powered attack submarines (SSNs, from ship submersible nuclear). TLAM/Ns have not been deployed since 1992, and will be retired in the near future.[26]

Nuclear warhead stockpile management and modernization

The total US stockpile of roughly 5100 warheads is organized in two overall categories: active and inactive warheads. The deployed category includes 2468 intact warheads (with all the components) that are deployed on operational delivery systems. The approximately 2600 non-deployed warheads are either (*a*) active in the 'responsive force' that can be deployed on operational delivery systems in a relatively short time, or (*b*) inactive in long-term storage with their limited-life components (e.g. tritium) removed. In addition, 3500–4500 other warheads are awaiting dismantlement.

The USA keeps nearly 5000 pits (cores) in storage at the Pantex Plant as a strategic reserve. Another 9000 pits held at Pantex make up most of the

---

[24] The sizes of the Russian and US inventories of non-strategic nuclear weapons are not limited by any legally binding arms control agreement, including the 2010 New START Treaty.

[25] All B61 bombs were apparently withdrawn from Ramstein Air Base, Germany, in 2005 and RAF Lakenheath, UK, in 2008. On the history and status of US nuclear weapons in Europe see Kristensen, H. M., 'U.S. nuclear weapons removed from the United Kingdom', FAS Strategic Security Blog, Federation of American Scientists, 26 June 2008, <http://www.fas.org/blog/ssp/2008/06/us-nuclear-weapons-withdrawn-from-the-united-kingdom.php>.

[26] Norris and Kristensen (note 23).

43 tonnes of weapon-grade plutonium previously declared in excess of military needs since 1993.[27] All of these pits come from retired warheads. Approximately 5000 canned assemblies (thermonuclear secondaries) are kept at the Oak Ridge Y-12 Plant, Tennessee.

III. Russian nuclear forces

As of January 2010 Russia had an estimated 4500 operational nuclear warheads (see table 8.3). Russia continues to reduce its strategic nuclear forces in accordance with its commitments under SORT and as part of a doctrinal shift away from a 'substantially redundant' (*suschestvenno izbytochnyi*) towards a 'minimally sufficient' (*garantirovanno dostatochnyi*) deterrence posture. Russia's new National Security Strategy, approved in May 2009, states that it will maintain parity with the USA in the area of offensive strategic weapons in the most cost-effective way.[28] According to a senior Russian military planner, Russia's strategic nuclear forces can guarantee 'minimally sufficient' deterrence until 2015–20 within the force ceilings imposed by SORT, even if the USA develops a ballistic missile defence (BMD) system. However, he added that the strategic forces would need qualitative improvements to enhance their survivability and ability to penetrate missile defences in the future.[29] As explained by a Russian missile designer, 'enhanced survivability' refers to the newer missile systems' ability to deliver both launch-on-warning and second-strike capabilities in response to a nuclear attack.[30] In light of these criteria, Russia has prioritized the development and deployment of a road-mobile ICBM with multiple independently-targetable re-entry vehicles (MIRVs) and a new type of SLBM.

Strategic bombers

Russia's strategic aviation units are grouped under the 37th Air Army of the Supreme High Command (Strategic) of the Russian Air Force. They include the 22nd Guards Heavy Bomber Division (Engels and Ryazan), with 13 Tu-160, 16 Tu-95MS16 and 7 Tu-95MS6 aircraft; and the 326th Heavy Bomber Division (Ukrainka), with 15 Tu-95MS16 and 25 Tu-95MS6 aircraft. The 37th Air Army also comprises four divisions of Tu-22M3

---

[27] On the USA's stocks of weapon-grade plutonium and HEU see appendix 8A.

[28] [National Security Strategy of the Russian Federation for the period until 2020], Presidential Decree no. 537, 12 May 2009, <http://www.scrf.gov.ru/documents/99.html> (in Russian).

[29] Umnov, S., [Russia's SNF: building up ballistic missile defence penetration capacities], *Voenno-Promyshlennyi Kur'er*, 8–14 Mar. 2006.

[30] Pulin, G., [Reliability of the nuclear shield], *Voenno-Promyshlennyi Kur'er*, 18–24 June 2008.

bombers.[31] In 2009 Russia continued to conduct regular strategic bomber patrols and announced that it had begun development of a new stealth strategic bomber, expected to enter service in 2025–30.[32]

Land-based ballistic missiles

The Russian Strategic Rocket Forces (SRF) consist of three missile armies: the 27th Guards Missile Army (five divisions, based in Vladimir), the 31st Missile Army (two divisions, based in Orenburg) and the 33rd Guards Missile Army (four divisions, based in Omsk).[33] In 2008 it was announced that the SRF would be reduced to two missile armies (four silo-based and five mobile divisions) by 1 January 2016.[34]

As of January 2010, Russia had on combat duty approximately 50 RS-20V Voevoda heavy ICBMs.[35] This is a silo-based, two-stage, liquid-propellant ICBM, which entered into service in 1988–92.[36] An older version, the RS-20B, was reportedly retired from service in 2009.[37] Instead of dismantlement, the SRF sometimes refurbishes RS-20Bs as Dnepr space launch vehicles (SLVs). On 30 July 2009 a Dnepr SLV put six commercial satellites into orbit.[38] At the end of 2009 the SRF extended the service life of the RS-20V to 23 years. This followed the successful launch on 24 December of an RS-20V from Dombarovsky missile base, Orenburg Region, to Kamchatka Peninsula.[39] Russia is reportedly planning to develop a new liquid-propellant heavy ICBM by 2016 as a future replacement for the RS-20V.[40]

As of January 2010 Russia had approximately 60 RS-18 missiles deployed.[41] The RS-18 is a silo-based, two-stage, liquid-propellant ICBM carrying up to six warheads, which entered into service in 1980.[42] Its ser-

---

[31] US Department of State, 'Russian Federation MOU data', July 2009, pp. 61–62; and 'Strategic aviation', Russian Strategic Nuclear Forces Blog, 5 Jan. 2010, <http://russianforces.org/aviation/>.

[32] 'Russia could double number of bombers on strategic patrols—general', RIA Novosti, 22 Dec. 2009, <http://en.rian.ru/russia/20091222/157325197.html>; and 'Russia to develop new strategic bomber by 2017', RIA Novosti, 23 Dec. 2009, <http://en.rian.ru/russia/20091223/157335991.html>.

[33] US Department of State (note 31).

[34] Isby, D. C., 'Russian SRF plans structural changes', Jane's Missiles and Rockets, vol. 13, no. 2 (Feb. 2009).

[35] Norris, R. S. and Kristensen, H. M., 'Nuclear notebook: Russian nuclear forces, 2010', Bulletin of the Atomic Scientists, vol. 66, no. 1 (Jan./Feb. 2010), p. 76.

[36] Lennox, D. (ed.), Jane's Strategic Weapon Systems, no. 51 (Jane's Information Group: Coulsdon, July 2009), pp. 160–62.

[37] [In 2009 SRF conducted three successful ICBM launches—General Shvaichenko], ARMS-TASS, 16 Dec. 2009, <http://armsshow.itar-tass.com/?page=article&aid=79161&cid=44>.

[38] Russian Ministry of Defence, [Launch of the RS-20B missile], 30 July 2009, <http://www.mil.ru/848/1045/1275/rvsn/19220/index.shtml?id=65401>.

[39] 'Russia test-fires Voyevoda ICBM', RIA Novosti, 24 Dec. 2009, <http://en.rian.ru/russia/2009 1224/157339099.html>.

[40] 'Russia says destroyed 9 ICBMs in 2009 under START 1 arms pact', RIA Novosti, 16 Dec. 2009, <http://en.rian.ru/russia/20091216/157256398.html>.

[41] Norris and Kristensen (note 35), p. 76.

[42] Lennox, ed. (note 36), pp. 159–60.

Table 8.3. Russian nuclear forces, January 2010

Type/Russian designation (NATO designation)	No. deployed	Year first deployed	Range (km)^a	Warhead loading	No. of warheads
Strategic offensive forces					**2 510**
Bombers	76				*844*
Tu-95MS6 (Bear-H6)	32	1981	6 500–10 500	6 x AS-15A ALCMs, bombs	192
Tu-95MS16 (Bear-H16)	31	1981	6 500–10 500	16 x AS-15A ALCMs, bombs	496
Tu-160 (Blackjack)	13	1987	10 500–13 200	12 x AS-15B ALCMs or AS-16 SRAMs, bombs	156
ICBMs	*331*				*1 090*
RS-20V Voevoda (SS-18 Satan)	~50	1992	11 000–15 000	10 x 500–800 kt	~500
RS-18 (SS-19 Stiletto)	~60	1980	10 000	6 x 400 kt	~360
RS-12M Topol (SS-25 Sickle)	~150	1985	10 500	1 x 800 kt	~150
RS-12M2 Topol-M (SS-27)	50	1997	10 500	1 x 800 kt	50
RS-12M1 Topol-M (SS-27)	18	2006	10 500	1 x (800 kt)	18
RS-24 (SS-27 Mod 2)	(3)	(2010–11)	10 500	4 x (400 kt)	(12)
SLBMs	*160*				*576*
RSM-50 Volna (SS-N-18 M1 Stingray)	64	1978	6 500	3 x 50 kt	192
RSM-54 Sineva (SS-N-23 Skiff)	96	1986/2007	9 000	4 x 100 kt	384
RSM-56 Bulava (SS-NX-30)	0	(2010–11)	>8 050	6 x (100 kt)	0
Strategic defensive forces					
ABMs^b	*~2150*				*~700*
53T6 (SH-08 Gazelle)	68	1986	..	1 x 10 kt	68
S-300 (SA-10/20 Grumble)	1900	1980	..	low kt	~600
S-400 Triumf (SA-21 Growler)	~200	2007	..	..	..
Non-strategic forces					
Land-based non-strategic bombers^c	*524*				*~650*
Tu-22M (Backfire)	124	1974	..	2 x AS-4 ASM, bombs	
Su-24 (Fencer)	400	1974	..	2 x bombs	
Naval non-strategic attack aircraft	*179*				*~240*
Tu-22M (Backfire)	58	1974	..	2 x AS-4 ASM, bombs	
Su-24 (Fencer)	58	1974	..	2 x bombs	
Be-12 (Mail)/Il-38 (May)	63	1967/68	..	1 x depth bomb	
SLCMs SS-N-9, SS-N-12, SS-N-19, SS-N-21, SS-N-22					*~280*
ASW and SAM weapons SS-N-15/16, SA-N-1/3/6, depth bombs, torpedoes^c					*~250*
Total defensive and non-strategic					**~2 120**
Total					**~4 630^d**

.. = not available or not applicable; ( ) = uncertain figure; ABM = anti-ballistic missiles; ALCM = air-launched cruise missile; ASM = air-to-surface missile; ASW = Anti-submarine warfare; ICBM = intercontinental ballistic missile; kt = kiloton; NATO = North Atlantic Treaty Organization; SAM = surface-to-air missile; SLBM = submarine-launched ballistic missile; SLCM = sea-launched cruise missile; SRAM = short-range attack missile; SSBN = nuclear-powered ballistic missile submarine.

[a] Aircraft range is for illustrative purposes only; actual mission range will vary according to flight profile and weapon loading.

[b] The 51T6 (SH-11 Gorgon) is no longer operational. The S-300P (SA-10 Grumble), S-300V (SA-12A Gladiator, SA-12B Giant) and S-400 may have some capability against some ballistic missiles. Only a third of 1900 deployed S-300s are counted as having nuclear capability.

[c] These figures assume that only half of land-based strike aircraft have nuclear missions. Surface ships are not estimated to be assigned nuclear torpedoes.

[d] An additional c. 7300 warheads are estimated to be in reserve or awaiting dismantlement for a total stockpile of c. 12 000 warheads.

Sources: US Department of State, START I Treaty Memoranda of Understanding, 1990–July 2009; US Air Force, National Air and Space Intelligence Center (NASIC), Ballistic and Cruise Missile Threat (NASIC: Wright-Patterson Air Force Base, OH, June 2009); US Central Intelligence Agency, National Intelligence Council, 'Foreign missile developments and the ballistic missile threat through 2015' (unclassified summary), Dec. 2001, <http://www.fas.org/spp/starwars/CIA-NIE.htm>; US Department of Defense, 'Proliferation: threat and response', Washington, DC, Jan. 2001, <http://www.fas.org/irp/threat/wmd.htm>; World News Connection, National Technical Information Service (NTIS), US Department of Commerce, various issues; Russian Strategic Nuclear Forces, <http://www.russianforces.org/>; International Institute for Strategic Studies, The Military Balance 2008 (Routledge: London, 2008); Cochran, T. B. et al., Nuclear Weapons Databook, vol. 4, Soviet Nuclear Weapons (Harper & Row: New York, 1989); Jane's Strategic Weapon Systems, no. 51 (Jane's Information Group: Coulsdon, July 2009); Proceedings, US Naval Institute, various issues; 'Nuclear notebook', Bulletin of the Atomic Scientists, various issues; and authors' estimates.

life was extended to 31 years as a result of test launches conducted in 2007 and 2008.[43]

Russia has approximately 150 RS-12M Topol ICBMs deployed in eight missile divisions.[44] The RS-12M is a road-mobile, three-stage, solid-propellant ICBM with a single warhead, which entered into service beginning in 1985.[45] It is expected to remain in service until 2019, following the completion of a service life extension programme.[46] As part of this programme, in 2009 there were successful test launches of the missile on 10 April from Plesetsk and on 10 December from Kapustin Yar.[47]

[43] 'Russia test launches RS-18 ICBM from Baikonur in Kazakhstan', RIA Novosti, 22 Oct. 2008, <http://en.rian.ru/russia/20081022/117885862.html>.

[44] Norris and Kristensen (note 35), p. 76.

[45] Lennnox (note 36), pp. 155–57.

[46] Isby, D. C., 'Mobile Topol-M production ends', Jane's Missiles and Rockets, vol. 13, no. 6 (June 2009), p. 6.

[47] Russian Ministry of Defence, [The successful test launch of the ICBM was conducted from the Kapustin Yar test range], 10 Dec. 2009, <http://www.mil.ru/848/1045/1275/rvsn/19220/index.shtml?id=69395>.

The RS-12M2/1 Topol-M missile is widely expected to become the backbone of the SRF once older missile types have been retired from service. It is a three-stage, solid-propellant ICBM that has been developed in both road-mobile (RS-12M1) and silo-based (RS-12M2) versions.[48] As of January 2010 Russia was believed to have 18 RS-12M1 and 50 RS-12M2 missiles in service.[49] The SRF has announced plans to introduce 10 more RS-12M2 and 9 more RS-12M1 missiles in 2010.[50]

Russia has developed and begun testing a missile designated as the RS-24, which is a RS-12M2/1 missile modified to carry three MIRVs.[51] Adding the MIRV capability to the existing single-warhead version of the missile was prohibited by the START Treaty. Statements made in 2009 by Russian military officials indicated that the missile would enter into service immediately after START's expiry, on 5 December 2009, and that the production of RS-12M1 might be abandoned in favour of the RS-24.[52] As of January 2010, however, the deployment of the RS-24 missile had not been announced by the military. Instead, more test launches were planned for 2010, and introduction of the missile into service was postponed until 2011.[53]

Ballistic missile submarines and sea-launched ballistic missiles

As of January 2010 the Russian Navy operated 12 SSBNs in its Northern and Pacific fleets. Of these, five are Delta III Class (Project 667BDR Kalmar) submarines, deployed with the Pacific Fleet.[54] Six Delta IV Class (Project 667BDRM Delfin) submarines are deployed with the Northern Fleet. Five of these have undergone a service-life extension overhaul which included the installation of the new modification of the RSM-54 Sineva missile. The K-18 *Karelia* returned to service in January 2010. The sixth Delta IV submarine—the K-407 *Novomoskovsk*—is expected to return to the fleet in 2010 after such an overhaul.[55] Russia also keeps in service one

[48] Lennnox (note 36), pp. 158–59.

[49] [In 2009 the second missile regiment equipped with mobile complexes 'Topol-M' will enter into service], ARMS-TASS, 17 Sep. 2009, <http://armstass.su/?page=article&aid=75694&cid=25>.

[50] [The number of 'Topol-M' ICBM regiments in service with the SRF will increase from 7 to 9 in 2010], PRIME-TASS, 10 Jan. 2010, <http://www.prime-tass.ru/news/0/{5840C86B-6F2C-40A4-98 88-F6243989E262}.uif>.

[51] 'RS-24 makes third successful flight', *Jane's Missiles and Rockets*, vol. 13, no. 1 (Jan. 2009), p. 3; and Nikolskii, A., [SRF wants to obtain the replacement for the 'Satan'], *Vedomosti*, 9 Dec. 2009, <http://www.vedomosti.ru/newsline/news/2009/12/09/903154>.

[52] Isby, D. C., 'Russia's MIRV RS-24s set for deployment during December', *Jane's Missiles and Rockets*, vol. 13, no. 12 (Dec. 2009), p. 10; and Isby (note 46).

[53] Nikolskii, A., [Three-headed missile is almost ready], *Vedomosti*, 15 Jan. 2009.

[54] Korotchenko, S., [Russia begins from here], *Voenno-Promyshlennyi Kur'er*, 22–28 Oct. 2008; and Saunders, S. (ed.), *Jane's Fighting Ships 2009–2010*, 112th edn (Jane's Information Group: Coulsdon, 2009), p. 652.

[55] [Northern Fleet's nuclear submarine 'Karelia' successfully concluded sea trials after modernization in Severodvinsk], ITAR-TASS, 18 Dec. 2009, <http://armstass.su/?page=article&aid=

Project 941 Akula (Typhoon Class) submarine for use as a test platform for the RSM-56 Bulava missile.

Russia is building three SSBNs of a new class, the Project 955 Borei. The lead boat in the class, the *Yurii Dolgorukii*, conducted a number of sea trials in 2009.[56] The second and third submarines, the *Aleksandr Nevskii* and the *Vladimir Monomakh*, have been under construction at the Sevmash shipyard since March 2004 and March 2006, respectively. Russia also plans to lay down the fourth SSBN of this class, the *Svyatitel Nikolai*, in 2010. The Project 955 SSBNs are designed to be armed with RSM-56 Bulava missiles.[57]

The troubled development of the Bulava, a three-stage, solid-propellant SLBM, received considerable attention from media and high-level officials in Russia in 2009. Once fitted on the Project 955 SSBNs, the Bulava is supposed to form the backbone of the future Russian naval deterrent force. During 2009 Bulava missiles were launched by the TK-208 *Dmitrii Donskoi* on 15 July and 9 December. Both attempts were high-profile failures.[58] This brought the total number of test flights of the Bulava to 12, with an additional 2 pop-up tests (i.e. tests of the mechanism which ejects the missile from the submarine). Only 2 of these are reported to have been completely successful.[59] The repeated failures are a major setback, not only for the Bulava development programme, but also for the plans to bring Project 955 submarines into service. The nuclear warheads to be carried by the Bulava reportedly were 'prepared [a] long time ago'.[60]

In 2009 Russia successfully conducted five underwater test launches of currently deployed types of SLBM. The K-443 *Svyatoi Georgii Pobedonosets* and K-44 *Ryazan'* conducted submerged launches of RSM-50 SLBMs on 6 and 7 October, respectively, from the Sea of Okhotsk to the Chizha test range in Arkhangelsk region.[61] On 13 July the K-84 *Yekaterinburg* launched an RSM-54 Sineva SLBM from a location near Franz Josef Land along a depressed trajectory to the Kura test site in Kamchatka. On 14 July the

79264&cid=25>; [Nuclear submarine 'Karelia' rejoined the Navy], *Izvestia*, 22 Jan. 2010; Saunders, ed. (note 54); and Isby, D. C., 'Russia announces construction of two new missile submarines', *Jane's Missiles and Rockets*, vol. 13, no. 6 (June 2009), p. 12.

[56] [SSBN 'Yuri Dolgoruky' has successfully completed the next stage of production tests], ARMS-TASS, 17 Nov. 2009, <http://armstass.su/?page=article&aid=77844&cid=25>.

[57] [Delay in construction of the 'Borei' submarine is not connected to the 'Bulava' trials], *Kommersant*, 21 Dec. 2009.

[58] [Yuri Solomonov could not carry 'Bulava'], *Kommersant*, 23 July 2009; and McKee, M., 'Strange "Norway spiral" was an out of control missile', *New Scientist*, 10 Dec. 2009.

[59] 'Bulava missile test history', Russian Strategic Nuclear Forces blog, 9 Dec. 2009, <http://russian forces.org/navy/slbms/bulava.shtml>.

[60] 'Bulava nuclear warhead ready long ago—Defense Ministry representative', ITAR-TASS, 8 Dec. 2009, Translation from Russian, World News Connection.

[61] Isby, D. C., 'Bulava tests face further delay', *Jane's Missiles and Rockets*, vol. 13, no. 12 (Dec. 2009), p. 7. The RSM-50 entered service in 1978 and is deployed on Delta III Class submarines. It has 2 liquid-fuelled stages and carries 3 warheads. Lennox, ed. (note 36), pp. 149–50.

K-117 *Bryansk* launched another Sineva from the North Pole region towards the Chizha test range.[62] On 1 November the K-117 *Bryansk* again launched a Sineva from the Barents Sea to Kura.[63]

Non-strategic nuclear weapons

Since the end of the cold war, Russia has significantly reduced its inventory of non-strategic nuclear weapons in implementation of two non-legally binding unilateral initiatives on non-strategic nuclear weapons, undertaken in 1991–92 together with parallel initiatives by the USA.[64] However, there is considerable uncertainty in estimates of this inventory, which continues to be characterized by a high degree of secrecy and a lack of transparency.[65] On the basis of the number of available delivery platforms, it is estimated that Russia has approximately 2000 operational warheads for delivery by air-defence missiles, tactical aircraft and naval cruise missiles, depth bombs and torpedoes.[66] In addition, Russia is believed to have up to several thousand non-strategic warheads held in reserve or awaiting dismantlement.

IV. British nuclear forces

The United Kingdom's nuclear deterrent consists exclusively of a sea-based component: Vanguard Class Trident SSBNs, Trident II (D5) SLBMs and associated warheads, and support infrastructure. In March 2009 the British Prime Minister, Gordon Brown, confirmed that the UK's inventory of 'operationally available warheads' had been reduced to fewer than 160.[67] These weapons are available for use by a fleet of four Trident SSBNs (see table 8.4). The UK leases the D5 SLBMs from the US Navy. Under a system of 'mingled asset ownership', the missiles to be loaded onto British submarines are randomly selected from the stockpile at the US Navy's Trident facility in Kings Bay, Georgia. The submarines then go to the Royal Naval Armaments Depot at Coulport, Scotland, where the missiles are fitted with

[62] Makeev Design Bureau, [Director General's note], *Konstruktor*, no. 7 (July 2009), p. 2. The Sineva (the Blue) SLBM was first test launched in 1983. On the upgraded Sineva version see Kile, S. N., Fedchenko, V. and Kristensen, H. M., 'World nuclear forces, 2008', *SIPRI Yearbook 2008*, pp. 378–79.

[63] Litovkin, D., ['Dolphin' hit a 'peg'], *Izvestia*, 2 Nov. 2009.

[64] See Fieldhouse, R., 'Nuclear weapon developments and unilateral reduction initiatives', *SIPRI Yearbook 1992*, pp. 72–73, 89–92.

[65] In 2007 the top Russian Ministry of Defence official responsible for nuclear weapon custody reported on the progress made in reducing this inventory but did not give specific numbers of warheads. Volgin, V., [Strategic monitoring], *Rossiiskaya Gazeta*, 31 Oct. 2007.

[66] Warheads for ships and submarines are stored on land in depots and can be deployed if necessary. See also Kile, Fedchenko and Kristensen (note 62), pp. 380–81.

[67] Brown, G., Speech on nuclear energy and non-proliferation, International Nuclear Fuel Cycle Conference, Lancaster House, London, 17 Mar. 2009, <http://www.number10.gov.uk/Page18631>.

nuclear warheads designed and manufactured at the Atomic Weapons Establishment (AWE), Aldermaston, England. The Trident fleet is based at Faslane, Scotland. On 26 May 2009, HMS *Victorious* successfully test-launched a D5 missile off the Atlantic coast of Florida as part of a demonstration and shakedown operation following a refuelling overhaul.[68]

Each SSBN is equipped with 16 D5 missiles carrying up to 48 warheads. The warhead is similar to the US W76 warhead and has an explosive yield of about 100 kt. It is believed that a number of the D5 missiles are deployed with only one warhead instead of three; this warhead may also have a greatly reduced explosive yield, possibly produced by the detonation of only the fission primary.[69] The reduced force-loading option is the result of a decision by the Ministry of Defence (MOD) in 1998 to give a 'sub-strategic', or limited-strike, role to the Trident fleet aimed at enhancing the credibility of the deterrent.[70] In 2002 the role of nuclear weapons was extended to include deterring 'leaders of states of concern and terrorist organisations'.[71]

In a posture known as Continuous at Sea Deterrence (CASD), one British SSBN is on patrol at all times.[72] The second and third SSBNs can be put to sea rapidly, but the British inventory does not include enough missiles to arm the fourth submarine. Since the end of the cold war, the SSBN on patrol has been kept at a level of reduced readiness with its missiles de-targeted and a 'notice to fire' measured in days.

The four Vanguard Class SSBNs will reach the end of their service lives from 2024.[73] In a plan approved by the British Parliament in 2007, the Royal Navy will renew the Trident system by replacing the existing submarines with a new class of SSBNs and equipping them with the modified D5LE SLBM being developed by the USA. The new submarine will enter into service in 2024 after testing and acceptance trials.[74] The scheduled in-

[68] Lockheed Martin, 'Lockheed Martin-built Trident II D5 missile achieves 127 successful test flights', Press release, 30 July 2009, <http://www.lockheedmartin.com/news/press_releases/2009/0730ssuk-trident.html>.

[69] Quinlan, M., 'The future of United Kingdom nuclear weapons: shaping the debate', *International Affairs*, vol. 82, no. 4 (July 2006).

[70] British Ministry of Defence (MOD), *The Strategic Defence Review: Modern Forces for the Modern World*, Cm 3999 (MOD: London, July 1998), para. 63.

[71] British Ministry of Defence, *The Strategic Defence Review: A New Chapter*, Cm 5566, vol. 1 (The Stationery Office: London, July 2002), para. 21.

[72] British Ministry of Defence and British Foreign and Commonwealth Office, *The Future of the United Kingdom's Nuclear Deterrent*, Cm 6994 (The Stationary Office: London, Dec. 2006), p. 27. See also Simpson, J. and Nielsen, J., 'The United Kingdom', eds H. Born, B. Gill and H. Hänggi, SIPRI, *Governing the Bomb: Civilian Control and Democratic Accountability of Nuclear Weapons* (Oxford University Press: Oxford, 2010)

[73] The lead ship of the class, HMS *Vanguard*, entered service in 1994. The original 25-year service life has been extended to 30 years.

[74] The MOD has been studying a further life-extension of the Vanguard SSBNs in case the new submarine's entry into service is delayed. Barrie, D., 'U.K. ponders further vanguard extension', *Aviation Week and Space Technology*, 21 Nov. 2008.

Table 8.4. British nuclear forces, January 2010

Type	Designation	No. deployed	Year first deployed	Range (km)^a	Warheads x yield	Warheads in stockpile
Submarine-launched ballistic missiles						
D5	Trident II	160	1994	>7 400	1–3 x 100 kt	225^b

^{a} Range is for illustrative purposes only; actual mission range will vary according to flight profile and weapon loading.

^{b} Up to 160 warheads are operationally available, including *c.* 144 to arm 48 missiles on 3 of 4 SSBNs. The total stockpile consists of no more than 225 warheads. Only 1 boat is on patrol at any time, with up to 48 warheads.

Sources: British Ministry of Defence (MOD), white papers, press releases and the MOD website, <http://www.mod.uk/>; British House of Commons, *Parliamentary Debates (Hansard)*; Norris, R. S. et al., *Nuclear Weapons Databook*, vol. 5, *British, French, and Chinese Nuclear Weapons* (Westview: Boulder, CO, 1994), p. 9; 'Nuclear notebook', *Bulletin of the Atomic Scientists*, various issues; and authors' estimate.

service date means that the British and US timetables for building a new generation of submarines and missiles to go on them are not in alignment. The US Navy has decided to extend the life of its existing D5 missiles to 2042, nearly two decades after the new generation of British submarines is scheduled to enter service. MOD officials have emphasized that design of the submarines' missile compartment has to be coordinated from the outset with the US Navy to ensure that it will be compatible with the design of the D5's successor.[75]

In 2009 the British Government appeared to back away from the idea of a 'like-for-like' replacement for the Vanguard Class submarines. In March 2009 Brown indicated that the new submarines would have 12 missile tubes rather than the 16 of the existing submarines.[76] In a 23 September 2009 speech to the UN General Assembly, Brown said that the UK was considering building only three Trident replacement submarines, rather than the planned four.[77] However, Brown gave no indication that the UK planned to reduce its stockpile of nuclear warheads, although he kept open the option of doing so 'consistent with [the UK's] national deterrence and with the progress of multilateral discussions'.[78] The option of reducing the SSBN force to three submarines had been included in a 2006 white paper on the future of the UK's strategic deterrent.[79] However, concerns had been raised about whether the smaller fleet could reliably sustain the CASD pos-

[75] Richardson, D., 'UK planning for Trident replacement takes shape', *Jane's Missiles and Rockets*, vol. 13, no. 5 (May 2009), p. 9.

[76] Brown (note 67).

[77] Brown, G., Speech to UN General Assembly, New York, 23 Sep. 2009, <http://www.un.org/ga/64/generaldebate/GB.shtml>.

[78] Brown (note 67).

[79] British Ministry of Defence and British Foreign and Commonwealth Office (note 72), p. 26.

ture. The concerns were raised again following a February 2009 collision between HMS *Vanguard* and the French SSBN *Le Triomphant* in the Bay of Biscay. Both submarines were forced to return to port for repairs.[80] Brown's statement at the UN came against the background of renewed political opposition during 2009 to the estimated procurement costs of the new submarines and associated infrastructure. In 2006 the cost of the planned four-boat fleet was estimated to be £15–20 billion ($28.5–38 billion).[81] A decision to reduce the new fleet to three submarines would save an estimated £3 billion ($5.7 billion).[82]

The British Government has yet to formally announce whether the nuclear warheads carried on the D5 SLBM will be refurbished or replaced. However, some press reports in 2008 indicated that a decision had already been taken to replace the existing stockpile of warheads, at an estimated total cost of more than £3 billion ($5.5 million).[83] The MOD has launched a long-term investment programme aimed at sustaining key skills and facilities at the AWE.[84]

V. French nuclear forces

France's nuclear forces consist of aircraft and SSBNs, carrying a total of about 300 warheads (see table 8.5). A 2008 white paper on defence and national security includes important clarifications concerning French nuclear forces. France will continue to rely on the 'principle of strict sufficiency' (corresponding to a 'minimum deterrence' policy) as a guarantor of its security, and the 'operational credibility' of the deterrent relies on 'permanent submarine patrols and airborne capability'.[85] France will also continue to sustain its nuclear weapon complex, including the research and development capabilities. In order to maintain the 'technical credibility' of its nuclear weapons in the absence of nuclear testing and facilities producing weapon-grade material, in 1996 France started a nuclear weapon simulation programme, employing the Laser Mégajoule (LMJ, megajoule laser), radiography and supercomputers.[86]

---

[80] 'France and UK admit to nuclear submarine collision in Atlantic', *Jane's Missiles and Rockets*, vol. 13, no. 4 (Apr. 2009), p. 16.

[81] British Ministry of Defence and British Foreign and Commonwealth Office (note 72), p. 26.

[82] Wintour, P. and Norton-Taylor, R., 'Brown offers to cut Trident nuclear submarines by a quarter', *The Guardian*, 23 Sep. 2009.

[83] Taylor, M., 'Britain plans to spend £3bn on new nuclear warheads', *The Guardian*, 25 July 2008.

[84] Reid, J., Secretary of State for Defence, 'Atomic Weapons Establishment', Written ministerial statement, House of Commons, *Hansard*, 19 July 2005, column C59WS.

[85] French Government, *Défense et sécurité nationale: Le livre blanc* [Defence and national security: the White Paper] (Odile Jacob: Paris, June 2008). English translation: French Government, *The French White Paper on Defence and National Security* (Odile Jacob: New York, 2008), pp. 161–63.

[86] French Government (note 85), p. 163.

Table 8.5. French nuclear forces, January 2010

Type	No. deployed	Year first deployed	Range (km)^a	Warheads x yield	Warheads in stockpile
Land-based aircraft					
Mirage 2000N	60	1988	2 750	1 x 300 kt ASMP 1 x .. kt ASMP-A	50
Rafale F3	–	(2010)	2 000	1 x .. kt ASMP-A	–
Carrier-based aircraft					
Super Étendard	24	1978	650	1 x 300 kt ASMP	10
Rafale MK3	–	(2010)	2 000	1 x .. kt ASMP-A	–
Submarine-launched ballistic missiles					
M45	48	1996	6 000^b	4–6 x 100 kt	240
M51	–	(2010)	6 000	4–6 x 100 kt	–
Total					**300^c**

.. = not available or not applicable; ( ) = uncertain figure; ASMP = Air–Sol Moyenne Portée (medium-range air-to-surface missile); ASMP-A = ASMP-Améliorée (improved ASMP).

^{a} Aircraft range is for illustrative purposes only; actual mission range will vary according to flight profile and weapon loading.

^{b} The range of the M45 is listed as only 4000 km in a 2001 report from the National Defence Commission of the French National Assembly.

^{c} The warhead stockpile will be reduced to fewer than 300 warheads in the near future. France does not have a reserve but may have a small inventory of spare warheads.

Sources: Sarkozy, N., French President, Speech on defence and national security, Porte de Versailles, 17 June 2008, <http://www.defense.gouv.fr/livre_blanc/>; French Ministry of Defence website, various policy papers, press releases and force profiles; French National Assembly, various defence bills; Norris, R. S. et al., *Nuclear Weapons Databook*, vol. 5, *British, French, and Chinese Nuclear Weapons* (Westview: Boulder, CO, 1994), p. 10; *Air Actualités*, various issues; *Aviation Week and Space Technology*, various issues; 'Nuclear notebook', *Bulletin of the Atomic Scientists*, various issues; and authors' estimates.

In 2009 France's sea-based strategic force consisted of a fleet of three operational Triomphant Class SSBNs—*Le Triomphant, Le Téméraire* and *Le Vigilant*. A fourth Triomphant Class SSBN, *Le Terrible,* is scheduled to enter service in July 2010.[87] All operational French SSBNs are armed with 16 Aérospatiale M45 missiles, which each carry up to six TN-75 warheads.[88] In 2010–15 the SSBNs will be gradually equipped with the longer-range M51.1 SLBM, a three-stage solid-propellant missile armed with up to six TN-75 warheads. The M51.1 is estimated to have a maximum range of 6000–8000 km.[89] The M51.1 missile had been successfully flight-tested in

[87] Saunders, ed. (note 54), p. 246.

[88] Norris, R. S. and Kristensen, H. M., 'Nuclear notebook: French nuclear forces, 2008', *Bulletin of the Atomic Scientists*, vol. 64, no. 4 (July/Aug. 2008).

[89] Lennox, ed. (note 36), p. 46; and 'France's nuclear-powered *Le Vigilant* prepares for patrol', *Jane's Missiles and Rockets*, vol. 9, no. 2 (Feb. 2005).

2006, 2007 and 2008 from a submerged launch platform.[90] On 27 January 2010 the missile was launched for the first time 'in real conditions' from the SSBN *Le Terrible*. The launch was reported as being successful.[91] France is developing another version of the M51 missile, the M51.2, which is designed to carry the new Tête Nucléaire Océanique (TNO, Oceanic Nuclear Warhead) and will supplant the M51.1 after 2015.[92]

In 2009 the air component of the French nuclear forces consisted of approximately 60 Mirage 2000N aircraft, equipping three squadrons; and about 24 Super Étendard aircraft deployed on the aircraft carrier *Charles de Gaulle*. The number of Mirage 2000N aircraft having a nuclear role will decrease following President Sarkozy's announcement in 2008 that France would reduce the airborne component of its nuclear forces by one-third.[93] Both types of aircraft carry the Air–Sol Moyenne Portée (ASMP, medium-range air-to-surface missile) cruise missile. A total of 90 ASMP missiles were produced, along with 80 TN81 300-kt warheads for use with them.[94]

The phasing-out of ASMPs will begin in 2011. A follow-on cruise missile, the ASMP-Améliorée (improved ASMP), completed 'operational evaluation firings' in March 2009 and was formally announced as operational on 1 October. As of January 2010, it was in service on the Mirage 2000N fighters of the 3/4 Limousin Fighter Squadron at Istres, and was due to become operational on the Dassault Rafale F3 in 2010. The missile's Tête Nucléaire Aeroportée (TNA, Airborne Nuclear Warhead) is the 'new medium-energy thermonuclear charge', the yield of which is not publicly known.[95]

VI. Chinese nuclear forces

China is estimated to have an arsenal of approximately 200 operational nuclear weapons for delivery mainly by ballistic missiles and aircraft (see table 8.6). Additional warheads may be in reserve, giving a total stockpile of about 240 warheads. The existence of tactical warheads is uncertain, although the testing series in the 1990s reportedly included tactical warhead designs. There are no credible reports indicating that the size of the Chinese nuclear stockpile has changed significantly in recent years.

---

[90] Kile, Fedchenko and Kristensen (note 3), pp. 363–64.

[91] 'French ballistic missile test called a success', Global Security Newswire, 27 Jan. 2010, <http://www.globalsecuritynewswire.org/gsn/nw_20100127_8630.php>.

[92] Lennox, ed. (note 36), p. 47.

[93] French Government (note 85), p. 112; and Sarkozy, N., French President, 'Presentation of SSBM "Le Terrible"', Speech, Cherbourg, 21 Mar. 2008, <https://pastel.diplomatie.gouv.fr/editorial/actual/ael2/bulletin.gb.asp?liste=20080331.gb.html>.

[94] Fiszer, M. and Gruszczynski,, J., 'French MoD to develop nuclear missile', *Journal of Electronic Defense*, vol. 26, no. 12 (Dec. 2003).

[95] Richardson, D., 'ASMP-A enters French Air Force service', *Jane's Missiles and Rockets*, vol. 13, no. 12 (Dec. 2009), p. 10.

Table 8.6. Chinese nuclear forces, January 2010

Type/Chinese designation (US designation)	No. deployed	Year first deployed	Range (km)^a	Warhead loading	No. of warheads
Land-based missiles^b	*134*				*134*
DF-3A (CSS-2)	12	1971	3 100^c	1 x 3.3 Mt	12
DF-4 (CSS-3)	12	1980	5 500	1 x 3.3 Mt	12
DF-5A (CSS-4)	20	1981	13 000	1 x 4–5 Mt	20
DF-21 (CSS-5)	60	1991	2 100^d	1 x 200–300 kt	60
DF-31 (CSS-10 Mod 1)	~15	2006	>7 200	1 x ..	15
DF-31A (CSS-10 Mod 2)	~15	2007	>11 200	1 x ..	15
SLBMs	*(36)*				*(36)*
JL-1 (CSS-N-3)	(12)	1986	>1 770	1 x 200–300 kt	(12)
JL-2 (CSS-NX-14)	(24)	(2010)	>7 200	1 x ..	(24)
Aircraft^e	*>20*				*(40)*
H-6 (B-6)	20	1965	3 100	1 x bomb	(20)
Attack (..)	..	1972– ..	..	1 x bomb	(20)
Cruise missiles	*150–350*				..
DH-10	150–350	2007	>1500	1 x ..	..^{f}
Total					**(~200)^g**

.. = not available or not applicable; ( ) = uncertain figure; SLBM = submarine-launched ballistic missile.

   ^{a} Aircraft range is for illustrative purposes only; actual mission range will vary.
   ^{b} China defines missile ranges as short-range, <1000 km; medium-range, 1000–3000 km; long-range, 3000–8000 km; and intercontinental range, >8000 km.
   ^{c} The range of the DF-3A may be greater than is normally reported.
   ^{d} The DF-21A (CSS-5 Mod 2) variant is believed to have a range of up to 2500 km.
   ^{e} Figures for aircraft are for nuclear-configured versions only.
   ^{f} The DH-10, which is also known by the Chinese designation CJ-10, may have a nuclear role. It is apparently employable from H-6 bombers and ground-based launchers.
   ^{g} Additional warheads are thought to be in storage to arm future DF-31, DF-31A and JL-2 missiles. The total stockpile is believed to comprise c. 240–300 warheads.

Sources: US Department of Defense (DOD), Office of the Secretary of Defense, *Military Power of the People's Republic of China*, various years; US Air Force, National Air and Space Intelligence Center (NASIC), various documents; US Central Intelligence Agency, various documents; US DOD, Office of the Secretary of Defense, *Proliferation: Threat and Response* (DOD: Washington, DC, Jan. 2001); Kristensen, H. M., Norris, R. S. and McKinzie, M. G., *Chinese Nuclear Forces and U.S. Nuclear War Planning* (Federation of American Scientists/Natural Resources Defense Council: Washington, DC, Nov. 2006); Norris, R. S. et al., *Nuclear Weapons Databook*, vol. 5, *British, French, and Chinese Nuclear Weapons* (Westview: Boulder, CO, 1994); 'Nuclear notebook', *Bulletin of the Atomic Scientists*, various issues; Google Earth; and authors' estimates.

At the same time, China has been changing the delivery systems for those warheads as part of its long-term modernization programme aimed at developing a more survivable force and more flexible nuclear deterrence and retaliatory options.[96] According to a 2009 report by the US Air Force, China has 'the most active and diverse ballistic missile development program in the world' and its 'ballistic missile force is expanding in both size and types of missiles'.[97]

Chinese land-based ballistic missiles are operated by the Second Artillery Corps (SAC) of the People Liberation Army (PLA). According to the data published annually by the US Department of Defense, in 2009 China's nuclear-capable missile arsenal consisted of the ageing liquid-fuelled DF-3A (Dong Feng, or East Wind) intermediate-range ballistic missile and the more modern road-mobile, solid-fuelled DF-21 medium-range ballistic missile (MRBM), which was assigned 'regional deterrence missions'.[98] In addition, China had two operationally deployed types of ICBM: the silo-based, liquid-fuelled DF-5A missile and the smaller, liquid-fuelled DF-4. The SAC is deploying modern mobile ICBM systems that are intended to enhance the survivability of the Chinese missile force by enabling the weapons to operate over a larger area. This includes the DF-31, a solid-propellant, road-mobile missile that was first deployed in 2006, as well as a longer-range (in excess of 11 200 km) variant, the DF-31A.[99] According to the USAF report, the new deployments means that the number of Chinese 'ICBM nuclear warheads capable of reaching the United States could expand to well over 100 during the next 15 years'.[100] However, the Chinese Government has reaffirmed that its nuclear posture adheres to the principle of a 'lean and effective strategic force' and to China's long-standing policy of no first use of nuclear weapons.[101]

According to China's 2008 defence white paper, the PLA Navy is working to enhance its 'capability of nuclear counterattacks'.[102] China has had difficulty in developing a sea-based nuclear deterrent. It built a single Type 092 (Xia Class) SSBN armed with 12 intermediate-range solid-fuel, single-warhead JL-1 (Ju Long, or Great Wave) SLBMs. The submarine has never conducted a deterrent patrol and is not thought to be fully operational.

[96] For a description of China's nuclear doctrine, and its plans for changing the operational status of the nuclear forces at 3 different levels of crisis, see Chinese State Council, *China's National Defense in 2008* (Information Office of the State Council of the People's Republic of China: Beijing, Jan. 2009), chapter VII. See also Gill, B. and Medeiros, E. S., 'China', eds Born, Gill and Hänggi (note 72)

[97] US Air Force, National Air and Space Intelligence Center (NASIC), *Ballistic and Cruise Missile Threat* (NASIC: Wright-Patterson Air Force Base, OH, Mar. 2009), p. 3.

[98] US Department of Defense (DOD), *Military Power of the People's Republic of China 2009*, Report to Congress (DOD: Washington, DC, Mar. 2009), p. 24. Although China has its own system for defining missile ranges (see table 8.6), the US DOD definitions are used here: short range = <1100 km; medium range = 1100–2750 km; intermediate range = 2750–5500 km; and intercontinental range = >5500 km.

[99] US Department of Defense (note 98).

[100] US Air Force (note 97), p. 3.

[101] Chinese State Council (note 96), chapter VII.

[102] Chinese State Council (note 96), chapter V.

China is currently building and deploying the Type 094 (Jin Class) SSBN. As of 2009, four submarines were reportedly in various stages of construction and outfitting, and a fifth had been commissioned but was not in service.[103] There have been reports indicating that one of the submarines had been deployed to a new base near Yulin on Hainan Island in the South China Sea.[104]

Each Jin Class SSBN will carry 12 three-stage, solid-propellant SLBMs, the JL-2, which is a sea-based variant of the DF-31 ICBM. The JL-2 has an estimated range of 7200 km, which means that it will have a true intercontinental range. It is believed to be armed with a single nuclear warhead, although there has been speculation that China might develop and deploy MIRVs on the missile.[105] The US DOD assessed in 2009 that the JL-2 would achieve an initial operational capability in 2009–10.[106] The same DOD report noted that the PLA Navy has 'only limited capacity to communicate with submarines at sea' and 'no experience in managing a SSBN fleet that performs strategic patrols'.[107]

It is thought that China has a small stockpile of nuclear bombs for delivery by aircraft. Although the PLA Air Force is not believed to have units whose primary purpose is to deliver the bombs, a declassified 1993 US Government report assesses that 'some units may be tasked for nuclear delivery as a contingency mission'.[108] The most likely aircraft for nuclear missions is the ageing H-6 bomber and possibly a more modern fighter-bomber aircraft. China is also a developing an air-launched version of a land-attack cruise missile, the DH-10 (also designated CJ-10) that may be for delivery by the H-6 aircraft. It is uncertain whether China has assigned a nuclear role to air- or ground-launched cruise missiles.

VII. Indian nuclear forces

The conservative estimate presented here is that India has an arsenal of 60–80 nuclear weapons. The figure is based on calculations of India's inventory of weapon-grade plutonium as well as the number of operational nuclear-capable weapon systems.[109]

In August 2009 Dr K. Santhanam, one of the key scientists associated with the nuclear tests conducted by India in May 1998, claimed that the

---

[103] Saunders, ed. (note 54), p. 128.

[104] Kristensen, H. M., 'New Chinese SSBN deploys to Hainan Island', 24 Apr. 2008, <http://www.fas.org/blog/ssp/2008/04/new-chinese-ssbn-deploys-to-hainan-island-naval-base.php>.

[105] See e.g. Saunders, ed. (note 54).

[106] US Department of Defense (note 98), p. 48.

[107] US Department of Defense (note 98), p. 24.

[108] US National Security Council, 'Report to Congress on status of China, India and Pakistan nuclear and ballistic missile programs', [28 July 1993], obtained under the US Freedom of Information Act by the Federation of American Scientists, <http://fas.org/irp/threat/930728-wmd.htm>.

[109] On India's stocks of fissile materials see appendix 8A.

hydrogen bomb test had been a fizzle (i.e. an inefficient detonation releasing less explosive energy than could be expected from theoretical calculations).[110] The statement has influenced the domestic debate on the need to conduct more nuclear tests. This option has become an increasingly costly one because it would jeopardize India's nuclear cooperation deals with the United States and other countries.[111]

Strike aircraft

At present, aircraft constitute the most mature component of India's nuclear strike capabilities (see table 8.7).[112] The Indian Air Force (IAF) has reportedly certified the Mirage 2000H Vajra (Divine Thunder) multi-role aircraft for delivery of nuclear gravity bombs. The IAF deploys two squadrons of Mirage 2000H aircraft at the Gwalior Air Force Station, Madhya Pradesh, in north-central India. In addition, it is believed that some of the IAF's four squadrons of Jaguar IS Shamsher (Sword) fighter-bombers may have a nuclear delivery role.[113] Other aircraft in the IAF's inventory that are potentially suitable for a nuclear role are the MiG-27 (Bahadur) and the Su-30MKI.

Land-based missiles

The Prithvi (Earth) short-range ballistic missile (SRBM) was India's sole operational ballistic missile for many years. A number of Prithvi I missiles are widely believed to have been modified to deliver nuclear warheads, although this has not been officially confirmed. The Prithvi I (SS-150) is a single-stage, road-mobile, liquid-fuel ballistic missile capable of delivering a 1000-kilogram warhead to a maximum range of 150 km. The first test of the missile was in 1988 and it was subsequently inducted into service by the Indian Army in 1994. It is currently deployed with the army's 333, 444 and 555 missile groups. The Prithvi II and Prithvi III SRBMs are not believed to be assigned nuclear weapon delivery roles.

Indian defence sources indicate that the family of longer-range Agni (Fire) ballistic missiles, which are designed to provide a quick-reaction nuclear capability, has largely taken over the Prithvi's nuclear role.[114] The

---

[110] Parashar, S., 'Kalam certifies Pokharan II, Santhanam stands his ground', *Times of India*, 28 Aug. 2009.

[111] On these deals see Anthony, I. and Bauer, S., 'Controls on security-related international transfers', *SIPRI Yearbook 2009*, pp. 467–71.

[112] Norris, R. S. and Kristensen, H. M., 'Nuclear notebook: India's nuclear forces', *Bulletin of the Atomic Scientists*, vol. 64, no. 5 (Nov./Dec. 2008).

[113] Norris and Kristensen (note 112).

[114] 'Prithvi SRBM', Bharat Rakshak Missiles, 12 Oct. 2009, <http://www.bharat-rakshak.com/MISSILES/ballistic/prithvi.html>.

Table 8.7. Indian nuclear forces, January 2010

Type	Range (km)[a]	Payload (kg)	Status
Aircraft			
Mirage 2000H Vajra	1 850	6 300	Has reportedly been certified for delivery of nuclear gravity bombs
Jaguar IS Shamsher	1 400	4 760	Some of 4 squadrons may have nuclear delivery role
Land-based ballistic missiles[b]			
Prithvi I (P-I)	150	800	Entered service in 1994; widely believed to have a nuclear delivery role; fewer than 50 launchers deployed; most recent test flight on 15 Apr. 2009
Agni I[c]	>700	1 000	Most recent Indian Army operational test in Mar. 2008; deployed with the Indian Army's 334 Missile Group
Agni II	>2 000	1 000	Army operational launches on 19 May and 23 Nov. 2009; both unsuccessful; operational status uncertain
Agni III	>3 000	1 500	Under development; test-launched 3 times, most recently on 7 Feb. 2010; induction expected in 2010–11
Agni IV	~5 000	..	Under development; test launch expected in 2010
Sea-based ballistic missiles			
Dhanush	350	500	Test-launched on 6 Mar. and 13 Dec. 2009; induction underway
K-15[d]	700	500–600	Under development; test-launched from submerged pontoon on 26 Feb. 2008

[a] Aircraft range is for illustrative purposes only; actual mission range will vary according to flight profile and weapon loading. Missile payloads may have to be reduced in order to achieve maximum range.

[b] India has also begun developing a subsonic cruise missile with a range of 1000 km, known as the Nirbhay (Fearless), which is rumoured to have a nuclear capability.

[c] The original Agni I, now known as the Agni, was a technology demonstrator programme that ended in 1996.

[d] According to unconfirmed Indian media reports, a land-based version of the K-15, known as the Shourya, was test-launched for the first time on 12 Nov. 2008.

Sources: Indian Ministry of Defence, annual reports and press releases; International Institute for Strategic Studies (IISS), *The Military Balance 2006–2007* (Routledge: London, 2007); US Air Force, National Air and Space Intelligence Center (NASIC), *Ballistic and Cruise Missile Threat* (NASIC: Wright-Patterson Air Force Base, OH, Mar. 2009); US Central Intelligence Agency, 'Unclassified report to Congress on the acquisition of technology relating to weapons of mass destruction and advanced conventional munitions, 1 January through 30 June 2002', Apr. 2003, <https://www.cia.gov/library/reports/archived-reports-1/>; US National Intelligence Council, 'Foreign missile developments and the ballistic missile threat through 2015' (unclassified summary), Dec. 2001, <http://www.dni.gov/nic/special_missilethreat2001.html>; 'Nuclear notebook', *Bulletin of the Atomic Scientists*, various issues; and Authors' estimates.

Agni was developed by India's Defence Research and Development Organisation (DRDO) as part of its integrated missile development programme. The Agni I is a single-stage, solid-fuel missile that can deliver a 1000 kg warhead to a maximum distance of 700–800 km. It is currently in service with the Indian Army's 334 Missile Group. The two-stage Agni II can deliver a similar payload to a maximum range of 2000 km.[115] During 2009 flight-tests of the Agni II missile took place in May and November. The tests were described as being 'not fully successful' in achieving performance goals.[116]

The two-stage, solid-fuel Agni III missile is expected to be able to deliver a 1500-kg payload to a range 3000–3500 km. The rocket represents several important technological advances in India's missile programme: it makes use of a flex-nozzle control system for rocket guidance, specially developed composite propellants, and guidance and control systems with fault-tolerant avionics.[117] The Agni III was most recently flight-tested in February 2010. DRDO officials declared the test to have been successful and stated that the Agni III was ready for induction into the armed forces.[118]

Sea-based missiles

India continues to develop two systems that will comprise the naval leg of its planned triad of nuclear forces. The first is the Dhanush (Bow) missile, a naval version of the Prithvi II that is under development by the DRDO.[119] The missile is launched from a stabilization platform mounted on surface ships and can reportedly carry a 500-kg warhead to a maximum range of 350 km.[120] It is designed to be able to hit both sea- and shore-based targets, but the system's operational utility may be limited by its relatively short range. A Dhanush missile was successfully tested in December 2009.[121]

The DRDO has tested components of an underwater missile launch system and is developing a two-stage ballistic missile that can be launched from a submerged submarine using a gas booster.[122] MOD statements have designated the missile as the K-15, although other Indian sources refer to it

---

[115] Chansoria, M., 'India's missile programme: augmenting firepower', *India Strategic*, Oct. 2009.
[116] Mallikarjun, Y., 'Agni-II test-fired', *The Hindu*, 20 May 2009; and 'Agni-II missile fails to clear night trial', *Times of India*, 24 Nov. 2009.
[117] Pant, H. V. and Gopalaswamy, B., 'Launch into the Ivy League', *Indian Express*, 1 May 2007.
[118] 'Agni 3 clears test, all set to be inducted into the armed forces', *Indian Express*, 8 Feb. 2010.
[119] Indian Ministry of Defence, 'Dhanush missile—test launch', Press release, 30 Mar. 2007, <http://pib.nic.in/release/release.asp?relid=26541>.
[120] '"Dhanush" missile successfully test-fired', *Times of India*, 14 Dec. 2009.
[121] Mallikarjun, Y. and Subramanian, T. S., 'Dhanush missile successfully test fired', *The Hindu*, 14 Dec. 2009.
[122] Associated Press, 'India developing submarine launched ballistic missiles', *International Herald Tribune*, 11 Sep. 2007; and Unnithan, S., 'The secret undersea weapon', *India Today*, 17 Jan. 2008.

as the Sagarika (Oceanic) project.[123] The new nuclear-capable missile will reportedly be able to deliver a 500-kg payload to a distance of up to 700 km.[124]

The K-15 is expected to be deployed on an indigenously constructed nuclear-powered submarine, which is being built for the Indian Navy at Visakhapatnam, Andhra Pradesh, under the Advanced Technology Vessel (ATV) project.[125] The first of these, the INS *Arihant*, was launched on 26 July 2009. The submarine will undergo sea-trials for up to two years and will be equipped with an unknown number of K-15 missiles.[126]

VIII. Pakistani nuclear forces[127]

Pakistan is estimated to possess 70–90 nuclear weapons that can be delivered by aircraft or ballistic missiles (see table 8.8). Its current nuclear arsenal is based on weapon designs using HEU, which is produced by a gas centrifuge uranium enrichment facility at the Kahuta Research Laboratories (also called the A. Q. Khan Research Laboratories), Punjab. There is considerable evidence that Pakistan is moving towards a plutonium-based arsenal. Plutonium-based warheads would normally be lighter and more compact than those using HEU to achieve the same yield. Such warheads could either be fitted onto smaller missiles, possibly including cruise missiles, or would give already deployed ballistic missiles longer ranges. The 50-megawatt-thermal Khushab I reactor, completed in 1998, is capable of producing about 10–12 kg of weapon-grade plutonium annually.[128] Pakistan is building two additional plutonium production reactors at the nuclear complex at Khushab, Punjab, one of which may have started operating in 2009.[129] These new reactors will increase Pakistan's plutonium-production

---

[123] In 2006 the Indian MOD stated that 'There is no missile project by name "Sagarika"'. Indian Ministry of Defence, 'Development and trials missiles', Press release, 2 Aug. 2006, <http://pib.nic.in/release/rel_print_page1.asp?relid=19395>.

[124] Subramanian, T. S., '"Sagarika" missile test-fired successfully', *The Hindu*, 27 Feb. 2008.

[125] Unnithan, S., 'Indigenous N-submarine in two years: Navy chief', *India Today*, 3 Dec. 2007.

[126] Subramanian, T. S., 'Nuclear submarine Arihant to be fitted with K-15 ballistic missiles', *The Hindu*, 27 July 2009.

[127] Norris, R. S. and Kristensen, H. M., 'Nuclear notebook: Pakistani nuclear forces, 2009', *Bulletin of the Atomic Scientists*, vol. 65, no. 5 (Sep./Oct. 2009).

[128] Mian, Z. et al., *Fissile Materials in South Asia: The Implications of the U.S.–India Nuclear Deal*, International Panel on Fissile Materials (IPFM) Research Report no. 1 (IPFM: Princeton, NJ, Sep. 2006). For Pakistan's current stocks of fissile materials see appendix 8A.

[129] Albright, D. and Brannan, P., 'Commercial satellite imagery suggests Pakistan is building a second much larger plutonium production reactor: is South Asia headed for a dramatic buildup in nuclear arsenals?', Institute for Science and International Security, 24 July 2006, <http://isis-online.org/isis-reports/category/pakistan/>; and Brannan, P., 'Steam emitted from second Khushan reactor cooling towers; Pakistan may have started operating second reactor', Imagery Brief, Institute for Science and International Security, 24 Mar. 2010, <http://isis-online.org/isis-reports/category/pakistan/>.

capability several-fold, provided that the country has sufficient capacity to reprocess spent fuel.[130]

International concerns about the custodial security of Pakistan's nuclear arsenal continued to grow in 2009.[131] There have been fears that nuclear weapons could be obtained by terrorists or misused by elements in the Pakistani Government. However, US officials have generally expressed confidence in the security of Pakistan's nuclear arsenal. It is widely believed that Pakistan's efforts to improve the security of its nuclear weapons have been ongoing and include some cooperation with the USA.[132]

Strike aircraft

In its nuclear weapon delivery role, the Pakistani Air Force is most likely to use the US-produced F-16 fighter aircraft. Pakistan had originally planned to spend $5.1 billion on buying F-16 aircraft. The financial constraints that the 2005 Kashmir earthquake imposed on Pakistan reduced the number of new aircraft that it could purchase from 36 to 18, which lowered the total value of the deal to $3.1 billion ($1.4 billion for the 18 new aircraft; $641 million for associated munitions; and $891 million on 46 Mid-Life Update kits for Pakistan's existing F-16 fleet).[133] In addition, the USA has provided Pakistan with 14 F-16s designated as Excess Defense Articles.

Land-based missiles

Pakistan has two land-based, short-range ballistic missiles that are believed to have nuclear delivery roles. The Ghaznavi (Hatf-3) is a single-stage, solid-propellant, road-mobile SRBM, which was inducted into service in 2004. The most recent reported test flight of the Ghaznavi was in February 2008.[134] The Shaheen I (Hatf-4) entered into service with the Pakistani Army in 2003. It was most recently test-launched in January 2008 during a training exercise conducted by the Army Strategic Force Command.[135]

---

[130] Albright and Brannan (note 129).

[131] Ahmed, I., 'Pakistan's nuclear weapons: how safe are they?', Institute for South Asian Studies (ISAS) Brief, National University of Singapore, 18 Nov. 2009, <http://www.isasnus.org/publications.htm>.

[132] Kerr, P. and Nikitin, M. B., *Pakistan's Nuclear Weapons: Proliferation and Security Issues*, Congressional Research Service (CRS) Report for Congress RL34248 (US Congress, CRS: Washington, DC, 9 Dec. 2009).

[133] Camp, D., US Department of State, 'Defeating al-Qaeda's Air Force: Pakistan's F-16 program in the fight against terrorism', Statement before the US House of Representatives Foreign Affairs Subcommittee on South Asia, 16 Sep. 2008, <http://2001-2009.state.gov/p/sca/ci/af/2008/109757.htm>.

[134] 'Ghaznavi missile launched', *Dawn*, 14 Feb. 2008.

[135] 'Pakistan tests ballistic missile', BBC News, 25 Jan. 2008, <http://news.bbc.co.uk/2/7208416.stm>.

Table 8.8. Pakistani nuclear forces, January 2010

Type	Range (km)[a]	Payload (kg)	Status
Aircraft			
F-16A/B	1 600	4 500	32 aircraft, deployed in 3 squadrons; most likely aircraft to have a nuclear delivery role
Ballistic missiles			
Ghaznavi (Hatf-3)	~400	500	Entered service with the Pakistani Army in 2004; fewer than 50 launchers deployed; most recent test launch on 13 Feb. 2008; believed to be a copy of the M-11 missile acquired from China in the 1990s
Shaheen I (Hatf-4)	>450[b]	750–1 000	Entered service with the Pakistani Army in 2003; fewer than 50 launchers deployed; most recent test launch on 25 Jan. 2008
Shaheen II (Hatf-6)	2 500	(~1 000)	First 2 army operational readiness launch on 19 and 21 Apr. 2008; expected to become operational soon[c]
Ghauri I (Hatf-5)	>1 200	700–1 000	Entered service with the Pakistani Army in 2003; fewer than 50 launchers deployed; test-launched on 1 Feb. 2008
Cruise missiles			
Babur (Hatf-7)	700[d]	..	Under development; test-launched on 6 May 2009; sea- and air-launched versions also under development
Ra'ad (Hatf-8)	350	..	Under development; air-launched; first 2 test launches on 25 Aug. 2007 and on 8 May 2008

.. = not available or not applicable; ( ) = uncertain figure.

[a] Aircraft range is for illustrative purposes only; actual mission range will vary according to flight profile and weapon loading. Missile payloads may have to be reduced in order to achieve maximum range.

[b] Some unofficial sources claim that the Shaheen I has a range of 600–1500 km.

[c] The 2 operational readiness tests suggest that the Shaheen II may be operational.

[d] Since 2006 the range of flight tests has increased from 500 km to 700 km, and the goal is now 1000 km.

Sources: US Air Force, National Air and Space Intelligence Center (NASIC), *Ballistic and Cruise Missile Threat* (NASIC: Wright-Patterson Air Force Base, OH, Mar. 2009); US Central Intelligence Agency, 'Unclassified report to Congress on the acquisition of technology relating to weapons of mass destruction and advanced conventional munitions, 1 January through 30 June 2002', Apr. 2003; US National Intelligence Council, 'Foreign missile developments and the ballistic missile threat through 2015' (unclassified summary), Dec. 2001, <http://www.dni.gov/nic/special_missilethreat2001.html>; International Institute for Strategic Studies, *The Military Balance 2006–2007* (Routledge: London, 2007); 'Nuclear notebook', *Bulletin of the Atomic Scientists*, various issues; and authors' estimates.

The Ghauri I (Hatf-5) is Pakistan's only medium-range ballistic missile. It is a road-mobile, liquid-fuelled, single-stage missile with a range of about 1200 km. The missile entered into service with the Pakistani Army in 2003 and was most recently test-launched in February 2008.[136] Pakistan continues to develop the two-stage, road-mobile, solid-propellant Shaheen II (Hatf-6) MRBM. It uses a two-stage, solid-propellant rocket motor and has a maximum range of 2500 km. It was first successfully tested on 9 March 2004 and the most recent tests of the missile were in April 2008.

Pakistan is continuing to develop its arsenal of cruise missiles. On 6 May 2009 it conducted the latest in a series of a flight tests of the nuclear-capable Babur (Hatf-7) cruise missile.[137] It is also reported to be developing air- and sea-launched versions of this missile.[138] The development of the Babur is believed to be a response to India's desire to acquire a missile defence system.[139] In addition, Pakistan is developing a nuclear-capable air-launched cruise missile, known as the Ra'ad (Hatf-8), which will have a range of 350 km. The Ra'ad's first test was in August 2007, and it was tested for the second time in May 2008.[140]

IX. Israeli nuclear forces

Israel continues to maintain its long-standing policy of nuclear ambiguity, neither officially confirming nor denying that it possesses nuclear weapons.[141] In 2009 this policy came under renewed international scrutiny when remarks made by officials in the new US Administration were interpreted as calling for Israel to join the NPT as a non-nuclear weapon state.[142]

The size of the Israeli nuclear weapon stockpile is unknown, but it is widely believed to consist of roughly 100 plutonium warheads. According to one estimate, Israel possessed 650 kg of military plutonium as of January 2009;[143] this is the equivalent of 130 warheads, assuming that each contains 5 kg of plutonium. Only part of this plutonium may have been used to produce weapons. It is estimated here that Israel has approximately 80 intact nuclear warheads, of which 50 are re-entry vehicles for delivery by ballistic missiles and the rest bombs for delivery by aircraft (see table 8.9). Many analysts believe that Israel has a recessed nuclear arsenal (i.e. one that requires some preparation before use). There has been speculation that Israel may have produced tactical nuclear weapons, including

[136] Ansari, U., 'Pakistan pushes to improve missile strike capability', *Defense News*, 17 Nov. 2008.
[137] Nasir, S. A., 'Babar missile test-fired last Wednesday', *The Nation* (Islamabad), 9 May 2009.
[138] 'Pakistan successfully test-fires Hataf-VII missile', *PakTribune*, 26 July 2007.
[139] 'Babur missile far superior to Indian Brahmos: Musharraf', *PakTribune*, 11 Aug. 2005.
[140] Khan, I. A., 'Cruise missile fired from aerial platform', *Dawn*, 9 May 2008.
[141] On the role of this policy in Israel's national security decision making see Cohen, A., 'Israel', eds Born, Gill and Hänggi (note 72).
[142] Lake, E., 'Secret U.S.–Israel nuclear accord in jeopardy', *Washington Times*, 6 May 2009.
[143] See appendix 8A this volume.

Table 8.9. Israeli nuclear forces, January 2010

Type	Range (km)^a	Payload (kg)	Status
Aircraft^b			
F-16A/B/C/D/I Falcon	1 600	5 400	205 aircraft in the inventory; some are believed to be certified for nuclear weapon delivery
Ballistic missiles^c			
Jericho II	1 500– 1 800	750– 1 000	*c.* 50 missiles; first deployed in 1990; test-launched on 27 June 2001
Jericho III	>4 000	1 000– 1 300	Test-launched on 17 Jan. 2008

^{a} Aircraft range is for illustrative purposes only; actual mission range will vary. Missile payloads may have to be reduced in order to achieve maximum range.

^{b} Some of Israel's 25 F-15I aircraft may also have a long-range nuclear delivery role.

^{c} The Shavit space launch vehicle, if converted to a ballistic missile, could deliver a 775-kg payload to a distance of 4000 km. The Jericho I, first deployed in 1973, is no longer operational.

Sources: Cohen, A. and Burr, W., 'Israel crosses the threshold', *Bulletin of the Atomic Scientists*, vol. 62, no. 3 (May/June 2006); Cohen, A., *Israel and the Bomb* (Columbia University Press: New York, 1998); Albright, D., Berkhout, F. and Walker, W., SIPRI, *Plutonium and Highly Enriched Uranium 1996: World Inventories, Capabilities and Policies* (Oxford University Press: Oxford, 1997); Lennox, D. (ed.), *Jane's Strategic Weapon Systems* (Jane's Information Group: Coulsdon, 2003); Fetter, S., 'Israeli ballistic missile capabilities', *Physics and Society*, vol. 19, no. 3 (July 1990)—for an updated analysis, see unpublished 'A ballistic missile primer', <http://www.publicpolicy.umd.edu/Fetter/Publications>; 'Nuclear notebook', *Bulletin of the Atomic Scientists*, various issues; and authors' estimates.

artillery shells and atomic demolition munitions, but this has never been documented. There have also been unsubstantiated rumours in recent years that Israel may have developed a nuclear-capable sea-launched cruise missile (SLCM), based on the US-made Harpoon missile, for its fleet of three Type 800 Dolphin Class diesel-electric attack submarines purchased from Germany. Israel has denied these rumours.[144]

X. North Korea's military nuclear capabilities

North Korea is widely believed to have produced and separated enough plutonium to build a small number of nuclear warheads. However, the amount of plutonium that North Korea has separated from the spent fuel of its 5-megawatt electric graphite-moderated research reactor at Yongbyon, and hence the number of warheads it may have produced, has been the

[144] Ben-David, A., 'Israel orders two more Dolphin subs', *Jane's Defense Weekly*, 30 Aug. 2006, p. 5; and Williams, D., 'Israeli sub sails Suez, signalling reach to Iran', Reuters, 3 July 2009, <http://www.reuters.com/article/idUSTRE5621XZ20090703>.

subject of controversy.[145] In addition, doubts persist about whether North Korea has the design and engineering skills needed to manufacture a fully functional operational nuclear weapon.[146] North Korea demonstrated a nuclear weapon capability by carrying out underground nuclear test explosions in October 2006 and May 2009.[147] In both cases the estimated yield of the test explosion was much lower than what the initial nuclear tests by nuclear weapon states have historically produced; this has led some experts to question if the detonation was fully successful.[148] According to the US intelligence community, the 2009 test 'was apparently more successful than the 2006 test'.[149]

On 26 June 2008 North Korea made a formal declaration of its nuclear programme. It declared that it held a stock of 30.8 kg of separated plutonium, but this did not include unextracted plutonium contained in irradiated fuel rods, material that remained in equipment at the Yongbyon facilities or was lost during reprocessing, and plutonium used in the October 2006 nuclear detonation.[150] North Korea reprocessed the rest of the fuel rods containing plutonium in 2009.[151] As of December 2009, North Korea's plutonium stockpile was estimated to be about 35 kg.[152] This would be sufficient to make seven nuclear weapons, assuming that each weapon uses 5 kg of plutonium.

Apart from its plutonium programme, North Korea has been suspected by the USA of pursuing an undeclared uranium enrichment programme aimed at producing HEU for use in nuclear weapons. In January 2009 there were renewed allegations by senior US officials that North Korea had an active programme for enriching uranium for military purposes.[153] In 2009 North Korea issued a number of statements acknowledging that it had an enrichment programme under way for producing fuel for future

[145] Among other uncertainties, it is unclear whether North Korea extracted plutonium from the spent fuel rods believed to have been removed from the reactor before the arrival of International Atomic Energy Agency inspectors in 1990.

[146] Sanger, D. E. and Broad, W. J., 'Small blast, or "big deal"? U.S. experts look for clues', *New York Times*, 11 Oct. 2006.

[147] See Fedchenko, V. and Ferm Hellgren, R., 'Nuclear explosions, 1945–2006', *SIPRI Yearbook 2007*; and appendix 8B.

[148] 'CIA says North Korea nuclear test a failure: report', Reuters, 28 Mar. 2007, <http://www.reuters.com/article/topNews/idUSSEO15521620070328>; and Park, J., 'The North Korean nuclear test: what the seismic data says', *Bulletin of the Atomic Scientists*, 26 May 2009.

[149] Blair, D. C., 'Annual threat assessment of the US Intelligence Community for the Senate Select Committee on Intelligence', Office of the Director of National Intelligence, 2 Feb. 2010, <http://www.dni.gov/testimonies/20100202_testimony.pdf>, p. 14.

[150] 'North Korea declares 31 kilogrammes of plutonium', Global Security Newswire, 24 Oct. 2008, <http://www.globalsecuritynewswire.org/gsn/ts_20081024_4542.php>; and Kile, S. N., 'Nuclear arms control and non-proliferation', *SIPRI Yearbook 2009*, pp. 397–402.

[151] See chapter 9 in this volume.

[152] See appendix 8A.

[153] Kessler, G., 'White House voices concern on North Korea and uranium', *Washington Post*, 8 Jan. 2009. In 2007 US intelligence officials had backed away from earlier claims that North Korea had a covert, production-scale uranium enrichment programme.

nuclear power reactors.[154] The US Director of National Intelligence reiterated in February 2010 that North Korea 'has pursued a uranium enrichment activity in the past, which we assess was for weapons'.[155]

XI. Conclusions

In 2009 there was an overall decline in the number of operational nuclear weapons deployed by the five legally recognized and four de facto nuclear weapon states. The decline was due primarily to the withdrawal from deployment of warheads on strategic nuclear delivery vehicles by Russia and the United States—which together account for more than 90 per cent of the world's inventory of nuclear weapons—pursuant to meeting the warhead limit set by the 2002 SORT Treaty. However, many of the Russian and US warheads withdrawn from service have been placed in storage and could be redeployed on delivery vehicles, since neither the 1991 START Treaty nor SORT requires warheads to be verifiably dismantled.

Despite signs of a further resurgence of public interest in nuclear disarmament in 2009, all of the legally recognized nuclear weapon states appeared determined to retain their nuclear arsenals for the indefinite future and were either modernizing their nuclear forces or had announced plans to do so. Among the de facto nuclear weapon states, India and Pakistan continued to expand their nuclear strike capabilities, while Israel appeared to be waiting to see how Iran's nuclear programme developed. There remained considerable uncertainty about North Korea's nuclear weapon capabilities.

---

[154] Korean Central News Agency (KCNA), 'DPRK Foreign Ministry vehemently refutes UNSC's "Presidential Statement"', 14 Apr. 2009, <http://www.kcna.co.jp/item/2009/200904/news14/2009 0414-23ee.html>; KCNA, 'UNSC urged to retract anti-DPRK steps', 29 Apr. 2009, <http://www. kcna.co.jp/item/2009/200904/news29/20090429-14ee.html>; KCNA, 'DPRK Foreign Ministry declares strong counter-measures against UNSC's "Resolution 1874"', 13 June 2009, <http://www. kcna.co.jp/item/2009/200906/news13/20090613-10ee.html>; and KCNA, 'DPRK Permanent Representative sends letter to president of UNSC', 4 Sep. 2009, <http://www.kcna.co.jp/item/2009/2009 09/news04/20090904-04ee.html>. For analysis of these statements see Pollack, J., 'Parsing enrichment in North Korea', Arms Control Wonk, 7 Sep. 2009, <http://www.armscontrolwonk.com/2456/ parsing-uranium-enrichment-in-north-korea>.

[155] Blair (note 149), p. 14.

Appendix 8A. Global stocks of fissile materials, 2009

ALEXANDER GLASER AND ZIA MIAN*

Tables 8A.1 and 8A.2 detail global stocks of highly enriched uranium and separated plutonium, respectively.

Table 8A.1. Global stocks of highly enriched uranium (HEU), 2009

	National stockpile (tonnes)[a]	Production status	Comments
China	20 ± 4^b	Stopped 1987–89	
France[c]	35 ± 6^b	Stopped early 1996	Includes 5.0 tonnes declared civilian
India[d]	0.6 ± 0.3^b	Continuing	
Israel[e]	0.1		
Pakistan	2.1 ± 0.4^b	Continuing	
Russia[f]	770 ± 300^b	Stopped 1987 or 1988	Includes 100 tonnes assumed to be reserved for naval and other reactor fuel; does not include 118 tonnes to be blended down
United Kingdom[g]	23.3 (declared)	Stopped 1963	Includes 1.4 tonnes declared civilian
United States[h]	508 (declared)	Stopped 1992	Includes 128 tonnes reserved for naval reactor fuel and 20 tonnes for other HEU reactor fuel; does not include 109 tonnes to be blended down or for disposition as waste
Non-nuclear weapon states[i]	~10		
Total	**~1370**[j]		**Not including 227 tonnes to be blended down**

[a] Most of this material is 90–93% enriched in uranium-235, which is typically considered as weapon grade. Important exceptions are noted where required. Blending down (i.e. reducing the concentration of uranium-235) of excess Russian and US weapon-grade HEU up to the end of 2009 and mid-2009, respectively, has been taken into account.

* International Panel on Fissile Materials, Princeton University.

[b] A 20% uncertainty is assumed in the figures for total stocks in China and Pakistan and for the military stockpile in France, and 50% for India. The uncertainty of 300 tonnes for Russia reflects a 20% uncertainty about total Russian HEU production, which may have been up to 1500 tonnes.

[c] France declared 5.0 tonnes of civilian HEU to the International Atomic Energy Agency (IAEA) as of the end of 2008; it is assumed here to be weapongrade, 93% enriched HEU, even though some of the material is in irradiated form. The 20% uncertainty in the estimate applies only to the military stockpile of 30 tonnes and does not apply to the declared stock of 5.0 tonnes.

[d] It is believed that India is producing HEU (93% enriched equivalent) at a rate of less than 0.1 tonnes each year for use as naval reactor fuel.

[e] Israel may have acquired c. 100 kg of weapon-grade HEU covertly in or before 1965 from the USA.

[f] As of Dec. 2009, 382 tonnes of Russia's weapon-grade HEU had been blended down. The estimate shown for the Russian reserve for naval reactors is the authors' estimate based on the size of the Russian fleet.

[g] This figure includes 21.9 tonnes of HEU as of 31 Mar. 2002, the average enrichments of which were not given. The UK declared a stock of 1.4 tonnes of civilian HEU to the IAEA as of the end of 2008.

[h] The amount of US HEU is given in actual tonnes, not 93% enriched equivalent. As of 30 Sep. 1996 the USA had an inventory of 741 tonnes of HEU containing 620 tonnes of uranium-235. To date, the USA has earmarked 233 tonnes of HEU for blending down. As of mid-2009 it had blended down 124 tonnes of this material; however, little if any of this HEU was weapon-grade.

[i] The 2008 IAEA Annual Report lists 267 significant quantities of HEU under comprehensive safeguards. This corresponds to 6.67 tonnes of uranium-235 in uranium. To reflect the uncertainty in the enrichment levels of this material, mostly in research reactor fuel, a total of 10 tonnes of HEU is assumed.

[j] This total is rounded to the nearest 5 tonnes.

Sources: International Panel on Fissile Materials (IPFM), Global Fissile Material Report 2009 (IPFM: Princeton, NJ, Oct. 2009), figure 1.2, p. 13; Institute for Science and International Security (ISIS), Global Stocks of Nuclear Explosive Materials (ISIS: Washington, DC, Dec. 2003); Albright, D., Berkhout, F. and Walker, W., SIPRI, Plutonium and Highly Enriched Uranium 1996: World Inventories, Capabilities and Policies (Oxford University Press: Oxford, 1997), p. 80, table 4.1; Israel: Myers, H., 'The real source of Israel's first fissile material', Arms Control Today, vol. 37, no. 8 (Oct. 2007), p. 56; Gilinsky, V., 'Israel's bomb', New York Review of Books, 13 May 2004; see also Gilinsky, V., 'Time for more NUMEC information', Arms Control Today, vol. 38, no. 5 (June 2008); Pakistan: Hibbs, M., 'Pakistan developed more powerful centrifuges', NuclearFuel, vol. 32, no. 3 (29 Jan. 2007); Hibbs, M., 'P-4 centrifuge raised intelligence concerns about post-1975 data theft', Nucleonics Week, 15 Feb. 2007; Russia: United States Enrichment Corporation, 'Megaton to megawatts', <http://www.usec.com/>; UK: British Ministry of Defence, 'Historical accounting for UK defence highly enriched uranium', Mar. 2006, <http://www.mod.uk/Defence Internet/AboutDefence/CorporatePublications/HealthandSafetyPublications/DepletedUranium/>; International Atomic Energy Agency (IAEA), Communication received from the United Kingdom of Great Britain and Northern Ireland concerning its policies regarding the management of plutonium, INFCIRC/549/Add.8/12, 15 Sep. 2009; USA: US Department of Energy (DOE), Highly Enriched Uranium, Striking a Balance: A Historical Report on the United States Highly Enriched Uranium Production, Acquisition, and Utilization Activities from 1945 through September 30, 1996 (DOE: Washington, DC, 2001); George, R. and Tousley, D., DOE, 'US highly enriched uranium disposition', Presentation to the Nuclear Energy Institute Nuclear Fuel Supply Forum, Washington, DC, 24 Jan. 2006; George, R., 'U.S. HEU disposition program', Institute of Nuclear Materials Management 50th Annual Meeting, Tucson, AZ, 13–19 July 2009; Non-nuclear weapon states: IAEA, Annual Report 2008 (IAEA: Vienna, 2009), table A4.

Table 8A.2. Global stocks of separated plutonium, 2009

Country	Military stocks as of January 2009 (tonnes)	Military production status	Civilian stocks as of January 2009, unless indicated (tonnes)
China	4 ± 0.8[a]	Stopped in 1991	0
France	5 ± 1.0[a]	Stopped in 1994	55.5 (does not include 28.3 foreign owned)
Germany	0		13 (in France, Germany and the UK)
India[b]	0.7 ± 0.14[a]	Continuing	6.8
Israel[c]	0.65 ± 0.13[a]	Continuing	0
Japan	0		47.6 (including a total of 38 in France and the UK)
North Korea[d]	0.035	Resumed in 2009	0
Pakistan[e]	0.1 ± 0.02[a]	Continuing	0
Russia[f]	145 ± 25 (34 declared excess)	Effectively stopped in 1997	46.5
Switzerland	0		<0.05
United Kingdom[g]	7.9 (4.4 declared excess)	Stopped in 1989	78.6 (includes 0.9 abroad but not 27.0 foreign owned)
United States[h]	92 (53.9 declared excess)	Stopped in 1988	0
Totals	**~255 (92 declared excess)**		**~248**

[a] An uncertainty of 20% is assumed for military plutonium stocks in China, France, India, Israel and Pakistan

[b] India is estimated to be producing c. 30 kg a year of weapon-grade plutonium from the CIRUS and Dhruva reactors. As part of the Indian–US Civil Nuclear Cooperation Initiative, India has included in the military sector much of the plutonium separated from its spent power-reactor fuel that is labelled civilian here. The 6.8 tonnes of civilian plutonium were not placed under safeguards in the 'India-specific' safeguards agreement signed by the Indian Government and the IAEA on 2 Feb. 2009.

[c] Israel is believed to still be operating the Dimona plutonium production reactor but may be using it primarily for tritium production.

[d] North Korea is reported to have declared a plutonium inventory of 31 kg in June 2008 and resumed production in 2009.

[e] Pakistan is estimated to be producing c. 10 kg a year of weapon-grade plutonium from its Khushab-1 reactor. Two additional plutonium production reactors are under construction at the same site.

[f] Russia is producing c. 0.5 tonnes of weapon-grade plutonium annually in its 1 remaining production reactor that continues to operate because it also produces heat and electricity for nearby communities. It is scheduled to be shut down in 2010. Russia has committed itself not to use this material for weapons. Russia does not include its plutonium declared as excess in its IAEA INFCIRC/549 statement.

^g The UK declared 83.0 tonnes of civilian plutonium (not including 27.0 tonnes of foreign-owned plutonium in the UK). This includes 4.4 tonnes of military plutonium declared excess. However, since this 4.4 tonnes is not designated for IAEA safeguarding, in this estimate it continues to be assigned to the military stocks and is not included in the civilian stocks.

^h In its IAEA INFCIRC/549 statement, the USA declared 53.9 tonnes of plutonium as excess for military purposes.

Sources: International Panel on Fissile Materials (IPFM), *Global Fissile Material Report 2009* (IPFM: Princeton, NJ, Oct. 2009), figure 1.3, p. 16; Institute for Science and International Security (ISIS), *Global Stocks of Nuclear Explosive Materials* (ISIS: Washington, DC, Dec. 2003); *Military production status*: Albright, D., Berkhout, F. and Walker, W., SIPRI, *Plutonium and Highly Enriched Uranium 1996: World Inventories, Capabilities and Policies* (Oxford University Press: Oxford, 1997); US Department of Energy (DOE), 'U.S. removes nine metric tons of plutonium from nuclear weapons stockpile', Press release, 17 Sep. 2007, <http://www.energy.gov/nationalsecurity/5500.htm>; *Civilian stocks (except for India)*: declarations by country to the International Atomic Energy Agency (IAEA) under INFCIRC/549, <http://www.iaea.org/Publications/Documents/>; *India*: Estimate based on assuming 50% of India's accumulated heavy-water reactor spent fuel has been reprocessed; and Mian, Z. et al., *Fissile Materials in South Asia and the Implications of the U.S.–India Nuclear Deal*, International Panel on Fissile Materials (IPFM) Research Report no. 1 (IPFM: Princeton, NJ, Sep. 2006); *North Korea*: Kessler, G., 'Message to U.S. preceded nuclear declaration by North Korea', *Washington Post*, 2 July 2008; *Russia*: Agreement between the Government of the United States of America and the Government of the Russian Federation concerning the Management and Disposition of Plutonium Designated as No Longer Required for Defense Purposes and Related Cooperation (Russian–US Plutonium Management and Disposition Agreement), signed on 1 Sep. 2000, <http://www.state.gov/documents/organization/18557.pdf>.

Appendix 8B. Nuclear explosions, 1945–2009

VITALY FEDCHENKO

I. Introduction

In May 2009 the Democratic People's Republic of Korea (DPRK, or North Korea) conducted what is widely believed to be a nuclear test explosion. This was North Korea's second nuclear explosion, following one conducted in October 2006, and brought the total number of nuclear explosions recorded since 1945 to 2054. This appendix describes the available information on the North Korean explosion and then presents up-to-date data on the number of nuclear explosions conducted since 1945.[1]

II. The nuclear test in North Korea

On 29 April 2009 North Korea's official news agency, the Korean Central News Agency (KCNA), issued a statement warning that the country was prepared to conduct a nuclear test explosion as a response to the imposition of sanctions by the United Nations Security Council.[2] On 25 May 2009 the Chinese and United States governments were reportedly given less than one hour's notice that North Korea would conduct a nuclear test.[3] The explosion itself took place at 00:54 UTC.[4] At 02:24 UTC the International Monitoring System (IMS) of the Comprehensive Nuclear-Test-Ban Treaty Organization Preparatory Commission (CTBTO) issued the first report to CTBTO member states on the time, location and magnitude of the event.[5] A few hours later the KCNA announced that North Korea had conducted 'one more successful underground nuclear test' that was 'on a new higher level in terms of its explosive power and technology'.[6]

The KCNA claim had to be verified by available technologies. The technologies used for verification of underground nuclear tests include seismology,

---

[1] For full details of how international researchers have sought to determine the explosion's nature, location and yield based on the available data see Fedchenko, V., 'North Korea's nuclear test explosion, 2009', SIPRI Fact Sheet, Dec. 2009, <http://books.sipri.org/product_info?c_product_id=397>.

[2] 'UNSC urged to retract anti-DPRK steps', Korean Central News Agency, 29 Apr. 2009, <http://www.kcna.co.jp/item/2009/200904/news29/20090429-14ee.html>. For further background see chapter 9, section IV, in this volume.

[3] 'NKorea informed US of nuclear test: official', Agence France-Presse, 25 May 2009, <http://www.google.com/hostednews/afp/article/ALeqM5gRTYYuI6qR20V2-SERacQVXo4Zhg>.

[4] UTC is Coordinated Universal Time, which approximates to Greenwich Mean Time (GMT).

[5] CTBTO, 'CTBTO's initial findings on the DPRK's 2009 announced nuclear test', Press release, 25 May 2009, <http://www.ctbto.org/press-centre/press-releases/2009/ctbtos-initial-findings-on-the-dprks-2009-announced-nuclear-test/>.

[6] 'KCNA report on one more successful underground nuclear test', Korean Central News Agency, 25 May 2009, <http://www.kcna.co.jp/item/2009/200905/news25/20090525-12ee.html>.

Table 8B.1. Data on North Korea's nuclear explosion, 25 May 2009

Source[a]	Origin time (UTC)	Latitude	Longitude	Error margin[b]	Body wave magnitude[c]
IDC, Vienna[d]	00:54:42.8	41.3110° N	129.0464° E	±9.6 km[e]	4.52
BJI, Beijing	00:54:43.10	41.3000° N	129.0000° E	..	4.6
CEME, Obninsk	00:54:40.9	41.29° N	129.07° E	..	5.0
NEIC, Denver	00:54:43	41.306° N	129.029° E	±3.8 km[f]	4.7
NORSAR, Karasjok	00:54:43	41.28° N	129.07° E	..	4.7

UTC = Coordinated Universal Time; km = kilometres; .. = data not available.

[a] Because of differences between estimates, particularly regarding the precise site of the explosion, data from 5 sources—1 internationally recognized body and 4 national bodies—is provided for comparison: IDC = Comprehensive Nuclear-Test-Ban Treaty Organization (CTBTO), International Data Centre, Vienna; BJI = China Earthquake Administration, Institute of Geophysics, Beijing; CEME = Russian Academy of Sciences, Geophysical Survey, Central Experimental Methodical Expedition, Obninsk, Kaluga oblast; NEIC = US Geological Survey, National Earthquake Information Center, Denver, CO; NORSAR = Norwegian national data centre for the CTBTO, Karasjok.

[b] The error margins are as defined by the data sources.

[c] Body wave magnitude indicates the size of the event. In order to give a reasonably correct estimate of the yield of an underground explosion, detailed information is needed (e.g. on the geological conditions in the area where the explosion took place). Body wave magnitude is therefore an unambiguous way of giving the size of an explosion.

[d] The IDC was 'in a test and provisional operation mode only' and only 75% of the monitoring stations in the CTBTO's International Monitoring System were contributing data at the time of the event.

[e] This figure is the length of the semi-major axis of the confidence ellipse.

[f] This figure is the horizontal location error, defined as the 'length of the largest projection of the three principal errors on a horizontal plane'.

Sources: IDC data: Excerpts from the CTBTO Reviewed Event Bulletin (REB) provided by the CTBTO Public Information Section and the Swedish Defence Research Agency (FOI); and CTBTO, 'CTBTO's initial findings on the DPRK's 2009 announced nuclear test', Press release, 25 May 2009, <http://www.ctbto.org/press-centre/press-releases/2009/ctbtos-initial-findings-on-the-dprks-2009-announced-nuclear-test/>; *BJI data*: International Seismological Centre (ISC), 'Event 13193113 North Korea', ISC On-line Bulletin, <http://www.isc.ac.uk/cgi-bin/web-db-v3?event_id=13193113>; *CEME data*: CEME, 'Information message on underground nuclear explosion conducted in North Korea on May 25, 2009', 26 May 2009, <http://www.ceme.gsras.ru/cgi-bin/info_quakee.pl?mode=1&id=125>; *NEIC data*: NEIC, 'Magnitude 4.7: North Korea', Preliminary Earthquake Report, 7 Aug. 2009, <http://earthquake.usgs.gov/eqcenter/recenteqsww/Quakes/us2009hbaf.php>; *NORSAR data*: NORSAR, 'Announced nuclear test by North Korea', Press release, <http://www.norsar.no/pc-61-99-Announced-Nuclear-Test-by-North-Korea.aspx>.

radionuclide monitoring and satellite imagery analysis.[7] Following the event, a combination of these technologies was employed by the IMS, individual states and many research institutions to verify whether there had indeed been an explosion and, if so, its characteristics such as location, yield and nature.

[7] US National Academy of Sciences, *Technical Issues Related to the Comprehensive Nuclear Test Ban Treaty* (National Academy Press: Washington, DC, 2002), pp. 39–41.

Seismic data recorded at monitoring stations around the world was used to estimate the time, location and size of the event (see table 8B.1). The recorded seismic wave patterns, the depth of the event (less than 1 km) and the fact that it occurred so close to the site of the 2006 nuclear test indicate that the 2009 event was an explosion rather than an earthquake.[8]

Based on the seismic data, most estimates of the yield of the explosion vary between 2 and 7 kilotons, which is 'about 5 times stronger' than the 2006 test.[9] In June 2009 the US Government estimated the yield as 'approximately a few kilotons', and non-governmental scientists tend to agree with this assessment.[10]

Seismic data alone is insufficient to confirm that an underground explosion is nuclear. Following North Korea's 2006 test, air sampling detected traces of radioxenon, which confirmed the nuclear nature of the explosion.[11] After the 2009 event no trace of radioxenon or other debris was reported to have been found.[12] Despite this, there is consensus among scientists and CTBTO officials that the explosion on 25 May 2009 in North Korea was most probably nuclear.[13] In order to establish the nuclear nature of the event with absolute certainty, on-site inspection is needed.[14]

Due to the absence of detected radioactive effluents from the explosion, it is not possible to establish whether the North Korean test in 2009 used uranium or plutonium. It is widely assumed that it used plutonium.[15] The extent to which the North Korean nuclear test was successful is also uncertain because, unlike in 2006, North Korea did not preannounce the expected yield of the explosion. Some experts have questioned the success of the test, because the several-kiloton yield of the North Korean device is still a few times smaller than the yield that the initial nuclear tests by nuclear weapon states have historically produced.[16]

---

[8] Pearce, R. G. et al., 'The announced nuclear test in the DPRK on 25 May 2009', *CTBTO Spectrum*, no. 13 (Sep. 2009), p. 27.

[9] MacKenzie, D., 'North Korea's nuke test could have positive outcome', *New Scientist*, 26 May 2009. The nuclear test explosion in 2006 was estimated to have had a yield under 1 kt. Fedchenko, V. and Ferm Hellgren, R., 'Nuclear explosions, 1945–2006', *SIPRI Yearbook 2007*, p. 553.

[10] US Office of the Director of National Intelligence, 'Statement by the Office of the Director of National Intelligence on North Korea's declared nuclear test on May 25, 2009', News Release no. 23-09, 15 June 2009, <http://www.dni.gov/press_releases/20090615_release.pdf>; and Kalinowski, M. B., 'Second nuclear test conducted by North Korea on 25 May 2009', Fact sheet, University of Hamburg, Carl Friedrich von Weizsäcker Centre for Science and Peace Research (ZNF), 27 May 2009, <http://www.znf.uni-hamburg.de/Factsheet_NK.pdf>.

[11] Fedchenko and Ferm Hellgren (note 9), p. 553; and Williams, D. L., 'Characterizing nuclear weapons explosions based upon collected radio-nuclide effluents', Memorandum, Massachusetts Institute of Technology, Department of Nuclear Science and Engineering, 21 Oct. 2006, <http://web.mit.edu/tyler9/www/Characterizing Nuclear Weapons Explosions.doc>.

[12] Pearce et al. (note 8), pp. 28–29.

[13] CTBTO, 'Experts sure about nature of the DPRK event', Press release, 12 June 2009, <http://www.ctbto.org/press-centre/highlights/2009/experts-sure-about-nature-of-the-dprk-event/>; and Clery, D., 'Verification experts puzzled over North Korea's nuclear test', *Science*, 19 June 2009.

[14] CTBTO, 'Homing in on the event', Press release, 29 May 2009, <http://www.ctbto.org/press-centre/highlights/2009/homing-in-on-the-event/>.

[15] See chapter 9, section IV, in this volume.

[16] Park, J., 'The North Korean nuclear test: what the seismic data says', *Bulletin of the Atomic Scientists*, 26 May 2009.

III. Estimated number of nuclear explosions, 1945–2009

Table 8B.2 lists the known nuclear explosions to date, including nuclear tests conducted in nuclear weapon test programmes, explosions carried out for peaceful purposes and the two nuclear bombs dropped on Hiroshima and Nagasaki in August 1945. The totals also include tests for safety purposes carried out by France, the Soviet Union and the USA, irrespective of the yield and of whether they caused a nuclear explosion.[17] The table does not include sub-critical experiments. Simultaneous detonations, also called salvo explosions, were carried out by the USA (from 1963) and the Soviet Union (from 1965), mainly for economic reasons.[18] Of the Soviet tests, 20 per cent were salvo experiments, as were 6 per cent of the US tests.

'Underground nuclear test' is defined by the 1990 Protocol to the 1974 Soviet–US Threshold Test-Ban Treaty (TTBT) as 'either a single underground nuclear explosion conducted at a test site, or two or more underground nuclear explosions conducted at a test site within an area delineated by a circle having a diameter of two kilometers and conducted within a total period of time of 0.1 second'.[19] 'Underground nuclear explosion' is defined by the 1976 Soviet–US Peaceful Nuclear Explosions Treaty (PNET) as 'any individual or group underground nuclear explosion for peaceful purposes'.[20] 'Group explosion' is defined as 'two or more individual explosions for which the time interval between successive individual explosions does not exceed five seconds and for which the emplacement points of all explosives can be inter-connected by straight line segments, each of which joins two emplacement points and each of which does not exceed 40 kilometers'.[21]

A number of moratoriums, both voluntary and legal, have been observed. The USSR, the UK and the USA observed a moratorium on testing from November 1958 to September 1961. The 1963 Partial Test-Ban Treaty (PTBT), which prohibits nuclear explosions in the atmosphere, in outer space and under water, entered into force on 10 October 1963.[22] The USSR observed a unilateral moratorium on testing between August 1985 and February 1987. The USSR and then Russia observed a moratorium on testing from January 1991 and the USA from October 1992, until they signed the Comprehensive Nuclear-Test-Ban Treaty (CTBT) on 24 September 1996; France observed a similar moratorium from April 1992 to September 1995. The CTBT, which has not yet entered into force, would prohibit the carrying out of any nuclear explosion.[23]

---

[17] In a safety experiment, or a safety trial, more or less fully developed nuclear devices are subjected to simulated accident conditions. The nuclear weapon core is destroyed by conventional explosives with no or very small releases of fission energy. The United Kingdom also carried out numerous safety tests, but they are not included in table 2 because of their high number.

[18] The USSR conducted simultaneous tests including as many as 8 devices on 23 Aug. 1975 and on 24 Oct. 1990 (the last Soviet test).

[19] 1999 TTBT Protocol, Section I, para. 2. For a summary and other details of the 1974 Treaty on the Limitation of Under-ground Nuclear Weapon Tests and its Protocol see annex A in this volume.

[20] PNET, Article II.a. For a summary and other details of the 1976 Treaty on Underground Nuclear Explosions for Peaceful Purposes see annex A in this volume.

[21] PNET (note 20), Article II.c.

[22] The parties include India, Pakistan, Russia, the UK and the USA. For a full list see annex A.

[23] The signatories include China, France, Russia, the UK and the USA. For a full list see annex A.

Table 8B.2. Estimated number of nuclear explosions, 1945–2009

a = atmospheric (or in a few cases underwater); u = underground.

Year	USA[a] a	u	Russia/ USSR a	u	UK[a] a	u	France a	u	China a	u	India a	u	Pakistan a	u	North Korea a	u	Total
1945	3	–	–	–	–	–	–	–	–	–	–	–	–	–	–	–	3
1946	2[b]	–	–	–	–	–	–	–	–	–	–	–	–	–	–	–	2
1947	–	–	–	–	–	–	–	–	–	–	–	–	–	–	–	–	–
1948	3	–	–	–	–	–	–	–	–	–	–	–	–	–	–	–	3
1949	–	–	1	–	–	–	–	–	–	–	–	–	–	–	–	–	1
1950	–	–	–	–	–	–	–	–	–	–	–	–	–	–	–	–	–
1951	15	1	2	–	–	–	–	–	–	–	–	–	–	–	–	–	18
1952	10	–	–	–	1	–	–	–	–	–	–	–	–	–	–	–	11
1953	11	–	5	–	2	–	–	–	–	–	–	–	–	–	–	–	18
1954	6	–	10	–	–	–	–	–	–	–	–	–	–	–	–	–	16
1955	17[b]	1	6[b]	–	–	–	–	–	–	–	–	–	–	–	–	–	24
1956	18	–	9	–	6	–	–	–	–	–	–	–	–	–	–	–	33
1957	27	5	16[b]	–	7	–	–	–	–	–	–	–	–	–	–	–	55
1958	62[c]	15	34	–	5	–	–	–	–	–	–	–	–	–	–	–	116
1959	–	–	–	–	–	–	–	–	–	–	–	–	–	–	–	–	–
1960	–	–	–	–	–	–	3	–	–	–	–	–	–	–	–	–	3
1961	–	10	58[b]	1	–	–	1	1	–	–	–	–	–	–	–	–	71
1962	39[b]	57	78	1	–	2	–	1	–	–	–	–	–	–	–	–	178
1963	4	43	–	–	–	–	–	3	–	–	–	–	–	–	–	–	50
1964	–	45	–	9	–	2	–	3	1	–	–	–	–	–	–	–	60
1965	–	38	–	14	–	1	–	4	1	–	–	–	–	–	–	–	58
1966	–	48	–	18	–	–	6	1	3	–	–	–	–	–	–	–	76
1967	–	42	–	17	–	–	3	–	2	–	–	–	–	–	–	–	64
1968	–	56		17	–	–	5	–	1	–	–	–	–	–	–	–	79
1969	–	46	–	19	–	–	–	–	1	1	–	–	–	–	–	–	67
1970	–	39	–	16	–	–	8	–	1	–	–	–	–	–	–	–	64
1971	–	24	–	23	–	–	5	–	1	–	–	–	–	–	–	–	53
1972	–	27	–	24	–	–	4	–	2	–	–	–	–	–	–	–	57
1973	–	24	–	17	–	–	6	–	1	–	–	–	–	–	–	–	48
1974	–	22	–	21	–	1	9	–	1	–	–	1	–	–	–	–	55
1975	–	22	–	19	–	–	–	2	–	1	–	–	–	–	–	–	44
1976	–	20	–	21	–	1	–	5	3	1	–	–	–	–	–	–	51
1977	–	20	–	24	–	–	–	9	1	–	–	–	–	–	–	–	54
1978	–	19	–	31	–	2	–	11	2	1	–	–	–	–	–	–	66
1979	–	15	–	31	–	1	–	10	1	–	–	–	–	–	–	–	58
1980	–	14	–	24	–	3	–	12	1	–	–	–	–	–	–	–	54
1981	–	16	–	21	–	1	–	12	–	–	–	–	–	–	–	–	50
1982	–	18	–	19	–	1	–	10	–	1	–	–	–	–	–	–	49
1983	–	18	–	25	–	1	–	9	–	2	–	–	–	–	–	–	55
1984	–	18	–	27	–	2	–	8	–	2	–	–	–	–	–	–	57
1985	–	17	–	10	–	1	–	8	–	–	–	–	–	–	–	–	36
1986	–	14	–	–	–	1	–	8	–	–	–	–	–	–	–	–	23
1987	–	14	–	23	–	1	–	8	–	1	–	–	–	–	–	–	47
1988	–	15	–	16	–	–	–	8	–	1	–	–	–	–	–	–	40
1989	–	11	–	7	–	1	–	9	–	–	–	–	–	–	–	–	28

Year	USA[a]		Russia/ USSR		UK[a]		France		China		India		Pakistan		North Korea		Total
	a	u	a	u	a	u	a	u	a	u	a	u	a	u	a	u	
1990	–	8	–	1	–	1	–	6	–	2	–	–	–	–	–	–	18
1991	–	7	–	–	–	1	–	6	–	–	–	–	–	–	–	–	14
1992	–	6	–	–	–	–	–	–	–	2	–	–	–	–	–	–	8
1993	–	–	–	–	–	–	–	–	–	1	–	–	–	–	–	–	1
1994	–	–	–	–	–	–	–	–	–	2	–	–	–	–	–	–	2
1995	–	–	–	–	–	–	–	5	–	2	–	–	–	–	–	–	7
1996	–	–	–	–	–	–	–	1	–	2	–	–	–	–	–	–	3
1997	–	–	–	–	–	–	–	–	–	–	–	–	–	–	–	–	–
1998	–	–	–	–	–	–	–	–	–	–	–	2[d]	–	2[d]	–	–	4
1999	–	–	–	–	–	–	–	–	–	–	–	–	–	–	–	–	–
2000	–	–	–	–	–	–	–	–	–	–	–	–	–	–	–	–	–
2001	–	–	–	–	–	–	–	–	–	–	–	–	–	–	–	–	–
2002	–	–	–	–	–	–	–	–	–	–	–	–	–	–	–	–	–
2003	–	–	–	–	–	–	–	–	–	–	–	–	–	–	–	–	–
2004	–	–	–	–	–	–	–	–	–	–	–	–	–	–	–	–	–
2005	–	–	–	–	–	–	–	–	–	–	–	–	–	–	–	–	–
2006	–	–	–	–	–	–	–	–	–	–	–	–	–	–	–	1	1
2007	–	–	–	–	–	–	–	–	–	–	–	–	–	–	–	–	–
2008	–	–	–	–	–	–	–	–	–	–	–	–	–	–	–	–	–
2009	–	–	–	–	–	–	–	–	–	–	–	–	–	–	–	1	1
Subtotal	217	815	219	496	21	24	50	160	23	22	–	3	–	2	–	2	
Total	1 032		715		45		210		45		3		2		2		2 054

Notes: This table is based on tables published in previous editions of the SIPRI Yearbook, most recently Fedchenko, V. and Ferm Hellgren, R., 'Nuclear explosions, 1945–2006', SIPRI Yearbook 2007, table 12B.2.

[a] All British tests from 1962 were conducted jointly with the USA at the US Nevada Test Site but are listed only under 'UK' in this table. Thus, the number of US tests is higher than shown. Safety tests carried out by the UK are not included in the table.

[b] 1 of these tests was carried out under water.

[c] 2 of these tests were carried out under water.

[d] India's detonations on 11 and 13 May 1998 are listed as 1 test for each date. The 5 detonations by Pakistan on 28 May 1998 are also listed as 1 test.

Sources: Swedish Defence Research Agency (FOI), various estimates, including information from the CTBTO International Data Centre and information from the Swedish National Data Centre provided to the author in Feb. 2007 and Oct. 2009; Reports from the Australian Seismological Centre, Australian Geological Survey Organisation, Canberra; US Department of Energy (DOE), United States Nuclear Tests: July 1945 through September 1992 (DOE: Washington, DC, 1994); Norris, R. S., Burrows, A. S. and Fieldhouse, R. W., Natural Resources Defense Council, Nuclear Weapons Databook, vol. 5, British, French and Chinese Nuclear Weapons (Westview: Boulder, CO, 1994); Direction des centres d'experimentations nucléaires (DIRCEN) and Commissariat à l'Énergie Atomique (CEA), Assessment of French Nuclear Testing (DIRCEN and CEA: Paris, 1998); Russian ministries of Atomic Energy and Defence, USSR Nuclear Weapons Tests and Peaceful Nuclear Explosions, 1949 through 1990 (Russian Federal Nuclear Center (VNIIEF): Sarov, 1996); and Natural Resources Defense Council, 'Archive of nuclear data', <http://www.nrdc.org/nuclear/nudb/datainx.asp>.

Part III. Non-proliferation, arms control and disarmament, 2009

9. Nuclear arms control and non-proliferation

SHANNON N. KILE

I. Introduction

The year 2009 saw new momentum behind global efforts to promote nuclear disarmament and non-proliferation. These efforts were given a boost in May 2009 when Russia and the United States began formal negotiations on a new strategic arms reduction treaty. Other developments included the consensus agreement reached in the 65-member Conference on Disarmament (CD) in Geneva to open negotiations on a fissile material cut-off treaty (FMCT) after a 12-year procedural impasse. The United Nations Security Council adopted a politically binding resolution that codified a broad consensus on a range of actions to promote nuclear disarmament and non-proliferation and to address the threat of nuclear terrorism. During the year two new nuclear weapon-free zone (NWFZ) treaties entered into force, one covering Central Asia and the other Africa.

At the same time, in 2009 little progress was made towards resolving the long-running controversies over the nuclear programmes of Iran and the Democratic People's Republic of Korea (DPRK, or North Korea), which have been the focus of international concerns about the spread of nuclear weapons. These concerns were heightened in 2009 by North Korea's decision to conduct a second nuclear test explosion and to resume the production of plutonium for nuclear weapons.

This chapter reviews these and other developments in nuclear arms control, disarmament and non-proliferation in 2009. Section II describes the opening of Russian–US negotiations on a strategic arms reduction treaty and the main points of contention in the talks. Section III describes developments related to Iran's nuclear programme and summarizes the findings of the International Atomic Energy Agency (IAEA) about the country's previously undeclared uranium enrichment plant whose existence was revealed in 2009. Section IV describes the impasse in the Six-Party Talks on the denuclearization of the Korean peninsula and North Korea's decisions to conduct a second nuclear test explosion and to restart its nuclear weapon production infrastructure. Section V summarizes international concerns about suspected undeclared nuclear activities in Syria and Myanmar. Sections VI and VII describe developments in multilateral disarmament and non-proliferation including the Central Asian and Afri-

Table 9.1. Summary of Russian–US nuclear arms reduction treaties' force limits

Treaty	Date of signature/ entry into force	Total treaty-accountable nuclear warheads	Total strategic nuclear delivery vehicles[a]	Expiration date
START I	31 July 1991/ 5 Dec. 1994[b]	6000	1600	5 Dec. 2009
START II	3 Jan. 1993/ ..[c]	3000–3500	None[d]	..
SORT	24 May 2002/ 1 June 2003	1700–2200	None	31 Dec. 2012
START follow-on	8 April 2010 ..	1500	800 (700 deployed)	10 years after entry into force

SORT = Strategic Offensive Reductions Treaty (Moscow Treaty); START = Strategic Arms Reduction Treaty.

[a] Strategic nuclear delivery vehicles are intercontinental ballistic missiles (ICBMs), submarine-launched ballistic missiles (SLBMs) and long-range bombers.

[b] In May 1992 Belarus, Kazakhstan and Ukraine signed the Lisbon Protocol with Russia and the USA, making all 5 countries parties to START I.

[c] The START II Treaty never entered into force.

[d] START II would have prohibited the deployment of multiple independently targetable re-entry vehicles (MIRVs) on ICBMs and limited parties to 1700–1750 SLBMs each.

Sources: Annex A; and White House, 'Joint Understanding for the START follow-on treaty', 8 July 2009, <http://www.whitehouse.gov/the_press_office/The-Joint-Understanding-for-The-Start-Follow-On-Treaty>.

can NWFZ treaties that entered into force in 2009. Section VIII presents the conclusions.

II. Russian–US strategic nuclear arms control

In 2009 Russia and the USA formally launched negotiations on a strategic arms reduction treaty to succeed the 1991 Treaty on the Reduction and Limitation of Strategic Offensive Arms (START Treaty).[1] The opening of the talks was a high priority for the Russian Government as well as for the new US Administration of President Barack Obama. In April Obama pledged to pursue a new treaty as part of a US commitment to a long-term vision of 'peace and security in a world without nuclear weapons'.[2]

The replacement of the START Treaty, which was set to expire on 5 December 2009, became an increasingly urgent issue for both Russia and

---

[1] For a summary and other details of the START Treaty see annex A in this volume.

[2] White House, 'Remarks by President Barack Obama, Hradcany Square, Prague, Czech Republic', 5 Apr. 2009, <http://www.whitehouse.gov/the_press_office/Remarks-By-President-Barack-Obama-In-Prague-As-Delivered/>.

the USA. This was because the START verification regime was the primary means by which the two countries monitor each other's strategic nuclear forces. The START regime included 13 types of on-site inspections as well as continuous monitoring activities, data exchanges and notifications regarding the parties' strategic nuclear forces and facilities.[3] It was also the basis for verifying the implementation of the additional nuclear force reductions mandated by the 2002 Strategic Offensive Reductions Treaty (SORT), which lacks its own verification provisions (see table 9.1).[4] Some arms control advocates pointed out that, if these arrangements were no longer to be observed, the strategic forces of Russia and the USA would become much less transparent to one another. This in turn would raise the risk of their respective nuclear force planning being driven by worst-case scenarios.[5]

On 1 April 2009 President Obama and Russian President Dmitry Medvedev issued a joint statement announcing their decision to begin talks on a 'new, comprehensive, legally binding agreement on reducing and limiting strategic offensive arms to replace the START Treaty'.[6] Bilateral talks followed on 24 April and negotiations opened on 22 May.[7]

In a Joint Understanding in July Obama and Medvedev reaffirmed their pledges to make further cuts in their countries' strategic offensive arms and to conclude 'at an early date' a new legally binding agreement to succeed the 1991 START Treaty.[8] The presidents proposed that each party reduce its strategic forces so that seven years after the treaty's entry into force the central limits would be 'in the range of 500–1100 for strategic nuclear delivery vehicles' (i.e. intercontinental ballistic missiles, ICBMs; submarine-launched ballistic missiles, SLBMs; and long-range bombers) and 'in the range of 1500–1675 for their associated warheads'.[9] The provisions for calculating these limits were to be agreed through further negotiations

---

[3] US Department of State, 'START: verification', Fact Sheet, 29 July 1991, <http://www.state.gov/www/global/arms/factsheets/wmd/nuclear/start1/strtveri.html>.

[4] For a summary of SORT (also called the Moscow Treaty) see annex A in this volume.

[5] Kimball, D., 'Jump-STARTing US–Russian disarmament', Arms Control Today, vol. 38, no. 9 (Apr. 2008), p. 3. Russian and US officials both emphasized the importance of preserving the START verification regime, albeit in a simplified form. Kile, S. N., 'Nuclear arms control and non-proliferation', SIPRI Yearbook 2009, p. 406.

[6] White House, 'Joint statement regarding further reductions in strategic offensive arms', 1 Apr. 2009, <http://www.whitehouse.gov/the_press_office/Joint-Statement-by-Dmitriy-A-Medvedev-and-Barack-Obama>.

[7] 'U.S., Russia set to open START talks May 19 in Moscow', RIA Novosti, 15 May 2009, <http://en.rian.ru/russia/20090515/155026763.html>. The delegations were led by US Assistant Secretary of State Rose Gottemoeller and Ambassador Anatoly Antonov, the Director of the Russian Foreign Ministry's Department of Security Affairs and Disarmament.

[8] White House, 'Joint Understanding for the START follow-on treaty', 8 July 2009, <http://www.whitehouse.gov/the_press_office/The-Joint-Understanding-for-The-Start-Follow-On-Treaty>.

[9] White House (note 8). Russia reportedly sought the lower limit of 500 delivery vehicles since it will have to eliminate a large number of obsolescent Soviet-era missiles over the next decade. MacAskill, E. and Harding, L., 'US and Russia close in on nuclear treaty', The Guardian, 15 Dec. 2009.

as were those on definitions, data exchanges, notifications, eliminations, inspections and verification procedures, and on confidence-building and transparency measures. The Joint Understanding stipulated that these measures were to be 'adapted, simplified, and made less costly, as appropriate, in comparison to the START Treaty'.[10] The treaty's duration would be 10 years unless it were superseded by a subsequent agreement.

Obama and Medvedev agreed that the new treaty would have a provision on the contentious issue of the 'interrelationship of strategic offensive and strategic defensive arms'.[11] Previous bilateral discussions of a post-START agreement had been complicated by Russian objections to the planned US deployment of missile defence interceptors and tracking radar at sites in the Czech Republic and Poland. Russia had insisted that the USA must first address Russia's concerns about the implications of the proposed missile defence system for its strategic nuclear deterrent before a new arms reduction agreement could be reached. According to US officials, the decision to include the provision linking strategic offensive and defensive forces reflected an understanding that missile defence issues would not be part of the negotiations on the post-START treaty.[12] The USA subsequently announced that it had shelved the planned missile defence system in the Czech Republic and Poland and would instead deploy elsewhere in Europe a reconfigured system designed to intercept short- and medium-range missiles. US officials denied that the decision was related to Russian objections to the system envisioned by the preceding US Administration.[13]

Principal issues of contention

Russia and the USA had held eight rounds of talks in Geneva by the end of 2009. The most significant substantive difference at the talks centred on specific monitoring activities for verifying the new numerical limits to be set by the post-START treaty. These included so-called non-reciprocal measures, in particular provisions for continuous portal monitoring by US inspectors at the Russian strategic missile production facility at Votkinsk.[14] These activities would not be reciprocal because the USA, unlike Russia, was no longer building new strategic missiles.[15] Russian also objected to

[10] White House (note 8).

[11] White House (note 8).

[12] Tauscher, E., US Under Secretary of State for Arms Control and International Security, Remarks to US Strategic Command Deterrence Symposium, Omaha, NE, 30 July 2009, <http://www.acronym.org.uk/docs/0907/doc11.htm>.

[13] Baker, P., 'White House scraps Bush's approach to missile shield', *New York Times*, 17 Sep. 2009.

[14] Grossman, E. M., 'U.S. treaty-monitoring presence at Russian missile plant winding down', Global Security Newswire, 20 Nov. 2009, <http://gsn.nti.org/gsn/nw_20091120_8953.php>.

[15] Russia had a reciprocal monitoring arrangement at what was then the Thiokol Strategic Operations facility in Utah before the US decision to halt the production of new missiles.

renewing the START Treaty's provisions for handling strategic missile flight-test data. Russia reportedly resisted renewing START's ban on the encryption of telemetry data from missile flight tests because it planned to introduce a new generation of strategic missiles while the USA had no plans to do so.[16]

In addition, Russia and the USA reportedly disagreed over whether to adjust the 'counting rules' used in the START Treaty (i.e. the rules for attributing a specific number of warheads to specific delivery vehicles regardless of whether those delivery vehicles carry fewer warheads). The USA pushed to modify these attribution rules and allow each side to use on-site inspections to count the number of warheads deployed on the other's delivery systems.[17] Russia countered that, without a set number of warheads per missile, what its inspectors find on individual missiles might not give adequate information about the US stockpile of operational warheads. This concern was related to Russia's insistence that a new treaty must effectively constrain the USA's considerable advantage over Russia in 'upload potential'—the ability to rapidly redeploy nuclear warheads held in storage on to strategic nuclear delivery vehicles. Russia's view was that a major shortcoming of SORT was that it did not 'lock in', or make irreversible, the mandated force reductions by requiring the parties to verifiably eliminate the warheads withdrawn from deployment.[18]

The previous US Administration's plans for deploying non-nuclear warheads on some strategic missile systems as part of the Strategic Command's Global Strike plan was another point of contention.[19] Russia wanted any future treaty limits to apply to US ICBMs and SLBMs that might be armed with conventional instead of nuclear munitions.[20]

---

[16] Collina, T. Z., 'START stalls; talks continue', *Arms Control Today*, vol. 40, no. 1 (Jan./Feb. 2010); and Grossman, E. M., 'Talks hit "sweet spot" for landing new START agreement, U.S. official says', Global Security Newswire, 13 Jan. 2010, <http://www.globalsecuritynewswire.org/gsn/nw_20100113_6737.php>.

[17] Collina, T. Z., 'START deadline looms; endgame begins', *Arms Control Today*, vol. 39, no. 9 (Nov. 2009).

[18] Diakov, A. and Miasnikov, E., 'On some aspects of the Joint Understanding for the START follow-on treaty, signed by U.S. and Russian presidents during the recent summit meeting', Moscow Centre for Arms Control, Energy and Environmental Studies, 7 Aug. 2009, <http://www.arms control.ru/pubs/en/adem080709e.pdf>, p. 3. In contrast to Russia, which had to eliminate ageing and obsolescent strategic missile delivery systems, the USA met the START-mandated limit on deployed strategic warheads largely by removing warheads carried on MIRVed missiles and placing them in storage. Russian experts noted that this would give the USA a significant advantage in the number of deployed strategic warheads if it chose to return to the previous missile loadings.

[19] See Kile, S. N., Fedchenko, V. and Kristensen, H., 'World nuclear forces, 2008', *SIPRI Yearbook 2008*, p. 370.

[20] Grossman, E. M., 'Russian experts question role of conventional "prompt Global Strike" weapons', Global Security Newswire, 7 Apr. 2009, <http://gsn.nti.org/gsn/nw_20090406_7955.php>.

Expiration of the START Treaty

By the late autumn of 2009 both Russia and the USA acknowledged that too many substantive issues and technical details remained unresolved for a new agreement to be concluded before the START Treaty expired.[21] With the expiration date looming, the two sides worked to complete a legally binding 'bridging mechanism', which would be in force until they finished a follow-on treaty, but they were unable to meet the deadline.[22] On 4 December presidents Obama and Medvedev issued a brief joint statement declaring their determination to continue working together 'to ensure that a new treaty on strategic arms enters into force at the earliest possible date'.[23]

The expiration of START meant that some of its verification procedures were discontinued. The most controversial of these was the end of the arrangement for US continuous monitoring activities at the Russian missile production facility at Votkinsk. This arrangement had been criticized in Russia as being excessively intrusive.[24] However, in the USA some Republican senators criticized the administration for having allowed the measure to lapse at a time when the Russian facility was producing new mobile ICBMs that are difficult for the USA to monitor through national technical means.[25]

A potential complication for the negotiations emerged when Russian Prime Minister Vladimir Putin linked Russia's signing of a follow-on treaty to new agreed limits on US missile defence plans.[26] This appeared to contradict statements made by US Administration officials that the two sides had agreed that missile defence issue would be addressed separately from the START follow-on accord.[27] In the USA, Putin's statement led to renewed political criticism of the Obama Administration's approach to the negotiations. In 2009 Republicans in the US Congress had sought to amend the 2010 National Defense Authorization Bill so as to prohibit spending to implement a START follow-on treaty unless the accord, among other things, placed no limitations on US missile defence capabilities and was

---

[21] Baker, P. and Levy, C. J., 'Arms treaty is likely to expire before new pact is set', *New York Times*, 3 Dec. 2009.

[22] 'START verification regime could outlast treaty', Global Security Newswire, 24 Nov. 2009, <http://www.globalsecuritynewswire.org/gsn/nw_20091124_5240.php>.

[23] White House, 'Joint statement by the President of the United States of America and the President of the Russian Federation on the expiration of the Strategic Arms Reduction Treaty (START)', 4 Dec. 2009, <http://www.whitehouse.gov/the-press-office/joint-statement-president-united-states-america-and-president-russian-federation-ex>.

[24] Poroskov, N., 'Goodbye Votkinsk', *Vremya Novostei*, 3 Dec. 2009.

[25] Kralev, N., 'U.S. to stop counting new missiles in Russia', *Washington Times*, 1 Dec. 2009.

[26] 'Vladimir Putin attacks US missile defence', BBC News, 29 Dec. 2009, <http://news.bbc.co.uk/2/hi/8433352.stm>.

[27] Tauscher (note 12).

accompanied by full funding for modernizing the US nuclear weapon production complex.[28]

The year ended without the conclusion of a new arms reduction agreement to replace the START Treaty. The two sides agreed to resume negotiations in Geneva in mid-January 2010.

III. Iran and nuclear proliferation concerns

In 2009 the controversy over the scope and nature of Iran's nuclear activities intensified with the revelation that Iran was building a previously undeclared uranium enrichment plant. In September Iran sent a letter to the IAEA Director General, Mohamed ElBaradei, informing the agency that Iran was building a second pilot enrichment facility, in addition to the one located at Natanz, to produce low-enriched uranium (LEU) for use as nuclear fuel.[29] The letter was sent to the IAEA shortly before US President Obama, French President Nicolas Sarkozy and British Prime Minister Gordon Brown convened a joint press conference to announce that Iran was building an undeclared enrichment plant and that their countries had been aware of the site for some time.[30]

According to US officials, the plant was located in an underground tunnel complex in the grounds of an Islamic Revolutionary Guards Corps base near the city of Qom. They expressed concern that the plant's size, configuration and location indicated that it might be used to produce highly enriched uranium (HEU) for a suspected nuclear weapon programme.[31] The plant's discovery also raised new suspicions about the possible existence of other undeclared nuclear facilities that were not subject to IAEA safeguards inspections.[32]

Iran denied that the facility, called the Fordow Fuel Enrichment Plant (FFEP) by the IAEA, was part of a covert nuclear weapon programme. In a letter to the agency in October Iran stated that the decision to build the plant came 'as a result of the augmentation of threats of military attacks against Iran'—an allusion to past Israeli and US statements that the use of

[28] Collina, T. Z., 'Administration pushes to finish "new START"', *Arms Control Today*, vol. 39, no. 7 (Sep. 2009).

[29] IAEA, Board of Governors, 'Implementation of the NPT safeguards agreement and relevant provisions of Security Council resolutions 1737 (2006), 1747 (2007), 1803 (2008) and 1835 (2008) in the Islamic Republic of Iran', Report by the Director General, GOV/2009/74, 16 Nov. 2009, p. 2. The letter indicated that the uranium would be enriched up to a level of 5% (in the isotope uranium-235). The IAEA documents cited here are available on the IAEA website, <http://www.iaea.org/>.

[30] Sanger, D. E. and Broad, W. J., 'U.S. and allies warn Iran over nuclear "deception"', *New York Times*, 26 Sep. 2009.

[31] White House, 'Background briefing by senior Administration officials on Iranian nuclear facility', 25 Sep. 2009, <http://www.whitehouse.gov/the_press_office/Background-Briefing-By-Senior-Administration-Officials-On-Iranian-Nuclear-Facility>.

[32] Lewis, J., 'Covert site in Iran', Arms Control Wonk, 25 Sep. 2009, <http://www.armscontrolwonk.com/2475/covert-site-in-iran>.

force against Iran's nuclear programme could not be ruled out. The letter stated that the Fordow site had been 'allocated' to the Atomic Energy Organization of Iran (AEOI) in the second half of 2007 and construction had begun at that time; the FFEP was scheduled to become operational in 2011. The letter explained that the site was being prepared as a 'contingency' plant so that enrichment activities would not be halted in the case of military attacks on Iran's pilot- and commercial-scale centrifuge plants at Natanz.[33]

On 26–27 October 2009 IAEA inspectors carried out a design information verification visit and confirmed that the plant was at an advanced stage of construction, although no centrifuges had been installed there. They also verified that the plant was configured to hold 16 cascades with a total of approximately 3000 centrifuges.[34] Iran told the IAEA that it planned to install only first-generation IR-1 centrifuges at Fordow. However, comments made by the director of the AEOI suggested that Iran would install a new generation of more efficient centrifuges there at a later date.[35] According to US officials, when fully operational the FFEP would have the capacity to produce enough HEU for 'one or two' nuclear weapons per year.[36]

IAEA questions and concerns

In November ElBaradei reported to the IAEA Board of Governors on safeguards implementation in Iran, highlighting several issues of concern regarding the Fordow plant. Although inspectors had confirmed that the layout of the facility matched the information provided in the design information questionnaire submitted by Iran in October, more information was needed to clarify the purpose of the facility. The report also questioned Iran's stated chronology of its work on the facility, noting that commercial satellite photos indicated that there had been construction at the site between 2002 and 2004 and that this had resumed in 2006. Whether all of these activities were associated with the construction of an enrichment plant was unclear.[37]

Regardless of when design work on the FFEP was authorized or construction began, Iran's failure to notify the IAEA of the new facility until

[33] IAEA, GOV/2009/74 (note 29), p. 3.
[34] IAEA, GOV/2009/74 (note 29), p. 2.
[35] Kalantari, H., 'Iran plans to use new centrifuge at nuclear plant', Reuters, 6 Oct. 2009, <http://www.reuters.com/article/idUSTRE5951Z920091006>.
[36] White House (note 31). The US Government's timeline was contested by 2 non-governmental analysts, who calculated that the plant would require up to 4 years to produce enough HEU for 1 weapon, if it started with natural uranium. Oelrich, I. and Barzashka, I., 'A technical evaluation of the Fordow fuel enrichment plant', *Bulletin of the Atomic Scientists*, 23 Nov. 2009.
[37] IAEA, GOV/2009/74 (note 29), p. 3.

September 2009 was 'inconsistent with its obligations under the Subsidiary Arrangements to its Safeguards Agreement'.[38] The report rejected the claims made by Iranian officials that they had not yet been required to inform the IAEA about the Fordow plant because Iran was currently implementing an older version of a safeguards subsidiary arrangement called Code 3.1.[39] The IAEA has stated repeatedly that no mechanism exists in Iran's safeguards agreement for its unilateral suspension of the modified Code 3.1 text that was agreed with the agency in 2003.[40]

In November the IAEA Board of Governors adopted a resolution that criticized Iran for not fulfilling its safeguards obligations and not complying with previous demands by the Board and the UN Security Council that it suspend all enrichment-related activities.[41] The resolution called on Iran to halt construction of the FFEP plant and to confirm that it had not 'taken a decision to construct, or authorize construction of, any other nuclear facility previously not declared to the Agency'. Iran was also urged to apply the modified Code 3.1 and to implement promptly the Additional Protocol.[42]

The resolution called on Iran to cooperate fully with the IAEA by 'providing such access and information that the Agency requests to resolve all outstanding issues concerning Iran's nuclear programme'. As detailed in ElBaradei's 16 November report to the Board, there remained a number of safeguards compliance issues 'of serious concern' that needed to be clarified to exclude the existence of possible military dimensions to Iran's

---

[38] In Feb. 2003, following the revelation of the previously undeclared enrichment plants at Natanz, Iran agreed to a modified text of its Subsidiary Arrangements General Part, Code 3.1, concerning the early provision of design information to the IAEA. This required Iran to provide the agency with design information for new nuclear facilities subject to safeguards 'as soon as the decision to construct, or to authorize construction, of such a facility has been taken, whichever is earlier'.

[39] In response to the UN Security Council's adoption of Resolution 1747, in Mar. 2007 Iran suspended its adherence to the modified Code 3.1 text. It reverted to the original version of the text agreed in 1976 under which Iran was required to submit design information for a new facility 'not later than 180 days before the facility is scheduled to receive nuclear material for the first time'.

[40] Iran has maintained that it could revert to the original version of the Code 3.1 text because the modified text had never been ratified by the Majlis (parliament). For a critical assessment of the Iranian claim see Acton, J. M., 'Iran violated international obligations on Qom facility', Carnegie Endowment of International Peace, Proliferation analysis, 25 Sep. 2009, <http://www.carnegie endowment.org/publications/index.cfm?fa=view&id=23884>.

[41] IAEA, Board of Governors, 'Implementation of the NPT safeguards agreement and relevant provisions of Security Council resolutions 1737 (2006), 1747 (2007), 1803 (2008) and 1835 (2008) in the Islamic Republic of Iran', Resolution, GOV/2009/82, 27 Nov. 2009. The resolution was rejected by 3 states (Cuba, Malaysia and Venezuela) and 6 states abstained (Afghanistan, Brazil, Egypt, Pakistan, South Africa and Turkey); 26 states voted in favour.

[42] IAEA, GOV/2009/82 (note 41), p. 2. In Dec. 2003 Iran had signed an Additional Protocol to its comprehensive safeguards agreement that gave IAEA inspectors enhanced powers to investigate possible undeclared nuclear activities. In Feb. 2006 Iran announced that it would no longer implement the protocol, which had yet to be ratified by the Majlis, in protest at the IAEA Board's decision to refer Iran's nuclear file to the UN Security Council.

nuclear programme.[43] The report noted that 'well over a year [had passed] since the Agency was last able to engage Iran' in discussions about the outstanding issues, in particular about allegations that Iran had carried out studies related to certain aspects of nuclear weapon design.[44] In addition to these alleged studies, suspicions that Iran was engaged in secret nuclear weapon design work were heightened when a Farsi-language document was published in a British newspaper that appeared to describe a programme to develop and test a key nuclear weapon component.[45]

In an apparent response to the IAEA Board's resolution, the Iranian Government announced on 29 November that it had approved plans for building 10 new uranium enrichment plants. The construction of 5 plants whose locations had already been decided would start within 2 months.[46]

Resumption of talks between Iran and the P5+1 states

Coinciding with the controversy over the plant at Fordow, in October Iran and the P5+1 states (the five permanent members of the UN Security Council—China, France, Russia, the United Kingdom and the USA—plus Germany) resumed negotiations, for the first time in more than a year, on the future of Iran's uranium enrichment programme. The talks appeared to achieve a breakthrough when the parties announced that they had reached an agreement in principle on a nuclear fuel supply deal: Iran would send 1200 kilograms of LEU—approximately 75 per cent of its total inventory of domestically produced LEU—to Russia for further enrichment.[47] France would then fabricate the Iranian LEU or Russian-origin enriched uranium into fuel for the Tehran Research Reactor (TRR).[48] That reactor was expected to run out of LEU fuel in 2010—a prospect that reportedly prompted Iran during the summer of 2009 to seek assistance in refuelling it.[49]

The proposed deal was greeted by Western countries as a useful confidence-building measure, since it would require Iran to ship most of its

[43] For a summary of these issues see Kile, S. N., 'Nuclear arms control and non-proliferation', *SIPRI Yearbook 2009*, pp. 395–96.

[44] IAEA, GOV/2009/74 (note 29), pp. 6–7.

[45] Philip, C., 'Secret document exposes Iran's nuclear trigger', *The Times*, 14 Dec. 2009. The document, which was dismissed by Iran as a fabrication, described a neutron initiator made out of uranium deutride that was designed to set off the explosion in a nuclear weapon.

[46] 'Iran "planning 10 new uranium enrichment sites"', BBC News, 29 Nov. 2009, <http://news.bbc.co.uk/2/hi/8385275.stm>; and 'Iran to build more uranium plants', Al Jazeera, 30 Nov. 2009, <http://english.aljazeera.net/news/middleeast/2009/11/20091129154255281852.html>.

[47] Erlanger, S. and Landler, M., 'Iran agrees to send enriched uranium to Russia', *New York Times*, 2 Oct. 2009.

[48] The TRR, which is used to produce medical isotopes, has been operating on Argentine fuel since 1993. The fuel in use is enriched to 19.7% in uranium-235. France and Russia are the only countries with the technical capability to fabricate fuel rods to the specifications required by the TRR.

[49] Porter, G., 'Iran's fuel for conflict', *Le Monde Diplomatique*, 9 Dec. 2009.

declared LEU stockpile out of the country by the end of 2009.[50] The material would be returned to Iran in the form of fuel plates, usable in the TRR but difficult to convert to weapon use. According to a number of official and non-governmental estimates, by early 2009 Iran had produced enough LEU to build at least one nuclear weapon if it chose to do so in the future.[51]

On 29 October Iran presented a counter-proposal to an IAEA-drafted plan that had been based on the P5+1 proposal.[52] Iran accepted in principle the idea of shipping domestically produced LEU abroad for enrichment, but it insisted that the shipments must be made in smaller batches over an undefined period of time. The offer reflected the Iranian Government's distrust over whether the Western countries would allow the return of the enriched fuel. The P5+1 proposal reportedly had become a politicized issue among the senior Iranian leadership, which was already deeply divided over the disputed results of the country's presidential elections in June 2009.[53]

Following repeated calls for Iran to clarify its position, the deal between Iran and the P5+1 collapsed the following month. Iranian Foreign Minister Manoucherh Mottaki announced that his country was not willing to send LEU abroad before the fuel intended for the TRR arrived in the country; Iran would consider a 'simultaneous exchange' on Iranian territory, on the Gulf island of Kish.[54] The new offer was dismissed by France, Germany and the UK (the 'European Union three', EU-3) and the USA as undermining the basic purpose of the original deal: namely, to bring Iran's stockpile of LEU below the level required to construct a nuclear weapon.[55]

The year ended without a fuel supply deal for the TRR. The breakdown of the talks led the USA to call for a tougher international approach to Iran, including the adoption of robust new sanctions. As 2010 began, however, signs appeared that the US calls would not enjoy the unanimous backing of the P5 states.[56]

---

[50] Erlanger and Landler (note 47); and Kalantari (note 35). According to several estimates, Iran would require c. 1 year to replace the 1200 kg of LEU at its current rate of production.

[51] Borger, J., 'Iran has enough enriched uranium to make bomb, IAEA says', *The Guardian*, 19 Feb. 2009; and 'Iran has enough nuclear fuel to make bomb: US', Reuters, 1 Mar. 2009, <http://www.reuters.com/article/idUSTRE5201GO20090301>.

[52] Blitz, J., Bozorgmehr, N. and Dombey, D., 'Iran seeks big changes to nuclear deal', *Financial Times*, 30 Nov. 2009; and Pouladi, F., 'Iran wants more talks on nuclear fuel deal', Agence France-Press, 30 Oct. 2009.

[53] 'Iran: too divided for a nuclear deal?', BBC News, 5 Nov. 2009, <http://news.bbc.co.uk/2/hi/8343990.stm>; and Porter (note 49).

[54] Hafezi, P., 'Iran rejects sending uranium abroad', Reuters, 18 Nov. 2009, <http://www.reuters.com/article/idUSTRE5AH2H820091118>.

[55] Erlanger, S., 'Frustration as Iran stalls on deal', *New York Times*, 20 Nov. 2009. See also Council of the European Union, 'Statement by Robert Cooper following the E3+3 meeting on Iran in Brussels', 20 Nov. 2009, <http://www.consilium.europa.eu/uedocs/cms_data/docs/pressdata/EN/declarations/111386.pdf>.

[56] MacFarquhar, N., 'Chinese envoy objects to more penalties for Iran', *New York Times*, 6 Jan. 2009.

IV. The impasse over North Korea's nuclear programme

In 2009 the Six-Party Talks remained stalemated over reviving a denuclearization plan for North Korea that had been agreed by the parties in 2007.[57] The plan set out a sequence of reciprocal steps, based on the principle of 'action-for-action', that were intended to pave the way for North Korea to verifiably 'abandon' its nuclear programme.[58] However, the deal broke down in the autumn of 2008 because of dispute between the two principal antagonists—North Korea and the USA—over how to verify the accuracy and completeness of North Korea's initial declaration of its nuclear facilities and plutonium production activities as required under the agreement.[59]

North Korea's resumption of ballistic missile and nuclear tests

In April 2009 North Korea's news agency reported that a three-stage rocket launched from the Musudan-ri missile facility on the north-east coast of the country had successfully carried into orbit a communications satellite.[60] In contrast to its previous launches of long-range rockets, North Korea had announced its intention to launch a civilian satellite several weeks before the event. The North Korean claim to have placed a satellite in orbit was dismissed by outside analysts because tracking data indicated that the rocket's third stage, along with the satellite payload, had crashed into the Pacific Ocean.[61] Japan, South Korea and the USA denounced the launch as an attempt by North Korea to continue flight testing its long-range Taepodong-2 ballistic missile following a failed test in 2006.[62]

Following protracted discussions, the UN Security Council unanimously adopted a presidential statement condemning North Korea's rocket launch, demanding that North Korea 'not conduct further launches' and reiterating that North Korea must fully comply with Resolution 1718 and suspend all ballistic missile activities.[63] The statement also called on the Security Coun-

---

[57] The Six-Party Talks began in Aug. 2003 as a Chinese diplomatic initiative aimed at resolving the controversy over how to address North Korea's suspected nuclear weapon programme. The 6 parties are China, Japan, North Korea, South Korea, Russia and the USA.

[58] For a description of the 2007 denuclearization plan see Kile, S. N., 'Nuclear arms control and non-proliferation', *SIPRI Yearbook 2008*, pp. 351–54.

[59] See Kile (note 5), pp. 399–402.

[60] Korean Central News Agency, 'KCNA on DPRK's successful launch of satellite Kwangmyong-song-2', 5 Apr. 2009, <http://www.kcna.co.jp/item/2009/200904/news05/20090405-11ee.html>.

[61] Broad, W. J., 'North Korea's missile launch was a failure, experts say', *New York Times*, 5 Apr. 2009.

[62] 'Defiant N Korea launches rocket', BBC News, 5 Apr. 2009, <http://news.bbc.co.uk/2/hi/7982874.stm>.

[63] United Nations, Security Council, Statement by the President, S/PRST/2009/7, 13 Apr. 2009. Resolution 1718 demanded that North Korea abandon all nuclear weapons as well as all existing

ell's Sanctions Committee on North Korea to implement the measures set out in Resolution 1718 that had been suspended on North Korea's return to the Six-Party Talks in late 2006.

North Korea denounced the statement as a US-led effort 'wantonly infringing upon the sovereignty of the DPRK' and the country's right under international law to develop a civilian satellite programme. In response to the Security Council's action North Korea announced that it would no longer participate in the Six-Party Talks and would not be bound by any agreements previously reached in the talks. It also would act to 'boost its nuclear deterrent for self-defence in every way'. In particular, it would restart the production of plutonium for nuclear weapons that been halted as part of the 2007 denuclearization agreement and would take measures 'to restore to their original state the nuclear facilities which had been disabled according to the agreement'.[64] North Korea subsequently announced that it had begun reprocessing the spent fuel rods from the graphite-moderated nuclear reactor at Yongbyon.[65]

International reaction to the second North Korean nuclear test explosion

In May 2009 North Korea's news agency reported that, for the second time, a successful underground nuclear test explosion had been carried out.[66] The previous test in October 2006 was widely considered to have been a failure because of its unexpectedly low explosive yield.[67] Although the test was not unexpected, the announcement was greeted by international condemnation.[68]

In June the UN Security Council unanimously approved Resolution 1874, which demanded that North Korea 'abandon all nuclear weapons and existing nuclear programmes in a complete, verifiable and irreversible

nuclear and ballistic missile programmes in a 'complete, verifiable and irreversible manner'. UN Security Council Resolution 1718, 14 Oct. 2006.

[64] Korean Central News Agency, 'DPRK Foreign Ministry vehemently refutes UNSC's "Presidential Statement"', 14 Apr. 2009, <http://www.kcna.co.jp/item/2009/200904/news14/20090414-23ee.html>.

[65] Korean Central News Agency, 'Foreign Ministry spokesman on reprocessing of spent fuel rods', 25 Apr. 2009, <http://www.kcna.co.jp/item/2009/200904/news25/20090425-20ee.html>.

[66] Korean Central News Agency, 'KCNA report on one more successful underground nuclear test', 25 May 2009, <http://www.kcna.co.jp/item/2009/200905/news25/20090525-12ee.html>.

[67] Based on the seismic data collected by several monitoring networks, non-governmental experts estimated that the explosive yield was c. 2–7 kilotons. The nuclear test explosion in 2006 was estimated to have a yield of under 1 kiloton. On the test explosion see appendix 8B in this volume.

[68] North Korea had issued a statement at the end of Apr. 2009 warning that it might conduct a nuclear test in response to the Security Council Sanctions Committee's decision to impose new restrictions on 3 major North Korean companies. Korean Central News Agency, 'UNSC urged to retract anti-DPRK steps', 29 Apr. 2009, <http://www.kcna.co.jp/item/2009/200904/news29/20090429-14ee.html>.

manner' and return to the Six-Party Talks.[69] In addition to imposing new financial sanctions on North Korea, the resolution called on UN member states to cooperate with the inspection of cargo travelling to and from North Korea. It gave them expanded authority to interdict ships on the high seas if there were 'reasonable grounds' to believe that the ships were carrying banned cargo, including equipment and materials for North Korea's nuclear and ballistic missile programmes. This provision brought the interdiction powers authorized by the Security Council into closer alignment with those of the US-led Proliferation Security Initiative (PSI).[70]

The North Korean Foreign Ministry denounced Resolution 1874 as 'yet another vile product of the US-led offensive of international pressure' aimed at undermining North Korea and its political system.[71] North Korea announced that, in light of the Security Council's action, it would move to weaponize all of the plutonium separated from the remaining spent fuel rods at Yongbyon.[72] The statement also said that North Korea had been developing experimental uranium enrichment technology for producing nuclear fuel for a future light-water reactor and would now 'commence' with enriching uranium. This attracted considerable international attention because it appeared to confirm longstanding suspicions that North Korea was secretly pursuing a uranium enrichment programme.[73]

In October 2009 the prospects for renewed diplomatic efforts appeared to brighten. North Korean leader Kim Jong Il reportedly said that his country would be prepared to return to the Six-Party Talks if it could first make progress in bilateral negotiations with the USA. US officials welcomed Kim's reported comments but emphasized that, while the USA was open to renewed bilateral dialogue with North Korea, it would not allow such discussions to replace the Six-Party Talks.[74]

---

[69] UN Security Council Resolution 1874, 12 June 2009. On the provisions of Resolution 1874 see appendix 12A in this volume.

[70] Announced by US President George W. Bush in May 2003, the PSI consists of a set of agreed principles under which participating countries are allowed to search aircraft and ships carrying suspect cargo and seize illegal weapons or missile and nuclear technologies. For an analysis of legal concerns arising from the PSI see Ahlström, C., 'The Proliferation Security Initiative: international law aspects of the Statement of Interdiction Principles', SIPRI Yearbook 2005, pp. 741–65.

[71] Korean Central News Agency, 'DPRK Foreign Ministry declares strong counter-measures to UNSC's "Resolution 1874"', 13 June 2009, <http://www.kcna.co.jp/item/2009/200906/news13/20090613-10ee.html>.

[72] On 3 Nov. 2009 North Korea announced that it had completed the reprocessing of the spent fuel rods. For further detail see chapter 8, section IX, in this volume.

[73] E.g. see Harden, B., 'North Korea says it will start enriching uranium', Washington Post, 13 June 2009. However, some non-governmental analysts pointed out that the North Korean statement did not explicitly refer to enriching uranium for use in nuclear weapons. Pollack, J., 'Mis-reporting North Korea', TotalWonkerr, 14 June 2009, <http://totalwonkerr.com/2038/mis-reporting-north-korea>.

[74] Thatcher, J., 'North Korea says ready to return to nuclear talks', Reuters, 6 Oct. 2009, <http://www.reuters.com/article/idUSSP48900020091006>.

There was a cautious improvement in the bilateral relations between North Korea and the USA during the remainder of 2009. These included the first visit to Pyongyang by Stephen Bosworth, the US special envoy to North Korea, on 8–10 December 2009.[75] After the visit, the North Korean Foreign Ministry stated that the country's leadership understood the need to resume the Six-Party Talks and had agreed to work with the USA to narrow the 'remaining differences'.[76] However, the year ended with no progress made towards restarting the talks, amid indications that North Korea was determined to retain its nascent nuclear arsenal for the indefinite future.

V. Proliferation concerns in Syria and Myanmar

Syria

In 2009 little progress was made in resolving the outstanding issues arising from the IAEA's investigation of a suspected undeclared nuclear facility located at al-Kibar, in eastern Syria. The site was destroyed by an Israeli air strike in September 2007.[77] The Israeli and US governments have alleged that Syria had been secretly constructing, with technical assistance from North Korea, a nuclear reactor said to be similar to the reactor that North Korea used to produce plutonium for a nuclear explosive device.[78] The Syrian Government has stated that the destroyed building was a disused military facility that had no connection to nuclear activities.[79]

In November the IAEA's Director General, Mohamed ElBaradei, reported to the Board of Governors that Syria continued to withhold the cooperation necessary for the agency to be able to confirm Syria's statements about the non-nuclear nature of the al-Kibar site.[80] Among other shortcomings, Syria had declined to provide information about its procurement of material and equipment that the IAEA believed could be used for building a reactor. Syria also continued to deny inspectors access to three

---

[75] 'Senior US envoy Bosworth begins talks in North Korea', BBC News, 8 Dec. 2009, <http://news.bbc.co.uk/2/hi/8400739.stm>.

[76] Korean Central News Agency, 'DPRK on US envoy's Pyongyang visit', 11 Dec. 2009, <http://www.kcna.co.jp/item/2009/200912/news11/20091211-12ee.html>.

[77] See Follath, E. and Stark, H., 'How Israel destroyed Syria's Al Kibar nuclear reactor', Der Spiegel, 2 Nov. 2009.

[78] US Office of the Director of National Intelligence, 'Background briefing with senior U.S. officials on Syria's covert nuclear reactor and North Korea's involvement', 24 Apr. 2008, <http://www.dni.gov/interviews.htm>. US intelligence officials acknowledged that they had only 'low confidence' that the site was part of a clandestine nuclear weapon programme since Syria did not possess a reprocessing facility or any of the other infrastructure needed for such a programme.

[79] 'Syria denies US allegations over nuclear reactor', Syria Today, May 2008.

[80] IAEA, Board of Governors, 'Implementation of the NPT safeguards agreement in the Syrian Arab Republic', Report by the Director General, GOV/2009/75, 16 Nov. 2009.

other locations that were suspected of having a 'functional relationship' to the activities at al-Kibar.[81]

The report also noted that the IAEA had made little progress in determining the origin of the anthropogenic (chemically processed) natural uranium particles, which are of a type not included in Syria's declared inventory, that were found in environmental samples taken by inspectors in 2008 at the al-Kibar site.[82] According to Syria, the particles are likely to have come from depleted-uranium (DU) munitions used by Israel in the attack on the site. Based on its analysis of the composition and the morphology of the particles, the IAEA assessed that there was a 'low probability' that the use of DU munitions could account for their presence.[83] The question of the particles' origin was important to the agency.[84] The uranium was in a form which must be declared by Syria to the IAEA under the country's safeguards agreement, and its presence raised doubt about the correctness and completeness of Syria's declaration.[85] In 2009 a similar safeguards compliance question arose when anthropogenic natural uranium particles, of a type not in Syria's declared inventory, were found in environmental samples taken from the hot cells of the country's single research reactor, in Damascus.[86]

Myanmar

In August 2009 an Australian newspaper reported that Myanmar was engaged in clandestine nuclear collaboration with North Korea. Dissident groups had previously made claims about covert nuclear sites in Myanmar, including reactors and uranium mines and mills.[87] The Australian story reported the construction of a secret nuclear reactor and plutonium reprocessing facility in caves at Naung Laing in the northern part of the country.[88] The alleged facilities were located near the site of a 10-megawatt

[81] IAEA, GOV/2009/75 (note 80), p. 3.

[82] IAEA, GOV/2009/75 (note 80), p. 2.

[83] IAEA, GOV/2009/75 (note 80), p. 2.

[84] One non-governmental expert, citing an unnamed source close to the IAEA, speculated that the particles came from nuclear fuel secretly imported by Syria from North Korea. Acton, J., 'Norks may have shipped Syria U fuel', Arms Control Wonk, 21 Nov. 2008, <http://www.armscontrolwonk.com/2106/new-evidence-of-nork-syria-link>.

[85] Agreement between the Government of the Syrian Arab Republic and the International Atomic Energy Agency for the application of safeguards in connection with the Treaty on the Non-proliferation of Nuclear Weapons, signed on 25 Feb. 1992, entered into force on 18 May 1992, reproduced in IAEA Information Circular INFCIRC/407, July 1992.

[86] See Albright, D. and Shire, J., 'IAEA Report on Iran', Institute for Science and International Security (ISIS) Report, 16 Nov. 2009; and Brannan, P., 'ISIS analysis of November 16, 2009 IAEA report on Syria', Institute for Science and International Security Reports, 16 Nov. 2009, <http://www.isis-online.org/isis-reports/detail/isis-analysis-of-november-6-2009-iaea-report-on-syria>.

[87] E.g. see Lintner, B., 'Tunnels, guns and kimchi: North Korea's quest for dollars: part 1', Yale-Global Online, 9 June 2009, <http://yaleglobal.yale.edu/content/NK-quest-for-dollars-part1>.

[88] McDonald, H., 'Revealed: Burma's nuclear bombshell', *Sydney Morning Herald*, 1 Aug. 2009.

nuclear reactor to be built by Russia under IAEA safeguards.[89] The newspaper cited two defectors as the source of the information about the secret facilities.

During the autumn of 2009 doubts arose about the report. According to one authoritative source, the IAEA had concluded that the suspect site was not a nuclear reactor but rather a non-nuclear industrial workshop or machinery plant. This conclusion was based on the absence of certain 'overhead signatures' for a reactor in satellite imagery and on 'specific information derived from first-hand knowledge of the site and its activities'.[90] A non-governmental organization examining the allegations emphasized that, while there remained 'valid suspicions about the existence' of such activities in Myanmar, 'the lack of specifics about many of the sites mentioned in the reports from opposition groups and defectors' made independent analysis of the claims 'very difficult'.[91]

VI. Developments related to multilateral treaties and initiatives

Fissile material cut-off treaty negotiations

In 2009 the Conference on Disarmament overcame a 12-year procedural impasse and adopted a programme of work, including an agreement to convene a working group to begin negotiations on an FMCT on the basis of the mandate adopted by the CD in 1995.[92] The CD also agreed to establish working groups for the other three core items on its agenda: nuclear disarmament, the prevention of an arms race in outer space, and negative security assurances.[93] In previous years, many member states or informal groups of states had insisted that progress towards an FMCT should be linked to simultaneous movement on the other core issues.

---

[89] Apart from this project, Myanmar is not known to have any significant nuclear facilities or to have conducted work in any area of the nuclear fuel cycle.

[90] Hibbs, M., 'IAEA probes Myanmar data, discourages new research reactor', *Nuclear Fuel*, vol. 34, no. 16 (10 Aug. 2009), pp. 3–5.

[91] Kelley, R., Scheel Stricker, A. and Brannan, P., 'Exploring claims about secret nuclear sites in Myanmar', Institute for Science and International Security (ISIS) Reports, 28 Jan. 2010, <http://www.isis-online.org/isis-reports/detail/exploring-claims-about-secret-nuclear-sites-in-myanmar/>.

[92] Conference on Disarmament, 'Decision for the establishment of a Programme of Work for the 2009 session', CD/1864, Geneva, 29 May 2009. The 1995 mandate (the so-called Shannon mandate) was to 'negotiate a non-discriminatory, multilateral and effectively verifiable treaty banning the production of fissile material for nuclear weapons or other nuclear explosive devices'. Conference on Disarmament, 'Report of Ambassador Gerald E. Shannon of Canada on consultations on the most appropriate arrangement to negotiate a treaty banning the production of fissile material for nuclear weapons or other nuclear explosive devices', CD/1299, 24 Mar. 1995.

[93] Conference on Disarmament, CD/1864 (note 92). Negative security assurances are commitments by the 5 legally recognized nuclear weapon states not to use, or threaten to use, nuclear weapons against non-nuclear weapon states parties to the NPT.

The CD's adoption of the programme of work gave rise to renewed optimism about the prospects for negotiating an FMCT. This was reinforced by the new US Administration's commitment to the goal of a verifiable treaty, in contrast to the position of its predecessor.[94] At the same, the decision to form a working group to open FMCT negotiations raised anew the dispute over the scope of a future treaty that had been left unresolved by the 1995 mandate.[95] One of the main points of contention has been whether an FMCT should ban only the future production of fissile material for weapon purposes or should also prevent existing stocks of such material from being used to manufacture new weapons. Some states, in particular Egypt and Pakistan, have demanded that the ban on future production of fissile material for weapon purposes should go beyond mandating a production cut-off and also cover existing stocks of such material. In contrast, the five legally recognized nuclear weapon states, along with India, have insisted that the mandate should apply only to future production of fissile material.[96]

Despite the adoption of the programme of work, the CD was unable to adopt a framework for implementing the programme before the end of the 2009 session, primarily due to procedural reservations from Pakistan.[97] In the absence of an implementation framework, the CD was unable to begin substantive work on any of the agenda items. This meant that the CD would have to adopt a new programme of work and implementation framework for its 2010 session, thereby raising the risk that some member states which have been traditionally lukewarm about an FMCT, such as Pakistan, might use procedural objections to block substantive work on it.

Preparatory Committee meeting for 2010 NPT Review Conference

The third and final meeting of the Preparatory Committee for the 2010 NPT Review Conference took place in New York on 4–15 May 2009.[98] The

---

[94] In 2006 the USA put forward a draft treaty text that omitted provisions for verification in accordance with the position of the Administration of President George W. Bush, announced in 2004, that an FMCT could not be effectively verified. See Kile, S. N., 'Nuclear arms control and non-proliferation', *SIPRI Yearbook 2007*, pp. 510–11.

[95] For a survey of issues related to the scope and verification of a future FMCT see International Panel of Fissile Materials (IPFM), *Global Fissile Material Report 2008: Scope and Verification of a Fissile Material (Cutoff) Treaty* (IPFM: Princeton, NJ, 11 Oct. 2008).

[96] Meyer, P., 'A fissile material (cut-off) treaty: some observations on scope and verification', *Disarmament Diplomacy*, no. 91 (summer 2009).

[97] Conference on Disarmament, 'Statement by Ambassador Zamir Akram, Permanent Representative of Pakistan, to the Conference on Disarmament', Geneva, 2 July 2009.

[98] The purpose of the Preparatory Committee meetings, which are held in the 3 years leading up to the quinquennial review conferences, is to 'consider principles, objectives and ways in order to promote the full implementation of the Treaty, as well as its universality, and to make recommendations thereon' to the review conferences. 'Strengthening the review process for the treaty', NPT/CONF.1995/32 (Part I), 11 May 1995.

meeting was characterized by a constructive atmosphere, which in the view of many observers reflected the new US Administration's positive approach to multilateral diplomacy and arms control.[99] A provisional agenda for the 2010 Review Conference was adopted by consensus, thereby averting a repeat of the procedural impasse that blocked most of the 2005 conference.[100] The parties also agreed on funding and organizational decisions, including the endorsement of Ambassador Libran Cabactulan of the Philippines for the presidency of the 2010 Review Conference.[101]

The Preparatory Committee meeting highlighted longstanding differences between the states parties on substantive matters related to the three main pillars of the NPT (nuclear energy, nuclear disarmament and non-proliferation). A consensus agreement was not reached on forwarding to the upcoming conference a set of substantive recommendations drafted by the chair. These had to do with nuclear disarmament and security assurances; regional issues, including the Middle East; and measures to strengthen compliance with non-proliferation undertakings. Some Non-Aligned Movement member states demanded action by the nuclear weapon states to take steps towards nuclear disarmament. Egypt took the lead in calling for renewed action to implement the resolution, adopted at the 1995 Review Conference, on the establishment of a weapons of mass destruction-free zone in the Middle East.[102]

New commitments to reducing nuclear dangers

New political commitments by world leaders to work towards nuclear disarmament and to support a broad framework of actions to reduce global nuclear dangers were made in 2009. Particular attention was given to expanding current efforts to enhance the safety and custodial security of weapon-usable nuclear material. Many of these efforts, notably the Group of Eight (G8) countries' Global Partnership against the Proliferation of Weapons and Materials of Mass Destruction, have focused on nuclear security activities on the territory of the former Soviet Union.[103]

In April 2009 US President Obama expressed particular concern about the risk of a nuclear weapon falling into the hands of a terrorist group—a

---

[99] Charbonneau, L., 'Obama boosts nuclear talks, split remains', Reuters, 15 May 2009, <http://www.reuters.com/article/latestCrisis/idUSN15244364>.

[100] For a summary of these issues see Kile, S. N., 'Nuclear arms control and non-proliferation', *SIPRI Yearbook 2006*, pp. 612–14.

[101] Final report of the Preparatory Committee for the 2010 Review Conference of the parties to the Treaty on the Non-Proliferation of Nuclear Weapons, NPT/CONF.2010/1, 20 May 2009.

[102] Johnson, R., 'Enhanced prospects for 2010: an analysis of the third PrepCom and the outlook for the 2010 NPT Review Conference', *Arms Control Today*, vol. 39, no. 5 (June 2009).

[103] The Global Partnership was established in 2002 to support cooperative projects, initially in Russia and Ukraine, aimed at addressing non-proliferation, disarmament, counterterrorism and nuclear safety issues. For a summary of recent activities see Kile (note 5), pp. 410–11.

scenario that he described as 'the most immediate and extreme threat to global security'.[104] Obama announced an ambitious international effort to secure 'all vulnerable nuclear material around the world' within four years and his intention to host a nuclear security summit meeting in 2010.

UN Security Council Resolution 1887

In September 2009 at a summit-level meeting chaired by President Obama and attended by 13 other heads of state or government, the United Nations Security Council unanimously adopted Resolution 1887.[105] The politically binding resolution expressed support for a broad range of steps to promote nuclear disarmament and to combat the spread of nuclear weapons, while eliding disagreements between member states over specific measures.

Although Resolution 1887 attracted considerable media attention because of its call to work towards a world without nuclear weapons, most of its substantive recommendations addressed non-proliferation and nuclear security measures. The resolution focused on strengthening legal and regulatory arrangements aimed at reducing the risk of illicit diversion of nuclear material. Resolution 1887 called for universal adherence to the 1980 Convention on the Physical Protection of Nuclear Material and Nuclear Facilities and its 2005 amendment, as well as the Convention for the Suppression of Acts of Nuclear Terrorism.[106] The resolution also called on states to share best practices in order to raise standards of nuclear security, with the aim of securing all vulnerable nuclear material within four years, and urged them to take 'all appropriate national measures ... to prevent proliferation financing and shipments, to strengthen export controls, to secure sensitive materials, and to control access to intangible transfers of technology'. In this context, the resolution recognized the need to give additional financial and other support for the sustainable implementation of UN Security Resolution 1540.[107]

The adoption of Resolution 1887 reflected a growing international recognition of the threat of nuclear terrorism and the need for cooperative action to address it. It also highlighted the emphasis that some countries, in particular the UK and the USA, have put on identifying nuclear security as a 'fourth pillar' of the NPT framework.[108] However, there has been concern in other countries that this emphasis on nuclear security will distract attention from the core goals of the NPT.

---

[104] White House (note 2).

[105] UN Security Council Resolution 1887, 24 Sep. 2009.

[106] For a description of the CPPNM see annex A in this volume.

[107] UN Security Council Resolution 1540, 28 Apr. 2004. See also Ahlström, C., 'United Nations Security Council Resolution 1540: non-proliferation by means of international legislation', *SIPRI Yearbook 2007*, pp. 460–76.

[108] E.g. see British Cabinet Office, *The Road to 2010: Addressing the Nuclear Question in the 21st Century*, Cmd 7675 (The Stationery Office: Norwich, 16 July 2009), p. 7.

VII. New nuclear weapon-free zones

Regional arrangements establishing nuclear weapon-free zones are important legal components of the global nuclear non-proliferation regime and supplement international efforts to prevent the emergence of new nuclear weapon states. In 2009 treaties establishing new NWFZs in Central Asia and in Africa entered into force (see table 9.2).

The Central Asian nuclear weapon-free zone

The Treaty on a Nuclear-Weapon-Free Zone in Central Asia (Treaty of Semipalatinsk) entered into force on 21 March 2009 after the final state party, Kazakhstan, deposited its instrument of ratification.[109] In 1997 the leaders of the five Central Asian states—Kazakhstan, Kyrgyzstan, Tajikistan, Turkmenistan and Uzbekistan—issued the Almaty Declaration, calling for the creation of a Central Asian nuclear-weapon-free zone. The treaty opened for signature in September 2006.[110]

The treaty's provisions are similar to those of other NWFZ agreements and oblige the parties not to conduct research on, develop, manufacture, stockpile or otherwise possess nuclear weapons and not to allow the use of their territory for the stationing of nuclear weapons.[111] It has several distinctive features as well. It is the first treaty to oblige the parties to conclude an Additional Protocol agreement with the IAEA and to follow the restrictions of the Comprehensive Nuclear-Test-Ban Treaty (CTBT), which has yet to come into force.[112] It also requires the parties to apply measures of physical protection to nuclear material and nuclear facilities on their territories in order to meet international standards—a reflection of concerns that Central Asia could become a source or transit corridor for the smuggling of nuclear materials. It also commits the parties to work to reverse environmental damage caused by the production and testing of former Soviet nuclear weapons in the region.

The protocol to the treaty, which provides for negative security assurances to the parties from the five legally recognized nuclear weapon states, had not been signed by any of these states as of 1 January 2010. China and Russia have supported adoption of the protocol, while France, the UK and the USA have expressed misgivings about it. The main concern of the latter

[109] United Nations, Office of Disarmament Affairs (UNODA), 'Fact Sheet: Treaty on Nuclear-Weapon-Free Zone in Central Asia', 20 Mar. 2009, <http://www.un.org/disarmament/WMD/Nuclear/NWFZ.shtml>.

[110] Parrish, S. and Potter, W., 'Central Asian states establish nuclear-weapon-free-zone despite US opposition', Center for Nonproliferation Studies (CNS) Research Report, Monterey Institute of International Studies, 8 Sep. 2006, <http://cns.miis.edu/stories/060905.htm>.

[111] For a summary and other details of the treaty see annex A in this volume.

[112] For a summary and other details of the CTBT see annex A in this volume.

Table 9.2. Nuclear weapon-free zone treaties

Treaty[a]	Zone of application	Date of signature	Date of entry into force
Treaty of Tlatelolco	Latin America, Caribbean	14 Feb. 1967	22 Apr. 1968
Treaty of Rarotonga	South Pacific	6 Aug. 1985	11 Dec. 1986
Treaty of Bangkok	South East Asia	15 Dec. 1995	27 Mar. 1997
Treaty of Pelindaba	Africa	11 Apr. 1996	15 July 2009
Treaty of Semipalatinsk	Central Asia	8 Sep. 2006	21 Mar. 2009

[a] In addition, certain uninhabited areas have been formally denuclearized: Antarctica (1959 Antarctic Treaty); outer space, the moon and other celestial bodies (1967 Outer Space Treaty); and the seabed and ocean floor (1971 Seabed Treaty).

Source: Annex A.

three governments has been that the treaty's language could be interpreted as allowing Russia to deploy nuclear weapons in the zone under certain circumstances, in accordance with the provisions of a prior defence agreement, the 1992 Treaty on Collective Security (Tashkent Treaty).[113]

The African nuclear weapon-free zone

The Treaty of Pelindaba, establishing an African NWFZ, entered into force on 15 July 2009, after Burundi had become the 28th state signatory to ratify it.[114] The treaty, named after the former South African nuclear weapon facility near Pretoria, opened for signature in Cairo in 1996. Its entry into force marked the culmination of over 40 years of activity within the African Union (AU) as well as the expansion of NWFZs to the entire southern hemisphere.

The treaty covers Africa, island state members of the AU and island territories considered by the AU to be part of Africa. In addition to containing provisions similar to those of other NWFZ agreements, the treaty provides for the parties to engage in peaceful nuclear activities while obliging them to conclude comprehensive safeguards agreements with the IAEA. The treaty also provides for the five legally recognized nuclear weapon states to give negative security assurances to the parties (Protocol I) and to pledge

---

[113] Kakatkar, M. and Pomper, M., 'Central Asian nuclear-weapon-free zone formed', *Arms Control Today*, vol. 39, no. 7 (Jan./Feb. 2009). Treaty on Collective Security, opened for signature 15 May 1992, entered into force 20 Apr. 1994, *United Nations Treaty Series*, vol. 1894 (1995). Four Central Asian parties to the Treaty of Semipalatinsk—Kazakhstan, Kyrgyzstan, Tajikistan and Uzbekistan— are also parties to the Collective Security Treaty and are members of the associated Collective Security Treaty Organization (CSTO). For a brief description of the CSTO see annex B in this volume.

[114] Harvey, C., 'African NWFZ treaty enters into force', *Arms Control Today*, vol. 39, no. 7 (Sep. 2009). The treaty has been signed by all 53 AU member states and Morocco. For a summary and other details of the Treaty of Pelindaba see annex A in this volume.

not to test or assist the testing of nuclear weapons within the zone (Protocol II).[115]

The entry into force of the Treaty of Pelindaba focused renewed attention on the dispute over whether the Africa NWFZ applies to the Indian Ocean island of Diego Garcia in the Chagos Archipelago.[116] The AU considers Diego Garcia and the surrounding islands to be part of Mauritius, an AU member state, and hence part of the African zone. However, the UK—which regards Diego Garcia, over which it exercises sovereignty, as part of the British Indian Ocean Territory—does not.[117] Under a series of bilateral agreements with the UK, the USA has built large naval and air installations on the island that support deployments of nuclear-capable attack submarines and long-range bombers. The USA has declared that neither the treaty nor protocols I and II apply to the activities on Diego Garcia of the USA, the UK or any other state not party to the treaty.[118]

VIII. Conclusions

In 2009 global efforts to promote nuclear disarmament and non-proliferation ahead of the 2010 NPT Review Conference gained new momentum. A potential breakthrough was made at the CD where the procedural impasse that had blocked the opening of negotiations on an FMCT was overcome. The prospects for bringing into force the CTBT were given a boost by a renewed US commitment to ratify the treaty. Greater political attention was also given to the challenge of enhancing the safety and custodial security of nuclear materials. The UN Security Council's adoption of Resolution 1887 reflected growing international recognition of the threat of nuclear terrorism and the need for cooperative action to address it.

Nonetheless, important challenges remained to the legal and normative underpinnings of the NPT regime. North Korea, which was a non-nuclear weapon state party to the NPT before announcing its formal withdrawal in 2003, conducted a second nuclear explosive test in 2009 and declared its intention to expand its military nuclear capabilities. In Iran safeguards compliance questions continued to be unresolved, which pointed to a possible military dimension to the country's nuclear programme.

---

[115] All 5 nuclear weapon states signed protocols I and II. They were ratified by China on 6 Sep. 1996; by France on 31 July 1997; and by the UK on 27 Feb. 2001.

[116] Sand, P. H., 'Diego Garcia: a thorn in the side of Africa's nuclear-weapon-free zone', *Bulletin of the Atomic Scientists*, 8 Oct. 2009.

[117] The UK qualified its signature of protocols I and II in 1996 by stating that it did 'not accept the inclusion of [the Chagos Archipelago] within the African nuclear-weapon-free zone' without the British Government's consent. See annex A in this volume.

[118] Russia has refused to ratify protocols I and II until it receives assurances from the USA that Diego Garcia will not be used for storing or transporting nuclear weapons. Harvey (note 114); and annex A in this volume.

Perhaps the most hopeful sign in 2009 was that top political leaders began 'thinking the unthinkable' and gave serious attention to formulating a long-term strategy for not only reducing the size and spread of nuclear arsenals, but eventually for eliminating them altogether. This was bolstered by the arrival of a new US Administration that embraced treaty-based arms control and disarmament and called for multilateral action to meet urgent proliferation challenges based on international law. As the year ended, the looming question was whether the rhetorical commitments that were heard in 2009 would be translated into concrete action.[119]

[119] On steps towards achieving a world free of nuclear weapons see chapter 1 in this volume.

10. Reducing security threats from chemical and biological materials

JOHN HART AND PETER CLEVESTIG*

I. Introduction

At the international, regional and national levels in 2009 states continued to develop strategies to prevent and remediate the effects of the possible misuse of chemical and biological materials. With some success, the parties to the 1993 Chemical Weapons Convention (CWC) and the 1972 Biological and Toxin Weapons Convention (BTWC) maintained their focus on capacity building, achieving universality of membership and effective implementation of national obligations, including those related to the security of dual-purpose materials.[1] In the United States, President Barack Obama's Administration presented its much anticipated policy on the BTWC in December 2009, while the European Union (EU) worked to develop a communication based on the recommendations of an EU chemical, biological, radiological and nuclear (CBRN) working group.

In 2009 India became the third state party to the CWC to complete the destruction of its chemical weapon stockpile. Iraq joined the convention and declared that it possesses chemical weapons. The parties to the BTWC met in 2009 to consider the enhancement of international cooperation, assistance and exchange in the life sciences and related technology for peaceful purposes, including the promotion of capacity building in disease surveillance, detection, diagnosis and biocontainment.

The implications of disease outbreaks, including those caused by a strain of H1N1 influenza and several anthrax deaths among heroin users in the United Kingdom, were evaluated by security analysts and government officials in the context of preparedness for and response to biological warfare. In 2009 states continued to develop mechanisms to license and oversee scientific research, the chemical industry and biotechnology, including for

---

[1] For summaries and other details of the Convention on the Prohibition of the Development, Production, Stockpiling and Use of Chemical Weapons and on Their Destruction and of the Convention on the Prohibition of the Development, Production and Stockpiling of Bacteriological (Biological) and Toxin Weapons and on Their Destruction see annex A in this volume.

* Dr Ian Anthony is the author of the subsection 'The European Union's Instrument for Stability and the CBRN Action Plan'.

companies that offer gene synthesis services, because of the security implications of these activities.

Section II of this chapter considers the threats posed by chemical and biological material. Sections III and IV discuss arms control and disarmament of, respectively, biological and chemical weapons. Section V reviews allegations of chemical and biological warfare (CBW) violations and prior programmes and activities. Activities related to prevention, response and remediation are considered in section VI. Section VII presents the conclusions.

II. The threats posed by chemical and biological material

Threat perceptions are less focused on the lethality of CBW agents. The threats posed by chemical and biological material can be categorized as those related to state security, population security and the security of critical infrastructure.[2] Each involves a distinct threat and policy response: protection of the state, the population and of critical infrastructure. Many of the specific policy responses arose from civil defence against nuclear weapon attack and have since increasingly been extended to include protection against natural disasters, attack by non-state actors and infectious disease outbreaks. When infectious disease is viewed in terms of population security, the intervention strategies may be formulated according to the requirements of prevention. In contrast, when critical infrastructure is the focus, the response strategy concentrates on preparedness.[3]

Biological threats can also be viewed in the wider context of the overall effects of disease burden, while chemical threats can be considered in terms of environmental pollution (e.g. the effects of toxic industrial chemicals released at low levels into the environment or large-scale releases in industrial accidents).[4] Many chemical and biological materials, even when developed or redirected for CBW purposes, do not ordinarily cause death. This is true of, for example, hallucinogenics such as lysergic acid diethylamide (LSD) and anti-crop agents such as rice blast (*Magnaporthe grisea*). Even CBW agents that are meant to cause death (e.g. *Bacillus anthracis*, the causative agent for anthrax) are generally less deadly than nuclear weapons and some conventional munitions (e.g. fuel air explosives or thermobaric bombs). It is also important to distinguish between acute and chronic toxic

[2] Based on Lakoff, A., 'From population to vital system: national security and the changing object of public health', eds A. Lakoff and S. J. Collier, *Biosecurity Interventions: Global Health and Security in Question* (Columbia University Press: New York, 2008), pp. 36–37.

[3] Lakoff (note 2), p. 37.

[4] Toxic industrial chemicals can be defined as having an LCt_{50} (lethal concentration for half of those exposed) of less than 100 000 mg-min/m^3 and being produced in amounts of over 30 tonnes annually at any given facility. Sun, Y. and Ong, K. Y., *Detection Technologies for Chemical Warfare Agents and Toxic Vapors* (CRC Press: Boca Raton, FL, 2005), p. 9.

effects.[5] For example, in 2004 Ukrainian presidential candidate Viktor Yushchenko was poisoned with a dioxin compound which, arguably, was selected partly because such cases of poisoning are rare and because of possible confusion between acute and chronic toxicity.

The type and nature of possible CBW violations is evolving and becoming more complex; they can be differentiated as technical or fundamental. CBW violation scenarios include: (a) traditional state weapon development programmes; (b) standby capacity by states for either traditional military or non-traditional agents; (c) non-lethal and less-than-lethal agents developed by states for law enforcement, peacekeeping and the like that may also serve as a basis for a standby capacity for faster CBW 'breakout'; and (d) non-state actor activity.

The CWC's declaration thresholds for the chemical industry are based on the concept of 'militarily significant' quantities (i.e. hundreds or thousands of tonnes). However, for non-state actors 'significant quantities' of chemical weapons are at the kilogram level. The term 'significant' is thus context dependent. Historically, it has referred to the amount of agent required to generate casualties or deaths with some degree of assurance for a military action or campaign.

Analyses of threats posed by non-state actors focus on capability and intent with ambiguous or competing conclusions.[6] The JASON Defense Advisory Group concluded that 'no credible approach' has been documented to 'anticipate the existence and characterization' of terrorism involving weapons of mass destruction (WMD) and that a 'significant deficiency in applying standard approaches from engineering and science' exists for predicting such events. False alarm rates and signal detection that are obscured by 'massive clutter' are responsible.[7] Chemical and biological terrorism threat assessments are therefore difficult to make due to the lack of intelligence indicators, incomplete data and excessive ambiguous or irrelevant data.

Legal and regulatory regimes can control chemical and biological agents through the use of select agent lists, catch-all clauses or a general purpose

---

[5] Sorg, O. et al., '2,3,7,8-tetrachlorodibenzo-p-dioxin (TCDD) poisoning in Victor Yushchenko: identification and measurement of TCDD metabolites', *The Lancet*, 3 Oct. 2009; and McKee, M., 'The poisoning of Victor Yushchenko', *The Lancet*, 3 Oct. 2009.

[6] Non-state actor acquisition and use of toxins is reviewed in Pita, R., 'Toxin weapons: from World War I to jihadi terrorism', *Toxin Reviews*, vol. 28, no. 4 (Nov. 2009), pp. 9–14. On the low frequency of attacks by non-state actors since 2001 see Boyd, D. et al., *Why Have We Not Been Attacked Again? Competing and Complementary Hypotheses for Homeland Attack Frequency*, ASCO Report no. 2008 007 (Defense Threat Reduction Agency, Advanced Systems Concepts Office: Fort Belvoir, VA, June 2008). Anne Stenersen, of the Terrorism and Political Violence Project at the Norwegian Defence Research Establishment (FFI), has reviewed al-Qaeda's CBRN capabilities and intentions based on extensive Arabic-language sources. Stenersen, A., *Al-Qaida's Quest for Weapons of Mass Destruction: The History Behind the Hype* (VDM Verlag: Saarbrücken, 2008).

[7] JASON Defense Advisory Group, *Rare Events* (Mitre Corporation: McLean, VA, Oct. 2009), p. 8.

criterion (GPC). The prohibitions against CBW in the BTWC and the CWC embody a GPC: all activities involving infectious biological material and toxic chemicals are prohibited except for peaceful, non-prohibited purposes. Placing an agent on a control list reflects in part whether it was considered for use as a CBW agent by prior state programmes. Ricin and saxitoxin, for example, were originally developed essentially for assassination purposes, not for their ability to kill large numbers of soldiers in the field.[8] As one analysis concludes: 'Ricin as a toxin is deadly but as an agent of bioterror is unsuitable and therefore does not warrant the press attention and subsequent public alarm that has been created'.[9]

The principal ways in which offensive CBW technologies could be disseminated are: state-to-state military contacts (publicized, discrete or secret); clandestine state programmes that import dual-purpose equipment, material and technology; and efforts by individuals and groups to acquire CBW expertise and material with possible state support. The challenge for arms control, disarmament and non-proliferation measures is how to take all these potential dissemination routes into account in order to ensure that the international prohibitions against CBW are effectively implemented.

III. Biological weapon arms control and disarmament

In 2006 the Sixth Review Conference of the Biological and Toxin Weapons Convention agreed an inter-sessional process for 2007–10 which consists of four meetings to be held in that period. In 2009 the Meeting of Experts took place on 24–28 August, and the Meeting of States Parties was held on 7–11 December.[10] The mandate of the 2009 meetings was to 'discuss, and promote common understanding and effective action on promoting capacity building in the fields of disease surveillance, detection, diagnosis, and containment of infectious diseases'.[11] The participants focused on the

---

[8] The Bulgarian dissident writer Georgi Markov was assassinated in London in 1978 by an unknown assailant using an imbrella to implant a pellet filled with ricin into his leg. Poli, M. A. et al., 'Ricin', ed. Z. F. Dembek, *Medical Aspects of Biological Warfare* (US Army, Office of the Surgeon General, Borden Institute: Washington, DC, 2007), p. 328; and US Senate, 'Unauthorized storage of toxic agents', Hearings before the Select Committee to Study Governmental Operations with Respect to Intelligence Activities, 16–18 Sep. 1975, <http://www.aarclibrary.org/publib/contents/church/contents_church_reports.htm>.

[9] Schep, L. J. et al., 'Ricin as a weapon of mass terror: separating fact from fiction', *Environment International*, vol. 35 (2009), p. 1270.

[10] See the website of the United Nations Office at Geneva <http://www.unog.ch/bwc>; and the 'Biological and Toxin Weapons Convention' website <http://www.opbw.org>. Daily reports and summaries of the Meeting of Experts and the Meeting of States Parties are available on the website of the BioWeapons Prevention Project, <http://www.bwpp.org/reports.html>. The parties have agreed to hold annual technical and political meetings between the 6th and 7th review conferences.

[11] BTWC Meeting of States Parties, 'Report of the meeting of states parties', document BWC/MSP/2009/5, 16 Dec. 2009.

recognition of infectious diseases as a global threat with potential severe implications for all states, regardless of whether such diseases have natural, deliberate or accidental causes.

Since the inception of confidence-building measure (CBM) data exchanges in 1986, 103 parties have participated; 62 parties submitted data on CBMs in 2009 (as of 1 November).[12] The Center for Arms Control and Non-Proliferation report on the biodefence programmes of selected states noted that annual US funding for research and development on counter-measures against biological agents had increased from $580 million in 2001 to over $3 billion by 2007. It also noted that the USA has spent or allocated almost $50 billion since 2001 to address biological weapon threats.[13]

The chairman of the Meeting of States Parties reported that no further states had joined the BTWC since 2008.[14] Various plenary statements referred to the importance of fully implementing Articles III and X of the BTWC. Developing states, in particular, have long emphasized the import-ance of the latter article, under which the parties undertake to facilitate and have the right to participate in the 'fullest possible exchange' of equip-ment, material and technology for peaceful purposes. Article III contains the prohibition against biological warfare, in which the parties undertake not to transfer directly or indirectly nor to assist, encourage or induce any actor to manufacture or acquire biological weapons.

A synthesis paper presented at the Meeting of States Parties itemizes the aims of enhancing international cooperation, assistance and exchange on the theme of the 2009 inter-sessional process topics. In addition it recog-nizes the necessity of: (a) addressing the problems, challenges and needs in developing international cooperation; (b) developing CBMs and inter-national, regional and bilateral cooperation to address the threats posed by infectious diseases; (c) creating the necessary infrastructure to support the establishment of core national public health capacities as required under the revised International Health Regulations (IHR) of the World Health Organization (WHO);[15] (d) developing human resources in conjunction

[12] Hamburg University, Research Group for Biological Arms Control, '2009 reader on publicly available CBMs', Dec. 2009, <http://www.biological-arms-control.org>, p. 1. See also McLaughlin, K. and Nixdorff, K. (eds), *BWPP Biological Weapons Reader* (BioWeapons Prevention Project (BWPP): Geneva, 2009); and BWPP, *Building a Global Ban: Why States Have Not Joined the BWC* (BWPP: Geneva, Apr. 2009).

[13] Center for Arms Control and Non-Proliferation, 'Ensuring compliance with the Biological Weapons Convention', Washington, DC, July 2009, <http://www.armscontrolcenter.org/policy/bio chem/articles/081709_ensuring_bwc_compliance/>.

[14] For a list of parties and signatories see annex A in this volume. The states that had neither signed nor ratified the convention were Angola, Cameroon, Chad, Comoros, Djibouti, Eritrea, Guinea, Israel, Kiribati, Marshall Islands, Mauritania, Micronesia, Mozambique, Namibia, Nauru, Niue, Samoa and Tuvalu.

[15] World Health Organization (WHO), *International Health Regulations (2005)*, 2nd edn (WHO: Geneva, 2005).

with infrastructural developments; and (e) improving standard operating procedures to enhance sustainability, support capacity building, and enhance quality controls and professional performance.[16]

Capacity building was prominently featured in the plenary statements, and Article X was highlighted, with accusations made of the denial of the transfer of materials such as reference samples and equipment (e.g. for calibrations) for peaceful purposes to and from states parties. India stated, for example, that it is 'a fact that denial of materials, equipment and technology related to peaceful uses of bio-technology continue[s] to exist and hamper legitimate uses of biological materials'.[17] The parties stressed that assistance providers do not understand the specific needs of recipient states but commended the current provision of educational support in Europe to students from developing countries. Reference was also made to the financial support of the Drugs for Neglected Diseases initiative.[18] On behalf of the EU, Sweden presented a work package for reporting assistance opportunities, while Cuba, on behalf of the Non-Aligned Movement, presented a proposal for a formal Article X implementation mechanism.[19]

On 9 December US Under Secretary of State Ellen O. Tauscher presented the USA's National Strategy for Countering Biological Threats.[20] She stated that the USA wished to 'reinvigorate' the convention as 'the premier forum for global outreach and coordination' against biological threats. Tauscher stated that the USA will support a 'rigorous, comprehensive program of cooperation, information exchange, and coordination that builds on and modifies as necessary' the BTWC's existing programme of work.[21] The revised US strategy focuses on: (a) the promotion of global health security to reduce the effect of disease outbreaks; (b) the establishment and strengthening of the international norm against the misuse of the life sciences; and (c) the implementation of a coordinated approach to 'influence,

---

[16] BTWC Meeting of States Parties, 'Synthesis of considerations, lessons, perspectives, recommendations, conclusions and proposals drawn from the presentations, statements, working papers and interventions on the topic under discussion at the meeting of experts', document BWC/MSP/2009/L.1, 16 Oct. 2009. On the IHRs see Raveché, B., 'International public health diplomacy: the case of global public health surveillance of avian influenza', *SIPRI Yearbook 2008*, pp. 456–69.

[17] Statement by Ambassador Hamid Ali Rao, Permanent Representative of India to the Conference on Disarmament, Meeting of States Parties to the BTWC, Geneva, 7 Dec. 2009.

[18] See the website of the Drugs for Neglected Diseases Initiative, <http://www.dndi.org>.

[19] BTWC Meeting of Experts, 'Striving towards a common format for reporting assistance opportunities and needs from states parties in areas with relevance for the BTWC: submitted by Sweden on behalf of the European Union', document BWC/MSP/2009/WP.6, 8 Dec. 2009; and BTWC Meeting of States Parties, 'The establishment of a mechanism for the full implementation of Article X of the convention: submitted by Cuba on behalf of the Group of the Non-aligned Movement and Other States', document BWC/MSP/2009/WP.2, 7 Dec. 2009.

[20] US National Security Council, *National Strategy for Countering Biological Threats* (White House: Washington, DC, Nov. 2009).

[21] US Department of State, 'Under Secretary for Arms Control and International Security Ellen Tauscher, Address to the annual meeting of the states parties to the Biological Weapons Convention', Geneva, 9 Dec. 2009, <http://www.state.gov/t/us/133335.htm>, pp. 3–4.

identify, inhibit, and interdict those who seek to misuse scientific progress to harm innocent people'.[22]

The Obama Administration has indicated that prevention is a major priority to which it is prepared to devote the corresponding necessary resources. It has also signalled the importance it places on the USA being proactively engaged in multilateral frameworks, as opposed to focusing on bilateral arrangements or 'coalitions of the willing'. The National Strategy for Countering Biological Threats encompasses a range of biorisks, including laboratory biosecurity and biosafety, and capacity building to assess the nature and origin of all disease outbreaks. The USA intends to assist resource-poor states to implement the revised IHRs. The regulations' revision indicates a shift in approach: biological weapon threats (i.e. deliberate disease outbreaks) are increasingly being considered by the WHO, which historically has avoided direct scrutiny of such threats.[23]

Some states parties reiterated their support for a legally binding protocol or verification mechanism for the BTWC. India, for example, stated its belief that 'only a multilaterally agreed mechanism for verification of compliance can provide the assurance of observance of compliance' and that a decision on strengthening the BTWC should be taken at the next review conference.[24] However, Tauscher noted that the USA would 'not seek to revive the negotiations on a verification protocol' to the BTWC because, after having reviewed previous efforts, it had determined that a 'legally binding protocol would not achieve meaningful verification or greater security'.[25]

IV. Chemical weapon arms control and disarmament

As of 31 December 2009, 188 states had ratified or acceded to the Chemical Weapons Convention, the principal international legal instrument against chemical warfare. Three states—Bahamas, the Dominican Republic and Iraq—became parties to the convention in 2009. A further two states—Israel and Myanmar—had signed but not ratified the convention, while five states had neither signed nor ratified the CWC.[26]

The Organisation for the Prohibition of Chemical Weapons (OPCW) continued its activities to maintain and improve implementation of the CWC, including strengthening chemical transfer control requirements. On 6–8 May a workshop for customs and border authorities in Eastern Europe

[22] US National Security Council (note 20), p. 4.

[23] Tucker, J. B., 'Seeking biosecurity without verification: the new US strategy on biothreats', *Arms Control Today*, vol. 40 (Jan./Feb. 2010), p. 6.

[24] Statement by Ambassador Hamid Ali Rao (note 17).

[25] US Department of State (note 21).

[26] The states that had not signed or ratified the CWC were Angola, Egypt, North Korea, Somalia and Syria. For a full list of parties and signatories see annex A in this volume.

on technical aspects of international transfer regimes affecting chemicals was organized by the OPCW and the Government of Belarus. The workshop considered the identification of chemicals relevant to the CWC, the Globally Harmonized System of Classification and Labelling of Chemicals, World Customs Organization recommendations, sources of information for customs officials and customs laboratories (e.g. the OPCW Handbook on Chemicals and the OPCW Central Analytical Database) and practical issues (e.g. customs software, risk assessment, and free trade ports and zones).[27]

In 2009 the OPCW released a revised Handbook on Chemicals to help the parties identify chemicals listed in the CWC's Annex on Chemicals. The handbook provides Chemical Abstracts Service (CAS) Registry numbers, International Union of Pure and Applied Chemistry and CAS chemical names, synonyms and World Customs Organization codes for more than 1300 scheduled chemicals and riot control agents that have been declared to the OPCW. However, the list is not comprehensive.[28]

The Conference of the States Parties and national implementation

The 14th Session of the Conference of the States Parties (CSP) to the CWC, held on 30 November–4 December 2009, approved the OPCW's 2010 Programme and Budget of €74 505 400 ($99.5 million), the fifth consecutive zero nominal growth budget.[29] Ambassador Ahmet Üzümcü of Turkey was elected by the CSP as the next director-general of the OPCW for the term 25 July 2010 to 24 July 2014.[30] The CSP also decided that mixtures of chemicals containing 1 per cent or less of a Schedule 2A or 2A* chemical need not be declared, a decision that affects the chemical industry.[31]

The OPCW continues to encourage the full and comprehensive implementation of the CWC's Article VII on national implementation measures. As of August 2009, 181 parties (96 per cent) had established or designated a national authority; 128 parties (68 per cent) had reported to the Technical

[27] OPCW, 'Call for nominations for a regional sensitisation workshop for customs and border authorities in Eastern Europe on the technical aspects of the transfers regime, Grodno, Belarus, 6–8 May 2009', Note by the Technical Secretariat, document S/743/2009, 10 Mar. 2009.

[28] OPCW, 'Handbook on Chemicals 2009 and language versions of the Declarations Handbook 2008', Note by the Technical Secretariat, document S/756/2009, 2 Apr. 2009; and OPCW, *Handbook on Chemicals (2009 Version)* (OPCW: The Hague, 2009), <http://www.opcw.org/our-work/national-implementation/declarations-adviser/handbook-on-chemicals/>.

[29] A total of €37 301 400 ($49.8 million) is allocated for verification. OPCW, 'Decision, programme and budget of the OPCW for 2010', document C-14/DEC.8, 2 Dec. 2009.

[30] OPCW, 'Decision, appointment of the director-general', document C-14/DEC.6, 2 Dec. 2009. An OPCW director-general may serve up to two 4-year terms. See Meier, O., 'Race is on for new head of OPCW', *Arms Control Today*, vol. 39, no. 7 (Sep. 2009), pp. 31–32.

[31] OPCW, 'Decision, guidelines regarding low-concentration limits for declarations of Schedule 2A and 2A* chemicals', document C-14/DEC.4, 2 Dec. 2009. See also Hart, J., 'The treatment of perfluorisobutylene under the Chemical Weapons Convention', *ASA Newsletter*, no. 88 (28 Feb. 2002), pp. 1, 20–23.

Secretarial the adoption of legislative and administrative measures to implement the CWC; and 86 parties (46 per cent) had adopted and reported on national legislation covering all key areas required by the CWC.[32]

Destruction of chemical weapons

The parties to the CWC that have declared chemical weapon stockpiles to the OPCW are Albania, India, Iraq, South Korea, Libya, Russia and the USA. As of 30 November 2009, of 71 194 agent tonnes of declared chemical weapons, 39 585 agent tonnes had been verifiably destroyed; of 8.67 million declared items and containers, 3.93 million had been destroyed.[33] As of the same date, 13 states had declared 70 former chemical weapon production facilities (CWPFs) of which 43 have been destroyed and 19 converted to peaceful purposes.[34] The CWC allows for the lifting of verification of CWPFs 10 years after they have been converted to peaceful purposes.[35] However, the Executive Council has yet to decide on the lifting of ongoing verification of such converted CWPFs.[36] At the end of 2010, when a two-year period of reduced chemical weapon destruction activity is envisaged, the OPCW's verification regime will face the challenge of how to utilize the organization's verification capacity (i.e. a percentage of its inspectors) given the fact that inspectors cannot be dismissed and re-employed on short notice.[37] In addition, a percentage of inspector salaries are paid by the states that receive inspections.

India completed the destruction of its Category 1 chemical weapons on 16 March, ahead of its extended deadline of 28 April 2009.[38] It became the third party to complete the destruction of its chemical weapon stockpile, after Albania and South Korea.

[32] OPCW, 'Note by the Director-General, report to the Conference of the States Parties at its fourteenth session on the status of implementation of Article VII of the Chemical Weapons Convention as at 19 August 2009', document C-14/DG.9, 21 Oct. 2009, p. 7.

[33] OPCW, 'Demilitarisation: chemical weapons declared and destroyed', 30 Nov. 2009, <http://www.opcw.org/our-work/demilitarisation>.

[34] The states are Bosnia and Herzegovina, China, France, India, Iran, Iraq, Japan, South Korea, Libya, Russia, Serbia, the United Kingdom and the USA. OPCW, 'Opening statement by the Director-General to the Conference of the States Parties at its fourteenth session', document C-14/DG.13, 30 Nov. 2009, para. 25.

[35] Chemical Weapons Convention (note 1), Verification Annex, Part V, para. 85.

[36] As of 30 Nov. 2009, 4 converted CWPFs in 2 states parties have passed the 10-year post-conversion verification threshold, and in 2010, 3 more CWPFs in 3 states parties are expected to pass it. OPCW (note 34), para. 27.

[37] Options for how to redirect inspectors' activities towards other OPCW work and for how to supplement the standing inspectorate with an 'inspector-on-call' system are being considered.

[38] India, 'Statement by India, 14th session of the Conference of the States Parties, Organization for the Prohibition of Chemical Weapons', The Hague, 30 Nov.–4 Dec. 2009, para. 10. The CWC places chemical weapons in 3 categories. 'Order of destruction' provisions are provided in CWC (note 1), Verification Annex, Part IV(A), paras 15–19.

In 2009 Iraq joined the CWC and declared that it possesses five former CWPFs and chemical weapons at the former Muthanna State Establishment.[39] The OPCW's preparations to send inspectors to carry out an initial inspection included meetings of OPCW officials in Jordan and inspection exercises.[40] In September 2009 Technical Secretariat officials travelled to the UK and the USA to review government documentation on Iraq's chemical munitions that were recovered and destroyed by British and US forces in 2003–2008.[41] On 1 July the US National Security Archive released transcripts of interrogations of former Iraqi President Saddam Hussein by the US Federal Bureau of Investigation (FBI) held in 2004, including those on nuclear, biological and chemical (NBC) weapons and threat perceptions.[42] The UN Office of Disarmament Affairs (ODA) also provided information obtained by the United Nations Special Commission on Iraq (UNSCOM) and the United Nations Monitoring, Verification and Inspection Commission (UNMOVIC).[43]

Because of the continued uncertain security situation in Iraq, it remained unclear when the OPCW would send inspectors. In addition, according to Charles A. Duelfer, who served as the Deputy Chairman of UNSCOM in 1993–2000 and headed the Iraq Survey Group from January 2004 until the group's disbanding later that year, the Muthanna facility contains 'dozens of buildings and bunkers . . . [and] UNSCOM, using the facilities at hand . . . destroyed 28,000 munitions, 480,000 liters of agent, 1.8 million liters of liquid chemical precursors, and a million kilograms of solid precursor chemicals'.[44] UNSCOM judged some containers and munitions to be too volatile to attempt to destroy; these were placed in a large bunker before it was 'finally, and permanently, sealed'. Duelfer describes the interior 'with its leaking sarin rounds, barrels with toxic agents, and assorted contaminated equipment' as 'a dark, lethal junkyard'. As of December 2009, Iraq and the OPCW Technical Secretariat had yet to finalize a detailed destruction plan which must then be forwarded to the Executive Council for its consideration and approval.

[39] OPCW (note 34), para. 26.

[40] OPCW official, Communication with the author, May 2009.

[41] OPCW (note 34), para. 28.

[42] 'Saddam Hussein talks to the FBI: twenty interviews and five conversations with "High Value Detainee #1" in 2004', National Security Archive Electronic Briefing Book no. 279, 1 July 2009, <http://www.gwu.edu/~nsarchiv/NSAEBB/NSAEBB279/index.htm>.

[43] The UNSCOM and UNMOVIC files are now in the custody of the UN's Archive and Records Management Section in the Department of Management, where they will remain sealed separately from other UN archival material for 30–60 years from 1 Mar. 2008. United Nations, 'Records and archives of the United Nations Monitoring, Verification and Inspection Commission', Secretary-General's bulletin, ST/SGB/2009/12, 1 Aug. 2009.

[44] Duelfer, C., Hide and Seek: The Search for the Truth in Iraq (PublicAffairs: New York, 2009), pp. 96–97.

The CSP granted a request by Libya to extend its intermediate and final chemical weapon destruction deadlines. Libya must now destroy its Category 1 chemical weapon stockpiles by 15 May 2011.[45]

With the completion of destruction of the chemical weapons at Kambarka on 27 March 2009, Russia's chemical weapon stockpile is now stored at five locations.[46] As of 25 November 2009 Russia had verifiably destroyed 18 000 tonnes or 45 per cent of its declared Category 1 chemical weapons (meeting its phase 3 extended deadline of 31 December 2009).[47] In May Russia began operating its fifth chemical weapon destruction facility (CWDF), at Shchuchye, and by December 5462 tonnes of organophosphorus nerve agents had been destroyed.[48] Destruction operations are also under way at the Leonidovka and Maradikovsky facilities. The last destruction facilities, at Kizner and Pochep, are expected to begin operation in 2010.[49]

The US chemical weapon stockpile is currently stored at six locations.[50] As of 31 October 2009 the USA had destroyed 18 516 agent tonnes of its Category 1 chemical weapons (67 per cent of its declared stockpile).[51] The USA estimates that by April 2012, the final CWC-mandated deadline, it will have destroyed 90 per cent of its stockpile; its current estimate for completing

[45] Its new intermediate destruction deadlines are: (a) phase 1 (1%) must be completed by 1 Nov. 2010; (b) phase 2 (20%) must be completed by 15 Dec. 2010; and (c) phase 3 (45%) must be completed by 31 Jan. 2011. OPCW, 'Decision, extension of the intermediate and final deadlines for the destruction by the Libyan Arab Jamahiriya of its Category 1 chemical weapons', document C-14/DEC.3, 2 Dec. 2009. On Libya's chemical weapon programme see Tucker, J., 'The rollback of Libya's chemical weapons program', *Nonproliferation Review*, vol. 16, no. 3 (Nov. 2009), pp. 363–84; and Hart, J. and Kile, S. N., 'Libya's renunciation of nuclear, biological and chemical weapons and ballistic missiles', *SIPRI Yearbook 2005*, pp. 629–48.

[46] Originally, Russia's chemical weapon stockpile was stored at Gorny, Saratov oblast; Kambarka, Udmurtia Republic; Kizner, Udmurtia Republic; Leonidovka, Penza oblast; Maradikovsky, Kirov oblast; Pochep, Bryansk oblast; and Shchuchye, Kurgan oblast. Destruction operations at Gorny and Kambarka have been completed. See [Destruction of chemical weapons in the Russian Federation] on the website of *Rossisskaya Gazeta*, <http://www.rg.ru/ximiya.html> (in Russian); and the website of *Khimicheskoe Razoruzhenia: Otkrity Elektronny Zhurnal*, <http://www.chemicaldisarmament.ru/> (in Russian). A chemist with the Soviet chemical defence establishment has published a history of the Soviet chemical weapon programme. Fedorov, L. A., [Chemical armament: war against one's own people: the tragic Russian experience], 3 vols (self-published: Moscow, Feb. 2009).

[47] OPCW (note 34), para. 14.

[48] Russian Government, *The Destruction of Chemical Weapons in the Russian Federation: To the Third Stage of the Implementation of the Chemical Weapons Convention* (ARMS-TASS Information Agency: Moscow, 2009), p. 4.

[49] Russian Federation, 'Statement by Mr. Victor Kholstov, Head of the Russian Delegation at the fourteenth session of the Conference of the States Parties to the Chemical Weapons Convention', The Hague, 30 Nov.–4 Dec. 2009, p. 2.

[50] The locations are Anniston, AL; Blue Grass, KY; Pine Bluff, AR; Pueblo, CO; Tooele, UT, and Umatilla, OR. Destruction operations have been completed at Aberdeen, MD; Johnston Atoll, west of Hawaii; and Newport, IN.

[51] OPCW (note 34), para. 15.

destruction operations at its last two storage facilities—at Pueblo, Colorado, and Blue Grass, Kentucky—are 2017 and 2021, respectively.[52]

Old, abandoned and sea-dumped chemical weapons

As of 30 November 2009 three countries—China, Italy and Panama—had declared that abandoned chemical weapons (ACWs) were present on their territories, and 13 countries had declared that they have possessed old chemical weapons (OCWs) since the convention's entry into force in 1997.[53]

China and Japan continued to prepare to destroy the chemical weapons that were abandoned in China by Japan during World War II. A mobile destruction facility (which has been constructed but not assembled) is expected to begin operation in Nanjing in 2010, and the two states and the OPCW Technical Secretariat have reached general agreement on the verification measures to be taken when the mobile unit is employed.[54] In 2009 survey work using ground-penetrating radar and further infrastructure work were carried out for a fixed CWDF to be constructed at Haerbaling, Jilin Province, the location of the largest number of ACWs.[55] In the 12 months preceding the CSP, Japan recovered and stored 2000 ACWs for later destruction.[56]

The US armed forces dumped chemical warfare materiel off Oahu, Hawaii, in 1933–46. In March 2009 the Hawai'i Undersea Military Munitions Assessment Project (HUMMA) collected water and sediment samples in suspected munition dump site areas.[57] In north-west Washington, DC, the US Army continued to search the Spring Valley neighbourhood for chemical weapons and related equipment and material (an operation it

[52] Weber, A. C., 'United States Chemical Demilitarization Program', Presented by the US Delegation to the 14th session of the Conference of the States Parties to the CWC, The Hague, 1 Dec. 2009, pp. 5, 11.

[53] OPCW (note 33). The countries that have declared OCWs to the OPCW are Austria, Australia, Belgium, Canada, France, Germany, Italy, Japan, Marshall Islands, Russia, Slovenia, the UK and the USA. ACWs are defined as chemical weapons that were abandoned by a state after 1 Jan. 1925 on the territory of another state without the permission of the latter. CWC (note 1), Article II, para. 6. OCWs are defined as chemical weapons that were produced before 1925 or chemical weapons produced between 1925 and 1946 that have deteriorated to such an extent that they are no longer usable in the manner in which they were designed. CWC (note 1), Article II, para. 5. See also 'The legacy of underwater munitions worldwide: policy and science of assessment, impacts and potential responses', *Marine Technology Society Journal*, Special issue, vol. 43, no. 4 (fall 2009).

[54] Delegation of China, 'Statement by Ambassador Zhang Jun, Head of the Chinese Delegation at the fourteenth session of the Conference of States Parties to the Chemical Weapons Convention', The Hague, 1 Dec. 2009, p. 2.

[55] Delegation of Japan, 'Statement by H. E. Mr. Minoru Shibuya, Ambassador of Japan and Permanent Representative of Japan to the OPCW at the fourteenth session of the Conference of the States Parties to the OPCW', The Hague, 30 Nov. 2009, p. 5.

[56] Delegation of Japan (note 55).

[57] Hawai'i Undersea Military Munitions Assessment Project, 'Current activities & progress', <http://hummaproject.com/activities.php>; and Garcia, S. S. et al., 'Discarded military munitions case study: ordnance reef (HI-06), Hawaii', *Marine Technology Society Journal*, Special issue, vol. 43, no. 4 (fall 2009), pp. 85–99.

began in 1994). In August it uncovered a World War I-era vial containing trace amounts of sulphur mustard.[58]

Nord Stream, a German–Russian business consortium which will construct and operate a 1200-kilometre gas pipeline linking Viborg, Russia, and Greifswald, Germany, issued an environmental assessment that identified three chemical munitions along the planned route of the pipeline off the coast of Denmark. Munitions that lie along the final route will be remediated.[59]

V. Allegations of violations and prior programmes and activities

In Afghanistan at least three attacks using poisonous fumes were made on girls' schools by alleged Taliban or al-Qaeda affiliates.[60] In 2009 at least 40 members of al-Qaeda in the Islamic Magrheb (AQIM) in Algeria were reported to have died of plague at a training camp in Tizi Ouzou; according to an unnamed US intelligence official, the incident resulted from 'an experiment with unconventional weapons [that] went awry'.[61]

In December 2009 in Chile, judge Alejandro Madrid ordered the arrest of six people, including four doctors, for their roles in the alleged assassination in 1982 of Eduardo Frei Montalva, a political opponent of President Augusto Pinochet. Madrid determined that the accused were involved in the administration of doses of thallium and sulphur mustard to Frei while he was a patient at the Santa Maria Clinic in Santiago: Frei underwent stomach surgery, after which he died.[62]

Periodically, discussions arise over whether white phosphorus is a chemical weapon. In 2009 a UN fact-finding mission, chaired by Richard Goldstone of South Africa, issued its report on the 2008–2009 Israeli military operations in the Gaza Strip. The report's authors accepted that white

[58] Ruane, M. E., 'Vial used for chemical agent mustard is uncovered', *Washington Post*, 13 Aug. 2009. The area, previously part of the grounds of American University, was used by the US Chemical Warfare Service during World War I for field testing of chemical weapons. Gordon, M. K., Sude, B. R. and Overbeck, R. A., 'Chemical testing in the Great War: the American University Experiment Station', *Washington History*, vol. 6, no. 1 (spring/summer 1994), pp. 29–45.
[59] Of the 35 munitions identified, 31 are located off the coast of Finland; 3 of the total are chemical munitions. Nord Stream, *Munitions: Conventional and Chemical*, Nord Stream Espoo Report: Key Issue Paper (Nord Stream: Zug, Feb. 2009), pp. 29–30.
[60] Winfield, G, 'Is this it?', *CBRNe World*, summer 2009, pp. 6–7.
[61] Pita, R., Gunaratna, R. and Henika, P., 'Al Qaeda in the Islamic Maghreb (AQIM) and the alleged production of the etiological agent of plague', *ASA Newsletter*, no. 131 (30 Apr. 2009), pp. 1, 21–22.
[62] 'Six arrested over "assassination" of former Chilean president', *Daily Telegraph*, 7 Dec. 2009; and Sanhueza, J. M., 'Detalles del auto de procesamiento médicos que lo operaron, Con bajas dosis de Talio y gas mostaza durante varios meses asesinaron a Frei' [Details of indictment against medical staff who operated by introducing doses of thallium and mustard gas over several months to assassinate Frei], *El Mostrador* (Santiago), 7 Dec. 2009.

phosphorus is not currently proscribed under international law but noted that Israeli armed forces 'were systematically reckless in determining its use in built-up areas'.[63] If white phosphorus is used to cause harm or death through its toxic properties, it would be covered by the CWC. However, if used as tracer rounds, the convention does not ban its use.[64]

The International Crisis Group's review of the literature on the chemical and biological weapon programmes of the Democratic People's Republic of Korea (DPRK, or North Korea), including Korean language sources, concluded that it 'possesses a large stockpile of chemical weapons and is suspected of maintaining a biological weapons program'.[65] In March North Korea was accused of obtaining 2000 confidential files, including the identity of 700 companies or state-run entities that manufacture toxic industrial chemicals and information on 1350 such chemicals, by hacking into the military Internet system of the Republic of Korea (South Korea). Questions were raised about the wisdom of South Korea's providing North Korea with computers and Internet technology training in the light of its alleged chemical and biological weapon programmes.[66]

Periodic allegations of the use of chemical weapons were made during the civil war in Sri Lanka between government forces and the Liberation Tigers of Tamil Eelam (LTTE or Tamil Tigers).[67] In March, after the Sri Lankan military recovered 17 respirators and 16 chemical protective suits, a Sri Lankan official stated that the LTTE had been employing 'chemical gases' against the government forces for two years.[68]

In the USA the National Academy of Sciences began a 15-month review of the scientific work underlying the investigation of the 2001 anthrax letter attacks in the USA to which the FBI will contribute $879 550.[69]

---

[63] United Nations, Human Rights Council, 'Human rights in Palestine and other occupied Arab territories', Report of the United Nations Fact-finding Mission on the Gaza Conflict (Goldstone Report), A/HRC/12/48, 25 Sep. 2009, p. 16.

[64] The term 'chemical weapon' is defined in CWC (note 1), Article II, para. 1.

[65] International Crisis Group (ICG), *North Korea's Chemical and Biological Weapons Programs*, Asia Report no. 167 (ICG: Brussels, 18 June 2009).

[66] 'N. Korean hackers infiltrated S. Korean military networks', *Chosun Ilbo*, 19 Oct. 2009.

[67] E.g. Hoffman, B., 'The first non-state use of a chemical weapon in warfare: the Tamil Tigers' assault on East Kiran', *Small Wars & Insurgencies*, vol. 20, nos 3–4 (Sep.–Dec. 2009), pp. 463–77. See also appendix 2A in this volume.

[68] 'Sri Lanka troops kill 12 more rebels: military', Agence France-Presse, 12 Mar. 2009; and Sri Lankan Ministry of Defence, 'LTTE plot for mass scale chemical attack barred [updated]', 13 Mar. 2009, <http://www.defence.lk/new.asp?fname=20090312_05>.

[69] Shane, S., 'F.B.I. to pay for anthrax inquiry review', *New York Times*, 7 May 2009. See also Hart, J. and Clevestig, P., 'Reducing security threats from chemical and biological materials', *SIPRI Yearbook 2009*, pp. 428–32.

VI. Prevention, response and remediation

On 25 May–5 June 2009 the European Chemical, Biological, Radioactive, Nuclear and Explosive Centre at the University of Umeå, Sweden, hosted a training course on the investigation of chemical, biological and toxin weapon use for experts who are available to the UN Secretary-General.[70] The UN Office of Disarmament Affairs currently maintains a roster of over 200 experts and 40 laboratories that have been nominated by 41 UN member states.[71] The ODA also continued to develop a biological incident database (the OPCW has primary responsibility for investigating alleged chemical weapon use).[72]

UN Security Council Resolution 1540 of 2004 requires states to adopt and enforce national laws criminalizing acts by any citizen or legal person engaged in developing, acquiring, manufacturing, possessing, transporting, transferring or using NBC weapons and their means of delivery.[73] In October 2009 the 1540 Committee, which was established pursuant to Resolution 1540, met for a comprehensive review of the resolution's implementation. UN member states and international and regional organizations shared experiences and expressed their views, and an open day was held at which non-governmental organizations (NGOs) that actively help a number of UN member states to implement the resolution could present their projects and ideas. However, representatives of informal bodies, such as the relevant export control regimes, were not invited to participate.[74] The meeting participants reviewed background reports on the status of implementation that had been prepared by the experts who support the work of the 1540 Committee.[75]

Many states indicated their desire to pursue practical, concrete measures to enhance Resolution 1540's implementation. However, other states highlighted problems, such as the lack of clear guidance and definitions to help

---

[70] United Nations, 'Experts to attend training course on investigation of chemical, biological, toxin weapons use, in Umeå, Sweden, 25 May–5 June', Press Release DC/3175, 22 May 2009, <http://www.un.org/News/Press/docs/2009/dc3175.doc.htm>.

[71] United Nations (note 70).

[72] On the database's format see UN Office for Disarmament Affairs and NGO Committee on Disarmament, Peace and Security, *Developing a Biological Incident Database*, UNODA Occasional Paper no. 15 (United Nations: New York, Mar. 2009), pp. 95–101.

[73] UN Security Council Resolution 1540, 28 Apr. 2004.

[74] The decision not to invite such participation was criticized by some states. Statement by Gary Quinlan, Ambassador and Permanent Representative of Australia to the United Nations Security Council Committee regarding the comprehensive review of the status of implementation of Resolution 1540, 1 Oct. 2009, <http://www.australiaun.org/unny/20091001_SC.html>. On the export control regimes see also chapter 12 in this volume.

[75] All but 1 of the reports is publicly available. The public reports include a regional analysis of implementation with examples of national and regional practices and experience sharing, and an assessment of the reporting template used to gather information on implementation in the light of information gathered up to 2008.

states understand how to meet the standard of appropriate and effective national laws that is established in the resolution.[76] The main organizer of the NGO open day concluded that more action at the national level to enhance implementation and a process to develop criteria and standards for compliance were both needed.[77]

The European Union's Instrument for Stability and the CBRN Action Plan

The EU undertakes internal and external policy actions. The EU Instrument for Stability and EU joint actions are examples of the latter, while the EU CBRN Action Plan is an example of internal policy action. An EU joint action in support of the BTWC will operate from May 2009 to April 2011. It consists of four projects: (a) promoting the universalization of the BTWC; (b) providing assistance to states parties for national implementation of the BTWC; (c) promoting the submission of CBM declarations on a regular basis by parties to the BTWC; and (d) providing support for the BTWC inter-sessional process.[78] The EU also launched a joint action in support of the World Health Organization that consists of two projects: promotion of biorisk reduction management through regional and national outreach; and strengthening the security and laboratory management practices against biological risks (a demonstration model for countries).[79] In December the European Commission concluded an agreement with the OPCW to carry out an EU joint action worth €2 110 000 ($2.8 million) to support OPCW activities over 18 months.[80]

On 8 April the European Commission agreed to allocate €225 million ($300 million) for the EU Instrument for Stability for the period 2009–11.

---

[76] The discussion is summarized in United Nations, Security Council, 'Review opens of implementation of Security Council Resolution 1540, compelling states to criminalize spread of mass destruction weapons to non-state actors', Press Release SC/9754, 30 Sep. 2009, <http://www.un.org/News/Press/docs/2009/sc9754.doc.htm>.

[77] Kraig, M. H., *United Nations Security Council Resolution 1540 at the Crossroads: The Challenges of Implementation* (Stanley Foundation: Muscatine, IA, 1 Oct. 2009).

[78] Council Joint Action 2008/858/CFSP of 10 Nov. 2008 in support of the Biological and Toxin Weapons Convention (BTWC), in the framework of the implementation of the EU Strategy against the Proliferation of Weapons of Mass Destruction, *Official Journal of the European Union*, L302, 13 Nov. 2008.

[79] Council Joint Action 2008/307/CFSP of 14 Apr. 2008 in support of the World Health Organization activities in the area of laboratory bio-safety and bio-security in the framework of the European Union Strategy against the proliferation of Weapons of Mass Destruction, *Official Journal of the European Union*, L106, 16 Apr. 2008.

[80] OPCW, 'OPCW Director-General welcomes continued EU support for OPCW activities', Press Release OPCW NEWS 60/2009, 15 Dec. 2009, <http://www.opcw.org/news/news/article/opcw-director-general-welcomes-continued-eu-support-for-opcw-activities/>; and Council Decision 2009/569/CFSP of 27 July 2009 on support for OPCW activities in the framework of the implementation of the EU Strategy against Proliferation of Weapons of Mass Destruction, *Official Journal of the European Union*, L197, 29 July 2009.

The money will support efforts to address the key threats that were identified in the 2003 European Security Strategy.[81] To implement the WMD component, EU assistance will continue to focus on redirecting scientists, export controls and 'illicit trafficking'. It will also support the development of safety and security culture when dealing with CBRN materials.[82]

In December 2009 the Council of the European Union adopted a CBRN Action Plan.[83] The plan's purpose is to contribute to the wider EU counter-terrorism effort, but it is designed using an 'all-hazard' approach that is intended to help prevent and mitigate incidents of accidental, natural or intentional origin. The action plan is one important element helping to implement the wider EU strategy to combat terrorism that was published in 2005.[84] The counterterrorism strategy defined four 'pillars' of action: terrorism prevention, the protection of critical infrastructure, the pursuit of terrorists and, should those measures fail, mounting an effective response to any act of mass impact terrorism that is carried out.

The action plan does not introduce new EU legislation. In December 2007 the Council decided that effective policies to address CBRN risks would be developed 'in close consultation with national authorities and, as appropriate, the industrial sectors concerned, academic institutions and other relevant stakeholders, notably with a view to ensuring the viability and proportionality of measures which may be required'.[85]

The counterterrorism effort built on work already carried out to elaborate a green paper in 2006 that pointed out basic elements that would be needed to strengthen biopreparedness.[86] Comments and discussion inside the EU institutions, and in particular within the Commission Directorate-General (DG) for Justice, Freedom and Security, expanded the portfolio of issues to include chemical security and radiological sources.[87] The task force worked on the principle of avoiding duplication of effort and there-

[81] 'A secure Europe in a better world: European Security Strategy', Brussels, 12 Dec. 2003.

[82] Council of the European Union, 'Instrument for stability: the EU's response to some of today's global threats', Press Release MEMO/09/164, 17 Apr. 2009, <http://europa.eu/rapid/pressReleases Action.do?reference=MEMO/09/164>.

[83] Council of the European Union, Council Conclusions on strengthening chemical, biological, radiological and nuclear (CBRN) security in the European Union: an EU CBRN action plan, document 15505/1/09, REV 1, Brussels, 12 Nov. 2009.

[84] Council of the European Union, The European Union Counter-Terrorism Strategy, document 14469/4/05 REV 4, Brussels 30 Nov. 2005.

[85] Council of the European Union, Council conclusions of 6 Dec. 2007 on addressing chemical, biological, radiological and nuclear risks and on bio-preparedness, 16589/07, 17 Dec. 2007.

[86] European Commission, 'Green paper on bio-preparedness', Brussels, COM(2007) 399, 11 July 2007.

[87] In contrast, nuclear security measures have been elaborated inside the EU over many years and are already enshrined in EU law.

fore gave relatively little attention to the security of radiological sources and chemical safety (issues being actively examined elsewhere in the EU).[88]

During 2008 and the first half of 2009 the Commission used an inter-disciplinary task force made up of both government and non-governmental experts to elaborate a communication on strengthening CBRN security that was presented to the EU member states in June 2009.[89] Consistent with the method of wide cooperation, the task force compiled and discussed existing good practices. The main effort was focused on biological risks as well as on chemical security. The approach to security and health built on work already carried out during the preparation of the green paper on bio-preparedness, and the June communication included an annex laying out a number of best practices that had already been identified.[90]

The December 2009 action plan eventually defined approximately 130 measures to prevent, detect and respond to CBRN threats and risks inside the EU.[91] The measures, which cover the entire spectrum of chemical, biological and radiological threats, will be implemented in phases. Projects that are allocated the highest priority will be initiated from mid-2009 to the end of 2010, although this period is also seen as a preparatory phase. The period 2011–12 is an enhanced implementation phase, and in 2013 the Commission plans to review progress and consider new projects. The Commission has concluded that the safety and security aspects of nuclear and radiological threats are already adequately covered by existing EU regulations but more work is needed on the chemical and biological side.[92]

In the first phase the first priority has been developing new lists of high-risk materials that require protection and special scrutiny. While controversial, given that lists developed in other initiatives that could serve as a point of reference exist, the Commission defended this approach by arguing that the existing lists are too narrowly defined for the purpose of counterterrorism. The narrow lists might, it is argued, even undermine efforts to promote security by creating an erroneous perception that only

[88] The Joint Research Centre of the Commission has made a study on radiological preparedness in the EU and chemical safety issues have been examined extensively, leading to the creation of a European Chemicals Agency (ECHA). See the website of ECHA at <http://echa.europa.eu/>.

[89] European Commission, 'Proposal for a new policy package on chemical, biological, radiological and nuclear (CBRN) security', Press Release MEMO/09/291, Brussels, 24 June 2009, <http://europa.eu/rapid/pressReleasesAction.do?reference=MEMO/09/291>.

[90] European Commission, 'Bridging security and health: towards the identification of good practices in the response to CBRN incidents and the security of CBR substances', 11480/09 ADD 3, Commission Staff Working Document, Brussels, 29 June 2009.

[91] Örnéus, P., 'EU statement at the comprehensive review of the status of implementation of Resolution 1540', New York, 30 Sep. 2009, <http://www.swedenabroad.com/Page___97653.aspx>.

[92] European Commission, 'The Commission proposes a new policy to enhance chemical, biological, radiological and nuclear security in the EU', Press Release IP/09/992, Brussels, 24 June 2009, <http://europa.eu/rapid/pressReleasesAction.do?reference=IP/09/992>.

these items need to be protected and monitored. The EU-specific list is also needed to help the Commission assess the economic impact of the measures contained in the action plan and to help develop budgets and allocate financing to implement the measures defined.

A second priority is to enhance security at facilities through the development of practical guidelines and good practice documents. Here the Commission intends to collate, assess and disseminate existing national and non-governmental products in order to create minimum standards across the EU. The third priority in the action plan is to assess the risks stemming from the transport of materials, where little action has so far been taken at the European level. The fourth priority is to develop detection equipment based on EU-wide trials, testing and certification. Standards adopted at the EU level are expected to have a powerful impact not only on the European market for such products, but also worldwide. The final priority in the first implementation phase is a dedicated effort to connect medical and research communities with the national authorities that are responsible for emergency planning and response (including first responders and law enforcement) in a more coherent and systematic manner.

To support these objectives the Commission intends to initiate a series of EU-wide projects to improve training, develop improved tools and strengthen personnel security. One of these projects will analyse the feasibility of mutual recognition of security clearances and qualifications across the EU as well as the development of common criteria for vetting procedures and background checks. This would include a common approach to visiting students and guest researchers and examination of whether or not a secure registry of personnel with access to the most sensitive items and technologies within the EU could be of value in counterterrorism. Finally, the projects under the action plan will be supported using financial instruments that are available to the DG for Justice, Freedom and Security as well as linking to the security research funds available under the Framework Programme for research that are administered within the Commission by the DG for Enterprise.

Scientific research

In 2009 attention continued to be focused on procedures for the oversight of gene synthesis and of the acquisition, handling and storage of biopharmaceuticals.[93] Such procedures are needed in order to help ensure that

---

[93] E.g. Jeremias, G., 'Regulating the worldwide transfer and use of biological dual-use goods: monitoring the trade of biological dual-use biological items', *Micromaterials and Nanomaterials*, Oct. 2009, pp. 32–36.

materials are not misused for CBW purposes. In November 2009 five gene synthesis companies established an International Gene Synthesis Consortium and a 'harmonized screening protocol for gene sequence & customer screening to promote biosecurity'.[94] The agreement covers five core components: (a) complete DNA sequence screening of every order for synthetic genes against a pathogen database, developed by the consortium, including screening of amino acid translated sequences;[95] (b) screening of customers to establish identity and clearance in accordance with national guidelines; (c) record keeping of all orders and customers for up to eight years; (d) order refusal at the liberty of the companies and the reporting to authorities of problematic orders; and (e) compliance with all applicable laws and regulations governing the synthesis, possession, transport, export and import of synthesized genes and other related products.[96] The same month the US Department of Health and Human Services issued for public comment a draft voluntary screening framework guidance for commercial providers of synthetic double-stranded DNA of 200 base pairs or more. The framework entails confirming the identity of customers, being aware of 'red flags' (e.g. unusual method of payment or shipping or labelling requests) and screening key nucleic acid segments based on select agents and toxins on the US Export Administration Regulation's Commerce Control List.[97] The Australia Group continued a 'particular focus on international developments' in synthetic biology and 'considered' an internal report on the implementation of possible oversight measures to ensure that synthetic biology is not misused.[98]

Chemical management and oversight

The American Chemical Society has asked the US Congress to make a regulatory distinction between university laboratories and industrial production sites in view of the relative threats posed by larger quantities of toxic chemicals, and the Congress continues to consider how standards and procedures for security vulnerability assessments of chemical facilities

---

[94] 'Gene-synthesis firms set up biosecurity protocol', *Genetic Engineering & Biotechnology News*, 18 Nov. 2009.

[95] 'Translated' refers to the conversion of the nucleic acid (DNA/RNA) sequence information into its corresponding amino acid (protein) sequence. Screening against US select agent lists will be included for all US domestic orders.

[96] International Gene Synthesis Consortium, 'Harmonized Screening Protocol: gene sequence and customer screening to promote biosecurity', <http://www.genesynthesisconsortium.org/Harmonized_Screening_Protocol.html>.

[97] US Department of Health and Human Services, Health and Human Services Department, 'Screening framework guidance for synthetic double-stranded DNA providers', *Federal Register*, vol. 74, no. 227 (27 Nov. 2009), pp. 62319–27.

[98] Australia Group, 'Media release: 2009 Australia Group Plenary', <http://www.australiagroup.net/en/agm_sept2009.html>. See also chapter 12, section III, in this volume.

should be applied.[99] Debate continues on whether and how information is sensitive and how such determinations should affect its public dissemination.[100] In 2009 it was revealed that US chemical security policy had been misused to prevent the release of information about an explosion at a chemical plant in August 2008.[101] Safety inspectors cancelled a briefing about the explosion because plant officials maintained that some information about the plant was protected from public disclosure under the 2002 Maritime Transportation Security Act.[102]

Disease surveillance and response and public health

In 2009 a new strain of influenza A emerged following a likely event of genetic reassortment.[103] This virus, which the WHO officially designated as a new strain in June, has an unusual genetic combination of material from swine, bird and human influenza viruses and is of a similar subtype (H1N1) to that of the 1918 Spanish influenza. Within the framework of the International Health Regulations, the WHO member states discussed whether the H1N1 outbreak should be designated a 'pandemic' because the definition of the term as understood by some states had not been met. The underlying issue was whether the term should be used in relation to the lethality or the geographic extent of the outbreak. In response, the WHO revised its definition of 'pandemic' in June and announced a 'phase six' outbreak.[104] The previous definition of pandemic was based on geographic spread, while the new WHO definition takes into greater account its severity.

[99] Hess, G., 'Chemical security bill wins approval', *Chemical & Engineering News*, vol. 87, no. 46 (16 Nov. 2009), p. 6.
[100] See Federation of American Scientists (FAS), 'Secrecy news blog', <http://www.fas.org/blog/secrecy/>; and US Department of the Army, *Classification of Former Chemical Warfare, Chemical and Biological Defense, and Nuclear, Biological, and Chemical Contamination Survivability Information* (Department of the Army: Washington, DC, 22 June 2005).
[101] Hamill, S. D., 'Safety panel cites errors in blast at chemical plant', *New York Times*, 23 Apr. 2009; and US House of Representatives, Committee on Energy and Commerce, 'Memorandum: supplemental information regarding the 2008 Bayer chemical plant explosion', 21 Apr. 2009, <http://energycommerce.house.gov/>.
[102] Ward, K., 'Board cancels hearing under Bayer pressure', *Charleston Gazette*, 25 Feb. 2009; and Maritime Transportation Security Act of 2002, US Public Law 107–295, signed into law on 25 Nov. 2002, <http://thomas.loc.gov/cgi-bin/query/z?c107:s1214:>.
[103] Novel Swine-Origin Influenza A (H1N1) Virus Investigation Team, 'Emergence of a novel swine-origin influenza A (H1N1) virus in humans', *New England Journal of Medicine*, vol. 360, no. 25 (18 June 2009), pp. 2605–15; and Malik Peiris, J. S., Poon, L. L. and Guan, Y., 'Emergence of a novel swine-origin influenza A virus (S-OIV) H1N1 virus in humans', *Journal of Clinical Virology*, vol. 45, no. 3 (July 2009), pp. 169–73.
[104] World Health Organization, Global Alert and Response, 'DG statement following the meeting of the Emergency Committee', 11 June 2009, <http://www.who.int/csr/disease/swineflu/4th_meeting_ihr/en/index.html>.

Health agencies in Scotland, UK, were alerted following the 16 December 2009 death of a heroin user in Glasgow, who tested positive for *Bacillus anthracis*.[105] A previous case of lethal anthrax infection in the UK had occurred in 2008 when a craftsman presumably contracted *B. anthracis* from animal hides that had been imported from Gambia.[106] Two years earlier, a similar fatal case of inhalation anthrax had occurred in Scotland, also involving imported animal hides for drums.[107] By 31 December six cases of anthrax had been confirmed in Glasgow, and three of these people died. Public health and police authorities suspected that the source was contaminated heroin. Bonemeal that had been imported from Afghanistan and used as a cutting agent in the heroin was suspected. The incident high-lighted the ability of the international narcotic trade to affect global health security, led to speculation about the nature of future biological threats and emphasized the need for faster microbial forensics capabilities.[108]

VII. Conclusions

An emphasis on control and oversight of chemical and biological materials implies reduced focus on traditional state military programmes. In add-ition, the international trade in biological and chemical materials and tech-nologies entails uncertainties and challenges. The negative effects of the signals that have been given to non-state actors by various threat assess-ment statements about the desirability of using chemical and biological weapons, and the anxiety that such use would provoke, could be mitigated by better understanding of the variability of the effects of CBRN weapons. Operational challenges associated with determining the volume and type of trade in dual-purpose material technology and intangible technology trans-fers can also inform threat assessments. This, in turn, would help to pro-mote a balanced understanding of the role of future CBW threats in inter-national peace and security.

---

[105] 'Anthrax found in Glasgow heroin users', BBC News, 18 Dec. 2009, <http://news.bbc.co.uk/2/hi/8419113.stm>.

[106] Anaraki, S. et al., 'Investigations and control measures following a case of inhalation anthrax in East London in a drum maker and drummer', *Eurosurveillance*, vol. 13, issue 51 (18 Dec. 2008).

[107] Riley, A., *Report on the Management of an Anthrax Incident in the Scottish Borders* (NHS Borders: Melrose, Dec. 2007).

[108] McNeil, D. G., 'Anthrax: in Scotland, six heroin users die of anthrax poisoning', *New York Times*, 11 Jan. 2010.

11. Conventional arms control

ZDZISLAW LACHOWSKI

I. Introduction

Endeavours to rejuvenate European conventional arms control intensified in 2009. The 1990 Treaty on Conventional Armed Forces in Europe (CFE Treaty) has been in abeyance since December 2007, when Russia uni-laterally 'suspended' its participation in the treaty.[1] However, the proposal by the President of Russia, Dmitry Medvedev, for a 'European security treaty' gave hope for progress. The European security dialogue that was initiated in 2008 continued in 2009, stressing the need to revitalize arms control and confidence- and security-building measures (CSBMs).[2] The subregional arms control framework in the Western Balkans continues to operate well and further steps have been taken to make it more self-reliant. However, the confidence-building and security-sharing efforts in Europe that focus on specific areas are in need of adaptation and upgrading.

Efforts to control 'inhumane weapons' continued in 2009, although with less dynamism than demonstrated in 2008 by the 'Oslo process' on cluster munitions.[3]

This chapter assesses major developments in conventional arms control in 2009. Section II discusses the status of and debate on European arms control. Section III addresses steps promoting 'soft' arms control measures to strengthen confidence and security, foster predictability and render practical disarmament assistance in the Organization for Security and Co-operation in Europe (OSCE) area. Section IV focuses on the control of 'inhumane' conventional weapons, while section V presents the con-clusions.

II. European arms control

The 1990 Treaty on Conventional Armed Forces in Europe is the most elaborate conventional arms control regime worldwide. Its implementation

---

[1] For a summary and other details of the CFE Treaty see annex A in this volume.

[2] OSCE, Corfu informal meeting of OSCE foreign ministers on the future of European security: Chair's concluding statement to the press, document CIO.GAL/83/09, 29 June 2009.

[3] See Lachowski, Z. and Post, S., 'Conventional arms control', *SIPRI Yearbook 2009*. The 'Oslo process' is the name given to the diplomatic activities and public campaign that resulted in the Con-vention on Cluster Munitions (CCM) in 2008. For a summary and other details of the CCM see annex A in this volume.

Table 11.1. Aggregate treaty-limited equipment holdings of the states parties to the Treaty on Conventional Armed Forces in Europe, as of 1 January 2010

Year	Tanks	ACVs	Artillery	Aircraft	Helicopters	Total
1990	58 282	77 402	47 573	14 311	3 437	201 005
1992	55 939	78 273	46 344	13 525	3 215	197 296
1995	33 217	51 349	33 324	10 174	2 749	130 813
2000	30 338	46 968	31 511	9 070	2 497	120 384
2010	20 979	38 599	24 677	6 110	1 750	92 115
Aggregate limits for all states parties						
	40 000	60 000	40 000	13 600	4 000	157 600
Decrease, 1990–2010						
	–37 303	–38 803	–22 896	–8 201	–1 687	–108 890

ACVs = armoured combat vehicle

Source: Treaty on Conventional Arms Control in Europe and the Concluding Act on the Negotiations on Personnel Strength of Conventional Armed Forces in Europe, Consolidated Matrix, JCG document JCG.TOI/1/10, 19 Mar. 2010.

has resulted in more than a 50 per cent decrease in the aggregate holdings of the treaty-limited equipment (TLE)—battle tanks, armoured combat vehicles, artillery of at least 100-mm calibre, combat aircraft and attack helicopters—of the parties (see table 11.1). However, it is built on an outdated bipolar concept: an equilibrium of major categories of heavy conventional armaments and equipment between the North Atlantic Treaty Organization (NATO) and the now defunct Warsaw Treaty Organization in its Atlantic-to-the-Urals area of application. The 1999 Agreement on Adaptation of the CFE Treaty would better respond to geopolitical shifts and new security circumstances and requirements.[4] The agreement has not entered into force because the NATO members and other states parties refuse to ratify it until Russia complies with the commitments it made at the 1999 OSCE Istanbul Summit.[5] The 1990 CFE Treaty and the associated agreed documents and decisions therefore remain binding on all parties, although Russia has 'suspended' its implementation of the CFE Treaty.

---

[4] For a summary and other details of the agreement see annex A in this volume. For the text of the CFE Treaty as amended by the Agreement on Adaptation see *SIPRI Yearbook 2000*, pp. 627–42.

[5] OSCE, 'Istanbul Summit Declaration', 17 Nov. 1999, paras 15–19; and OSCE, 'Final Act of the Conference of the States Parties to the Treaty on Conventional Armed Forces in Europe', 17 Nov. 1999, Annex 14. These texts are reproduced in *SIPRI Yearbook 2000*, pp. 642–46; and OSCE, 'Istanbul Document 1999', <http://www.osce.org/item/15853.html>, pp. 46–54, 236–59. With regard to the outstanding issues Russia committed itself: (*a*) to reduce its military equipment in Georgia; (*b*) to withdraw all Russian troops and ammunition from the territory of Moldova; and (*c*) to eliminate its stocks of ammunition and military equipment in the Trans-Dniester region of Moldova.

A European security architecture and conventional arms control

A European security dialogue was initiated at the 2008 Helsinki Ministerial Council, and in June 2009 the Organization for Security and Co-operation in Europe foreign ministers' meeting in Corfu, Greece, stressed the urgent need to revitalize arms control and CSBMs. The meeting launched a wide-ranging dialogue on European security that became known as the 'Corfu process', and 11 additional meetings of that type were held in 2009. These meetings prepared the agenda for the OSCE Ministerial Meeting in Athens, Greece, in December and for future meetings. The 'strategic dimension' of arms control, including the CFE Treaty, CSBMs and a broad range of security challenges and threats was one of the five broad areas that were addressed.[6]

In June 2008 Medvedev had presented a plan to hold a mid-2009 European summit to elaborate a legally binding European security pact.[7] Thus, the faltering dialogue on the context and scope of the future of conventional arms control was conducted with the Russian President's proposal in mind, although, initially, the relation of the draft European security treaty to the CFE Treaty and to CSBMs was unclear.

After the August 2008 Georgia–Russia conflict, Medvedev announced a doctrine of 'privileged interests' for Russia's neighbouring regions, which would potentially further hamper the prospects of the European arms control regime.[8] Medvedev later urged OSCE participating states to guarantee 'equal security' organized on Russia's terms.[9] 'Hard' (armament limitation-related) security was emphasized as a determining factor and, regardless of its actions in the Georgia–Russia conflict, these positions also gave indications of how Russia would address conventional arms control issues. The Russian proposal for a new Euro-Atlantic security treaty, published in November 2009, fell far short of the announced wide security agenda and focused instead on establishing a mechanism of consultations and conferences to address the concerns of any member state about possible threats to its security from other parties.[10]

---

[6] See OSCE, Corfu process: Reinforced Permanent Council, document CIO.GAL/179/09, 23 Nov. 2009.

[7] President of Russia, 'Speech at meeting with German political, parliamentary and civic leaders', Berlin, 5 June 2008, <http://www.kremlin.ru/eng/sdocs/speeches.shtml?stype=82912>. For more discussion of the Euro-Atlantic security setting in 2009 see chapter 4 in this volume.

[8] Interview given by Dmitry Medvedev to television channels Channel One, Rossiya, NTV, Sochi, Russia, 31 Aug. 2008, <http://kremlin.ru/eng/text/speeches/2008/08/31/1850_type82912type82916_206003.shtml>. On the Georgia–Russia conflict see Stepanova, E., 'Trends in armed conflicts: one-sided violence against civilians', *SIPRI Yearbook 2009*, pp. 57–60.

[9] President of Russia, 'Speech at World Policy Conference', Evian, France, 8 Oct. 2008, <http://eng.kremlin.ru/speeches/2008/10/08/2159_type82912type82914_207457.shtml>.

[10] European security treaty, Unofficial translation, Draft, President of Russia, 29 Nov. 2009, <http://eng.kremlin.ru/text/docs/2009/11/223072.shtml>.

Soon after the inauguration of Barack Obama as United States President, his administration restarted the strategic arms control dialogue with Russia.[11] In February 2009 the Russian Deputy Foreign Minister, Alexander Grushko, stated that the arms control aspects of a European security treaty would not replace the CFE Treaty and other Europe-related arms control accords.[12] The details of the proposed treaty's arms control arrangements were spelled out by Russian officials at various meetings during the first half of 2009, and legally binding disarmament measures were stressed as crucial elements.

At the same time, meetings of OSCE high officials and experts were being held to discuss the state of the OSCE and to muster support for conventional arms control. The OSCE ambassadors debated the future of European security and the OSCE's role, stressing that the goal of the OSCE participating states should be to build on and strengthen the existing OSCE principles, provisions and commitments ('Helsinki Plus' or 'OSCE Plus') rather than seeking to replace them as proposed by Russia ('Helsinki II').[13] Most participating states pointed to revitalization of arms control and CSBMs as an urgent priority. An Austrian workshop on European security dialogue discussed the concept of 'multipolarity' and its failure to address issues such as low-intensity conflicts and the future of the CFE.[14] A meeting of experts in June in Germany that was intended to provide new impetus to the CFE discussion had little tangible success. Nevertheless, at an informal ambassadorial meeting devoted to arms control and CSBMs the significance of those topics was re-emphasized not only by the CFE states parties, but also by non-signatories of the treaty.[15]

Russia's draft security treaty proposed involving all of the major international structures in the Euro-Atlantic region, in contrast to the proposed Helsinki Plus discussion, which prioritized the OSCE. The two approaches overlapped but were not necessarily congruent. The Russian Foreign Minister, Sergei Lavrov, presented a general outline of the security treaty,

[11] Biden, J. R., Speech at the 45th Munich Security Conference, Munich, 7 Feb. 2009, <http://www.securityconference.de/Joseph-R-Biden.234+M52b89fcdf08.0.html>; and White House, 'Remarks by President Barack Obama, Prague, Czech Republic, 5 May 2009, <http://www.whitehouse.gov/the_press_office/Remarks-By-President-Barack-Obama-In-Prague-As-Delivered/>. See also chapters 4 and 9 in this volume.

[12] OSCE, Forum for Security Cooperation and Permanent Council, document FSC-PC.DEL/9/2009, 18 Feb. 2009.

[13] OSCE, 'Debate on the future of European security and the role of the OSCE', Ambassadors' retreat, Stegersbach, 24–25 Apr. 2009, Summary by the Greek Chairmanship, 27 Apr. 2009, document CIO.GAL/53/09, 27 Apr. 2009. The predecessor of the OSCE was established at the 1975 Helsinki Conference. Russia has tended to use the terms 'Helsinki II' and 'Helsinki Plus' interchangeably.

[14] OSCE, 'Expert meeting on a European security dialogue', Palais Niederösterreich, Vienna, 8 May 2009.

[15] OSCE, 'Corfu process: Vienna informal meetings at ambassadors' level, 22 September 2009', Chair's perception paper, document CIO.GAL/132/09, 24 Sep. 2009.

emphasizing its priority of hard security, at the OSCE's Annual Security Review Conference (ASRC) in June 2009.[16]

Another Russian representative at the ASRC elaborated on the arms control elements of a draft treaty, including three conceptual clusters (within the arms control 'bloc') dealing with: (a) the basic objectives, (b) the guiding principles for negotiation of new accords, and (c) the required criteria for reaching new understandings.[17]

The basic objectives included lower levels of armed forces and military activities of a non-provocative character; strengthened regional stability by preventing the military domination of any state or group of states; assistance to stabilize crisis situations; and pursuit of 'reasonable sufficiency' by banning the permanent stationing of substantial combat forces on the territory of another state.

The guiding principles stressed: (a) arms control, confidence building, restraint and reasonable sufficiency in military development; (b) sovereignty and equal rights in negotiations carried out on a voluntary basis; and (c) respect for and recognition of the security interests of the future parties to such a treaty.

The required criteria were: a balanced approach and reciprocity; militarily significant arms control obligations; increased transparency regarding military forces and activities; avoidance of financial and economic burdens in the security building process; verifiability; and adaptability.

Russia proposed starting a 'programme for immediate action', similar to the programme of the early 1990s, aimed at updating, reformulating and extending the scope of the Vienna Document 1999 on Confidence- and Security-Building Measures.[18] Russia also advocated adapting and updating the 1999 Platform for Cooperative Security, which promotes non-hierarchical relations among international organizations in the Euro-Atlantic region. Both proposals were supported by the members of the Collective Security Treaty Organization (CSTO).[19]

---

[16] OSCE, Annual Security Review Conference, Delegation of the Russian Federation, 'The challenges of "hard security" in the Euro-Atlantic region: the role of the OSCE in establishing a stable and effective security system', Statement by Sergei Lavrov, Russian Minister for Foreign Affairs, at the opening session of the OSCE Annual Security Review Conference, Vienna, 23 June 2009.

[17] See e.g. OSCE, 'Collective security or new confrontation: who is choosing what', Statement by Professor Vyacheslav Kulebyakin at the 2009 Annual Security Review Conference, Working Session II, Politico-military aspects of security: arms control arrangements and confidence-building measures in the OSCE area, Vienna, 19 June 2009.

[18] See Conference on Security and Co-operation in Europe, Helsinki Document 1992: The Challenges of Change, Programme for Immediate Action annex, Helsinki, 10 July 1992, <http://www.osce.org/mc/13017.html>. For a summary of the Vienna Document 1999 see annex A in this volume.

[19] Statement by the CSTO member states at the OSCE Forum for Security Cooperation, document FSC.DEL/208/09, 18 Nov. 2009. In late Sep. 2009, the CSTO foreign ministers meeting in New York supported the Russian initiative for a European security treaty and called for a meeting of leaders of the CSTO, NATO, the European Union, the Commonwealth of Independent States and the OSCE as a first step. For a brief description of the CSTO see annex B in this volume.

Competing views on revival of the CFE regime

In an attempt to keep the CFE treaty regime alive, despite Russia's suspension, in December 2008 the German Foreign Minister, Frank-Walter Steinmeier, invited high-ranking experts from CFE countries to Germany to make a 'new beginning'.[20] Lavrov responded at the 2008 Helsinki Ministerial Council that a solution to the impasse, based on NATO's 'parallel actions' package—proposals by the Western states in 2007–2008 for step-by-step ratification of the Agreement on Adaptation accompanied by consistent implementation of Russia's Istanbul commitments[21]—was 'quite amorphous', in contrast to 'a plan of carefully outlined Russian actions'. [22] He also praised Germany's ideas that were 'similarly oriented' to the Russian plan. In response, the Western states parties to the CFE Treaty continued to urge Russia to address the crisis on the basis of NATO's parallel action package as the most promising approach and criticized the incompleteness of the data provided by Russia.

Although it is preoccupied with nuclear disarmament issues, policy and negotiation, the USA has promised to help resolve the deadlock with Russia over the CFE Treaty. A senior official of the Department of State's Bureau of Verification and Compliance stated that the issue would be a top priority.[23] However, swift progress on the issue appeared unrealistic.

The NATO Summit Declaration on Alliance Security that was adopted in April 2009 reconfirmed the NATO stance on the CFE Treaty regime that was agreed at the March 2008 North Atlantic Council (NAC) Bucharest Summit: NATO's parallel actions package addresses all of Russia's concerns.[24]

In 2009, as in previous years, Russia refused to provide complete data, submit notifications and receive inspections under the CFE Treaty regime. However, its declarations and documents in 2009 demonstrated a degree of cautious search for agreement. NATO promised to provide its annual information exchange in 2009, called on Russia to do the same and warned that not reciprocating 'could make it difficult' for NATO to provide information

[20] Speech by Federal Foreign Minister, Dr Frank-Walter Steinmeier, at the OSCE Ministerial Council in Helsinki on 4 Dec. 2008, document MC.DEL/14/08, 4 Dec. 2008.

[21] Socor, V., '"Action for action" on the CFE Treaty: opportunity and risk', *Eurasia Daily Monitor*, 9 Oct. 2007; and NATO, NAC Statement on CFE, Press Release 2008(047), 28 Mar. 2008, <http://www.nato.int/docu/pr/2008/p08-047e.html>. See also Lachowski and Post (note 3), pp. 446–48.

[22] Russian Ministry of Foreign Affairs, Information and Press Department, Speech by Russian Minister of Foreign Affairs Sergei Lavrov at the 16th Meeting of the OSCE Ministerial Council, Helsinki, 5 Dec. 2008, <http://www.ln.mid.ru>.

[23] Gottemoeller, R., Assistant Secretary of State-designate for the Bureau of Verification and Compliance, Testimony before the US Senate Foreign Relations Committee, 26 Mar. 2009, <http://www.foreign.senate.gov/testimony/2009/GottemoellerTestimony090326p.pdf>.

[24] NATO, Declaration on Alliance Security issued by the Heads of State and Government participating in the meeting of the North Atlantic Council in Strasbourg/Kehl, 4 Apr. 2009, <http://www.nato.int/cps/en/natolive/news_52838.htm>, para. 57.

to Russia in the future. At the same time, the NATO states declared that they were prepared for intensive efforts to find a way forward to salvage the CFE regime.[25]

In contrast to the general character of NATO's parallel actions package, Russia has submitted several documents that spell out its ideas for a European arms control regime in detail. In May 2009 the Russian delegation submitted a document entitled 'Restoring the viability of the CFE Treaty: a way forward' in the Joint Consultative Group (JCG).[26] Russia's declared belief was that the treaty regime might be salvaged while work on the Russian–US draft package solution progressed. The 12-point Russian aide-memoire presented the Russian standpoint, elaborated in detail on demands and suggestions that had been contained in earlier documents and added new proposals.

1. Russia expected the 'most reliable guarantees' that the Agreement on Adaptation would be ratified within the agreed timeframe.

2. Russia stressed the inclusion of certain provisions in the package concerning the provisional application of the adapted treaty regime.[27]

3. As 'an absolutely essential prerequisite' for agreement, territorial (flank) subceilings that apply to Russia would be abandoned.[28] Russia would, however, be ready to negotiate additional confidence-building measures (CBMs) on a reciprocal basis with other partners. Its motivation for abolishing the flank limitations was because they hinder the 'fight against terrorism'. The Russian proposal would extend flank limitations to the entire European territory of Russia. Turning Russia's entire European territory into a flank area would allegedly create equal rights and obligations for Russia and the other flank CFE Treaty states parties and strengthen the regime through the territorial extension of the flank area.[29] While such a compromise would favour Russia (by giving it a free hand to concentrate TLE near its borders in strategic areas), the limitation on deployments that exceed territorial ceilings would be retained for the other flank states.

[25] OSCE, Statement by the delegation of Denmark, 17th Meeting of the OSCE Ministerial Council, document MC.DEL/78/09, 2 Dec. 2009.

[26] Joint Consultative Group, document JCG.JOUR/693, Annex 3, attachment, 5 May 2009.

[27] Russia originally envisaged a 2-step approach: a 9-month period when the states parties would be guided by a political commitment to observe the adapted CFE Treaty; then, if the regime has not yet entered into force, the commencement of provisional application.

[28] The flank (or Article V) zone was a space of strategic importance (along with Central Europe) along the lines of confrontation between the two blocs. In the wake of the break-up of the Soviet Union the significance and role of the flank zone was essentially changed compared with the circumstances in which it was negotiated and agreed.

[29] Kulebyakin, V., 'European security and the Treaty on Conventional Armed Forces in Europe', eds W. Zellner, H.-J. Schmidt and G. Neuneck, *Die Zukunft konventioneller Rüstungskontrolle in Europe, The Future of Conventional Arms Control in Europe* (Nomos: Baden-Baden, 2009), p. 249.

4. The agreed reduced levels of TLE for NATO members would enter into force along with the provisional application of the adapted treaty regime.

5. The concrete terms for accession to the treaty regime by new NATO members would be attached to the package solution.

6. The definition of 'substantial combat forces' would also be appended to the draft package.[30]

7. A decision should be adopted at the start of negotiations on further modernization of the adapted CFE Treaty regime after its entry into force. Such a decision would also contain a model list of issues to be considered.

8. Russia requested that a draft decision be agreed and appended to the Russian–US package solution, approving and supporting the continuation of the current 'peacekeeping' operation in Moldova.[31] Later, this draft decision would be submitted to the OSCE Permanent Council for approval.

9. Russia could consider undertaking certain transparency measures regarding Moldova and the 'Trans-Caucasus' (apparently referring to Abkhazia and South Ossetia), depending on the situation at the time.

10. The proposal could be approved in the final document of a new extraordinary conference of the states parties to the CFE Treaty.

11. Once the Agreement on Adaptation has entered into force or begun to be applied provisionally, Russia would resume its implementation. As a gesture of goodwill, it would consider reciprocal transparency measures on a bilateral basis prior to the entry into force of the Agreement on Adaptation or its provisional application.

12. Russia stressed the need for dialogue with the USA on the CFE Treaty to elaborate the details of the Russian–US draft package. Russia is also open to dialogue with other states parties, for example in the JCG.

The Russian initiative was immediately supported by Belarus as an important step towards addressing the CFE Treaty crisis. Other states, par-

---

[30] Russia has long demanded that NATO clarify the meaning of the term 'substantial combat forces', which was contained in its 1997 pledge not to undertake 'additional permanent stationing of substantial combat forces'. Russia submitted its proposed parameters for (the combat brigade-level) 'substantial combat forces' in 2008. See Lachowski and Post (note 3), p. 448.

[31] The declaration of 18 Mar. 2009 by the Moldovan President, the separatist Trans-Dniester leader and the Russian President complicated realization of the Istanbul commitment regarding full and unconditional withdrawal of Russian military forces from Moldova. Consenting to the 'advisability of transforming [the Russian troops] into a peace guaranteeing operation under the aegis of the OSCE following the Transdniestrian settlement', Moldova weakened its negotiating position on Trans-Dniester in future endeavours and undermined the Western position in CFE talks. 'Joint Declaration adopted following talks between President of the Russian Federation Dmitry Medvedev, and President of the Republic of Moldova Vladimir Voronin and Head of Transdniestria Igor Smirnov', Barvikha, 18 Mar. 2009, document 431-18-03-2009, <http://www.ln.mid.ru/brp_4.nsf/english>. See also Socor, V., 'Voronin–Medvedev accord demolishes Moldova's negotiating position on Transnistria', *Eurasia Daily Monitor*, 20 Mar. 2009. On the peace operation in Trans-Dniester see appendix 3A, table 3A.2, in this volume.

ticularly those that are NATO members, expressed reservations, stressing the value of NATO's parallel actions package. What seemed important was not the assertive language but the apparent willingness of Russia to return to the negotiating table. While some of the proposals, such as the substantial combat forces issue and accession of new members, appear easy to address, other demands are difficult to tackle (e.g. 'bloc-to-Russia' parity and the issues related to Russia's Istanbul pledges). The flank issue, spelled out in absolute terms by Russia, is bound to put NATO and other interested states parties to the most challenging test of principle.

The 'readaptation' debate: the focal points

By the end of 2009 NATO had not formulated an official position on updating the CFE regime ('readaptation'). Instead, experts and analysts have tried to fill that gap with ideas and suggestions, pointing to the critical issues related to ensuring European military stability.[32] Some basic views and propositions for resolving the CFE crisis can be identified, although the final outcome of future CFE talks remains uncertain.

The consensus of the current debate is that continuity, rather than a radical change (i.e. a different arms control regime), is preferable and that the 'readapted' CFE Treaty should be an integral part of the European security architecture. The all-embracing character of the regime is no longer perceived as valid. While the 'all-European' system is deemed workable in general, regional and local threats and challenges call for more subtle and tailored arrangements, of both a legal and a political nature.

Irrespective of its undeniable merits, the Agreement on Adaptation is no longer satisfactory in view of the changed situation, particularly with regard to subregional challenges. Debate centres on whether it is advisable to ratify the agreement and move to negotiating an updated (readapted) treaty, or to move directly to negotiation of a new treaty regime.[33] Russia's May 2009 aide-memoire suggests that the former approach is now acceptable to it. In general, NATO's parallel actions package is also accepted by Russia as the basis for talks, albeit with reservations and preconditions.

The dilemma of linking the adapted treaty with Russia's fulfilment of its Istanbul commitments must be resolved. Even if NATO is willing to show a

---

[32] On 'readapting' the treaty regime see eds Zellner, Schmidt and Neuneck (note 29), especially Champenois, P.-E., 'CFE in the current strategic environment', pp. 199–206; Grand, C., 'European security and conventional arms control: an agenda for the 21st century', pp. 144–51; Richter, W., 'Ways out of the crisis: approaches for the preservation of the CFE regime', pp. 347–65; and Zellner, W., 'Conventional arms control in Europe at the strategic and sub-regional levels: the balance of military capabilities—a valid concept?', pp. 475–83.

[33] It is e.g. claimed that Russia would not accept the adapted treaty in its current shape, while NATO and the remaining states parties would not agree to a treaty that is partially non-applicable and soon to be changed. Richter (note 32), pp. 362–63.

degree of flexibility, complete renunciation of Russia's Istanbul pledges appears unacceptable.[34] In this context, a deal for decoupling the strategic (i.e. the CFE Treaty's area of application) and subregional levels from each other has been suggested.[35]

Russia's aim to re-establish military balance with the West must be taken into account. In any event, Russia's CFE holdings will decrease in number, whether or not the planned military reform that started in 2008 is feasible: Russia cannot afford to maintain outmoded and costly arsenals.[36] Growing anxiety about NATO's supremacy in conventional armaments explains the rationale for Russia's demand for further cuts. The NATO states' ceilings under the Agreement on Adaptation are higher than their actual holdings. As a goodwill gesture and a sign of self-restraint, the national and territorial ceilings of the NATO states could be lowered while not compromising the security needs of individual states parties or of NATO.

A politically binding sufficiency rule rather than parity in the Russia–NATO ratio has been suggested as a balance-of-force solution. Such an approach would mean that the aggregate NATO potential would not exceed that of Russia by a certain percentage.[37] Another view stresses the relevance of regional balances of forces, while questioning the global relevance of reasonable sufficiency.[38]

Destabilizing force concentrations should be further limited, including in border areas and conflict zones. The flexibility mechanisms of the adapted treaty should be revised in order to constrain their maximum utilization. The concern was raised as early as the 1997–99 CFE adaptation talks: if all of Europe were to become a CFE area, new parties and small countries together could amass destabilizing TLE of the magnitude of several army corps.[39] To promote regional stability it has been proposed that military safety zones with reduced levels of TLE be developed, for example along the borders of states that are engaged in dispute.[40] The term 'substantial combat forces' should be clarified and defined in terms of numerical parameters and areas, and possibly legally anchored in the CFE Treaty.

The flank issue is at the centre of the dispute, and new subregional approaches have been advocated to address the situation.[41] Breaking up Russia's total flank limitations into a number of TLE ceilings in various

[34] Richter (note 32), 349–50.
[35] Zellner (note 32), p. 479.
[36] See also chapter 7, section II, in this volume.
[37] Zellner (note 32), p. 483.
[38] Champenois (note 32), p. 205.
[39] Richter (note 32), p. 351.
[40] Richter (note 32), pp. 361–62.
[41] Zellner (note 32), p. 481; and Champenois (note 32), p. 205. Swimming against the tide, a former Russian top CFE negotiator advocates the adapted CFE Treaty and its flank solution. Chernov, V., 'The collapse of the CFE Treaty and the prospects for conventional arms control in Europe', eds Zellner, Schmidt and Neuneck (note 29), p. 187.

Russian oblasts and in certain regions of neighbouring countries has been proposed. However, if Russia were to lift the flank restrictions, the West could respond in a similar manner. Thus, Russia must decide whether it is worth acting unilaterally. Establishing terms of accession for the Baltic states in the run-up to approval of the Agreement on Adaptation that are similar to those for the Central European states and additional transparency measures have also been suggested.[42]

Various CBMs in the CFE context (e.g. voluntary non-deployment of combat forces on the territories of other states, stronger linkage of the CFE regime with counterterrorism efforts; and engaging Russia in joint peace operations) have also been proposed.[43]

Readaptation would create opportunities for the international community: new technological developments and categories of conventional weapons and forces that are having an increasing impact on tactical and strategic security could be addressed. It could also give the European Union (EU) the chance to reconsider its reluctance to address traditional arms control in its entirety.[44]

Subregional arms control in the Western Balkans

Currently, the 1996 Agreement on Sub-Regional Arms Control (Florence Agreement) is the only fully functional 'hard' arms control agreement in Europe. The political situation in the region in 2009 has not obviously affected the sense of military security that derives from the Dayton Accords. Armaments limited by the Florence Agreement have been destroyed voluntarily since the end of the official reduction period in 1997. By November 2009 the parties had scrapped or converted a total of 9228 heavy weapons. By November 2009, 621 inspections had been conducted, including some 130 reduction inspections or visits.[45]

The agreement on a two-phase ownership plan, proposed by the Personal Representative of the OSCE Chairperson, is politically important.[46] The parties to the Florence Agreement have long sought the attainment of full autonomy in its implementation. Phase 1 envisages the transfer

---

[42] Zellner (note 32), pp. 481–82. Russia would like the Baltic states to be covered by the flank regime.

[43] See 'Discussion note on the Treaty on Conventional Forces in Europe', *Euro-Atlantic Security: One Vision, Three Paths* (EastWest Institute: New York, June 2009), pp. 8–9.

[44] See Neuneck, G., 'Conventional arms control in Europe–structural stability and new weapons developments', pp. 515–30, and Schmidt, H.-J., 'The European Union and its growing importance for conventional arms control', eds Zellner, Schmidt and Neuneck (note 29), pp. 491–96.

[45] Periotto, C. (Brig. Gen.), 'Report to the 17th OSCE Ministerial Council. Implementation of the Agreement on Sub-regional Arms Control (Article IV, Annex 1-B, Dayton Peace Accords)', document MC.GAL/10/09, 9 Nov. 2008. For a summary of the Florence Agreement see annex A in this volume. The text of the Dayton Agreement is available at <http://www.oscebih.org/overview/gfap/eng/>.

[46] Periotto (note 45).

of technical functions that are currently provided by the Office of the Personal Representative to the parties, preferably by the end of 2011. Full responsibility for implementation could then be transferred to the parties if the political situation permits (phase 2). In 2009 this schedule was approved by the Contact Group comprising France, Germany, Italy, Russia, the United Kingdom and the USA, as well as representatives of the EU. The parties to the Florence Agreement have expressed reservations only of a technical and financial nature.

III. Building military security cooperation in the OSCE area[47]

For decades European military confidence and security building has been a unique practice and experiment. In 2009 the OSCE participants continued to focus on its operational, 'soft', arms control dimension.[48] Reports were submitted to the Ministerial Meeting at the end of the year on military confidence building and security, cooperation in the field of small arms and light weapons (SALW), reduction in stockpiles of conventional ammunition (SCA), and the Code of Conduct on Politico-Military Aspects of Security (COC).[49] Significantly, in 2009 the general level of implementation of information exchanges under the norm- and standard-setting regimes was lower and less compliant in timing than in previous years. The normative efforts of the confidence-enhancing measures have also dwindled. With the aim of strengthening cooperation between the OSCE Forum for Security Co-operation (FSC) and the OSCE Permanent Council as part of the revamped concept of comprehensive and indivisible security, these bodies held five joint meetings in 2009.

---

[47] For a list of states participating in OSCE see annex B in this volume. The OSCE area covers Europe, from the Atlantic to the Urals, and Central Asia.

[48] Soft arms control denotes a variety of military confidence building measures. See e.g. Lachowski, Z., *Confidence- and Security-Building Measures in the New Europe*, SIPRI Research Report no. 18 (Oxford University Press: Oxford, 2004), pp. 1–2.

[49] For an overview of developments in 2009 see OSCE, 'Letter from the Chairperson of the Forum for Security Cooperation to the Prime Minister and the Minister for Foreign Affairs of Greece, Chairperson of the 17th Meeting of the Ministerial Council', document MC.GAL/4/09/Rev.2, 19 Nov. 2009; OSCE, Forum for Security Co-operation, 'Efforts in the field of arms control agreements and confidence-and security-building measures in accordance with its mandate', Chairperson's Progress Report to the 17th Meeting of the Ministerial Council, Athens, Dec. 2009, document FSC.DEL/200/09/Rev.1, 9 Nov. 2009; OSCE, Forum for Security Co-operation, 'The continuing implementation of the OSCE Document on Small Arms and Light Weapons', Chairperson's Progress Report to the 17th Meeting of the Ministerial Council, document FSC.DEL/191/09/Rev.2, 9 Nov. 2009; OSCE, Forum for Security Co-operation, 'The continuing implementation of the OSCE Document on Stockpiles of Conventional Ammunition', Chairperson's Progress Report to the 17th Meeting of the Ministerial Council, document MC.GAL/8/09, 11 Nov. 2009; and OSCE, Forum for Security Co-operation, 'Efforts to further improve the implementation of the Code of Conduct on Politico-Military Aspects of Security', Chairperson's Progress Report to the 17th Meeting of the Ministerial Council, document MC.GAL/7/09, 11 Nov. 2009.

Confidence- and security-building measures

Overall, formal implementation of CSBMs under the Vienna Document 1999 has remained high and relatively stable for several years.[50] While the CFE Treaty regime is suspended, the number of inspections and evaluation visits under the politically binding Vienna Document in 2009 was similar to that of 2008, with Russia being the most active requesting country.[51] However, the crisis in building confidence and security at the subregional level was underscored by Russia's request in January 2009 for an evaluation visit to a military formation and the inspection of a specified area on the (unoccupied) territory of Georgia, just months after the August 2008 conflict. Both requests were rejected by Georgia as 'cynical' and *force majeure* in Georgian–Russian relations was announced by Georgia until the end of the occupation of Abkhazia and South Ossetia.[52]

Poland objected to the Belarusian–Russian military exercises held in September 2009, the biggest Russian-led manoeuvres in Europe since 1999.[53] Although formal notification of the manoeuvres was given in the correct way, the size of the two parallel war games—'Zapad-2009' and 'Ladoga-2009', which were given the collective name 'Osen-2009'—was just under the permitted observation thresholds.[54] Thus, some of the concerned states were not able to properly monitor the exercises.[55]

[50] OSCE, FSC.DEL/200/09/Rev.1 (note 49).

[51] The respective numbers are: 109 inspections in 2008 and 96 in 2009; and 75 evaluation visits in 2008 and 65 in 2009. In 2009 Russia carried out 23 inspections and 19 evaluation visits. OSCE, Conflict Prevention Centre, 'Annual CPC survey on CSBM information exchanged in 2009', document FSC.GAL/3/10, 20 Jan. 2010.

[52] On 26 Jan. 2009 the European Union Monitoring Mission in Georgia (EUMM) signed a Memorandum of Understanding with the Georgian Ministry of Defence containing a unilateral confidence-building measure stipulating certain restrictions on the movements of the Georgian armed forces in the vicinity of the administrative boundary lines of Abkhazia and South Ossetia and giving advance information of movements to the EUMM. EU Monitoring Mission in Georgia, 'EUMM and Georgian Ministry of Defence sign Memorandum of Understanding', Tbilisi, Press release, 26 Jan. 2009, <http://www.eumm.eu/en/press_and_public_information/press_releases/796/>. Under paragraphs 78 and 120 of the Vienna Document 1999, if the receiving or visiting state is prevented from accepting or carrying out an inspection or evaluation visit, it shall explain in detail the reasons without delay. On the Vienna Document 1999 see annex A in this volume. Many participating states consider *force majeure* an obstacle preventing more openness.

[53] Poland reportedly alerted NATO's Secretary General to the offensive nature of the Russian exercise. 'Sikorski: rosyjskie manewry blisko naszych granic sa niepokojace' [Sikorski: the Russian manoeuvres close to our borders give rise to concern], *Gazeta Wyborcza* (Warsaw), 12 Nov. 2009.

[54] According to the notification made by Belarus, Zapad-2009 employed 12 500 troops, in contrast to the 13 000-troop threshold; 228 battle tanks, in contrast to the 300-tank threshold; 470 armoured combat vehicles (ACV), in contrast to the 500-ACV threshold; and 234 multiple rocket launchers (MRLS), in contrast to the 250-artillery pieces threshold. The parallel Russian-notified 'Ladoga' exercise nearby in Russia employed 7400 troops, 150 tanks and 100 ACVs.

[55] The scenario assumed a rising of ethnic Poles in western Belarus and an attack by Lithuanian terrorists in the Russian Kaliningrad exclave. The observation was subject to some constraints by the Belarusian/Russian side, such as the timeframe (1 day of observation).

A noteworthy event took place under the 1992 Treaty on Open Skies regime. In September, Georgia and Russia, together with a team from the United Kingdom, carried out two joint overflights over each other's territory.[56]

Numerous proposals were submitted to the FSC in 2009, but only one led to a new decision.[57] The meeting of the heads of the verification centres was held separately from the annual implementation assessment meeting (AIAM) on 14 December; its conclusions were presented at the March 2010 AIAM. The new practice of holding a separate meeting should enable issues, concrete proposals and initiatives to be better developed in the run-up to the AIAM.

A Russian 'food-for-thought' paper on the implementation of the Vienna Document 1999 blamed the poor record of CSBM implementation on lack of political will and the lessened interest in such measures of a significant number of the OSCE participating states.[58] The Russian paper stated that more than half of the Vienna Document provisions exist only on paper and the loss of importance of the document is alarming. In an effort to update the Vienna Document regime, Russia urged other states to address the long-standing proposals on naval activities, rapid reaction forces, verification and compulsory notification of major military activities. Russia also suggested that specific deadlines for the individual reviews be established.

In the run-up to the Athens Ministerial Council, Belarus and Russia submitted a draft ministerial decision concerning the Vienna Document 1999 that aimed at convincing the FSC to conduct a review of the Vienna Document with a focus on 'targeted' improvements. The Athens Ministerial Council called on the FSC in 2010 to intensify the security dialogue, including on the role of arms control and CSBMs, and to explore ways of strengthening the OSCE's politico-military toolbox, including the Vienna Document 1999.[59]

Small arms, stockpiles of ammunition and toxic rocket fuel

The prolonged crisis in the field of security cooperation could not but affect the SALW and SCA dimensions. The issues of small arms and excessive surplus ammunition are interrelated and increasingly share similar norm-

---

[56] 'Georgia-UK-Russia joint surveillance flights', Civil.ge, Daily News Online, Tbilisi, 9 Oct. 2009, <http://www.civil.ge/eng/_print.php?id=21554>. For a summary and other details of the Treaty on Open Skies see annex A in this volume.

[57] OSCE, Decision no. 8/09, Best Practice Guide for Implementation of the Vienna Document 1999 Chapter IV, Contacts, document FSC.DOC.8/09, 14 Oct. 2009.

[58] OSCE, Delegation of the Russian Federation, 'Food-for-thought paper—analysis of the implementation of the Vienna Document 1999: Initial remarks', document FSC.AIAM/2/09, 20 Feb. 2009.

[59] OSCE, Ministerial Council Decision no. 16/09, Issues relevant to the Forum for Security Co-operation, document MC.DEC/16/09, 2 Dec. 2009.

ativo and practical features. Coordination of efforts with international organizations has been intensified in both areas. When applicable, the scope of meetings on SALW and SCA have been expanded to accommodate other relevant projects and issues. Since 2003 the OSCE had received 29 requests for assistance from 14 countries regarding enhancement of the management and security of stockpiles of SALW and conventional ammunition or the destruction of surpluses. In 2009 the OSCE and the UN Development Programme (UNDP) finalized negotiations on financial and legal mechanisms to facilitate the joint implementation of projects concerning SALW and SCA.[60]

The 2000 OSCE Document on Small Arms and Light Weapons and other relevant documents are instruments for addressing SALW problems, fostering transparency and confidence among the participating states, and helping to contain regional crises and conflicts and to combat terrorism and organized crime.[61] In 2001–2008 OSCE participating states destroyed approximately 8.6 million small arms, and in 2009 the participating states pledged nearly €434 000 ($600 000) for OSCE SALW projects.[62]

The September 2009 OSCE review meeting pointed to problems and challenges in the implementation of the SALW Document, such as the lack of adequate legislation and procedures regarding SALW and ammunition, the discrepancy between donors' concerns and beneficiaries' needs and the lack of harmonized international standards, and to the need to considerably update the document.[63] In the area of normative cooperation in 2009, work focused on updating FSC Decision 15/02 on expert advice on implementation of section V, 'Early warning, conflict prevention, crisis management and post-conflict rehabilitation', of the SALW Document.[64] The practical help given to OSCE participating states has resulted in SALW assistance

---

[60] OSCE, document FSC.DEL/191/09/Rev.2 (note 49); and OSCE, document MC.GAL/8/09 (note 49).

[61] OSCE, Forum for Security Co-operation, OSCE Document on Small Arms and Light Weapons, 24 Nov. 2000, <http://www.osce.org/fsc/13281.html>. The other documents include OSCE, *Handbook of Best Practices on Small Arms and Light Weapons* (OSCE: Vienna, 2003); OSCE, Forum for Security Co-operation, 'Standard elements of end-user certificates and verification procedures for SALW exports', Decision no. 5/04, document FSC/DEC/5/04, 17 Nov. 2004; OSCE, Forum for Security Co-operation, 'Principles on the control of brokering in small arms and light weapons', Decision no. 8/04, document FSC/DEC/8/04, 24 Nov. 2004; and OSCE, Ministerial Council, 'OSCE principles for export controls of man-portable air defence systems', Decision no. 8/04, document MC.DEC/8/04, 7 Dec. 2004.

[62] OSCE, FSC.DEL/191/09/Rev.2 (note 49), annex C.

[63] See OSCE Meeting to Review the OSCE Document on Small Arms and Light Weapons and its supplementary decisions, Vienna, 22 and 23 Sep. 2009, Consolidated Summary, document FSC.GAL/109/09, 20 Oct. 2009.

[64] OSCE, Decision 11/09, Update on FSC Decision 15/02 on expert advice on implementation of Section V of the Document on Small Arms and Light Weapons, document FSC/DEC/11/09, 25 Nov. 2009.

projects in Belarus, Cyprus, Kyrgyzstan and Tajikistan that were carried out in 2008–2009.[65]

Unsecured or uncontrolled stockpiles of conventional ammunition and toxic liquid rocket fuel components (mainly melange) pose cross-dimensional security, humanitarian, economic and environmental risks. Under the 2003 SCA Document, any OSCE state that has identified a security risk to its surplus stockpiles and needs help to address such a risk may request the assistance of the international community through the OSCE.[66] The strong tendency to sell, rather than to destroy, SCA as the method of disposal has continued. The OSCE therefore faces the challenge of changing this preference and of introducing specific export criteria.[67] In 2009, participating states pledged approximately €1.2 million ($1.7 million) for SCA projects, around half as much as in the preceding year.

Requests for destruction assistance and stockpile management and security remain the most dynamic area of implementation. Projects in Albania and Tajikistan were completed in 2009, while another project in Albania (demilitarization of ammunition) started. The melange project in Ukraine, one of the largest OSCE extra-budgetary projects, has decisively entered the stage of implementation—by the end of 2010 more than 3000 tonnes of melange will have been transported to a chemical destruction facility in Russia for neutralization.

Others projects are in the initial phases of implementation and will start when sufficient funding is available. The OSCE concluded discussions with Kazakhstan on enhancing its capacity for testing propellants, and a project proposal was developed. The Ukrainian project proposal to provide specialized equipment for clearance of unexploded ordnance was also completed. The Comprehensive Programme on SALW and SCA in Moldova is approaching completion. In Georgia, all ongoing and planned projects were suspended in 2009 as a result of the closing of the OSCE Mission to Georgia, but ways are being sought to renew them.

The Code of Conduct on Politico-Military Aspects of Security

The 1994 Code of Conduct on Politico-Military Aspects of Security is the norm-setting document on the cooperative behaviour and mutual responsibilities of states in the OSCE region and the democratic control of their armed forces. It also addresses politico-military relations within states.[68]

---

[65] The projects in Cyprus and Tajikistan have been successfully completed; the project in Belarus is in progress; and the project plan for Kyrgyzstan has been finalized.

[66] OSCE, 'OSCE Document on Stockpiles of Conventional Ammunition', document FSC. DOC/1/03, 19 Nov. 2003.

[67] OSCE, document MC.GAL/8/09 (note 49).

[68] OSCE, 'Code of Conduct on Politico-Military Aspects of Security', document DOC.FSC/1/95, 3 Dec. 1994.

Information exchange on the implementation of the Code generally remains high.[69] It was agreed to postpone the deadline for replies to the questionnaire from 15 April to 15 June 2009 in order to allow the participating states to use the new questionnaire (see below) should they choose to do so.[70]

In April 2009 the FSC adopted a decision on a technical update of the questionnaire.[71] The questionnaire consists of three main sections: (a) interstate elements (account of measures to prevent and combat terrorism; stationing of armed forces on foreign territory; and implementation of other international commitments to the COC); (b) intrastate elements (national planning and decision-making processes; existing structures and processes; procedures related to the personnel of various military forces; and implementation of other political norms, principles, decisions and international humanitarian law); and (c) public access and contact information. The update's 24 sub-items are meant to deliver more structured, clearer, concise and less duplicative information than its predecessor. A number of new sub-items have been introduced, such as those on national efforts to prevent and combat terrorism; on arms control, disarmament and CSBMs; and on issues concerning international humanitarian law. Participating OSCE states are also requested to provide information on military, paramilitary and internal security forces as well as on intelligence services and police.[72]

'Practical disarmament': NATO-assisted munitions destruction

The NATO Maintenance and Supply Agency (NAMSA) is NATO's principal logistics support management agency.[73] NAMSA's main task is to assist NATO states by organizing common procurement and supply of spare parts, and arranging maintenance and repair services for the weapon systems in their inventories. NAMSA has taken the lead in many demilitarization projects. Agreements have also been reached for NAMSA to support non-NATO states under the Partnership for Peace (PFP). NATO's PFP Trust Fund was established in 2000 under the 1997 Anti-Personnel Mine

---

[69] OSCE, document MC.GAL/7/09 (note 49).

[70] OSCE, Decision no. 1/09 postponing the 2009 Annual Information Exchange on the OSCE Code of Conduct on Politico-Military Aspects of Security, document FSC/DEC/1/09, 11 Mar. 2009.

[71] OSCE, 'Technical update of the questionnaire of the Code of Conduct', document FSC.DEC/2/09, 1 Apr. 2009. The questionnaire was originally elaborated in 1998 and updated in 2003.

[72] In their interpretative statements, 17 participating states declared their intention to expand their replies with information on women, peace and security; 5 called on other states to include statements on their democratic political control of private military and security companies; and 1 state underlined the voluntary character of additional information regarding national efforts to prevent and combat terrorism (question 1.4). OSCE, document MC.GAL/7/09 (note 49), attachments 1, 2 and 3.

[73] On NAMSA's aims, tasks and activities see <http://www.namsa.nato.int/>.

(APM) Convention originally to assist PFP countries with the safe destruction of stocks of APMs; later it was extended to include the destruction of
SALW and surplus munitions, and to cover other defence reform-related
activities.

By February 2009, 24 NATO members, 14 PFP states, 2 contact states
(Australia and Japan), several international organizations (the EU, the
OSCE and the UNDP) and one non-governmental organization (Milieu-
kontakt International) had contributed to the 15 Trust Fund projects
managed by NAMSA. By 2009 NAMSA had completed eight Trust Fund
demilitarization projects on schedule, and it is the executing agent for
another seven ongoing projects. In 2000–2007, within six projects more
than 4.1 million APMs were destroyed in Albania, Belarus, Moldova, Serbia
and Montenegro, Tajikistan and Ukraine. Moreover, 28 000 surplus SALW
were destroyed in Serbia and Montenegro; 11 500 tonnes of SALW munitions were scrapped in Albania; and 250 cubic metres of rocket fuel were
neutralized in Moldova.[74]

Under the ongoing projects launched or continued in 2009, destruction
is planned of 400 000 SALW and 300 man-portable air defence systems
(MANPADS) in Ukraine, and 27 000 SALW and 1000 MANPADS in
Kazakhstan. In Georgia the project provided for the destruction of more
than 1000 air-to-surface unguided missiles and 7700 anti-hail rockets.
During phase 1 of the Ukraine II project 15 000 tonnes of SCA will be
destroyed.[75]

IV. Control of inhumane weapons

Since the mid-1990s 'inhumane weapons' have captured international
attention as their military utility has been increasingly questioned and the
humanitarian and economic harm they cause widely denounced. Several
international agreements not only regulate or ban the use of APMs, explosive remnants of war (ERW) and cluster munitions, but also seek to limit
the effects of armed conflict on civilians.

The 1981 Certain Conventional Weapons (CCW) Convention restricts or
prohibits the use of specific categories of weapons that are deemed to cause
unnecessary or unjustifiable suffering to combatants or to affect civilians
indiscriminately.[76] The Ottawa process to ban APMs, outside the CCW
framework, resulted in the APM Convention, which seeks to eliminate all

---

[74] NATO Maintenance and Supply Agency, 'Latest news, facts & figures', <http://www.namsa.
nato.int/Demil/news_e.htm>.

[75] Altogether 136 tonnes of munitions and 1.5 million SALW are earmarked for destruction.

[76] For a summary and other details of the Convention on the Prohibitions or Restrictions on the
Use of Certain Conventional Weapons which may be Deemed to be Excessively Injurious or to have
Indiscriminate Effects (CCW, also known as the 'Inhumane Weapons' Convention) and of its
5 protocols see annex A in this volume.

such weapons.[77] Until recently, the 2003 Protocol V of the CCW Convention was the only international legislation covering ERW, including cluster munitions. Using the APM Convention as a model, the Oslo process stigmatized cluster munitions and the Convention on Cluster Munitions (CCM) banning them was signed in Oslo in December 2008 and will enter into force on 1 August 2010.

Cluster munitions in the context of the CCW Convention

As a consequence of international pressure, many of the main users, producers and possessors of stockpiles of cluster munitions have opted to continue dialogue in the CCW Convention framework, rather than join the Oslo process. The issue of cluster munitions has been on the CCW agenda since the 2006 CCW Review Conference. In August 2009, after informal consultations within the Group of Governmental Experts (GGE), its chairman, Gustavo Ainchil, presented a Draft Protocol on Cluster Munitions that could eventually become a sixth protocol to the CCW Convention.[78]

The meeting of the CCW High Contracting Parties on 12–13 November 2009 focused on the issue of cluster munitions. The states parties pledged to continue negotiations informed by the chairman's consolidated text of the draft protocol, the cluster munitions document and other proposals by delegations. The aim remains to conclude the negotiations as rapidly as possible.[79]

Explosive remnants of war

The CCW Convention's Protocol V on Explosive Remnants of War recognizes the humanitarian problems caused by ERW and covers post-conflict remedial measures to minimize their occurrence, effects and the risk they pose. Sixty-two states parties were bound by the protocol at the end of 2009, and during the year 11 more states became parties.[80] Italy and Saudi Arabia announced that they have ratified Protocol V and will soon deposit their instruments of ratification with the UN Secretary-General. Universality of the protocol remains the focus of discussion.

---

[77] For a summary and other details of the Convention on the Prohibition of the Use, Stockpiling, Production and Transfer of Anti-Personnel Mines and on their Destruction see annex A in this volume.

[78] CCW, 'Draft protocol on cluster munitions', Presented by the Chairperson of the CCW Group of Governmental Experts, CCW/MSP/2009/WP.1, 21 Oct. 2009. CCW documents are available on the website of the United Nations Office at Geneva, <http://www.unog.ch/ccw/>.

[79] See CCW, 'Cluster munitions: consolidated text', document CCW/GGE/2009-II/2, Annex I, 22 Apr. 2009; and UN Office at Geneva, News and Media, 'Parties to Conventional Weapons Convention decide to continue negotiations on cluster munitions', 19 Nov. 2009.

[80] For a list of parties to Protocol V see annex A in this volume.

During the Third Conference of the High Contracting Parties to Protocol V in Geneva in November 2009, the parties were called on to make full use of the convention's implementation mechanism in order to facilitate assistance and improve knowledge of the scope of the problem of ERW and ways of tackling it. Stronger measures under the Plan of Action on Victim Assistance that was adopted in 2008 were advocated. Other topics included: (*a*) clearance, removal and destruction of ERW; (*b*) cooperation, assistance and requests for assistance; (*c*) national reporting; and (*d*) generic preventive measures. A meeting of experts of the parties to Protocol V will be held in April 2010 on these issues and on the web-based information system for implementation of the protocol. The Fourth Conference of the High Contracting Parties will meet in November 2010.[81]

Mines

No new parties joined the 156 states parties to the APM Convention in 2009. Although some key producers and users of anti-personnel mines—especially China, India, Pakistan, Russia and the USA—have not signed the convention, it is regarded as one of the most successful multilateral conventional arms control agreements. About 44 million APMs have been destroyed under the APM Convention by a total of 86 states parties that have completed the destruction of their stockpiles. As of mid-2009 approximately 12 million APMs were estimated to remain to be destroyed by four parties to the convention—Belarus (3.4 million), Greece (1.4 million), Turkey (1.3 million) and Ukraine (6.1 million)—and an estimated 160 million APMs are stockpiled by non-party states.[82] Myanmar and Russia, both non-parties to the convention, continued to use APMs in 2008–2009, as did non-state armed groups in at least seven countries.

Three states parties—Belarus, Greece and Turkey—all with large stockpiles of APMs, failed to meet their 1 March 2008 destruction deadlines, and all three remained in serious violation of the convention. The 2009 deadlines for completing the destruction of APMs in mined areas were extended for 15 parties. In 2009, 4 additional parties—Argentina, Cambodia, Tajikistan and Uganda—requested similar extensions for periods ranging from 3 to 10 years. At the end of 2009, Albania, Greece, Rwanda and Zambia were declared to be mine-free countries.[83]

Representatives of parties to the APM Convention, states not party, international organizations, UN agencies, the International Committee of

[81] UN Office at Geneva, News and Media, 'States forge further efforts at strengthening implementation of protocol on explosive remnants of war', 19 Nov. 2009.

[82] International Campaign to Ban Landmines, *Landmine Monitor Report 2009: Toward a Mine-Free World* (Mines Action Canada: Ottawa, 2009).

[83] Each state party to the convention is required to destroy its stockpile of APMs within 4 years and to clear all mined areas under its jurisdiction or control within 10 years.

the Red Cross and the International Campaign to Ban Landmines met in Cartagena, Colombia, from 29 November to 4 December 2009, for the Second Review Conference of the APM Convention. The review conference aimed to assess challenges in the universalization and full implementation of the convention and evaluated the progress made since the 2004 First Review Conference. Notably, after conflicting official statements in November, the USA, a non-party to the APM Convention, participated in the Cartagena Summit on a Mine-Free World on 30 November–1 December, the first time it has attended such a meeting. The head of the US delegation informed the participants that the US Administration has initiated a comprehensive landmine policy review.[84]

Improvised explosive devices

Improvised explosive devices (IEDs), also known as roadside bombs, are widely used in terrorist actions and other unconventional warfare. Their use has remained an acute problem in conflicts. A group of experts, established in 2008 by the CCW Annual Conference of the parties to Amended Protocol II, which prohibits mines, booby traps and other devices, met in April 2009 to explore the issue of IEDs. The 11th Annual Conference, held in November 2009, appointed two coordinators to carry out the work of the experts group: to consider IEDs, and to review the operation and status of Amended Protocol II with regard to protection of civilians against the indiscriminate effects of mines.[85]

V. Conclusions

The prospects for advances in European arms control appeared better in 2009 than in preceding years, even though the CFE Treaty regime remained in limbo. As part of the Corfu process, the significance of arms control for European security was reacknowledged by all OSCE participating states. These states expressed strong political will for change. At the Athens Ministerial Council they reaffirmed their desire to overcome the long-standing deadlock in the main regimes—the CFE Treaty and the Vienna Document on CSBMs—and perhaps integrate or link them more

---

[84] Abramson, J., 'In a first, U.S. attends landmine meeting', *Arms Control Today*, vol. 40, no. 1 (Jan./Feb. 2010). The USA claimed to be unable to meet its national defence needs and its security commitments to friends and allies if it signed the convention. Although a non-party, the USA has been in substantial compliance with most of the APM Convention's provisions. It has not deployed APMs since 1991, banned their export in 1992 and stopped manufacturing them in 1997. The USA has also spent $1.5 billion in demining and related activities since 1993. It has promised to end all use of persistent landmines by the end of 2010 while continuing to use so-called smart mines.

[85] CCW, 'Improvised explosive devices (IEDs)', 11 Annual Conference of the High Contracting Parties, document CCW/AP.II/CONF.11/2, 19 Oct. 2009; and UN Office at Geneva, News and Media, 'States parties to CCW Amended Protocol II on mines and explosive devices prohibition decide to continue work on improvised explosive devices', 19 Nov. 2009.

closely to other security-related endeavours in the OSCE area. Solutions will require innovation and determination as well as the ability to compromise. In relation to broader security, Russia insists on convening a Euro-Atlantic summit with the aim of crowning it with a European security treaty. The Western states demonstrated caution and restraint, making their consent contingent on the adequacy of the substance and scope of an eventual agreement. The current US Administration has embarked on a thorough review of the US arms control agenda, and in February 2010 a Special Envoy for Conventional Armed Forces in Europe was appointed to start consultations with NATO, European partners and Russia on the future of the CFE regime.

European security-related measures that are associated with arms control aim to respond to traditional as well as new threats and to risks and challenges. However, progress as regards the Vienna Document regime's CSBMs remains at a standstill. The OSCE participants strive to counter cross-dimensional threats that are increasingly of a local and subregional nature. With the decreased norm-setting activity, the practical assistance given to the Euro-Atlantic states through the implementation of select projects remains a chief activity in the improvement of security and stability in the OSCE region.

Humanitarian tools continue to predominate in the tackling of global challenges in the conventional arms control field. The grass-roots 'processes' and conventions as well as the traditional intergovernmental treaties and protocols compete, yet continue to have a mutually reinforcing moral impact as they strive to address the problems of human suffering and the betterment of living conditions in conflict-ridden areas and throughout the world.

12. Controls on security-related international transfers

SIBYLLE BAUER AND IVANA MIĆIĆ

I. Introduction

Changing patterns and increasing complexity characterized the nature of both the legal trade of dual-use items and the illicit procurement of material and technology for weapons of mass destruction (WMD) over the past decade.[1] The use of intermediaries, front companies and diversion or trans-shipment points has multiplied the number and kind of actors and activities that are involved in security-related transfers. The term 'export controls' continues to be commonly used to describe the control of security-related items. However, the term 'transfer controls' more accurately reflects reality as it relates to, among other things, controls on brokering, transit, trans-shipment, financial flows and technical assistance (e.g. manual services and the oral transfer of 'know-how'). The term transfer controls also includes the intangible transfer of technology (ITT)—the transmission of technology through intangible means, such as the transfer of technical information via electronic means—a category of transfers that places new demands on controls from both a legal and practical enforcement perspective.

The focus of non-proliferation efforts has shifted from the physical movement of goods to analysis of which elements of a transaction are relevant to, and should be subject to, controls. These developments not only create challenges, but also offer new opportunities for international cooperation. The simple supplier–recipient paradigm is no longer adequate, and the questions 'who produces?' and 'who procures?' have been expanded to include 'who is involved along the way?' Furthermore, the constant pressure to facilitate and speed up legitimate trade through the minimization of constraints, delays, costs and administrative burdens shrinks the amount of time available for enforcement intervention. This highlights the need for international cooperation, and also emphasizes that such control and intervention decisions must be rooted in solid national and international law.

While there is a common basis in United Nations Security Council Resolution 1540 for efforts to prevent WMD proliferation, different legal trad-

---

[1] Dual-use items are goods and technologies that have both civilian and military applications.

SIPRI Yearbook 2010: Armaments, Disarmament and International Security

itions as well as policy priorities and perceptions face both common challenges of practical implementation and common requirements based on international law. The resulting obligations raise questions of how to legally conceptualize and define terms such as brokering, transit, transshipment and effective penalties for breaches, and whether a common understanding across a region and internationally can, and should, be found.

While this chapter focuses on controls on dual-use items, controls on the transfer of items specially designed and developed for military use are also covered. Section II summarizes recent updates to controls on proliferation-sensitive goods and technologies in UN forums. Section III describes the functional areas of a number of export control regimes and provides information on recent developments in those regimes. Section IV examines how the European Union (EU) is addressing transfer control challenges at the EU and member state levels. The conclusions are presented in section V. Appendix 12A outlines developments in the imposition and application of multilateral arms embargoes in 2009.

II. United Nations Security Council resolutions on transfers of proliferation-sensitive items

UN Security Council Resolution 1540, which was drawn up to prevent access by non-state actors to WMD and to nuclear and radiological materials, is now widely used as the generic legal basis for promoting and demanding international export control standards.[2] The resolution established the 1540 Committee, which works with UN member states to implement the resolution.[3] The Committee's eighth programme identified five main areas of work and set-up working groups, open to all Security Council delegations, whose tasks were broken into four categories: (*a*) monitoring

---

[2] Resolution 1540 imposes binding obligations on all states to establish domestic controls to prevent the proliferation of WMD weapons and their means of delivery, including by establishing 'appropriate controls over related materials'. UN Security Council Resolution 1540, 28 Apr. 2004. UN Security Council resolutions are available at <http://www.un.org/sc/>. On the legal controversy around the UN Security Council as a legislator under Article VII of the UN Charter see Ahlström, C., 'United Nations Security Council Resolution 1540: non-proliferation by means of international legislation', *SIPRI Yearbook 2007*, pp. 460–73.

[3] Resolution 1810 extended the mandate of the 1540 Committee until 2011. United Nations, 1540 Committee, Programme of work of the Security Council Committee established pursuant to Resolution 1540 (2004) from 1 February 2009 to 31 January 2010, Annex to S/2009/124, 4 Mar. 2009; and UN Security Council Resolution 1810, 25 Apr. 2008. See also UN Security Council Resolution 1673, 27 Apr. 2006; and Anthony, I. and Bauer, S., 'Controls on security-related international transfers', *SIPRI Yearbook 2009*, p. 460. On the 1540 Committee see <http://www.un.org/sc/1540/> and chapter 10, section VI, in this volume.

and implementation, (b) assistance, (c) cooperation with international organizations and (d) transparency and outreach.[4]

On 24 September 2009, at a UN Security Council summit chaired by US President Barack Obama and attended by 13 other heads of state or government, the UN Security Council unanimously adopted Resolution 1887, which aims to promote nuclear disarmament and to combat the spread of nuclear weapons.[5] While the resolution urges states to take 'all appropriate national measures … to strengthen export controls … and to control access to intangible transfers of technology', it does not specify these measures.

International efforts to prevent the proliferation of nuclear, biological and chemical (NBC) weapons and their delivery systems have increasingly focused on non-state actors and on the programmes of a small number of states. The UN Security Council has adopted a series of resolutions that contain restrictions or prohibitions on the transfer of controlled items to Iran and to the Democratic People's Republic of Korea (DPRK, or North Korea).[6] As of January 2010 consensus on additional or stronger sanctions on Iran had not been reached because of diverging political and economic interests. UN Security Council Resolution 1874, which was adopted in response to North Korea's nuclear test of 25 May 2009, gives member states broader powers to inspect cargo, consistent with international law, if they have 'reasonable grounds' to believe that a vessel contains items that are prohibited under the resolution and to seize and dispose of such items.[7] This resolution incorporates principles introduced by the 2003 Proliferation Security Initiative (PSI), which Obama proposed become a durable international institution.[8]

On 2 December 2009 the UN General Assembly agreed a timetable for negotiating an arms trade treaty by 2012.[9]

---

[4] The 5 main areas of work focus on reviewing implementation of Resolution 1540, increasing information on implementation, promoting implementation, enhancing cooperation and encouraging states to provide financial assistance. United Nations, S/2009/124 (note 3), pp. 7–8.

[5] UN Security Council Resolution 1887, 24 Sep. 2009. See also chapter 9 in this volume.

[6] For details see appendix 12A.

[7] UN Security Council Resolution 1874, 12 June 2009. On the provisions of this resolution see appendix 12A. On the explosion see appendix 8B and chapter 9 in this volume.

[8] White House, 'Remarks by President Barack Obama, Hradcany Square, Prague, Czech Republic', 5 Apr. 2009, <http://www.whitehouse.gov/the_press_office/Remarks-By-President-Barack-Obama-In-Prague-As-Delivered/>. On the PSI see Ahlström, C., 'The Proliferation Security Initiative: international law aspects of the Statement of Interdiction Principles', *SIPRI Yearbook 2005*, pp. 741–67.

[9] UN General Assembly Resolution 64/48, 2 Dec. 2009.

Table 12.1. Participation in multilateral weapon and technology transfer control regimes, as of 1 January 2010

State	Zangger Committee	NSG	Australia Group	MTCR	Wassenaar Arrangement
Argentina	x	x	x	x	x
Australia	x	x	x	x	x
Austria	x	x	x	x	x
Belarus		x			
Belgium	x	x	x	x	x
Brazil		x		x	
Bulgaria	x	x	x	x	x
Canada	x	x	x	x	x
China	x	x			
Croatia	x	x	x		x
Cyprus		x	x		
Czech Republic	x	x	x	x	x
Denmark	x	x	x	x	x
Estonia		x	x		x
Finland	x	x	x	x	x
France	x	x	x	x	x
Germany	x	x	x	x	x
Greece	x	x	x	x	x
Hungary	x	x	x	x	x
Iceland		x*	x	x	
Ireland	x	x	x	x	x
Italy	x	x	x	x	x
Japan	x	x	x	x	x
Kazakhstan	x	x			
Korea, South	x	x	x	x	x
Latvia		x	x		x
Lithuania		x	x		x
Luxembourg	x	x	x	x	x
Malta		x	x		x
Netherlands	x	x	x	x	x
New Zealand		x	x	x	x
Norway	x	x	x	x	x
Poland	x	x	x	x	x
Portugal	x	x	x	x	x
Romania	x	x	x		x
Russia	x	x		x	x
Slovakia	x	x	x		x
Slovenia	x	x	x		x
South Africa	x	x		x	x
Spain	x	x	x	x	x
Sweden	x	x	x	x	x
Switzerland	x	x	x	x	x
Turkey	x	x	x	x	x
United Kingdom	x	x	x	x	x
Ukraine	x	x	x	x	x
Unites States	x	x	x	x	x
European Commission	o	o	x		
Total membership	**37**	**46**	**41**	**34**	**40**

NSG = Nuclear Suppliers Group; MTCR = Missile Technology Control Regime; o = observer; x = member/participant; * = joined in 2009.

III. Developments in multilateral export control regimes

Four informal multilateral arrangements worked within their specific fields to strengthen transfer control cooperation in 2009: the Australia Group (AG), the Missile Technology Control Regime (MTCR), the Nuclear Suppliers Group (NSG) and the Wassenaar Arrangement on Export Controls for Conventional Arms and Dual-Use Goods and Technologies (WA). The states participating in these arrangements and in the Zangger Committee are listed in table 12.1.[10]

Purpose and set-up

Specific events that demonstrated the use, or potential use, of WMD and concern about the increase in WMD programmes created political will to establish the AG, MTCR and NSG. The AG was established in the light of international concern about the use of chemical weapons in the 1980–88 Iran–Iraq War. At first, AG participants cooperated to maintain and develop their national controls to prevent the export of chemicals that might be used for, or diverted to, chemical weapon programmes. The participating states now seek to prevent the intentional or inadvertent supply of materials or equipment to chemical or biological weapon programmes.[11] The MTCR works to prevent the proliferation of unmanned delivery systems capable of delivering WMD.[12] The NSG aims to prevent the proliferation of nuclear weapons by controlling transfers of nuclear and nuclear-related material, equipment, software and technology.[13] While the AG, MTCR and NSG focus on WMD and their delivery systems, the WA promotes transparency and the exchange of information and views on transfers of conventional arms and related dual-use goods and technologies. It encourages responsible behaviour and seeks to prevent 'destabilizing accumulations' of such items.[14]

The common purpose of all four regimes is to strengthen the national transfer control systems of participating states—as well as those of non-

[10] The Zangger Committee participants seek to take account of the effect of 'changing security aspects' on the 1968 Treaty on the Non-Proliferation Proliferation of Nuclear Weapons (Non-Proliferation Treaty, NPT) and to 'adapt export control conditions and criteria' in that light, although it is not formally part of the NPT regime. For basic information on the AG, the MTCR, the NSG, the WA and the Zangger Committee see annex B in this volume. For a summary and other details of the NPT see annex A in this volume.

[11] See the AG website, <http://www.australiagroup.net/>.

[12] See the MTCR website, <http://www.mtcr.info/>.

[13] On the NSG see Anthony, I., Ahlström, C. and Fedchenko, V., *Reforming Nuclear Export Controls: The Future of the Nuclear Suppliers Group*, SIPRI Research Report no. 22 (Oxford University Press: Oxford, 2007); and the NSG website, <http://www.nuclearsuppliersgroup.org/>.

[14] The term 'destabilizing accumulations' lends itself to varying interpretation, although states have made efforts to establish common standards through best practice documents. See the WA website, <http://www.wassenaar.org/>.

participating states—in order to prevent the spread of NBC weapons and their means of delivery. They differ mostly in the type of controlled items they cover and their specific dynamics, which are to a large degree due to the differences in membership.

Unlike the AG and the NSG, the MTCR does not derive its rationale from an international treaty.[15] However, UN Security Council resolutions 1718 and 1737 incorporate the MTCR control list and thus make it binding on all UN members with regard to transfers to Iran and North Korea.[16] The MTCR is complemented by the Hague Code of Conduct against Ballistic Missile Proliferation, which has much wider participation.[17]

The regimes are similar operationally and organizationally. They are informal agreements that operate on consensus and are not legally binding. Members apply regime principles and guidelines through their national legislation and systems. Policy, enforcement and licensing officials as well as technical experts meet in different groups within the regimes and report to the respective plenary (the decision-making body); this allows authorities involved in export controls at the national level to participate to some degree in the regimes. The technical working groups prepare changes to the control lists that are annually adopted by each plenary. Apart from the AG, which is always chaired by Australia, the regime chair rotates among participating states on an annual basis. Although the quality of information exchange and the ability to take effective decisions within regimes vary (e.g. in the plenary's ability to agree on a public statement), the regimes are essential not only for the drawing up of guidelines and control lists but also for the facilitation of international cooperation and networking.[18]

Common themes discussed in the regimes include ITT, effective law enforcement, end-use controls and engagement with non-participating

[15] The AG derives its rationale from the 1972 Biological and Toxin Weapons Convention (BTWC) and the 1993 Chemical Weapons Convention (CWC), and the NSG from the 1968 NPT. In practice, the BTWC has a weaker link to the AG due to the convention's lack of institutionalization. For summaries and other details of the BTWC, the CWC and the NPT see annex A in this volume.

[16] UN Security Council Resolution 1718, 14 Oct. 2006; UN Security Council Resolution 1737, 23 Dec. 2006; and Anthony, I. and Bauer, S., 'Controls on security-related international transfers', *SIPRI Yearbook 2007*, pp. 658–63.

[17] As of 1 Jan. 2010 there were 130 signatories to the Hague Code of Conduct (HCOC). For a list of signatories and a summary of the HCOC see annex B in this volume.

[18] E.g. it was agreed at the 2009 MTCR plenary to approach individual countries to remind them of their obligations under UN Security Council resolutions 1718, 1737, 1747, 1803 and 1874, but consensus could not be achieved on naming individual national missile programmes considered to be of concern in the press release. German Government, *Bericht der Bundesregierung zum Stand der Bemühungen um Rüstungskontrolle, Abrüstung und Nichtverbreitung sowie über die Entwicklung der Streitkräftepotentiale (Jahresabrüstungsbericht 2009)* [Federal Government report on progress on arms control, disarmament, non-proliferation and development of the capabilities of the armed forces (annual disarmament report 2009)] (German Government: Berlin, 12 Jan. 2010), p. 93; UN Security Council Resolution 1747, 24 Mar. 2007; and UN Security Council Resolution 1803, 3 Mar. 2008. No public statement from the MTCR plenary was issued in 2009. Statements from previous years are accessible on the MTCR website, <http://www.mtcr.info>.

states. Regime members exchange information on proliferation challenges and risks (including sensitive end-users, international procurement networks and state-sponsored procurement efforts) as well as on policies towards particular regions or states. They also circulate among themselves export licence applications that have been denied. The various working-level groups aim to strengthen national control systems by exchanging information, experiences, challenges and lessons learned from proliferation cases. Changes in global security have shifted the regimes' focus from state programmes and recipients to specific regions, countries and non-state actors. The demands in UN Security Council Resolution 1540 for brokering and transit controls have been taken up in regime discussions.

While the original focus was on drawing up common control lists, members proceeded to agree on effective national procedures and legal provisions, and now also develop best practice guides. Through outreach, regime members promote the principles, guidelines and control lists; non-members can choose to adhere to them without joining the regimes.

Cross-regime evolution, trends and challenges

Control lists and best practices

From the beginning, a key function of these multilateral arrangements has been the updating of their respective control lists, and over the past 20 years, control list updates have tended to be minor and specific. A regime's control list becomes legally binding once it is incorporated into national or supranational law. Efforts are under way in the AG and WA to make the lists more user-friendly for both industry and government authorities.[19] Combining the different regime lists into a consolidated list, as has been done by the EU, is one way of increasing user-friendliness.

The regimes' technical working groups have the challenging task of adapting lists to keep pace with rapid technological developments, easier access to technology and more sophisticated procurement methods (see the discussion of ITT below). In an effort to address this, the regimes have adopted WMD end-use clauses for unlisted items (the so-called catch-all mechanism); this control can be applied to items that are not listed in national or supranational law but that could still be diverted or used for WMD-related purposes. This mechanism allows countries expanded controls on proliferation-sensitive transfers. Moreover, the time lag between regime decisions and national implementation creates additional risks and

---

[19] Wassenaar Arrangement, '2009 plenary meeting of the Wassenaar Arrangement on Export Controls for Conventional Arms and Dual-use Goods and Technologies', Public statement, Vienna, 3 Dec. 2009, <http://www.wassenaar.org/publicdocuments/index_PD09.html>; and Leahy, J., 'Day one: regime updates: Australia Group', 10th International Export Control Conference, Istanbul, 25–27 June 2009, <http://exportcontrol.org/pastconferences/2705c.aspx>.

reinforces the importance of catch-all controls. An interesting aspect is the criteria for including items in the lists (e.g. whether the criteria are based on the traditional export control goals or also include counterterrorism considerations).

Regimes continue to refine their respective control lists and to assess the possible end-uses of currently uncontrolled items. Since 2007 the AG has maintained a particular focus on international developments in the field of synthetic biology.[20] In 2009 the AG 'considered a report from its specialist technical advisory group in this area' and 'agreed to broaden the scope of the advisory group to include a range of evolving technologies'. The AG list now includes software. The WA plenary amended the control list, among other things, for information security (encryption) and reception equipment for global navigation satellite systems.[21]

Over time, the scope of the regimes has expanded to include agreement on effective national procedures and legal provisions as well as the development of best practice guides, which complement already existing enforcement officers' handbooks. Topics discussed and agreed in the guidelines are often the result of national legislation and practice already in place. For example, in 2009 the AG and the NSG agreed a best practices guide on effective end-use controls that is based on a German proposal which was adopted by the WA in 2007 and has also been introduced in the MTCR.[22] The guide aims to provide a more comprehensive approach to end-use controls by going beyond end-use certificates. It includes both the obligations of exporters and government authorities, and covers the pre-licensing, licensing and post-licensing phase. This example also demonstrates one approach to coordinating regime efforts: introducing similar documents and approaches in the different regimes.

The intangible transfer of technology

ITT refers to both the transfer of knowledge and skills by a person (e.g. technical assistance, research papers presented at conferences etc.) and the transfer of technology via non-physical form (e.g. via fax, email, software or telephone). ITT can be, but is not necessarily, accompanied by a transfer of physical items. The term ITT encompasses information required for the development, production, use and repair of an item. Basic scientific research or information in the public domain is exempt from ITT controls, although drawing the line can be difficult in practice.

Due to its intangible nature, ITT is extremely challenging to control. Ways to approach ITT controls include company audits, visa screening and

---

[20] Australia Group, '2009 Australia Group plenary', Media release, 25 Sep. 2009, <http://www.australiagroup.net/en/agm_sept2009.html>.
[21] Wassenaar Arrangement (note 19).
[22] German Government (note 18), p. 91.

raising awareness within industry and academia.[23] Possible ITT providers include retired academics and technical experts, who may be motivated by money or prestige to share sensitive knowledge. The existence of ITT controls illustrates the overall move away from classical export control and the supplier–recipient paradigm.

In 2008, after the AG adopted 'enhanced measures' to deal with ITT in 2007, AG participants agreed that ITT is 'an area of increasing priority in the defence against the proliferation of chemical and biological weapons capabilities' and exchanged information on national measures for screening visa applications as a means of countering ITT of concern.[24] In 2009 the AG decided to produce an ITT booklet by 2010.[25] The guide aims to clarify the scope of ITT controls and the different ways that technology can be transferred. It also explores related control options for customs enforcement. In its 2009 plenary statement, the AG 'noted the ongoing importance of engaging industry and academic sectors in support of the Group's work'.[26]

At the 2003 MTCR plenary, the participating states agreed to take steps to develop national procedures to subject MTCR-controlled ITT to export controls, in accordance with their national legislation. The ITT issue was also discussed in 2004 and 2005. In 2006 it was agreed that transfers, as mentioned in the MTCR Guidelines for Sensitive Missile-Relevant Transfers, 'comprise tangible as well as intangible transfers'.[27]

In 2009 the NSG 'elaborated best-practice guides to be used by Participating Governments internally and for outreach activities' to address the challenges posed by intangible transfer of technology and end-use control.[28] The Hungarian NSG chair for 2009–10 announced a focus on ITT issues.[29]

In 2006 the WA agreed 'Best Practices for implementing intangible technology transfer controls'.[30] These include the 'provision of training to export control enforcement authorities on appropriate investigative tech-

---

[23] Recent ITT discussions tended to focus on visa-screening for students and professors. See e.g. Anthony and Bauer (note 3), p. 463.

[24] All statements are available on the Australia Group website, <http://www.australiagroup.net>.

[25] Wingren, L.-E., Swedish ambassador to Bosnia and Herzegovina, 'EU statement by the presidency on behalf of the European Union at the Australia Group plenary session', Paris, 22 Sep. 2009, <http://www.se2009.eu/fr/reunions_actualites/2009/9/22/statement_at_the_plenary_session_of_th e_australia_group>. Funding for the ITT guide is being provided by South Korea.

[26] Australia Group (note 46).

[27] MTCR, 'Plenary meeting of the Missile Technology Control Regime', Press release, Copenhagen, 2–6 Oct. 2006, <http://www.mtcr.info/english/press/copenhagen.html>; and MTCR, Guidelines for Sensitive Missile-Relevant Transfers, <http://www.mtcr.info/english/guidetext.htm>.

[28] Nuclear Suppliers Group (note 35).

[29] Stefan, L., 'Day one: regime updates: Nuclear Suppliers Group', 10th International Export Control Conference (note 19).

[30] Wassenaar Arrangement, 'Best practices for implementing intangible transfer of technology controls', Vienna, 6 Dec. 2006, <http://www.wassenaar.org/publicdocuments/index_PD06.html>.

niques to uncover violations of national controls on ITT exports or access to such specialist expertise'; the appropriate 'surveillance or monitoring, pursuant to national laws and regulations, of entities that are suspected . . . of making unauthorized intangible transfers of controlled technology' and the 'sanctioning by national authorities of those under their jurisdiction that have transferred controlled technology by intangible means in violation of export controls'.

Enforcement and penalties

Enforcement as an essential element of an effective export control system has received more attention in recent years, although the necessary practical steps of resource allocation as well as the complementary legal, institutional and procedural changes are only gradually being put in place. Penalties to prevent, deter and punish violations of transfer control laws are an important part of enforcement and a precondition for increasing the shift of responsibility from the licensing authority to the exporter. Resolution 1540 requires each UN member state to put effective and appropriate penalties in place, which raises the question of how these terms are to be defined and translated into national provisions. Similarly, EU member states are starting to discuss national approaches to put effective, dissuasive and proportionate penalties in place, as required by EU law.[31]

The AG requires members to implement 'an effective export control system which provides national controls for all items on the AG common control lists and is supported by adequate licensing and enforcement regimes' and to create 'legal penalties and sanctions for contravention of controls' and be 'willing to enforce them'.[32] NSG members should have in place legal measures to ensure the effective implementation of NSG guidelines, including enforcement measures and penalties for violations.[33] The WA's best practices for effective enforcement include the designation of law enforcement responsibilities in the relevant areas, the provision of ade-

---

[31] Council Regulation (EC) No 428/2009 of 5 May 2009 setting up a Community regime for the control of exports, transfer, brokering and transit of dual-use items, *Official Journal of the European Union*, L134, 29 May 2009. The same requirement was already included in Council Regulation (EC) No. 1334/2000 of 22 June 2000 setting up a Community regime for the control of exports of dual-use items and technology, *Official Journal of the European Communities*, L159, 30 June 2000. See also section IV below; and Wetter, A., *Enforcing European Union Law on Exports of Dual-use Goods*, SIPRI Research Report 24 (Oxford University Press: Oxford, 2009). On effective and appropriate penalties as they relate to Resolution 1540 and to the EU and EU member states see section II above and section IV below.

[32] Australia Group, 'Australia Group Membership', [n.d.], <http://www.australiagroup.net/en/membership.html>.

[33] International Atomic Energy Agency, 'Guidelines for nuclear transfers', Information Circular INFCIRC/254/Rev.9/Part.1, 7 Nov. 2007, p. 4; and International Atomic Energy Agency, 'Guidelines for transfers of nuclear-related dual-use equipment, materials, software, and related technology', Information Circular INFCIRC/254/Rev.7/Part 2, 20 Mar. 2006, p. 2.

quate resources and training for enforcement officers, and the assurance 'that national laws and regulations have statutes of limitations sufficiently long to permit the detection and prosecution of export control violations'. They also emphasize the importance of mutual legal and customs assistance and international investigation and prosecution cooperation, and the need to establish 'effective penalties'.[34]

Membership

The only regime to accept new members in 2009 was the NSG, which admitted Iceland.[35] A number of applications are pending in the WA; no new members have been admitted since South Africa joined in early 2006. For example, Serbia has submitted a request for membership of the WA and intends also to submit a request for membership of the NSG.[36] Applications are also pending in the AG.

China and Croatia have applied for MTCR membership.[37] Kazakhstan, which is 'consistently pursuing the policy of becoming the integral part of the international export control regimes', has declared joining the MTCR a priority and submitted an official application for membership in June 2003.[38] Kazakhstan declared in 2009 that it already follows the MTCR Guidelines and Technical Annex.[39] As of 2009 four other countries had declared their unilateral adherence to the MTCR.[40] Under the Indian–US Civil Nuclear Cooperation Initiative, signed on 10 October 2008, India is required to adhere to MTCR guidelines.[41] India is already committed to 'harmonisation and adherence' to MTCR guidelines under the terms of an Indian–US joint statement.[42]

[34] Wassenaar Arrangement, 'Best practices for effective enforcement' (1 Dec. 2000), *Basic Document* (Wassenaar Arrangement: Vienna, Jan. 2010), pp. 49–50.

[35] Nuclear Suppliers Group, 'NSG plenary meeting', Press statement, Budapest, 11–12 June 2009, <http://www.nuclearsuppliersgroup.org/Leng/PRESS/2009-10-Budapest.pdf>.

[36] Starcevic, F., Permanent representative of Serbia to the United Nations in New York, Statement at First Committee General Debate, 9 Oct. 2009, <http://www.un.int/serbia/Statements/52.pdf>.

[37] Croatian Ministry of Foreign Affairs and European Integration, 'Multilateral relations', <http://www.mfa.hr/MVP.asp?pcpid=1239>. China submitted its application for MTCR membership in 2004. US Department of Defense, Defense Treaty Inspection Readiness Program, 'Missile Technology Control Regime (MTCR)', <http://dtirp.dtra.mil/TIC/synopses/mtcr.cfm>.

[38] Abusseitov, K., Permanent representative of Kazakhstan at the Conference on Disarmament, Statement, Geneva, 7 Aug. 2007, <http://www.unog.ch/>.

[39] Kazakh Government, 'On Kazakhstan's efforts to join [the] Missile Technology Control Regime', Press release, London, 10 Nov. 2009, <http://www.kazembassy.org.uk/press_releases.html>.

[40] Those countries are Israel, Romania, Slovakia and the Former Yugoslav Republic of Macedonia (FYROM).

[41] US Department of Defense (note 37). See also Anthony and Bauer (note 3).

[42] Indian Government and US Government, 'India–U.S. joint statement', Press release, Washington, DC, 18 July 2005, <http://www.indianembassy.org/press_release/2005/July/21.htm>.

A number of EU member states do not yet participate in all four regimes.[43] Decisions on whether to accept new members are made on both technical and political grounds (i.e. on the basis of broader policy issues rather than on export control-specific ones) and on issues related to the exchange of sensitive information (both denials and intelligence information access). Formally, new members are considered if they have an effective export control system and enforcement, and are compliant with international treaties. In some cases, the question of whether the applicant is a supplier (e.g. for the Nuclear Suppliers Group, as the name indicates) or a producer (e.g. for the WA, as specifically mentioned by its membership criterion) is also considered. The AG requires members to be a manufacturer, exporter or trans-shipper of AG-controlled items.[44] Such membership requirements may become less significant over time as the importance of brokering and transit controls increases and as information about the denial of permits for interceptions gains importance.

One example of political considerations that could influence the decision of membership is Cyprus, which states that Turkey is vetoing its membership in the export control regimes.[45] The regimes are less driven by a common political goal and shared threat perceptions than before. Rather, the issue of membership expansion illustrates the conflicting political interests within the regimes that have influenced their atmosphere and functionality. A broader question is how to balance the need to increase the number of countries benefitting from enhanced access to information and contact networks through regime membership with the risk that an increase in the number of members could reduce the regimes' effectiveness.

Outreach

For a number of years, all the regimes have engaged with non-participating states through outreach visits, participation in international conferences and the organization of specialized seminars. They have also increased their transparency and made the documents agreed at plenary meetings (e.g. guidelines, best practice guides, plenary statements and control lists) available on their websites. Outreach activities aim to broaden the acceptance and implementation of agreed export control principles and raise awareness among non-participating states. The AG specifically stresses that 'international acceptance of Australia Group controls and practices are in part a result of the Group's extensive outreach to non-members and

[43] Of the 27 EU member states, 8—Cyprus, Estonia, Latvia, Lithuania, Malta, Romania, Slovakia and Slovenia—are not part of the MTCR and 1—Cyprus—is not a WA participant.

[44] Australia Group, 'Australia Group membership', <http://www.australiagroup.net/en/member ship.html>.

[45] Cypriot Ministry of Foreign Affairs, 'Turkey's attempts to exclude Cyprus' membership', <http://www.mfa.gov.cy/mfa/mfa2006.nsf/All/826CB014C0CDE8DEC22571B100229450>.

other international bodies'.[46] Depending on the regime and the country in question, outreach can function as an alternative to membership or assist in preparation for membership.

The quantity and nature of outreach activities reflect (*a*) the respective chair's ambitions and priorities; (*b*) the proactive efforts by non-participating, interested or membership-seeking countries; and (*c*) the reflection of regime cycles. There tend to be more inward-looking periods, when participating states are preoccupied by unresolved internal difficulties and times when there is consensus and enough energy for the regimes to focus outward. The work necessarily depends on threat perceptions and political agendas (e.g. the current greater focus on nuclear rather than on chemical weapons).

Outreach activities are conducted in different ways. For example, the AG plenary in 2008 endorsed strategies to improve the focus of outreach activities and better coordinate efforts.[47] For outreach purposes, the AG's website is available in Arabic, Chinese, English, French, German, Spanish and Russian. The AG favours a regional approach and has reached out to over 50 countries (many of them in Asia).[48]

Following requests for technical assistance, an MTCR technical outreach meeting for 15 non-participating states was organized in 2009, and a similar meeting is planned for 2010.[49] A German proposal for a paper on missile threats to be used for outreach events awaits consensus.[50] The MTCR has also emphasized outreach to industry.[51]

In 2009 the NSG held bilateral outreach talks with Albania, Bosnia and Herzegovina, Egypt, India, Indonesia, Israel, Former Yugoslav Republic of Macedonia, Malaysia, Mexico, Montenegro, Pakistan, Serbia, Singapore, Thailand and the United Arab Emirates.[52] As noted in an NSG statement, the 'Chair and the other Troika members were mandated to continue contacts with Non-NSG Participating Governments and International Organisations ... to inform them on recent developments within the Group, to assist partners in their efforts to enhance their export controls and to facilitate adherence to the NSG Guidelines.'[53] The 2009–10 Hungarian chair has announced a special focus on the Western Balkans.[54]

---

[46] Australia Group (note 20). See also chapter 10 in this volume.

[47] Leahy (note 19).

[48] Australia Group, '2006 Australia Group plenary', Media release, 12–15 June 2006, <http://www.australiagroup.net/en/agm_june2006.html>.

[49] Quinn (note 51); and German Government (note 18), p. 93.

[50] German Government (note 18), p. 93.

[51] Quinn, J., 'Day one: regime updates: Missiles Technology Control Regime', 10th International Export Control Conference (note 19).

[52] German Government (note 18), p. 88.

[53] Nuclear Suppliers Group (note 35). The NSG Troika includes the current, previous and upcoming chairs.

[54] Stefan (note 29).

In 2009 WA outreach activities included post-plenary briefings, interaction with industry and bilateral outreach to a number of non-participating states. The plenary decided to conduct a technical briefing on changes to the WA control lists for several non-participating states in 2010.[55]

Nuclear-specific issues

While the non-proliferation community is still digesting the repercussions of the NSG decision to exempt India from its guidelines and anticipating the possible impact on 2010 NPT Review Conference, the NSG member states that are pursuing civil-nuclear interests are focusing on practical issues to be resolved.[56] The 2009 NSG plenary discussions focused on 'the proliferation implications of the nuclear test by North Korea, and Iran's nuclear programme'.[57]

The NSG has yet to agree on new guidelines that would make the International Atomic Energy Agency (IAEA) safeguards contained in the Additional Protocol a precondition for receiving nuclear exports.[58] The main obstacle to agreement is that not all NSG members have signed the Additional Protocol.[59] Lack of consensus on these guidelines in the NSG reflect in large part some countries' concern that the guidelines will forestall or limit their options for developing civil nuclear programmes in the future. At its July 2009 summit, the Group of Eight (G8) industrialized countries agreed, with the NSG not yet reaching consensus, to implement the NSG's proposed guidelines in the next year. Among other things, the G8 countries' agreement would mean that they could not export sensitive nuclear technology (i.e. for enrichment and reprocessing).[60] The increased demand for nuclear energy and the anticipated spread of dual-use nuclear technology

[55] Wassenaar Arrangement (note 19), p. 1.

[56] Anthony and Bauer (note 3), pp. 466–71; and Horner, D., 'Indian–U.S. nuclear trade still faces hurdles', *Arms Control Today*, vol. 40, no. 3 (Jan./Feb. 2010).

[57] Zanathy, G. M., Hungarian ambassador to Austria, 'Opening remarks, NSG transparency seminar', New York, 15 Oct. 2009, <http://www.nuclearsuppliersgroup.org/Leng/05-pubblic.htm>. See also chapter 9 in this volume.

[58] An Additional Protocol is a legal document granting the IAEA inspection authority that complements that provided in underlying safeguards agreements. Comprehensive safeguards are based on a combination of nuclear material accountancy, complemented by containment and surveillance techniques (e.g. tamper-proof seals and cameras that the IAEA installs at facilities to monitor activities on a continuous basis). EU and US governments endorsed the NSG's efforts 'to reach agreement on strengthened export controls on enrichment and reprocessing technologies and on making the Additional Protocol a standard for nuclear supply'. See 'Declaration on non-proliferation and disarmament', EU–US Summit Declaration, 3 Nov. 2009, <http://www.se2009.eu/polopoly_fs/1.21999!menu/standard/file/st15351-re01.en09.pdf>, Annex 3.

[59] German Government (note 18), p. 89. For a list of states that have signed an Additional Protocol see annex A in this volume.

[60] G8 Summit, 'L'Aquila statement on non-proliferation', Declaration, L'Aquila, 8 July 2009, <http://www.g8italia2009.it/G8/Home/Summit/G8-G8_Layout_locale-1199882116809_Atti.htm>.

will have a strong impact on non-proliferation and also on future nuclear export controls.

IV. Supply-side and cooperative measures in the European Union

The full implications of the entry into force of the Lisbon Treaty on 1 December 2009 for non-proliferation and export control policies are yet to become clear.[61] The EU will no longer be divided into three pillars: one supranational (known as the Community) and two intergovernmental (one dealing with foreign and security policy and the other with police and judicial cooperation in criminal matters). Nevertheless, a division of competences between member states and the EU remains. The new high representative for foreign affairs and security policy, Catherine Ashton, together with the Council of the EU (the Council), will determine what level of priority to assign to non-proliferation and export control issues and the way in which the new European External Action Service and other actors dealing with these issues will be structured and resourced. One of the known legal implications is that future revisions to dual-use regulations will come under the co-decision procedure (now to be called the normal procedure), which puts the European Parliament in a very powerful position.

In the conventional arms export control area, 2009 was characterized by the national implementation of decisions made in 2008 at the EU level. In December 2008, the EU's Common Rules Governing Control of Exports of Military Technology and Equipment (Common Rules) replaced the EU Code of Conduct on Arms Exports that had been agreed 10 years earlier.[62] There were also major developments in the legislation governing EU dual-use export controls in 2009.

The Intra-Community Transfers Directive, which was approved by the European Parliament in December 2008, was adopted on 6 May 2009 and entered into force in June 2009.[63] It anticipates the use of global and

---

[61] On the Lisbon Treaty see chapter 4, section III, in this volume.

[62] Council Common Position 2008/944/CFSP of 8 Dec. 2008 defining common rules governing control of exports of military technology and equipment, *Official Journal of the European Union*, L335, 13 Dec. 2008, pp. 99–103; and Council of the European Union, EU Code of Conduct on Arms Exports, 8675/2/98 Rev. 2, Brussels, 5 June 1998. On the impact of the EU Code of Conduct see Bauer, S. and Bromley, M., *The European Union Code of Conduct on Arms Exports: Improving the Annual Report*, SIPRI Policy Paper no. 8 (SIPRI: Stockholm, Nov. 2004); Bromley, M. and Brzoska, M., 'Towards a common, restrictive EU arms export policy? The impact of the EU Code of Conduct on major conventional arms exports', *European Foreign Affairs Review*, vol. 13, no. 3 (2008), pp. 333–56; and Bromley, M., *The Impact on Domestic Policy of the EU Code of Conduct on Arms Exports: The Czech Republic, the Netherlands and Spain*, SIPRI Policy Paper no. 21 (SIPRI: Stockholm, May 2008).

[63] Directive 2009/43/EC of the European Parliament and of the Council of 6 May 2009 simplifying terms and conditions of transfers of defence-related products within the Community, *Official*

general licences for transfers of military equipment within the EU (instead of licences authorizing individual transactions) and the introduction of a certification scheme for recipient companies. Member states are required to implement the directive within two years and apply implementing provisions by 2012.

Recast of the European Union dual-use regulation

EU Regulation 428/2009 regulating the export, brokering and transit of dual-use items, including software and technology, entered into force on 27 August 2009.[64] The new provisions are the result of over two years of negotiation by the 27 EU member states and replaces Regulation 1334/2000.[65] The new law brings the EU in line with the requirements of UN Security Council Resolution 1540 regarding brokering, transit and trans-shipment controls.[66] Although there were EU-wide controls for dual-use items previously, there were none for brokering and transit. However, some member states already had national provisions in place for brokering and transit. Germany, for example, has used an individual intervention clause (*Einzeleingriff*) to give national authorities the legal power to interdict a border-crossing transaction.[67] German authorities can also use the recently introduced option of preventive seizure.[68]

Regulation 428/2009 establishes a legal possibility for the national authorities to prohibit the transit of listed dual-use items under certain conditions. The transit of listed dual-use items through the EU can be prohibited if the items are or may be intended for a WMD end-use. However, the new regulation includes no EU-wide possibility to stop the transit of unlisted items, although other EU customs and national provisions may apply. In addition, countries can introduce a licensing requirement at national level. The wording of the new transit provision is identical to the legal construction used for the catch-all WMD end-use provisions in the

Journal of the European Union, L146, 10 June 2009, pp. 1–36. See also Anthony and Bauer (note 3), pp. 476–78.

[64] Council Regulation (EC) no. 428/2009 (note 31). See also section III above; Wetter (note 31); and Council of the European Union, 'Security-related export controls I: dual use items and technology', <http://www.consilium.europa.eu/showPage.aspx?id=408&lang=en>.

[65] Council Regulation (EC) no. 1334/2000 (note 31).

[66] The EU defines trans-shipment as a sub-category of transit.

[67] This is possible if there is agreement by 3 ministries (Economy, Foreign Affairs and Finance) that this is necessary in order to (a) 'guarantee the vital security interests of the Federal Republic of Germany', (b) 'prevent a disturbance of the peaceful coexistence between nations', or (c) 'prevent a major disruption of the foreign relations of the Federal Republic of Germany'. Außenwirtschaftsgesetz [Foreign Trade and Payments Act], 28 Apr. 1961, as amended most recently on 19 Dec. 2009, <http://bundesrecht.juris.de/awg/index.html>, Article 2.

[68] Gesetz über das Zollkriminalamt und die Zollfahndungsämter (Zollfahndungsdienstgesetz, ZFdG) [Law on the customs criminological office and the customs investigation offices (Customs Investigation Service Law)], <http://bundesrecht.juris.de/zfdg/BJNR320210002.html>, Article 35b.

same document, with one significant difference: Article 4 applies to exports of unlisted items to a WMD end-use, while the new Article 6 applies to the transit of listed items to a WMD end-use. Although Regulation 428/2009 establishes the legal powers of the state to intervene and defines the obligations of the exporter and, newly, the broker, it does not impose obligations on the person conducting the transit; hence the role of the transit actor is not legally defined.

The regulation's legal end-use construction is also used for the control of brokering activities. It defines brokering as 'the negotiation or arrangement of transactions for the purchase, sale or supply of dual-use items from a third country to any other third country, or the selling or buying of dual-use items that are located in third countries for their transfer to another third country'.[69] Ancillary services (e.g. insurance) are explicitly excluded. If a broker has been informed by the competent authorities that the items in question are or may be intended for a WMD end-use, the brokering requires an authorization. If a broker is aware that listed dual-use items are intended for a WMD end-use, he or she must notify the competent authorities.[70] The regulation explicitly gives member states the possibility to expand both the brokering and transit provisions at the national level, for example, through extraterritorial controls and an expanded range of items.

While UN Security Council Resolution 1540 was the main motivation for the revision of Regulation 1334/2000, many other issues were also put on the table once discussions were opened. This partly accounts for the length of the discussions. Another reason was the number of issues generated by the 2004 Peer Review.[71] Furthermore, legal reviews take time, even at national level, and in this instance agreement had to be reached between 27 countries. For example, the decision either to make all dual-use transits subject to a licensing requirement or to prohibit a small number of dual-use transits with a suspected WMD end-use has very different practical implications for EU member states, depending on the volume of transits (in general) and dual-use transits (in particular) through their territory. The discussions revealed the lack of international or EU-wide agreement on definitions of the terms 'brokering', 'transit' and 'trans-shipment', and implementation of their related 1540 requirements. Some issues were left to national discretion, such as how to proceed once a transit is stopped or interrupted.

Regulation 428/2009 is directly applicable in all 27 member states. It requires each state to take the necessary steps to implement and enforce the regulation and to put in place effective, proportionate and dissuasive

[69] Council Regulation (EC) no. 428/2009 (note 31), Article 2. 'Third countries' are all countries outside the EU.
[70] Council Regulation (EC) no. 428/2009 (note 31), Article 5.
[71] Anthony, I. and Bauer, S., 'Transfer controls', *SIPRI Yearbook 2005*, pp. 699–719.

sanctions for violations and national laws to implement the regulation. This major task for member states started in 2009 and will continue in the coming years. Prior to EU accession, candidate countries are required to align themselves with the EU *acquis*.[72] The revision therefore affects accession, candidate and potential candidate countries.

Combating the proliferation of weapons of mass destruction

The 'New lines for action by the European Union in combating the proliferation of weapons of mass destruction and their delivery systems' (New Lines) of December 2008 further develops and complements the EU's 2003 WMD Strategy.[73] The New Lines set ambitious goals to achieve by the end of 2010. Among these is the 'better use' for the EU of WMD clauses in agreements with third countries, a concept that was first introduced by the EU's 2003 WMD Strategy.[74] During 2009 a WMD clause was agreed with Central American countries, China, South Korea, Indonesia, Iraq and the Gulf Cooperation Council.[75] The EU–Syria Association Agreement, which includes a WMD clause, is awaiting entry into force.[76] Negotiations with Brunei Darussalam, Libya, Malaysia, the Philippines, Russia, Singapore, Thailand and Viet Nam are ongoing.[77] However, the record so far is mixed and the differences in the wording of the clause in each case illustrate that proliferation norms are easily compromised where economic interests are at stake.[78] At the same time, the EU has actively initiated and funded cooperative projects to combat proliferation, including in the area of export controls.

---

[72] The *acquis communautaire* is the body of common rights and obligations that is binding on all EU member states.

[73] Council of the European Union, Council Conclusions and new lines for action by the European Union in combating the proliferation of weapons of mass destruction and their delivery systems, 17172/08, Brussels, 17 Dec. 2008; and Council of the European Union, 'EU Strategy against Proliferation of Weapons of Mass Destruction', Brussels, 12 Dec. 2003, <http://europa.eu/legislation_summaries/foreign_and_security_policy/cfsp_and_esdp_implementation/l33234_en.htm>.

[74] The EU introduced the non-proliferation clause, also known as the WMD clause, in 2003 as a way to encourage its non-EU partners to enhance their participation in and implementation of multilateral non-proliferation instruments. Grip, L., 'The EU non-proliferation clause: a preliminary assessment', SIPRI Background Paper, Nov. 2009, <http://books.sipri.org/product_info?c_product_id=394>.

[75] Council of the European Union, Six-monthly progress report on the implementation of the EU Strategy against the proliferation of weapons of mass destruction (2009/I), 11490/09, Brussels, 26 June 2009, p. 36.

[76] Delegation of the European Union to Syria, 'EU–Syria Association Agreement', <http://www.delsyr.ec.europa.eu/en/eu_and_syria_new/cooperation_agreements_and_priorities_2.htm>.

[77] Council of the European Union, Six-monthly progress report on the implementation of the EU Strategy against the proliferation of weapons of mass destruction (2009/II), 17387/09, Brussels, 9 Dec. 2009, p. 5.

[78] Grip (note 74).

Cooperation with non-European Union partner countries on export control

In December 2009 the Council adopted a decision in support of continued EU activities that promote the control of conventional arms exports and the principles and criteria of the Common Rules among third countries.[79] The 2009 decision will fund regional seminars on conventional arms export control in accession, candidate and European Neighbourhood Policy (ENP) countries during 2010 and 2011. This initiative, unlike the 2008 joint action, will also support staff exchanges and visits by officials from partner countries to export control authorities in the EU. The two-year project will be implemented by the German Office of Economics and Export Controls (Bundesamt für Wirtschaft und Ausfuhrkontrolle, BAFA).

The initiative complements the EU assistance and cooperation programmes in the dual-use area that are funded through the EU budget and also implemented by BAFA, in close cooperation with other EU member states. The main difference between conventional and dual-use outreach initiatives is the financial gap: dual-use export control cooperation has had consistent funding since 2005 for an ever-increasing number of countries, while the conventional export control area has only had ad hoc financing for individual activities and at a much lower level.[80] The dual-use activities are funded by one of the EU financial instruments for external action, the Instrument for Stability (IFS). The IFS's Multi-annual Indicative Programme for 2009–11, adopted on 8 April 2009, provides €123 million ($171 million) for chemical, biological, radiological and nuclear (CBRN) risk mitigation, including strengthening export control and combating illicit trafficking.[81] Additional funding to combat such trafficking is available from other parts of the IFS.

---

[79] Council Decision 2009/1012/CFSP, which provided €787 000 for conventional outreach initiatives for 2010–11, is a follow-on to the Mar. 2008 joint action on outreach on the then EU Code of Conduct on Arms Exports, which provided €500 500 towards conventional outreach initiatives for 2008–2009. Council Joint Action 2008/230/CFSP of 17 Mar. 2008 on support for EU activities in order to promote the control of arms exports and the principles and criteria of the EU Code of Conduct on arms exports among third countries, *Official Journal of the European Union*, L75, 18 Mar. 2008, pp. 81–85; and Council Decision 2009/1012/CFSP of 22 Dec. 2009 on support for EU activities in order to promote the control of arms exports and the principles and criteria of Common Position 2008/944/CFSP among third countries, *Official Journal of the European Union*, L348, 29 Dec. 2009, pp. 16–20. On Council Joint Action 2008/230/CFSP see also Anthony and Bauer (note 3), pp. 473–74.

[80] The IFS's indicative budget for 2009–11 proposed €6–10 million for 'assistance and cooperation on export control on dual-use goods'. European Commission, 'The Instrument for Stability: Multi-annual Indicative Programme 2009–2011', Brussels, 8 Apr. 2009, C(2009)2641, <http://ec.europa.eu/external_relations/ifs/docs/>, p. 19. On the funding of conventional outreach activities for 2008–11 see note 79.

[81] European Commission (note 80).

V. Conclusions

The multiplicity of actors involved in proliferation-sensitive transactions and their inherent complexity requires adjustments not just of the concepts and language, but also of related laws as well as licensing and enforcement mechanisms. These also necessitate stronger international cooperation because even those states that do not produce dual-use items may be involved (e.g. as transit and trans-shipment points or through the jurisdiction over their nationals who act as brokers and freight forwarders). International cooperation and assistance increasingly overlap, and there is a need to move beyond the supplier–recipient paradigm and towards cooperative arrangements. The export control regimes cannot escape from this trend. Transparency and outreach to non-members have become essential functions of the regimes. Further challenges will be posed by the need for licensing and enforcement practices and legal provisions to keep pace with technological developments. While traditional export control set-ups do not fully address proliferation's complexity, they are adjusting.

Appendix 12A. Multilateral arms embargoes, 2009

PIETER D. WEZEMAN AND NOEL KELLY

I. Introduction

There were 29 mandatory multilateral arms embargoes in force in 2009, directed at a total of 17 targets, including governments, non-governmental forces and a transnational network. The United Nations imposed 12 of these embargoes, the European Union (EU) imposed 16 and the Economic Community of West African States (ECOWAS) imposed 1.[1]

During 2009 the UN Security Council imposed its first new arms embargo since 2006, on Eritrea. The UN widened the arms embargo on the Democratic People's Republic of Korea (DPRK, or North Korea) and lifted the arms embargo on the Government of Liberia.

Nine of the 16 EU embargoes were straightforward implementations of UN arms embargoes.[2] In addition, two EU arms embargoes differed from UN embargoes in their scope or coverage and five did not have UN counterparts.[3] In 2009 the EU imposed a new arms embargo on Guinea and lifted its arms embargo on Uzbekistan. ECOWAS imposed a new arms embargo on Guinea.

Section II of this appendix gives details of the developments in UN arms embargoes in 2009 and section III covers developments in the EU and ECOWAS. Table 12A.1 provides details of all the multilateral arms embargoes in force in 2009. This appendix does not cover the formal and informal unilateral arms embargoes that individual states impose.

II. Developments in United Nations arms embargoes

In December 2009 the UN Security Council imposed open-ended sanctions on Eritrea.[4] This was a reaction to the findings by the latest UN Monitoring Group on Somalia that Eritrea had provided political, financial and logistical support

---

[1] In addition, voluntary embargoes on Armenia and Azerbaijan that were imposed in 1992 by the Organization for Security and Co-operation in Europe (OSCE) and in 1993 by the UN were still in force. They were not enforced by all OSCE participating states and all UN member states. Conference on Security and Co-operation in Europe, Committee of Senior Officials, Statement, annex 2 to Journal of the Eighth Meeting of the Committee, 13 Mar. 1992; and UN Security Council Resolution 853, 29 July 1993. All UN documents cited here are available at <http://documents.un.org/>.

[2] These were the embargoes on al-Qaeda, the Taliban and associated individuals and entities, the Democratic Republic of the Congo (non-governmental forces, NGF), Côte d'Ivoire, Iraq (NGF), North Korea, Lebanon (NGF), Liberia, Sierra Leone (NGF) and Somalia.

[3] The 2 EU embargoes that differed from UN embargoes were those on Iran, which covered more weapon types than the UN embargo, and on Sudan, which covered the country as a whole whereas the UN embargo applied only to the Darfur region. The 5 EU embargoes with no UN counterpart were those on China, Guinea, Myanmar, Uzbekistan and Zimbabwe.

[4] UN Security Council Resolution 1907, 23 Dec. 2009.

to armed groups in Somalia and to Eritrea's refusal to withdraw its armed forces from territory disputed by Eritrea and Djibouti and engage in diplomatic dialogue about this issue. The sanctions include an embargo on transfers of all arms and related materiel and services to and from Eritrea.

Since 2005 the UN Monitoring Group on Somalia has reported that Eritrea has supported, including with arms supplies, groups in Somalia fighting the Somali Transitional Federal Government.[5] Although the Security Council amended the embargo on Somalia in November 2008 to specify that sanctions should be applied to all entities that violated the embargo, this did not lead to specific action against any violator.[6] In May 2009 the Intergovernmental Authority on Development (IGAD) and the African Union (AU) accused Eritrea of supporting armed groups in Somalia and called on the UN to impose sanctions on Eritrea.[7] The Security Council discussed possible sanctions against Eritrea several times before Uganda circulated a draft resolution in November 2009.[8] In early December 2009 the president of the Security Council indicated that negotiations over the proposed sanctions within the Council were difficult, commenting that sanctions were a 'thorny issue'.[9] However, on 23 December Resolution 1907 obtained broad support and passed with 13 votes in favour, with China abstaining and Libya voting against.[10]

In reaction to a nuclear test explosion and ballistics missile tests by North Korea, in June 2009 the UN Security Council unanimously amended existing sanctions on North Korea imposed in 2006.[11] It extended the embargo from supplies of most major arms to North Korea to include all arms and related materiel, except for small arms and light weapons. Furthermore, the embargo on procurement of arms from North Korea was extended to include all arms, without exception. The resolution also established a panel of experts to mon-

---

[5] United Nations, Security Council, Report of the Monitoring Group on Somalia pursuant to Security Council resolution 1639 (2005), annex to S/2006/229, 4 May 2006, pp. 10–13. This and subsequent reports of the Monitoring Group on Somalia are available at <http://www.un.org/sc/committees/751/mongroup.shtml>.

[6] UN Security Council Resolution 1844, 20 Nov. 2008, para 8(b).

[7] Intergovernmental Authority on Development (IGAD), Communiqué of the 33rd Extra-ordinary session (Extra-ord. no. 1) of the IGAD Council of Ministers on the security and political situation in the subregion in particular Somalia, Addis Ababa, 20 May 2009, <http://www.igad.org/index.php?option=com_content&task=view&id=265&Itemid=96>; and African Union, Peace and Security Council, 190th meeting, Communiqué, 22 May 2009, <http://www.africa-union.org/root/au/index/index_may09.htm>. For a brief description of IGAD see annex B in this volume. Its members are Djibouti, Eritrea, Ethiopia, Kenya, Somalia, Sudan and Uganda.

[8] United Nations, Security Council, 6158th meeting, S/PV.6158, 9 July 2009; United Nations, Security Council, 6197th meeting, S/PV.6197, 8 Oct. 2009; and Charbonneau, L., 'Move at UN to sanction Eritrea over Somalia links', Reuters, 19 Nov. 2009, <http://www.reuters.com/article/idUSN19531413>.

[9] United Nations, 'Press conference by Security Council president', 2 Dec. 2009, <http://www.un.org/News/briefings/docs/2009/091202_SCPres.doc.htm>.

[10] United Nations, Security Council, 6254th meeting, S/PV.6254, 23 Dec. 2009.

[11] UN Security Council Resolution 1874, 12 June 2009. The 2006 embargo on arms imports and exports was limited to battle tanks, armoured combat vehicles, large calibre artillery systems, combat aircraft, attack helicopters, warships, missiles or missile systems as defined for the purpose of the United Nations Register of Conventional Arms, or related materiel including spare parts. UN Security Council Resolution 1718, 14 Oct. 2006. On North Korea's nuclear test see appendix 8B and chapter 9, section IV, in this volume.

CONTROLS ON INTERNATIONAL TRANSFERS 469

itor the implementation of the sanctions. Of the 12 UN arms embargoes, only 3—those on Iran, Iraq and Lebanon—now lack an associated panel of experts.

In December 2009 Security Council Resolution 1903 lifted the arms embargo on the Government of Liberia for a trial period of one year.[12] The Liberian Government had been subject to UN arms embargoes since 1992, although from 2005 the Sanctions Committee on Liberia regularly authorized exemptions that allowed the transfer of arms to Liberia for use by the government's security forces.[13] The Sanctions Committee on Liberia must still be notified in advance of shipments of arms and related materials to the Liberian Government. Resolution 1903 also extended the arms embargo on all non-governmental entities and individuals operating in Liberia for 12 months.

Inspections and embargo violations

The resolutions imposing arms embargoes on Eritrea, Iran and North Korea include specific calls for UN member states to inspect on their territory any suspected cargo transported by air or ship to or from the embargoed countries.[14] In addition, the 2009 resolution amending sanctions on North Korea calls on UN member states to inspect vessels, with the consent of the flag state, on the high seas if they have reasonable grounds to believe that prohibited items are on board. If the flag state does not consent to inspection on the high seas, the resolution requires the flag state to direct the vessel to a port for the required inspection. If the flag state does not do so, the member state requesting the inspection should submit a report to the embargo committee.[15] China and Russia voted in favour of the resolution, but expressed their reservations about this unprecedented element in a UN embargo and stressed that the resolution does not allow the use of force.[16]

During 2009 cargo inspections led to the uncovering of several violations of the UN embargoes on arms exports from Iran and North Korea. In February Cyprus reported that it had found arms and ammunition from Iran destined for Syria on a Cypriot-flagged ship chartered by the Islamic Republic of Iran Shipping Lines (IRISL).[17] In October US troops boarded a German-flagged ship chartered by IRISL in the Gulf of Suez and found eight containers of casings for small arms ammunition on their way from Iran to Syria. The ship was redirected to Malta, where the weapons were offloaded.[18] In November Israel

[12] Security Council Resolution 1903, 17 Dec. 2009.

[13] United Nations, Security Council, Final report of the Panel of Experts on Liberia submitted pursuant to paragraph 4 of Security Council Resolution 1854 (2008), annex to S/2009/640, 11 Dec. 2009, pp. 41–43.

[14] UN Security Council Resolution 1907 (note 4), para. 7; UN Security Council Resolution 1803, 3 Mar. 2008, para. 11; and Security Council Resolution 1874 (note 11), para. 11.

[15] Security Council Resolution 1874 (note 11), paras 12–13.

[16] United Nations, Security Council, 6141st meeting, S/PV.6141, 12 June 2009, pp. 3, 8.

[17] United Nations, Security Council, 6142nd meeting, S/PV.6142, 15 June 2009; and United Nations, Security Council, 'Implementation assistance notice', 24 July 2009, <http://www.un.org/sc/committees/1737/selecdocs.shtml>.

[18] United Nations, Security Council, 6235th meeting, S/PV.6235, 10 Dec. 2009; and 'German ship transporting arms for Iran', Der Spiegel, 12 Oct. 2009.

reported that it had intercepted, with 'the consent of the relevant authorities', 36 containers with arms originating from Iran on-board an Antiguan and Barbudan-flagged IRISL-operated ship in the Mediterranean.[19] In July the US Navy tracked on the high seas a North Korean ship suspected of carrying arms to Myanmar but made no attempt to inspect it. The ship turned back to North Korea without offloading cargo.[20] Rocket propelled grenades and parts for conventional arms destined for Iran were found in August in the United Arab Emirates (UAE) on a Bahamian-flagged ship originating from North Korea.[21] In November South Africa seized a shipment of spare parts for tanks on a ship sailing from North Korea to the Republic of the Congo.[22] Finally, in December 35 tonnes of arms originating from North Korea were found in a Georgian-registered aircraft detained in Thailand.[23]

In the case of the UN arms embargoes on al-Qaeda, the Taliban and associated individuals and entities, the Democratic Republic of the Congo, Somalia and the Darfur region of Sudan, continuous violations since the imposition of the sanctions have been reported by UN panels of experts, including significant violations in 2009.[24] In 2009 for the first time the UN Group of Experts on Côte d'Ivoire reported significant violations of the UN arms embargo on the country. It reported that all parties in the conflict were rearming and strongly suspected that significant quantities of small arms and related ammunition had been systematically supplied in 2008 and 2009 from the territory of Burkina Faso to Ivorian rebel forces.[25]

III. Developments in other multilateral arms embargoes

During 2009 the political situation in Guinea deteriorated, culminating on 28 September 2009 in the killing of over 150 demonstrators by Guinean soldiers.[26] In response to these developments, the International Contact Group on Guinea recommended that the international community impose sanctions on Guinea, including an arms embargo.[27] Soon afterwards ECOWAS and the EU—

---

[19] United Nations (note 18); and Government of Antigua and Barbuda, 'Antigua Department of Marine Services and Merchant Shipping launches investigation into ammunitions find aboard the Antigua and Barbuda flagged vessel the Motor Vessel "Francop"', Press release, 9 Nov. 2009, <http://www.ab.gov.ag/gov_v2/government/pressreleases/pressreleases2009/prelease_2009Nov09 _1.html>.

[20] Kirk, D., 'Storm over North Korea–Iran arms vessel', Asia Times, 1 Sep. 2009; and Choe, S., 'South Korea says freighter from north turns back', New York Times, 6 July 2009.

[21] Kirk (note 20).

[22] 'South Africa reports seizing banned North Korea weapons', BBC News, 26 Feb. 2010, <http://news.bbc.co.uk/2/hi/8539408.stm>.

[23] McCartan, B., 'Weapons seizure hits North Korea hard', Asia Times, 22 Dec. 2009.

[24] Reports by the panels of experts can be found on the website of the UN Security Council sanctions committees, <http://www.un.org/sc/committees/>.

[25] United Nations, Security Council, Final report of the Group of Experts on Côte d'Ivoire pursuant to paragraph 11 of Security Council Resolution 1842 (2008), annex to S/2009/521, 9 Oct. 2009.

[26] Aziakou, G., 'Guinea mayhem was "crime against humanity": UN report', AFP, 21 Dec. 2009, <http://www.google.com/hostednews/afp/article/ALeqM5iAtFl4yvbtRin3uNtL4F0idhGo1Q>.

[27] Final Communique, 8th Session of the International Contact group on Guinea (ICG-G), 12 Oct. 2009, <http://www.africa-union.org/root/AU/Conferences/2009/october/Communique[1]_ICG-G. pdf>. The Contact Group is co-chaired by the AU and ECOWAS commissions and also involves the

two participants in the Contact Group imposed arms embargoes on Guinea. The ECOWAS arms embargo, imposed on 17 October 2009, was only the second that it had imposed on one of its member states.[28] The EU imposed its sanctions on Guinea on 27 October 2009, including an arms embargo.[29]

On 27 October 2009 the EU decided not to renew its sanctions, including an arms embargo, on Uzbekistan, in order 'to encourage the Uzbek authorities to take further substantive steps to improve the rule of law and the human rights situation'.[30] The EU had concluded that sufficient change had occurred in Uzbekistan, even though a key demand in the EU sanctions had not been met, namely an independent international inquiry into the 'excessive, disproportionate and indiscriminate use of force by the Uzbek security forces' during demonstrations in Andijan in May 2005.[31]

Other EU arms embargoes included in sanctions related to human rights were not changed. The formation in 2009 of a power-sharing government in Zimbabwe was not enough progress for the EU to lift any of its sanctions on the country.[32]

Community of Sahelo-Saharan States (CEN-SAD), the EU, the Mano River Union, the Organisation of the Islamic Conference, the International Organisation of La Francophonie and the UN, as well as the chairs of the AU Peace and Security Council and of ECOWAS, and the permanent and the African members of the UN Security Council.

[28] ECOWAS, Extraordinary Summit of ECOWAS heads of state and government, Final communiqué, Abuja, 17 Oct. 2009. The first ECOWAS arms embargo was imposed on Togo from 19 to 26 Feb. 2005.

[29] Council Common Position 2009/788/CFSP of 27 Oct. 2009 concerning restrictive measures against the Republic of Guinea, *Official Journal of the European Union*, L281, 28 Oct. 2009.

[30] Council of the European Union, 2971st meeting, General Affairs and External Relations, Press Release 14658/09 (Presse 299), Luxembourg, 27 Oct. 2009.

[31] Council Common Position 2005/792/CFSP of 14 Nov. 2005 concerning restrictive measures against Uzbekistan, *Official Journal of the European Union*, L299, 16 Nov. 2005.

[32] Bearak, B., 'Europeans to keep sanctions on Zimbabwe', *New York Times*, 13 Sep. 2009.

Table 12A.1. Multilateral arms embargoes in force during 2009

Target[a]	Date embargo first imposed	Principal instruments establishing or amending embargo[b]	Developments during 2009
United Nations arms embargoes			
Al-Qaeda, the Taliban and associated individuals and entities	19 Dec. 2000	UNSCRs 1333, 1390	Extended until 30 June 2011 by UNSCR 1904, 17 Dec. 2009
Democratic Republic of the Congo (NGF)	28 July 2003	UNSCRs 1493, 1596, 1807	Extended until 30 Nov. 2010 by UNSCR 1896, 30 Nov. 2009
Côte d'Ivoire	15 Nov. 2004	UNSCR 1572	Extended until 31 Oct. 2010 by UNSCR 1893, 29 Oct. 2009
Eritrea	23 Dec. 2009	UNSCR 1907	New embargo
Iran (technology related to nuclear weapon delivery systems)[c]	23 Dec. 2006	UNSCR 1737	
Iraq (NGF)	6 Aug. 1990	UNSCRs 661, 1483, 1546	
North Korea[d]	15 July 2006	UNSCRs 1695, 1718	Amended by UNSCR 1874, 12 June 2009
Lebanon (NGF)	11 Aug. 2006	UNSCR 1701	
Liberia (NGF)[e]	22 Dec. 2003	UNSCRs 1521, 1683	Amended and extended until 17 Dec. 2010 by UNSCR 1903, 17 Dec. 2009
Sierra Leone (NGF)	8 Oct. 1997	UNSCRs 1132, 1171	
Somalia[f]	23 Jan. 1992	UNSCRs 733, 1725	
Sudan (Darfur)	30 July 2004	UNSCR 1556, 1591	
European Union arms embargoes			
Al-Qaeda, the Taliban and associated individuals and entities	17 Dec. 1996	CPs 96/746/CFSP, 2001/154/CFSP, 2002/402/CFSP	
China	27 June 1989	European Council declaration	
Democratic Republic of the Congo (NGF)	7 Apr. 1993	Declaration, CPs 2003/680/CFSP, 2005/440/CFSP, 2008/369/CFSP	
Côte d'Ivoire	13 Dec. 2004	CP 2004/852/CFSP	
Guinea	27 Oct. 2009	CP 2009/788/CFSP	New embargo
Iran	27 Feb. 2007	CPs 2007/140/CFSP, 2007/246/CFSP	

Iraq (NGF)	4 Aug. 1990	Declaration, CPs 2003/495/CFSP, 2004/553/CFSP	Extended until 31 Dec. 2009 by CP 2009/175/CFSP, 5 Mar. 2009
North Korea	20 Nov. 2006	CP 2006/795/CFSP	Amended by CP 2009/573/CFSP, 27 July 2009
Lebanon (NGF)	15 Sep. 2006	CP 2006/625/CFSP	
Liberia	7 May 2001	CPs 2001/357/CFSP, 2004/137/CFSP, 2005/518/CFSP	
Myanmar[g]	29 July 1991	GAC declaration, CPs 96/635/CFSP 2003/297/CFSP	Extended until 30 Apr. 2010 by CP 2009/351/CFSP, 27 Apr. 2009
Sierra Leone (NGF)	29 June 1998	CP 98/409/CFSP	
Somalia	10 Dec. 2002	CP 2002/960/CFSP	Amended by CP 2009/138/CFSP, 16 Feb. 2009
Sudan	15 Mar. 1994	CPs 94/165/CFSP, 2004/31/CFSP, 2005/411/CFSP	
Uzbekistan[h]	14 Nov. 2005	CP 2005/792/CFSP	Expired on 13 Nov. 2009
Zimbabwe	18 Feb. 2002	CP 2002/145/CFSP	Extended until 20 Feb. 2010 by CP 2009/68/CFSP, 26 Jan. 2009
Economic Community of West African States (ECOWAS) arms embargoes			
Guinea	17 Oct. 2009	ECOWAS statement	New embargo

CP = Council Common Position; GAC = General Affairs Council; NGF = non-governmental forces; UNSCR = UN Security Council Resolution.

[a] The target may have changed since the first imposition of the sanctions. The target stated here is as at the end of 2009.

[b] The earlier instruments may have been amended or repealed by subsequent instruments.

[c] UNSCR 1747, 24 Mar. 2007, calls on member states to exercise 'vigilance and restraint in the direct and indirect supply, sale or transfers to Iran of conventional arms' and placed a mandatory embargo on exports of conventional arms from Iran but does not impose a mandatory embargo on transfers of conventional arms to Iran.

[d] UNSCR 1874 calls on UN member states to exercise vigilance over the direct or indirect supply, sale or transfer to North Korea of small arms and light weapons (SALW) and obligates them to notify the relevant UN sanctions committee at least 5 days prior to selling, supplying or transferring SALW to North Korea.

[e] Liberia has been the target of UN arms embargoes since 1992, with related but different objectives. Prior to the passing of UNSCR 1903, the Sanctions Committee on Liberia could authorize exemptions from the arms embargo for transfers of arms and military equipment, technical training and assistance to the Liberian Government in accordance with UNSCR 1683, 13 June 2006.

ᶠ UNSCR 1725 exempted African Union (AU) and Intergovernmental Authority on Development (IGAD) forces present in Somalia from the arms embargo and allows them to help facilitate the re-establishment of Somali national security forces. UNSCR 1772, 20 Aug. 2007, allows more explicitly the supply of arms by states solely for the purpose of helping develop Somali security sector institutions, in the absence of a negative decision by the Sanctions Committee.

ᵍ The EU and its member states first imposed an arms embargo on Myanmar in 1990.

ʰ The General Affairs and External Relations Council decided on 27 Oct. 2009 not to renew any of the sanctions against Uzbekistan.

Sources: United Nations, 'UN Security Council Sanctions Committees', <http://www.un.org/sc/committees/>; and Council of the European Union, 'List of EU embargoes on arms exports', 16105/09, 13 Nov. 2009.

Annexes

Annex A. Arms control and disarmament agreements

Annex B. International security cooperation bodies

Annex C. Chronology 2009

Annex A. Arms control and disarmament agreements

NENNE BODELL

This annex lists multi- and bilateral treaties, conventions, protocols and agreements relating to arms control and disarmament. Unless otherwise stated, the status of agreements and of their parties and signatories is as of 1 January 2010.

Notes

1. The agreements are divided into universal treaties (i.e. multilateral treaties open to all states; section I), regional treaties (i.e. multilateral treaties open to states of a particular region; section II) and bilateral treaties (section III). Within each section the agreements are listed in the order of the date on which they were adopted, signed or opened for signature (multilateral agreements) or signed (bilateral agreements). The date on which they entered into force and the depositary for multilateral treaties are also given.

2. The main source of information is the lists of signatories and parties provided by the depositaries of the treaties. In lists of parties and signatories, states whose name appears in italics have ratified, acceded or succeeded to, or signed the agreement since 1 January 2009.

3. For some major treaties, the substantive parts of the most important reservations, declarations or interpretive statements made in connection with a state's signature, ratification, accession or succession are given in notes below the entry.

4. States and organizations listed as parties have ratified, acceded to or succeeded to the agreements. Former non-self-governing territories, upon attaining statehood, sometimes make general statements of continuity to all agreements concluded by the former governing power. This annex lists as parties only those new states that have made an uncontested declaration on continuity or have notified the depositary of their succession. The Russian Federation continues the international obligations of the Soviet Union. Serbia continues the international obligations of the State Union of Serbia and Montenegro.

5. Unless stated otherwise, the multilateral agreements listed in this annex are open to all states or to all states in the respective zone (or region) for signature, ratification, accession or succession. Not all the signatories and parties are United Nations members. Taiwan, while not recognized as a sovereign state by many countries, is listed as a party to the agreements that it has ratified.

6. Where possible, the location of an accurate copy of the treaty text is given. This may be provided by a treaty depositary, an agency or secretariat connected with the treaty, or in the *United Nation Treaty Series*. The *United Nation Treaty Series* is available online at <http://treaties.un.org/>.

I. Universal treaties

Protocol for the Prohibition of the Use in War of Asphyxiating, Poisonous or Other Gases, and of Bacteriological Methods of Warfare (1925 Geneva Protocol)

Signed at Geneva on 17 June 1925; entered into force on 8 February 1928; depositary French Government

The protocol declares that the parties agree to be bound by the prohibition on the use of these weapons in war.

Parties (137): Afghanistan, Albania, Algeria, Angola, Antigua and Barbuda, Argentina, Australia, Austria, Bahrain, Bangladesh, Barbados, Belgium, Benin, Bhutan, Bolivia, Brazil, Bulgaria, Burkina Faso, Cambodia, Cameroon, Canada, Cape Verde, Central African Republic, Chile, China, *Costa Rica*, Côte d'Ivoire, Croatia, Cuba, Cyprus, Czech Republic, Denmark, Dominican Republic, Ecuador, Egypt, Equatorial Guinea, Estonia, Ethiopia, Fiji, Finland, France, Gambia, Germany, Ghana, Greece, Grenada, Guatemala, Guinea-Bissau, Holy See, Hungary, Iceland, India, Indonesia, Iran, Iraq, Ireland, Israel, Italy, Jamaica, Japan, Jordan, Kenya, Korea (North), Korea (South), Kuwait, Laos, Latvia, Lebanon, Lesotho, Liberia, Libya, Liechtenstein, Lithuania, Luxembourg, Madagascar, Malawi, Malaysia, Maldives, Malta, Mauritius, Mexico, Monaco, Mongolia, Morocco, Nepal, Netherlands, New Zealand, Nicaragua, Niger, Nigeria, Norway, Pakistan, Panama, Papua New Guinea, Paraguay, Peru, Philippines, Poland, Portugal, Qatar, Romania, Russia, Rwanda, Saint Kitts and Nevis, Saint Lucia, Saint Vincent and the Grenadines, Saudi Arabia, Senegal, Serbia, Sierra Leone, Slovakia, Slovenia, Solomon Islands, South Africa, Spain, Sri Lanka, Sudan, Swaziland, Sweden, Switzerland, Syria, Taiwan, Tanzania, Thailand, Togo, Tonga, Trinidad and Tobago, Tunisia, Turkey, Uganda, UK, Ukraine, Uruguay, USA, Venezuela, Viet Nam, Yemen

Signed but not ratified (1): El Salvador

Note: On joining the protocol, some states entered reservations which upheld their right to employ chemical or biological weapons against non-parties to the protocol, against coalitions which included non-parties or in response to the use of these weapons by a violating party. Many of these states have withdrawn these reservations, particularly after the conclusion of the 1972 Biological and Toxin Weapons Convention and the 1993 Chemical Weapons Convention since the reservations are incompatible with their obligation under the conventions.

In addition to these, 'explicit', reservations, a number of states that made a declaration of succession to the protocol on gaining independence inherited 'implicit' reservations from their respective predecessor states. For example, these 'implicit' reservations apply to the states that gained independence from France and the UK before the latter states withdrew or amended their reservations. States that acceded (rather than succeeded) to the protocol did not inherit reservations in this way.

Protocol text: International Committee of the Red Cross, International Humanitarian Law, <http://www.icrc.org/ihl.nsf/FULL/280?OpenDocument>

Convention on the Prevention and Punishment of the Crime of Genocide (Genocide Convention)

Adopted at Paris by the UN General Assembly on 9 December 1948; entered into force on 12 January 1951; depositary UN Secretary-General

Under the convention any commission of acts intended to destroy, in whole or in part, a national, ethnic, racial or religious group as such is declared to be a crime punishable under international law.

Parties (141): Afghanistan, Albania*, Algeria*, Andorra, Antigua and Barbuda, Argentina*, Armenia, Australia, Austria, Azerbaijan, Bahamas, Bahrain*, Bangladesh*, Barbados, Belarus*, Belgium, Belize, Bolivia, Bosnia and Herzegovina, Brazil, Bulgaria*, Burkina Faso, Burundi, Cambodia, Canada, Chile, China*, Colombia, Comoros, Congo (Democratic Republic of the), Costa Rica, Côte d'Ivoire, Croatia, Cuba, Cyprus, Czech Republic, Denmark, Ecuador, Egypt, El Salvador, Estonia, Ethiopia, Fiji, Finland, France, Gabon, Gambia, Georgia, Germany, Ghana, Greece, Guatemala, Guinea, Haiti, Honduras, Hungary*, Iceland, India*, Iran, Iraq, Ireland, Israel, Italy, Jamaica, Jordan, Kazakhstan, Korea (North), Korea (South), Kuwait, Kyrgyzstan, Laos, Latvia, Lebanon, Lesotho, Liberia, Libya, Liechtenstein, Lithuania, Luxembourg, Macedonia (Former Yugoslav Republic of), Malaysia*, Maldives, Mali, Mexico, Moldova, Monaco, Mongolia*, Montenegro*, Morocco*, Mozambique, Myanmar*, Namibia, Nepal, Netherlands, New Zealand, Nicaragua, *Nigeria*, Norway, Pakistan, Panama, Papua New Guinea, Paraguay, Peru, Philippines*, Poland*, Portugal*, Romania*, Russia*, Rwanda*, Saint Vincent and the Grenadines, Saudi Arabia, Senegal, Serbia*, Seychelles, Singapore*, Slovakia, Slovenia, South Africa, Spain*, Sri Lanka, Sudan, Sweden, Switzerland, Syria, Tanzania, Togo, Tonga, Trinidad and Tobago, Tunisia, Turkey, Uganda, UK, Ukraine*, United Arab Emirates, Uruguay, USA*, Uzbekistan, Venezuela*, Viet Nam*, Yemen*, Zimbabwe

* With reservation and/or declaration.

Signed but not ratified (1): Dominican Republic

Convention text: United Nations Treaty Collection, <http://treaties.un.org/Pages/CTCTreaties.aspx?id=4>

Geneva Convention (IV) Relative to the Protection of Civilian Persons in Time of War

Signed at Geneva on 12 August 1949; entered into force on 21 October 1950; depositary Swiss Federal Council

The Geneva Convention (IV) establishes rules for the protection of civilians in areas covered by war and in occupied territories. This convention was formulated at the Diplomatic Conference held from 21 April to 12 August 1949. Other conventions adopted at the same time were: Convention (I) for the Amelioration of the Condition of the Wounded and Sick in Armed Forces in the Field; Convention (II) for the Amelioration of the Condition of the Wounded, Sick and Shipwrecked Members of Armed Forces at Sea; and Convention (III) Relative to the Treatment of Prisoners of War.

Parties (194): Afghanistan, Albania*, Algeria, Andorra, Angola*, Antigua and Barbuda, Argentina, Armenia, Australia*, Austria, Azerbaijan, Bahamas, Bahrain, Bangladesh*, Barbados*, Belarus, Belgium, Belize, Benin, Bhutan, Bolivia, Bosnia and Herzegovina, Botswana, Brazil, Brunei Darussalam, Bulgaria, Burkina Faso, Burundi, Cambodia, Cameroon, Canada, Cape Verde, Central African Republic, Chad, Chile, China*, Colombia, Comoros, Congo (Democratic Republic of the), Congo (Republic of the), Cook Islands, Costa Rica, Côte d'Ivoire, Croatia, Cuba, Cyprus, Czech Republic*, Denmark, Djibouti, Dominica, Dominican Republic, Ecuador, Egypt, El Salvador, Equatorial Guinea, Eritrea, Estonia, Ethiopia, Fiji, Finland, France, Gabon, Gambia, Georgia, Germany*, Ghana, Greece, Grenada, Guatemala, Guinea, Guinea-Bissau*, Guyana, Haiti, Holy See, Honduras, Hungary, Iceland, India, Indonesia, Iran*, Iraq, Ireland, Israel*, Italy, Jamaica, Japan, Jordan, Kazakhstan, Kenya, Kiribati, Korea (North)*, Korea (South)*, Kuwait*, Kyrgyzstan, Laos, Latvia, Lebanon, Lesotho, Liberia, Libya, Liechtenstein, Lithuania, Luxembourg, Macedonia (Former Yugoslav Republic of)*, Madagascar, Malawi, Malaysia, Maldives, Mali, Malta, Marshall Islands,

Mauritania, Mauritius, Mexico, Micronesia, Moldova, Monaco, Mongolia, Montenegro, Morocco, Mozambique, Myanmar, Namibia, Nauru, Nepal, Netherlands, New Zealand*, Nicaragua, Niger, Nigeria, Norway, Oman, Pakistan*, Palau, Panama, Papua New Guinea, Paraguay, Peru, Philippines, Poland, Portugal*, Qatar, Romania, Russia*, Rwanda, Saint Kitts and Nevis, Saint Lucia, Saint Vincent and the Grenadines, Samoa, San Marino, Sao Tome and Principe, Saudi Arabia, Senegal, Serbia, Seychelles, Sierra Leone, Singapore, Slovakia, Slovenia, Solomon Islands, Somalia, South Africa, Spain, Sri Lanka, Sudan, Suriname*, Swaziland, Sweden, Switzerland, Syria, Tajikistan, Tanzania, Thailand, Timor-Leste, Togo, Tonga, Trinidad and Tobago, Tunisia, Turkey, Turkmenistan, Tuvalu, Uganda, UK*, Ukraine*, United Arab Emirates, Uruguay*, USA*, Uzbekistan, Vanuatu, Venezuela, Viet Nam*, Yemen*, Zambia, Zimbabwe

Note: In 1989 the Palestine Liberation Organization (PLO) informed the depositary that it had decided to adhere to the four Geneva conventions and the protocols of 1977.
* With reservation and/or declaration.

Convention text: Swiss Federal Department of Foreign Affairs, <http://www.eda.admin.ch/eda/fr/home/topics/intla/intrea/chdep/warvic/gvaciv.html>

Protocol I Additional to the 1949 Geneva Conventions, and Relating to the Protection of Victims of International Armed Conflicts

Protocol II Additional to the 1949 Geneva Conventions, and Relating to the Protection of Victims of Non-International Armed Conflicts

Opened for signature at Bern on 12 December 1977; entered into force on 7 December 1978; depositary Swiss Federal Council

The protocols confirm that the right of parties that are engaged in international or non-international armed conflicts to choose methods or means of warfare is not unlimited and that the use of weapons or means of warfare that cause superfluous injury or unnecessary suffering is prohibited.

Parties to Protocol I (169) and Protocol II (165): Afghanistan, Albania, Algeria*, Angola[1]*, Antigua and Barbuda, Argentina*, Armenia, Australia*, Austria*, Bahamas, Bahrain, Bangladesh, Barbados, Belarus*, Belgium*, Belize, Benin, Bolivia*, Bosnia and Herzegovina*, Botswana, Brazil*, Brunei Darussalam, Bulgaria*, Burkina Faso*, Burundi, Cambodia, Cameroon, Canada*, Cape Verde*, Central African Republic, Chad, Chile*, China*, Colombia*, Comoros, Congo (Democratic Republic of the)*, Congo (Republic of the), Cook Islands*, Costa Rica*, Côte d'Ivoire, Croatia, Cuba, Cyprus*, Czech Republic*, Denmark*, Djibouti, Dominica, Dominican Republic, Ecuador, Egypt*, El Salvador*, Equatorial Guinea, Estonia, Ethiopia, Fiji, Finland*, France*, Gabon, Gambia, Georgia, Germany*, Ghana, Greece*, Grenada, Guatemala, Guinea*, Guinea-Bissau, Guyana, Haiti, Holy See, Honduras, Hungary*, Iceland*, Ireland*, Italy*, Jamaica, Japan*, Jordan, Kazakhstan, Kenya, Korea (North)[1], Korea (South)*, Kuwait, Kyrgyzstan, Laos*, Latvia, Lebanon, Lesotho, Liberia, Libya, Liechtenstein*, Lithuania*, Luxembourg*, Macedonia (Former Yugoslav Republic of)*, Madagascar*, Malawi, Maldives, Mali*, Malta*, Mauritania, Mauritius*, Mexico[1], Micronesia, Moldova, Monaco, Mongolia*, Montenegro, Mozambique, Namibia*, Nauru, Netherlands*, New Zealand*, Nicaragua, Niger, Nigeria, Norway*, Oman, Palau, Panama*, Paraguay*, Peru, Philippines[2], Poland*, Portugal*, Qatar*,

Romania*, Russia*, Rwanda*, Saint Kitts and Nevis, Saint Lucia, Saint Vincent and the Grenadines, Samoa, San Marino, Sao Tome and Principe, Saudi Arabia*, Senegal, Serbia*, Seychelles*, Sierra Leone, Slovakia*, Slovenia*, Solomon Islands, South Africa, Spain*, Sudan, Suriname, Swaziland, Sweden*, Switzerland*, Syria*[1], Tajikistan*, Tanzania, Timor-Leste, Togo*, Tonga*, Trinidad and Tobago*, Tunisia, Turkmenistan, Uganda, UK*, Ukraine*, United Arab Emirates*, Uruguay*, Uzbekistan, Vanuatu, Venezuela, Viet Nam[1], Yemen, Zambia, Zimbabwe

* With reservation and/or declaration.
[1] Party only to Protocol I.
[2] Party only to Protocol II.

Protocol texts: Swiss Federal Department of Foreign Affairs, <http://www.eda.admin. ch/eda/fr/home/topics/intla/intrea/chdep/warvic.html>

Antarctic Treaty

Signed at Washington, DC, on 1 December 1959; entered into force on 23 June 1961; depositary US Government

The treaty declares the Antarctic an area to be used exclusively for peaceful purposes. It prohibits any measure of a military nature in the Antarctic, such as the establishment of military bases and fortifications, and the carrying out of military manoeuvres or the testing of any type of weapon. The treaty bans any nuclear explosion as well as the disposal of radioactive waste material in Antarctica. The treaty provides a right of on-site inspection of all stations and installations in Antarctica to ensure compliance with its provisions.

In accordance with Article IX, consultative meetings are convened at regular intervals to exchange information and hold consultations on matters pertaining to Antarctica, as well as to recommend to the governments measures in furtherance of the principles and objectives of the treaty.

The treaty is open for accession by UN members or by other states invited to accede with the consent of all the parties entitled to participate in the consultative meetings provided for in Article IX. States demonstrating their interest in Antarctica by conducting substantial scientific research activity there, such as the establishment of a scientific station or the despatch of a scientific expedition, are entitled to become consultative members.

Parties (47): Argentina[†], Australia[†], Austria, Belarus, Belgium[†], Brazil[†], Bulgaria[†], Canada, Chile[†], China[†], Colombia, Cuba, Czech Republic, Denmark, Ecuador[†], Estonia, Finland[†], France[†], Germany[†], Greece, Guatemala, Hungary, India[†], Italy[†], Japan[†], Korea (North), Korea (South)[†], Monaco, Netherlands[†], New Zealand[†], Norway[†], Papua New Guinea, Peru[†], Poland[†], Romania, Russia[†], Slovakia, South Africa[†], Spain[†], Sweden[†], Switzerland, Turkey, UK[†], Ukraine[†], Uruguay[†], USA[†], Venezuela

[†] This state is a consultative member under Article IX of the treaty.

Treaty text: Secretariat of the Antarctic Treaty, <http://www.ats.aq/e/ats_treaty.htm>

The Protocol on Environmental Protection (**1991 Madrid Protocol**) entered into force on 14 January 1998.

Protocol text: Secretariat of the Antarctic Treaty, <http://www.ats.aq/e/ats_protocol.htm>

Treaty Banning Nuclear Weapon Tests in the Atmosphere, in Outer Space and Under Water (Partial Test-Ban Treaty, PTBT)

Signed at Moscow by three original parties on 5 August 1963 and opened for signature by other states at London, Moscow and Washington, DC, on 8 August 1963; entered into force on 10 October 1963; depositaries British, Russian and US governments

The treaty prohibits the carrying out of any nuclear weapon test explosion or any other nuclear explosion: (*a*) in the atmosphere, beyond its limits, including outer space, or under water, including territorial waters or high seas; and (*b*) in any other environment if such explosion causes radioactive debris to be present outside the territorial limits of the state under whose jurisdiction or control the explosion is conducted.

Parties (125): Afghanistan, Antigua and Barbuda, Argentina, Armenia, Australia, Austria, Bahamas, Bangladesh, Belarus, Belgium, Benin, Bhutan, Bolivia, Bosnia and Herzegovina, Botswana, Brazil, Bulgaria, Canada, Cape Verde, Central African Republic, Chad, Chile, Colombia, Congo (Democratic Republic of the), Costa Rica, Côte d'Ivoire, Croatia, Cyprus, Czech Republic, Denmark, Dominican Republic, Ecuador, Egypt, El Salvador, Equatorial Guinea, Fiji, Finland, Gabon, Gambia, Germany, Ghana, Greece, Guatemala, Guinea-Bissau, Honduras, Hungary, Iceland, India, Indonesia, Iran, Iraq, Ireland, Israel, Italy, Jamaica, Japan, Jordan, Kenya, Korea (South), Kuwait, Laos, Lebanon, Liberia, Libya, Luxembourg, Madagascar, Malawi, Malaysia, Malta, Mauritania, Mauritius, Mexico, Mongolia, Morocco, Myanmar, Nepal, Netherlands, New Zealand, Nicaragua, Niger, Nigeria, Norway, Pakistan, Panama, Papua New Guinea, Peru, Philippines, Poland, Romania, Russia, Rwanda, Samoa, San Marino, Senegal, Serbia, Seychelles, Sierra Leone, Singapore, Slovakia, Slovenia, South Africa, Spain, Sri Lanka, Sudan, Suriname, Swaziland, Sweden, Switzerland, Syria, Taiwan, Tanzania, Thailand, Togo, Tonga, Trinidad and Tobago, Tunisia, Turkey, Uganda, UK, Ukraine, Uruguay, USA, Venezuela, Yemen, Zambia

Signed but not ratified (11): Algeria, Burkina Faso, Burundi, Cameroon, Ethiopia, Haiti, Mali, Paraguay, Portugal, Somalia, Viet Nam

Treaty text: United Nations Treaty Series, vol. 480 (1963)

Treaty on Principles Governing the Activities of States in the Exploration and Use of Outer Space, Including the Moon and Other Celestial Bodies (Outer Space Treaty)

Opened for signature at London, Moscow and Washington, DC, on 27 January 1967; entered into force on 10 October 1967; depositaries British, Russian and US governments

The treaty prohibits the placing into orbit around the earth of any object carrying nuclear weapons or any other kind of weapons of mass destruction, the installation of such weapons on celestial bodies, or the stationing of them in outer space in any other manner. The establishment of military bases, installations and fortifications, the testing of any type of weapons and the conduct of military manoeuvres on celestial bodies are also forbidden.

Parties (108): Afghanistan, Algeria, Antigua and Barbuda, Argentina, Australia, Austria, Bahamas, Bangladesh, Barbados, Belarus, Belgium, Benin, Brazil, Brunei Darussalam,

Bulgaria, Burkina Faso, Canada, Chile, China, Cuba, Cyprus, Czech Republic, Denmark, Dominica, Dominican Republic, Ecuador, Egypt, El Salvador, Equatorial Guinea, Fiji, Finland, France, Germany, Greece, Grenada, Guinea-Bissau, Hungary, Iceland, India, Indonesia, Iraq, Ireland, Israel, Italy, Jamaica, Japan, Kazakhstan, Kenya, Korea (South), Kuwait, Laos, Lebanon, Libya, Luxembourg, Madagascar, Mali, Mauritius, Mexico, Mongolia, Montenegro, Morocco, Myanmar, Nepal, Netherlands, New Zealand, Niger, Nigeria, Norway, Pakistan, Papua New Guinea, Peru, Poland, Portugal, Romania, Russia, Saint Kitts and Nevis, Saint Lucia, Saint Vincent and the Grenadines, San Marino, Saudi Arabia, Seychelles, Sierra Leone, Singapore, Slovakia, Solomon Islands, South Africa, Spain, Sri Lanka, Swaziland, Sweden, Switzerland, Syria, Taiwan, Thailand, Togo, Tonga, Tunisia, Turkey, Uganda, UK, Ukraine, United Arab Emirates, Uruguay, USA, Venezuela, Viet Nam, Yemen, Zambia

Signed but not ratified (27): Bolivia, Botswana, Burundi, Cameroon, Central African Republic, Colombia, Congo (Democratic Republic of the), Congo (Republic of the), Ethiopia, Gambia, Ghana, Guyana, Haiti, Holy See, Honduras, Iran, Jordan, Lesotho, Macedonia (Former Yugoslav Republic of), Malaysia, Nicaragua, Panama, Philippines, Rwanda, Serbia, Somalia, Trinidad and Tobago

Treaty text: United Nations Treaty Series, vol. 610 (1967)

Treaty on the Non-Proliferation of Nuclear Weapons (Non-Proliferation Treaty, NPT)

Opened for signature at London, Moscow and Washington, DC, on 1 July 1968; entered into force on 5 March 1970; depositaries British, Russian and US governments

The treaty prohibits the transfer by a nuclear weapon state—defined in the treaty as those which have manufactured and exploded a nuclear weapon or other nuclear explosive device prior to 1 January 1967—to any recipient whatsoever of nuclear weapons or other nuclear explosive devices or of control over them, as well as the assistance, encouragement or inducement of any non-nuclear weapon state to manufacture or otherwise acquire such weapons or devices. It also prohibits the receipt by non-nuclear weapon states from any transferor whatsoever, as well as the manufacture or other acquisition by those states, of nuclear weapons or other nuclear explosive devices.

The parties undertake to facilitate the exchange of equipment, materials and scientific and technological information for the peaceful uses of nuclear energy and to ensure that potential benefits from peaceful applications of nuclear explosions will be made available to non-nuclear weapon parties to the treaty. They also undertake to pursue negotiations in good faith on effective measures relating to cessation of the nuclear arms race at an early date and to nuclear disarmament, and on a treaty on general and complete disarmament.

Non-nuclear weapon states undertake to conclude safeguard agreements with the International Atomic Energy Agency (IAEA) with a view to preventing diversion of nuclear energy from peaceful uses to nuclear weapons or other nuclear explosive devices. A Model Protocol Additional to the Safeguards Agreements, strengthening the measures, was approved in 1997; Additional Safeguards Protocols are signed by states individually with the IAEA.

A Review and Extension Conference, convened in 1995 in accordance with the treaty, decided that the treaty should remain in force indefinitely.

Parties (190): Afghanistan[†], Albania[†], Algeria[†], Andorra, Angola, Antigua and Barbuda[†], Argentina[†], Armenia[†], Australia[†], Austria[†], Azerbaijan[†], Bahamas[†], Bahrain, Bangladesh[†], Barbados[†], Belarus[†], Belgium[†], Belize[†], Benin, Bhutan[†], Bolivia[†], Bosnia and Herzegovina[†], Botswana, Brazil[†], Brunei Darussalam[†], Bulgaria[†], Burkina Faso[†], Burundi, Cambodia[†], Cameroon[†], Canada[†], Cape Verde, Central African Republic, Chad, Chile[†], China[†], Colombia, Comoros, Congo (Democratic Republic of the)[†], Congo (Republic of the), Costa Rica[†], Côte d'Ivoire[†], Croatia[†], Cuba[†], Cyprus[†], Czech Republic[†], Denmark[†], Djibouti, Dominica[†], Dominican Republic[†], Ecuador[†], Egypt[†], El Salvador[†], Equatorial Guinea, Eritrea, Estonia[†], Ethiopia[†], Fiji[†], Finland[†], France[†], Gabon, Gambia[†], Georgia, Germany[†], Ghana[†], Greece[†], Grenada[†], Guatemala[†], Guinea, Guinea-Bissau, Guyana[†], Haiti, Holy See[†], Honduras[†], Hungary[†], Iceland[†], Indonesia[†], Iran[†], Iraq[†], Ireland[†], Italy[†], Jamaica[†], Japan[†], Jordan[†], Kazakhstan[†], Kenya, Kiribati[†], Korea (South)[†], Kuwait[†], Kyrgyzstan[†], Laos[†], Latvia[†], Lebanon[†], Lesotho[†], Liberia, Libya[†], Liechtenstein[†], Lithuania[†], Luxembourg[†], Macedonia[†] (Former Yugoslav Republic of), Madagascar[†], Malawi[†], Malaysia[†], Maldives[†], Mali[†], Malta[†], Marshall Islands, Mauritania, Mauritius[†], Mexico[†], Micronesia, Moldova, Monaco[†], Mongolia[†], Montenegro, Morocco[†], Mozambique, Myanmar[†], Namibia[†], Nauru[†], Nepal[†], Netherlands[†], New Zealand[†], Nicaragua[†], Niger, Nigeria[†], Norway[†], Oman, Palau, Panama, Papua New Guinea[†], Paraguay[†], Peru[†], Philippines[†], Poland[†], Portugal[†], Qatar, Romania[†], Russia[†], Rwanda, Saint Kitts and Nevis[†], Saint Lucia[†], Saint Vincent and the Grenadines[†], Samoa[†], San Marino[†], Sao Tome and Principe, Saudi Arabia, Senegal[†], Serbia[†], Seychelles[†], Sierra Leone, Singapore[†], Slovakia[†], Slovenia[†], Solomon Islands[†], Somalia, South Africa[†], Spain[†], Sri Lanka[†], Sudan[†], Suriname[†], Swaziland[†], Sweden[†], Switzerland[†], Syria[†], Taiwan, Tajikistan[†], Tanzania[†], Thailand[†], Timor-Leste, Togo, Tonga[†], Trinidad and Tobago[†], Tunisia[†], Turkey[†], Turkmenistan, Tuvalu[†], Uganda, UK[†], Ukraine[†], United Arab Emirates[†], Uruguay[†], USA[†], Uzbekistan[†], Vanuatu, Venezuela[†], Viet Nam[†], Yemen[†], Zambia[†], Zimbabwe[†]

[†] Party with safeguards agreements in force with the IAEA, as required by the treaty, or concluded by a nuclear weapon state, as defined in the treaty, on a voluntary basis.

Treaty text: International Atomic Energy Agency, INFCIRC/140, 22 Apr. 1970, <http://www.iaea.org/Publications/Documents/Treaties/npt.html>

Additional Safeguards Protocols in force (93): Afghanistan, Armenia, Australia, Austria, Azerbaijan, Bangladesh, Belgium, Botswana, Bulgaria, Burkina Faso, Burundi, Canada, *Central African Republic*, Chile, China, *Colombia*, Comoros, Congo (Democratic Republic of the), Croatia, Cuba, Cyprus, Czech Republic, Denmark, Ecuador, El Salvador, Estonia, Fiji, Finland, France, Georgia, Germany, Ghana, Greece, Guatemala, Haiti, Holy See, Hungary, Iceland, Indonesia, Ireland, Italy, Jamaica, Japan, Jordan, Kazakhstan, Korea (South), Kuwait, Latvia, Libya, Lithuania, Luxembourg, Macedonia (Former Yugoslav Republic of), Madagascar, Malawi, Mali, Malta, Marshall Islands, *Mauritania*, Mauritius, Monaco, Mongolia, Netherlands, New Zealand, Nicaragua, Niger, Nigeria, Norway, Palau, Panama, Paraguay, Peru, Poland, Portugal, Romania, Russia, Seychelles, Singapore, Slovakia, Slovenia, South Africa, Spain, Sweden, Switzerland, Tajikistan, Tanzania, Turkey, Turkmenistan, Uganda, UK, Ukraine, Uruguay, *USA*, Uzbekistan

Notes: On 6 Feb. 2007 Iran informed the IAEA that it would no longer act in accordance with the provisions of its unratified Additional Safeguards Protocol. Taiwan, although it has not concluded a safeguards agreement, has agreed to apply the measures contained in the 1997 Model Additional Safeguards Protocol.

Model Additional Safeguards Protocol text: International Atomic Energy Agency, INFCIRC/540 (corrected), Sep. 1997, <http://www.iaea.org/OurWork/SV/Safeguards/sg_protocol.html>

Treaty on the Prohibition of the Employment of Nuclear Weapons and other Weapons of Mass Destruction on the Seabed and the Ocean Floor and in the Subsoil thereof (Seabed Treaty)

Opened for signature at London, Moscow and Washington, DC, on 11 February 1971; entered into force on 18 May 1972; depositaries British, Russian and US governments

The treaty prohibits implanting or emplacing on the seabed and the ocean floor and in the subsoil thereof beyond the outer limit of a 12-mile (19-kilometre) seabed zone any nuclear weapons or any other types of weapons of mass destruction as well as structures, launching installations or any other facilities specifically designed for storing, testing or using such weapons.

Parties (97): Afghanistan, Algeria, Antigua and Barbuda, Argentina, Australia, Austria, Bahamas, Belarus, Belgium, Benin, Bosnia and Herzegovina, Botswana, Brazil[1], Bulgaria, Canada[2], Cape Verde, Central African Republic, China, Congo (Republic of the), Côte d'Ivoire, Croatia, Cuba, Cyprus, Czech Republic, Denmark, Dominican Republic, Equatorial Guinea, Ethiopia, Finland, Germany, Ghana, Greece, Guatemala, Guinea-Bissau, Hungary, Iceland, India[3], Iran, Iraq, Ireland, Italy[4], Jamaica, Japan, Jordan, Korea (South), Laos, Latvia, Lesotho, Libya, Liechtenstein, Luxembourg, Malaysia, Malta, Mauritius, Mexico[5], Mongolia, Montenegro, Morocco, Nepal, Netherlands, New Zealand, Nicaragua, Niger, Norway, Panama, Philippines, Poland, Portugal, Qatar, Romania, Russia, Rwanda, Saint Kitts and Nevis, Saint Vincent and the Grenadines, Sao Tome and Principe, Saudi Arabia, Serbia[6], Seychelles, Singapore, Slovakia, Slovenia, Solomon Islands, South Africa, Spain, Swaziland, Sweden, Switzerland, Taiwan, Togo, Tunisia, Turkey[7], UK, Ukraine, USA, Viet Nam[8], Yemen, Zambia

[1] It is the understanding of Brazil that the word 'observation', as it appears in para. 1 of Article III of the treaty, refers only to observation that is incidental to the normal course of navigation in accordance with international law.

[2] Canada declared that Article I, para. 1, cannot be interpreted as indicating that any state has a right to implant or emplace any weapons not prohibited under Article I, para. 1, on the seabed and ocean floor, and in the subsoil thereof, beyond the limits of national jurisdiction, or as constituting any limitation on the principle that this area of the seabed and ocean floor and the subsoil thereof shall be reserved for exclusively peaceful purposes. Articles I, II and III cannot be interpreted as indicating that any state but the coastal state has any right to implant or emplace any weapon not prohibited under Article I, para. 1 on the continental shelf, or the subsoil thereof, appertaining to that coastal state, beyond the outer limit of the seabed zone referred to in Article I and defined in Article II. Article III cannot be interpreted as indicating any restrictions or limitation upon the rights of the coastal state, consistent with its exclusive sovereign rights with respect to the continental shelf, to verify, inspect or effect the removal of any weapon, structure, installation, facility or device implanted or emplaced on the continental shelf, or the subsoil thereof, appertaining to that coastal state, beyond the outer limit of the seabed zone referred to in Article I and defined in Article II.

[3] The accession by India is based on its position that it has full and exclusive rights over the continental shelf adjoining its territory and beyond its territorial waters and the subsoil thereof. There cannot, therefore, be any restriction on, or limitation of, the sovereign right of India as a coastal state to verify, inspect, remove or destroy any weapon, device, structure, installation or facility, which might be implanted or emplaced on or beneath its continental shelf by any other country, or to take such other steps as may be considered necessary to safeguard its security.

[4] Italy stated, inter alia, that in the case of agreements on further measures in the field of disarmament to prevent an arms race on the seabed and ocean floor and in their subsoil, the question of the delimitation of the area within which these measures would find application shall have to be examined and solved in each instance in accordance with the nature of the measures to be adopted.

[5] Mexico declared that the treaty cannot be interpreted to mean that a state has the right to emplace weapons of mass destruction, or arms or military equipment of any type, on the continental shelf of Mexico. It reserves the right to verify, inspect, remove or destroy any weapon, structure,

installation, device or equipment placed on its continental shelf, including nuclear weapons or other weapons of mass destruction.

[6] In 1974 the Ambassador of Yugoslavia transmitted to the US Secretary of State a note stating that in the view of the Yugoslav Government, Article III, para. 1, of the treaty should be interpreted in such a way that a state exercising its right under this article shall be obliged to notify in advance the coastal state, in so far as its observations are to be carried out 'within the stretch of the sea extending above the continental shelf of the said state'. The USA objected to the Yugoslav reservation, which it considered incompatible with the object and purpose of the treaty.

[7] Turkey declared that the provisions of Article II cannot be used by a state party in support of claims other than those related to disarmament. Hence, Article II cannot be interpreted as establishing a link with the UN Convention on the Law of the Sea. Furthermore, no provision of the Seabed Treaty confers on parties the right to militarize zones which have been demilitarized by other international instruments. Nor can it be interpreted as conferring on either the coastal states or other states the right to emplace nuclear weapons or other weapons of mass destruction on the continental shelf of a demilitarized territory.

[8] Viet Nam stated that no provision of the treaty should be interpreted in a way that would contradict the rights of the coastal states with regard to their continental shelf, including the right to take measures to ensure their security.

Signed but not ratified (20): Bolivia, Burundi, Cambodia, Cameroon, Colombia, Costa Rica, Gambia, Guinea, Honduras, Lebanon, Liberia, Madagascar, Mali, Myanmar, Paraguay, Senegal, Sierra Leone, Sudan, Tanzania, Uruguay

Treaty text: *United Nations Treaty Series*, vol. 955 (1974)

Convention on the Prohibition of the Development, Production and Stockpiling of Bacteriological (Biological) and Toxin Weapons and on their Destruction (Biological and Toxin Weapons Convention, BTWC)

Opened for signature at London, Moscow and Washington, DC, on 10 April 1972; entered into force on 26 March 1975; depositaries British, Russian and US governments

The convention prohibits the development, production, stockpiling or acquisition by other means or retention of microbial or other biological agents or toxins whatever their origin or method of production of types and in quantities that have no justification of prophylactic, protective or other peaceful purposes, as well as weapons, equipment or means of delivery designed to use such agents or toxins for hostile purposes or in armed conflict. The destruction of the agents, toxins, weapons, equipment and means of delivery in the possession of the parties, or their diversion to peaceful purposes, should be effected not later than nine months after the entry into force of the convention for each country. The parties hold annual political and technical meetings to strengthen implementation of the convention. The Seventh Review Conference, to be held in 2011, will consider whether and how to implement further measures to strengthen the regime.

Parties (164): Afghanistan, Albania, Algeria, Antigua and Barbuda, Argentina, Armenia, Australia, Austria*, Azerbaijan, Bahamas, Bahrain*, Bangladesh, Barbados, Belarus, Belgium, Belize, Benin, Bhutan, Bolivia, Bosnia and Herzegovina, Botswana, Brazil, Brunei Darussalam, Bulgaria, Burkina Faso, Cambodia, Canada, Cape Verde, Chile, China*, Colombia, Congo (Democratic Republic of the), Congo (Republic of the), Cook Islands, Costa Rica, Croatia, Cuba, Cyprus, Czech Republic*, Denmark, Dominica, Dominican Republic, Ecuador, El Salvador, Equatorial Guinea, Estonia, Ethiopia, Fiji, Finland, France, Gabon, Gambia, Georgia,

Germany, Ghana, Greece, Grenada, Guatemala, Guinea-Bissau, Holy See, Honduras, Hungary, Iceland, India*, Indonesia, Iran, Iraq, Ireland*, Italy, Jamaica, Japan, Jordan, Kazakhstan, Kenya, Korea (North), Korea (South)*, Kuwait*, Kyrgyzstan, Laos, Latvia, Lebanon, Lesotho, Libya, Liechtenstein, Lithuania, Luxembourg, Macedonia (Former Yugoslav Republic of), Madagascar, Malaysia*, Maldives, Mali, Malta, Mauritius, Mexico*, Moldova, Monaco, Mongolia, Montenegro, Morocco, Netherlands, New Zealand, Nicaragua, Niger, Nigeria, Norway, Oman, Pakistan, Palau, Panama, Papua New Guinea, Paraguay, Peru, Philippines, Poland, Portugal, Qatar, Romania, Russia, Rwanda, Saint Kitts and Nevis, Saint Lucia, Saint Vincent and the Grenadines, San Marino, Sao Tome and Principe, Saudi Arabia, Senegal, Serbia, Seychelles, Sierra Leone, Singapore, Slovakia*, Slovenia, Solomon Islands, South Africa, Spain, Sri Lanka, Sudan, Suriname, Swaziland, Sweden, Switzerland*, Taiwan, Tajikistan, Thailand, Timor-Leste, Togo, Tonga, Trinidad and Tobago, Tunisia, Turkey, Turkmenistan, Uganda, UK*, Ukraine, United Arab Emirates, Uruguay, USA, Uzbekistan, Vanuatu, Venezuela, Viet Nam, Yemen, Zambia, Zimbabwe

* With reservation and/or declaration.

Signed but not ratified (13): Burundi, Central African Republic, Côte d'Ivoire, Egypt, Guyana, Haiti, Liberia, Malawi, Myanmar, Nepal, Somalia, Syria, Tanzania

Treaty text: *United Nations Treaty Series*, vol. 1015 (1976)

Convention on the Prohibition of Military or Any Other Hostile Use of Environmental Modification Techniques (Enmod Convention)

Opened for signature at Geneva on 18 May 1977; entered into force on 5 October 1978; depositary UN Secretary-General

The convention prohibits military or any other hostile use of environmental modification techniques having widespread, long-lasting or severe effects as the means of destruction, damage or injury to states party to the convention. The term 'environmental modification techniques' refers to any technique for changing—through the deliberate manipulation of natural processes—the dynamics, composition or structure of the earth, including its biota, lithosphere, hydrosphere and atmosphere, or of outer space. The understandings reached during the negotiations, but not written into the convention, define the terms 'widespread', 'long-lasting' and 'severe'.

Parties (73): Afghanistan, Algeria, Antigua and Barbuda, Argentina, Armenia, Australia, Austria, Bangladesh, Belarus, Belgium, Benin, Brazil, Bulgaria, Canada, Cape Verde, Chile, China*, Costa Rica, Cuba, Cyprus, Czech Republic, Denmark, Dominica, Egypt, Finland, Germany, Ghana, Greece, Guatemala, Hungary, India, Ireland, Italy, Japan, Kazakhstan, Korea (North), Korea (South)*, Kuwait, Lithuania, Laos, Malawi, Mauritius, Mongolia, Netherlands*, New Zealand, Nicaragua, Niger, Norway, Pakistan, Panama, Papua New Guinea, Poland, Romania, Russia, Saint Lucia, Saint Vincent and the Grenadines, Sao Tome and Principe, Slovakia, Slovenia, Solomon Islands, Spain, Sri Lanka, Sweden, Switzerland, Tajikistan, Tunisia, UK, Ukraine, Uruguay, USA, Uzbekistan, Viet Nam, Yemen

* With declaration.

Signed but not ratified (16): Bolivia, Congo (Democratic Republic of the), Ethiopia, Holy See, Iceland, Iran, Iraq, Lebanon, Liberia, Luxembourg, Morocco, Portugal, Sierra Leone, Syria, Turkey, Uganda

Convention text: United Nations Treaty Collection, <http://treaties.un.org/Pages/CTCTreaties. aspx?id=26>

Convention on the Physical Protection of Nuclear Material and Nuclear Facilities

Original convention opened for signature at New York and Vienna on 3 March 1980; entered into force on 8 February 1987; convention amended in 2005; depositary IAEA Director General

The amended convention obligates the parties to protect nuclear facilities and material used for peaceful purposes while in storage as well as transport. The amendments will take effect 30 days after they have been ratified, accepted or approved by two-thirds of the states parties to the convention.

Parties to the original convention (142): Afghanistan, Albania, Algeria*, Andorra*, Antigua and Barbuda, Argentina*, Armenia, Australia, Austria*, Azerbaijan*, Bahamas, Bangladesh, Belarus, Belgium*, Bolivia, Bosnia and Herzegovina, Botswana, Brazil, Bulgaria, Burkina Faso, Cambodia, Cameroon, Canada, Cape Verde, Central African Republic, Chile, China*, Colombia, Comoros, Congo (Democratic Republic of the), Costa Rica, Croatia, Cuba*, Cyprus*, Czech Republic, Denmark, Djibouti, Dominica, *Dominican Republic*, Ecuador, El Salvador*, Equatorial Guinea, Estonia, Euratom*, Fiji, Finland*, France*, Gabon, Georgia, Germany, Ghana, Greece*, Grenada, Guatemala*, Guinea, Guinea-Bissau, Guyana, Honduras, Hungary, Iceland, India*, Indonesia*, Ireland*, Israel*, Italy*, Jamaica, Japan, *Jordan*, Kazakhstan, Kenya, Korea (South)*, Kuwait*, Latvia, Lebanon, Libya, Liechtenstein, Lithuania, Luxembourg*, Macedonia (Former Yugoslav Republic of), Madagascar, Mali, Malta, Marshall Islands, Mauritania, Mexico, Moldova, Monaco, Mongolia, Montenegro, Morocco, Mozambique*, Namibia, Nauru, Netherlands*, New Zealand, Nicaragua, Niger, Nigeria, *Niue*, Norway*, Oman*, Pakistan*, Palau, Panama, Paraguay, Peru*, Philippines, Poland, Portugal*, Qatar*, Romania*, Russia*, Rwanda, Saint Kitts and Nevis, *Saudi Arabia*, Senegal, Serbia, Seychelles, Slovakia, Slovenia, South Africa*, Spain*, Sudan, Swaziland, Sweden*, Switzerland*, Tajikistan, Tanzania, Togo, Tonga, Trinidad and Tobago, Tunisia, Turkey*, Turkmenistan, Uganda, UK*, Ukraine, United Arab Emirates, Uruguay, USA, Uzbekistan, Yemen

   * With reservation and/or declaration.

Signed but not ratified (1): Haiti

Convention text: International Atomic Energy Agency, INFCIRC/274/Rev.1, May 1980, <http://www.iaea.org/Publications/Documents/Conventions/cppnm.html>

Ratifications, acceptances or approvals of the amended convention deposited (33): Algeria, *Antigua and Barbuda*, Australia, Austria, Bulgaria, *Chile, China*, Croatia, *Estonia*, Fiji, Gabon, Hungary, India, *Jordan*, Kenya, Libya, *Liechtenstein, Lithuania*, Mauritania, Moldova, *Niger*, Nigeria, *Norway*, Poland, Romania, Russia, Seychelles, *Slovenia*, Spain, Switzerland, Turkmenistan, Ukraine, *United Arab Emirates*

Amendment text: International Atomic Energy Agency, Board of Governors, GOV/INF/2005/10-GC(49)/INF/6, 6 Sep. 2005, <http://www.iaea.org/Publications/Documents/Conventions/cppnm.html>

Convention on Prohibitions or Restrictions on the Use of Certain Conventional Weapons which may be Deemed to be Excessively Injurious or to have Indiscriminate Effects (CCW Convention, or 'Inhumane Weapons' Convention)

The convention, with protocols I, II and III, opened for signature at New York on 10 April 1981; entered into force on 2 December 1983; depositary UN Secretary-General

The convention is an 'umbrella treaty', under which specific agreements can be concluded in the form of protocols. In order to become a party to the convention a state must ratify at least two of the protocols.

The amendment to Article I of the original convention was opened for signature at Geneva on 21 November 2001. It expands the scope of application to non-international armed conflicts. The amended convention entered into force on 18 May 2004.

Protocol I prohibits the use of weapons intended to injure by fragments which are not detectable in the human body by X-rays.

Protocol II prohibits or restricts the use of mines, booby-traps and other devices.

Amended Protocol II, which entered into force on 3 December 1998, reinforces the constraints regarding anti-personnel mines.

Protocol III restricts the use of incendiary weapons.

Protocol IV, which entered into force on 30 July 1998, prohibits the employment of laser weapons specifically designed to cause permanent blindness to unenhanced vision.

Protocol V, which entered into force on 12 November 2006, recognizes the need for measures of a generic nature to minimize the risks and effects of explosive remnants of war.

Parties to the original convention and protocols (111): Albania, Argentina*, Australia, Austria, Bangladesh, Belarus, Belgium, Benin[1], Bolivia, Bosnia and Herzegovina, Brazil, Bulgaria, Burkina Faso, Cambodia, Cameroon, Canada*, Cape Verde, Chile[1], China*, Colombia, Costa Rica, Croatia, Cuba, Cyprus*, Czech Republic, Denmark, Djibouti, Ecuador, El Salvador, Estonia[1], Finland, France*, Gabon[1], Georgia, Germany, Greece, Guatemala, Guinea-Bissau, Holy See*, Honduras, Hungary, Iceland, India, Ireland, Israel*[2], Italy*, Jamaica[1], Japan, Jordan[1], *Kazakhstan*[1], Korea (South)[3], Laos, Latvia, Lesotho, Liberia, Liechtenstein, Lithuania[1], Luxembourg, Macedonia (Former Yugoslav Republic of), Madagascar, Maldives[1], Mali, Malta, Mauritius, Mexico, Moldova, Monaco[3], Mongolia, Montenegro, Morocco[4], Nauru, Netherlands*, New Zealand, Nicaragua[1], Niger, Norway, Pakistan, Panama, Paraguay, Peru[1], Philippines, Poland, Portugal, *Qatar*[1], Romania*, Russia, Saudi Arabia[1], Senegal[5], Serbia, Seychelles, Sierra Leone[1], Slovakia, Slovenia, South Africa, Spain, Sri Lanka, Sweden, Switzerland, Tajikistan, Togo, Tunisia, Turkey*[3], Turkmenistan[2], Uganda, UK*, Ukraine, *United Arab Emirates*[1], Uruguay, USA*, Uzbekistan, Venezuela

* With reservation and/or declaration.
[1] Party only to 1981 Protocols I and III.
[2] Party only to 1981 Protocols I and II.
[3] Party only to 1981 Protocol I.
[4] Party only to 1981 Protocol II.
[5] Party only to 1981 Protocol III.

Signed but not ratified the original convention and protocols (5): Afghanistan, Egypt, Nigeria, Sudan, Viet Nam

Parties to the amended convention and original protocols (72): Albania, Argentina, Australia, Austria, Belarus, Belgium, Bosnia and Herzegovina, Bulgaria, Burkina Faso, Canada, Chile, China, *Colombia, Costa Rica*, Croatia, Cuba, Czech Republic, Denmark, *Ecuador*, El Salvador, Estonia, Finland, France, *Georgia*, Germany, Greece, *Guatemala*, Guinea-Bissau, Holy See*, Hungary, Iceland, India, Ireland, Italy, Jamaica, Japan, Korea (South), Latvia, Liberia, Liechtenstein, Lithuania, Luxembourg, Macedonia (Former Yugoslav Republic of), Malta, Mexico*, Moldova, Montenegro, Netherlands, Nicaragua, Niger, Norway, Panama, Paraguay, Peru, Poland, Portugal, Romania, Russia, Serbia, Sierra Leone, Slovakia, Slovenia, Spain, Sri Lanka, Sweden, Switzerland, *Tunisia*, Turkey, UK, Ukraine, *Uruguay, USA*

* With reservation and/or declaration.

Parties to Amended Protocol II (93): Albania, Argentina, Australia, Austria*, Bangladesh, Belarus*, Belgium*, Bolivia, Bosnia and Herzegovina, Brazil, Bulgaria, Burkina Faso, Cambodia, Cameroon, Canada, Cape Verde, Chile, China*, Colombia, Costa Rica, Croatia, Cyprus, Czech Republic, Denmark*, Ecuador, El Salvador, Estonia, Finland*, France*, *Georgia*, Germany*, Greece*, Guatemala, Guinea-Bissau, Holy See, Honduras, Hungary*, Iceland, India, Ireland*, Israel*, Italy*, Jamaica, Japan, Jordan, Korea (South)*, Latvia, Liberia, Liechtenstein*, Lithuania, Luxembourg, Macedonia (Former Yugoslav Republic of), Madagascar, Maldives, Mali, Malta, Moldova, Monaco, Morocco, Nauru, Netherlands*, New Zealand, Nicaragua, Niger, Norway, Pakistan*, Panama, Paraguay, Peru, Philippines, Poland, Portugal, Romania, Russia*, Senegal, Seychelles, Sierra Leone, Slovakia, Slovenia, South Africa*, Spain, Sri Lanka, Sweden, Switzerland, Tajikistan, Tunisia, Turkey, Turkmenistan, UK*, Ukraine*, Uruguay, USA*, Venezuela

* With reservation and/or declaration.

Parties to Protocol IV (96): Albania, Argentina, Australia*, Austria*, Bangladesh, Belarus, Belgium*, Bolivia, Bosnia and Herzegovina, Brazil, Bulgaria, Burkina Faso, Cambodia, Cameroon, Canada*, Cape Verde, Chile, China, Colombia, Costa Rica, Croatia, Cyprus, Czech Republic, Denmark, Ecuador, El Salvador, Estonia, Finland, France, Georgia, Germany*, Greece*, Guatemala, Guinea-Bissau, Holy See, Honduras, Hungary, Iceland, India, Ireland*, Israel*, Italy*, Jamaica, Japan, *Kazakhstan*, Latvia, Liberia, Liechtenstein*, Lithuania, Luxembourg, Macedonia (Former Yugoslav Republic of), Madagascar, Maldives, Mali, Malta, Mauritius, Mexico, Moldova, Mongolia, Montenegro, Morocco, Nauru, Netherlands*, New Zealand, Nicaragua, Niger, Norway, Pakistan, Panama, Paraguay, Peru, Philippines, Poland*, Portugal, *Qatar*, Romania, Russia, Saudi Arabia, Serbia, Seychelles, Sierra Leone, Slovakia, Slovenia, South Africa*, Spain, Sri Lanka, Sweden*, Switzerland*, Tajikistan, Tunisia, Turkey, UK*, Ukraine, Uruguay, *USA*, Uzbekistan

* With reservation and/or declaration.

Parties to Protocol V (62): Albania, Australia, Austria, Belarus, Bosnia and Herzegovina, Bulgaria, *Canada*, Chile, *Costa Rica*, Croatia, Czech Republic, Denmark, *Ecuador*, El Salvador, Estonia, Finland, France, Georgia, Germany, Guatemala, Guinea-Bissau, Holy See*, Hungary, Iceland, India, Ireland, Jamaica, Korea (South), *Latvia*, Liberia, Liechtenstein, Lithuania, Luxembourg, Macedonia (Former Yugoslav Republic of), Madagascar, *Mali*, Malta, Moldova, Netherlands, New Zealand, Nicaragua, Norway, *Pakistan*, Paraguay, *Peru*, Portugal, *Qatar*, Romania, Russia, Senegal, Sierra Leone, Slovakia, Slovenia, Spain, Sweden, Switzerland, Tajikistan, Tunisia, Ukraine, *United Arab Emirates*, Uruguay, *USA*

* With reservation and/or declaration.

Convention and protocol texts (original and amendments): United Nations Treaty Collection, <http://treaties.un.org/Pages/CTCTreaties.aspx?id=26>

Convention on the Prohibition of the Development, Production, Stockpiling and Use of Chemical Weapons and on their Destruction (Chemical Weapons Convention, CWC)

Opened for signature at Paris on 13 January 1993; entered into force on 29 April 1997; depositary UN Secretary-General

The convention prohibits the development, production, acquisition, transfer, stockpiling and use of chemical weapons. The CWC regime consists of four 'pillars': disarmament, non-proliferation, assistance and protection against chemical weapons, and international cooperation on the peaceful uses of chemistry.

Each party undertakes to destroy its chemical weapons by 29 April 2012. Old and abandoned chemical weapons will continue to be destroyed as they are uncovered from, for example, former battlefields.

Parties (188): Afghanistan, Albania, Algeria, Andorra, Antigua and Barbuda, Argentina, Armenia, Australia, Austria, Azerbaijan, *Bahamas*, Bahrain, Bangladesh, Barbados, Belarus, Belgium, Belize, Benin, Bhutan, Bolivia, Bosnia and Herzegovina, Botswana, Brazil, Brunei Darussalam, Bulgaria, Burkina Faso, Burundi, Cambodia, Cameroon, Canada, Cape Verde, Central African Republic, Chad, Chile, China, Colombia, Comoros, Congo (Democratic Republic of the), Congo (Republic of the), Cook Islands, Costa Rica, Côte d'Ivoire, Croatia, Cuba, Cyprus, Czech Republic, Denmark, Djibouti, Dominica, *Dominican Republic*, Ecuador, El Salvador, Equatorial Guinea, Eritrea, Estonia, Ethiopia, Fiji, Finland, France, Gabon, Gambia, Georgia, Germany, Ghana, Greece, Grenada, Guatemala, Guinea, Guinea-Bissau, Guyana, Haiti, Holy See, Honduras, Hungary, Iceland, India, Indonesia, Iran, *Iraq*, Ireland, Italy, Jamaica, Japan, Jordan, Kazakhstan, Kenya, Kiribati, Korea (South), Kuwait, Kyrgyzstan, Laos, Latvia, Lebanon, Lesotho, Liberia, Libya, Liechtenstein, Lithuania, Luxembourg, Macedonia (Former Yugoslav Republic of), Madagascar, Malawi, Malaysia, Maldives, Mali, Malta, Marshall Islands, Mauritania, Mauritius, Mexico, Micronesia, Moldova, Monaco, Mongolia, Montenegro, Morocco, Mozambique, Namibia, Nauru, Nepal, Netherlands, New Zealand, Nicaragua, Niger, Nigeria, Niue, Norway, Oman, Pakistan, Palau, Panama, Papua New Guinea, Paraguay, Peru, Philippines, Poland, Portugal, Qatar, Romania, Russia, Rwanda, Saint Kitts and Nevis, Saint Lucia, Saint Vincent and the Grenadines, Samoa, San Marino, Sao Tome and Principe, Saudi Arabia, Senegal, Serbia, Seychelles, Sierra Leone, Singapore, Slovakia, Slovenia, Solomon Islands, South Africa, Spain, Sri Lanka, Sudan, Suriname, Swaziland, Sweden, Switzerland, Tajikistan, Tanzania, Thailand, Timor-Leste, Togo, Tonga, Trinidad and Tobago, Tunisia, Turkey, Turkmenistan, Tuvalu, Uganda, UK, Ukraine, United Arab Emirates, Uruguay, USA, Uzbekistan, Vanuatu, Venezuela, Viet Nam, Yemen, Zambia, Zimbabwe

Signed but not ratified (2): Israel, Myanmar

Convention text: United Nations Treaty Collection, <http://treaties.un.org/Pages/CTCTreaties.aspx?id=26>

Comprehensive Nuclear-Test-Ban Treaty (CTBT)

Opened for signature at New York on 24 September 1996; not in force; depositary UN Secretary-General

The treaty would prohibit the carrying out of any nuclear weapon test explosion or any other nuclear explosion, and urges each party to prevent any such nuclear explosion at any place under its jurisdiction or control and refrain from causing, encouraging or in any way participating in the carrying out of any nuclear weapon test explosion or any other nuclear explosion.

The treaty will enter into force 180 days after the date of the deposit of the instruments of ratification of the 44 states listed in an annex to the treaty. All the 44 states possess nuclear power reactors and/or nuclear research reactors.

States whose ratification is required for entry into force (44): Algeria, Argentina, Australia, Austria, Bangladesh, Belgium, Brazil, Bulgaria, Canada, Chile, China*, Colombia, Congo (Democratic Republic of the), Egypt*, Finland, France, Germany, Hungary, India*, Indonesia*, Iran*, Israel*, Italy, Japan, Korea (North)*, Korea (South), Mexico, Netherlands, Norway, Pakistan*, Peru, Poland, Romania, Russia, Slovakia, South Africa, Spain, Sweden, Switzerland, Turkey, UK, Ukraine, USA*, Viet Nam

* Has not ratified the treaty.

Ratifications deposited (151): Afghanistan, Albania, Algeria, Andorra, Antigua and Barbuda, Argentina, Armenia, Australia, Austria, Azerbaijan, Bahamas, Bahrain, Bangladesh, Barbados, Belarus, Belgium, Belize, Benin, Bolivia, Bosnia and Herzegovina, Botswana, Brazil, Bulgaria, Burkina Faso, Burundi, Cambodia, Cameroon, Canada, Cape Verde, Chile, Colombia, Congo (Democratic Republic of the), Cook Islands, Costa Rica, Côte d'Ivoire, Croatia, Cyprus, Czech Republic, Denmark, Djibouti, Dominican Republic, Ecuador, El Salvador, Eritrea, Estonia, Ethiopia, Fiji, Finland, France, Gabon, Georgia, Germany, Greece, Grenada, Guyana, Haiti, Holy See, Honduras, Hungary, Iceland, Ireland, Italy, Jamaica, Japan, Jordan, Kazakhstan, Kenya, Kiribati, Korea (South), Kuwait, Kyrgyzstan, Laos, Latvia, Lebanon, Lesotho, *Liberia*, Libya, Liechtenstein, Lithuania, Luxembourg, Macedonia (Former Yugoslav Republic of), Madagascar, Malawi, Malaysia, Maldives, Mali, Malta, *Marshall Islands*, Mauritania, Mexico, Micronesia, Moldova, Monaco, Mongolia, Montenegro, Morocco, Mozambique, Namibia, Nauru, Netherlands, New Zealand, Nicaragua, Niger, Nigeria, Norway, Oman, Palau, Panama, Paraguay, Peru, Philippines, Poland, Portugal, Qatar, Romania, Russia, Rwanda, Saint Kitts and Nevis, Saint Lucia, *Saint Vincent and the Grenadines*, Samoa, San Marino, Senegal, Serbia, Seychelles, Sierra Leone, Singapore, Slovakia, Slovenia, South Africa, Spain, Sudan, Suriname, Sweden, Switzerland, Tajikistan, Tanzania, Togo, Tunisia, Turkey, Turkmenistan, Uganda, UK, Ukraine, United Arab Emirates, Uruguay, Uzbekistan, Vanuatu, Venezuela, Viet Nam, Zambia

Signed but not ratified (31): Angola, Brunei Darussalam, Central African Republic, Chad, China, Comoros, Congo (Republic of the), Egypt, Equatorial Guinea, Gambia, Ghana, Guatemala, Guinea, Guinea-Bissau, Indonesia, Iran, Iraq, Israel, Myanmar, Nepal, Papua New Guinea, Sao Tome and Principe, Solomon Islands, Sri Lanka, Swaziland, Thailand, Timor-Leste, *Trinidad and Tobago*, USA, Yemen, Zimbabwe

Treaty text: United Nations Treaty Collection, <http://treaties.un.org/Pages/CTCTreaties. aspx?id=26>

Convention on the Prohibition of the Use, Stockpiling, Production and Transfer of Anti-Personnel Mines and on their Destruction (APM Convention)

Opened for signature at Ottawa on 3–4 December 1997 and at New York on 5 December 1997; entered into force on 1 March 1999; depositary UN Secretary-General

The convention prohibits anti-personnel mines (APMs), which are defined as mines designed to be exploded by the presence, proximity or contact of a person and which will incapacitate, injure or kill one or more persons.

Each party undertakes to destroy all its stockpiled APMs as soon as possible but not later that four years after the entry into force of the convention for that state party. Each party also undertakes to destroy all APMs in mined areas under its jurisdiction or control not later than 10 years after the entry into force of the convention for that state party.

Parties (156): Afghanistan, Albania, Algeria, Andorra, Angola, Antigua and Barbuda, Argentina*, Australia*, Austria*, Bahamas, Bangladesh, Barbados, Belarus, Belgium, Belize, Benin, Bhutan, Bolivia, Bosnia and Herzegovina, Botswana, Brazil, Brunei Darussalam, Bulgaria, Burkina Faso, Burundi, Cambodia, Cameroon, Canada*, Cape Verde, Central African Republic, Chad, Chile*, Colombia, Comoros, Congo (Democratic Republic of the), Congo (Republic of the), Cook Islands, Costa Rica, Côte d'Ivoire, Croatia, Cyprus, Czech Republic*, Denmark, Djibouti, Dominica, Dominican Republic, Ecuador, El Salvador, Equatorial Guinea, Eritrea, Estonia, Ethiopia, Fiji, France, Gabon, Gambia, Germany, Ghana, Greece*, Grenada, Guatemala, Guinea, Guinea-Bissau, Guyana, Haiti, Holy See, Honduras, Hungary, Iceland, Indonesia, Iraq, Ireland, Italy, Jamaica, Japan, Jordan, Kenya, Kiribati, Kuwait, Latvia, Lesotho, Liberia, Liechtenstein, Lithuania*, Luxembourg, Macedonia (Former Yugoslav Republic of), Madagascar, Malawi, Malaysia, Maldives, Mali, Malta, Mauritania, Mauritius*, Mexico, Moldova, Monaco, Montenegro*, Mozambique, Namibia, Nauru, Netherlands, New Zealand, Nicaragua, Niger, Nigeria, Niue, Norway, Palau, Panama, Papua New Guinea, Paraguay, Peru, Philippines, Portugal, Qatar, Romania, Rwanda, Saint Kitts and Nevis, Saint Lucia, Saint Vincent and the Grenadines, Samoa, San Marino, Sao Tome and Principe, Senegal, Serbia*, Seychelles, Sierra Leone, Slovakia, Slovenia, Solomon Islands, South Africa*, Spain, Sudan, Suriname, Swaziland, Sweden*, Switzerland*, Tajikistan, Tanzania, Thailand, Timor-Leste, Togo, Trinidad and Tobago, Tunisia, Turkey, Turkmenistan, Uganda, UK*, Ukraine, Uruguay, Vanuatu, Venezuela, Yemen, Zambia, Zimbabwe

* With reservation and/or declaration.

Signed but not ratified (2): Marshall Islands, Poland

Convention text: United Nations Treaty Collection, <http://treaties.un.org/Pages/CTCTreaties.aspx?id=26>

Convention on Cluster Munitions

Adopted at Dublin on 30 May 2008; opened for signature at Oslo on 3 December 2008; will enter into force on 1 August 2010; depositary UN Secretary-General

The convention's objectives are to prohibit the use, production, transfer and stockpiling of cluster munitions that cause unacceptable harm to civilians, and to establish a framework for cooperation and assistance that ensures adequate provision of care and rehabilitation for victims, clearance of contaminated areas, risk reduction education and destruction of stockpiles. The convention does not apply to mines.

Parties as of 1 April 2010 (30): Albania, Austria, Belgium*, Burkina Faso[1], Burundi, Croatia, *Denmark*[1], France, Germany, Holy See*, Ireland, *Japan, Laos, Luxembourg, Macedonia (Former Yugoslav Republic of), Malawi, Malta, Mexico, Moldova*[1], *Montenegro*[1], New Zealand, Nicaragua, Niger, Norway, San Marino, Sierra Leone, Slovenia, Spain, Uruguay, Zambia

  * With reservation and/or declaration.
  [1] Deposited instruments of ratification in Jan.–Mar. 2010.

Signed but not ratified as of 1 April 2010 (74): Afghanistan, Angola, Australia, Benin, Bolivia, Bosnia and Herzegovina, Botswana, Bulgaria, *Cameroon*, Canada, Cape Verde, Central African Republic, Chad, Chile, Colombia, Comoros, *Congo (Democratic Republic of the)*, Congo (Republic of the), Cook Islands, Costa Rica, Côte d'Ivoire, *Cyprus*, Czech Republic, *Dominican Republic*, Ecuador, El Salvador, Fiji, Gambia, Ghana, Guatemala, Guinea, Guinea-Bissau, *Haiti*, Honduras, Hungary, Iceland, Indonesia, *Iraq*, Italy, *Jamaica*, Kenya, Lebanon, Lesotho, Liberia, Liechtenstein, Lithuania, Madagascar, Mali, Monaco, Mozambique, Namibia, Nauru, Netherlands, *Nigeria*, Palau, Panama, Paraguay, Peru, Philippines, Portugal, Rwanda, *Saint Vincent and the Grenadines*, Samoa, Sao Tome and Principe, Senegal, Somalia, South Africa, Sweden, Switzerland, Tanzania, Togo, *Tunisia*, Uganda, UK

Convention text: United Nations Treaty Collection, <http://treaties.un.org/Pages/CTCTreaties. aspx?id=26>

II. Regional treaties

Treaty for the Prohibition of Nuclear Weapons in Latin America and the Caribbean (Treaty of Tlatelolco)

Original treaty opened for signature at Mexico City on 14 February 1967; entered into force on 22 April 1968; treaty amended in 1990, 1991 and 1992; depositary Mexican Government

The treaty prohibits the testing, use, manufacture, production or acquisition by any means, as well as the receipt, storage, installation, deployment and any form of possession of any nuclear weapons by Latin American and Caribbean countries.

The parties should conclude agreements individually with the IAEA for the application of safeguards to their nuclear activities. The IAEA has the exclusive power to carry out special inspections.

The treaty is open for signature by all the independent states of the Latin American and Caribbean zone as defined in the treaty.

Under *Additional Protocol I* states with territories within the zone (France, the Netherlands, the United Kingdom and the United States) undertake to apply the statute of military denuclearization to these territories.

Under *Additional Protocol II* the recognized nuclear weapon states—China, France, Russia, the United Kingdom and the United States—undertake to respect the statute of military denuclearization of Latin America and the Caribbean and not to contribute to acts involving a violation of the treaty, nor to use or threaten to use nuclear weapons against the parties to the treaty.

Parties to the original treaty (33)· Antigua and Barbuda, Argentina[1], Bahamas, Barbados[1], Belize[2], Bolivia, Brazil[1], Chile[1], Colombia[1], Costa Rica[1], Cuba[1], Dominica, Dominican Republic[3], Ecuador[1], El Salvador[1], Grenada[4], Guatemala[1], Guyana[1], Haiti, Honduras, Jamaica[1], Mexico[1], Nicaragua[3], Panama[1], Paraguay[1], Peru[1], Saint Kitts and Nevis, Saint Lucia, Saint Vincent and the Grenadines, Suriname[1], Trinidad and Tobago, Uruguay[1], Venezuela[1]

[1] Has ratified the amendments of 1990, 1991 and 1992.
[2] Has ratified the amendments of 1990 and 1992 only.
[3] Has ratified the amendment of 1992 only.
[4] Has ratified the amendment of 1990 only.

Parties to Additional Protocol I (4): France[1], Netherlands, UK[2], USA[3]

Parties to Additional Protocol II (5): China[4], France[5], Russia[6], UK[2], USA[7]

[1] France declared that Protocol I shall not apply to transit across French territories situated within the zone of the treaty, and destined for other French territories. The protocol shall not limit the participation of the populations of the French territories in the activities mentioned in Article 1 of the treaty, and in efforts connected with the national defence of France. France does not consider the zone defined in the treaty as established in accordance with international law; it cannot, therefore, agree that the treaty should apply to that zone.

[2] When signing and ratifying protocols I and II, the UK made the following declarations of understanding: The signing and ratification by the UK could not be regarded as affecting in any way the legal status of any territory for the international relations of which the UK is responsible, lying within the limits of the geographical zone established by the treaty. Should any party to the treaty carry out any act of aggression with the support of a nuclear weapon state, the UK would be free to reconsider the extent to which it could be regarded as bound by the provisions of Protocol II.

[3] The USA ratified Protocol I with the following understandings: The provisions of the treaty do not affect the exclusive power and legal competence under international law of a state adhering to this Protocol to grant or deny transit and transport privileges to its own or any other vessels or aircraft irrespective of cargo or armaments; the provisions do not affect rights under international law of a state adhering to this protocol regarding the exercise of the freedom of the seas, or regarding passage through or over waters subject to the sovereignty of a state. The declarations attached by the USA to its ratification of Protocol II apply also to Protocol I.

[4] China declared that it will never send its means of transportation and delivery carrying nuclear weapons into the territory, territorial sea or airspace of Latin American countries.

[5] France stated that it interprets the undertaking contained in Article 3 of Protocol II to mean that it presents no obstacle to the full exercise of the right of self-defence enshrined in Article 51 of the UN Charter; it takes note of the interpretation by the Preparatory Commission for the Denuclearization of Latin America according to which the treaty does not apply to transit, the granting or denying of which lies within the exclusive competence of each state party in accordance with international law. In 1974 France made a supplementary statement to the effect that it was prepared to consider its obligations under Protocol II as applying not only to the signatories of the treaty, but also to the territories for which the statute of denuclearization was in force in conformity with Protocol I.

[6] On signing and ratifying Protocol II, the USSR stated that it assumed that the effect of Article 1 of the treaty extends to any nuclear explosive device and that, accordingly, the carrying out by any party of nuclear explosions for peaceful purposes would be a violation of its obligations under Article 1 and would be incompatible with its non-nuclear weapon status. For states parties to the treaty, a solution to the problem of peaceful nuclear explosions can be found in accordance with the provisions of Article V of the NPT and within the framework of the international procedures of the IAEA. It declared that authorizing the transit of nuclear weapons in any form would be contrary to the objectives of the treaty.

Any actions undertaken by a state or states parties to the treaty which are not compatible with their non-nuclear weapon status, and also the commission by one or more states parties to the treaty of an act of aggression with the support of a state which is in possession of nuclear weapons or together with such a state, will be regarded by the USSR as incompatible with the obligations of those countries under the treaty. In such cases it would reserve the right to reconsider its obligations under Protocol II. It further reserves the right to reconsider its attitude to this protocol in the event of any actions on the part of other states possessing nuclear weapons which are incompatible with their obligations under the said protocol.

[7] The USA signed and ratified Protocol II with the following declarations and understandings: Each of the parties retains exclusive power and legal competence to grant or deny non-parties transit and transport privileges. As regards the undertaking not to use or threaten to use nuclear weapons against the parties, the USA would consider that an armed attack by a party, in which it was assisted by a nuclear weapon state, would be incompatible with the treaty.

Original treaty text: *United Nations Treaty Series*, vol. 634 (1968)

Amended treaty text: Agency for the Prohibition of Nuclear Weapons in Latin America and the Caribbean, <http://www.opanal.org/opanal/Tlatelolco/P-Tlatelolco-i.htm>

South Pacific Nuclear Free Zone Treaty (Treaty of Rarotonga)

Opened for signature at Rarotonga on 6 August 1985; entered into force on 11 December 1986; depositary Secretary General of the Pacific Islands Forum Secretariat

The treaty prohibits the manufacture or acquisition of any nuclear explosive device, as well as possession or control over such device by the parties anywhere inside or outside the zone defined in an annex. The parties also undertake not to supply nuclear material or equipment, unless subject to IAEA safeguards, and to prevent in their territories the stationing as well as the testing of any nuclear explosive device and undertake not to dump, and to prevent the dumping of, radioactive waste and other radioactive matter at sea anywhere within the zone. Each party remains free to allow visits, as well as transit, by foreign ships and aircraft.

The treaty is open for signature by the members of the Pacific Islands Forum.

Under *Protocol 1* France, the United Kingdom and the United States undertake to apply the treaty prohibitions relating to the manufacture, stationing and testing of nuclear explosive devices in the territories situated within the zone for which they are internationally responsible.

Under *Protocol 2* China, France, Russia, the United Kingdom and the United States undertake not to use or threaten to use a nuclear explosive device against the parties to the treaty or against any territory within the zone for which a party to Protocol 1 is internationally responsible.

Under *Protocol 3* China, France, Russia, the United Kingdom and the United States undertake not to test any nuclear explosive device anywhere within the zone.

Parties (13): Australia, Cook Islands, Fiji, Kiribati, Nauru, New Zealand, Niue, Papua New Guinea, Samoa, Solomon Islands, Tonga, Tuvalu, Vanuatu

Parties to Protocol 1 (2): France, UK; *signed but not ratified (1)*: USA

Parties to Protocol 2 (4): China, France[1], Russia, UK[2]; *signed but not ratified (1)*: USA

Parties to Protocol 3 (4): China, France, Russia, UK; *signed but not ratified (1)*: USA

[1] France declared that the negative security guarantees set out in Protocol 2 are the same as the Conference on Disarmament declaration of 6 Apr. 1995 referred to in UN Security Council Resolution 984 of 11 Apr. 1995.

[2] On ratifying Protocol 2 in 1997, the UK declared that nothing in the treaty affects the rights under international law with regard to transit of the zone or visits to ports and airfields within the zone by ships and aircraft. The UK will not be bound by the undertakings in Protocol 2 in case of an invasion or any other attack on the UK, its territories, its armed forces or its allies, carried out or

sustained by a party to the treaty in association or alliance with a nuclear weapon state or if a party violates its non-proliferation obligations under the treaty.

Treaty text: United Nations Treaty Series, vol. 1445 (1987)

Treaty on Conventional Armed Forces in Europe (CFE Treaty)

Original treaty signed at Paris on 19 November 1990; entered into force on 9 November 1992; depositary Dutch Government

The treaty sets ceilings on five categories of treaty-limited equipment (TLE)— battle tanks, armoured combat vehicles, artillery of at least 100-mm calibre, combat aircraft and attack helicopters—in an area stretching from the Atlantic Ocean to the Ural Mountains (the Atlantic-to-the-Urals, ATTU).

The treaty was negotiated and signed by the member states of the Warsaw Treaty Organization and NATO within the framework of the Conference on Security and Co-operation in Europe (from 1995 the Organization for Security and Co-operation in Europe, OSCE).

The **1992 Tashkent Agreement**, adopted by the former Soviet republics with territories within the ATTU area of application (with the exception of Estonia, Latvia and Lithuania) and the **1992 Oslo Document** (Final Document of the Extraordinary Conference of the States Parties to the CFE Treaty) introduced modifications to the treaty required because of the emergence of new states after the break-up of the Soviet Union.

Parties (30): Armenia, Azerbaijan, Belarus, Belgium, Bulgaria, Canada, Czech Republic, Denmark, France, Georgia, Germany, Greece, Hungary, Iceland, Italy, Kazakhstan, Luxembourg, Moldova, Netherlands, Norway, Poland, Portugal, Romania, Russia[1], Slovakia, Spain, Turkey, UK, Ukraine, USA

[1] On 14 July 2007 Russia declared its intention to suspend its participation in the CFE Treaty and associated documents and agreements, which took effect on 12 Dec. 2007.

The first Review Conference of the CFE Treaty adopted the **1996 Flank Document**, which reorganized the flank areas geographically and numerically, allowing Russia and Ukraine to deploy TLE in a less constraining manner.

Original (1990) treaty text: Organization for Security and Co-operation in Europe, <http://www.osce.org/item/13752.html?html=1>

Consolidated (1993) treaty text: Dutch Ministry of Foreign Affairs, <http://www.minbuza.nl/en/treaties/004285>

Flank Document text: Organization for Security and Co-operation in Europe, <http://www.osce.org/item/13755.html?html=1>, annex A

Concluding Act of the Negotiation on Personnel Strength of Conventional Armed Forces in Europe (CFE-1A Agreement)

Signed by the parties to the CFE Treaty at Helsinki on 10 July 1992; entered into force simultaneously with the CFE Treaty; depositary Dutch Government

The politically binding agreement sets ceilings on the number of personnel of the conventional land-based armed forces of the parties within the ATTU area.

Agreement text: Organization for Security and Co-operation in Europe, <http://www. osce.org/item/13753.html?html=1>

Agreement on Adaptation of the CFE Treaty

Signed by the parties to the CFE Treaty at Helsinki on 19 November 1999; not in force; depositary Dutch Government

The agreement would replace the CFE Treaty bloc-to-bloc military balance with regional balance, establish individual state limits on TLE holdings and provide for a new structure of limitations and new military flexibility mechanisms, flank sub-limits and enhanced transparency. It would open the CFE regime to all the other European states. It will enter into force when it has been ratified by all the signatories. The **1999 Final Act**, with annexes, contains politically binding arrangements with regard to Georgia, Moldova and Central Europe, and withdrawals of armed forces from foreign territories.

Ratifications deposited (3): Belarus, Kazakhstan, Russia*[1]

Note: Ukraine has ratified the 1999 Agreement on Adaptation of the CFE Treaty but has not deposited its instruments with the depositary.
   * With reservation and/or declaration.
   [1] On 14 July 2007 Russia declared its intention to suspend its participation in the CFE Treaty and associated documents and agreements, which took effect on 12 Dec. 2007.

Agreement text: Organization for Security and Co-operation in Europe, <http://www. osce.org/item/13760.html?html=1>

Treaty text as amended by 1999 agreement: SIPRI Yearbook 2000, pp. 627–42

Final Act text: Organization for Security and Co-operation in Europe, <http://www. osce.org/item/13761.html?html=1>

Treaty on Open Skies

Opened for signature at Helsinki on 24 March 1992; entered into force on 1 January 2002; depositaries Canadian and Hungarian governments

The treaty obligates the parties to submit their territories to short-notice unarmed surveillance flights. The area of application stretches from Vancouver, Canada, eastward to Vladivostok, Russia.

The treaty was negotiated between the member states of the Warsaw Treaty Organization and NATO. It was opened for signature by the NATO member states, former member states of the Warsaw Treaty Organization and the states of the former Soviet Union (except for Estonia, Latvia and Lithuania). For six months after entry into force of the treaty, any other participating state of the Organization for Security and Co-operation in Europe could apply for accession to the treaty, and from 1 July 2002 any state can apply to accede to the treaty.

Parties (34): Belarus, Belgium, Bosnia and Herzegovina, Bulgaria, Canada, Croatia, Czech Republic, Denmark, Estonia, Finland, France, Georgia, Germany, Greece, Hungary, Iceland, Italy, Latvia, Lithuania, Luxembourg, Netherlands, Norway, Poland, Portugal, Romania, Russia, Slovakia, Slovenia, Spain, Sweden, Turkey, UK, Ukraine, USA

Signed but not ratified (1): Kyrgyzstan

Treaty text: Canada Treaty Information, <http://www.treaty-accord.gc.ca/text-texte.asp?id= 102747>

Treaty on the Southeast Asia Nuclear Weapon-Free Zone (Treaty of Bangkok)

Signed at Bangkok on 15 December 1995; entered into force on 27 March 1997; depositary Thai Government

The treaty prohibits the development, manufacture, acquisition or testing of nuclear weapons inside or outside the zone as well as the stationing and transport of nuclear weapons in or through the zone. Each state party may decide for itself whether to allow visits and transit by foreign ships and aircraft. The parties undertake not to dump at sea or discharge into the atmosphere anywhere within the zone any radioactive material or waste or dispose of radioactive material on land. The parties should conclude an agreement with the IAEA for the application of full-scope safeguards to their peaceful nuclear activities.

The zone includes not only the territories but also the continental shelves and exclusive economic zones of the states parties.

The treaty is open for all states of South East Asia.

Under a *Protocol* to the treaty, China, France, Russia, the United Kingdom and the United States are to undertake not to use or threaten to use nuclear weapons against any state party to the treaty. They should further undertake not to use nuclear weapons within the South East Asia nuclear weapon-free zone. The protocol will enter into force for each state party on the date of its deposit of the instrument of ratification.

Parties (10): Brunei Darussalam, Cambodia, Indonesia, Laos, Malaysia, Myanmar, Philippines, Singapore, Thailand, Viet Nam

Protocol: no signatures, no parties

Treaty and protocol texts: ASEAN Secretariat, <http://www.aseansec.org/5181.htm>

African Nuclear-Weapon-Free Zone Treaty (Treaty of Pelindaba)

Signed at Cairo on 11 April 1996; entered into force on 15 July 2009; depositary Secretary-General of the African Union

The treaty prohibits the research, development, manufacture and acquisition of nuclear explosive devices and the testing or stationing of any nuclear explosive device. Each party remains free to allow visits and transit by foreign ships and aircraft. The treaty also prohibits any attack against nuclear installations. The parties undertake not to dump or permit the dumping of radioactive waste and other radioactive matter anywhere within the zone. Each party should individually conclude an agreement with the IAEA for the application of comprehensive safeguards to their peaceful nuclear activities.

The zone includes the territory of the continent of Africa, island states members of the African Union (AU) and all islands considered by the AU to be part of Africa.

The treaty is open for signature by all the states of Africa.

Under *Protocol I* China, France, Russia, the United Kingdom and the United States are to undertake not to use or threaten to use a nuclear explosive device against the parties to the treaty.

Under *Protocol II* China, France, Russia, the United Kingdom and the United States are to undertake not to test nuclear explosive devices within the zone.

Under *Protocol III* states with territories within the zone for which they are internationally responsible are to undertake to observe certain provisions of the treaty with respect to these territories. This protocol is open for signature by France and Spain.

The protocols entered into force simultaneously with the treaty for those protocol signatories that had deposited their instruments of ratification.

Parties (29): Algeria, Benin, Botswana, Burkina Faso, *Burundi*, Côte d'Ivoire, Equatorial Guinea, Ethiopia, Gabon, Gambia, Guinea, Kenya, Lesotho, Libya, Madagascar, *Malawi*, Mali, Mauritania, Mauritius, Mozambique, Nigeria, Rwanda, Senegal, South Africa, Swaziland, Tanzania, Togo, *Tunisia*, Zimbabwe

Signed but not ratified (25): Angola, Cameroon, Cape Verde, Central African Republic, Chad, Comoros, Congo (Democratic Republic of the), Congo (Republic of the), Djibouti, Egypt, Eritrea, Ghana, Guinea-Bissau, Liberia, Morocco, Namibia, Niger, Sahrawi Arab Democratic Republic (Western Sahara), Sao Tome and Principe, Seychelles, Sierra Leone, Somalia, Sudan, Uganda, Zambia

Protocol I, ratifications deposited (3): China, France[1], UK[2]; *signed but not ratified (2):* Russia[3], USA[4]

Protocol II, ratifications deposited (3): China, France, UK[2]; *signed but not ratified (2):* Russia[3], USA[4]

Protocol III, ratifications deposited (1): France

[1] France stated that the Protocols did not affect its right to self-defence, as stipulated in Article 51 of the UN Charter. It clarified that its commitment under Article 1 of Protocol I was equivalent to the negative security assurances given by France to non-nuclear weapon states parties to the NPT, as confirmed in its declaration made on 6 Apr. 1995 at the Conference on Disarmament, and as referred to in UN Security Council Resolution 984 of 11 Apr. 1995.

[2] The UK stated that it did not accept the inclusion of the British Indian Ocean Territory within the African nuclear-weapon-free zone without its consent, and did not accept, by its adherence to

Protocols I and II, any legal obligations in respect of that territory. Moreover, it would not be bound by its undertaking under Article 1 of Protocol I in case of an invasion or any other attack on the UK, its dependent territories, its armed forces or other troops, or its allies or a state towards which it had a security commitment, carried out or sustained by a party to the treaty in association or alliance with a nuclear weapon state, or if any party to the treaty was in material breach of its own non-proliferation obligations under the treaty.

[3] Russia stated that as long as a military base of a nuclear state was located on the islands of the Chagos archipelago these islands could not be regarded as fulfilling the requirements put forward by the treaty for nuclear-weapon-free territories. Moreover, since certain states declared that they would consider themselves free from the obligations under the protocols with regard to the mentioned territories, Russia could not consider itself to be bound by the obligations under Protocol I in respect to the same territories. Russia interpreted its obligations under Article 1 of Protocol I as follows: It would not use nuclear weapons against a state party to the treaty, except in the case of invasion or any other armed attack on Russia, its territory, its armed forces or other troops, its allies or a state towards which it had a security commitment, carried out or sustained by a non-nuclear weapon state party to the treaty, in association or alliance with a nuclear weapon state.

[4] The USA stated, with respect to Protocol I, that it would consider an invasion or any other attack on the USA, its territories, its armed forces or other troops, or its allies or on a state towards which it had a security commitment, carried out or sustained by a party to the treaty in association or alliance with a nuclear-weapon state, to be incompatible with the treaty party's corresponding obligations. The USA also stated that neither the treaty nor Protocol II would apply to the activities of the UK, the USA or any other state not party to the treaty on the island of Diego Garcia or elsewhere in the British Indian Ocean Territory. Therefore, no change was required in the operations of US armed forces in Diego Garcia and elsewhere in these territories.

Treaty text: African Union, <http://www.africa-union.org/root/AU/Documents/Treaties/treaties.htm>

Agreement on Sub-Regional Arms Control (Florence Agreement)

Adopted at Florence and entered into force on 14 June 1996

The agreement was negotiated under the auspices of the OSCE in accordance with the mandate in Article IV of Annex 1-B of the 1995 General Framework Agreement for Peace in Bosnia and Herzegovina (Dayton Agreement). It sets numerical ceilings on armaments of the former warring parties. Five categories of heavy conventional weapons are included: battle tanks, armoured combat vehicles, heavy artillery (75 mm and above), combat aircraft and attack helicopters. The limits were reached by 31 October 1997; by that date 6580 weapon items, or 46 per cent of pre-June 1996 holdings, had been destroyed. By 1 January 2010, a further 2650 items had been destroyed voluntarily. The implementation of the agreement is monitored and assisted by the OSCE's Personal Representative of the Chairman-in-Office, the Contact Group (France, Germany, Italy, Russia, the United Kingdom and the United States) and supported by other OSCE supporting states.

In 2006 the number of parties fell from five to three with the dissolution of the defence ministries of the sub-national entities of Bosnia and Herzegovina. The remaining parties agreed on six legally binding amendments in March 2006. The number of parties rose to four in 2007, following the independence of Montenegro.

Parties (4): Bosnia and Herzegovina, Croatia, Montenegro, Serbia

Agreement text: OSCE Mission to Bosnia and Herzegovina, <http://www.oscebih.org/documents/11-eng.pdf>

Inter-American Convention Against the Illicit Manufacturing of and Trafficking in Firearms, Ammunition, Explosives, and Other Related Materials

Adopted at Washington, DC, on 13 November 1997; opened for signature at Washington, DC, on 14 November 1997; entered into force on 1 July 1998; depositary General Secretariat of the Organization of American States

The purpose of the convention is to prevent, combat and eradicate the illicit manufacturing of and trafficking in firearms, ammunition, explosives and other related materials; and to promote and facilitate cooperation and the exchange of information and experience among the parties.

Parties (30): Antigua and Barbuda, Argentina*, Bahamas, Barbados, Belize, Bolivia, Brazil, Chile, Colombia, Costa Rica, Dominica, *Dominican Republic*, Ecuador, El Salvador, Grenada, Guatemala, Guyana, Haiti, Honduras, Mexico, Nicaragua, Panama, Paraguay, Peru, Saint Kitts and Nevis, Saint Lucia, Suriname, Trinidad and Tobago, Uruguay, Venezuela

   * With reservation.

Signed but not ratified (4): Canada, Jamaica, Saint Vincent and the Grenadines, USA

Convention text: Organization of American States, <http://www.oas.org/juridico/english/treaties/a-63.html>

Inter-American Convention on Transparency in Conventional Weapons Acquisitions

Adopted at Guatemala City on 7 June 1999; entered into force on 21 November 2002; depositary General Secretariat of the Organization of American States

The objective of the convention is to contribute more fully to regional openness and transparency in the acquisition of conventional weapons by exchanging information regarding such acquisitions, for the purpose of promoting confidence among states in the Americas.

Parties (13): Argentina, Brazil, Canada, Chile, *Dominican Republic*, Ecuador, El Salvador, Guatemala, Nicaragua, Paraguay, Peru, Uruguay, Venezuela

Signed but not ratified (8): Bolivia, Colombia, Costa Rica, Dominica, Haiti, Honduras, Mexico, USA

Convention text: Organization of American States, <http://www.oas.org/juridico/english/treaties/a-64.html>

Vienna Document 1999 of the Negotiations on Confidence- and Security-Building Measures

Adopted by the participating states of the Organization for Security and Co-operation in Europe at Istanbul on 16 November 1999; entered into force on 1 January 2000

The Vienna Document 1999 builds on the 1986 Stockholm Document on Confidence- and Security-Building Measures (CSBMs) and Disarmament in Europe and previous Vienna Documents (1990, 1992 and 1994). The Vienna Document

1990 provided for annual exchange of military information, military budget exchange, risk reduction procedures, a communication network and an annual CSBM implementation assessment. The Vienna Documents 1992 and 1994 extended the area of application and introduced new mechanisms and parameters for military activities, defence planning and military contacts.

The Vienna Document 1999 introduces regional measures aimed at increasing transparency and confidence in bilateral, multilateral and regional contexts and some improvements, in particular regarding the constraining measures.

Document text: Organization for Security and Co-operation in Europe, <http://www.osce.org/item/4251.html?html=1>

ECOWAS Convention on Small Arms, Light Weapons, their Ammunition and Other Related Materials

Adopted by the member states of the Economic Community of West African States (ECOWAS) at Abuja, on 14 June 2006; entered into force on 29 September 2009; depositary President of the ECOWAS Commission

The convention obligates the parties to prevent and combat the excessive and destabilizing accumulation of small arms and light weapons in the 15 ECOWAS member states.

Parties (9*): *Benin*, Burkina Faso, *Liberia*, Mali, Niger, *Nigeria*, Senegal, Sierra Leone, *Togo*

Signed but not ratified (6): Cape Verde, Côte d'Ivoire, Gambia*, Ghana, Guinea*, Guinea-Bissau

  * According to unconfirmed media reports, Gambia has ratified the convention and Guinea has ratified but not deposited its instrument.

Convention text: ECOWAS Small Arms Control Programme, <http://www.ecosap.ecowas.int/en/ecosap/strategic_docs/convention/convention_small_arms.pdf>

Treaty on a Nuclear-Weapon-Free Zone in Central Asia (Treaty of Semipalatinsk)

Signed at Semipalatinsk on 8 September 2006; entered into force on 21 March 2009; depositary Kyrgyz Government

The treaty obligates the parties not to conduct research on, develop, manufacture, stockpile or otherwise acquire, possess or have control over any nuclear weapons or other nuclear explosive device by any means anywhere.

Under a *Protocol* China, France, Russia, the United Kingdom and the United States are to undertake not to use or threaten to use a nuclear explosive device against the parties to the treaty. This Protocol will enter into force for each party on the date of its deposit of its instrument of ratification.

Parties (5): *Kazakhstan*, Kyrgyzstan, *Tajikistan*, *Turkmenistan*, Uzbekistan

Protocol: no signatures, no parties

Treaty text: United Nations, Office for Disarmament Affairs, Status of Multilateral Arms Regulation and Disarmament Agreements, <http://disarmament.un.org/treatystatus.nsf>

III. Bilateral treaties

Treaty on the Limitation of Anti-Ballistic Missile Systems (ABM Treaty)

Signed by the Soviet Union and the United States at Moscow on 26 May 1972; entered into force on 3 October 1972; not in force from 13 June 2002

The parties—Russia and the USA—undertook not to build nationwide defences against ballistic missile attack and to limit the development and deployment of permitted strategic missile defences. The treaty prohibited the parties from giving air defence missiles, radars or launchers the technical ability to counter strategic ballistic missiles and from testing them in a strategic ABM mode.

The **1974 Protocol** to the ABM Treaty introduced further numerical restrictions on permitted ballistic missile defences.

In 1997 Belarus, Kazakhstan, Russia, Ukraine and the USA signed a memorandum of understanding designating Belarus, Kazakhstan and Ukraine as parties to the treaty along with Russia as successor states of the Soviet Union and a set of Agreed Statements specifying the demarcation line between strategic missile defences (which are not permitted under the treaty) and non-strategic or theatre missile defences (which are permitted under the treaty). The set of 1997 agreements on anti-missile defence were ratified by Russia in April 2000, but because the USA did not ratify them they did not enter into force. On 13 December 2001 the USA announced its withdrawal from the treaty, which came into effect on 13 June 2002.

Treaty and protocol texts: US Department of State, <http://www.state.gov/t/isn/trty/16332.htm>

Treaty on the Limitation of Underground Nuclear Weapon Tests (Threshold Test-Ban Treaty, TTBT)

Signed by the Soviet Union and the United States at Moscow on 3 July 1974; entered into force on 11 December 1990

The parties—Russia and the USA—undertake not to carry out any underground nuclear weapon test having a yield exceeding 150 kilotons. The 1974 verification protocol was replaced in 1990 with a new protocol.

Treaty and protocol texts: United Nations Treaty Series, vol. 1714 (1993)

Treaty on Underground Nuclear Explosions for Peaceful Purposes (Peaceful Nuclear Explosions Treaty, PNET)

Signed by the Soviet Union and the United States at Moscow and Washington, DC, on 28 May 1976; entered into force on 11 December 1990

The parties—Russia and the USA—undertake not to carry out any individual underground nuclear explosion for peaceful purposes having a yield exceeding 150 kilotons or any group explosion having an aggregate yield exceeding 150 kilotons; and not to carry out any group explosion having an aggregate yield exceeding 1500 kilotons unless the individual explosions in the group could be identified and measured by agreed verification procedures. The 1976 verification protocol was replaced in 1990 with a new protocol.

Treaty text: United Nations Treaty Series, vol. 1714 (1993)

Treaty on the Elimination of Intermediate-Range and Shorter-Range Missiles (INF Treaty)

Signed by the Soviet Union and the United States at Washington, DC, on 8 December 1987; entered into force on 1 June 1988

The treaty obligated the original parties—the Soviet Union and the USA—to destroy all ground-launched ballistic and cruise missiles with a range of 500–5500 kilometres (intermediate-range, 1000–5500 km; and shorter-range, 500–1000 km) and their launchers by 1 June 1991. A total of 2692 missiles were eliminated by May 1991. In 1994 treaty membership was expanded to include Belarus, Kazakhstan and Ukraine. For 10 years after 1 June 1991 on-site inspections were conducted to verify compliance. The use of surveillance satellites for data collection has continued after the end of on-site inspections on 31 May 2001.

Treaty text: US Department of State, <http://www.state.gov/t/vci/trty/102360.htm>

Treaty on the Reduction and Limitation of Strategic Offensive Arms (START I Treaty)

Signed by the Soviet Union and the United States at Moscow on 31 July 1991; entered into force on 5 December 1994; expired on 5 December 2009

The treaty obligated the original parties—the Soviet Union and the USA—to make phased reductions in their offensive strategic nuclear forces over a seven-year period. It sets numerical limits on deployed strategic nuclear delivery vehicles (SNDVs)—ICBMs, SLBMs and heavy bombers—and the nuclear warheads they carry. In the Protocol to Facilitate the Implementation of the START Treaty (**1992 Lisbon Protocol**), which entered into force on 5 December 1994, Belarus, Kazakhstan and Ukraine also assumed the obligations of the former Soviet Union under the treaty.

Note: The treaty expired on 5 Dec. 2009 without an agreement on an extension or replacement being reached by the parties until the 2010 New START Treaty was signed on 8 Apr. 2010.

Treaty and protocol texts: US Department of State, <http://www.state.gov/t/isn/18535.htm>

Treaty on Further Reduction and Limitation of Strategic Offensive Arms (START II Treaty)

Signed by Russia and the United States at Moscow on 3 January 1993; not in force

The treaty would have obligated the parties to eliminate their MIRVed ICBMs and reduce the number of their deployed strategic nuclear warheads to no more than 3000–3500 each (of which no more than 1750 may be deployed on SLBMs) by 1 January 2003. On 26 September 1997 the two parties signed a *Protocol* to the treaty providing for the extension until the end of 2007 of the period of implementation of the treaty.

Note: The treaty was ratified by the US Senate and the Russian Parliament, but the two parties never exchanged the instruments of ratification. The treaty thus never entered into force. On 14 June 2002, as a response to the taking effect on 13 June of the USA's withdrawal from the ABM Treaty, Russia declared that it would no longer be bound by the START II Treaty.

Treaty and protocol text: US Department of State, <http://www.state.gov/t/vci/trty/102887.htm>

Treaty on Strategic Offensive Reductions (SORT Treaty, Moscow Treaty)

Signed by Russia and the United States at Moscow on 24 May 2002; entered into force on 1 June 2003

The treaty obligates the parties to reduce the number of their operationally deployed strategic nuclear warheads so that the aggregate numbers do not exceed 1700–2200 for each party by 31 December 2012.

Note: The treaty will be terminated on the entry into force of the 2010 New START Treaty.

Treaty text: US Senate, *The Moscow Treaty*, Treaty Document 107-8 (Government Printing Office: Washington, DC, 2002)

Treaty on Measures for the Further Reduction and Limitation of Strategic Offensive Arms (New START Treaty, Prague Treaty)

Signed by Russia and the United States at Prague on 8 April 2010; not in force

The treaty will obligate the parties each to reduce their number of (*a*) deployed ICBMs, SLBMs and heavy bombers to 700; (*b*) warheads on deployed ICBMs and SLBMs and warheads counted for deployed heavy bombers to 1550; and (*c*) deployed and non-deployed ICBM launchers, SLBM launchers and heavy bombers to 800. The reductions must be achieved within seven years of the treaty's entry into force; a Bilateral Consultative Commission will resolve questions about compliance and other implementation issues. A *Protocol* to the treaty contains verifications mechanisms.

The treaty, which must be ratified by the Russian Federal Assembly and the US Senate, follows on from the 1991 Treaty on the Reduction and Limitation of Strategic Offensive Arms (START I Treaty) and will supersede the 2002 Treaty on Strategic Offensive Reductions (SORT Treaty). It will remain in force for 10 years unless superseded earlier by a subsequent agreement.

Treaty text: US Department of State, <http://www.state.gov/documents/organization/140035.pdf>

Annex B. International security cooperation bodies

NENNE BODELL

This annex describes the main international organizations, intergovernmental bodies, treaty-implementing bodies and transfer control regimes whose aims include the promotion of security, stability, peace or arms control and lists their members or participants as of 1 January 2010.

The member states of the United Nations and organs within the UN system are listed first, followed by all other organizations in alphabetical order. Not all members or participants of these organizations are UN member states. States that joined or first participated in the organization during 2009 are shown in italics. The address of an Internet site with information about each organization is provided where available. On the arms control and disarmament agreements mentioned here, see annex A.

United Nations (UN)

The UN, the world intergovernmental organization, was founded in 1945 through the adoption of its Charter. Its headquarters are in New York, USA. The six principal UN organs are the General Assembly, the Security Council, the Economic and Social Council (ECOSOC), the Trusteeship Council (which suspended operation in 1994), the International Court of Justice (ICJ) and the secretariat. The UN also has a large number of specialized agencies and other autonomous bodies.

UN member states (192) and year of membership

Afghanistan, 1946
Albania, 1955
Algeria, 1962
Andorra, 1993
Angola, 1976
Antigua and Barbuda, 1981
Argentina, 1945
Armenia, 1992
Australia, 1945
Austria, 1955
Azerbaijan, 1992
Bahamas, 1973
Bahrain, 1971
Bangladesh, 1974
Barbados, 1966
Belarus, 1945

Belgium, 1945
Belize, 1981
Benin, 1960
Bhutan, 1971
Bolivia, 1945
Bosnia and Herzegovina, 1992
Botswana, 1966
Brazil, 1945
Brunei Darussalam, 1984
Bulgaria, 1955
Burkina Faso, 1960
Burundi, 1962
Cambodia, 1955
Cameroon, 1960
Canada, 1945

Cape Verde, 1975
Central African Republic, 1960
Chad, 1960
Chile, 1945
China, 1945
Colombia, 1945
Comoros, 1975
Congo, Democratic Republic of the, 1960
Congo, Republic of the, 1960
Costa Rica, 1945
Côte d'Ivoire, 1960
Croatia, 1992
Cuba, 1945
Cyprus, 1960

Czech Republic, 1993
Denmark, 1945
Djibouti, 1977
Dominica, 1978
Dominican Republic, 1945
Ecuador, 1945
Egypt, 1945
El Salvador, 1945
Equatorial Guinea, 1968
Eritrea, 1993
Estonia, 1991
Ethiopia, 1945
Fiji, 1970
Finland, 1955
France, 1945
Gabon, 1960
Gambia, 1965
Georgia, 1992
Germany, 1973
Ghana, 1957
Greece, 1945
Grenada, 1974
Guatemala, 1945
Guinea, 1958
Guinea-Bissau, 1974
Guyana, 1966
Haiti, 1945
Honduras, 1945
Hungary, 1955
Iceland, 1946
India, 1945
Indonesia, 1950
Iran, 1945
Iraq, 1945
Ireland, 1955
Israel, 1949
Italy, 1955
Jamaica, 1962
Japan, 1956
Jordan, 1955
Kazakhstan, 1992
Kenya, 1963
Kiribati, 1999
Korea, Democratic People's
    Republic of (North Korea),
    1991
Korea, Republic of (South
    Korea), 1991
Kuwait, 1963
Kyrgyzstan, 1992
Laos, 1955

Latvia, 1991
Lebanon, 1945
Lesotho, 1966
Liberia, 1945
Libya, 1955
Liechtenstein, 1990
Lithuania, 1991
Luxembourg, 1945
Macedonia, Former Yugoslav
    Republic of, 1993
Madagascar, 1960
Malawi, 1964
Malaysia, 1957
Maldives, 1965
Mali, 1960
Malta, 1964
Marshall Islands, 1991
Mauritania, 1961
Mauritius, 1968
Mexico, 1945
Micronesia, 1991
Moldova, 1992
Monaco, 1993
Mongolia, 1961
Montenegro, 2006
Morocco, 1956
Mozambique, 1975
Myanmar, 1948
Namibia, 1990
Nauru, 1999
Nepal, 1955
Netherlands, 1945
New Zealand, 1945
Nicaragua, 1945
Niger, 1960
Nigeria, 1960
Norway, 1945
Oman, 1971
Pakistan, 1947
Palau, 1994
Panama, 1945
Papua New Guinea, 1975
Paraguay, 1945
Peru, 1945
Philippines, 1945
Poland, 1945
Portugal, 1955
Qatar, 1971
Romania, 1955
Russia, 1945
Rwanda, 1962

Saint Kitts and Nevis, 1983
Saint Lucia, 1979
Saint Vincent and the
    Grenadines, 1980
Samoa, 1976
San Marino, 1992
Sao Tome and Principe, 1975
Saudi Arabia, 1945
Senegal, 1960
Serbia, 2000
Seychelles, 1976
Sierra Leone, 1961
Singapore, 1965
Slovakia, 1993
Slovenia, 1992
Solomon Islands, 1978
Somalia, 1960
South Africa, 1945
Spain, 1955
Sri Lanka, 1955
Sudan, 1956
Suriname, 1975
Swaziland, 1968
Sweden, 1946
Switzerland, 2002
Syria, 1945
Tajikistan, 1992
Tanzania, 1961
Thailand, 1946
Timor-Leste, 2002
Togo, 1960
Tonga, 1999
Trinidad and Tobago, 1962
Tunisia, 1956
Turkey, 1945
Turkmenistan, 1992
Tuvalu, 2000
Uganda, 1962
UK, 1945
Ukraine, 1945
United Arab Emirates, 1971
Uruguay, 1945
USA, 1945
Uzbekistan, 1992
Vanuatu, 1981
Venezuela, 1945
Viet Nam, 1977
Yemen, 1947
Zambia, 1964
Zimbabwe, 1980

Website: <http://www.un.org/>

UN Security Council

Permanent members (the P5): China, France, Russia, UK, USA

Non-permanent members (10): Austria*, Bosnia and Herzegovina**, Brazil**, Gabon**, Japan*, Lebanon**, Mexico*, Nigeria**, Turkey*, Uganda*

> *Note*: Non-permanent members are elected by the UN General Assembly for two-year terms.
> * Member in 2009–10.
> ** Member in 2010–11.

Website: <http://www.un.org/sc/>

Conference on Disarmament (CD)

The CD is a multilateral arms control negotiating body that is intended to be the single multilateral disarmament negotiating forum of the international community. It has been enlarged and renamed several times since 1959. It is not a UN body but reports to the UN General Assembly. It is based in Geneva, Switzerland.

Members (65): Algeria, Argentina, Australia, Austria, Bangladesh, Belarus, Belgium, Brazil, Bulgaria, Cameroon, Canada, Chile, China, Colombia, Congo (Democratic Republic of the), Cuba, Ecuador, Egypt, Ethiopia, Finland, France, Germany, Hungary, India, Indonesia, Iran, Iraq, Ireland, Israel, Italy, Japan, Kazakhstan, Kenya, Korea (North), Korea (South), Malaysia, Mexico, Mongolia, Morocco, Myanmar, Netherlands, New Zealand, Nigeria, Norway, Pakistan, Peru, Poland, Romania, Russia, Senegal, Slovakia, South Africa, Spain, Sri Lanka, Sweden, Switzerland, Syria, Tunisia, Turkey, UK, Ukraine, USA, Venezuela, Viet Nam, Zimbabwe

Website: <http://www.unog.ch/disarmament/>

International Atomic Energy Agency (IAEA)

The IAEA is an intergovernmental organization within the UN system. It is endowed by its Statute, which entered into force in 1957, to promote the peaceful uses of atomic energy and ensure that nuclear activities are not used to further any military purpose. Under the 1968 Non-Proliferation Treaty and the nuclear weapon-free zone treaties, non-nuclear weapon states must accept IAEA nuclear safeguards to demonstrate the fulfilment of their obligation not to manufacture nuclear weapons. Its headquarters are in Vienna, Austria.

Members (151): Afghanistan, Albania, Algeria, Angola, Argentina, Armenia, Australia, Austria, Azerbaijan, *Bahrain*, Bangladesh, Belarus, Belgium, Belize, Benin, Bolivia, Bosnia and Herzegovina, Botswana, Brazil, Bulgaria, Burkina Faso, *Burundi*, *Cambodia**, Cameroon, Canada, Central African Republic, Chad, Chile, China, Colombia, Congo (Democratic Republic of the), *Congo (Republic of the)*, Costa Rica, Côte d'Ivoire, Croatia, Cuba, Cyprus, Czech Republic, Denmark, Dominican Republic, Ecuador, Egypt, El Salvador, Eritrea, Estonia, Ethiopia, Finland, France, Gabon, Georgia, Germany, Ghana, Greece, Guatemala, Haiti, Holy See, Honduras, Hungary, Iceland, India, Indonesia, Iran, Iraq, Ireland, Israel, Italy, Jamaica, Japan, Jordan,

Kazakhstan, Kenya, Korea (South), Kuwait, Kyrgyzstan, Latvia, Lebanon, *Lesotho*, Liberia, Libya, Liechtenstein, Lithuania, Luxembourg, Macedonia (Former Yugoslav Republic of), Madagascar, Malawi, Malaysia, Mali, Malta, Marshall Islands, Mauritania, Mauritius, Mexico, Moldova, Monaco, Mongolia, Montenegro, Morocco, Mozambique, Myanmar, Namibia, Nepal, Netherlands, New Zealand, Nicaragua, Niger, Nigeria, Norway, *Oman*, Pakistan, Palau, Panama, Paraguay, Peru, Philippines, Poland, Portugal, Qatar, Romania, Russia, Saudi Arabia, Senegal, Serbia, Seychelles, Sierra Leone, Singapore, Slovakia, Slovenia, South Africa, Spain, Sri Lanka, Sudan, Sweden, Switzerland, Syria, Tajikistan, Tanzania, Thailand, Tunisia, Turkey, Uganda, UK, Ukraine, United Arab Emirates, Uruguay, USA, Uzbekistan, Venezuela, Viet Nam, Yemen, Zambia, Zimbabwe

Notes: North Korea was a member of the IAEA until June 1994. In addition to the above-named states, Cape Verde, Papua New Guinea, Rwanda and Togo have had their membership approved by the IAEA General Conference; it will take effect once the state deposits the necessary legal instruments with the IAEA.

* Cambodia withdrew from the IAEA in Mar. 2003 but rejoined in Nov. 2009.

Website: <http://www.iaea.org/>

African Union (AU)

The AU was formally established in 2001 when the Constitutive Act of the African Union entered into force. In 2002 it replaced the Organization for African Unity. Membership is open to all African states. The AU promotes unity, security and conflict resolution, democracy, human rights, and political, social and economic integration in Africa. The Peace and Security Council (PSC) is a standing decision-making organ for the prevention, management and resolution of conflicts. The AU's headquarters are in Addis Ababa, Ethiopia.

Members (53): Algeria, Angola, Benin, Botswana, Burkina Faso, Burundi, Cameroon, Cape Verde, Central African Republic, Chad, Comoros, Congo (Democratic Republic of the), Congo (Republic of the), Côte d'Ivoire, Djibouti, Egypt, Equatorial Guinea, Eritrea, Ethiopia, Gabon, Gambia, Ghana, Guinea*, Guinea-Bissau, Kenya, Lesotho, Liberia, Libya, Madagascar**, Malawi, Mali, Mauritania, Mauritius, Mozambique, Namibia, Niger***, Nigeria, Rwanda, Western Sahara (Sahrawi Arab Democratic Republic, SADR), Sao Tome and Principe, Senegal, Seychelles, Sierra Leone, Somalia, South Africa, Sudan, Swaziland, Tanzania, Togo, Tunisia, Uganda, Zambia, Zimbabwe

* Guinea's membership of the AU was suspended in Dec. 2008.
** Madagascar's membership was suspended in Mar. 2009.
*** Niger's membership was suspended in Feb. 2010.

Website: <http://www.africa-union.org/>

Asia–Pacific Economic Cooperation (APEC)

APEC was established in 1989 to enhance open trade and economic prosperity in the Asia–Pacific region. Security and political issues, including combating terrorism, non-proliferation of weapons of mass destruction and effective transfer control systems, have been increasingly discussed since the mid-1990s. Its seat is in Singapore.

Member economies (21): Australia, Brunei Darussalam, Canada, Chile, China, Hong Kong, Indonesia, Japan, Korea (South), Malaysia, Mexico, New Zealand, Papua New Guinea, Peru, Philippines, Russia, Singapore, Taiwan, Thailand, USA, Viet Nam

Website: <http://www.apec.org/>

Association of Southeast Asian Nations (ASEAN)

ASEAN was established in 1967 to promote economic, social and cultural development as well as regional peace and security in South East Asia. The seat of the secretariat is in Jakarta, Indonesia.

Members (10): Brunei Darussalam, Cambodia, Indonesia, Laos, Malaysia, Myanmar, Philippines, Singapore, Thailand, Viet Nam

Website: <http://www.aseansec.org/>

ASEAN Regional Forum (ARF)

The ARF was established in 1994 to address security issues.

Participants (27): The ASEAN member states and Australia, Bangladesh, Canada, China, European Union, India, Japan, Korea (North), Korea (South), Mongolia, New Zealand, Pakistan, Papua New Guinea, Russia, Sri Lanka, Timor-Leste, USA

Website: <http://www.aseanregionalforum.org/>

ASEAN Plus Three (APT)

The APT cooperation began in 1997, in the wake of the Asian financial crisis, and was institutionalized in 1999. It aims to foster economic, political and security cooperation and financial stability among its members.

Participants (13): The ASEAN member states and China, Japan, Korea (South)

Website: <http://www.aseansec.org/20182.htm>

East Asia Summit (EAS)

The East Asia Summit started in 2005 as a regional forum for dialogue on strategic, political and economic issues with the aim of promoting peace, stability and economic prosperity in East Asia. The annual meetings are held in connection with the ASEAN summits.

Participants (16): The ASEAN member states and Australia, China, India, Japan, Korea (South), New Zealand

Website: <http://www.dfat.gov.au/asean/eas/>

Australia Group (AG)

The AG is a group of states, formed in 1985, that seeks to prevent the intentional or inadvertent supply of materials or equipment to chemical or biological weapon programmes by sharing information on proliferation cases and strategies to manage them, including the harmonization of transfer controls.

Participants (41): Argentina, Australia, Austria, Belgium, Bulgaria, Canada, Croatia, Cyprus, Czech Republic, Denmark, Estonia, European Commission, Finland, France, Germany, Greece, Hungary, Iceland, Ireland, Italy, Japan, Korea (South), Latvia, Lithuania, Luxembourg, Malta, Netherlands, New Zealand, Norway, Poland, Portugal, Romania, Slovakia, Slovenia, Spain, Sweden, Switzerland, Turkey, UK, Ukraine, USA

Website: <http://www.australiagroup.net/>

Collective Security Treaty Organization (CSTO)

The CSTO was formally established in 2002–2003 by six signatories of the 1992 Collective Security Treaty. It aims to promote cooperation among its members. An objective is to provide a more efficient response to strategic problems such as terrorism and narcotics trafficking. Its seat is in Moscow, Russia.

Members (7): Armenia, Belarus, Kazakhstan, Kyrgyzstan, Russia, Tajikistan, Uzbekistan

Website: <http://www.dkb.gov.ru/>

Commonwealth of Independent States (CIS)

The CIS was established in 1991 as a framework for multilateral cooperation among former Soviet republics. Its headquarters are in Minsk, Belarus.

Members (11): Armenia, Azerbaijan, Belarus, Kazakhstan, Kyrgyzstan, Moldova, Russia, Tajikistan, Turkmenistan, Ukraine, Uzbekistan

Note: Georgia withdrew from the CIS on 18 Aug. 2009.

Website: <http://www.cis.minsk.by/>

Commonwealth of Nations

Established in its current form in 1949, the Commonwealth is an organization of developed and developing countries whose aim is to advance democracy, human rights, and sustainable economic and social development within its member states and beyond. Its secretariat is in London, UK.

Members (54): Antigua and Barbuda, Australia, Bahamas, Bangladesh, Barbados, Belize, Botswana, Brunei Darussalam, Cameroon, Canada, Cyprus, Dominica, Fiji*, Gambia, Ghana, Grenada, Guyana, India, Jamaica, Kenya, Kiribati, Lesotho, Malawi, Malaysia, Maldives, Malta, Mauritius, Mozambique, Namibia, Nauru, New Zealand, Nigeria, Pakistan, Papua New Guinea, *Rwanda*, Saint Kitts and Nevis, Saint Lucia, Saint Vincent and the Grenadines, Samoa, Seychelles, Sierra Leone, Singapore, Solomon Islands, South Africa, Sri Lanka, Swaziland, Tanzania, Tonga, Trinidad and Tobago, Tuvalu, Uganda, UK, Vanuatu, Zambia

* Fiji's membership of the Commonwealth was suspended on 1 Sep. 2009.

Website: <http://www.thecommonwealth.org/>

Communauté Économiques d'États de l'Afrique Centrale (CEEAC, Economic Community of Central African States, ECCAS)

CEEAC was established in 1983 to promote political dialogue, create a customs union and establish common policies in Central Africa. Its secretariat is in Libreville, Gabon. The Council for Peace and Security in Central Africa (COPAX) is a mechanism for promoting joint political and military strategies for conflict prevention, management and resolution in Central Africa.

Members (10): Angola, Burundi, Cameroon, Central African Republic, Chad, Congo (Democratic Republic of the), Congo (Republic of the), Equatorial Guinea, Gabon, Sao Tome and Principe

Website: <http://www.ceeac-eccas.org/>

Comprehensive Nuclear-Test-Ban Treaty Organization (CTBTO)

The CTBTO will become operational when the 1996 Comprehensive Nuclear-Test-Ban Treaty (CTBT) has entered into force. It will resolve questions of compliance with the treaty and act as a forum for consultation and cooperation among the states parties. A Preparatory Commission was established to prepare for the work of the CTBTO, in particular by establishing the International Monitoring System, consisting of seismic, hydro-acoustic, infrasound and radionuclide stations from which data is transmitted to the CTBTO International Data Centre. Its seat is in Vienna, Austria.

Signatories to the CTBT (182): See annex A

Website: <http://www.ctbto.org/>

Conference on Interaction and Confidence-building Measures in Asia (CICA)

Initiated in 1992, CICA was established by the 1999 Declaration on the Principles Guiding Relations among the CICA Member States, as a forum to enhance security cooperation and confidence-building measures among the member states. It also promotes economic, social and cultural cooperation.

Members (20): Afghanistan, Azerbaijan, China, Egypt, India, Iran, Israel, Jordan, Kazakhstan, Korea (South), Kyrgyzstan, Mongolia, Pakistan, Palestine, Russia, Tajikistan, Thailand, Turkey, United Arab Emirates, Uzbekistan

Website: <http://www.s-cica.org/>

Council for Security Cooperation in the Asia Pacific (CSCAP)

CSCAP was established in 1993 as an informal, non-governmental process for regional confidence building and security cooperation through dialogue and consultation on security matters in the Asia–Pacific region.

Member committees (21): Australia, Brunei Darussalam, Cambodia, Canada, China, CSCAP Europe, India, Indonesia, Japan, Korea (North), Korea (South), Malaysia, Mongolia, New Zealand, Papua New Guinea, Philippines, Russia, Singapore, Thailand, USA, Viet Nam

Website: <http://www.cscap.org/>

Council of Europe (COE)

Established in 1949, the Council is open to membership of all European states that accept the principle of the rule of law and guarantee their citizens' human rights and fundamental freedoms. Its seat is in Strasbourg, France. Among its organs are the European Court of Human Rights and the Council of Europe Development Bank.

Members (47): Albania, Andorra, Armenia, Austria, Azerbaijan, Belgium, Bosnia and Herzegovina, Bulgaria, Croatia, Cyprus, Czech Republic, Denmark, Estonia, Finland, France, Georgia, Germany, Greece, Hungary, Iceland, Ireland, Italy, Latvia, Liechtenstein, Lithuania, Luxembourg, Macedonia (Former Yugoslav Republic of), Malta, Moldova, Monaco, Montenegro, Netherlands, Norway, Poland, Portugal, Romania, Russia, San Marino, Serbia, Slovakia, Slovenia, Spain, Sweden, Switzerland, Turkey, UK, Ukraine

Website: <http://www.coe.int/>

Council of the Baltic Sea States (CBSS)

The CBSS was established in 1992 as a regional intergovernmental organization for cooperation among the states of the Baltic Sea region. Its secretariat is in Stockholm, Sweden.

Members (12): Denmark, Estonia, European Commission, Finland, Germany, Iceland, Latvia, Lithuania, Norway, Poland, Russia, Sweden

Website: <http://www.cbss.org/>

Economic Community of West African States (ECOWAS)

ECOWAS was established in 1975 to promote trade and cooperation and con-tribute to development in West Africa. In 1981 it adopted the Protocol on Mutual Assistance in Defence Matters. Its executive secretariat is in Lagos, Nigeria.

Members (15): Benin, Burkina Faso, Cape Verde, Côte d'Ivoire, Gambia, Ghana, Guinea*, Guinea-Bissau, Liberia, Mali, Niger**, Nigeria, Senegal, Sierra Leone, Togo

 * Guinea was suspended from participation in the activities of ECOWAS on 10 Jan. 2009.
 ** Niger was suspended from participation in the activities of the ECOWAS on 21 Oct. 2009.

Website: <http://www.ecowas.int/>

European Union (EU)

The EU is an organization of European states that cooperate in a wide field, including a single market with free movement of people, goods, services and capital, a common currency for some members, and a Common Foreign and

Security Policy (CFSP). Its main bodies are the European Council, the Council of the European Union, the European Commission and the European Parliament. The CFSP and the Common Security and Defence Policy (CSDP) are coordinated by the High Representative of the Union for Foreign Affairs and Security Policy. The 2007 Treaty of Lisbon, which modernizes the way in which the EU functions, entered into force on 1 December 2009. The EU's seat is in Brussels, Belgium.

Members (27): Austria, Belgium, Bulgaria, Cyprus, Czech Republic, Denmark, Estonia, Finland, France, Germany, Greece, Hungary, Ireland, Italy, Latvia, Lithuania, Luxembourg, Malta, Netherlands, Poland, Portugal, Romania, Slovakia, Slovenia, Spain, Sweden, UK

Website: <http://europa.eu/>

European Atomic Energy Community (Euratom, or EAEC)

Euratom was created by the 1957 Treaty Establishing the European Atomic Energy Community (Euratom Treaty) to promote the development of nuclear energy for peaceful purposes and to administer the multinational regional safeguards system covering the EU member states. The Euratom Supply Agency, located in Luxembourg, has the task of ensuring a regular and equitable supply of ores, source materials and special fissile materials to EU member states.

Members (27): The EU member states

Website: <http://ec.europa.eu/euratom/>

European Defence Agency (EDA)

The EDA is an agency of the EU, under the direction of the Council. It was established in 2004 to help develop European defence capabilities, to promote European armaments cooperation and to work for a strong European defence technological and industrial base. The EDA's decision-making body is the Steering Board, composed of the defence ministers of the participating member states and the EU's High Representative for Foreign Affairs and Security Policy (as head of the agency). The EDA is located in Brussels, Belgium.

Participating member states (26): Austria, Belgium, Bulgaria, Cyprus, Czech Republic, Estonia, Finland, France, Germany, Greece, Hungary, Ireland, Italy, Latvia, Lithuania, Luxembourg, Malta, Netherlands, Poland, Portugal, Romania, Slovakia, Slovenia, Spain, Sweden, UK

Website: <http://eda.europa.eu/>

Group of Eight (G8)

The G8 is a group of (originally seven) leading industrialized countries that have met informally, at the level of head of state or government, since the 1970s. The G8 Global Partnership against the Spread of Weapons and Materials of Mass Destruction, launched in 2002, addresses non-proliferation, disarmament, counterterrorism and nuclear safety issues.

Members (8): Canada, France, Germany, Italy, Japan, Russia, UK, USA

Website: <http://www.g8.gc.ca/>

Gulf Cooperation Council (GCC)

Formally called the Cooperation Council for the Arab States of the Gulf, the GCC was created in 1981 to promote regional integration in such areas as economy, finance, trade, administration and legislation and to foster scientific and technical progress. The members also cooperate in areas of foreign policy and military and security matters. The Supreme Council is the highest GCC authority. Its headquarters are in Riyadh, Saudi Arabia

Members (6): Bahrain, Kuwait, Oman, Qatar, Saudi Arabia, United Arab Emirates

Website: <http://www.gcc-sg.org/>

Hague Code of Conduct against Ballistic Missile Proliferation (HCOC)

The 2002 HCOC is subscribed to by a group of states that recognize its principles, primarily the need to prevent and curb the proliferation of ballistic missile systems capable of delivering weapons of mass destruction and the importance of strengthening multilateral disarmament and non-proliferation mechanisms. The Austrian Ministry of Foreign Affairs, Vienna, Austria, acts as the HCOC secretariat.

Subscribing states (130): Afghanistan, Albania, Andorra, Argentina, Armenia, Australia, Austria, Azerbaijan, Belarus, Belgium, Benin, Bosnia and Herzegovina, Bulgaria, Burkina Faso, Burundi, Cambodia, Cameroon, Canada, Cape Verde, Chad, Chile, Colombia, Comoros, Cook Islands, Costa Rica, Croatia, Cyprus, Czech Republic, Denmark, Dominican Republic, Ecuador, El Salvador, Eritrea, Estonia, Ethiopia, Fiji, Finland, France, Gabon, Gambia, Georgia, Germany, Ghana, Greece, Guatemala, Guinea, Guinea-Bissau, Guyana, Haiti, Holy See, Honduras, Hungary, Iceland, Ireland, Italy, Japan, Jordan, Kazakhstan, Kenya, Kiribati, Korea (South), Latvia, Liberia, Libya, Liechtenstein, Lithuania, Luxembourg, Macedonia (Former Yugoslav Republic of), Madagascar, Malawi, Maldives, Mali, Malta, Marshall Islands, Mauritania, Micronesia, Moldova, Monaco, Mongolia, Montenegro, Morocco, Mozambique, Netherlands, New Zealand, Nicaragua, Niger, Nigeria, Norway, Palau, Panama, Papua New Guinea, Paraguay, Peru, Philippines, Poland, Portugal, Romania, Russia, Rwanda, Samoa, San Marino, Senegal, Serbia, Seychelles, Sierra Leone, Slovakia, Slovenia, South Africa, Spain, Sudan, Suriname, Sweden, Switzerland, Tajikistan, Tanzania, Timor-Leste, Tonga, Tunisia, Turkey, Turkmenistan, Tuvalu, Uganda, UK, Ukraine, Uruguay, USA, Uzbekistan, Vanuatu, Venezuela, Zambia

Website: <http://www.bmeia.gv.at/index.php?id=64664&L=1>

Intergovernmental Authority on Development (IGAD)

Initiated in 1986 as the Intergovernmental Authority on Drought and Development, IGAD was formally established in 1996 to promote peace and stability in the Horn of Africa and to create mechanisms for conflict prevention, management and resolution. Its secretariat is in Djibouti.

Members (7): Djibouti, Eritrea, Ethiopia, Kenya, Somalia, Sudan, Uganda

Website: <http://www.igad.int/>

International Criminal Court (ICC)

The ICC is an independent, permanent international criminal court dealing with questions of genocide, war crimes and crimes against humanity. The court's statute was adopted in Rome in 1998 and entered into force on 1 July 2002. Its seat is at The Hague, the Netherlands.

Parties (110): Afghanistan, Albania, Andorra, Antigua and Barbuda, Argentina, Australia, Austria, Barbados, Belgium, Belize, Benin, Bolivia, Bosnia and Herzegovina, Botswana, Brazil, Bulgaria, Burkina Faso, Burundi, Cambodia, Canada, Central African Republic, Chad, *Chile*, Colombia, Comoros, Congo (Democratic Republic of the), Congo (Republic of the), Cook Islands, Costa Rica, Croatia, Cyprus, *Czech Republic*, Denmark, Djibouti, Dominica, Dominican Republic, Ecuador, Estonia, Fiji, Finland, France, Gabon, Gambia, Georgia, Germany, Ghana, Greece, Guinea, Guyana, Honduras, Hungary, Iceland, Ireland, Italy, Japan, Jordan, Kenya, Korea (South), Latvia, Lesotho, Liberia, Liechtenstein, Lithuania, Luxembourg, Macedonia (Former Yugoslav Republic of), Madagascar, Malawi, Mali, Malta, Marshall Islands, Mauritius, Mexico, Mongolia, Montenegro, Namibia, Nauru, Netherlands, New Zealand, Niger, Nigeria, Norway, Panama, Paraguay, Peru, Poland, Portugal, Romania, Saint Kitts and Nevis, Saint Vincent and the Grenadines, Samoa, San Marino, Senegal, Serbia, Sierra Leone, Slovakia, Slovenia, South Africa, Spain, Suriname, Sweden, Switzerland, Tajikistan, Tanzania, Timor-Leste, Trinidad and Tobago, Uganda, UK, Uruguay, Venezuela, Zambia

Website: <http://www.icc-cpi.int/>

Joint Compliance and Inspection Commission (JCIC)

The JCIC was the forum established by the 1991 START I Treaty in which the parties exchanged data, resolved questions of compliance, clarified ambiguities and discussed ways to improve implementation of the treaty. It convened at the request of at least one of the parties. It ceased to exist with the expiry of the treaty on 5 December 2009. On entry into force of the 2010 Russian–US New START Treaty, a Bilateral Consultative Commission will be established.

Parties to the START I Treaty (5): See annex A

Joint Consultative Group (JCG)

The JCG was established by the 1990 Treaty on Conventional Armed Forces in Europe (CFE Treaty) to promote the objectives and implementation of the treaty by reconciling ambiguities of interpretation and implementation. Its seat is in Vienna, Austria.

Parties to the CFE Treaty (30): See annex A

Website: <http://www.osce.org/item/13517.html>

League of Arab States

Also known as the Arab League, it was established in 1945. Its principal object-ive is to form closer union among Arab states and foster political and economic cooperation. An agreement for collective defence and economic cooperation among the members was signed in 1950. Its Permanent Headquarters are in Cairo, Egypt.

Members (22): Algeria, Bahrain, Comoros, Djibouti, Egypt, Iraq, Jordan, Kuwait, Lebanon, Libya, Mauritania, Morocco, Oman, Palestine, Qatar, Saudi Arabia, Somalia, Sudan, Syria, Tunisia, United Arab Emirates, Yemen

Website: <http://www.arableagueonline.org/>

Missile Technology Control Regime (MTCR)

The MTCR is an informal group of countries that seek to coordinate national export licensing efforts aimed at preventing the proliferation of missile systems capable of delivering weapons of mass destruction. The countries apply the Guidelines for Sensitive Missile-Relevant Transfers.

Partners (34): Argentina, Australia, Austria, Belgium, Brazil, Bulgaria, Canada, Czech Republic, Denmark, Finland, France, Germany, Greece, Hungary, Iceland, Ireland, Italy, Japan, Korea (South), Luxembourg, Netherlands, New Zealand, Norway, Poland, Portugal, Russia, South Africa, Spain, Sweden, Switzerland, Turkey, UK, Ukraine, USA

Website: <http://www.mtcr.info/>

Non-Aligned Movement (NAM)

NAM was established in 1961 as a forum for consultations and coordination of positions in the United Nations on political, economic and arms control issues among non-aligned states.

Members (118): Afghanistan, Algeria, Angola, Antigua and Barbuda, Bahamas, Bahrain, Bangladesh, Barbados, Belarus, Belize, Benin, Bhutan, Bolivia, Botswana, Brunei Darussalam, Burkina Faso, Burundi, Cambodia, Cameroon, Cape Verde, Central African Republic, Chad, Chile, Colombia, Comoros, Congo (Democratic Republic of the), Congo (Republic of the), Côte d'Ivoire, Cuba, Djibouti, Dominica, Dominican Republic, Ecuador, Egypt, Equatorial Guinea, Eritrea, Ethiopia, Gabon, Gambia, Ghana, Grenada, Guatemala, Guinea, Guinea-Bissau, Guyana, Haiti, Honduras, India, Indonesia, Iran, Iraq, Jamaica, Jordan, Kenya, Korea (North), Kuwait, Laos, Lebanon, Lesotho, Liberia, Libya, Madagascar, Malawi, Malaysia, Maldives, Mali, Mauritania, Mauritius, Mongolia, Morocco, Mozambique, Myanmar, Namibia, Nepal, Nicaragua, Niger, Nigeria, Oman, Pakistan, Palestine Liberation Organization, Panama, Papua New Guinea, Peru, Philippines, Qatar, Rwanda, Saint Kitts and Nevis, Saint Lucia, Saint Vincent and the Grenadines, Sao Tome and Principe, Saudi Arabia, Senegal, Seychelles, Sierra Leone, Singapore, Somalia, South Africa, Sri Lanka, Sudan, Suriname, Swaziland, Syria, Tanzania, Thailand, Timor-Leste, Togo, Trinidad and Tobago, Tunisia, Turkmenistan, Uganda, United Arab Emirates, Uzbekistan, Vanuatu, Venezuela, Viet Nam, Yemen, Zambia, Zimbabwe

Website: <http://www.namegypt.org/>

North Atlantic Treaty Organization (NATO)

NATO was established in 1949 by the North Atlantic Treaty (Washington Treaty) as a Western defence alliance. Article 5 of the treaty defines the members' commitment to respond to an armed attack against any party to the treaty. Its headquarters are in Brussels, Belgium.

Members (28): *Albania*, Belgium, Bulgaria, Canada, *Croatia*, Czech Republic, Denmark, Estonia, France*, Germany, Greece, Hungary, Iceland, Italy, Latvia, Lithuania, Luxembourg, Netherlands, Norway, Poland, Portugal, Romania, Slovakia, Slovenia, Spain, Turkey, UK, USA

   * France rejoined the integrated military structures of NATO during 2009.

Website: <http://www.nato.int/>

Euro-Atlantic Partnership Council (EAPC)

The EAPC brings together NATO and its Partnership for Peace (PFP) partners for dialogue and consultation. It is the overall political framework for the bilateral PFP programme.

Members (50): The NATO member states and Armenia, Austria, Azerbaijan, Belarus, Bosnia and Herzegovina, Finland, Georgia, Ireland, Kazakhstan, Kyrgyzstan, Macedonia (Former Yugoslav Republic of), Malta, Moldova, Montenegro, Russia, Serbia, Sweden, Switzerland, Tajikistan, Turkmenistan, Ukraine, Uzbekistan

Website: <http://www.nato.int/cps/en/natolive/topics_49276.htm>

NATO–Russia Council (NRC)

The NRC was established in 2002 as a mechanism for consultation, consensus building, cooperation, and joint decisions and action on security issues, focusing on areas of mutual interest identified in the 1997 NATO–Russia Founding Act on Mutual Relations, Cooperation and Security and new areas, such as terrorism, crisis management and non-proliferation.

Participants (29): The NATO member states and Russia

Website: <http://www.nato-russia-council.info/>

NATO–Ukraine Commission (NUC)

The NUC was established in 1997 for consultations on political and security issues, conflict prevention and resolution, non-proliferation, arms transfers and technology transfers, and other subjects of common concern.

Participants (29): The NATO member states and Ukraine

Website: <http://www.nato.int/issues/nuc/>

Nuclear Suppliers Group (NSG)

The NSG, formerly also known as the London Club, was established in 1975. It coordinates national transfer controls on nuclear materials according to its Guidelines for Nuclear Transfers (London Guidelines, first agreed in 1978), which contain a 'trigger list' of materials that should trigger IAEA safeguards when they are to be exported for peaceful purposes to any non-nuclear weapon state, and the Guidelines for Transfers of Nuclear-Related Dual-Use Equipment, Materials, Software and Related Technology (Warsaw Guidelines).

Participants (46): Argentina, Australia, Austria, Belarus, Belgium, Brazil, Bulgaria, Canada, China, Croatia, Cyprus, Czech Republic, Denmark, Estonia, Finland, France, Germany, Greece, Hungary, *Iceland*, Ireland, Italy, Japan, Kazakhstan, Korea (South), Latvia, Lithuania, Luxembourg, Malta, Netherlands, New Zealand, Norway, Poland, Portugal, Romania, Russia, Slovakia, Slovenia, South Africa, Spain, Sweden, Switzerland, Turkey, UK, Ukraine, USA

Website: <http://www.nuclearsuppliersgroup.org/>

Open Skies Consultative Commission (OSCC)

The OSCC was established by the 1992 Open Skies Treaty to resolve questions of compliance with the treaty.

Parties to the Open Skies Treaty (34): See annex A

Website: <http://www.osce.org/item/13516.html>

Organisation Conjointe de Coopération en matière d'Armement (OCCAR, Organisation for Joint Armament Cooperation)

OCCAR was established in 1996, with legal status since 2001, by France, Germany, Italy and the UK. Its aim is to provide more effective and efficient arrangements for the management of specific collaborative armament programmes. Its headquarters are in Bonn, Germany.

Members (6): Belgium, France, Germany, Italy, Spain, UK

Website: <http://www.occar-ea.org/>

Organisation for Economic Co-operation and Development (OECD)

Established in 1961, the OECD's objectives are to promote economic and social welfare by coordinating policies among the member states. Its headquarters are in Paris, France.

Members (30): Australia, Austria, Belgium, Canada, Czech Republic, Denmark, Finland, France, Germany, Greece, Hungary, Iceland, Ireland, Italy, Japan, Korea (South), Luxembourg, Mexico, Netherlands, New Zealand, Norway, Poland, Portugal, Slovakia, Spain, Sweden, Switzerland, Turkey, UK, USA

Website: <http://www.oecd.org/>

Organization for Democracy and Economic Development–GUAM

GUAM is a group of four states, established to promote stability and strengthen security, whose history goes back to 1997. The Organization was established in 2006. The members cooperate to promote social and economic development and trade in eight working groups. Its secretariat is in Kyiv, Ukraine.

Members (4): Azerbaijan, Georgia, Moldova, Ukraine

Website: <http://guam-organization.org/>

Organization for Security and Co-operation in Europe (OSCE)

The Conference on Security and Co-operation in Europe (CSCE), which had been initiated in 1973, was renamed the OSCE in 1995 as a primary instrument of comprehensive and cooperative security for early warning, conflict prevention, crisis management and post-conflict rehabilitation in its area. Its headquarters are in Vienna, Austria. Its Forum for Security Co-operation (FSC), also in Vienna, deals with arms control and confidence- and security-building measures. The OSCE comprises several institutions, all located in Europe.

Participants (56): Albania, Andorra, Armenia, Austria, Azerbaijan, Belarus, Belgium, Bosnia and Herzegovina, Bulgaria, Canada, Croatia, Cyprus, Czech Republic, Denmark, Estonia, Finland, France, Georgia, Germany, Greece, Holy See, Hungary, Iceland, Ireland, Italy, Kazakhstan, Kyrgyzstan, Latvia, Liechtenstein, Lithuania, Luxembourg, Macedonia (Former Yugoslav Republic of), Malta, Moldova, Monaco, Montenegro, Netherlands, Norway, Poland, Portugal, Romania, Russia, San Marino, Serbia, Slovakia, Slovenia, Spain, Sweden, Switzerland, Tajikistan, Turkey, Turkmenistan, UK, Ukraine, USA, Uzbekistan

Website: <http://www.osce.org/>

Organisation for the Prohibition of Chemical Weapons (OPCW)

The OPCW was established by the 1993 Chemical Weapons Convention to oversee implementation of the convention and resolve questions of compliance. Its seat is in The Hague, the Netherlands.

Parties to the Chemical Weapons Convention (188): See annex A

Website: <http://www.opcw.org/>

Organization of American States (OAS)

The OAS is a group of states in the Americas that adopted its charter in 1948, with the objective of strengthening peace and security in the western hemisphere. The general secretariat is in Washington, DC, USA.

Members (35): Antigua and Barbuda, Argentina, Bahamas, Barbados, Belize, Bolivia, Brazil, Canada, Chile, Colombia, Costa Rica, Cuba*, Dominica, Dominican Republic, Ecuador, El Salvador, Grenada, Guatemala, Guyana, Haiti, Honduras**, Jamaica, Mexico, Nicaragua, Panama, Paraguay, Peru, Saint Kitts and Nevis, Saint Lucia, Saint Vincent and the Grenadines, Suriname, Trinidad and Tobago, Uruguay, USA, Venezuela

* By a resolution of 3 June 2009, the 1962 resolution that excluded Cuba from the OAS ceased to have effect; according to the 2009 resolution, Cuba's participation in the organization 'will be the result of a process of dialogue'.

** On 5 July 2009 Honduras was suspended from active participation in the OAS.

Website: <http://www.oas.org/>

Organization of the Black Sea Economic Cooperation (BSEC)

BSEC was established in 1992. Its aims are to ensure peace, stability and prosperity and to promote and develop economic cooperation and progress in the Black Sea region. Its permanent secretariat is in Istanbul, Turkey.

Members (12): Albania, Armenia, Azerbaijan, Bulgaria, Georgia, Greece, Moldova, Romania, Russia, Serbia, Turkey, Ukraine

Website: <http://www.bsec-organization.org/>

Organization of the Islamic Conference (OIC)

The OIC was established in 1969 by Islamic states to promote cooperation among the members and to support peace, security and the struggle of the people of Palestine and all Muslim people. Its secretariat is in Jeddah, Saudi Arabia.

Members (57): Afghanistan, Albania, Algeria, Azerbaijan, Bahrain, Bangladesh, Benin, Brunei Darussalam, Burkina Faso, Cameroon, Chad, Comoros, Côte d'Ivoire, Djibouti, Egypt, Gabon, Gambia, Guinea, Guinea-Bissau, Guyana, Indonesia, Iran, Iraq, Jordan, Kazakhstan, Kuwait, Kyrgyzstan, Lebanon, Libya, Malaysia, Maldives, Mali, Mauritania, Morocco, Mozambique, Niger, Nigeria, Oman, Pakistan, Palestine, Qatar, Saudi Arabia, Senegal, Sierra Leone, Somalia, Sudan, Suriname, Syria, Tajikistan, Togo, Tunisia, Turkey, Turkmenistan, Uganda, United Arab Emirates, Uzbekistan, Yemen

Website: <http://www.oic-oci.org/>

Organismo para la Proscripción de las Armas Nucleares en la América Latina y el Caribe (OPANAL, Agency for the Prohibition of Nuclear Weapons in Latin America and the Caribbean)

OPANAL was established by the 1967 Treaty of Tlatelolco to resolve, together with the IAEA, questions of compliance with the treaty. Its seat is in Mexico City, Mexico.

Parties to the Treaty of Tlatelolco (33): See annex A

Website: <http://www.opanal.org/>

Pacific Islands Forum

The Forum was founded in 1971 by a group of South Pacific states that proposed the South Pacific Nuclear Free Zone, embodied in the 1985 Treaty of Rarotonga. As well as monitoring implementation of the treaty, the Forum provides a venue for informal discussions on a wide range of issues. The secretariat is in Suva, Fiji.

Members (16): Australia, Cook Islands, Fiji, Kiribati, Marshall Islands, Micronesia, Nauru, New Zealand, Niue, Palau, Papua New Guinea, Samoa, Solomon Islands, Tonga, Tuvalu, Vanuatu

Website: <http://www.forumsec.org/>

Regional Cooperation Council

The RCC was launched in 2008 as the successor of the Stability Pact for South Eastern Europe that was initiated by the EU at the 1999 Conference on South Eastern Europe. It promotes mutual cooperation and European and Euro-Atlantic integration of South Eastern Europe in order to inspire development in the region for the benefit of its people. It focuses on six priority areas: economic and social development, energy and infrastructure, justice and home affairs, security cooperation, building human capital, and parliamentary cooperation. Its secretariat is based in Sarajevo and its Liaison Office in Brussels.

Members (45): Albania, Austria, Bosnia and Herzegovina, Bulgaria, Canada, Council of Europe, Council of Europe Development Bank, Croatia, Czech Republic, Denmark, European Bank for Reconstruction and Development, European Investment Bank, European Union, Germany, Finland, France, Greece, Hungary, Ireland, Italy, Latvia, Macedonia (Former Yugoslav Republic of), Moldova, Montenegro, North Atlantic Treaty Organization, Norway, Organisation for Economic Co-operation and Development, Organization for Security and Co-operation in Europe, Poland, Romania, Serbia, Slovakia, Slovenia, South East European Cooperative Initiative, Spain, Sweden, Switzerland, Turkey, UK, United Nations, UN Economic Commission for Europe, UN Development Programme, UN Interim Administration Mission in Kosovo, USA, World Bank

Website: <http://www.rcc.int/>

Shanghai Cooperation Organisation (SCO)

The SCO's predecessor group, the Shanghai Five, was founded in 1996; it was renamed the SCO in 2001 and opened for membership of all states that support its aims. The member states cooperate on confidence-building measures and regional security and in the economic sphere. The SCO secretariat is in Beijing, China.

Members (6): China, Kazakhstan, Kyrgyzstan, Russia, Tajikistan, Uzbekistan

Website: <http://www.sectsco.org/>

Six-Party Talks

The talks are a forum for multilateral negotiations on North Korea's nuclear programme. They are held in Beijing and are chaired by China.

Participants (6): China, Japan, Korea (North), Korea (South), Russia, USA

Southeast European Cooperative Initiative (SECI)

SECI was initiated by the USA in coordination with the EU in 1996 to promote cooperation and stability among the countries of South Eastern Europe and facilitate their accession into European structures. The SECI secretariat is located in the OSCE offices in Vienna, Austria.

Members (13): Albania, Bosnia and Herzegovina, Bulgaria, Croatia, Greece, Hungary, Macedonia (Former Yugoslav Republic of), Moldova, Montenegro, Romania, Serbia, Slovenia, Turkey

Website: <http://www.secinet.info/>

Southern African Development Community (SADC)

SADC was established in 1992 to promote regional economic development and the fundamental principles of sovereignty, peace and security, human rights and democracy. The Organ on Politics, Defence and Security Cooperation (OPDS) is intended to promote peace and security in the region. The secretariat is in Gaborone, Botswana.

Members (15): Angola, Botswana, Congo (Democratic Republic of the), Lesotho, Madagascar*, Malawi, Mauritius, Mozambique, Namibia, Seychelles, South Africa, Swaziland, Tanzania, Zambia, Zimbabwe

   * Madagascar was suspended from all organs of the SADC in Mar. 2009.

Website: <http://www.sadc.int/>

Special Verification Commission (SVC)

The Commission was established by the 1987 Treaty on the Elimination of Intermediate-Range and Shorter-Range Missiles (INF Treaty) as a forum to resolve compliance questions and measures necessary to improve the viability and effectiveness of the treaty.

Parties to the INF Treaty (5): See annex A

Sub-Regional Consultative Commission (SRCC)

The SRCC was established by the 1996 Agreement on Sub-Regional Arms Control (Florence Agreement) as the forum in which the parties resolve questions of compliance with the agreement.

Parties to the Florence Agreement (4): See annex A

Website: <http://www.osce.org/item/13692.html>

Unión de Naciones Suramericanas (UNASUR, Union of South American Nations)

UNASUR will be fully established on the entry into force of its 2008 Constitutive Treaty. It will be an intergovernmental organization with the aim of strengthening regional integration, political dialogue, economic development and coordination in defence matters among its member states. Its headquarters will be in Quito, Ecuador. UNASUR will gradually replace the Andean Community and the Mercado Común del Sur (MERCOSUR, Southern Common Market). The South American Defence Council (Consejo de Defensa Suramericano, CDS) was approved by the member states in December 2008 and had its first meeting in March 2009. The objectives of the CDS are to consolidate South America as a zone of peace and to create a regional identity and strengthen regional cooperation in defence issues.

Members (12): Argentina, Bolivia, Brazil, Chile, Colombia, Ecuador, Guyana, Paraguay, Peru, Suriname, Uruguay, Venezuela

Websites: <http://www.pptunasur.com/>, <http://www.cdsunasur.org/>

Wassenaar Arrangement (WA)

The Wassenaar Arrangement on Export Controls for Conventional Arms and Dual-Use Goods and Technologies was formally established in 1996. It aims to prevent the acquisition of armaments and sensitive dual-use goods and technologies for military uses by states whose behaviour is cause for concern to the member states. Its secretariat is in Vienna, Austria.

Participants (40): Argentina, Australia, Austria, Belgium, Bulgaria, Canada, Croatia, Czech Republic, Denmark, Estonia, Finland, France, Germany, Greece, Hungary, Ireland, Italy, Japan, Korea (South), Latvia, Lithuania, Luxembourg, Malta, Netherlands, New Zealand, Norway, Poland, Portugal, Romania, Russia, Slovakia, Slovenia, South Africa, Spain, Sweden, Switzerland, Turkey, UK, Ukraine, USA

Website: <http://www.wassenaar.org/>

Western European Union (WEU)

The WEU was established by the 1954 Modified Brussels Treaty. Its seat is in Brussels, Belgium. The WEU's operational activities (the Petersberg Tasks) were transferred to the EU in 2000. The WEU's residual tasks include collective defence commitments, institutional dialogue and support for armaments cooperation.

Note: On 31 Mar. 2010 the parties to the Modified Brussels Treaty decided to terminate the treaty and, consequently, to close the WEU by June 2011.

Members (10): Belgium, France, Germany, Greece, Italy, Luxembourg, Netherlands, Portugal, Spain, UK

Website: <http://www.weu.int/>

Zangger Committee

Established in 1971–74, the Nuclear Exporters Committee, called the Zangger Committee, is a group of nuclear supplier countries that meets informally twice a year to coordinate transfer controls on nuclear materials according to its regularly updated trigger list of items which, when exported, must be subject to IAEA safeguards. It complements the work of the Nuclear Suppliers Group.

Members (37): Argentina, Australia, Austria, Belgium, Bulgaria, Canada, China, Croatia, Czech Republic, Denmark, Finland, France, Germany, Greece, Hungary, Ireland, Italy, Japan, Kazakhstan, Korea (South), Luxembourg, Netherlands, Norway, Poland, Portugal, Romania, Russia, Slovakia, Slovenia, South Africa, Spain, Sweden, Switzerland, Turkey, UK, Ukraine, USA

Website: <http://www.zanggercommittee.org/>

Annex C. Chronology 2009

NENNE BODELL

This chronology lists the significant events in 2009 related to armaments, disarmament and international security. The dates are according to local time. Keywords are indicated in the right-hand column. Definitions of the abbreviations can be found on pages xxi–xxiv.

2 Jan.	Sri Lankan Government forces capture the town of Kilinochchi, in the north of Sri Lanka, following heavy fighting with the Liberation Tigers of Tamil Eelam (LTTE) rebels. Kilinochchi has been held by the LTTE since 1999 and is an important political symbol for the Sri Lankan Government.	Sri Lanka
3–18 Jan.	Following massive Israeli air strikes on the Gaza Strip since the offensive started on 27 Dec. 2008, Israeli ground forces enter the area. Heavy fighting takes places in Gaza City between the Israeli forces and Hamas. According to Palestinian and human rights groups, up to 1400 Palestinians have been killed since the offensive began; 13 Israelis have been killed. (See also *18 Jan.* and *16 Oct.*)	Israel; Gaza Strip
15 Jan.	The 3000 Ethiopian forces supporting the Transitional Federal Government (TFG) of Somalia withdraw completely from Mogadishu, Somalia, two years after the Ethiopian intervention to oust Islamist rebels.	Somalia; Ethiopia
18 Jan.	On 17 Jan. Israeli Prime Minister Ehud Olmert announces a unilateral ceasefire in the Gaza Strip from 18 Jan., declaring that Israel has achieved the goals it set when launching the military operation on 27 Dec. 2008. On 18 Jan. Hamas declares its own truce, demanding the withdrawal of Israeli troops from the Gaza Strip within one week and the opening of all crossings for the entry of humanitarian aid and food. On 21 Jan. Israel completes its troop withdrawal from the Gaza Strip.	Israel; Gaza Strip
20 Jan.	Rwandan troops cross into eastern Democratic Republic of the Congo (DRC) to assist Congolese Government forces in their military operations against the Rwandan Hutu Democratic Liberation Forces of Rwanda (Forces démocratiques de libération du Rwanda, FDLR) rebels. During the joint military operation the National Congress for People's Defence (Congrès National pour la Défense du Peuple, CNDP) rebel leader Laurent Nkunda is arrested on 22 Jan. when fleeing into Rwanda.	DRC; Rwanda

21 Jan.	The Israeli armed forces announces that it will investigate the allegations made by several NGOs that it used white phosphorus illegally during its three-week military operation in the Gaza Strip. Under Protocol III of the 1981 Certain Conventional Weapons Convention, the use of white phosphorus as an incendiary weapon is not allowed in areas where civilians are concentrated. The 1993 Chemical Weapons Convention (CWC) also bans it from being employed in a manner that is meant to cause death or other harm through its toxic properties.	Israel; Laws of war
22 Jan.	US President Barack Obama signs executive orders closing the US detention camp at Guantánamo Bay, Cuba, within a year; closing the Central Intelligence Agency's secret prisons; requiring a review of military trials for terror suspects; and requiring all interrogations to follow the non-coercive methods specified in the US Army Field Manual.	USA
25 Jan.	Sri Lankan Government forces capture Mullaitivu, the last stronghold of the Liberation Tigers of Tamil Eelam (LTTE) rebels in north-eastern Sri Lanka. The International Committee of the Red Cross (ICRC) estimates that 250 000 civilians are trapped by the fighting and warns of a major humanitarian crisis.	Sri Lanka
26 Jan.	The first trial at the International Criminal Court (ICC) opens in The Hague, Netherlands. At the trial the leader of the Union of Congolese Patriots (Union des Patriotes Congolais, UPC), Thomas Lubanga Dyilo, is charged with committing war crimes, consisting of enlisting and conscripting children under the age of 15 years and using them to participate actively in hostilities in the Democratic Republic of the Congo (DRC) between 2002 and 2003. Lubanga Dyilo was arrested in 2006.	ICC; DRC
27–28 Jan.	Hamas breaks the ceasefire declared on 18 Jan. by attacking an Israeli frontier patrol; Israel responds immediately by renewing its air strikes on the Gaza Strip border with Egypt.	Israel; Gaza Strip
30 Jan.	The North Korean Committee for the Peaceful Reunification of Korea declares that all military and political agreements with South Korea are 'dead', accusing the South Korean Government of having pushed relations to the 'brink of a war'.	North Korea; South Korea
3 Feb.	Iran launches its first domestically built satellite into orbit. Iran states that the satellite is meant for research and telecommunications purposes, but Western states express concern that the technology could be used in the development of ballistic missiles.	Iran; Satellites
6 Feb.	A British and a French submarine, both carrying ballistic missiles with nuclear warheads, collide in the middle of the Atlantic Ocean. Both countries report no injuries.	France; UK; Submarines

6 Feb.   Kyrgyzstan announces its decision to close the US military   Kyrgyzstan;
base at Manas, near Bishkek. The Manas base was set up in   USA; Military
2001 to assist the US military operations against al-Qaeda and   bases
the Taliban in Afghanistan. The decision is reversed on
25 June when the Kyrgyz Parliament ratifies a treaty allowing
the base to serve as a key support base and transit hub for
NATO forces in Afghanistan. (See also *13 Oct.*)

16 Feb.   The provincial government of the North West Frontier Prov-   Pakistan; Islam
ince of Pakistan and a local militant leader, Sufi Mohammad,
sign an agreement (the Nizam-e-Adal regulation) creating a
separate system of justice based on sharia law in the
Malakand division, which includes the Swat Valley region.
The agreement is an attempt to stop the Taliban uprising that
started in the region in 2007. Pakistani President Asif Ali
Zardari claims that peace has to be restored in the Swat
Valley before he approves the regulation.

17 Feb.   Meeting in Doha, Qatar, the Sudanese Government and the   Sudan; Darfur
Justice and Equality Movement (JEM) rebel group in Darfur
sign a declaration of good intent, under which the parties
agree to end attacks on refugee camps in the region and to
exchange prisoners. The negotiations will continue under the
auspices of the Government of Qatar.

17 Feb.   The trial of the former Khmer Rouge leader, Kaing Guek Eav   Cambodia; War
('Duch') opens at the Extraordinary Chambers in the Courts   crimes
of Cambodia (ECCC) in Phnom Penh. Duch is charged with
crimes against humanity during the 1975–79 'Democratic
Kampuchea' period. The ECCC was set up by the UN and the
Government of Cambodia in 2003. On 31 Mar. Duch admits
his responsibility for crimes committed at Tuol Sleng prison.

17 Feb.   US President Barack Obama authorizes the deployment of an   USA;
additional 17 000 military personnel to Afghanistan. The   Afghanistan
troops will be deployed to 'meet urgent security needs' in
southern Afghanistan.

4 Mar.   The Pre-Trial Chamber I of the International Criminal Court   Sudan; Darfur;
(ICC), The Hague, Netherlands, issues a warrant for the   War crimes;
arrest of Sudanese President Omar Hassan al-Bashir on   ICC; NGOs; Aid
charges of crimes against humanity and war crimes in Darfur.
This is the first arrest warrant ever issued by the ICC for a sit-
ting head of state. In response, the Sudanese authorities order
10 foreign humanitarian agencies, to leave Sudan.

4 Mar.   Meeting in Brussels, the foreign ministers of the NATO   NATO; Russia;
member states agree that the formal cooperation with Russia   NATO–Russia
in the NATO–Russia Council, suspended in Aug. 2008 as a   Council
protest against Russia's war with Georgia, will resume.

6–8 Mar.	A Chinese Navy ship, maritime surveillance aircraft and fishing vessels conduct manoeuvres and drop debris in close proximity to the USNS *Impeccable*, a civilian-operated ship conducting surveillance for the US Navy near Hainan, where China maintains a naval base. The USA accuses China of dangerous and illegal conduct; China charges the USA with violating Chinese laws regarding its disputed exclusive economic zone.	China; USA
11 Mar.	French President Nicolas Sarkozy announces that France will return to the integrated military command of NATO, which it withdrew from in 1966 due to a controversy over US influence in Europe.	France; NATO
15 Mar.	The European Union's EUFOR Tchad/RCA peacekeeping mission hands over its operations to the UN Mission in the Central African Republic and Chad (MINURCAT) in accordance with UN Security Council Resolution 1834 (2008).	EU; UN; CAR; Chad; Sudan
17 Mar.	Meeting with Russian Defence Ministry officials, President Dmitry Medvedev announces that Russia will begin a comprehensive military rearmament from 2011. Its primary task will be to enhance the combat preparedness of the Russian forces, especially the strategic nuclear forces. Medvedev expresses concerns over NATO's expansion close to Russia's borders.	Russia; Armed forces
17 Mar.	Two US female journalists, together with their Chinese guide, are detained by North Korean soldiers at the China–North Korea border when reporting on North Korean refugees in north-eastern China. In June the two women are sentenced to 12 years of hard labour. On 4 Aug. the two are pardoned and released following mediation by former US President Bill Clinton.	North Korea; China; USA
19 Mar.	China and Viet Nam agree to set up a hotline between their foreign ministries, and to focus on negotiations to solve the outstanding maritime issues in order to maintain peace and stability in the South China Sea.	China; Viet Nam; CBMs
21 Mar.	Following ratification by Kazakhstan on 11 Dec. 2008, the 2006 Treaty on a Nuclear-Weapon-Free-Zone in Central Asia (Treaty of Semipalatinsk) enters into force.	Central Asia; NWFZ
23 Mar.	Meeting in Goma, Democratic Republic of the Congo (DRC), the Congolese Government, the National Congress for People's Defence (Congrès National pour la Défense du Peuple, CNDP) and other armed rebel groups in North and South Kivu provinces sign peace agreements. The agreements envisage an end to hostilities, transformation of armed groups into political parties, the return of displaced persons and refugees to their homes, and integration into national political life of the leaders of all armed groups.	DRC

24 Mar.	French Defence Minister Hervé Morin announces that France will compensate those suffering health problems linked to radiation and resulting from the more than 200 nuclear weapon tests that France carried out from 1960 to 1996 in Algeria and Polynesia. France has previously not recognized any link between the testing and radiation-related sickness.	France; Nuclear testing; Radiation
27 Mar.	US President Barack Obama presents the new US strategy for Afghanistan and Pakistan. Its goal is to disrupt, dismantle and defeat al-Qaeda in both countries and to prevent their return in the future. A standing, trilateral dialogue between Afghanistan, Pakistan and the USA will be launched together with enhanced intelligence sharing and military cooperation; US troops will be deployed to train Afghan security forces; and substantial assistance will be given to rebuild the Afghan civilian infrastructure, assisted by the UN and international aid organizations. Ambassador Richard Holbrooke is appointed the US special representative for Afghanistan and Pakistan. (See also *1 Dec.*)	USA; Afghanistan; Pakistan
27 Mar.	A bomb explodes at a mosque in Jamrud, in the Khyber region, Pakistan, killing at least 48 people and injuring more than 70. The sectarian violence linked to al-Qaeda and Afghan and Pakistani Taliban groups has escalated across Pakistan since an attack on the Sri Lankan cricket team in Lahore on 3 Mar.	Pakistan; Terrorism
30 Mar.	The Manawan police training academy in Lahore, Pakistan, is attacked by gunmen from the Pakistani Taliban group led by Baitullah Mehsud. The attack kills several civilians, policemen and insurgents. After eight hours of heavy fighting the security forces recapture the academy. Mehsud states that the attack is in retaliation for the continued US unmanned aerial vehicle (UAV) air strikes and there will be further attacks 'until the Pakistani government stops supporting the Americans'. There have been more than 35 US air strikes in North and South Waziristan since Aug. 2008, killing around 340 people.	Pakistan; Terrorism
1 Apr.	Meeting in London, Russian President Dmitry Medvedev and US President Barack Obama issue two joint statements on further reducing and limiting strategic offensive weapons in accordance with the obligations under Article VI of the 1968 Treaty on the Non-Proliferation of Nuclear Weapons (NPT). They decide to replace the 1991 Strategic Arms Reduction Treaty (START) with a new legally binding agreement before the START Treaty expires in Dec. 2009; to agree to work bilaterally and internationally to resolve regional conflicts; to support the continued Six-Party Talks on North Korea's nuclear programme; and to start a dialogue on security and stability in Europe.	Russia; USA; Arms control
1 Apr.	Albania and Croatia become members of the North Atlantic Treaty Organization (NATO).	NATO; Enlargement; Albania; Croatia

1 Apr.	After taking office, the new Israeli Foreign Minister, Avigdor Lieberman, states that the Israeli Government is not bound by the commitments made by its predecessors, such as the 2007 Annapolis Agreement for a two-state solution of the Israeli–Palestinian conflict, but only by the 2003 Road Map for Peace.

Israel; Palestinian territories

3–4 Apr.	At its 60th anniversary summit meeting in Strasbourg, France, and Kehl, Germany, NATO issues the Strasbourg–Kehl Summit Declaration launching the process to develop a new Strategic Concept to define NATO's longer-term role in the new security environment of the 21st century. It decides to modernize its capabilities; engage with other international organizations and countries, including on missions and operations; and welcomes the French decision to fully participate in NATO. It adopts the Declaration on Alliance Security, reaffirming the basic values, principles and purposes of the alliance. Danish Prime Minister Anders Fogh Rasmussen is appointed NATO's next Secretary General.

NATO

5 Apr.	North Korea launches a missile carrying a satellite from its launching site, Musudan-ri, on the east coast of the country. North Korean officials claim that the launch was successful and that the satellite is in orbit. Reports from South Korea claim that the missile has broken up and fallen into the sea. (See also *13 Apr.*)

North Korea; Missiles

5 Apr.	In a speech in Prague, Czech Republic, US President Barack Obama outlines his vision of a nuclear weapon-free world. He pledges to reduce the US nuclear weapon stockpile, to work to bring the 1996 Comprehensive Nuclear-Test-Ban Treaty (CTBT) into force, to make new efforts to secure sensitive nuclear materials within four years, and to engage with Iran by presenting it with a choice between access to peaceful nuclear energy or isolation by maintaining its current nuclear strategy. Obama states that as long as Iran poses a potential nuclear threat, the USA will continue to work on the missile defence system to be situated in Poland and the Czech Republic.

Nuclear weapons; Nuclear disarmament

13 Apr.	The UN Security Council unanimously adopts a statement condemning North Korea's 5 Apr. missile launch as a contravention of Security Council Resolution 1718 (2006), and demands that North Korea not conduct further launches. On 14 Apr. North Korea responds that it is permanently leaving the Six-Party Talks on its nuclear programme; informs the IAEA that it will no longer cooperate with the agency; asks nuclear inspectors to leave the country immediately; and states that it is taking steps to reactivate its partially dismantled nuclear facility at Yongbyon.

North Korea; Nuclear programme; IAEA; UN

16 Apr.	Russia's Anti-terrorist Committee announces that the 1999 decree authorizing the 'counterterrorism' operation in Chechnya is rescinded in order 'to create conditions to further normalize the situation' in the republic.

Chechnya; Russia

16 Apr.	Following the release of four memos on the techniques used by Central Intelligence Agency (CIA) agents to interrogate terrorism suspects, issued by the Office of Legal Counsel between 2002 and 2005, US President Barack Obama states that agents who used these techniques in good faith on legal advice from the Department of Justice will not be subject to prosecution.	USA; Laws of war
20–23 Apr.	More than 100 000 civilians flee the last stronghold of the Liberation Tigers of Tamil Eelam (LTTE) rebels as the Sri Lankan Government forces continue their 'final offensive' against the rebels in the north of the country. The rebels claim that the government forces have killed and injured several thousand civilians. On 22 Apr. the army claims that two senior LTTE rebels have surrendered, and after a meeting in the UN Security Council UN officials accuse the LTTE of using civilians as human shields and urge them to lay down their weapons.	Sri Lanka
21 Apr.	Following a ceremony on 18 Apr. where the leader of the Party for the Liberation of the Hutu People–National Liberation Forces (Parti pour la libération du peuple Hutu–Forces nationales de libération, Palipehutu–FNL) rebel group, Agathon Rwasa, surrendered his weapons and uniform to the African Union (AU), the AU starts to disarm 21 000 Palipehutu–FNL rebels as part of the 2006 peace agreement. At the same time, the rebel group officially becomes a political party under the new, non-ethnic name FNL.	Burundi
23 Apr.	In three separate suicide bomb attacks, in Baghdad and Diyala Province, Iraq, at least 80 people are killed and 120 more are injured.	Iraq; Terrorism
25 Apr.	Following the UN Sanctions Committee's decision on 24 Apr. to impose sanctions on three North Korean companies involved in the arms trade, and to update the list of goods and technologies already banned, North Korea's state media report that reprocessing of spent nuclear fuels rods has been resumed at the Yongbyon reactor. On 29 Apr. North Korea threatens to conduct nuclear missile tests unless the UN apologizes for its condemnation of the 5 Apr. rocket launch.	North Korea; Nuclear programme; UN; Sanctions
30 Apr.	Abkhazia, Russia and South Ossetia sign an agreement under which Russia pledges to protect the borders of Abkhazia and South Ossetia until they have established their own border service. The agreement is for five years, with an automatic extension for another five years. The EU, NATO and the USA condemn it as a breach of the Aug. 2008 Georgia–Russia agreement brokered by the EU.	Russia; Abkhazia; South Ossetia
5 May	The International Committee of the Red Cross (ICRC) confirms that US air strikes in Farah, Afghanistan, targeted at Taliban militants, have killed 'dozens' of civilians. Afghan officials claim that as many as 150 people have been killed.	USA; Afghanistan; Taliban

5–8 May	The Pakistani Government claims that Taliban militants have broken the peace agreement signed on 16 Feb. and launches an army offensive in an attempt to eliminate 4000–5000 Taliban militants from the Swat Valley, Pakistan. The UN High Commissioner for Refugees (UNHCR) estimates that 550 000 people have been displaced in the Swat Valley region since Aug. 2008 due to the escalating violence, and that the new fighting will displace thousands more.	Pakistan; Taliban; Terrorism
6 May–1 June	NATO holds, under the Partnership for Peace (PFP) programme, a series of military exercises in Georgia. Russia calls the exercises 'an overt provocation'.	NATO; Georgia; Russia
17 May	The Liberation Tigers of Tamil Eelam (LTTE) rebels announce that the 'battle has reached its bitter end' and that they are laying down their arms, thus ending a 26-year conflict. On 18 May Sri Lankan Government forces kill the LTTE's founder, Velupillai Prabhakaran, together with other top LTTE leaders. For the first time since 1983 the government armed forces now control all of Sri Lanka's territory. On 19 May President Mahinda Rajapaksa formally declares peace in the country.	Sri Lanka
19–21 May	Officials from the Russian and US governments meet in Moscow, Russia, to start talks on the follow-on treaty for the 1991 Strategic Arms Reduction Treaty (START), which will expire in Dec. 2009.	Russia; USA; Arms control
25 May	North Korea carries out a underground nuclear weapon test in Kilju, Hamgyong province. North Korea states that the test was successfully conducted 'as part of the measures to bolster up its nuclear deterrent for self-defence'. The international community condemns the test.	North Korea; Nuclear weapons; Nuclear testing
26 May	France opens a military base in the United Arab Emirates (UAE), its first permanent base in the Middle East. The base will host up to 500 French troops.	France; UAE; Military bases
26 May	Former rebels the New Forces (Forces Nouvelles de Côte d'Ivoire, FNCI) hand over 10 zones in the north of Côte d'Ivoire to civilian administrators appointed by President Laurent Gbagbo. The handover is part of the 2007 Ouagadougou Political Accord and its complementary agreements.	Côte d'Ivoire
27 May	Following South Korea's announcement on 26 May that it will fully join the US-led Proliferation Security Initiative (PSI), North Korea announces that it is no longer bound by the terms of the 1953 ceasefire agreement. North Korea states that South Korea's actions are a 'declaration of war'.	North Korea; South Korea; PSI
27 May	A suicide bomb attack on a police building in Lahore, Pakistan, kills at least 26 people and injures more than 200. The Pakistani Taliban claim responsibility for the attack and state that it is a response to the ongoing military operation in the Swat Valley. (See *5–8 May*.)	Pakistan; Taliban; Terrorism

23 May	After 12 years of stalemate the Conference on Disarmament (CD), Geneva, Switzerland, adopts by consensus document CD/1863 containing a programme of work for its 2009 session. According to the document the CD will establish working groups on nuclear disarmament and non-proliferation issues, including a fissile material cut-off treaty (FMCT).

CD; Arms control

12 June	The UN Security Council unanimously adopts Resolution 1874, condemning North Korea's nuclear weapon test on 25 May; strengthening the sanctions against the country by blocking funding for nuclear, missile and proliferation activities; widening the ban on arms imports and exports; and calling on member states to inspect and destroy all banned cargo to and from North Korea if there are reasonable grounds to suspect a violation. Following the adoption of the resolution, on 13 June North Korea declares that it will weaponize its extracted plutonium stock and start enriching uranium.

UN; North Korea; WMD

13 June	Following the presidential election in Iran on 12 June, in which President Mahmoud Ahmadinejad is re-elected, hundreds of thousands of people take to the streets to protest against what they perceive as a fraudulent election. At least eight people are killed and several wounded by security forces in the largest demonstrations since the 1979 Iranian revolution.

Iran

14 June	Israeli Prime Minister Benjamin Netanyahu announces that Israel is ready to endorse the creation of a Palestinian state as long as it is demilitarized and the Palestinians accept Israel as a Jewish state with Jerusalem as the capital. Palestinian officials reject the Israeli conditions for a two-state solution.

Israel; Palestinian territories

17 June	Following a North Korean threat of a 'thousandfold' retaliation against the USA and its allies if provoked, Chinese President Hu Jintao and Russian President Dmitry Medvedev issue a statement urging North Korea to return to negotiations on its nuclear programme. The two leaders express 'serious concerns' over the escalating tensions on the Korean peninsula.

North Korea; China; Russia; WMD

27 June	The first NATO–Russia Council meeting at the ministerial level since 2008 is held on Corfu, Greece. It agrees to restart the military-to-military contacts between NATO and Russia, even though 'fundamental differences remain on Georgia'.

NATO; Russia; NATO–Russia Council

28 June	Meeting on Corfu, Greece, the Organization for Security and Co-operation in Europe (OSCE) foreign ministers launch the Corfu Process to advance the dialogue on European security challenges.

OSCE

28 June	Manuel Zelaya, President of Honduras, is overthrown in a military coup and forced to leave the country. The coup sparks large demonstrations both for and against Zelaya, and several people are injured. The Organization of American States (OAS), the UN and the countries in the region condemn the coup and the OAS suspends Honduras from its activities. Mediation talks in July, led by Costa Rican President Oscar Arias, end without result. The EU and the USA suspend their aid to Honduras.	Honduras; OAS
30 June	The withdrawal of US combat troops from cities and villages in Iraq is completed and their security duties are handed over to Iraqi forces. Approximately 131 000 US troops remain in Iraq.	Iraq; USA
30 June	The UN Observer Mission in Georgia (UNOMIG) and the OSCE Mission to Georgia withdraw from Georgia after Russia's refusal to extend their mandates. UNOMIG has been deployed in Abkhazia since 1993, and the OSCE Mission has been in South Ossetia since 1992.	UN; OSCE; Georgia; Peacekeeping operations
2 July	US and Afghan forces launch Operation Khanjar, a major offensive against Taliban militants in Helmand province, south-western Afghanistan, involving 4000 US and 650 Afghan soldiers.	USA; Afghanistan
2–4 July	North Korea test-fires four short-range cruise missiles and seven short-range ballistic missiles. On 6 July the UN Security Council condemns the tests as violations of three existing resolutions and as posing a threat to regional and international security.	UN; North Korea; Missiles
5–26 July	Around 150 people are killed and more than 800 injured in ethnic riots between Muslim Uighurs and Han Chinese in Urumqi, Xinjiang, China. More than 1400 people are arrested. The Uighurs protest against the Han Chinese control of the province, and the protests are among the most serious since the Tiananmen Square protests in 1989. On 7 July the Chinese authorities deploy thousands of security forces to attempt to end the growing violence. Even after the violence ends, the Chinese Government severely curbs civil liberties in Xinjiang, including Internet access, at least until Feb. 2010.	China; Ethnic minorities
6 July	In Moscow US President Barack Obama and Russian President Dmitry Medvedev sign the Joint Understanding for the START Follow-on Treaty, committing their countries to reduce strategic warhead numbers to 1500–1675 and strategic delivery vehicles to 500–1100. The reductions are to be achieved within seven years of the new treaty being signed, which is to occur before the START Treaty expires in Dec. 2009, and to include 'effective' verification measures. Obama and Medvedev issue a joint statement on missile defence issues, agreeing to a joint study on ballistic missile threats and establishing the Joint Data Exchange Center to serve as the basis for a multilateral missile-launch notification regime. (See also *5 Dec.*)	Russia; USA; Arms control; Missiles

15 July	Following Burundi's ratification, on 22 June, the 1996 African Nuclear-Weapon-Free Zone Treaty (Treaty of Pelindaba) enters into force.	Africa; NWFZ
16 July	British Prime Minister Gordon Brown issues a statement on nuclear non-proliferation together with the new British strategy, *Road to 2010*, outlining how the UK will play a leading role in tackling nuclear issues.	UK; Nuclear weapons
18 Aug.	Georgia's withdrawal from the Commonwealth of Independent States (CIS) takes effect. President Mikheil Saakashvili announced the withdrawal in Aug. 2008 following the Georgian–Russian conflict.	Georgia; CIS
19 Aug.	A series of bomb attacks in Baghdad, Iraq, kills 95 people and injures about 300. Iraqi Prime Minister Nouri Maliki orders a security review.	Iraq; Terrorism
1 Sep.	The Commonwealth of Nations fully suspends Fiji from the organization after its lack of progress towards a return to constitutional democracy since the 2006 military coup. Fiji was partly suspended from the organization in Dec. 2006.	Fiji; Commonwealth of Nations
4 Sep.	At least 90 people, including many civilians, are killed in a NATO air strike in Kunduz province, northern Afghanistan, when the International Security Assistance Force (ISAF) attacks two fuel tankers, previously hijacked by the Taliban.	Afghanistan; NATO
9 Sep.	The chief prosecutor at the International Criminal Court (ICC) announces that the ICC has started a preliminary investigation of alleged war crimes in Afghanistan. The examination focuses on the actions of the US-led coalition forces, the Taliban and al-Qaeda.	Afghanistan; ICC
17 Sep.	US President Barack Obama announces a revision of the USA's 2007 plan for missile defence deployment in the Czech Republic and Poland. He recommends a new 'phased, adaptive approach' to missile defence, based on revised assessments of Iranian missile plans: Iran is more rapidly developing short- and medium-range ballistic missiles than previously projected. Advances have also been made in US capabilities and technologies.	USA; Missile defence
17 Sep.	More than 80 people are killed in a government air raid on a camp for displaced persons in northern Yemen. Government officials claim that rebels fired from the camp. Violence in Yemen has escalated since government forces launched an operation targeting Shia rebels (the Houthi) in Aug.	Yemen; Terrorism
21 Sep.	The International Atomic Energy Agency (IAEA) receives information from the Iranian authorities regarding a 'new pilot fuel enrichment plant' near Qom. On 25 Sep. US President Barack Obama, French President Nicolas Sarkozy and British Prime Minister Gordon Brown claim that Iran has been covertly building the uranium enrichment facility for several years. In Mar. 2008 the UN Security Council threatened to impose sanctions on Iran unless it stops all uranium enrichment activities.	UN; IAEA; Iran

24 Sep.	The UN Security Council, with 14 heads of state and government present, unanimously adopts Resolution 1887, the first comprehensive action on nuclear issues since the mid-1990s. The Security Council reaffirms its strong support for the 1968 Treaty on the Non-Proliferation of Nuclear Weapons (NPT); calls on states not yet signatories to the treaty to accede to it; and calls on the states parties to fully comply with their obligations and to set realistic goals to strengthen the treaty at the 2010 NPT Review Conference.	UN; NPT
28 Sep.	An opposition protest meeting against the military leader Moussa Dadis Camara in Conakry, Guinea, ends in a violent attack on the demonstrators by Guinean security forces. More than 150 people are killed and over 1000 are injured according to a local human rights organization. The international community condemns the excessive violence used. On 17 Oct. the Economic Community of West African States (ECOWAS) imposes an arms embargo on Guinea, and on 27 Oct. the Council of the EU adopts Common Position 2009/788/CFSP concerning restrictive measures against the Republic of Guinea, including an arms embargo.	Guinea; ECOWAS; EU; Arms embargoes
29 Sep.	The 2006 Economic Community of West African States (ECOWAS) Convention on Small Arms, Light Weapons, Their Ammunition and Other Related Materials enters into force following Benin's deposit of the ninth instrument of ratification.	ECOWAS; SALW
30 Sep.	The Independent International Fact-Finding Mission on the Conflict in Georgia (IIFFMCG), commissioned by the Council of the EU in Dec. 2008, presents the results of its investigation of the origins and development of the 2008 conflict in Georgia. The report concludes that the conflict was started by a Georgian attack that was not justified by international law; that the attack followed months of provocation; and that both Georgia and Russia violated international humanitarian law.	Georgia; Russia; EU
1 Oct.	The UN Security Council permanent members (China, France, Russia, the UK and the USA), Germany (the P5+1), and Iran meet in Geneva, Switzerland, for the first talks on the Iranian nuclear programme since July 2008. The meeting ends with an agreement to hold further discussions before the end of Oct., and with Iran agreeing to allow inspectors from the International Atomic Energy Agency (IAEA) to visit its new enrichment facility.	UN; Germany; Iran
8 Oct.	The African Union (AU) Panel on Darfur, established to find a peaceful solution to the conflict in Darfur, Sudan, and headed by former South African President Thabo Mbeki, submits its report to the AU in Addis Ababa, Ethiopia. The AU Peace and Security Council summit, held on 29 Oct. in Abuja, Nigeria, endorses the report and its recommendations, including one to establish a new court consisting of Sudanese and foreign judges to bring justice to Darfur.	AU; Sudan; Darfur

13 Oct.	The final French and Spanish troops leave the Manas airbase, near Bishkek, Kyrgyzstan. The Kyrgyz Government had cancelled the agreements on the use of the base by France and Spain in Mar. 2009.	Kyrgyzstan; France; Spain; Military bases
13 Oct.	China and Russia sign, in Beijing, a detailed agreement on advance notification of ballistic missile and carrier rocket launches. The agreement builds upon a previous mutual non-targeting agreement and a Shanghai Cooperation Organization pact on notification of missile launches and other military activity in border areas.	China; Russia; Missiles
16 Oct.	The UN Human Rights Council adopts, by a vote of 25–6, with 11 abstentions, Resolution A/HRC/S-12/L.1, endorsing the recommendations made in Richard Goldstone's report on the Israeli offensive in the Gaza Strip in Dec. 2008–Jan. 2009. The report accuses both Israel and Palestinian militants of war crimes and demands that the parties investigate the allegations, or the cases will be referred to the International Criminal Court (ICC).	UN; Israel; Gaza Strip; War crimes
17 Oct.	The Pakistani Army launches a massive air and ground offensive against al-Qaeda and Taliban rebels in South Waziristan. At least 20 000 people flee the region. Nearly 200 people have been killed in suicide bombings and attacks throughout Pakistan since 26 Sep.	Pakistan; Terrorism
23 Oct.	The International Atomic Energy Agency (IAEA) proposal of 21 Oct. for a draft agreement under which Iran would send its enriched uranium to France and Russia to be turned into nuclear fuel for Iran's research reactor is approved by France, Russia and the USA. Iran responds to the IAEA on 29 Oct., citing 'technical and economic considerations' related to the proposal. On 25 Oct. a team of IAEA inspectors begins an inspection of the previously secret Fordow uranium enrichment facility near Qom, Iran.	IAEA; Iran
25 Oct.	Two coordinated car bombs close to ministry buildings in Baghdad, Iraq, kill more than 150 people and injure around 500. The attacks are the bloodiest in Baghdad since Apr. 2007. The Islamic State of Iraq, a militant group linked to al-Qaeda, claims responsibility for the attacks, but this is not independently verified.	Iraq; Terrorism
26 Oct.	The trial of the former Bosnian Serb leader Radovan Karadzic opens at the International Criminal Tribunal for the former Yugoslavia (ICTY), The Hague, Netherlands. Karadzic, who is charged with war crimes and crimes against humanity during the 1992–95 war in Bosnia and Herzegovina, was taken to the ICTY in 2008.	Bosnia and Herzegovina; ICTY
27 Oct.	Meeting in Brussels, the Council of the EU lifts its arms embargo against Uzbekistan, imposed in 2005, after Uzbekistan releases some political prisoners and abolishes the death penalty. The Council will also closely and continuously monitor the human rights situation in Uzbekistan and review its decision within a year.	EU; Arms embargo; Uzbekistan

28 Oct.	Six international UN personnel are killed and several wounded in two attacks by Taliban militants in Kabul, Afghanistan. The attacks are the deadliest on UN staff in Afghanistan since 2001.	UN; Afghanistan; Terrorism
28 Oct.	A large explosion in a market place in Peshawar, Pakistan, kills at least 57 people and injures up to 200. The number of bomb attacks in Pakistan has increased since the military operations against Taliban militants in South Waziristan started. (See 17 Oct.)	Pakistan; Terrorism
30 Oct.	The UN First Committee adopts by a vote of 153–1, with 19 abstentions (Zimbabwe voted against), Resolution A/C.1/ 64/L.38/Rev.1, setting a timetable for the negotiation of an arms trade treaty. A UN conference on an arms trade treaty will be held in 2012 to elaborate a legally binding instrument for the transfer of conventional arms.	UN; Arms trade; Treaties
2 Nov.	North Korea states that it would return to the Six-Party Talks on its nuclear programme if the USA agrees to hold bilateral negotiations first. On 3 Nov. the North Korean official news agency announces that the reprocessing of 8000 spent nuclear fuel rods to extract weapon-grade plutonium is completed.	North Korea; Nuclear programme
4 Nov.	Israeli naval forces seize a cargo ship bound for Lebanon off the coast of Cyprus. The ship contains hundreds of tonnes of weapons in containers marked 'I.R. Iran Shipping Lines Group'. Israel claims that the cargo originated in Iran—in contravention of UN sanctions on arms exports from Iran— and was bound for Hezbollah forces in Lebanon, and that it proves Israeli allegations of arms smuggling by Iran and Syria. Syria denies the allegations; Iran, Lebanon and Hezbollah do not comment on the incident.	Iran; Syria; UN; Sanctions; Lebanon; Israel
5 Nov.	Saudi Arabia launches massive bombing raids against Yemeni rebels along the border between the two countries, following the killing of a Saudi soldier on 4 Nov. The Yemeni Government has been fighting the Houthi rebel group since 2004, but the violence has escalated throughout the year, and raises fears that al-Qaeda members have found refuge in Yemen.	Yemen; Saudi Arabia
10 Nov.	North and South Korean warships exchange fire at the disputed Yellow Sea border between the two countries.	North Korea; South Korea
27 Nov.	A bomb on the Nevsky Express train causes it to crash between Moscow and St Petersburg, killing 27 people and injuring about 100. On 2 Dec. a group of Islamists, linked to Chechen rebels, from the North Caucasus claim responsibility for the attack.	Russia; Terrorism

29 Nov. State media in Iran report on the government-approved plans to build 10 new uranium enrichment plants, similar in size to the main facility at Natanz. The Iranian announcement follows the adoption by the International Atomic Energy Agency (IAEA) of Resolution GOV/2009/82 on 27 Nov., urging Iran to fully comply with all of it obligations under several UN Security Council and IAEA resolutions. The UK and the USA condemn the Iranian move.   Iran; Nuclear programme; UN; IAEA

29 Nov. Russian President Dmitry Medvedev presents his draft European security treaty, which was originally proposed in June 2008, to the EU, NATO and the Organization for Security and Co-operation in Europe (OSCE). According to a Russian Government statement, the proposal's goal is 'to create a single, indivisible space in the sphere of military-political security in the Euro-Atlantic region'.   Europe; Security

1 Dec. US President Barack Obama announces his decision to send an additional 30 000 troops to Afghanistan, bringing US force strength to more than 100 000 troops. The aim of the deployment is to defeat al-Qaeda, reverse the Taliban's momentum, and strengthen the capacity of the Afghan security forces and government in order to achieve a responsible transition of power. The mission is to last 18 months, and troops should begin to withdraw in July 2011. Obama also calls for more international allied forces, and on 4 Dec. the Secretary General of NATO, Anders Fogh Rasmussen, states that at least 25 NATO countries will send 7000 extra troops to Afghanistan.   USA; Afghanistan

1 Dec. The 2007 Treaty of Lisbon enters into force. It provides the EU with reformed institutions—including a permanent President of the European Council and a High Representative for Foreign Affairs and Security Policy—and working methods to tackle global challenges such as climate change, security and sustainable development.   EU

5 Dec. The 1991 Strategic Arms Reduction Treaty (START) expires. On 4 Dec. a Joint US–Russian Statement on the Expiration of the START Treaty is issued in which the two states express their commitment to continue to work together in the spirit of the treaty and their firm intention to ensure that a new treaty on strategic weapons enters into force at the earliest possible date.   Russia; USA; START Treaty; Arms control

8 Dec. A series of car bombs kills at least 127 people and wound over 400 in Baghdad, Iraq. The al-Qaeda-led insurgency is blamed for the attacks.   Iraq; Terrorism

9 Dec. US President Barack Obama releases the National Strategy for Countering Biological Threats, which addresses the challenges of the proliferation of biological weapons and their use by terrorists. It focuses on promoting global health security, combating infectious disease, establishing and reinforcing norms against the misuse of the life sciences, and instituting coordinated activities to hinder such misuse.   USA; Biological weapons

12 Dec.	A Georgian cargo aircraft carrying weapons from North Korea is seized while refuelling in Bangkok, Thailand. The final destination of the weapons is unclear.	North Korea; Weapons; Illegal trade
3 Dec.	The UN Security Council adopts, by a vote of 13–1, with Libya voting against and China abstaining, Resolution 1907, imposing an arms embargo on Eritrea because of its role in Somalia and its refusal to withdraw armed forces following the conflict with Djibouti in June 2008. It is the first new UN arms embargo since 2006.	UN; Eritrea; Arms embargo
25 Dec.	An attempted terrorist attack occurs on a passenger flight from Amsterdam, Netherlands, bound for Detroit, Michigan, USA. The suspect, Umar Farouk Abdulmutallab, carries explosive chemicals sewn into his underwear and claims he is acting on behalf of al-Qaeda in Yemen.	USA; Terrorism; Yemen

About the authors

Dr Ian Anthony (United Kingdom) is SIPRI Research Coordinator and Director of the SIPRI Arms Control and Non-proliferation Programme. His SIPRI publications include *Reforming Nuclear Export Controls: The Future of the Nuclear Suppliers Group*, SIPRI Research Report no. 22 (2007, co-author), *Reducing Threats at the Source: A European Perspective on Cooperative Threat Reduction*, SIPRI Research Report no. 19 (2004) and *Russia and the Arms Trade* (1998, editor). He has contributed to the SIPRI Yearbook since 1988.

Alyson J. K. Bailes (United Kingdom) is a Visiting Professor at the University of Iceland, specializing in security studies. After a 30-year career in the British Diplomatic Service she was Director of SIPRI from 2002 to 2007. She has written extensively on European, Nordic and Arctic security issues; her latest book is an anthology of speeches, *Through European Eyes* (University of Iceland Press, 2009). She has contributed to the SIPRI Yearbook since 2003.

Dr Sibylle Bauer (Germany) is Head of SIPRI's Export Control Project and Senior Researcher with the Arms Control and Non-proliferation Programme. Previously, she was a Researcher with the Institute for European Studies in Brussels. Her extensive publications on export control and armaments issues include *The European Union Code of Conduct on Arms Exports: Improving the Annual Report*, SIPRI Policy Paper no. 8 (2004, co-author) and chapters in *The Arms Trade* (Routledge, 2010) and *From Early Warning To Early Action? The Debate on the Enhancement of the EU's Crisis Response Capability Continues* (European Commission, 2008, as co-author). She has contributed to the SIPRI Yearbook since 2004.

Dr Stephanie Blair (Canada) is an Associated Senior Research Fellow at SIPRI and co-director of the SIPRI Project on the Civilian Contribution to Peace Operations. She served in both the OSCE Kosovo Verification Mission and the UN Interim Administration Mission in Kosovo (UNMIK), was on the team that established the Lester B. Pearson Canadian International Peacekeeping Training Centre (PPC), and co-founded the International Association of Peacekeeping Training Centres (IAPTC). She received her PhD in War Studies from King's College London. She is the author or co-author of several articles and publications on peacekeeping and stability operations.

Nenne Bodell (Sweden) is Director of the SIPRI Library and Documentation Department and of the SIPRI Arms Control and Disarmament Documentary Survey Programme. She has contributed to the SIPRI Yearbook since 2003.

Mark Bromley (United Kingdom) is a Researcher with the SIPRI Arms Transfers Programme, where his work focuses on European arms exports and export controls and South American arms acquisitions. Previously, he was a Policy

Analyst for the British American Security Information Council (BASIC). His publications include 'The Europeanisation of arms export policy in the Czech Republic, Slovakia, and Poland', *European Security* (June 2007), *The Impact on Domestic Policy of the EU Code of Conduct on Arms Exports: The Czech Republic, the Netherlands and Spain*, SIPRI Policy Paper no. 21 (May 2008), and *Air Transport and Destabilizing Commodity Flows*, SIPRI Policy Paper no. 24 (May 2009, co-author). He has contributed to the SIPRI Yearbook since 2004.

Dr Peter Clevestig (Sweden) is a Senior Researcher with the Chemical and Biological Security Project of the SIPRI Arms Control and Non-proliferation Programme. His research interests include laboratory biosecurity and policies, biological warfare and bioterrorism, microbial forensics and dual-use research of concern. He has authored several scientific articles and book chapters on bioterrorism, security aspects of emerging biotechnology and disease surveillance. He is the author of the *Handbook of Applied Biosecurity for Life Science Laboratories* (2009). He has contributed to the SIPRI Yearbook since 2008.

Dr Andrew Cottey (United Kingdom) is Senior Lecturer and Jean Monnet Chair in European Political Integration, Department of Government, University College Cork. He has been a NATO Research Fellow, a Research Associate at the International Institute for Strategic Studies and a Guest Researcher at SIPRI. His publications include *Security in the New Europe* (Palgrave Macmillan, 2007), *Reshaping Defence Diplomacy: New Roles for Military Cooperation and Assistance*, Adelphi Paper 365 (Oxford University Press/International Institute for Strategic Studies, 2004) and *Subregional Cooperation in the New Europe: Building Security, Prosperity and Solidarity from the Barents to the Black Sea* (Macmillan/EastWest Institute, 1999). He contributed to the SIPRI Yearbook in 2003, 2004 and 2006.

Vitaly Fedchenko (Russia) is a Researcher with the SIPRI Arms Control and Non-proliferation Programme, with responsibility for nuclear security issues and the political, technological and educational dimensions of nuclear arms control and non-proliferation. Previously, he was a visiting researcher at SIPRI and worked at the Center for Policy Studies in Russia and the Institute for Applied International Research in Moscow. He is the author or co-author of several publications on nuclear forensics, nuclear security and verification, and the international nuclear fuel cycle, including *Reforming Nuclear Export Controls: The Future of the Nuclear Suppliers Group*, SIPRI Research Report no. 22 (2007, co-author). He has contributed to the SIPRI Yearbook since 2005.

Dr Bates Gill (United States) is the seventh Director of SIPRI. Before joining SIPRI in October 2007, he held the Freeman Chair in China Studies at the Center for Strategic and International Studies in Washington, DC. He previously served as a Senior Fellow in Foreign Policy Studies and inaugural Director of the Center for Northeast Asian Policy Studies at the Brookings Institution. He has a long record of research and publication on international and regional security issues, particularly regarding arms control, non-proliferation, strategic nuclear relations, peacekeeping and military–technical development, especially with regard to China and Asia. His most recent publications include *Asia's New Multilateralism: Cooperation, Competition, and the Search for Community* (Columbia University Press, 2009, co-editor) and *Rising Star: China's New Security Diplomacy* (Brookings, 2007, revised edition 2010).

Dr Alexander Glaser (Germany) is Assistant Professor at the Woodrow Wilson School of Public and International Affairs and in the Department of Mechanical and Aerospace Engineering at Princeton University. He is a participant in the university's Program on Science and Global Security and works with the International Panel on Fissile Materials, which publishes the annual *Global Fissile Material Report*. He received his PhD in physics in 2005 from Darmstadt University of Technology, Germany. Between 2001 and 2003 he was an SSRC/MacArthur Fellow with the Security Studies Program at the Massachusetts Institute of Technology. During 2000 and 2001 he was an adviser to the German Federal Ministry of Environment and Reactor Safety. He is associate editor of *Science & Global Security*. He has contributed to the SIPRI Yearbook since 2007.

Dr Bharath Gopalaswamy (India) is a Researcher with the SIPRI Arms Control and Non-proliferation Programme. Previously, he was a postdoctoral associate at Cornell University's Peace Studies Program where he worked on the technical aspects of foreign policy issues. He has a PhD in mechanical engineering with a specialization in numerical acoustics. He has worked at the Indian Space Research Organisation's High-Altitude Test Facilities and for EADS Astrium.

James E. Goodby (United States) is a Research Fellow at Stanford University's Hoover Institution and a Non-Resident Senior Fellow at the Brookings Institution. He is the author and editor of several books dealing with control of nuclear weapons and European security issues. As a US Foreign Service Officer he served as ambassador to Finland, head of the US delegation to the Stockholm Conference on confidence-building measures in Europe, vice-chair of the US START delegation, Special Representative of the President for Nuclear Security and Disarmament, and held diplomatic assignments with US missions to NATO and the European Communities.

Lotta Harbom (Sweden) is a Research Assistant with the Uppsala Conflict Data Program at the Department of Peace and Conflict Research, Uppsala University. She has contributed to the SIPRI Yearbook since 2005.

John Hart (United States) is a Senior Researcher and Head of the Chemical and Biological Security Project of the SIPRI Arms Control and Non-proliferation Programme. He is also a doctoral candidate in military sciences at the Finnish National Defence University. His publications include *Chemical*

Weapon Destruction in Russia: Political, Legal and Technical Aspects (1998, co-editor) and *Historical Dictionary of Nuclear, Biological and Chemical Warfare* (Scarecrow Press, 2007, co-author). His recent publications include a chapter on WMD inspection and verification regimes in *Combating Weapons of Mass Destruction: the Future of International Non-Proliferation Policy* (University of Georgia Press, 2009, co-author). He has contributed to the SIPRI Yearbook in 1997, 1998 and since 2002.

Dr Paul Holtom (United Kingdom) is the Director of the SIPRI Arms Transfers Programme. Previously, he was a Research Fellow with the University of Glamorgan Centre for Border Studies. His most recent publications include *Transparency in Transfers of Small Arms and Light Weapons: Reports to the United Nations Register of Conventional Arms, 2003–2006*, SIPRI Policy Paper no. 22 (2008), *Implementation of the EU Common Position on the Control of Arms Brokering* (SEESAC, 2009) and 'Nothing to report: the lost promise of the UN Register of Conventional Arms', *Contemporary Security Policy* (April 2010). He has contributed to the SIPRI Yearbook since 2007.

Dr Olawale Ismail (Nigeria) is a Researcher with the SIPRI Military Expenditure and Arms Production Programme and Project Coordinator for the SIPRI Africa Security and Governance Project. He holds a PhD in peace studies from the University of Bradford. He previously worked with the Conflict, Security and Development Group (CSDG), King's College London and for the SIPRI Project on Budgeting for the Military Sector in Africa. His recent publications include *Post-War Regimes and State Reconstruction in Liberia and Sierra Leone* (CODESRIA, 2009, co-author), *Dynamics of Post-conflict Reconstruction and Peace Building in West Africa: Between Change and Security* (Nordic Africa Institute, 2009) and 'The dialectics of "junctions" and "bases": youth, "securocommerce" and the crises of order in downtown Lagos', *Security Dialogue* (2009).

Dr Susan T. Jackson (USA) joined SIPRI's Military Expenditure and Arms Production Programme in July 2009 as Head of the Arms Production Project. She holds a PhD from the University of Arizona on the linkages between state and corporate global competitiveness and military spending. Prior to graduate school, she worked for the Foreign Policy Studies programme of the Brookings Institution in Washington, DC. She lived in Turkey for more than three years, where her work included editing and translating for a daily economic and political news digest for business executives.

Krister Karlsson (USA) was an intern with the SIPRI Armed Conflict and Conflict Management Programme in 2009–10. He is completing a master's degree at the Uppsala University Department of Peace and Conflict Research.

Noel Kelly (Ireland) has been a Research Assistant with the SIPRI Military Expenditure and Arms Production and Arms Transfers programmes since

January 2008. He is responsible for the electronic archive common to these three research areas and maintains the SIPRI reporting system for military expenditure. He contributed to the SIPRI Yearbook in 2009.

Shannon N. Kile (USA) is a Senior Researcher and Head of the Nuclear Weapons Project of the SIPRI Arms Control and Non-proliferation Programme. His principal areas of research are nuclear arms control and non-proliferation with a special interest in Iran and North Korea. He has contributed to numerous SIPRI publications, including chapters on nuclear arms control and nuclear forces and weapon technology for the SIPRI Yearbook since 1995. His recent publications include, as editor, *Europe and Iran: Perspectives on Non-proliferation*, SIPRI Research Report no. 21 (2005).

Hans M. Kristensen (Denmark) is Director of the Nuclear Information Project at the Federation of American Scientists (FAS). He is co-author of the 'Nuclear notebook' column in the *Bulletin of the Atomic Scientists*. His recent publications include 'Counter-proliferation in US nuclear strategy', in *US Nuclear Strategy and the Implications for Global Security* (Dalhouse University: Centre for Foreign Policy Studies, 2009), and *Obama and the Nuclear War Plan* (FAS, 2010). He has contributed to the SIPRI Yearbook since 2001.

Dr Zdzislaw Lachowski (Poland) is a Senior Fellow with the SIPRI Euro-Atlantic Security Programme. His research interests include the problems of European military security and arms control as well as European politico-military integration. He is the co-editor of *International Security in a Time of Change: Threats–Concepts–Institutions* (Nomos, 2004), author of *Confidence- and Security-Building Measures in the New Europe*, SIPRI Research Report no. 18 (2004) and *Foreign Military Bases in Eurasia*, SIPRI Policy Paper no. 18 (2007), and lead author of *Tools for Building Confidence on the Korean Peninsula* (2007). He has contributed to the SIPRI Yearbook since 1992.

Tim Macintyre (Australia) is Head of Global Research at the Institute for Economics and Peace, which produces the Global Peace Index. His role is to commission, direct and manage research for the Institute as well as oversee publication of periodical materials. Prior to joining the Institute, he was employed by research companies Gartner and the Economist Intelligence Unit. He holds a master's degree in international studies from the University of Sydney and a Bachelor of Commerce (international business) from the University of Adelaide.

Zia Mian (Pakistan/United Kingdom) is a physicist with Princeton University's Program on Science and Global Security, where he directs the Project on Peace and Security in South Asia. For the past decade his work has focused on nuclear weapons, arms control and disarmament, and nuclear energy issues in Pakistan and India. He has previously worked at the Union of Concerned Scientists, the Sustainable Development Policy Institute and Quaid-e-Azam

University, Islamabad. He contributed to the SIPRI Yearbook in 2003 and in 2007–2009.

Ivana Mićić (Belgium) is a Researcher with the SIPRI Arms Control and Non-proliferation Programme with expertise in export control and on South Eastern Europe. She plays a key role in implementing and developing SIPRI's projects on strengthening capacities to investigate and prosecute export control violations in South Eastern Europe and strengthening export controls systems.

Dr Sam Perlo-Freeman (United Kingdom) is a Senior Researcher with the SIPRI Military Expenditure and Arms Production Programme, responsible for monitoring data on military expenditure worldwide. Previously, he was a Senior Lecturer at the University of the West of England, working in the field of defence and peace economics. His recent publications include 'The demand for military expenditure in developing countries: hostility vs. capability', *Defence and Peace Economics* (August 2008, co-author), and a chapter on the UK's arms industry in *The Global Arms Trade: A Handbook* (Routledge, 2009). He contributed to the SIPRI Yearbook in 2003, 2004, 2008 and 2009.

Camilla Schippa (Italy) is a Director of the Institute for Economics and Peace, where she manages the development of the Global Peace Index as well as the research carried out internationally on and around the index. Until early 2008 she was chief of office of the United Nations Office for Partnerships, where she guided the creation of strategic alliances between the UN and corporations, foundations and philanthropists.

Kirsten Soder (Germany) was a Researcher with the SIPRI Armed Conflict and Conflict Management Programme. Since 2006 she has managed the SIPRI Multilateral Peace Operations Database and contributed to the SIPRI Yearbook and the Center on International Cooperation's Annual Review of Global Peace Operations. She has contributed to the SIPRI Yearbook since 2007.

Carina Solmirano (Argentina) is a Researcher with the SIPRI Military Expenditure and Arms Production Programme responsible for monitoring military expenditure in Latin America, the Middle East and South Asia. Prior to joining SIPRI, she worked at the Josef Korbel School of International Studies at the University of Denver, Colorado, where she is a doctoral candidate. She has also worked on arms control issues at the Argentine NGO Asociacion para Politicas Publicas and as an adviser at the Argentine Senate.

Dr Ekaterina Stepanova (Russia) is a Lead Researcher on armed conflicts, terrorism and the political economy of conflicts at the Institute of the World Economy and International Relations (IMEMO) of the Russian Academy of Sciences. She also lectures at the European University in Saint Petersburg (EUSP) and at the European Peace University (EPU) in Austria. In 2007–2009, she led the SIPRI Armed Conflict and Conflict Management Programme. She is the author of four monographs, including *Terrorism in Asymmetrical Conflict: Ideological and Structural Aspects*, SIPRI Research Report no. 23 (2008), also published in Spanish (Argentinian Ministry of Defence, 2009) and Russian (Nauchnaya kniga, 2010). The latest of her co-edited volumes is *Terrorism: Patterns of Internationalization* (Sage, 2009). She serves on the editorial boards of the journals *Terrorism and Political Violence* and *Security Index*. She has contributed to the SIPRI Yearbook since 2008.

Professor Peter Wallensteen (Sweden) has held the Dag Hammarskjöld Chair in Peace and Conflict Research at Uppsala University since 1985 and has been the Richard G. Starmann Sr Research Professor of Peace Studies at the University of Notre Dame since 2006. He directs the Uppsala Conflict Data Program and the Special Program on the Implementation of Targeted Sanctions. The second, updated edition of his book *Understanding Conflict Resolution: War, Peace and the Global System* (Sage) was published in 2007. He is co-editor of *International Sanctions: Between Words and Wars in the Global System* (Frank Cass, 2005) and *Third Parties in Conflict Prevention* (Gidlunds, 2008). He has contributed to the SIPRI Yearbook since 1988.

Pieter D. Wezeman (Netherlands) is a Senior Researcher with the SIPRI Arms Transfers Programme. He rejoined SIPRI in 2006, having previously worked at the institute from 1994 to 2003. From 2003 to 2006 he was a Senior Analyst for the Dutch Ministry of Defence in the field of proliferation of conventional and nuclear weapon technology. He contributed to the SIPRI Yearbook in 1995–2003 and since 2007.

Siemon T. Wezeman (Netherlands) is a Senior Fellow with the SIPRI Arms Transfers Programme, where he has worked since 1992. Among his publications are several relating to international transparency in arms transfers, *The Future of the United Nations Register of Conventional Arms*, SIPRI Policy Paper no. 4 (August 2003), and *Cluster Weapons: Necessity or Convenience?* (Pax Christi Netherlands, 2005, co-author). He has contributed to the SIPRI Yearbook since 1993.

Sharon Wiharta (Indonesia) is a Senior Researcher with the SIPRI Armed Conflict and Conflict Management Programme, where she leads research on peacekeeping and peacebuilding issues. Her particular areas of interest are transitional justice and efforts to re-establish the rule of law in post-conflict situations. She is currently co-directing the SIPRI Project on the Civilian Contribution to Peace Operations. Her publications include *Peace Operations: Trends, Progress and Prospects* (Georgetown University Press, 2008, co-editor), *The Transition to a Just Order: Establishing Local Ownership after Conflict* (Folke Bernadotte Academy, 2007, co-author) and *The Effectiveness of Foreign Military Assets in Natural Disaster Response* (2007, lead author). She has contributed to the SIPRI Yearbook since 2002.

Errata

SIPRI Yearbook 2009: Armaments, Disarmament and International Security

Page 2, line 40	*For* '2532 contributors' *read* '32 contributors'
Page 102, line 29	*For* '37 000-strong' *read* '3700-strong'
Page 143, entry 3	*For* 'EU Advisory Mission for Security Sector Reforms in Guinea-Bissau' *read* 'EU Advisory Mission for Security Sector Reform in Guinea-Bissau'
Page 156, note 103, line 3	*For* '1992 Ohrid Framework Agreement' *read* '2001 Ohrid Framework Agreement'
Page 336, line 19	*For* 'import' *read* 'import or export'
Page 414, footnote 4	*Israel should be added to the list of states that have neither signed nor ratified the BTWC*
Pages 421–22, footnote 48	*For* 'The CWC requires that all recovered ACWs must be destroyed by 29 April 2012.' *read* 'The CWC requires that all chemical weapons be destroyed by 2007 but allows for this deadline to be extended. In the case of ACWs in China the deadline was extended to 2012 at the request of China and Japan. This deadline might be further extended.'
Page 472, line 25	*For* 'Criterion 3' *read* 'Criterion 2'

SIPRI Yearbook 2010: Armaments, Disarmament and International Security

Errata for this printed edition of *SIPRI Yearbook 2010* will appear at <http://www.sipri.org/yearbook/> and in *SIPRI Yearbook 2011*. The online edition of *SIPRI Yearbook 2010* at <http://www.sipriyearbook.org/> will be updated as errata are discovered.

Index